New York

2007

ExxonMobil
Travel Publications

Acknowledgements

We gratefully acknowledge the help of our representatives for their efficient and perceptive inspections of the lodging and dining establishments listed; the establishments' proprietors for their cooperation in showing their facilities and providing information about them; and the many users of previous editions who have taken the time to share their experiences. Mobil Travel Guide is also grateful to all the talented writers who contributed entries to this book.

www.mobiltravelguide.com

Front cover photo: Niagara Falls, Skyline of New York City, Statue of Liberty by Shutterstock

ISBN: 0-7627-4259-3 or 978-0-7627-4259-2

ISSN: 1550-1930

Manufactured in China.

10 9 8 7 6 5 4 3 2 1

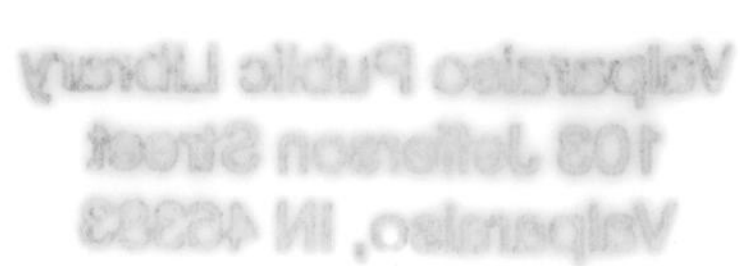

Contents

Maps

New York

MAP SYMBOLS

TRANSPORTATION

CONTROLLED ACCESS HIGHWAYS

- Freeway
- Tollway
- Under Construction
- Interchange and Exit Number

OTHER HIGHWAYS

- Primary Highway
- Secondary Highway
- Divided Highway
- Other Paved Road
- Unpaved Road (Check conditions locally)

HIGHWAY MARKERS

- Interstate Route
- U.S. Route
- State or Provincial Route
- County or Other Route
- Trans-Canada Highway
- Canadian Provincial Autoroute
- Mexican Federal Route

OTHER SYMBOLS

- Distances along Major Highways (Miles in U.S.; kilometers in Canada and Mexico)
- Tunnel; Pass
- Auto Ferry; Passenger Ferry

OTHER MAP FEATURES

- Time Zone Boundary
- Mountain Peak; Elevation (in Feet) — Mt. Olympus 7,965
- Perennial; Intermittent River

RECREATION

- National Park
- National Forest; National Grassland
- Other Large Park or Recreation Area
- Small State Park with and without Camping
- Military Lands
- Indian Reservation
- Trail
- Ski Area
- Point of Interest

CITIES AND TOWNS

- National Capital
- State or Provincial Capital
- Cities, Towns, and Populated Places (Type size indicates relative importance)
- Urban Area (State and province maps only)
- Large Incorporated Cities (City maps only)

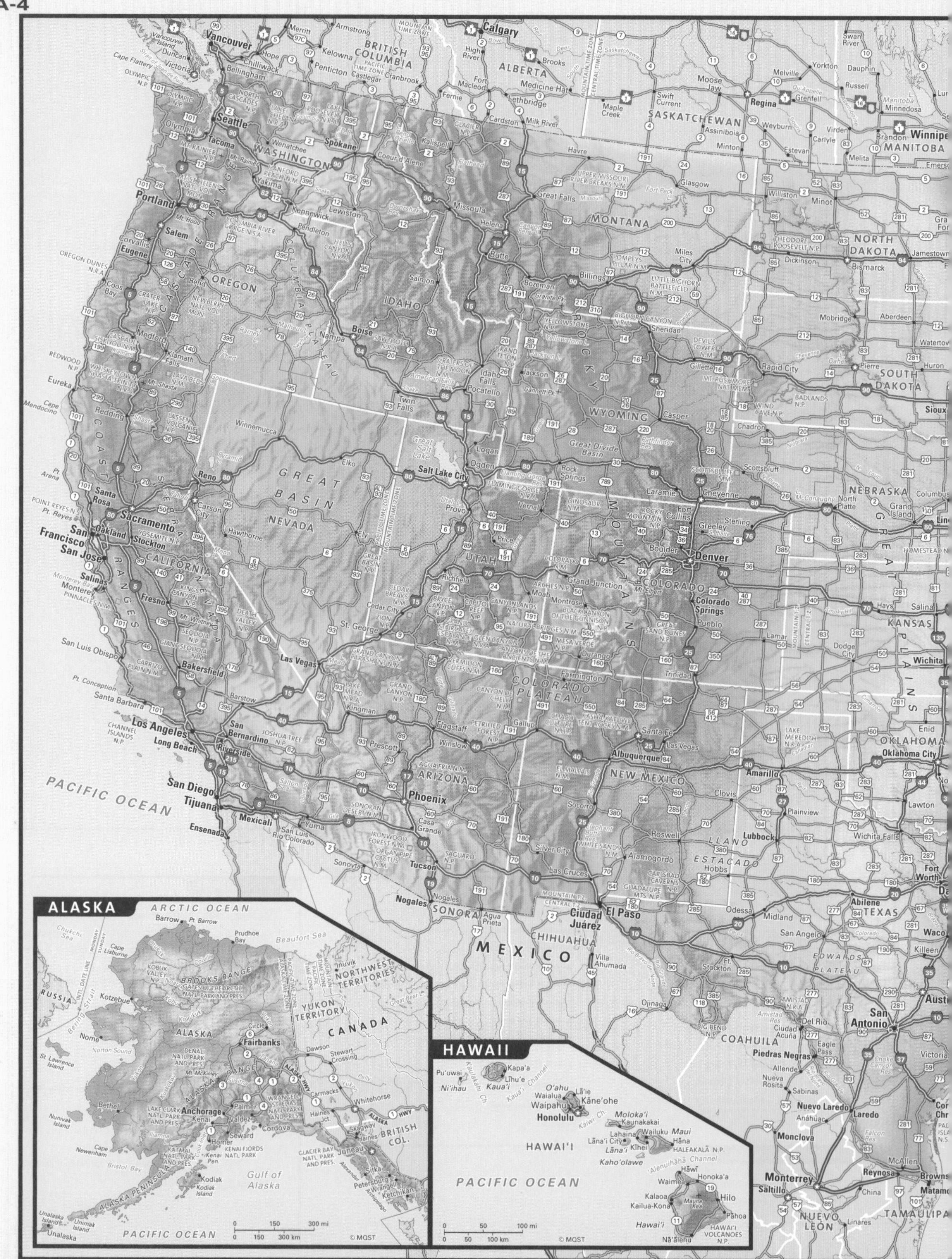
BRITISH COLUMBIA
ALBERTA
SASKATCHEWAN
MANITOBA
WASHINGTON
OREGON
IDAHO
MONTANA
WYOMING
NORTH DAKOTA
SOUTH DAKOTA
NEBRASKA
KANSAS
OKLAHOMA
TEXAS
NEW MEXICO
COLORADO
UTAH
NEVADA
CALIFORNIA
ARIZONA
MEXICO
SONORA
CHIHUAHUA
COAHUILA
NUEVO LEÓN
TAMAULIPA
PACIFIC OCEAN
GREAT BASIN
COLORADO PLATEAU
COLUMBIA PLATEAU
LLANO ESTACADO
EDWARDS PLATEAU
GREAT PLAINS
CASCADE RANGE
SIERRA NEVADA
COAST RANGES
ROCKY MOUNTAINS
Vancouver
Calgary
Regina
Winnipe
Seattle
Tacoma
Spokane
Portland
Salem
Eugene
Boise
Missoula
Helena
Butte
Great Falls
Billings
Bismarck
Pierre
Rapid City
Casper
Cheyenne
Denver
Colorado Springs
Pueblo
Salt Lake City
Provo
Ogden
Reno
Carson City
Sacramento
Oakland
San Francisco
San Jose
Stockton
Fresno
Bakersfield
Los Angeles
Long Beach
San Bernardino
Riverside
San Diego
Tijuana
Mexicali
Las Vegas
Phoenix
Tucson
Flagstaff
Albuquerque
Santa Fe
El Paso
Ciudad Juárez
Amarillo
Lubbock
Oklahoma City
Wichita
San Antonio
Laredo
Nuevo Laredo
Monterrey
Saltillo
ALASKA
ARCTIC OCEAN
BROOKS RANGE
ALASKA RANGE
YUKON TERRITORY
NORTHWEST TERRITORIES
CANADA
RUSSIA
Barrow
Fairbanks
Anchorage
Juneau
Nome
Kodiak
Gulf of Alaska
PACIFIC OCEAN
© MQST
HAWAII
Kaua'i
O'ahu
Honolulu
Moloka'i
Maui
Lāna'i
Kaho'olawe
Hawai'i
Hilo
PACIFIC OCEAN
© MQST

CANADA
ONTARIO
QUÉBEC
NEW BRUNSWICK
MAINE
MINNESOTA
WISCONSIN
MICHIGAN
IOWA
ILLINOIS
INDIANA
OHIO
PENNSYLVANIA
NEW YORK
VT
NH
MASS
CT
R.I.
NEW JERSEY
MD
DE.
WEST VIRGINIA
VIRGINIA
KENTUCKY
TENNESSEE
NORTH CAROLINA
SOUTH CAROLINA
GEORGIA
FLORIDA
ALABAMA
MISSISSIPPI
LOUISIANA
ARKANSAS
MISSOURI
OZARK PLATEAU
APPALACHIAN MOUNTAINS
Lake Superior
Lake Michigan
Lake Huron
Lake Ontario
Lake Erie
ATLANTIC OCEAN
GULF OF MEXICO
BAHAMAS
EASTERN TIME ZONE
CENTRAL TIME ZONE
Thunder Bay
Sault Ste. Marie
Sudbury
Toronto
Ottawa
Montreal
Québec
Minneapolis
St. Paul
Duluth
Milwaukee
Madison
Chicago
Detroit
Cleveland
Buffalo
Pittsburgh
Columbus
Indianapolis
Cincinnati
Louisville
Lexington
St. Louis
Kansas City
Des Moines
Memphis
Nashville
Knoxville
Chattanooga
Atlanta
Birmingham
Montgomery
Jackson
New Orleans
Baton Rouge
Mobile
Houston
Galveston
Shreveport
Little Rock
Tallahassee
Jacksonville
Orlando
Tampa
St. Petersburg
Miami
Fort Lauderdale
West Palm Beach
Key West
Savannah
Charleston
Columbia
Charlotte
Raleigh
Durham
Greensboro
Winston-Salem
Richmond
Norfolk
Virginia Beach
Washington, DC
Baltimore
Philadelphia
New York
Newark
Hartford
Providence
Boston
Albany
Syracuse
Rochester
Portland
Augusta
Nassau
© MAPQUEST
0
150
300 mi
0
150
300 km

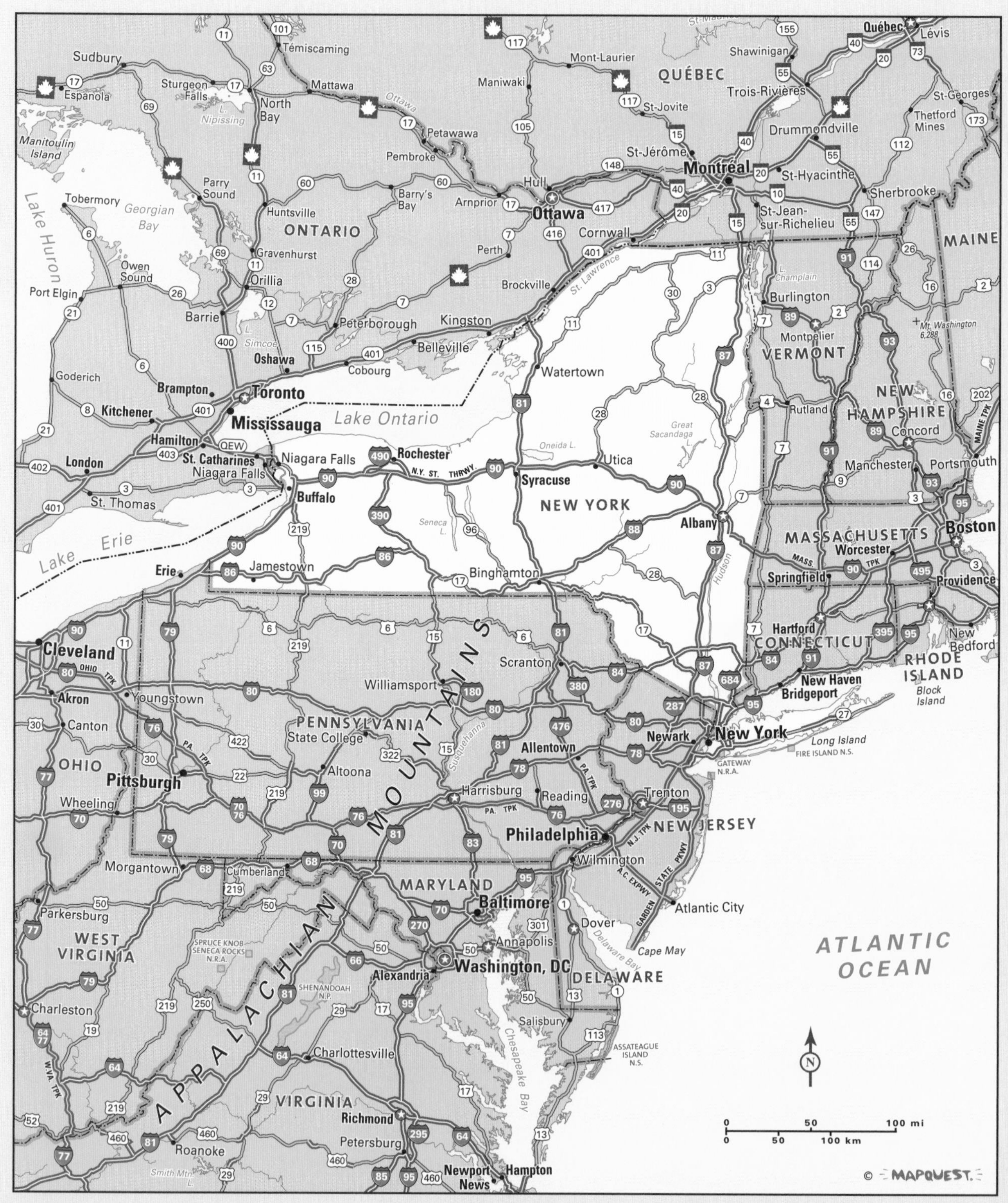
QUÉBEC
ONTARIO
NEW YORK
VERMONT
NEW HAMPSHIRE
MAINE
MASSACHUSETTS
CONNECTICUT
RHODE ISLAND
PENNSYLVANIA
NEW JERSEY
DELAWARE
MARYLAND
OHIO
WEST VIRGINIA
VIRGINIA
APPALACHIAN MOUNTAINS
ATLANTIC OCEAN
Lake Huron
Georgian Bay
Lake Ontario
Lake Erie
L. Nipissing
L. Simcoe
L. Champlain
Great Sacandaga L.
Oneida L.
Seneca L.
Smith Mtn. L.
St. Lawrence
Ottawa
Hudson
Susquehanna
Delaware Bay
Chesapeake Bay
Long Island
Block Island
Manitoulin Island
Sudbury
Espanola
Sturgeon Falls
North Bay
Témiscaming
Mattawa
Petawawa
Pembroke
Mont-Laurier
Maniwaki
St-Jovite
St-Jérôme
Montréal
Trois-Rivières
Shawinigan
Québec
Lévis
Drummondville
St-Hyacinthe
Sherbrooke
St-Jean-sur-Richelieu
St-Georges
Thetford Mines
Hull
Ottawa
Arnprior
Barry's Bay
Huntsville
Parry Sound
Tobermory
Owen Sound
Port Elgin
Gravenhurst
Orillia
Barrie
Perth
Cornwall
Brockville
Kingston
Peterborough
Belleville
Cobourg
Oshawa
Goderich
Brampton
Toronto
Mississauga
Kitchener
Hamilton
St. Catharines
Niagara Falls
London
St. Thomas
Buffalo
Rochester
Syracuse
Utica
Watertown
Albany
Binghamton
Jamestown
Erie
Burlington
Montpelier
Mt. Washington 6,288
Rutland
Concord
Manchester
Portsmouth
Boston
Worcester
Springfield
Providence
Hartford
New Bedford
New Haven
Bridgeport
New York
Newark
FIRE ISLAND N.S.
GATEWAY N.R.A.
Cleveland
Akron
Youngstown
Canton
Pittsburgh
Wheeling
Scranton
Williamsport
State College
Altoona
Allentown
Reading
Harrisburg
Philadelphia
Trenton
Wilmington
Atlantic City
Cape May
Dover
Morgantown
Cumberland
Baltimore
Annapolis
Washington, DC
Alexandria
Parkersburg
SPRUCE KNOB SENECA ROCKS N.R.A.
SHENANDOAH N.P.
Charleston
Charlottesville
Salisbury
ASSATEAGUE ISLAND N.S.
Richmond
Petersburg
Roanoke
Newport News
Hampton
N.Y. ST. THRWY.
OHIO TPK
PA. TPK
MASS TPK
N.J. TPK
GARDEN STATE PKWY
A.C. EXPWY
W.VA. TPK
MAINE TPK
QEW
0 50 100 mi
0 50 100 km
N
© MAPQUEST.

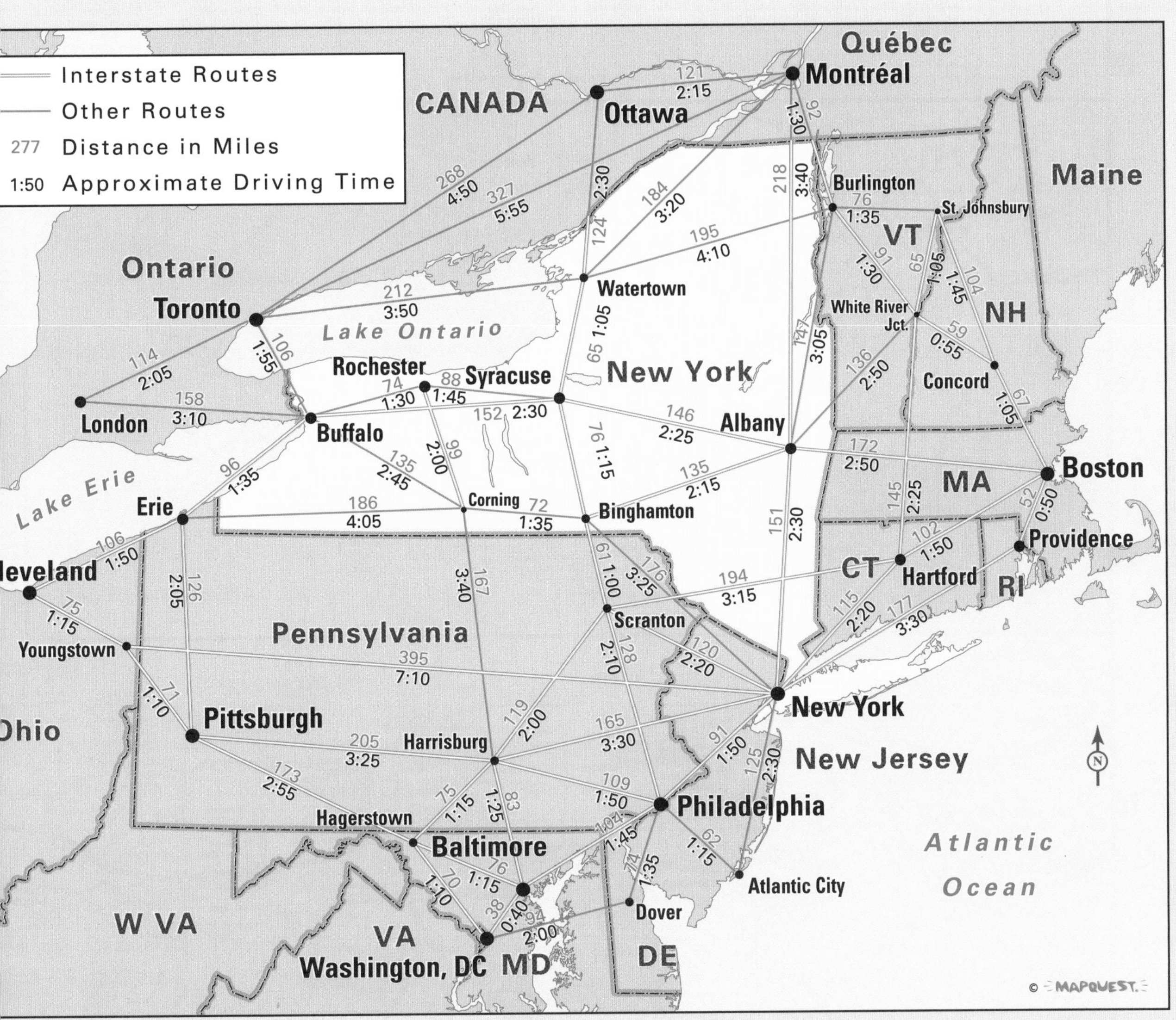
Interstate Routes
Other Routes
277 Distance in Miles
1:50 Approximate Driving Time
Québec
Montréal
Ottawa
CANADA
Maine
Burlington
St. Johnsbury
VT
NH
Ontario
Toronto
Watertown
Lake Ontario
White River Jct.
New York
Rochester
Syracuse
Concord
London
Buffalo
Albany
Boston
MA
Lake Erie
Erie
Corning
Binghamton
Providence
CT
Hartford
RI
Cleveland
Pennsylvania
Scranton
Youngstown
New York
Ohio
Pittsburgh
Harrisburg
New Jersey
Philadelphia
Hagerstown
Baltimore
Atlantic
Ocean
Atlantic City
Dover
W VA
VA
Washington, DC
MD
DE
© MAPQUEST.

New York

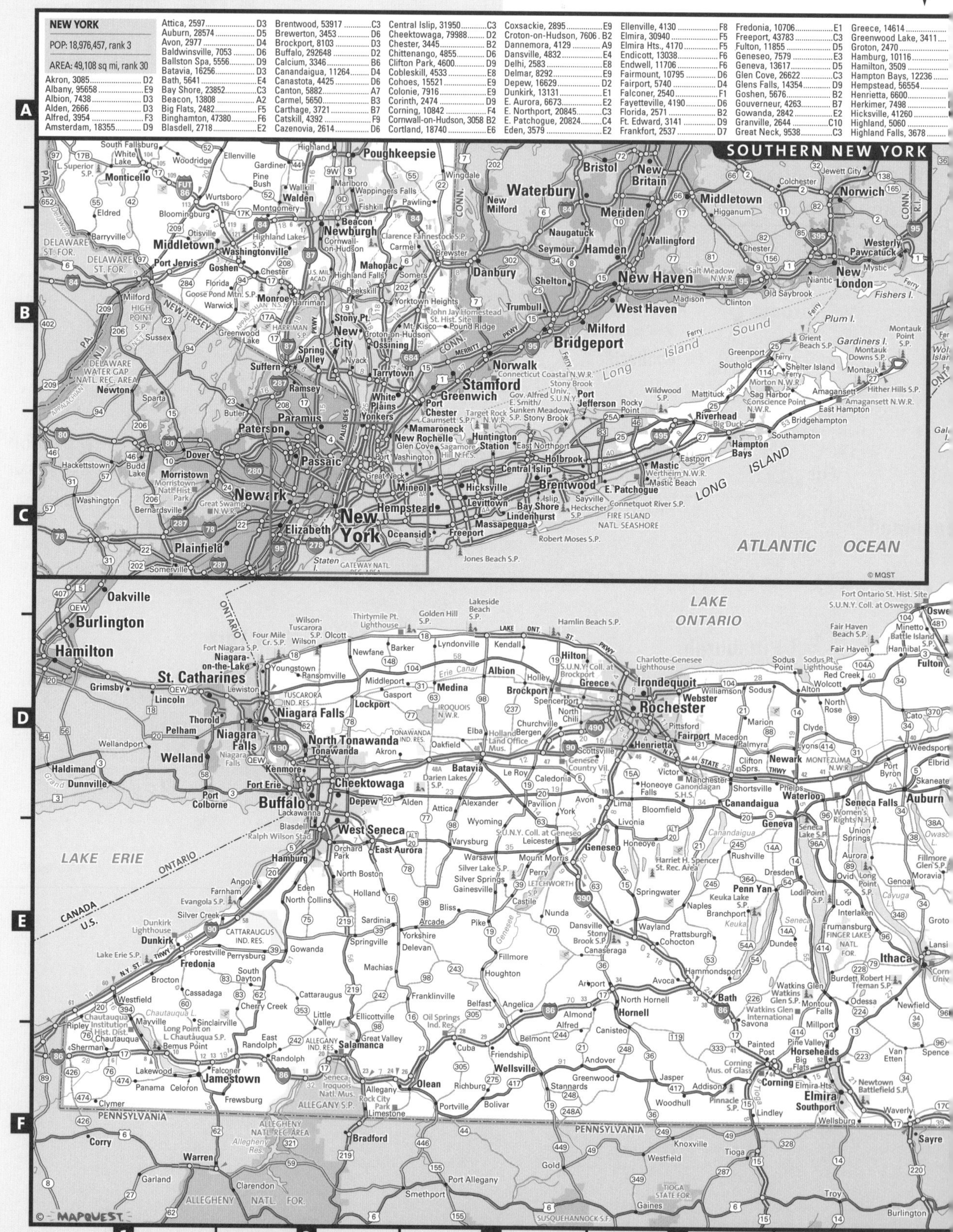

NEW YORK

POP: 18,976,457, rank 3

AREA: 49,108 sq mi, rank 30

Akron, 3085 ... D2
Albany, 95658 ... E9
Albion, 7438 ... D3
Alden, 2666 ... D3
Alfred, 3954 ... F3
Amsterdam, 18355 ... D9
Attica, 2597 ... D3
Auburn, 28574 ... D5
Avon, 2977 ... D4
Baldwinsville, 7053 ... D6
Ballston Spa, 5556 ... D9
Batavia, 16256 ... D3
Bath, 5641 ... E4
Bay Shore, 23852 ... C3
Beacon, 13808 ... A2
Big Flats, 2482 ... F5
Binghamton, 47380 ... F6
Blasdell, 2718 ... E2
Brentwood, 53917 ... C3
Brewerton, 3453 ... D6
Brockport, 8103 ... D3
Buffalo, 292648 ... D2
Calcium, 3346 ... B6
Canandaigua, 11264 ... D4
Canastota, 4425 ... D6
Canton, 5882 ... A7
Carmel, 5650 ... B3
Carthage, 3721 ... B7
Catskill, 4392 ... F9
Cazenovia, 2614 ... D6
Central Islip, 31950 ... C3
Cheektowaga, 79988 ... D2
Chester, 3445 ... B2
Chittenango, 4855 ... D6
Clifton Park, 4600 ... D9
Cobleskill, 4533 ... E8
Cohoes, 15521 ... E9
Colonie, 7916 ... E9
Corinth, 2474 ... D9
Corning, 10842 ... F4
Cornwall-on-Hudson, 3058 B2
Cortland, 18740 ... E6
Coxsackie, 2895 ... E9
Croton-on-Hudson, 7606 . B2
Dannemora, 4129 ... A9
Dansville, 4832 ... E4
Delhi, 2583 ... E8
Delmar, 8292 ... E9
Depew, 16629 ... D2
Dunkirk, 13131 ... E1
E. Aurora, 6673 ... E2
E. Northport, 20845 ... C3
E. Patchogue, 20824 ... C4
Eden, 3579 ... E2
Ellenville, 4130 ... F8
Elmira, 30940 ... F5
Elmira Hts., 4170 ... F5
Endicott, 13038 ... F6
Endwell, 11706 ... F6
Fairmount, 10795 ... D6
Fairport, 5740 ... D4
Falconer, 2540 ... F1
Fayetteville, 4190 ... D6
Florida, 2571 ... B2
Ft. Edward, 3141 ... D9
Frankfort, 2537 ... D7
Fredonia, 10706 ... E1
Freeport, 43783 ... C3
Fulton, 11855 ... D5
Geneseo, 7579 ... E3
Geneva, 13617 ... D5
Glen Cove, 26622 ... C3
Glens Falls, 14354 ... D9
Goshen, 5676 ... B2
Gouverneur, 4263 ... B7
Gowanda, 2842 ... E2
Granville, 2644 ... C10
Great Neck, 9538 ... C3
Greece, 14614 ...
Greenwood Lake, 3411 ...
Groton, 2470 ...
Hamburg, 10116 ...
Hamilton, 3509 ...
Hampton Bays, 12236 ...
Hempstead, 56554 ...
Henrietta, 6600 ...
Herkimer, 7498 ...
Hicksville, 41260 ...
Highland, 5060 ...
Highland Falls, 3678 ...

New York

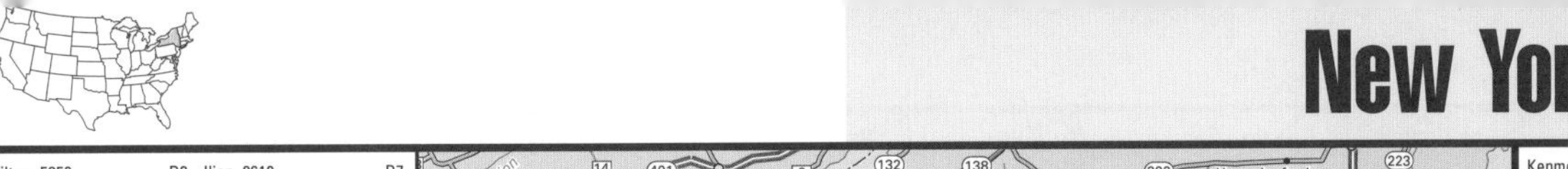

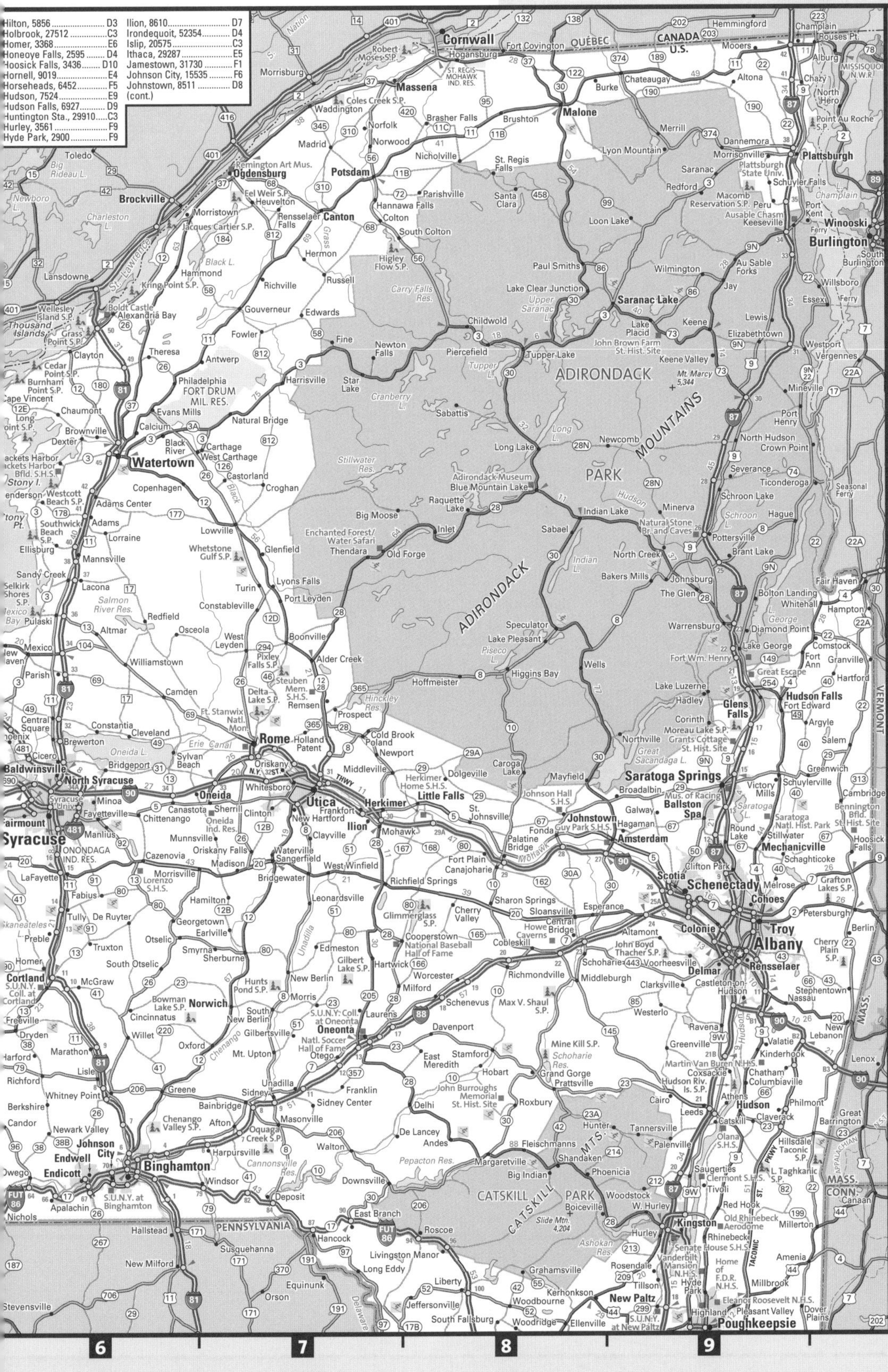

A
B
C
D
E
F
6
7
8
9
10
Cornwall
Massena
Malone
Plattsburgh
Ogdensburg
Brockville
Canton
Potsdam
Burlington
Winooski
Saranac Lake
Lake Placid
Tupper Lake
ADIRONDACK PARK
ADIRONDACK MOUNTAINS
Watertown
Rome
Utica
Herkimer
Little Falls
Ilion
Oneida
Syracuse
North Syracuse
Johnstown
Amsterdam
Saratoga Springs
Glens Falls
Hudson Falls
Schenectady
Troy
Albany
Cohoes
Colonie
Rensselaer
Delmar
Oneonta
Norwich
Cortland
Binghamton
Johnson City
Endicott
Endwell
Hudson
Catskill
Kingston
New Paltz
Poughkeepsie
CATSKILL PARK
CATSKILL MTS.
QUÉBEC
CANADA
U.S.
PENNSYLVANIA
VERMONT
MASS.
CONN.

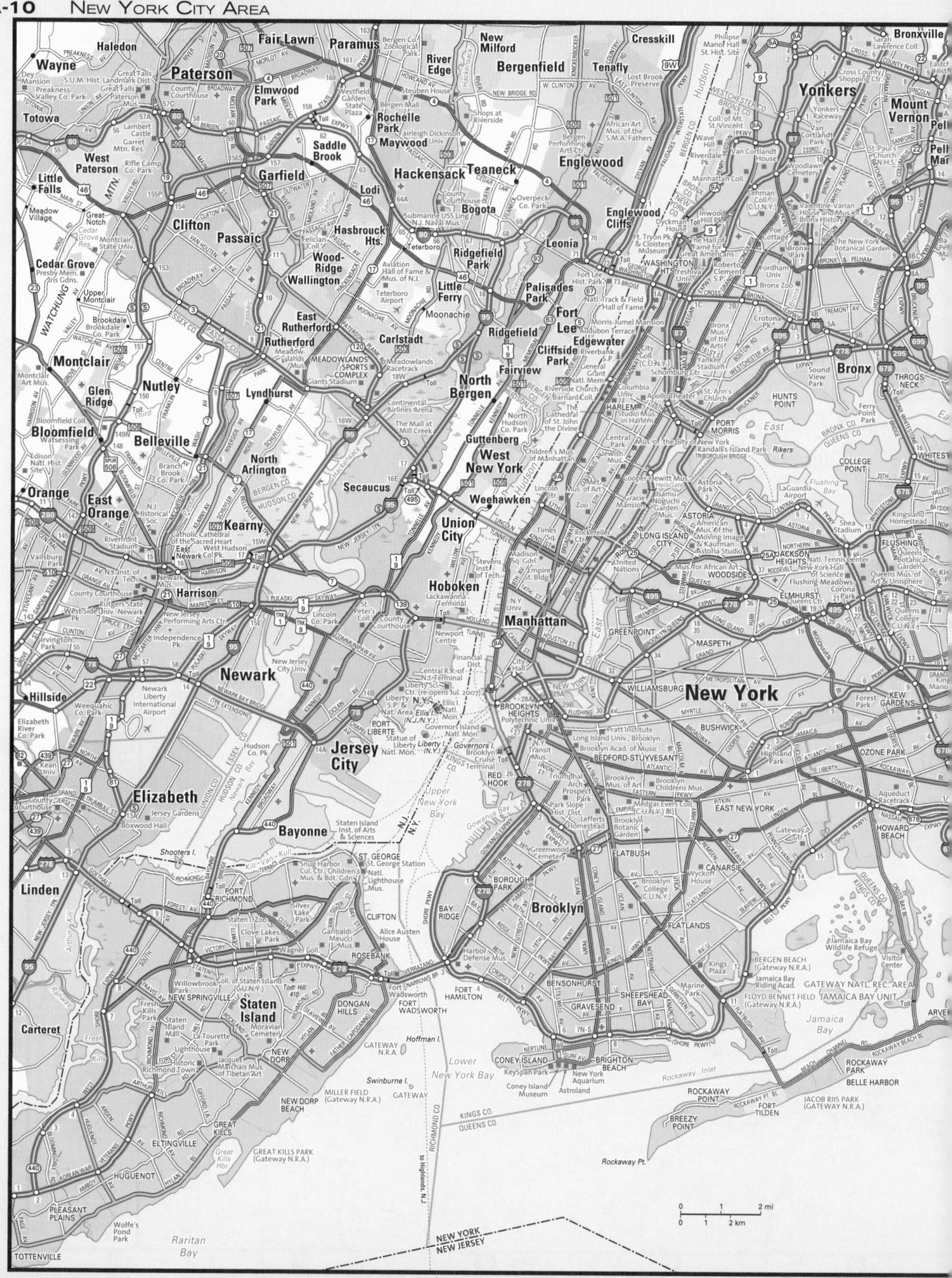
Fair Lawn
Paramus
New Milford
Cresskill
Bronxville
Haledon
Wayne
Paterson
River Edge
Bergenfield
Tenafly
Yonkers
Mount Vernon
Elmwood Park
Totowa
Rochelle Park
Maywood
Saddle Brook
Englewood
West Paterson
Little Falls
Garfield
Hackensack
Teaneck
Lodi
Clifton
Bogota
Englewood Cliffs
Passaic
Hasbrouck Hts.
Leonia
Cedar Grove
Wood-Ridge
Wallington
Ridgefield Park
Little Ferry
Palisades Park
Fort Lee
East Rutherford
Moonachie
Carlstadt
Rutherford
Ridgefield
Edgewater
Montclair
Cliffside Park
Fairview
Bronx
Glen Ridge
Nutley
Lyndhurst
North Bergen
Bloomfield
Belleville
Guttenberg
West New York
North Arlington
Secaucus
Weehawken
Orange
East Orange
Kearny
Union City
Hoboken
Harrison
Manhattan
Newark
New York
Hillside
Jersey City
Elizabeth
Bayonne
Linden
Brooklyn
Staten Island
Carteret
Lower New York Bay
Raritan Bay
Jamaica Bay
Rockaway Inlet
Rockaway Pt.
NEW YORK
NEW JERSEY
0 1 2 mi
0 1 2 km

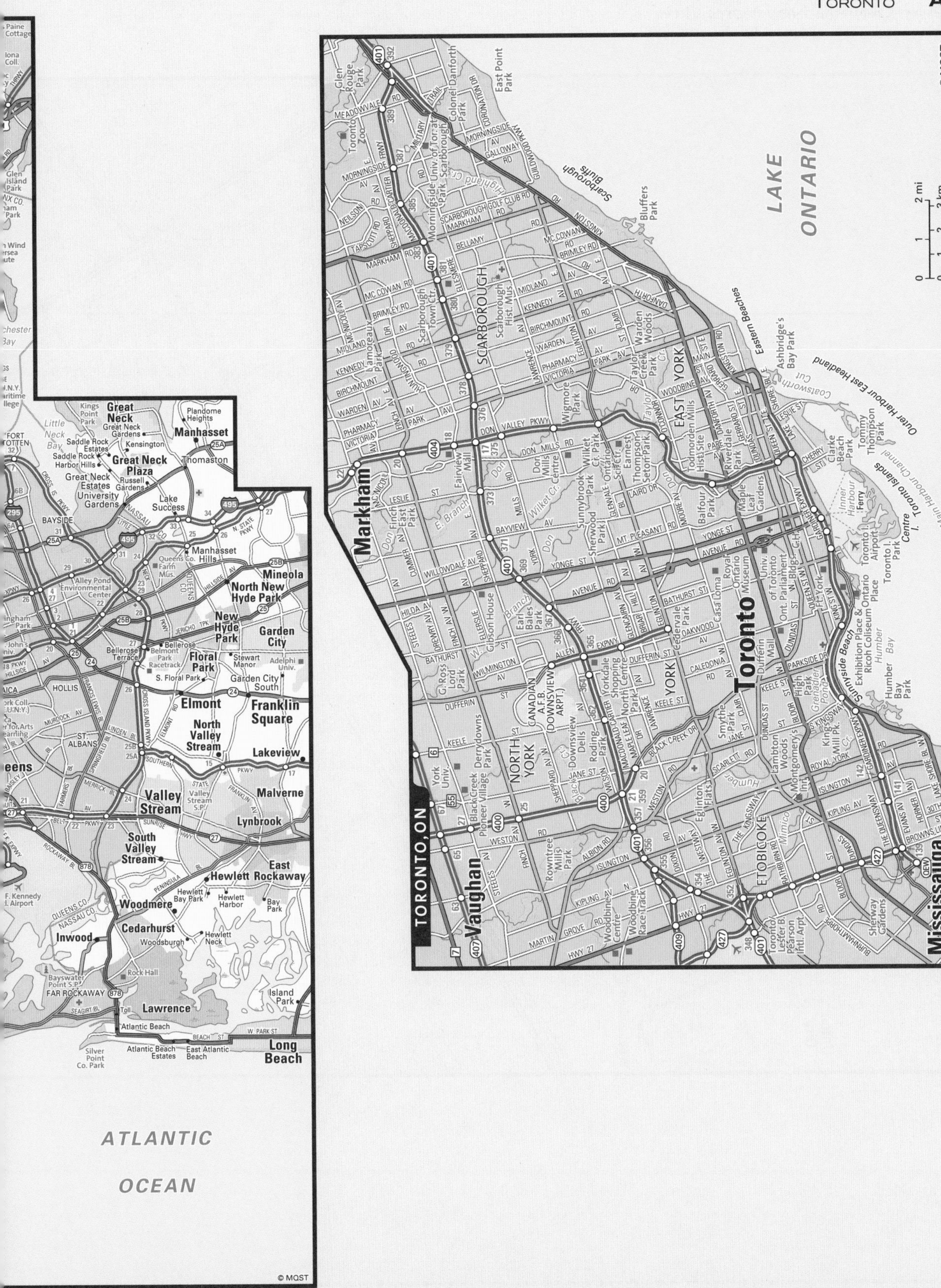
TORONTO, ON
LAKE ONTARIO
Toronto
Markham
Vaughan
Mississauga
SCARBOROUGH
EAST YORK
NORTH YORK
YORK
ETOBICOKE
Scarborough Bluffs
Bluffers Park
East Point Park
Glen Rouge Park
Toronto Zoo
Eastern Beaches
Ashbridge's Bay Park
Coatsworth Cut
Outer Harbour East Headland
Tommy Thompson Park
Clarke Beach Park
Toronto Islands
Main Harbour Channel
Inner Harbour
Ferry
Toronto I. Airport
Centre I.
Toronto I. Park
Ontario Place
Exhibition Place & Ricoh Coliseum
Humber Bay
Humber Bay Park
Sunnyside Beach
High Park
Grenadier Pond
Casa Loma
Royal Ontario Museum
Univ. of Toronto
Ont. Parliament
Maple Leaf Gardens
Riverdale Park
Todmorden Mills Hist. Site
Ontario Science Ctr.
Wilket Cr. Park
Earnest Thompson Seton Park
Sunnybrook Park
Sherwood Park
Don Mills Centre
Fairview Mall
Scarborough Town Ctr.
Scarborough Hist. Mus.
Univ. of Toronto Scarborough
Morningside Park
Colonel Danforth Park
Wigmore Park
Taylor Creek Park
Warden Woods
Yorkdale Shopping Centre
Downsview Dells
Roding Park
Earl Bales Park
Gibson House
G. Ross Lord Park
York Univ.
Black Creek Pioneer Village
Derrydowns Park
Canadian A.F.B. (Downsview Arpt.)
Rowntree Mills Park
Woodbine Centre
Woodbine Racetrack
Toronto Lester B. Pearson Intl. Arpt.
Eglinton Flats
Lambton Woods
Montgomery's Inn
Smythe Park
Kingsway
Mill Pk.
Sherway Gardens
Balfour Park
Cedarvale Park
Lamoreaux Park
Finch East Park
Kings Point Park
Great Neck
Great Neck Gardens
Great Neck Plaza
Great Neck Estates
Plandome Heights
Manhasset
Thomaston
Kensington
Saddle Rock
Saddle Rock Estates
Harbor Hills
Russell Gardens
University Gardens
Lake Success
Little Neck Bay
Bayside
Manhasset Hills
Queens Co. Farm Mus.
Alley Pond Environmental Center
North New Hyde Park
Mineola
New Hyde Park
Garden City
Bellerose
Bellerose Terrace
Belmont Park Racetrack
Floral Park
S. Floral Park
Stewart Manor
Adelphi Univ.
Garden City South
Elmont
Franklin Square
North Valley Stream
Hollis
St. Albans
Lakeview
Valley Stream
Valley Stream S.P.
Malverne
Lynbrook
South Valley Stream
East Rockaway
Hewlett
Hewlett Bay Park
Hewlett Harbor
Bay Park
Woodmere
Cedarhurst
Inwood
Woodsburgh
Hewlett Neck
Rock Hall
Bayswater Point S.P.
Far Rockaway
Lawrence
Island Park
Atlantic Beach
Atlantic Beach Estates
East Atlantic Beach
Long Beach
Silver Point Co. Park
ATLANTIC OCEAN
© MQST
© MQST

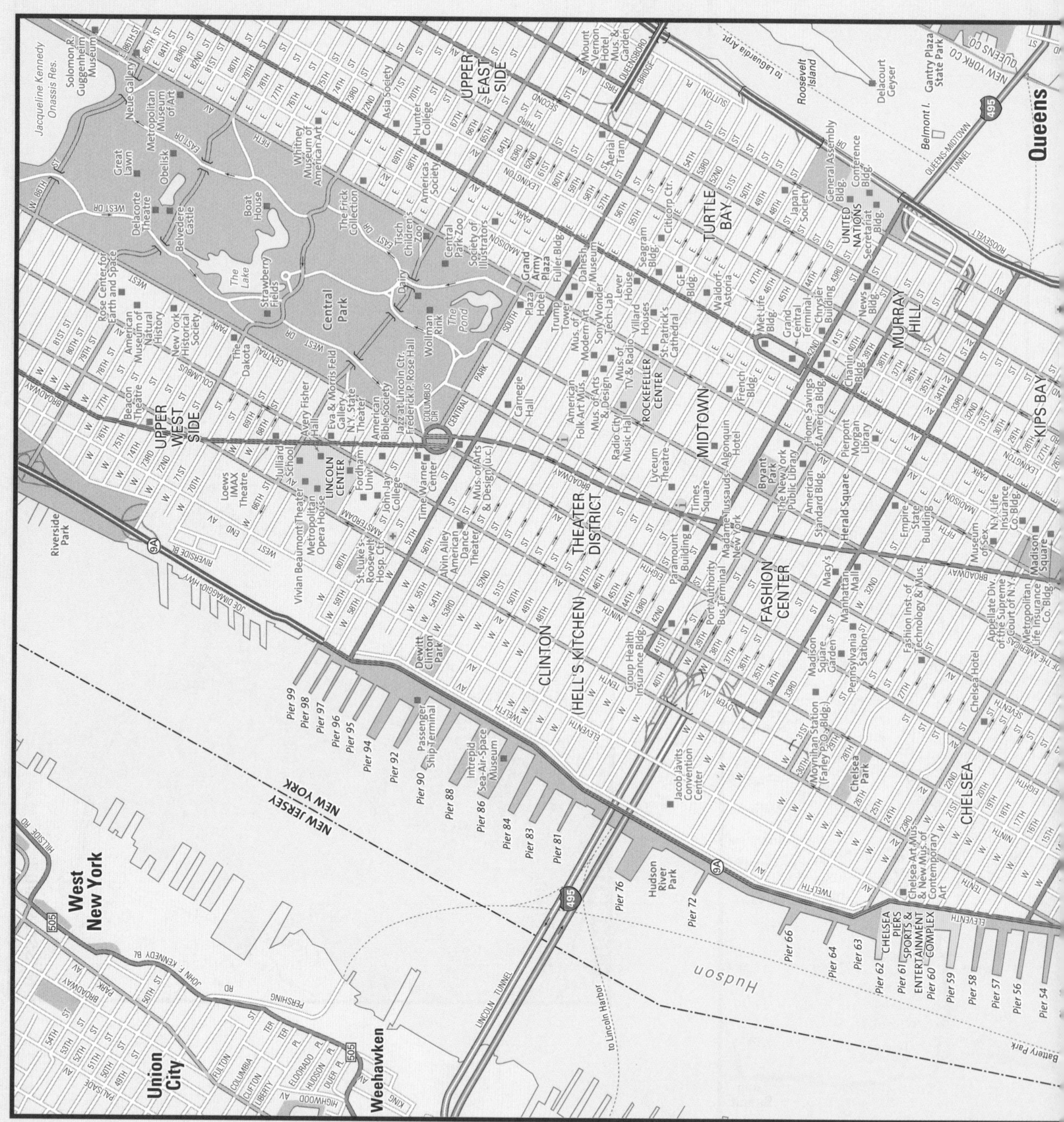

UPPER EAST SIDE
UPPER WEST SIDE
Central Park
The Lake
The Pond
Great Lawn
Jacqueline Kennedy Onassis Res.
Solomon R. Guggenheim Museum
Neue Gallery
Metropolitan Museum of Art
Obelisk
Delacorte Theatre
Belvedere Castle
Boat House
Strawberry Fields
Whitney Museum of American Art
Asia Society
Hunter College
Americas Society
The Frick Collection
Tisch Children's Zoo
Central Park Zoo
Society of Illustrators
Dairy
Wollman Rink
Rose Center for Earth and Space
American Museum of Natural History
New York Historical Society
The Dakota
Beacon Theatre
Lincoln Center
Julliard School
Metropolitan Opera House
Vivian Beaumont Theater
Avery Fisher Hall
Fordham Univ.
John Jay College
American Bible Society
Time Warner Center
Columbus Cir
Carnegie Hall
Loews IMAX Theatre
Riverside Park
St. Luke's Roosevelt Hosp. Ctr.
Alvin Ailey American Dance Theater
Mus. of Arts & Design (u.c.)
Grand Army Plaza
Plaza Hotel
Trump Tower
Fuller Bldg.
Mus. of Modern Art
Sony Wonder Tech. Lab
American Folk Art Mus.
Mus. of Arts & Design
Mus. of TV & Radio
Radio City Music Hall
ROCKEFELLER CENTER
St. Patrick's Cathedral
Villard Houses
Lever House
Seagram Bldg.
Citicorp Ctr.
GE Bldg.
Waldorf-Astoria
TURTLE BAY
Japan Society
UNITED NATIONS
General Assembly Bldg.
Conference Bldg.
Secretariat Bldg.
Met Life Bldg.
Grand Central Terminal
Chrysler Building
News Bldg.
MURRAY HILL
MIDTOWN
French Bldg.
Algonquin Hotel
Lyceum Theatre
Times Square
Madame Tussauds New York
Paramount Building
THEATER DISTRICT
CLINTON (HELL'S KITCHEN)
Port Authority Bus Terminal
Group Health Insurance Bldg.
Bryant Park
The New York Public Library
Home Savings of America Bldg.
Chanin Bldg.
Pierpont Morgan Library
American Standard Bldg.
Herald Square
Macy's
Empire State Building
FASHION CENTER
Manhattan Mall
Madison Square Garden
Pennsylvania Station
Moynihan Station (Farley P. O. Bldg.)
Fashion Inst. of Technology & Mus.
Museum of Sex
N.Y. Life Insurance Co. Bldg.
Madison Square
Appellate Div. of the Supreme Court of N.Y.
Metropolitan Life Insurance Co. Bldg.
Chelsea Hotel
Chelsea Park
CHELSEA
KIPS BAY
Chelsea Art Mus. & New Mus. of Contemporary Art
CHELSEA PIERS SPORTS & ENTERTAINMENT COMPLEX
Jacob Javits Convention Center
Dewitt Clinton Park
Passenger Ship Terminal
Intrepid Sea-Air-Space Museum
Hudson River Park
Pier 99
Pier 98
Pier 97
Pier 96
Pier 95
Pier 94
Pier 92
Pier 90
Pier 88
Pier 86
Pier 84
Pier 83
Pier 81
Pier 76
Pier 72
Pier 66
Pier 64
Pier 63
Pier 62
Pier 61
Pier 60
Pier 59
Pier 58
Pier 57
Pier 56
Pier 54
Hudson
NEW YORK
NEW JERSEY
LINCOLN TUNNEL
QUEENS-MIDTOWN TUNNEL
QUEENSBORO BRIDGE
Roosevelt Island
Belmont I.
Delacourt Geyser
Gantry Plaza State Park
Queens
to LaGuardia Arpt.
Aerial Tram
Mount Vernon Hotel Mus. & Garden
West New York
Union City
Weehawken
to Lincoln Harbor
JOE DIMAGGIO HWY
JOHN F. KENNEDY BL

GREENPOINT
WILLIAMSBURG
East
WILLIAMSBURG BRIDGE
Bushwick Inlet
NEW YORK CO.
KINGS CO.
Wallabout Bay
BROOKLYN NAVY YARD
FORT GREENE
Barry Park
Brooklyn
D.U.M.B.O
BROOKLYN HEIGHTS
Cadman Plaza
U.S. Court House
N.Y.C. COLL. OF TECH. (C.U.N.Y.)
Plymouth Church of the Pilgrims
Brooklyn Historical Society
Empire-Fulton Ferry S.P.
MANHATTAN BRIDGE
BROOKLYN BRIDGE
BROOKLYN-QUEENS EXPWY
BROOKLYN-BATTERY TUNNEL
STUYVESANT TOWN
GRAMERCY PARK
Gramercy Pk. (private)
Stuyvesant Square
Bellevue Hosp. Ctr.
V.A. Med. Ctr.
Beth Israel Medical Center
Cabrini Medical Ctr.
Tompkins Square
Ukrainian Museum
EAST VILLAGE
East River Park
Hamilton Fish Park
LOWER EAST SIDE
Seward Park
Union Sq.
Con Edison Building
THE COOPER UNION
Foundation Bldg.
Merchant's House Museum
Public Theater
Grace Church
NOHO
NOLITA
LITTLE ITALY
CHINATOWN
Columbus Park
New Mus. of Contemporary Art (u.c.)
Lower East Side Tenement Mus. N.H.S.
Eldridge St. Project
Mus. of the Chinese in the Americas
Theodore Roosevelt Birthplace N.H.S.
Forbes Galleries
Salmagundi Club
Jefferson Market Ct. Hse.
Macdougal Alley
Washington Square
Washington Arch
NEW YORK UNIV.
GREENWICH VILLAGE
WEST VILLAGE
Sheridan Square
St. Vincent's Hosp. & Medical Ctr.
SOHO
Guggenheim Mus. SoHo
MoCCA
Hudson River Park
Hudson Park
N.Y.C. Fire Museum
TRIBECA
Hudson Square
Criminal Courts Bldg.
Foley Sq.
N.Y. Supreme & Co. Court
U.S. Ct. Hse.
Municipal Bldg.
City Hall
African Burial Ground Natl. Mon.
Old N.Y. Co. Ct. Hse.
Woolworth Bldg.
Pace Univ. N.Y.C. Campus
St. Paul's Chapel
WORLD TRADE CENTER SITE
WORLD FINANCIAL CENTER
Winter Garden
Irish Hunger Memorial
N.Y. Mercantile Exchange
BATTERY PARK CITY
Downtown Athletic Club
Skyscraper Mus.
Mus. of Jewish Heritage
Castle Clinton Natl. Mon.
Battery Park
New York Unearthed
Fraunces Tavern
Natl. Mus. of the American Indian
Mus. of Am. Financial Hist.
FINANCIAL DISTRICT
Federal Hall Natl. Mem.
New York Stock Exchange
Fed. Res. Bank
Trinity Church
Cunard Bldg.
World Port New York
SOUTH ST. SEAPORT
Seaport Mus.
Pier 17 Pavilion
Street of Ships
NYC Police Mus.
Pier 51
Pier 49
Pier 46
Pier 45
Pier 42
Pier 40
Pier 32
Pier 26
Pier 25
HOLLAND TUNNEL
to Hoboken, N.J.
to Ellis I.
to Liberty I.
to Port Liberte, N.J.
to Staten I.
to Staten Island
to Highlands, N.J.
0 0.25 0.5 mi
0 0.25 0.5 0.75 km
© MQST

Distances in chart are in miles. To convert miles to kilometers, multiply the distance in miles by 1.609

Example:
New York, NY to Boston, MA = 215 miles or 346 kilometers (215 x 1.609)

	ALBUQUERQUE, NM	ATLANTA, GA	BALTIMORE, MD	BILLINGS, MT	BIRMINGHAM, AL	BISMARCK, ND	BOISE, ID	BOSTON, MA	BUFFALO, NY	BURLINGTON, VT	CHARLESTON, SC	CHARLESTON, WV	CHARLOTTE, NC	CHEYENNE, WY	CHICAGO, IL	CINCINNATI, OH	CLEVELAND, OH	DALLAS, TX	DENVER, CO	DES MOINES, IA	DETROIT, MI	EL PASO, TX	HOUSTON, TX	INDIANAPOLIS, IN	JACKSON, MS	KANSAS CITY, MO	LAS VEGAS, NV	LITTLE ROCK, AR	LOS ANGELES, CA	LOUISVILLE, KY	MEMPHIS, TN	MIAMI, FL	MILWAUKEE, WI	MINNEAPOLIS, MN	MONTRÉAL, QC	NASHVILLE, TN	NEW ORLEANS, LA	NEW YORK, NY	OKLAHOMA CITY, OK	OMAHA, NE	ORLANDO, FL	PHILADELPHIA, PA	PHOENIX, AZ	PITTSBURGH, PA	PORTLAND, ME	PORTLAND, OR	RAPID CITY, SD	RENO, NV	RICHMOND, VA	ST. LOUIS, MO	SALT LAKE CITY, UT	SAN ANTONIO, TX	SAN DIEGO, CA	SAN FRANCISCO, CA	SEATTLE, WA	TAMPA, FL	TORONTO, ON	VANCOUVER, BC	WASHINGTON,DC	WICHITA, KS
ALBUQUERQUE, NM		1490	1902	991	1274	1333	966	2240	1808	2178	1793	1568	1649	538	1352	1409	1619	754	438	1091	1608	263	994	1298	1157	894	578	900	806	1320	1033	2155	1426	1339	2172	1248	1276	2015	546	973	1934	1954	466	1670	2338	1395	841	1020	1876	1051	624	818	825	1111	1463	1949	1841	1597	1896	707
ATLANTA, GA	1490		679	1889	150	1559	2218	1100	910	1158	317	503	238	1482	717	476	726	792	1403	967	735	1437	800	531	386	801	2067	528	2237	419	389	661	813	1129	1241	242	473	869	944	989	440	782	1868	676	1197	2647	1511	2440	527	549	1916	1000	2166	2618	2705	455	958	2838	636	989
BALTIMORE, MD	1902	679		1959	795	1551	2401	422	370	481	583	352	441	1665	708	521	377	1399	1690	1031	532	2045	1470	600	1032	1087	2445	1072	2705	602	933	1109	805	1121	564	716	1142	192	1354	1168	904	104	2366	246	520	2830	1626	2623	152	841	2100	1671	2724	2840	2775	960	565	2908	38	1276
BILLINGS, MT	991	1889	1959		1839	413	626	2254	1796	2181	2157	1755	2012	455	1246	1552	1597	1433	554	1007	1534	1255	1673	1432	1836	1088	965	1530	1239	1547	1625	2554	1175	839	2093	1648	1955	2049	1227	904	2333	2019	1199	1719	2352	889	379	960	2053	1341	548	1500	1302	1176	816	2348	1762	949	1953	1067
BIRMINGHAM, AL	1274	150	795	1839		1509	2170	1215	909	1241	466	578	389	1434	667	475	725	647	1356	919	734	1292	678	481	241	753	1852	381	2092	369	241	812	763	1079	1289	194	351	985	729	941	591	897	1723	763	1313	2599	1463	2392	678	501	1868	878	2021	2472	2657	606	958	2791	758	838
BISMARCK, ND	1333	1559	1551	413	1509		1039	1846	1388	1773	1749	1347	1604	594	838	1144	1189	1342	693	675	1126	1597	1582	1024	1548	801	1378	1183	1702	1139	1337	2224	767	431	1685	1315	1734	1641	1136	616	2003	1611	1662	1311	1944	1301	320	1372	1645	1053	960	1599	1765	1749	1229	2018	1354	1362	1545	934
BOISE, ID	966	2218	2401	626	2170	1039		2697	2239	2624	2520	2182	2375	737	1708	1969	2040	1711	833	1369	1977	1206	1952	1852	2115	1376	760	1808	1033	1933	1954	2883	1748	1465	2535	1976	2234	2491	1506	1234	2662	2462	993	2161	2795	432	930	430	2496	1628	342	1761	1096	646	500	2677	2204	633	2395	1346
BOSTON, MA	2240	1100	422	2254	1215	1846	2697		462	214	1003	741	861	1961	1003	862	654	1819	2004	1326	741	2465	1890	940	1453	1427	2757	1493	3046	964	1353	1529	1100	1417	313	1136	1563	215	1694	1463	1324	321	2706	592	107	3126	1921	2919	572	1181	2395	2092	3065	3135	3070	1380	570	3204	458	1616
BUFFALO, NY	1808	910	370	1796	909	1388	2239	462		375	899	431	695	1502	545	442	197	1393	1546	868	277	2039	1513	508	1134	995	2299	1066	2572	545	927	1425	642	958	397	716	1254	400	1262	1005	1221	414	2274	217	560	2667	1463	2460	485	749	1936	1665	2632	2677	2612	1276	106	2745	384	1184
BURLINGTON, VT	2178	1158	481	2181	1241	1773	2624	214	375		1061	782	919	1887	930	817	567	1763	1931	1253	652	2409	1916	878	1479	1366	2684	1437	2957	915	1297	1587	1027	1343	92	1086	1588	299	1632	1390	1383	371	2644	587	233	3052	1848	2845	630	1119	2322	2036	3020	3062	2997	1438	419	3130	517	1554
CHARLESTON, SC	1793	317	583	2157	466	1749	2520	1003	899	1061		468	204	1783	907	622	724	1109	1705	1204	879	1754	1110	721	703	1102	2371	900	2554	610	760	583	1003	1319	1145	543	783	773	1248	1290	379	685	2184	642	1101	2948	1824	2741	428	850	2218	1310	2483	2934	2973	434	1006	3106	539	1291
CHARLESTON, WV	1568	503	352	1755	578	1347	2182	741	431	782	468		265	1445	506	209	255	1072	1367	802	410	1718	1192	320	816	764	2122	745	2374	251	606	994	601	918	822	395	926	515	1022	952	790	454	2035	217	839	2610	1422	2403	322	512	1880	1344	2393	2620	2571	845	537	2705	346	953
CHARLOTTE, NC	1649	238	441	2012	389	1604	2375	861	695	919	204	265		1637	761	476	520	1031	1559	1057	675	1677	1041	575	625	956	2225	754	2453	464	614	730	857	1173	1003	397	713	631	1102	1144	525	543	2107	438	959	2802	1678	2595	289	704	2072	1241	2405	2759	2827	581	802	2960	397	1145
CHEYENNE, WY	538	1482	1665	455	1434	594	737	1961	1502	1887	1783	1445	1637		972	1233	1304	979	100	633	1241	801	1220	1115	1382	640	843	1076	1116	1197	1217	2147	1012	881	1799	1240	1502	1755	773	497	1926	1725	1004	1425	2059	1166	305	959	1760	892	436	1046	1179	1176	1234	1941	1468	1368	1659	613
CHICAGO, IL	1352	717	708	1246	667	838	1708	1003	545	930	907	506	761	972		302	346	936	1015	337	283	1543	1108	184	750	532	1768	662	2042	299	539	1382	89	409	841	474	935	797	807	474	1161	768	1819	467	1101	2137	913	1930	802	294	1406	1270	2105	2146	2062	1176	510	2196	701	728
CINCINNATI, OH	1409	476	521	1552	475	1144	1969	862	442	817	622	209	476	1233	302		253	958	1200	599	261	1605	1079	116	700	597	1955	632	2215	106	493	1141	398	714	815	281	820	636	863	736	920	576	1876	292	960	2398	1219	2191	530	350	1667	1231	2234	2407	2368	935	484	2501	517	785
CLEVELAND, OH	1619	726	377	1597	725	1189	2040	654	197	567	724	255	520	1304	346	253		1208	1347	669	171	1854	1328	319	950	806	2100	882	2374	356	742	1250	443	760	588	531	1070	466	1073	806	1045	437	2085	136	751	2469	1264	2262	471	560	1738	1481	2437	2478	2413	1101	303	2547	370	995
DALLAS, TX	754	792	1399	1433	647	1342	1711	1819	1393	1763	1109	1072	1031	979	936	958	1208		887	752	1218	647	241	913	406	554	1331	327	1446	852	466	1367	1010	999	1772	681	525	1589	209	669	1146	1501	1077	1246	1917	2140	1077	1933	1309	635	1410	271	1375	1827	2208	1161	1441	2342	1362	367
DENVER, CO	438	1403	1690	554	1356	693	833	2004	1546	1931	1705	1367	1559	100	1015	1200	1347	887		676	1284	701	1127	1088	1290	603	756	984	1029	1118	1116	2069	1055	924	1843	1162	1409	1799	681	541	1847	1744	904	1460	2102	1261	404	1054	1688	855	531	946	1092	1271	1329	1862	1512	1463	1686	521
DES MOINES, IA	1091	967	1031	1007	919	675	1369	1326	868	1253	1204	802	1057	633	337	599	669	752	676		606	1283	992	481	931	194	1429	567	1703	595	720	1632	378	246	1165	725	1117	1121	546	136	1411	1091	1558	791	1424	1798	629	1591	1126	436	1067	1009	1766	1807	1822	1426	834	1956	1025	390
DETROIT, MI	1608	735	532	1534	734	1126	1977	741	277	652	879	410	675	1241	283	261	171	1218	1284	606		1799	1338	318	960	795	2037	891	2310	366	752	1401	380	697	564	541	1079	622	1062	743	1180	592	2074	292	838	2405	1201	2198	627	549	1675	1490	2373	2415	2350	1194	233	2483	526	984
EL PASO, TX	263	1437	2045	1255	1292	1597	1206	2465	2039	2409	1754	1718	1677	801	1543	1605	1854	647	701	1283	1799		758	1489	1051	1085	717	974	801	1499	1112	1959	1617	1530	2363	1328	1118	2235	737	1236	1738	2147	432	1893	2563	1767	1105	1315	1955	1242	864	556	730	1181	1944	1753	2032	2087	2008	898
HOUSTON, TX	994	800	1470	1673	678	1582	1952	1890	1513	1916	1110	1192	1041	1220	1108	1079	1328	241	1127	992	1338	758		1033	445	795	1474	447	1558	972	586	1201	1193	1240	1892	801	360	1660	449	910	980	1572	1188	1366	1988	2381	1318	2072	1330	863	1650	200	1487	1938	2449	995	1561	2583	1433	608
INDIANAPOLIS, IN	1298	531	600	1432	481	1024	1852	940	508	878	721	320	575	1115	184	116	319	913	1088	481	318	1489	1033		675	485	1843	587	2104	112	464	1196	279	596	872	287	826	715	752	618	975	655	1764	370	1038	2280	1101	2073	641	239	1549	1186	2122	2290	2249	990	541	2383	596	674
JACKSON, MS	1157	386	1032	1836	241	1548	2115	1453	1134	1479	703	816	625	1382	750	700	950	406	1290	931	960	1051	445	675		747	1735	269	1851	594	211	915	835	1151	1514	423	185	1223	612	935	694	1135	1482	988	1550	2544	1458	2337	914	505	1813	644	1780	2232	2612	709	1183	2746	996	771
KANSAS CITY, MO	894	801	1087	1088	753	801	1376	1427	995	1366	1102	764	956	640	532	597	806	554	603	194	795	1085	795	485	747		1358	382	1632	516	536	1466	573	441	1359	559	932	1202	348	188	1245	1141	1360	857	1525	1805	710	1598	1085	252	1074	812	1695	1814	1872	1259	1028	2007	1083	192
LAS VEGAS, NV	578	2067	2445	965	1852	1378	760	2757	2299	2684	2371	2122	2225	843	1768	1955	2100	1331	756	1429	2037	717	1474	1843	1735	1358		1478	274	1874	1611	2733	1808	1677	2596	1826	1854	2552	1124	1294	2512	2500	285	2215	2855	1188	1035	442	2444	1610	417	1272	337	575	1256	2526	2265	1390	2441	1276
LITTLE ROCK, AR	900	528	1072	1530	381	1183	1808	1493	1066	1437	900	745	754	1076	662	632	882	327	984	567	891	974	447	587	269	382	1478		1706	526	140	1190	747	814	1446	355	455	1262	355	570	969	1175	1367	920	1590	2237	1093	2030	983	416	1507	600	1703	2012	2305	984	1115	2439	1036	464
LOS ANGELES, CA	806	2237	2705	1239	2092	1702	1033	3046	2572	2957	2554	2374	2453	1116	2042	2215	2374	1446	1029	1703	2310	801	1558	2104	1851	1632	274	1706		2126	1839	2759	2082	1951	2869	2054	1917	2820	1352	1567	2538	2760	369	2476	3144	971	1309	519	2682	1856	691	1356	124	385	1148	2553	2538	1291	2702	1513
LOUISVILLE, KY	1320	419	602	1547	369	1139	1933	964	545	915	610	251	464	1197	299	106	356	852	1118	595	366	1499	972	112	594	516	1874	526	2126		386	1084	394	711	920	175	714	739	774	704	863	678	1786	394	1062	2362	1215	2155	572	264	1631	1125	2144	2372	2364	878	589	2497	596	705
MEMPHIS, TN	1033	389	933	1625	241	1337	1954	1353	927	1297	760	606	614	1217	539	493	742	466	1116	720	752	1112	586	464	211	536	1611	140	1839	386		1051	624	940	1306	215	396	1123	487	724	830	1035	1500	780	1451	2382	1247	2175	843	294	1652	739	1841	2144	2440	845	975	2574	896	597
MIAMI, FL	2155	661	1109	2554	812	2224	2883	1529	1425	1587	583	994	730	2147	1382	1141	1250	1367	2069	1632	1401	1959	1201	1196	915	1466	2733	1190	2759	1084	1051		1478	1794	1671	907	874	1299	1609	1654	232	1211	2390	1167	1627	3312	2176	3105	954	1214	2581	1401	2688	3140	3370	274	1532	3504	1065	1655
MILWAUKEE, WI	1426	813	805	1175	763	767	1748	1100	642	1027	1003	601	857	1012	89	398	443	1010	1055	378	380	1617	1193	279	835	573	1808	747	2082	394	624	1478		337	939	569	1020	894	880	514	1257	865	1892	564	1198	2063	842	1970	899	367	1446	1343	2145	2186	1991	1272	607	2124	799	769
MINNEAPOLIS, MN	1339	1129	1121	839	1079	431	1465	1417	958	1343	1319	918	1173	881	409	714	760	999	924	246	697	1530	1240	596	1151	441	1677	814	1951	711	940	1794	337		1255	886	1337	1211	793	383	1573	1181	1805	881	1515	1727	606	1839	1216	621	1315	1257	2014	2055	1654	1588	924	1788	1115	637
MONTRÉAL, QC	2172	1241	564	2093	1289	1685	2535	313	397	92	1145	822	1003	1799	841	815	588	1772	1843	1165	564	2363	1892	872	1514	1359	2596	1446	2869	920	1306	1671	939	1255		1094	1632	383	1625	1300	1466	454	2637	607	282	2963	1758	2756	714	1112	2232	2043	2931	2972	2907	1522	330	3041	600	1547
NASHVILLE, TN	1248	242	716	1648	194	1315	1976	1136	716	1086	543	395	397	1240	474	281	531	681	1162	725	541	1328	801	287	423	559	1826	355	2054	175	215	907	569	886	1094		539	906	703	747	686	818	1715	569	1234	2405	1269	2198	626	307	1675	954	2056	2360	2463	701	764	2597	679	748
NEW ORLEANS, LA	1276	473	1142	1955	351	1734	2234	1563	1254	1588	783	926	713	1502	935	820	1070	525	1409	1117	1079	1118	360	826	185	932	1854	455	1917	714	396	874	1020	1337	1632	539		1332	731	1121	653	1245	1548	1108	1660	2663	1643	2431	1002	690	1932	560	1846	2298	2731	668	1302	2865	1106	890
NEW YORK, NY	2015	869	192	2049	985	1641	2491	215	400	299	773	515	631	1755	797	636	466	1589	1799	1121	622	2235	1660	715	1223	1202	2552	1262	2820	739	1123	1299	894	1211	383	906	1332		1469	1258	1094	91	2481	367	313	2920	1716	2713	342	956	2189	1861	2839	2929	2864	1150	507	2998	228	1391
OKLAHOMA CITY, OK	546	944	1354	1227	729	1136	1506	1694	1262	1632	1248	1022	1102	773	807	863	1073	209	681	546	1062	737	449	752	612	348	1124	355	1352	774	487	1609	880	793	1625	703	731	1469		463	1388	1408	1012	1124	1792	1934	871	1727	1331	505	1204	466	1370	1657	2002	1403	1295	2136	1350	161
OMAHA, NE	973	989	1168	904	941	616	1234	1463	1005	1390	1290	952	1144	497	474	736	806	669	541	136	743	1236	910	618	935	188	1294	570	1567	704	724	1654	514	383	1300	747	1121	1258	463		1433	1228	1440	928	1561	1662	525	1455	1263	440	932	927	1630	1672	1719	1448	971	1853	1162	307
ORLANDO, FL	1934	440	904	2333	591	2003	2662	1324	1221	1383	379	790	525	1926	1161	920	1045	1146	1847	1411	1180	1738	980	975	694	1245	2512	969	2538	863	830	232	1257	1573	1466	686	653	1094	1388	1433		1006	2169	963	1422	3091	1955	2884	750	993	2360	1180	2467	2918	3149	82	1327	3283	860	1434
PHILADELPHIA, PA	1954	782	104	2019	897	1611	2462	321	414	371	685	454	543	1725	768	576	437	1501	1744	1091	592	2147	1572	655	1135	1141	2500	1175	2760	678	1035	1211	865	1181	454	818	1245	91	1408	1228	1006		2420	306	419	2890	1686	2683	254	895	2160	1774	2779	2900	2835	1062	522	2968	140	1330
PHOENIX, AZ	466	1868	2366	1199	1723	1662	993	2706	2274	2644	2184	2035	2107	1004	1819	1876	2085	1077	904	1558	2074	432	1188	1764	1482	1360	285	1367	369	1786	1500	2390	1892	1805	2637	1715	1548	2481	1012	1440	2169	2420		2136	2804	1335	1308	883	2343	1517	651	987	358	750	1513	2184	2307	1655	2362	1173
PITTSBURGH, PA	1670	676	246	1719	763	1311	2161	592	217	587	642	217	438	1425	467	292	136	1246	1460	791	292	1893	1366	370	988	857	2215	920	2476	394	780	1167	564	881	607	569	1108	367	1124	928	963	306	2136		690	2590	1386	2383	341	611	1859	1519	2494	2599	2534	1019	321	2668	240	1046
PORTLAND, ME	2338	1197	520	2352	1313	1944	2795	107	560	233	1101	839	959	2059	1101	960	751	1917	2102	1424	838	2563	1988	1038	1550	1525	2855	1590	3144	1062	1451	1627	1198	1515	282	1234	1660	313	1792	1561	1422	419	2804	690		3223	2019	3016	670	1279	2493	2189	3162	3233	3168	1478	668	3301	556	1714
PORTLAND, OR	1395	2647	2830	889	2599	1301	432	3126	2667	3052	2948	2610	2802	1166	2137	2398	2469	2140	1261	1798	2405	1767	2381	2280	2544	1805	1188	2237	971	2362	2382	3312	2063	1727	2963	2405	2663	2920	1934	1662	3091	2890	1335	2590	3223		1268	578	2925	2057	771	2322	1093	638	170	3106	2633	313	2824	1775
RAPID CITY, SD	841	1511	1626	379	1463	320	930	1921	1463	1848	1824	1422	1678	305	913	1219	1264	1077	404	629	1201	1105	1318	1101	1458	710	1035	1093	1309	1215	1247	2176	842	606	1758	1269	1643	1716	871	525	1955	1686	1308	1386	2019	1268		1151	1720	963	628	1335	1372	1368	1195	1970	1429	1328	1620	712
RENO, NV	1020	2440	2623	960	2392	1372	430	2919	2460	2845	2741	2403	2595	959	1930	2191	2262	1933	1054	1591	2198	1315	2072	2073	2337	1598	442	2030	519	2155	2175	3105	1970	1839	2756	2198	2431	2713	1727	1455	2884	2683	883	2383	3016	578	1151		2718	1850	524	1870	642	217	755	2899	2426	898	2617	1568
RICHMOND, VA	1876	527	152	2053	678	1645	2496	572	485	630	428	322	289	1760	802	530	471	1309	1688	1126	627	1955	1330	641	914	1085	2444	983	2682	572	843	954	899	1216	714	626	1002	342	1331	1263	750	254	2343	341	670	2925	1720	2718		834	2194	1530	2684	2934	2869	805	660	3003	108	1274
ST. LOUIS, MO	1051	549	841	1341	501	1053	1628	1181	749	1119	850	512	704	892	294	350	560	635	855	436	549	1242	863	239	505	252	1610	416	1856	264	294	1214	367	621	1112	307	690	956	505	440	993	895	1517	611	1279	2057	963	1850	834		1326	968	1875	2066	2125	1008	782	2259	837	441
SALT LAKE CITY, UT	624	1916	2100	548	1868	960	342	2395	1936	2322	2218	1880	2072	436	1406	1667	1738	1410	531	1067	1675	864	1650	1549	1813	1074	417	1507	691	1631	1652	2581	1446	1315	2232	1675	1932	2189	1204	932	2360	2160	651	1859	2493	771	628	524	2194	1326		1419	754	740	839	2375	1902	973	2094	1044
SAN ANTONIO, TX	818	1000	1671	1500	878	1599	1761	2092	1665	2036	1310	1344	1241	1046	1270	1231	1481	271	946	1009	1490	556	200	1186	644	812	1272	600	1356	1125	739	1401	1343	1257	2043	954	560	1861	466	927	1180	1774	987	1519	2189	2322	1335	1870	1530	968	1419		1285	1737	2275	1195	1714	2410	1635	624
SAN DIEGO, CA	825	2166	2724	1302	2021	1765	1096	3065	2632	3020	2483	2393	2405	1179	2105	2234	2437	1375	1092	1766	2373	730	1487	2122	1780	1695	337	1703	124	2144	1841	2688	2145	2014	2931	2056	1846	2839	1370	1630	2467	2779	358	2494	3162	1093	1372	642	2684	1875	754	1285		508	1271	2481	2601	1414	2720	1531
SAN FRANCISCO, CA	1111	2618	2840	1176	2472	1749	646	3135	2677	3062	2934	2620	2759	1176	2146	2407	2478	1827	1271	1807	2415	1181	1938	2290	2232	1814	575	2012	385	2372	2144	3140	2186	2055	2972	2360	2298	2929	1657	1672	2918	2900	750	2599	3233	638	1368	217	2934	2066	740	1737	508		816	2933	2643	958	2834	1784
SEATTLE, WA	1463	2705	2775	816	2657	1229	500	3070	2612	2997	2973	2571	2827	1234	2062	2368	2413	2208	1329	1822	2350	1944	2449	2249	2612	1872	1256	2305	1148	2364	2440	3370	1991	1654	2907	2463	2731	2864	2002	1719	3149	2835	1513	2534	3168	170	1195	755	2869	2125	839	2275	1271	816		3164	2577	140	2769	1843
TAMPA, FL	1949	455	960	2348	606	2018	2677	1380	1276	1438	434	845	581	1941	1176	935	1101	1161	1862	1426	1194	1753	995	990	709	1259	2526	984	2553	878	845	274	1272	1588	1522	701	668	1150	1403	1448	82	1062	2184	1019	1478	3106	1970	2899	805	1008	2375	1195	2481	2933	3164		1383	3297	916	1448
TORONTO, ON	1841	958	565	1762	958	1354	2204	570	106	419	1006	537	802	1468	510	484	303	1441	1512	834	233	2032	1561	541	1183	1028	2265	1115	2538	589	975	1532	607	924	330	764	1302	507	1295	971	1327	522	2307	321	668	2633	1429	2426	660	782	1902	1714	2601	2643	2577	1383		2711	563	1217
VANCOUVER, BC	1597	2838	2908	949	2791	1362	633	3204	2745	3130	3106	2705	2960	1368	2196	2501	2547	2342	1463	1956	2483	2087	2583	2383	2746	2007	1390	2439	1291	2497	2574	3504	2124	1788	3041	2597	2865	2998	2136	1853	3283	2968	1655	2668	3301	313	1328	898	3003	2259	973	2410	1414	958	140	3297	2711		2902	1977
WASHINGTON, DC	1896	636	38	1953	758	1545	2395	458	384	517	539	346	397	1659	701	517	370	1362	1686	1025	526	2008	1433	596	996	1083	2441	1036	2702	596	896	1065	799	1115	600	679	1106	228	1350	1162	860	140	2362	240	556	2824	1620	2617	108	837	2094	1635	2720	2834	2769	916	563	2902		1272
WICHITA, KS	707	989	1276	1067	838	934	1346	1616	1184	1554	1291	953	1145	613	728	785	995	367	521	390	984	898	608	674	771	192	1276	464	1513	705	597	1655	769	637	1547	748	890	1391	161	307	1434	1330	1173	1046	1714	1775	712	1568	1274	441	1044	624	1531	1784	1843	1448	1217	1977	1272	

A Word to Our Readers

Travelers are on the roads in great numbers these days. They're exploring the country on day trips, weekend getaways, business trips, and extended family vacations, visiting major cities and small towns along the way. Because time is precious and the travel industry is ever-changing, having accurate, reliable travel information at your fingertips is critical. Mobil Travel Guide has been providing invaluable insight to travelers for more than 45 years, and we are committed to continuing this service well into the future.

The Mobil Corporation (known as Exxon Mobil Corporation since a 1999 merger) began producing the Mobil Travel Guide books in 1958, following the introduction of the US interstate highway system in 1956. The first edition covered only five Southwestern states. Since then, our books have become the premier travel guides in North America, covering all 50 states and Canada.

Since its founding, Mobil Travel Guide has served as an advocate for travelers seeking knowledge about hotels, restaurants, and places to visit. Based on an objective process, we make recommendations to our customers that we believe will enhance the quality and value of their travel experiences. Our trusted Mobil One- to Five-Star rating system is the oldest and most respected lodging and restaurant inspection and rating program in North America. Most hoteliers, restaurateurs, and industry observers favorably regard the rigor of our inspection program and understand the prestige and benefits that come with receiving a Mobil Star rating.

The Mobil Travel Guide process of rating each establishment includes:

- Unannounced facility inspections
- Incognito service evaluations for Mobil Four-Star and Mobil Five-Star properties
- A review of unsolicited comments from the general public
- Senior management oversight

For each property, more than 450 attributes, including cleanliness, physical facilities, and employee attitude and courtesy, are measured and evaluated to produce a mathematically derived score, which is then blended with the other elements to form an overall score. These quantifiable scores allow comparative analysis among properties and form the basis that we use to assign our Mobil One- to Five-Star ratings.

This process focuses largely on guest expectations, guest experience, and consistency of service, not just physical facilities and amenities. It is fundamentally a relative rating system that rewards those properties that continually strive for and achieve excellence each year. Indeed, the very best properties are consistently raising the bar for those that wish to compete with them. These properties proactively respond to consumers' needs even in today's uncertain times.

Only facilities that meet Mobil Travel Guide's standards earn the privilege of being listed in the guide. Deteriorating, poorly managed establishments are deleted. A Mobil Travel Guide listing constitutes a positive quality recommendation; every listing is an accolade, a recognition of achievement. Our Mobil One- to Five-Star rating system highlights its level of service. Extensive in-house research is constantly underway to determine new additions to our lists.

- The Mobil Five-Star Award indicates that a property is one of the very best in the country and consistently provides gracious and courteous service, superlative quality in its facility, and a unique ambience. The lodgings and restaurants at the Mobil Five-Star level consistently and proactively respond to consumers' needs and continue their commitment to excellence, doing so with grace and perseverance.
- Also highly regarded is the Mobil Four-Star Award, which honors properties for outstanding achievement in overall facility and for providing very strong service levels in all areas. These

award winners provide a distinctive experience for the ever-demanding and sophisticated consumer.

- The Mobil Three-Star Award recognizes an excellent property that provides full services and amenities. This category ranges from exceptional hotels with limited services to elegant restaurants with a less-formal atmosphere.
- A Mobil Two-Star property is a clean and comfortable establishment that has expanded amenities or a distinctive environment. A Mobil Two-Star property is an excellent place to stay or dine.
- A Mobil One-Star property is limited in its amenities and services but focuses on providing a value experience while meeting travelers' expectations. The property can be expected to be clean, comfortable, and convenient.

Allow us to emphasize that we do not charge establishments for inclusion in our guides. We have no relationship with any of the businesses and attractions we list and act only as a consumer advocate. In essence, we do the investigative legwork so that you won't have to.

Keep in mind, too, that the hospitality business is ever-changing. Restaurants and lodgings—particularly small chains and stand-alone establishments—change management or even go out of business with surprising quickness. Although we make every effort to double-check information during our annual updates, we nevertheless recommend that you call ahead to make sure the place you've selected is still open and offers all the amenities you're looking for. We've provided phone numbers; when available, we also list fax numbers and Web site addresses.

We hope that your travels are enjoyable and relaxing and that our books help you get the most out of every trip you take. If any aspect of your accommodation, dining, or sightseeing experience motivates you to comment, please drop us a line. We depend a great deal on our readers' remarks, so you can be assured that we will read your comments and assimilate them into our research. General comments about our books are also welcome. You can write to us at Mobil Travel Guide, 7373 N Cicero Ave, Lincolnwood, IL 60712, or send an e-mail to info@mobiltravelguide.com.

Take your Mobil Travel Guide books along on every trip you take. We're confident that you'll be pleased with their convenience, ease of use, and breadth of dependable coverage.

Happy travels!

How to Use This Book

The Mobil Travel Guide Regional Travel Planners are designed for ease of use. Each state has its own chapter, beginning with a general introduction that provides a geographical and historical orientation to the state and gives basic statewide tourist information, from climate to calendar highlights to seatbelt laws. The remainder of each chapter is devoted to travel destinations within the state—mainly cities and towns, but also national parks and tourist areas—which, like the states, are arranged in alphabetical order.

The following sections explain the wealth of information you'll find about those travel destinations: information about the area, things to see and do there, and where to stay and eat.

Maps and Map Coordinates

At the front of this book in the full-color section, we have provided state maps as well as maps of selected larger cities to help you find your way around once you leave the highway. You'll find a key to the map symbols on the Contents page at the beginning of the map section.

Next to most cities and towns throughout the book, you'll find a set of map coordinates, such as C-2. These coordinates reference the maps at the front of this book and help you find the location you're looking for quickly and easily.

Destination Information

Because many travel destinations are close to other cities and towns where travelers might find additional attractions, accommodations, and restaurants, we've included cross-references to those cities and towns when it makes sense to do so. We also list addresses, phone numbers, and Web sites for travel information resources—usually the local chamber of commerce or office of tourism—as well as pertinent statistics and, in many cases, a brief introduction to the area. Information about airports, ground transportation, and suburbs is included for large cities.

Driving Tours and Walking Tours

The driving tours that we include for many states are usually day trips that make for interesting side excursions, although they can be longer. They offer you a way to get off the beaten path and visit an area that travelers often overlook. These trips frequently cover areas of natural beauty or historical significance.

Each walking tour focuses on a particularly interesting area of a city or town. Again, these tours can provide a break from everyday tourist attractions. The tours often include places to stop for meals or snacks.

What to See and Do

Mobil Travel Guide offers information about nearly 20,000 museums, art galleries, amusement parks, historic sites, national and state parks, ski areas, and many other types of attractions. A white star on a black background ★ signals that the attraction is a must-see—one of the best in the area. Because municipal parks, public tennis courts, swimming pools, and small educational institutions are common to most towns, they generally are not mentioned.

Following an attraction's description, you'll find the months, days, and, in some cases, hours of operation; the address/directions, telephone number, and Web site (if there is one); and the admission price category. The following are the ranges we use for admission fees, based on one adult:

- **FREE**
- **$** = Up to $5
- **$$** = $5.01-$10
- **$$$** = $10.01-$15
- **$$$$** = Over $15

Special Events

Special events are either annual events that last only a short time, such as festivals and fairs, or longer, seasonal events such as horse racing, theater, and summer concerts. Our Special Events listings also include infrequently occurring occasions that mark certain dates or events, such as a centennial or other commemorative celebration.

Listings

Lodgings, spas, and restaurants are usually listed under the city or town in which they're located. Make sure to check the related cities and towns that appear right beneath a city's heading for additional options, especially if you're traveling to a major metropolitan area that includes many suburbs. If a property is located in a town that doesn't have its own heading, the listing appears under the town nearest it, with the address and town given immediately after the establishment's name. In large cities, lodgings located within 5 miles of major commercial airports may be listed under a separate "Airport Area" heading that follows the city section.

LODGINGS

Travelers have different wants and needs when it comes to accommodations. To help you pinpoint properties that meet your particular needs, Mobil Travel Guide classifies each lodging by type according to the following characteristics.

Mobil Rated Lodgings

- **Limited-Service Hotel.** A limited-service hotel is traditionally a Mobil One-Star or Mobil Two-Star property. At a Mobil One-Star hotel, guests can expect to find a clean, comfortable property that commonly serves a complimentary continental breakfast. A Mobil Two-Star hotel is also clean and comfortable but has expanded amenities, such as a full-service restaurant, business center, and fitness center. These services may have limited staffing and/or restricted hours of use.
- **Full-Service Hotel.** A full-service hotel traditionally enjoys a Mobil Three-Star, Mobil Four-Star, or Mobil Five-Star rating. Guests can expect these hotels to offer at least one full-service restaurant in addition to amenities such as valet parking, luggage assistance, 24-hour room service, concierge service, laundry and/or dry-cleaning services, and turndown service.
- **Full-Service Resort.** A resort is traditionally a full-service hotel that is geared toward recreation and represents a vacation and holiday destination. A resort's guest rooms are typically furnished to accommodate longer stays. The property may offer a full-service spa, golf, tennis, and fitness facilities or other leisure activities. Resorts are expected to offer a full-service restaurant and expanded amenities, such as luggage assistance, room service, meal plans, concierge service, and turndown service.
- **Full-Service Inn.** An inn is traditionally a Mobil Three-Star, Mobil Four-Star, or Mobil Five-Star property. Inns are similar to bed-and-breakfasts (see below) but offer a wider range of services, most significantly a full-service restaurant that serves at least breakfast and dinner.

Specialty Lodgings

Mobil Travel Guide recognizes the unique and individualized nature of many different types of lodging establishments, including bed-and-breakfasts, limited-service inns, and guest ranches. For that reason, we have chosen to place our stamp of approval on the properties that fall into these two categories in lieu of applying our traditional Mobil Star ratings.

- **B&B/Limited-Service Inn.** A bed-and-breakfast (B&B) or limited-service inn is traditionally an owner-occupied home or residence found in a residential area or vacation destination. It may be a structure of historic significance. Rooms are often individually decorated, but telephones, televisions, and private bathrooms may not be available in every room. A B&B typically serves only breakfast to its overnight guests, which is included in the room rate. Cocktails and refreshments may be served in the late afternoon or evening.
- **Guest Ranch.** A guest ranch is traditionally a rustic, Western-themed property that specializes in stays of three or more days. Horseback riding is often a feature, with stables and trails found on the property. Facilities can range from clean, comfortable establishments to more luxurious facilities.

Mobil Star Rating Definitions for Lodgings

- ★★★★★ : A Mobil Five-Star lodging provides consistently superlative service in an exceptionally distinctive luxury environment, with expanded services. Attention to detail is evident

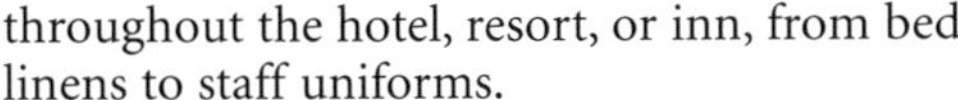

throughout the hotel, resort, or inn, from bed linens to staff uniforms.

- ★★★★ : A Mobil Four-Star lodging provides a luxury experience with expanded amenities in a distinctive environment. Services may include, but are not limited to, automatic turndown service, 24-hour room service, and valet parking.
- ★★★ : A Mobil Three-Star lodging is well appointed, with a full-service restaurant and expanded amenities, such as a fitness center, golf course, tennis courts, 24-hour room service, and optional turndown service.
- ★★ : A Mobil Two-Star lodging is considered a clean, comfortable, and reliable establishment that has expanded amenities, such as a full-service restaurant on the premises.
- ★ : A Mobil One-Star lodging is a limited-service hotel, motel, or inn that is considered a clean, comfortable, and reliable establishment.

Information Found in the Lodging Listings

Each lodging listing gives the name, address/location (when no street address is available), neighborhood and/or directions from downtown (in major cities), phone number(s), fax number, total number of guest rooms, and seasons open (if not year-round). Also included are details on business, luxury, recreational, and dining facilities at the property or nearby. A key to the symbols at the end of each listing can be found on the page following the "A Word to Our Readers" section.

For every property, we also provide pricing information. Because lodging rates change frequently, we list a pricing category rather than specific prices. The pricing categories break down as follows:

- **$** = Up to $150
- **$$** = $151-$250
- **$$$** = $251-$350
- **$$$$** = $351 and up

All prices quoted are in effect at the time of publication; however, prices cannot be guaranteed. In some locations, short-term price variations may exist because of special events, holidays, or seasonality. Certain resorts have complicated rate structures that vary with the time of year; always confirm rates when making your plans.

Because most lodgings offer the following features and services, information about them does not appear in the listings:

- Year-round operation
- Bathroom with tub and/or shower in each room
- Cable television in each room
- In-room telephones
- Cots and cribs available
- Daily maid service
- Elevators
- Major credit cards accepted

SPAS

Mobil Travel Guide is pleased to announce its newest category: hotel and resort spas. Until now, hotel and resort spas have not been formally rated or inspected by any organization. Every spa selected for inclusion in this book underwent a rigorous inspection process similar to the one Mobil Travel Guide has been applying to lodgings and restaurants for more than four decades. After spending a year and a half researching more than 300 spas and performing exhaustive incognito inspections of more than 200 properties, we narrowed our list to the 48 best spas in the United States and Canada.

Mobil Travel Guide's spa ratings are based on objective evaluations of more than 450 attributes. Approximately half of these criteria assess basic expectations, such as staff courtesy, the technical proficiency and skill of the employees, and whether the facility is maintained properly and hygienically. Several standards address issues that impact a guest's physical comfort and convenience, as well as the staff's ability to impart a sense of personalized service and anticipate clients' needs. Additional criteria measure the spa's ability to create a completely calming ambience.

The Mobil Star ratings focus on much more than the facilities available at a spa and the treatments it offers. Each Mobil Star rating is a cumulative score achieved from multiple inspections that reflects the spa management's attention to detail and commitment to consumers' needs.

Mobil Star Rating Definitions for Spas

- ★★★★★ : A Mobil Five-Star spa provides consistently superlative service in an exceptionally distinctive luxury environment with extensive amenities. The staff at a Mobil Five-Star spa provides extraordinary service above and beyond the traditional spa experience, allowing guests to achieve the highest level of relaxation and pampering. A Mobil Five-Star spa offers an extensive array of treatments, often incorporating international themes and products. Attention to detail is evident throughout the spa, from arrival to departure.
- ★★★★ : A Mobil Four-Star spa provides a luxurious experience with expanded amenities in an elegant and serene environment. Throughout the spa facility, guests experience personalized service. Amenities might include, but are not limited to, single-sex relaxation rooms where guests wait for their treatments, plunge pools and whirlpools in both men's and women's locker rooms, and an array of treatments, including at a minimum a selection of massages, body therapies, facials, and a variety of salon services.
- ★★★ : A Mobil Three-Star spa is physically well appointed and has a full complement of staff to ensure that guests' needs are met. It has some expanded amenities, such as, but not limited to, a well-equipped fitness center, separate men's and women's locker rooms, a sauna or steam room, and a designated relaxation area. It also offers a menu of services that at a minimum includes massages, facial treatments, and at least one other type of body treatment, such as scrubs or wraps.

RESTAURANTS

All Mobil Star rated dining establishments listed in this book have a full kitchen and offer seating at tables; most offer table service.

Mobil Star Rating Definitions for Restaurants

- ★★★★★ : A Mobil Five-Star restaurant offers one of few flawless dining experiences in the country. These establishments consistently provide their guests with exceptional food, superlative service, elegant décor, and exquisite presentations of each detail surrounding a meal.
- ★★★★ : A Mobil Four-Star restaurant provides professional service, distinctive presentations, and wonderful food.
- ★★★ : A Mobil Three-Star restaurant has good food, warm and skillful service, and enjoyable décor.
- ★★ : A Mobil Two-Star restaurant serves fresh food in a clean setting with efficient service. Value is considered in this category, as is family friendliness.
- ★ : A Mobil One-Star restaurant provides a distinctive experience through culinary specialty, local flair, or individual atmosphere.

Information Found in the Restaurant Listings

Each restaurant listing gives the cuisine type, street address (or directions if no address is available), phone and fax numbers, Web site (if available), meals served, days of operation (if not open daily year-round), and pricing category. Information about appropriate attire is provided, although it's always a good idea to call ahead and ask if you're unsure; the meaning of "casual" or "business casual" varies widely in different parts of the country. We also indicate whether the restaurant has a bar, whether a children's menu is offered, and whether outdoor seating is available. If reservations are recommended, we note that fact in the listing. When valet parking is available, it is noted in the description. In many cases, self-parking is available at the restaurant or nearby.

Because menu prices can fluctuate, we list a pricing category rather than specific prices. The pricing categories are defined as follows, per diner, and assume that you order an appetizer or dessert, an entrée, and one drink:

- **$** = $15 and under
- **$$** = $16-$35
- **$$$** = $36-$85
- **$$$$** = $86 and up

Again, all prices quoted are in effect at the time of publication, but prices cannot be guaranteed.

SPECIAL INFORMATION FOR TRAVELERS WITH DISABILITIES

The Mobil Travel Guide 🄳 symbol indicates that an establishment is not at least partially accessible to people with mobility problems. When the 🄳 symbol follows a listing, the establishment is not equipped with facilities to accommodate people using wheelchairs or crutches or otherwise needing easy access to doorways and rest rooms. Travelers with severe mobility problems or with hearing or visual impairments may or may not find the facilities they need. Always phone ahead to make sure hat an establishment can meet your needs.

Understanding the Symbols

What to See and Do

★	=	One of the top attractions in the area
$	=	Up to $5
$$	=	$5.01 to $10
$$$	=	$10.01 to $15
$$$$	=	Over $15

Lodgings

$	=	Up to $150
$$	=	$151 to $250
$$$	=	$251 to $350
$$$$	=	Over $350

Restaurants

$	=	Up to $15
$$	=	$16 to $35
$$$	=	$36 to $85
$$$$	=	Over $85

Lodging Star Definitions

★★★★★ A Mobil Five-Star lodging establishment provides consistently superlative service in an exceptionally distinctive luxury environment with expanded services. Attention to detail is evident throughout the hotel/resort/inn from the bed linens to the staff uniforms.

★★★★ A Mobil Four-Star lodging establishment is a hotel/resort/inn that provides a luxury experience with expanded amenities in a distinctive environment. Services may include, but are not limited to, automatic turndown service, 24-hour room service, and valet parking.

★★★ A Mobil Three-Star lodging establishment is a hotel/resort/inn that is well appointed, with a full-service restaurant and expanded amenities, such as, but not limited to, a fitness center, golf course, tennis courts, 24-hour room service, and optional turndown service.

★★ A Mobil Two-Star lodging establishment is a hotel/resort/inn that is considered a clean, comfortable, and reliable establishment, but also has expanded amenities, such as a full-service restaurant on the premises.

★ A Mobil One-Star lodging establishment is a limited-service hotel or inn that is considered a clean, comfortable, and reliable establishment.

Restaurant Star Definitions

★★★★★ A Mobil Five-Star restaurant is one of few flawless dining experiences in the country. These restaurants consistently provide their guests with exceptional food, superlative service, elegant décor, and exquisite presentations of each detail surrounding the meal.

★★★★ A Mobil Four-Star restaurant provides professional service, distinctive presentations, and wonderful food.

★★★ A Mobil Three-Star restaurant has good food, warm and skillful service, and enjoyable décor.

★★ A Mobil Two-Star restaurant serves fresh food in a clean setting with efficient service. Value is considered in this category, as is family friendliness.

★ A Mobil One-Star restaurant provides a distinctive experience through culinary specialty, local flair, or individual atmosphere.

Symbols at End of Listings

- Facilities for people with disabilities not available
- Pets allowed
- Ski in/ski out access
- Golf on premises
- Tennis court(s) on premises
- Indoor or outdoor pool
- Fitness room
- Major commercial airport within 5 miles
- Business center

Making the Most of Your Trip

A few hardy souls might look back with fondness on a trip during which the car broke down, leaving them stranded for three days, or a vacation that cost twice what it was supposed to. For most travelers, though, the best trips are those that are safe, smooth, and within budget. To help you make your trip the best it can be, we've assembled a few tips and resources.

Saving Money

ON LODGING

Many hotels and motels offer discounts—for senior citizens, business travelers, families, you name it. It never hurts to ask—politely, that is. Sometimes, especially in the late afternoon, desk clerks are instructed to fill beds, and you might be offered a lower rate or a nicer room to entice you to stay. Simply ask the reservation agent for the best rate available. Also, make sure to try both the toll-free number and the local number. You may be able to get a lower rate from one than from the other.

Timing your trip right can cut your lodging costs as well. Look for bargains on stays over multiple nights, in the off-season, and on weekdays or weekends, depending on the location. Many hotels in major metropolitan areas, for example, have special weekend packages that offer leisure travelers considerable savings on rooms; they may include breakfast, cocktails, and/or dinner discounts.

Another way to save money is to choose accommodations that give you more than just a standard room. Rooms with kitchen facilities enable you to cook some meals yourself, reducing your restaurant costs. A suite might save money for two couples traveling together. Even hotel luxury levels can provide good value, as many include breakfast or cocktails in the price of a room.

State and city taxes, as well as special room taxes, can increase your room rate by as much as 25 percent per day. We are unable to include information about taxes in our listings, but we strongly urge you to ask about taxes when making reservations so that you understand the total cost of your lodgings before you book them.

Watch out for telephone-usage charges that hotels frequently impose on long-distance, credit-card, and other calls. Before phoning from your room, read the information given to you at check-in, and then be sure to review your bill carefully when checking out. You won't be expected to pay for charges that the hotel didn't spell out. Consider using your cell phone if you have one; or, if public telephones are available in the hotel lobby, your cost savings may outweigh the inconvenience of using them.

Here are some additional ways to save on lodgings:

- Stay in B&B accommodations. They're generally less expensive than standard hotel rooms, and the complimentary breakfast cuts down on food costs.
- If you're traveling with children, find lodgings at which kids stay free.
- When visiting a major city, stay just outside the city limits; these rooms are usually less expensive than those in downtown locations.
- Consider visiting national parks during the low season, when prices of lodgings near the parks drop by 25 percent or more.
- When calling a hotel, ask whether it is running any special promotions or if any discounts are available; many times reservationists are told not to volunteer these deals unless they're specifically asked about them.
- Check for hotel packages; some offer nightly rates that include a rental car or discounts on major attractions.

ON DINING

There are several ways to get a less expensive meal at an expensive restaurant. Early-bird dinners are popular in many parts of the country and offer considerable savings. If you're interested in visiting a Mobil Four- or Five-Star establishment, consider going at lunchtime. Although the prices are probably still relatively high at midday, they may be half of those at dinner, and you'll experience the same ambience, service, and cuisine.

ON ENTERTAINMENT

Although many national parks, monuments, seashores, historic sites, and recreation areas may be visited free of charge, others charge an entrance fee and/or a usage fee for special services and facilities. If you plan to make several visits to national recreation areas, consider one of the following money-saving programs offered by the National Park Service:

- **National Parks Pass.** This annual pass is good for entrance to any national park that charges an entrance fee. If the park charges a per-vehicle fee, the pass holder and any accompanying passengers in a private noncommercial vehicle may enter. If the park charges a per-person fee, the pass applies to the holder's spouse, children, and parents as well as the holder. It is valid for entrance fees only; it does not cover parking, camping, or other fees. You can purchase a National Parks Pass in person at any national park where an entrance fee is charged; by mail from the National Park Foundation, PO Box 34108, Washington, DC 20043-4108; by calling toll-free 888/467-2757; or at www.nationalparks.org. The cost is $50.
- **Golden Eagle Sticker.** When affixed to a National Parks Pass, this hologram sticker, available to people who are between 17 and 61 years of age, extends coverage to sites managed by the US Fish and Wildlife Service, the US Forest Service, and the Bureau of Land Management. It is good until the National Parks Pass to which it is affixed expires and does not cover usage fees. You can purchase one at the National Park Service, the Fish and Wildlife Service, or the Bureau of Land Management fee stations. The cost is $15.
- **Golden Age Passport.** Available to citizens and permanent US residents 62 and older, this passport is a lifetime entrance permit to fee-charging national recreation areas. The fee exemption extends to those accompanying the permit holder in a private noncommercial vehicle or, in the case of walk-in facilities, to the holder's spouse and children. The passport also entitles the holder to a 50 percent discount on federal usage fees charged in park areas, but not on concessions. Golden Age Passports must be obtained in person and are available at most National Park Service units that charge an entrance fee. The applicant must show proof of age, such as a driver's license or birth certificate (Medicare cards are not acceptable proof). The cost is $10.
- **Golden Access Passport.** Issued to citizens and permanent US residents who are physically disabled or visually impaired, this passport is a free lifetime entrance permit to fee-charging national recreation areas. The fee exemption extends to those accompanying the permit holder in a private noncommercial vehicle or, in the case of walk-in facilities, to the holder's spouse and children. The passport also entitles the holder to a 50 percent discount on usage fees charged in park areas, but not on concessions. Golden Access Passports must be obtained in person and are available at most National Park Service units that charge an entrance fee. Proof of eligibility to receive federal benefits (under programs such as Disability Retirement, Compensation for Military Service-Connected Disability, and the Coal Mine Safety and Health Act) is required, or an affidavit must be signed attesting to eligibility.

A money-saving move in several large cities is to purchase a **CityPass.** If you plan to visit several museums and other major attractions, CityPass is a terrific option because it gets you into several sites for one substantially reduced price. Currently, CityPass is available in Boston, Chicago, Hollywood, New York, Philadelphia, San Francisco, Seattle, southern California (which includes Disneyland, SeaWorld, and the San Diego Zoo), and Toronto. For more information or to buy one, call toll-free 888/330-5008 or visit www.citypass.net. You can also buy a CityPass from any participating CityPass attraction.

Here are some additional ways to save on entertainment and shopping:

- Check with your hotel's concierge for various coupons and special offers; they often have two-for-one tickets for area attractions and coupons for discounts at area stores and restaurants.
- Purchase same-day concert or theater tickets for half-price through the local cheap-tickets outlet, such as TKTS in New York or Hot Tix in Chicago.

- Visit museums on their free or "by donation" days, when you can pay what you wish rather than a specific admission fee.
- Save receipts from purchases in Canada; visitors to Canada can get a rebate on federal taxes and some provincial sales taxes.

ON TRANSPORTATION

Transportation is a big part of any vacation budget. Here are some ways to reduce your costs:

- If you're renting a car, shop early over the Internet; you can book a car during the low season for less, even if you'll be using it in the high season.
- Rental car discounts are often available if you rent for one week or longer and reserve in advance.
- Get the best gas mileage out of your vehicle by making sure that it's properly tuned up and keeping your tires properly inflated.
- Travel at moderate speeds on the open road; higher speeds require more gasoline.
- Fill the tank before you return your rental car; rental companies charge to refill the tank and do so at prices of up to 50 percent more than at local gas stations.
- Make a checklist of travel essentials and purchase them before you leave; don't get stuck buying expensive sunscreen at your hotel or overpriced film at the airport.

FOR SENIOR CITIZENS

Always call ahead to ask if a discount is being offered, and be sure to carry proof of age. Additional information for mature travelers is available from the American Association of Retired Persons (AARP), 601 E St NW, Washington, DC 20049; phone 202/434-2277; www.aarp.org.

Tipping

Tips are expressions of appreciation for good service. However, you are never obligated to tip if you receive poor service.

IN HOTELS

- Door attendants usually get $1 for hailing a cab.
- Bell staff expect $2 per bag.
- Concierges are tipped according to the service they perform. Tipping is not mandatory when you've asked for suggestions on sightseeing or restaurants or for help in making dining reservations. However, a tip of $5 is appropriate when a concierge books you a table at a restaurant known to be difficult to get into. For obtaining theater or sporting event tickets, $5 to $10 is expected.
- Maids should be tipped $1 to $2 per day. Hand your tip directly to the maid, or leave it with a note saying that the money has been left expressly for the maid.

IN RESTAURANTS

Before tipping, carefully review your check for any gratuity or service charge that is already included in your bill. If you're in doubt, ask your server.

- Coffee shop and counter service waitstaff usually receive 15 percent of the bill, before sales tax.
- In full-service restaurants, tip 18 percent of the bill, before sales tax.
- In fine restaurants, where gratuities are shared among a larger staff, 18 to 20 percent is appropriate.
- In most cases, the maitre d' is tipped only if the service has been extraordinary, and only on the way out. At upscale properties in major metropolitan areas, $20 is the minimum.
- If there is a wine steward, tip $20 for exemplary service and beyond, or more if the wine was decanted or the bottle was very expensive.
- Tip $1 to $2 per coat at the coat check.

AT AIRPORTS

Curbside luggage handlers expect $1 per bag. Car-rental shuttle drivers who help with your luggage appreciate a $1 or $2 tip.

Staying Safe

The best way to deal with emergencies is to avoid them in the first place. However, unforeseen situations do happen, so you should be prepared for them.

IN YOUR CAR

Before you head out on a road trip, make sure that your car has been serviced and is in good working order. Change the oil, check the battery and belts, make sure that your windshield washer fluid is full and your tires are properly inflated (which can also improve your gas mileage). Other inspections recommended by the vehicle's manufacturer should also be made.

Next, be sure you have the tools and equipment needed to deal with a routine breakdown:

- Jack
- Spare tire
- Lug wrench
- Repair kit
- Emergency tools
- Jumper cables
- Spare fan belt
- Fuses
- Flares and/or reflectors
- Flashlight
- First-aid kit
- In winter, a windshield scraper and snow shovel

Many emergency supplies are sold in special packages that include the essentials you need to stay safe in the event of a breakdown.

Also bring all appropriate and up-to-date documentation—licenses, registration, and insurance cards—and know what your insurance covers. Bring an extra set of keys, too, just in case.

En route, always buckle up! In most states, wearing a seatbelt is required by law.

If your car does break down, do the following:

- Get out of traffic as soon as possible—pull well off the road.
- Raise the hood and turn on your emergency flashers or tie a white cloth to the roadside door handle or antenna.
- Stay in your car.
- Use flares or reflectors to keep your vehicle from being hit.

IN YOUR HOTEL

Chances are slim that you will encounter a hotel or motel fire, but you can protect yourself by doing the following:

- Once you've checked in, make sure that the smoke detector in your room is working properly.
- Find the property's fire safety instructions, usually posted on the inside of the room door.
- Locate the fire extinguishers and at least two fire exits.
- Never use an elevator in a fire.

For personal security, use the peephole in your room door and make sure that anyone claiming to be a hotel employee can show proper identification. Call the front desk if you feel threatened at any time.

PROTECTING AGAINST THEFT

To guard against theft wherever you go:

- Don't bring anything of more value than you need.
- If you do bring valuables, leave them at your hotel rather than in your car.
- If you bring something very expensive, lock it in a safe. Many hotels put one in each room; others will store your valuables in the hotel's safe.
- Don't carry more money than you need. Use traveler's checks and credit cards or visit cash machines to withdraw more cash when you run out.

For Travelers with Disabilities

To get the kind of service you need and have a right to expect, don't hesitate when making a reservation to question the management about the availability of accessible rooms, parking, entrances, restaurants, lounges, or any other facilities that are important to you, and confirm what is meant by "accessible."

The Mobil Travel Guide [D] symbol indicates establishments that are not at least partially accessible to people with special mobility needs (people using wheelchairs or crutches or otherwise needing easy access to buildings and rooms). Further information about these criteria can be found in the earlier section "How to Use This Book."

A thorough listing of published material for travelers with disabilities is available from the Disability Bookshop, Twin Peaks Press, Box 129, Vancouver, WA 98666; phone 360/694-2462; disabilitybookshop.virtualave.net. Another reliable organization is the Society for Accessible Travel & Hospitality (SATH), 347 Fifth Ave, Suite 610, New York, NY 10016; phone 212/447-7284; www.sath.org.

Important Toll-Free Numbers and Online Information

Hotels

Adams Mark 800/444-2326
www.adamsmark.com

America's Best Value Inn 888/315-2378
www.americasbestvalueinn.com

AmericInn 800/634-3444
www.americinn.com

AmeriHost Inn 800/434-5800
www.amerihostinn.com

Amerisuites 800/833-1516
www.amerisuites.com

Baymont Inns 800/621-1429
www.baymontinns.com

Best Inns & Suites 800/237-8466
www.bestinn.com

Best Western 800/780-7234
www.bestwestern.com

Budget Host Inn 800/283-4678
www.budgethost.com

Candlewood Suites 888/226-3539
www.candlewoodsuites.com

Clarion Hotels 800/252-7466
www.choicehotels.com

Comfort Inns and Suites 800/252-7466
www.comfortinn.com

Country Hearth Inns 800/848-5767
www.countryhearth.com

Country Inns & Suites 800/456-4000
www.countryinns.com

Courtyard by Marriott 800/321-2211
www.courtyard.com

Crowne Plaza Hotels and Resorts 800/227-6963
www.crowneplaza.com

Days Inn 800/544-8313
www.daysinn.com

Delta Hotels 800/268-1133
www.deltahotels.com

Destination Hotels & Resorts 800/434-7347
www.destinationhotels.com

Doubletree Hotels 800/222-8733
www.doubletree.com

Drury Inn 800/378-7946
www.druryhotels.com

Econolodge 800/553-2666
www.econolodge.com

Embassy Suites 800/362-2779
www.embassysuites.com

ExelInns of America 800/367-3935
www.exelinns.com

Extended StayAmerica 800/398-7829
www.extendedstayhotels.com

Fairfield Inn by Marriott 800/228-2800
www.fairfieldinn.com

Fairmont Hotels 800/441-1414
www.fairmont.com

Four Points by Sheraton 888/625-5144
www.fourpoints.com

Four Seasons 800/819-5053
www.fourseasons.com

Hampton Inn 800/426-7866
www.hamptoninn.com

Hard Rock Hotels, Resorts, and Casinos 800/473-7625
www.hardrockhotel.com

Harrah's Entertainment 800/427-7247
www.harrahs.com

Hawthorn Suites 800/527-1133
www.hawthorn.com

Hilton Hotels and Resorts (US) 800/774-1500
www.hilton.com

Holiday Inn Express 800/465-4329
www.hiexpress.com

Holiday Inn Hotels and Resorts 800/465-4329
www.holiday-inn.com

Homestead Studio Suites 888/782-9473
www.extendedstayhotels.com

Homewood Suites 800/225-5466
www.homewoodsuites.com

Howard Johnson 800/406-1411
www.hojo.com

Hyatt 800/633-7313
www.hyatt.com

Inns of America 800/826-0778
www.innsofamerica.com

InterContinental 888/424-6835
www.intercontinental.com

Joie de Vivre 800/738-7477
www.jdvhospitality.com

Kimpton Hotels 888/546-7866
www.kimptonhotels.com

Knights Inn 800/843-5644
www.knightsinn.com

La Quinta 800/531-5900
www.lq.com

Le Meridien. 800/543-4300
www.lemeridien.com
Leading Hotels of the World. 800/223-6800
www.lhw.com
Loews Hotels 800/235-6397
www.loewshotels.com
MainStay Suites 800/660-6246
www.mainstaysuites.com
Mandarin Oriental 800/526-6566
www.mandarinoriental.com
Marriott Hotels, Resorts, and Suites 800/228-9290
www.marriott.com
Microtel Inns & Suites 800/771-7171
www.microtelinn.com
Millennium & Copthorne Hotels 866/866-8086
www.millenniumhotels.com
Motel 6. . . . . .800/466-8356
www.motel6.com
Omni Hotels 800/843-6664
www.omnihotels.com
Pan Pacific Hotels and Resorts. 800/327-8585
www.panpacific.com
Park Inn & Park Plaza 888/201-1801
www.parkinn.com
The Peninsula Group . . . . Contact individual hotel
www.peninsula.com
Preferred Hotels & Resorts Worldwide. 800/323-7500
www.preferredhotels.com
Quality Inn. 800/228-5151
www.qualityinn.com
Radisson Hotels 800/333-3333
www.radisson.com
Raffles International Hotels and Resorts. 800/637-9477
www.raffles.com
Ramada Plazas, Limiteds, and Inns. 800/272-6232
www.ramada.com
Red Lion Inns. 800/733-5466
www.redlion.com
Red Roof Inns. 800/733-7663
www.redroof.com
Regent International 800/545-4000
www.regenthotels.com
Relais & Chateaux 800/735-2478
www.relaischateaux.com
Renaissance Hotels 888/236-2427
www.renaissancehotels.com
Residence Inn 800/331-3131
www.residenceinn.com
Ritz-Carlton. 800/241-3333
www.ritzcarlton.com
RockResorts. 888/367-7625
www.rockresorts.com
Rodeway Inn. 800/228-2000
www.rodeway.com
Rosewood Hotels & Resorts. 888/767-3966
www.rosewoodhotels.com
Select Inn 800/641-1000
www.selectinn.com
Sheraton 888/625-5144
www.sheraton.com
Shilo Inns 800/222-2244
www.shiloinns.com
Shoney's Inn. 800/552-4667
www.shoneysinn.com
Signature/Jameson Inns. .800/822-5252
www.jamesoninns.com
Sleep Inn. 877/424-6423
www.sleepinn.com
Small Luxury Hotels of the World. 800/525-4800
www.slh.com
Sofitel. 800/763-4835
www.sofitel.com
SpringHill Suites 888/236-2427
www.springhillsuites.com
St. Regis Luxury Collection. 888/625-5144
www.stregis.com
Staybridge Suites. 800/238-8000
www.staybridge.com
Summit International 800/457-4000
www.summithotelsandresorts.com
Super 8 Motels 800/800-8000
www.super8.com
The Sutton Place Hotels. 866/378-8866
www.suttonplace.com
Swissôtel. 800/637-9477
www.swissotels.com
TownePlace Suites. 888/236-2427
www.towneplace.com
Travelodge 800/578-7878
www.travelodge.com
Vagabond Inns. 800/522-1555
www.vagabondinn.com
W Hotels 888/625-5144
www.whotels.com
Wellesley Inn and Suites. 800/444-8888
www.wellesleyinnandsuites.com

WestCoast Hotels 800/325-4000
www.westcoasthotels.com
Westin Hotels & Resorts 800/937-8461
www.westinhotels.com
Wingate Inns 800/228-1000
www.thewingateinns.com
Woodfin Suite Hotels 800/966-3346
www.woodfinsuitehotels.com
WorldHotels 800/223-5652
www.worldhotels.com
Wyndham Hotels & Resorts 800/996-3426
www.wyndham.com

Airlines

Air Canada 888/247-2262
www.aircanada.com
AirTran 800/247-8726
www.airtran.com
Alaska Airlines 800/252-7522
www.alaskaair.com
American Airlines 800/433-7300
www.aa.com
ATA 800/435-9282
www.ata.com
Continental Airlines 800/523-3273
www.continental.com
Delta Air Lines 800/221-1212
www.delta.com
Frontier Airlines 800/432-1359
www.frontierairlines.com
Hawaiian Airlines 800/367-5320
www.hawaiianairlines.com
Jet Blue Airlines 800/538-2583
www.jetblue.com
Midwest Airlines 800/452-2022
www.midwestairlines.com
Northwest Airlines 800/225-2525
www.nwa.com
Southwest Airlines 800/435-9792
www.southwest.com
Spirit Airlines 800/772-7117
www.spiritair.com
United Airlines 800/241-6522
www.united.com
US Airways 800/428-4322
www.usairways.com

Car Rentals

Advantage 800/777-5500
www.arac.com
Alamo 800/327-9633
www.alamo.com
Avis 800/831-2847
www.avis.com
Budget 800/527-0700
www.budget.com
Dollar 800/800-4000
www.dollar.com
Enterprise 800/325-8007
www.enterprise.com
Hertz 800/654-3131
www.hertz.com
National 800/227-7368
www.nationalcar.com
Payless 800/729-5377
www.paylesscarrental.com
Rent-A-Wreck.com 800/535-1391
www.rentawreck.com
Thrifty 800/847-4389
www.thrifty.com

Mobil Travel Guide 2007 **Five-Star** Award Winners

CALIFORNIA

Lodgings

The Beverly Hills Hotel, *Beverly Hills*
Chateau du Sureau, *Oakhurst*
Four Seasons Hotel San Francisco, *San Francisco*
Hotel Bel-Air, *Los Angeles*
The Peninsula Beverly Hills, *Beverly Hills*
Raffles L'Ermitage Beverly Hills, *Beverly Hills*
St. Regis Monarch Beach Resort & Spa, *Dana Point*
St. Regis San Francisco, *San Francisco*
The Ritz-Carlton, San Francisco, *San Francisco*

Restaurants

The Dining Room, *San Francisco*
The French Laundry, *Yountville*

COLORADO

Lodgings

The Broadmoor, *Colorado Springs*
The Little Nell, *Aspen*

CONNECTICUT

Lodging

The Mayflower Inn, *Washington*

DISTRICT OF COLUMBIA

Lodging

Four Seasons Hotel Washington, DC *Washington*

FLORIDA

Lodgings

Four Seasons Resort Palm Beach, *Palm Beach*
The Ritz-Carlton Naples, *Naples*
The Ritz-Carlton, Palm Beach, *Manalapan*

GEORGIA

Lodgings

Four Seasons Hotel Atlanta, *Atlanta*
The Lodge at Sea Island Golf Club, *St. Simons Island*

Restaurants

The Dining Room, *Atlanta*
Seeger's, *Atlanta*

HAWAII

Lodging

Four Seasons Resort Maui, *Wailea, Maui*

ILLINOIS

Lodgings

Four Seasons Hotel Chicago, *Chicago*
The Peninsula Chicago, *Chicago*
The Ritz-Carlton, A Four Seasons Hotel, *Chicago*

Restaurants

Alinea, *Chicago*
Charlie Trotter's, *Chicago*

MAINE

Restaurant

The White Barn Inn, *Kennebunkport*

MASSACHUSETTS

Lodgings

Blantyre, *Lenox*
Four Seasons Hotel Boston, *Boston*

NEVADA

Lodging

Tower Suites at Wynn, *Las Vegas*

Restaurants

Alex, *Las Vegas*
Joel Robuchon at the Mansion, *Las Vegas*

NEW YORK

Lodgings

Four Seasons, Hotel New York, *New York*
Mandarin Oriental, *New York*
The Point, *Saranac Lake*
The Ritz-Carlton New York, Central Park, *New York*
The St. Regis, *New York*

Restaurants

Alain Ducasse, *New York*
Jean Georges, *New York*
Masa, *New York*
per se, *New York*

NORTH CAROLINA

Lodging

The Fearrington House Country Inn, *Pittsboro*

PENNSYLVANIA

Restaurant

Le Bec-Fin, *Philadelphia*

SOUTH CAROLINA

Lodging

Woodlands Resort & Inn, *Summerville*

Restaurant

Dining Room at the Woodlands, *Summerville*

TENNESSEE

Lodging

The Hermitage, *Nashville*

TEXAS

Lodging

The Mansion on Turtle Creek, *Dallas*

VERMONT

Lodging

Twin Farms, *Barnard*

VIRGINIA

Lodgings

The Inn at Little Washington, *Washington*
The Jefferson Hotel, *Richmond*

Restaurant

The Inn at Little Washington, *Washington*

Mobil Travel Guide has been rating establishments with its Mobil One- to Five-Star system since 1958. Each establishment awarded the Mobil Five-Star rating is one of the best in the country. Detailed information on each award winner can be found in the corresponding regional edition listed on the back cover of this book.

Four- and Five-Star Establishments in New York

★★★★★ Lodgings

Four Seasons Hotel New York, *New York*
Mandarin Oriental, New York, *New York*
The Point, *Saranac Lake*
The Ritz-Carlton New York, Central Park, *New York*
The St. Regis, *New York*

★★★★ Lodgings

The Carlyle, *New York*
The Lowell, *New York*
The Mercer, *New York*
The New York Palace, *New York*
The Peninsula New York, *New York*
The Pierre New York, A Taj Hotel, *New York*
The Ritz-Carlton New York, Battery Park, *New York*
Trump International Hotel & Tower, *New York*

★★★★★ Restaurants

Alain Ducasse, *New York*
Jean Georges, *New York*
Masa, *New York*
per se, *New York*

★★★★ Restaurants

Asiate, *New York*
Atelier, *New York*
Aureole, *New York*
Blue Hills at Stone Barns, *Pocantico Hills*
Bouley, *New York*
Daniel, *New York*
Danube, *New York*
Four Seasons Restaurant, *New York*
Gilt, *New York*
Gotham Bar & Grill, *New York*
Gramercy Tavern, *New York*
Kai, *New York*
La Grenouille, *New York*
Le Bernardin, *New York*
March, *New York*
Picholine, *New York*
Sugiyama, *New York*

★★★★★ Spa

Mandarin Oriental New York, *New York*

★★★★ Spas

The Peninsula Spa at the Peninsula New York, *New York*
The Spa at Emerson Place, Emerson Inn & Spa, *Mount Tremper*
Four Seasons Hotel New York Spa, *New York*

New York

When Giovanni da Verrazano entered New York Harbor in 1524, the Native Americans of the state were at constant war with one another. But around 1570, under Dekanawidah and Hiawatha, they formed the Iroquois Confederacy (the first League of Nations) and began to live in peace. They were known as the Five Nations and called themselves the "Men of Men."

In 1609, Samuel de Champlain explored the valley of the lake that bears his name, and Henry Hudson sailed up the river that bears his. There was a trading post at Fort Nassau (Albany) in 1614. New Amsterdam (now New York City) was founded in 1625.

Wars with the Native Americans and French kept the area in turmoil until after 1763. During the Revolution, New York's eastern part was a seesaw of military action and occupation. After the war, Washington was inaugurated president in 1789, and the seat of federal government was established in New York City. As late as 1825, much of New York's central area was swampy wilderness.

Governor DeWitt Clinton envisioned a canal extending from the Hudson River at Albany to Buffalo to develop the state and give needed aid to its western farmers. Started in 1817 and finished in 1825, the Erie Canal became the gateway to the West and was the greatest engineering work of its time, reducing the cost of freight between Buffalo and New York City from $100 to $5 a ton. Enlarged and rerouted, it is now part of the New York State Canal system, 527 miles used mainly for recreational boating.

Industry grew because water power was available; trade and farming grew because of the Erie Canal and its many branches. The state has given the nation four native-born presidents (Van Buren, Fillmore, and both Roosevelts) and two who built their careers here (Cleveland and Arthur).

In addition to being a delightful state in which to tour or vacation, New York has New York City, one of the great cosmopolitan centers of the world.

Population: 17,990,456
Area: 54,471 square miles
Elevation: 0-5,344 feet
Peak: Mount Marcy (Essex County)
Entered Union: Eleventh of original 13 states (July 26, 1788)
Capital: Albany
Motto: Ever upward
Nickname: Empire State
Flower: Rose
Bird: Bluebird
Tree: Sugar Maple
Fair: August-September in Syracuse
Time Zone: Eastern
Web Site: www.iloveny.state.ny.us

Fun Facts:

- The New York Stock Exchange began in 1792 when 24 brokers met under a buttonwood tree facing 68 Wall Street.
- New York was the first state to require license plates on automobiles.
- The first pizzeria in the country was opened in New York City in 1895 by Gennaro Lombardi.
- As late as the 1840s, thousands of pigs roamed Wall Street to consume garbage–an early sanitation system.
- Downtown Manhattan was the nation's first capital.

Calendar Highlights

MARCH

St. Patrick's Day Parade *(Manhattan). Along Fifth Ave.* New York's biggest parade; approximately 100,000 marchers.

April

Central New York Maple Festival *(Cortland). Phone 607/849-3812.* A variety of events demonstrate the process of making maple syrup; also arts and crafts, hay rides, and entertainment.

MAY

Tulip Festival *(Albany). Washington Park. Phone 518/434-2032.* Three-day event includes the crowning of the Tulip Queen, as well as arts, crafts, food, vendors, children's rides, and entertainment. Over 50,000 tulips throughout the park.

July

Rochester Music Fest *(Rochester). Brown Square Park. Phone 800/677-7282.* Three-day celebration of American music. Nationally and internationally known jazz, blues, country, and folk musicians.

Stone House Day *(Kingston). In Hurley. Phone 845/331-4121.* Tour of ten privately owned colonial stone houses led by costumed guides; old Hurley Reformed Church and burying ground; antique show; re-creation of American Revolution military encampment; and country fair.

AUGUST

America's Fair *(Buffalo). Phone 716/649-3900.* One of the oldest and largest fairs in the nation. Entertainment, rides, games, exhibits, agricultural and livestock shows.

New York State Fair *(Syracuse). State Fairgrounds. Phone 315/487-7711.* The only state fair in New York. Agricultural, animal, and commercial exhibits; midway concerts.

US Open *(Queens). Box office phone 718/760-6200. www.usopen.org.* One of the bigger tennis tournaments of the year.

SEPTEMBER

Adirondack Canoe Classic *(Saranac Lake). Phone Chamber of Commerce 518 /891-1990 or toll-free 800/347-1992.* Ninety-mile race from Old Forge to Saranac Lake for canoes, kayaks, and guideboats.

NOVEMBER

Macy's Thanksgiving Day Parade *(Manhattan). Down Broadway to 34th St, from W 77th St and Central Park W. Phone Macy's Special Events, 212/494-4495.* Floats, balloons, television and movie stars.

NYC Marathon *(Manhattan). Phone 212/423-2249. www.ingnycmarathon.com.* Major city marathon with more than 25,000 runners.

When to Go/Climate

New York State is large, and the weather is varied. The northern and western parts of the state experience more extreme temperaturescold, snowy winters and cool summers. Winters are long, especially near the Great Lakes. The Adirondacks, too, can have frigid winters, but fall foliage is magnificent, and summer temperatures and humidity are ideal. Spring thunderstorms frequently travel the Hudson River Valley, and summers here, as well as in New York City and its environs, are hot and humid.

AVERAGE HIGH/LOW TEMPERATURES (°F)

New York

Jan 38/25	**May** 72/54	**Sep** 76/60
Feb 40/27	**Jun** 80/63	**Oct** 65/50
Mar 50/35	**Jul** 85/68	**Nov** 54/41
Apr 61/44	**Aug** 84/67	**Dec** 43/31

Syracuse

Jan 31/14	**May** 68/46	**Sep** 72/51
Feb 33/15	**Jun** 77/54	**Oct** 60/41
Mar 43/25	**Jul** 82/59	**Nov** 48/33
Apr 56/36	**Aug** 79/58	**Dec** 32/21

Adirondack Park

From Albany, take Route 9 north to Glens Falls and Lake George Village. Described as "the most queenly of American lakes," Lake George is 44 square miles of deep blue water dotted with 225 islands; opportunities for water recreation abound in this vacation mecca. Fresh powder awaits winter travelers north on Route 28 at the Gore Mountain Ski Area in North Creek.

Farther north on Route 28 is Adirondack Park, which is bordered by Lake Champlain on the east, the Black River on the west, the St. Lawrence River on the north, and the Mohawk River valley on the south. At 6 million acres, Adirondack State Park is the largest US Park outside of Alaska (9,000 square miles). Six million acresthat's the size of New Jersey and Rhode Island combined. Just imagine the recreational opportunities availableyou could spend days here and not even scratch the surface of all there is to see and do. Whitewater raft on the Hudson, Moose, or Black rivers. Climb one of the 46 peaks in the Adirondack Range. Feeling adventurous? Have a go at Mount Marcy, also known as Cloud Splitter, which is the highest peak in the range at 5,344 feet. Not a climber? Try canoeing, fishing, or mountain biking instead.

Be sure to make time for a visit to Enchanted Forest/Water Safari (off Route 28 in Old Forge; phone 315/369-6145)especially if you are traveling with children. After all, there's no better place to spend a hot day than at New Yorks largest water theme park. Challenging adventure slides are sure to be a hit with older kids, while Tadpole Hole and Pygmy Pond keep the tots cool and happy. Enchanted Forest entertains with the Treetop Skyride and the Enchanted Forest Railroad, and Magical Escapades offers such distractions as bumper cars, a Ferris wheel, and tilt-a-whirl. If that's not enough excitement for one day, stop next door at Calypsos Cove where you will find miniature golf, go-karts, batting cages, bumper boats, and an arcade.

The next stop is Blue Mountain Lake. Take the 3-mile trail to the summit of Blue Mountain (3,800 feet) for spectacular views of Adirondack Park. Then head to the Adirondack Museum for a taste of Adirondack history and modes of life. Housed in 20 buildings on 30 acres, the museum also showcases one of the best boat collections in the world, including sail canoes, steamboats, and the famous Adirondack guide boat.

Head south on Route 28 back to Lake George. Take Route 9N to Bolton Landing and Ticonderoga, home of Fort Mt. Hope and Fort Ticonderoga (ca 1755). Head south on 22 to Whitehall, then follow the Champlain Canal and Hudson River down Route 4. Stop in Saratoga Springs to visit Saratoga National Historical Park, the National Museum of Racing and Hall of Fame, and Saratoga Spa State Park. Continue on Route 4 to return to Albany. **(Approximately 280 miles)**

Escape to Long Island

Long Island is a world unto itselfespecially off the Long Island Expressway. A mix of city sophistication and rural simplicity, Long Island is a playground for New Yorkers, who find the state parks, wildlife sanctuaries, and small towns refreshing. From New York City, take Southern Parkway 27 to Freeport, then Meadowbrook Parkway south. Stop and visit the beautiful white beaches of Jones Beach State Park for some fun in the sun. Unwind by swimming in the cool waters of the Atlantic, fishing, boating, exploring the nature and bike trails, golfing, or playing softball or shuffleboard. Then continue east on the Parkway along the Atlantic Ocean to JFK Wildlife Sanctuary, Cedar Beach in Gilgo Beach State Park, and Oak Beach. Cross over Robert Moses Bridge for a trip to Robert Moses State Park, located on the western end of Fire Island National Seashore. The pristine white-sand beach located here features such amenities as rest rooms, showers, lifeguards, concession, and picnic areas. Camping is available farther east at Watch Hill. Ranger-led interpretive canoe programs and nature walks begin at the Watch Hill visitor center. Stop in at the picturesque Fire Island Light Station to visit the ground-floor museum, which houses exhibits on shipwrecks and offshore rescues. (The lighthouse can be toured if reservations are made in advance.) From there, backtrack across the bridge to Robert Moses Causeway. Take Parkway 27A east to Bay Shore to visit 690-acre Bayard Cutting Arboretum. Continue through Islip and East Islip back to 27 (Sunrise Expressway), connecting with 27A again to Shinnecock Indian Reservation and Southampton.

One of the oldest English settlements in New York, Southampton was settled in 1640 by colonists from Massachusetts. Today, it is a blue-blood resort, with old, established homes and swanky boutiques along Job's Lane and Main Street and luxurious beach cottages and Victorian gingerbread mansions. Tour the Old Halsey House, the oldest English frame house in New York. Parrish Art Museum features 19th- and 20th-century American art, as well as Japanese woodblock prints and changing exhibits. Southampton Historical Museum includes a fantastic collection of Indian artifacts.

Continue on to East Hampton, a fashionable resort town with lots to see and do. Take a guided tour of the 1806 windmill at Hook Mill; visit the Guild Hall Museum for a look at regional art; explore Historic Mulford Farm, a living history farm museum with costumed interpreters; or make an appointment to tour Jackson Pollocks home and studio. The nearby town of Amagansett is home to the Town Marine Museumsure to be a hit with the anglers in your family. Exhibits explore commercial and sportfishing, whaling, fishing techniques, and underwater archeology. At the very tip of Long Island is Montauk, home to Hither Hills State Park and Montauk Point State Park. Be sure to tour the Montauk Point Lighthouse Museum before taking the Long Island Expressway back to Manhattan.
(Approximately 275 miles)

Exploring the Finger Lakes Region

This scenic, rolling region is marked by 11 finger-shaped lakes, named for the tribes of the Six Nations of Iroquois. According to Native American legend, the lakes were formed when God placed his hands on some of the most beautiful land ever created. The landscape features dazzling waterfalls, wild gorges and glens spanned by trestle bridges, steep hills and fairy-tale valleys, spring-fed lakes, sand beaches, and richly forested state parks. Area recreational opportunities include fascinating hiking, boating, and fishing on all 11 lakes.

The towns of the Finger Lakes region have a penchant for classical Greek and Latin namesRomulus, Homer, Etna, Ovid, Camillus, Marcellus, Sparta, Sempronius, Vesper, Scipiovillesuggesting rural sophistication and architectural flamboyance. The public buildings and mansions on the wide, shady streets of Ithaca, Skaneateles, Seneca Falls, Penn Yan, Geneva, and Canandaigua celebrate every architectural fad from 1840-1910, including Greek and Gothic Revival, Italianate, Georgian, Federal, Queen Anne, Richardsonian Romanesque, Beaux Arts, and Art Deco styles. If architecture isn't your thing, you can attend wine tastings and festivals at local vineyards or learn everything there is to know about enology (the science of winemaking) and viticulture (grape harvesting, fermentation, bottling, riddling racks, French oak barrels, tartrates, and yeasts) by taking the vineyard tours.

From Rochester, head south on Route 96 to Canandaigua, where you will find Sonnenberg Gardens and Mansion and Finger Lakes Race Track. Spend some time exploring the 50-acre estate at Sonnenberg, which includes the 40-room mansion, nine formal gardens, ponds, and a green house conservatory. Continue east on Route 5 to Geneva, which is located on Seneca Lake, the deepest and widest of the Finger Lakes.

Seneca Lake is known for its large concentration of lake trout, so this is a great place to cast your fishing lines into the water. If you are traveling over Memorial Day weekend, you'll catch the National Trout Derby here. Otherwise, head to Seneca Lake State Park, where the kids can take a swim or play at the playground while you try to catch the evenings dinner. From there, follow Route 14 south along Seneca Lake to Penn Yan for a look at the local architecture. The Windmill Farm and Craft Market, where Mennonites arrive in horse and buggy to sell farm produce and hand-made crafts, is also worth a stop. Children will enjoy Fullager Farms Family Farm and Petting Zoo, a working dairy farm that offers such diversions as pony rides, hay rides, and a petting zoo. Farther south on Route 14 is scenic Watkins Glen. Take some time to explore Watkins Glen Gorge, a glacier-made chasm complete with waterfalls. Several foot trails trace the rim of the gorge; stairs and bridges allow you to explore the inside of the chasm. Along the same lines, the nearby town of Montour Falls features 156-foot Chequaga Falls. If you are looking to do more fishing, stop at Catharine Creek where rainbow trout are abundant. From Watkins Glen, head south on 224 and north on 13 to Ithaca on picturesque Cayuga Lake. Visit Cornell Plantations Botanical Gardens, Sapsucker Woods Bird Sanctuary, and Moosewood Caf. Those traveling with children might want to check out the Sciencenter, home to over 100 hands-on science exhibits. Talk a walk along Sagan Planetwalk, an outdoor scale model of the solar system located on the grounds of Sciencenterit stretches for almost a mile! Children and adults alike will enjoy a visit to Fall Creek Gorge; the falls here stand almost as high as those at Niagara. This is a good place to pause for a scenic picnic. Round out your tour of the Finger Lakes Region by taking 348/90 north and 20 west to Seneca Falls. The big draw here is the Womens Rights National Historic Park, which honors such womens rights activists as Elizabeth Cady Stanton, Amelia Bloomer, Lucretia Mott, and Susan B. Anthony. Return to Rochester via 20 west and 96 west. **(Approximately 220 miles)**

MEANDERING ALONG LAKE ERIE

This tour winds along Lake Erie through fertile vineyard country and charming villages that seem lost in time in this surprisingly pastoral corner of the Empire State. Begin in Buffalo, with an architectural tour of Frank Lloyd Wright houses or a trip to the Albright-Knox Art Gallery. Children may better appreciate a trip to Buffalo Zoological Gardens where they can see over 2,000 animals in indoor and outdoor exhibits that include a tropical gorilla habitat. There is also a children's petting zoo. The Buffalo Museum of Science is another popular spot among those traveling with children. In addition to a Discovery Zone designed especially for kids, the museum features such exhibits as Dinosaurs & Co. and Insect World, which are bound to fascinate the younger generation. Stop in Allentown for a bite to eat before taking Route 5 southwest along Lake Erie to the lovely vacation city of Dunkirk. Visit Lake Erie State Park, where you can stroll the bluffs, swim, fish, and do some first-class bird-watching. Camp sites and cabins provide rustic accommodations for those looking to stay the night. A trip to Dunkirk Lighthouse is next on the agenda; take the guided tour for a fascinating history of the Great Lakes. Pushing on, stop in the charming town of Fredonia before continuing on Route 5 to Westfield, where you will take 394 south to Mayville and Chautauqua, home of beautiful Lake Chautauqua. Visit the world-famous Chautauqua Institution, a summer center for arts, education, religion, and recreation. Then follow 474 west to the small village of Panama.

You'll want to make time to explore the otherworldly boulders, cliffs, caves, crevices, and passages at Panama Rocks Park. This strange 25-acre rock outcropping is comprised of Paleozoic sea islands compressed into quartz conglomerate; boulders here are over 60 feet high. This enchanted world will delight and intrigue everyone in your group. Relax with a snack in the lovely picnic grove; the snack bar here offers a menu of fun and tasty picnic foods. Spend a leisurely hour on a self-guided tour of the 1-mile hiking trail (maps are provided). Pause often to photograph the sights (400 ISO film works best in these low-light conditions)the most spectacular scenery is along the lower portion of the trail. Keep in mind that the trail is too rough to accommodate strollers or wheelchairs. If you are feeling adventurous, allow extra time for off-trail explorationthis is the best way to experience the cliffs and crevices of this strange world. Other popular activities here include repelling and bird-watching.

Round out your trip by heading east on 474 to Jamestown and the Lucy-Desi Museum, which features exhibits and a video presentation on the lives and careers of Desi Arnaz and Jamestown native Lucille Ball. **(Approximately 110 miles)**

THE THOUSAND ISLANDS

From Syracuse, cross the Erie Canal on Route 48. Follow the Oswego Canal route (48 to 481) to the Fort Ontario State Historical Site, where you can explore military life as it was in the 1860s. For more history, head next to the H. Lee White Marine Museum. Continuing on, take 104 east to Mexico Bay, then follow 3 north to Sackets Harbor and Sackets Harbor Battlefield State Historical Site. In nearby Watertown, visit the Sci-Tech Center, a hands-on science museum sure to be a hit with the kids. Ever wonder how maple syrup is made? A visit to the American Maple Museum should answer all your questions about this sweet, sticky stuff. Continue on 12E to Clayton, where three state parks offer swimming, fishing, boating, and camping. Stop in at the Thousand Islands Museum to learn more about the history of this scenic region. The Antique Boat Museum may be of interest to the nautically minded in your group; the Antique Boat Show takes place here in August.

Our last stop is Alexandria Bay and the Thousand Islands. Described by French explorer Count Frontenac as "a Fairyland, that neither pen nor tongue of man may even attempt to describe," these 1,793-odd islands and islets, some only big enough to hold an American flag and others several acres in size, lie along the world's longest unprotected international border. When the International Boundary Commission divided up the islands (1817-1822), Canada got roughly 2/3 of them. The United States got the larger islands, including Wellesley and Grindstone, as well as the deep-water channel to Lake Ontario and the other Great Lakes.

Each of the Thousand Islands in the St. Lawrence River is a little kingdom with a story. On Zavikon, you can see the shortest international bridge in the world. Only 10 meters long, the bridge connects a Canadian cottage with an American flag on a pole. On Heart Island, you can tour the melancholy ruins of the half-finished Boldt Castle. Self-made millionaire George Boldt began building the $2,500,000 castle as a gift for his beloved young wife in the 1890s; he abandoned it to ruin when she died in 1904.

What better way to experience the Thousand Islands than out on the water? Boat tours and canoe expeditions explore the sheltered natural wonders of the islands. Sailboat charters and scuba dives are available to see the many shipwrecks off Kingston, including the *Horace Tabor* (1867), a 46-meter sailboat built in Michigan, and the *Steamer Comet* (1848), a 337-ton paddlewheeler built in Portsmouth.

On land, visit the Aqua Zoo (phone 315/482-5771), a privately owned aquarium that displays hundreds of varieties of marine life, including piranhas, alligators, and sharksoh my! Head up into the air with a hot-air balloon or helicopter ride for gorgeous aerial views of the islands. **(Approximately 215 miles)**

THE HAMPTONS

A series of charming hamlets and pristine villages stud Long Island's east end like jeweled beads strung on a flat, 50-mile-long, farm-green ribbon. These include Bridgehampton, East Hampton, Hampton Bays, Southampton, and Westhampton Beach. Other Hampton communities have less obvious place names: Amagansett, Eastport, East Quogue, Montauk, Sag Harbor, Wainscott, and Water Mill. The strand begins at Eastport—about 70 miles east of Manhattan—and continues eastward out to Montauk on the South Fork, a narrow strip of Long Island bordered by the Atlantic Ocean to the south and by the quiet waters of Peconic Bay and Gardiner's Bay to the north.

The Italian explorer Giovanni da Verrazano first sighted the region in 1524. In 1609, it is likely that Henry Hudson saw it too, but landed instead on western Long Island, closer to what is now New York City. A Dutch trader first stepped ashore at Montauk in 1614, and began to trade with indigenous Montauket Indians. English settlers—mostly farmers and fishermen—began arriving in 1664 and, during the colonial period that followed, created the wonderful villages that appeal to so many today. Organized around village greens, their shingled saltbox houses have deeply slanted thatched roofs and are separated by low white picket fences. In the 1800s, the whaling, fishing, and ship-building industries flourished and added a new dimension to the trade of the area, especially in the still-scenic port of Sag Harbor, on the northern coast of the South Fork.

The unusual combination of pastoral and marine abundance, along with seaside splendor, attracts an enormously varied population of second-home owners, weekenders, and visitors who join the local farmers, baymen, business owners, and an army of service personnel. Among them are scions, settlers' descendents, trendsetters, has-beens, wannabes, and recognizable names in the worlds of art, communications, design, fashion, finance, industry, media, and politics.

The Hamptons "season" has lengthened beyond its former Memorial Day to Labor Day summer period, although that's unquestionably still the time when beach lovers, boaters, swimmers, surfers, and singles flock eastward. During July and August, the height of the social season, celebrities attract benefactors to charity events, celebrity watchers get an eyeful, and day-trippers seek fun in the sun. During the months before and after summer, there's far less traffic on Route 27 (Montauk Highway, also called Main Street within the villages), the main east-west road.

From early spring through Indian summer, nature lovers hike, ride, boat, walk, shop, and dine in the area's fabulous restaurants (where reservations are recommended year-round). In October, there are vineyards to visit, pumpkins to pick, and Halloween festivals with hayrides, music, and book signings. In times past, shops posted sale signs by late September and closed from fall to spring; now, they are bustling with holiday merchandise in December and filled with shoppers, even on crisp winter weekends. Like many shops, galleries, and antique stores, movies, theatrical performances, and museums are open on weekends from spring until the New Year.

Most visitors drive to the Hamptons from New York City by traveling due east on the Long Island Expressway. Others take the Hampton Jitney (phone toll-free 800/936-0440) or the LIRR train (phone 631/231-5477 or 516/822-5477) from Manhattan. Many visitors fly to the Hamptons via Islip MacArthur (ISP) airport on Long Island; JFK International and La Guardia (LGA) in Queens, New York; and Newark Airport in New Jersey (NRK). There are also small, mostly private airfields in Shirley, Westhampton Beach, and East Hampton. Others take ferries to the Hamptons. One ferry departs from Bridgeport, Connecticut and goes to Port Jefferson, Long Island; another departs from New London, Rhode Island via Orient Point to Shelter Island and Sag Harbor; other ferries go to Montauk from Block Island, Newport, New London, and Mystic. Public transportation is ideal for visitors who plan to enjoy the Hamptons mostly on foot or bicycle (taxis are readily available).

What to See and Do in the Hamptons

Beaches

The primary Hamptons attraction is the silky-soft, sandy Atlantic Ocean beachfront (the sands facing the bay have a different texture). People head to beaches to walk, bird-watch and, in some places, to ride; they sunbathe, read, socialize, and play volleyball, and use the beach as a launching pad to swim and surf. The ocean borders one side of the beach; on the other, dusty miller-spotted mounds of dunes separate the beach from stately mansions, grand estates, and private clubs.

Many beaches provide lifeguards, rest rooms, showers, and snack bars; some have volleyball courts. All are open to the public and easily accessible to walkers and bikers. Parking, however, usually requires a vehicular fee for Suffolk County and New York State beaches (and parks with beaches) and a local permit for individual town beaches. (Nonresident permits are available in local communities and some innkeepers even make them available to their guests.

Natural Parks, Refuges, and Preserves

The rural landscape portrayed by artists who have lived in or visited the Hamptons also lures nature lovers with its sand-swept shores, hiking trails, rivers, ponds, bays, and ocean. Throughout the seasons, about 145 species of birds—including American oystercatchers, greater yellowlegs, egrets and songbirds, terns, willets, and black skimmers—can be found on beaches, in nature preserves, and in wildlife refuges. Bird watchers can find endangered piping plovers as well as ospreys in nests on the beaches. Pheasant, geese, wild duck, blue heron, red-tail hawks, and deer also populate nature refuges.

A number of New York State Parks have open camping areas (for the Long Island regional office, phone 631/669-1000 or 631/951-3440); the most popular is Hither Hills State Park, on the ocean in Montauk. Suffolk County Parks span a range from the Theodore Roosevelt County Park (Montauk Highway, Montauk; phone 631/852-7878), which offers horseback riding, biking, canoeing, camping, fishing, seasonal hunting, and beach access, to Shinnecock East County Park (Dune Road, Southampton; phone 631/852-8899), which flanks the eastern border of the Shinnecock Inlet and is a favorite spot for striped bass fishing and outer beach camping. There are parklands in Southampton and East Hampton townships, as well as nature preserves, wildlife refuges, and nature trails. Some of the 28 preserves on the South Fork require a guide to accompany visitors (phone 631/329-7689). The pristine and peaceful Montauk Dunes, Nature and Wildlife Preserves, and hiking trails like the Greenbelt Trail Conference (phone 631/380-0753) are idyllic for hikers.

Boating

The boating season extends more than six months, depending upon the sport, and centers in various harbors, ports, and bays. Offshore fishermen reach the ocean from marinas at the western edge of the Hamptons, at Shinnecock Inlet, and Montauk. Private chartered sportfishing yachts of all sizes, commercial fishing fleets, and public "head" boats are available to visitors. Kayaks, canoes, and small fishing boats are available for rent at many locations, and those who trailer small boats can use public marinas. Sailors dock or moor off Sang Harbor or in Three Mile Harbor and cruise Peconic Bay, Shelter Island; or follow the Atlantic to Block Island, Nantucket, Martha's Vineyard, Cape Cod, or Fire Island.

The Montauk Point Lighthouse

The Montauk Point Lighthouse, the oldest New York State lighthouse, is located within a 724-acre state park at the easternmost point of the South Fork on a site where the Royal Navy used signal bonfires to alert ships during the American Revolution. In 1792, the land, at the edge of a high oceanfront bluff, was purchased for $255.12. The 80-foot sand-stone lighthouse, completed in 1796, cost $22,500. Visitors can climb its 137 spiral steps and visit the park's Lost at Sea memorial, museum, and gift shop. Other activities include hiking on the dune-swept nature trails, watching ospreys and bald eagles, and searching for cormorants, loons, and harbor seals.

Farm Stands

Farm-stand shopping is an integral part of Hampton life. Wise shoppers browse the many farm stands for the best produce, including asparagus in May and strawberries in June. Local farms provide a plethora of flowers, homemade pies and jams, and superb fresh produce: berries, peaches, potatoes, greens, melons, pumpkins, and Long Island's succulent white, tiny-kernel sweet corn.

Wineries

When Moses Fournier planted his French grapes during the pre-colonial period, little did he imagine that vintners and visitors would be drawn to the region hundreds of years later for the same qualities that lured him: sunshine and fertile soil. Today, wine tastings and winery tours are popular in the Hamptons, particularly in the fall and on rainy weekends. Winemaking dates back almost 30 years on Long Island, and the region received a special designation as an American Viticultural Area on July 16, 2001. This assures that the grape-growing region has specific, ideal wine-making characteristics, including the right climate and soil conditions. Through there are fewer South Fork wineries than North Fork ones, visiting these wineries is always a pleasant way to spend an afternoon. Channing Daughters Winery (1927 Scuttle Hole Road, Bridgehampton; phone 631/537-7224), one of the newer wineries, opened its tasting room in 1998. A large chateau is the home of Duck Walk Vineyards (162 Montauk Highway, Water Mill; phone 631/726-555) where Dr. Heroditus Damianos of Pindar Vineyards grows local grapes and produces wine. Sagpond Vineyards (Sagg Road, Sagaponack; phone 631/537-5106) was the first winery to produce estate-bottled wines. Finally, Domaine Wolffer Chardonnay is named for its owner, Christian Wolffer, who built a stunning winery where tastings and sales take place under soaring ceilings.

Visitors willing to spend an extra hour (each way) traveling to Long Island's Wine Country on the North Fork will find the experience more than worthwhile. (*Beware:* this trip can take much longer on busy summer days.) The North Fork's two main roads run for 30 miles west to east, but there are a number of wineries near Greenport. Follow the grape cluster signs on Main Road (Route 25) and on Sound Avenue (North Road/Route 48). Among the top Main Road wineries are Bedell Cellars, Bidwell Vineyards, Corey Creek Vineyards, Gristina Vineyards, Lenz Winery, Paumonok Vineyards, Pellegrini Vineyards, and Pindar Vineyards. Pugliese Vineyards is on Bridge Lane in Cutchogue, one of the many short north/south roads that connects the two east/west arteries. On Sound Avenue, Hargrave Vineyards and Palmer Vineyards offer award-winning selections.

Art in the Hamptons

The history of art in the Hamptons can be traced back to the Montauket and Shinnecock Indians, who transformed seashells into wonderful wampum that they used to trade with 17th-century colonists. By the 1870s, the area's luminous light, fertile farmlands and sandy shores lured painters to a rural countryside that reminded them of Europe. The artists—Winslow Homer, Edwin Austin Abbey, John Twachtman, and William Merritt Chase—called themselves "The Tile Club" and created what became the second-oldest art colony in America. As time passed, artists continued to flock eastward. Childe Hassam arrived in the 1920s. In the 1940s, Jackson Pollock and Lee Krasner, Willem and Elaine de Kooning, and Robert Motherwell reinterpreted the landscape according to their individual sensitivity. Abstract Expression attracted more artists and the first of dozens of art galleries opened. (This first gallery is now known as the Elaine Benson Gallery and Sculpture Garden, on Main Street, Bridgehampton; phone 631/537-5513.) Artists from the New York School displayed their work and exhibitions, including pop artist Larry Rivers, cubist Fernand Leger, abstract painter Harry Kramer, glass artist Dale Chihuly, sculptor Louise Nevelson, ceramist Toshiko Takaezu, and jeweler David Yurman.

Most of the art galleries are found in the villages of Southampton, Westhampton Beach, and, primarily, in East Hampton. On just one tiny passageway between Main Street and the public parking lot in East Hampton, art lovers can stop in to Vered (68 Park Place Passage; phone 631/324-3308) and see work by Marc Chagall, Pablo Picasso, Henri Matisse, Ben Shahn, David Hockney, and Louise Nevelson. The Wallace Gallery, across the Passage (37A Main Street; phone 631/329-4516), displays a retrospective of local landscapes and seascapes that reflect the authentic history of the region, including work by east-end artists Edward Lamson Henry, Thomas Moran, and Childe Hassam.

Guild Hall (158 Main Street, East Hampton; phone 631/324-0806) provides exciting lectures, films, music, and live theatrical performances at the John Drew Theater. Its fine art exhibitions often focus on regional artists. Parrish Art Museum, (25 Job's Lane, Southampton; phone 631/283-2118) has the largest public collection of the works of William Merritt Chase and Fairfield Porter. This leading cultural institution offers changing exhibitions, lectures, films, and concerts, as well as children's events. Its sculpture garden and arboretum provide a pleasant refuge from the shops on Job's Lane. Art aficionados flock to the Ossorio Foundation (164 Mariner Drive, Southampton; phone 631/287-2020) and to the Pollock-Krasner House and Study Center (830 Fireplace Road, East Hampton; phone 631/324-4949).

Antiques

There are antique shops all along Route 27A (Montauk Highway, also called Main Street within the villages). Most display desirably timeless English and French country pieces, such as large tables, chests, armoires and side tables. Many shops also specialize in selling wonderful accessories to furnish fabulous (second) homes designed to entertain guests. Happily, there are also dealers who search out rare and exciting American pieces from the 18th and 19th centuries. The villages of Amagansett and Bridgehampton are especially known for their antique shops.

Theater

The area's cultural life is enriched by local performers who appear in productions at the Westhampton Beach Performing Arts Center (Main Street, Westhampton Beach; phone 631/288-1500), John Drew Theatre at Guild Hall (158 Main Street, East Hampton; phone 631/ 324-0806), and at Bay Street Theater (Sag Harbor; phone 631/725-9500). Mitzi Pazer of Pazer Production presents a series of four staged readings of new plays followed by refreshments at The Playwright's Theatre of East Hampton (LTV Studios, 75 Industrial Road, Wainscott; phone 631/324-5373). What is particularly special about this production is the cast, which has included such actors as Phyllis Newman, Tammy Grimes, and Ben Gazzara.

Historic Attractions

There are 19 historic districts and 65 houses, buildings, and sites (even a wrecked ship) that are listed on the National Register of Historic Places. East Hampton, considered one of America's most beautiful villages, is a fascinating combination of colonial charm and 21st-century sophistication.

It boasts more than luxurious inns, fabulous shops, art galleries, fine restaurants, and theater. Among its many historic attractions is the Hook Windmill at the eastern edge of town. Although crude windmills were built to grind corn as early as 1664, Nathaniel Dominy IV built this one in 1806, and it still stands as a fine example of the many historic windmills built in the area. The East Hampton Historical Society also conducts walking tours that are highly recommended (phone 631/324-6850) and include Home Sweet Home (14 James Lane; phone 631/324-0713), the boyhood home of John Howard Payne, who wrote his famous poem about this darling saltbox house, which was built in 1650.

Sag Harbor, sometimes called the "unhamptony" Hampton because of its low-key ambiance, has a few more shops today, but maintains its port-town ambience. The Sag Harbor Whaling and Historical Museum is housed in a gracious Greek Revival mansion (Main and Garden streets; phone 631/725-0770) and features a collection of whaling paraphernalia, ship models, a boat collection, artifacts, and toys.

Special Events

Events in the Hamptons range from traditional small-town parades to sophisticated major productions and appeal to a wide variety of interests. Garden lovers plan their trips for the early spring daffodil season when Jack Lenor Larson opens Longhouse to visitors (Hands Creek Road, East Hampton; phone 631/329-3568). The Longhouse Foundation also operates tours, seminars, workshops, and dance and musical performances.

The summer season traditionally begins in mid-May with an emerging artists show at the Elaine Benson Gallery in conjunction with the John Steinbeck Meet the Writers Book Fair. This is an opportunity to meet many of the famous authors who sign and sell their books to benefit Southampton College's John Steinbeck writing program and library. During Memorial Day weekend, the annual Potatohampton Minithon 10k run takes place in Bridgehampton. In June, on a Sunday afternoon, pleasure boats and commercial fishing vessels parade past a reviewing stand in Montauk for the annual Blessing of the Fleet (phone 516/537-0500). Prize fishing tournaments are held in Montauk throughout the fishing season. Traditional parades with schoolchildren and local fire departments march on July 4th, and spectacular fireworks follow in East Hampton and Montauk. Throughout July, there are countless events in the area. Some of the most popular are the Guild Hall Clothesline

Art Sale (158 Main Street, East Hampton; phone 631/324-0806), the annual Quilt Show and Sale (Water Mill; phone 631/726-4625) and The Ladies Village Improvement Society Sale (Gardiner Brown House, 95 Main Street; phone 631/324-1220). The "ladies" raise funds to beautify and safeguard the village of East Hampton at a fabulous flea market that is considered one of the summer's main events. In August, the Artists and Writers Softball Game draws crowds to watch the serious celebrities at bat, and people flock to the Lighthouse Weekend in Montauk (phone 631/688-2544), where there's a festival with a variety of events, including big band music, fife and drum corps, and face painting. The Music Festival of the Hamptons (phone toll-free 800/644-4418) is a ten-day period of classical music concert performances.

Throughout August, the Bridgehampton Polo Club matches attract crowds. Labor Day weekend is time for two of the area's most important annual events. The Hampton Classic Horse Show (240 Snake Hollow Road of Route 27; phone 631/537-3177) attracts over 40,000 spectators, including horse aficionados, breeders, trainers, riders, fans, and countless celebrities whose family members compete. They gather on the 60-acre show grounds to watch the 1,200 national competitors—including US Equestrian Team championship riders and Olympic veteran jumpers—strut their stuff. The event goes beyond the competition; there's a petting farm and pony care for kids and boutique garden with 36 vendors. At the Shinnecock Powwow (Montauk Highway, 8 miles east of Hampton Bays, 2 miles east of Southampton village; phone 631/283-6143), Native Americans gather to demonstrate Tribal rituals, dance, artifacts, and crafts. Some traditional Native American dishes are also served.

In mid-October, along with a number of winery events, the annual Hamptons International Film Festival comes to East Hampton (Sag Harbor Cinema, UA Theater, and Guild Hall, East Hampton; phone 631/324-4600). Venues at The Spotlight Film Series show advance screenings of major films. Sometimes, a star introduces the film, such as when Ed Harris introduced Pollock, a movie about Jackson Pollock, an artist who lived in the Hamptons. Roger Ebert taught three master classes about Citizen Kane in 2001. Major sections of the festival include American Independent Films (feature length narratives and documentaries plus shorts), World Cinema Films, Cuban Films, and a Student Film Competition. One $25,000 prize goes to the international filmmaker who made the best film about conflict and resolution.

Parks and Recreation

Water-related activities, hiking, riding, various other sports, picnicking and visitor centers, as well as camping, are available in many of New York's parks and recreation areas. There are more than 200 outdoor state recreation facilities, including state parks, forest preserves, and similar areas. For information about recreation areas within the Adirondack and Catskill forest preserves, contact the Department of Environmental Conservation, 50 Wolf Rd, Albany 12233-4790; phone 518/457-2500. For information about other state parks and recreation areas, contact Office of Parks, Recreation and Historic Preservation, Albany 12238; phone 518/474-0456. The state also provides funds for maintenance of 7,300 miles of trails for snowmobiling. Reservations for all state-operated campgrounds and cabins can be made by calling 800/456-CAMP. There is a $4 fee for boat launching at some state parks. Pets on leash where allowed. The basic fee for camping is $13/night; additional charges for amenities and hookups (electric and sewer). Call or write for detailed information about individual parks.

FISHING AND HUNTING

New York state offers excellent fishing and hunting opportunities, with a wide variety of lengthy seasons. Write or phone for detailed information about fees and regulations. Contact the NYS Department of Environmental Conservation, License Sales Office-Room 151, 50 Wolf Rd, Albany 12233-4790, phone 518/402-8843, for the most current fees and a mail-order license application and fishing/hunting regulations guides. *The Conservationist* is the department's official illustrated bimonthly periodical on New York State natural resources; contact PO Box 1500, Latham, NY 12110-9983 for a subscription ($10 per year).

Driving Information

Safety belts are mandatory for all persons in the front seat of a vehicle. Children under 7 years of age must be in approved passenger restraints anywhere in a vehicle; ages 4-9 may use regulation safety belts; ages 3 and under must use approved child safety seats. For more information, phone 518/474-5111.

INTERSTATE HIGHWAY SYSTEM

The following alphabetical listing of New York towns in this book shows that these cities are within 10 miles of the indicated interstate highways. Check a highway map for the nearest exit.

Highway Number	Cities/Towns within 10 Miles
Interstate 81	Alexandria Bay, Binghamton, Clayton, Cortland, Syracuse, Watertown.
Interstate 84	Brewster, Fishkill, Middletown, Newburgh, Port Jervis.
Interstate 87	Albany, Ausable Chasm, Bolton Landing, Catskill, Diamond Point, Glen Falls, Hartsdale, Hudson, Kingston, Lake George Village, Lake Luzerne, Monroe, Newburgh, New Paltz, New York, Nyack, Plattsburgh, Poughkeepsie, Rouses Point, Saratoga Springs, Saugerties, Schroon Lake, Spring Valley, Stony Point, Tarrytown, Troy, Warrensburg, Woodstock, Yonkers.
Interstate 88	Bainbridge, Binghamton, Oneonta.
Interstate 90	Albany, Amsterdam, Auburn, Batavia, Buffalo, Canaan, Canajoharie, Canandaigua, Canastota, Dunkirk, Geneva, Herkimer, Ilion, Johnstown, Oneida, Palmyra, Rochester, Rome, Schenectady, Seneca Falls, Syracuse, Troy, Utica, Victor, Waterloo.
Interstate 95	Mamaroneck, White Plains.

Additional Visitor Information

The *I Love New York Winter Travel & Ski Guide* and the *I Love New York Travel Guide* (covering upstate New York, Long Island, and New York City) may be obtained from the State Department of Economic Development, Division of Tourism, PO Box 2603, Albany 12220-0603; phone 518/474-4116 or 800/225-5697; www.iloveny.com.

Adirondack Park (B-8)

See also Blue Mountain Lake, Lake George Village, Lake Placid, Long Lake, Old Forge

14 miles NW of Amsterdam on Hwy 30.

The Adirondack Mountains are protected under an 1885 law establishing the forest preserve and an 1892 law creating Adirondack Park. The state now owns more than 2 1/2 million of the nearly 6 million acres of the park, a wilderness mountain area with streams and lakes. There are 42 public campgrounds of varying size, a 125-mile canoe route from Old Forge to the Saranacs, and 750 miles of marked foot trails among the pines and spruces. Hunting and fishing are permitted under state regulations. Detailed camping information may be obtained from the Department of Environmental Conservation, Bureau of Recreation, 50 Wolf Rd, Room 679, Albany 12233-5253. Phone 518/457-2500. www.adirondacks.org

Afton

Restaurant

★ ★ **RIVER CLUB.** *1 Maple St, Afton (13730). Phone 607/639-3060.* American menu. Dinner. Closed Mon-Wed; Dec 25. Bar. Children's menu. Converted railroad depot overlooking river. Outdoor seating. **$$**

Albany (E-9)

See also Canaan, Coxsackie, Howes Cave, Schenectady, Troy

Settled 1624
Population 95,658
Elevation 150 ft
Area Code 518
Information Albany County Convention & Visitors Bureau, 25 Quackenbush Sq, 12207; phone 518/434-1217 or toll-free 800/258-3582
Web Site www.albany.org

Albany is situated on the Hudson River, where Henry Hudson ended the voyage of the *Half Moon* in 1609. It was settled by Dutch-speaking Walloons from Holland, Norwegians, Danes, Germans, and Scots during the patronship of Kiliaen Van Rensselaer and was named in honor of the Duke of Kent and Albany when the British took over the city in 1664. Despite the French and Indian War, Albany was a thriving fur-trading center in 1754. Albany's General Philip Schuyler commanded the northern defenses in the Revolution and, according to Daniel Webster, was "second only to Washington in the services he performed for his country."

Albany has been a transportation center since Native American trail days. Robert Fulton's steamboat, the *Clermont,* arrived here from Jersey City in 1807. The Erie Canal opened in 1825; by 1831, 15,000 canal boats and 500 ocean-going ships crowded Albany's docks.

Politics is a colorful part of the business of New York's capital city. Located on the western bank of the Hudson River and at the crossroads of major state highways, Albany is now a hub of transportation, business, industry, and culture.

What to See and Do

Albany Institute of History and Art. *125 Washington Ave, Albany (12210). 1 block W of capitol. Phone 518/463-4478. www.albanyinstitute.org.* Victorian salon, colonial exhibits, traveling and changing exhibits; Hudson-Mohawk Valley paintings and sculpture; contemporary art; changing exhibits and programs promote fine arts as well as regional history; research library with archival material. (Wed-Sat 10 am-5 pm, Sun noon-5 pm; closed holidays) **$$**

Ausable Chasm. *1 mile N of Keesville; 12 miles S of Plattsburgh off I-87.* www.*ausablechasm.com.* This scenic gorge, accessible from Highway 9, was opened to the public in 1870. It is one of the oldest tourist attractions in the United States. Ausable (Aw-SAY-bl) Chasm leads eastward toward Lake Champlain for about a mile and a half. This spectacular gorge is 20 to 50 feet wide and from 100 to 200 feet deep. The Ausable River plunges in falls and rapids past curious rock formations, each with its own name: Pulpit Rock, Elephant's Head, Devil's Oven, Jacob's Well, the Cathedral. Paths and bridges crisscross the chasm. Camping is available on the grounds.

Activities. Game room, glassblower's shop, craft shops, picnic area, and playground. (July-Aug, daily) Cross-country ski center (winter).

Self-guided walking tour. *25 Quackenbush Sq, Albany (12207).* To midway point of stream and guided boat ride through "flume" rapids. (Memorial Day weekend-Columbus Day, daily) **$$$$**

Crailo State Historic Site. *9 1/2 Riverside Ave, Rensselaer (12144). 1 1/2 blocks S of Hwys 9 and 20. Phone 518/463-8738.* Eighteenth-century Dutch house, now a museum of Dutch culture in the Hudson Valley. Exhibits and audiovisual presentation explain the history and development of Dutch settlements in America. (Early-Apr-Oct: Wed-Sat 10 am-5 pm; tours begin on hour and half hour, last tour begins at 4:30 pm; Nov-Mar: by appointment) **$**

Dutch Apple Cruises Inc. *Madison Ave and Broadway, Albany (12201). Phone 518/463-0220. www.dutchapplecruises.com.* Scenic cruises on the Hudson River with a view of the Capital District. Sightseeing, dinner/entertainment, and Sun brunch cruises (by reservation). (May-Oct, daily) **$$$**

Empire State Plaza. *Madison and State sts, Albany (12230). NY State Thrwy, exit 23. Phone 518/474-2418.* A 98-acre, 11-building complex providing office space for state government, cultural, and convention facilities; New York State Modern Art Collection on view. On 42nd floor is the Tower Building observation deck (daily). **FREE**

Historic Cherry Hill. *523 1/2 S Pearl St, Albany (12202). Phone 518/434-4791. www.historiccherryhill.org.* (1787) Georgian-style farmhouse built for Philip Van Rensselaer, a prominent merchant farmer. Lived in by four generations of descendants until 1963. Nine period rooms of original furnishings and personal belongings from the 18th to 20th centuries. Gardens. Tours (Apr-June, Oct-Dec: Tues-Fri noon, 1 pm, 2 pm, 3 pm, Sat 10 am, 11 am, noon, 1 pm, 2 pm, 3 pm, Sun 1 pm, 2 pm, 3 pm; July-Sept: Tues-Sat 10 am, 11 am, noon, 1 pm, 2 pm, 3 pm, Sun 1 pm, 2 pm, 3 pm; closed Jan-Mar, also holidays). **$**

New York State Museum. *Cultural Education Center of the Empire State Plaza, Madison and State sts, Albany (12230). Phone 518/474-5877. www.nysm.nysed.gov.* Life-size dioramas, photo murals, and thousands of objects illustrate the relationship between people and nature in New York state. Three major halls detailing life in metropolitan New York, the Adirondacks, and upstate New York. Special exhibits of photography, art, history, nature, science, and Native Americans. Working carousel. Memorial to the World Trade Center. Cafeteria. Entertainment, classes, and films. (Daily 9:30 am-5 pm; closed Jan 1, Thanksgiving, Dec 25) **DONATION**

Rensselaerville. *63 Huyck Rd, Rensselaerville (12147). 27 miles SW via Hwy 443 to end of Hwy 85. Phone 518/797-3783.* Village, established in 1787, has restored homes, inns, churches, gristmill. Nature preserve and biological research station. Also here is the Rensselaerville Institute, offering cultural programs and a conference center for educational and business meetings.

Schuyler Mansion State Historic Site. *32 Catherine St, Albany (12202). Phone 518/434-0834.* (1761) Georgian mansion, home of Philip Schuyler, general of the Revolutionary War and US senator. Alexander Hamilton married Schuyler's daughter here, and other prominent early leaders visited here. Tours begin on the hour. Last tour begins at 4 pm (fee). (Apr-Oct: Wed-Sun 10 am-5 pm; July-Aug: Tues; Nov-Mar: by appointment, Tues-Fri 10 am-4 pm; closed holidays except Memorial Day, July 4, Labor Day) **$$$**

Shaker Heritage Society. *875 Watervliet Shaker Rd, Albany (12211). Phone 518/456-7890.* Located on the site of the first Shaker settlement in America. Grounds, 1848 Shaker Meeting House, orchard, and cemetery where founder Mother Ann Lee is buried. Gift shop. Tours (June-Oct: Sat 11:30 am and 1:30 pm) ($) (Feb-Oct: Tues-Sat 9:30 am-4 pm; Nov-Dec: Mon-Sat 10 am-4 pm) **FREE**

State Capitol. *Empire State Plaza, State and Swan sts, Albany (12242). Phone 518/474-2418. assembly.state.ny.us.* A $25,000,000 granite "French" chateau. Legislative session begins the Wednesday after the first Monday in Jan. Guided tours (daily). **FREE**

Ten Broeck Mansion. *9 Ten Broeck Pl, Albany (12210). Phone 518/436-9826. www.tenbroeck.org.* (1798) Brick Federal house with Greek Revival additions; built by General Abraham Ten Broeck, it was also the home of the prominent Olcott family. Contains collection of period furniture, fine arts, three period bathrooms (1890s), and changing exhibits of the Albany County Historical Association; also lawn and herb garden during summer. (May-Dec, Thurs-Sun afternoons; closed holidays) **$$**

University at Albany, State University of New York. *Washington and Western aves, Albany (12222). E of NY State Thrwy, exit 24. Phone 518/442-3300. www.albany.edu.* (1844) (13,000 students) A 382-acre campus; art gallery; performing arts center; 1 million-volume library; nuclear accelerator; atmospheric science research center; carillon tower.

Special Events

First Night. *Downtown. Phone 518/434-2032.* Celebration of the arts with music performances and fireworks to welcome the new year. Dec 31.

Tulip Festival. *Washington Park, Albany (12207). Willett St between State St and Madison Ave. Phone 518/434-2032.* Mother's Day weekend.

Limited-Service Hotels

★ ★ **BEST WESTERN SOVEREIGN HOTEL-ALBANY.** *1228 Western Ave, Albany (12203). Phone 518/489-2981; toll-free 888/963-7666; fax 518/489-8967. www.bestwestern.com.* 195 rooms, 5 story. Pets accepted; fee. Complimentary full breakfast. Check-in 2 pm, check-out noon. Wireless Internet access. Restaurant, bar. Fitness room. Indoor pool, outdoor pool. Airport transportation available. Business center. **$**

★ ★ **COURTYARD BY MARRIOTT.** *168 Wolf Rd, Albany (12205). Phone 518/482-8800; toll-free 800/321-2211; fax 518/482-0001. www.courtyard.com.* 78 rooms, 3 story. Check-in 3 pm, check-out noon. High-speed Internet access. Fitness room. Indoor pool, whirlpool. Airport transportation available. **$$**

★ **HAMPTON INN.** *10 Ulenski Dr, Albany (12205). Phone 518/438-2822; toll-free 800/426-7866; fax 518/438-2931. www.hamptoninn. com.* 153 rooms, 5 story. Complimentary continental breakfast. Check-in 2 pm, check-out noon. Outdoor pool. Airport transportation available. **$**

★ ★ **HOLIDAY INN.** *205 Wolf Rd, Albany (12205). Phone 518/458-7250; toll-free 800/465-4329; fax 518/458-7377. www.holiday-inn. com.* 312 rooms, 6 story. Pets accepted. Check-in 4 pm, check-out noon. High-speed Internet access. Restaurant, bar. Children's activity center. Fitness room. Indoor pool, outdoor pool, whirlpool. Business center. **$**

Full-Service Hotels

★ ★ **CENTURY HOUSE HOTEL.** *997 New Loudon Rd, Latham (12110). Phone 518/785-0931; toll-free 888/674-6873; fax 518/785-3274. www.thecentury-house.com.* The Century House offers its guests a pool, restaurant, nature trails, a tennis court, complimentary breakfast, and much more. The rooms are elegantly decorated with colonial style and cherry wood furnishing. 68 rooms, 2 story. Pets accepted, some restrictions; fee. Complimentary full breakfast. Check-out noon. Restaurant, bar. Fitness room. Outdoor pool. Tennis. **$**

★ ★ ★ **CROWNE PLAZA.** *State and Lodge sts, Albany (12207). Phone 518/462-6611; toll-free 800/227-6963; fax 518/462-2901. www.albanycityct.crowneplaza. com.* This hotel is located near the Capitol Building, Empire State Plaza, and the Pepsi Arena.384 rooms, 15 story. Check-in 4 pm, check-out 11 am. High-speed Internet access, wireless Internet access. Two restaurants, two bars. Fitness room. Indoor pool, whirlpool. Airport transportation available. Business center. **$$**

★ ★ ★ **DESMOND HOTEL AND CONFERENCE CENTER.** *660 Albany Shaker Rd, Albany (12211). Phone 518/869-8100; toll-free 800/448-3500; fax 518/869-7659. www.desmondhotels.com.* With lush green indoor courtyards and elegantly decorated rooms, this hotel offers old-world charm. 323 rooms, 4 story. Pets accepted, some restrictions. Check-in 4 pm, check-out noon. High-speed Internet access. Two restaurants, two bars. Fitness room. Indoor pool, children's pool. Airport transportation available. **$$**

★ ★ ★ **MARRIOTT ALBANY.** *189 Wolf Rd, Albany (12205). Phone 518/458-8444; toll-free 800/228-9290; fax 518/458-7365. www.marriott.com.* This hotel is located five minutes from the Albany International Airport and 20 minutes from downtown Albany. 360 rooms, 8 story. Check-in 4 pm, check-out noon. High-speed Internet access. Restaurant, bar. Fitness room. Indoor pool, outdoor pool, whirlpool. **$$**

Full-Service Inn

★ ★ ★ **GREGORY HOUSE COUNTRY INN.** *3016 Hwy 43, Averill Park (12018). Phone 518/674-3774; fax 518/674-8916. www.gregoryhouse.com.* This country inn, located near Albany and Troy, offers 12 rooms and a fine dining restaurant. Guests can visit the nearby Tanglewood in Lenox, which is the summer home of the Boston Symphony. 12 rooms, 2 story. Complimentary continental breakfast. Check-in 2 pm, check-out 11 am. Restaurant, bar. Outdoor pool. **$**

Specialty Lodging

MANSION HILL INN. *115 Philip St at Park Ave, Albany (12202). Phone 518/465-2038; toll-free 888/299-0455; fax 518/434-2313. www.mansionhill.com.* 8 rooms, 2 story. Pets accepted. Complimentary full breakfast. Check-in 4 pm, check-out 11:30 am. Restaurant. **$$**

THE MORGAN STATE HOUSE. *393 State St, Albany (12210). Phone 888/427-6063; toll-free 888/427-6063; fax 518/463-1316. www.statehouse.com.* 6 rooms. Complimentary full breakfast. Check-in 3 pm, check-out noon. **$$**

Restaurants

★ BONGIORNO'S. *23 Dove St, Albany (12210). Phone 518/462-9176; fax 518/465-0846.* Italian menu. Lunch, dinner. Closed Sun; holidays. Bar. Casual attire. Reservations recommended. **$$**

★ ★ ★ JACK'S OYSTER HOUSE. *42 State St, Albany (12207). Phone 518/465-8854; fax 518/434-2134. www.jacksoysterhouse.com.* This downtown landmark has been dishing out seafood to local politicians, businessmen, and families since 1913. And it knows its history: look for the enormous photos of historic Albany. (And don't miss the fresh Maine lobster!) American, seafood menu. Lunch, dinner. Bar. Children's menu. Casual attire. Reservations recommended. **$$$**

★ ★ ★ LA SERRE. *14 Green St, Albany (12207). Phone 518/463-6056; fax 518/463-3830.* Truffle mousse pat and escargot are among the appetizer options at this upscale continental establishment, located inside a beautiful historic building that dates back to the 1840s. Also on the menu: Angus beef, New Zealand lamb and "Veal La Serre." French menu. Lunch, dinner. Closed Sun; holidays. Bar. Business casual attire. Reservations recommended. Outdoor seating. **$$$**

★ ★ ★ MANSION HILL. *115 Philip St, Albany (12202). Phone 518/465-2038; toll-free 888/299-0455; fax 518/434-2313. www.mansionhill.com.* The inn bills itself as "Albany's best kept secret," and for once there's truth in advertising. A typical meal at this downtown bed-and-breakfast, run by the Stofelano family since 1984, might include homemade ravioli, pan-roasted half duckling or chicken tenderloins. American menu. Breakfast, dinner. Closed Sun; holidays. Casual attire. Outdoor seating. **$$$**

★ ★ ★ SCRIMSHAW. *660 Albany-Shaker Rd, Albany (12211). Phone 518/869-8100; fax 518/869-7659. www.desmondhotels.com.* Found inside the elegant Desmond Hotel, this restaurant serves a broad selection of seafood (even oysters on the half shell). There are also several surf 'n' turf options as well as the "Scrimshaw Potato"— whipped potatoes inside a puff pastry shell. American, seafood menu. Dinner. Closed Sun; holidays. Bar. Business casual attire. Reservations recommended. **$$**

Alexandria Bay (B-6)

See also Clayton

Population 1,088
Elevation 284 ft
Area Code 315
Zip 13607
Information Chamber of Commerce, 11 Market St, Box 365; phone 315/482-9531, toll-free 800/541-2110, or 888-432-7884
Web Site www.alexbay.org

Resort center of the Thousand Islands, Alexandria Bay overlooks a cluster of almost 1,800 green islands divided by intricate waterways. The islands range in size from a few square inches, a handful of rocks with a single tree, to several miles in length.

What to See and Do

Boldt Castle. *Collins Landing, Alexandria Bay (13607). On Heart Island. Phone 315/482-9724; toll-free 800/847-5263. www.boldtcastle.com.* George C. Boldt came from Prussia in the 1860s and became the most successful hotel magnate in America, managing the Waldorf-Astoria in New York City and owning the Bellevue-Stratford in Philadelphia. The castle was a $2,500,000 present to his wife, who died in 1904; the castle was never completed. Other structures here include the dove cote, which housed fancy fowl; Italian garden, Alster Tower power house, and the yacht house. Slide show in main castle; craft demonstrations and exhibits on first floor. **Note:** Structure and grounds now being restored. (Early May-mid-Oct, daily 10 am-6:30 pm; to 7:30 pm in Jul-Aug) **$$**

Kring Point State Park. *25950 Kring Point Rd, Alexandria Bay (13679). 6 miles NE on Hwy 12, then W on Kring Point Rd. Phone 315/482-2444.* Swimming beach, bathhouse, fishing, boating (launch, dock); picnicking, cabins, tent and trailer sites, cross-country skiing. (Early May-Columbus Day)

Rockport Boat Lines. *2 miles E of Thousand Islands International Bridge, off Thousand Islands Pkwy E in Rockport, Ontario. Phone 613/659-3402; toll-free*

800/563-8687. A one-hour tour through the islands. (May-Oct, daily)

Thousand Islands Skydeck. *Hill Island RR 1, Alexandria Bay (KOE 1LO). Phone 613/659-2335.* Between the spans of the Thousand Islands International Bridge, on Hill Island, Lansdowne, Ontario.

Uncle Sam Boat Tours. *47 James St, Alexandria Bay (13607). Phone 315/482-2611; toll-free 800/253-9229. www.usboattours.com.* Two-hour cruises wind through scenic islands; dinner and luncheon cruises (May-Oct). All tours stop at Boldt Castle.

Wellesley Island. *44927 Cross Island Rd, Fine View (13640). Across Thousand Islands International Bridge. Phone 315/482-2722.* On the island are three state parks: **Wellesley Island.** Swimming beach, bathhouse, fishing, boating (ramp, marina); nature center, hiking, golf, cross-country skiing, snowmobiling, picnicking, playground, concession, trailer sites. Standard fees. **DeWolf Point.** Swimming, fishing, boating (ramp); tent and trailer sites, cabins. Standard fees. **Waterson Point.** Accessible only by boat. Fishing, boat anchorage; camping, picnicking.

Limited-Service Hotel

★ LEDGES RESORT MOTEL. *71 Anthony St, Alexandria Bay (13607). Phone 315/482-9334; fax 315/482-9334. www.thousandislands.com/ledges.* 27 rooms. Closed mid-Oct-early May. Pets accepted, some restrictions. Complimentary continental breakfast. Check-out 11 am. Outdoor pool. **$**

Full-Service Resorts

★ ★ BONNIE CASTLE RESORT. *Outer Holland St, Alexandria Bay (13607). Phone 315/482-4511; toll-free 800/955-4511; fax 315/482-9600. www.bonniecastle.com.* This hotel takes full advantage of its location on the St. Lawrence River. Visitors will enjoy a riverside bar and grill, live entertainment on weekends, indoor and outdoor pools, and a location within walking distance from restaurants and shopping. 128 rooms, 3 story. Check-in 2 pm, check-out 11 am. Restaurant, bar. Fitness room. Indoor pool, outdoor pool, whirlpool. Tennis. Airport transportation available. **$**

★ ★ EDGEWOOD RESORT. *Edgewood Park Dr, Alexandria Bay (13607). Phone 315/482-9922; toll-free 800/334-3996; fax 315/482-5210.* Built in 1886; extensive grounds on riverfront; boat tours. 160 rooms, 2 story. Check-out 11 am. Restaurant, bar. Outdoor pool. **$**

★ ★ PINE TREE POINT RESORT. *70 Anthony St, Alexandria Bay (13607). Phone 315/482-9911; toll-free 888/756-3229; fax 315/482-6420. www.pinetreepointresort.com.* 96 rooms. Closed Nov-Apr. Check-out 11 am. Restaurant, bar. Outdoor pool, whirlpool. **$**

★ ★ ★ RIVEREDGE RESORT HOTEL. *17 Holland St, Alexandria Bay (13607). Phone 315/482-9917; toll-free 800/365-6987; fax 315/482-5010. www.riveredge.com.* Found on the St. Lawrence River, this resort offers many rooms with a river view as well as casual and fine dining; an indoor and an outdoor pool and Jacuzzi; and a dock with power, water, and cable hook ups. 129 rooms, 4 story. Pets accepted, some restrictions; fee. Check-in 3 pm, check-out 11 am. Restaurant, bar. Fitness room. Indoor pool, outdoor pool, whirlpool. **$$**

Restaurants

★ ★ CAVALLARIO'S STEAK & SEAFOOD HOUSE. *24 Church St, Alexandria Bay (13607). Phone 315/482-9867; fax 315/482-2160.* American menu. Dinner. Closed early Nov-mid-Apr. Bar. Children's menu. Valet parking. **$$$**

★ ★ ★ THE CRYSTAL DINING ROOM. *31 Holland St, Alexandria Bay (13607). Phone 315/482-4511; fax 315/482-5036. www.bonniecastle.com.* The Crystal Dining Room is located in the Bonnie Castle Resort, and it overlooks the St. Lawrence River. A mirrored baby grand piano sets the atmosphere in the elaborately adorned restaurant, which serves a simple menu with plenty of fresh seafood. American menu. Breakfast, lunch, dinner. Closed Dec 25. Bar. Children's menu. Outdoor seating. **$$**

★ ★ ★ JACQUES CARTIER. *17 Holland St, Alexandria Bay (13607). Phone 315/482-9917; fax 315/482-5010. www.riveredge.com.* Located at the Riveredge Resort, this restaurant upholds the timeless traditions of continental dining: tableside preparations of caesar salad and flaming desserts. From mid-May to mid-October (the restaurant is closed during the off season), patrons enjoy rich seafood dishes and con-

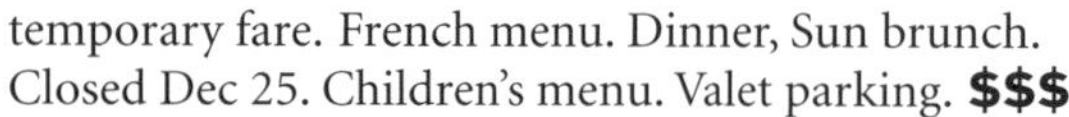

temporary fare. French menu. Dinner, Sun brunch. Closed Dec 25. Children's menu. Valet parking. **$$$**

Allegany State Park (F-2)

See also Olean

At Salamanca on Hwy 17.

This 65,000-acre park is one of the most complete recreation areas in the United States. It borders on the Allegany Indian Reservation and the Kinzua Reservoir in New York and the Allegheny National Forest in Pennsylvania. It has more than 85 miles of hiking trails and many scenic drives through rolling hills. The park is open all year and has a museum, seasonal stores, and two restaurants. Swimming at Quaker and Red House lakes, bathhouses, boat rentals, fishing; hunting, sports fields, tennis, 25 miles of groomed cross-country ski trails, 55 miles of snowmobile trails, tobogganing; picnicking, refreshment stands; tent and trailer sites (Apr-Dec, most with electricity), cabins.

Amagansett (C-5)

See also East Hampton, Montauk, Sag Harbor

Population 1,067
Elevation 40 ft
Area Code 631
Zip 11930
Information East Hampton Chamber of Commerce, 79A Main St, East Hampton 11937; phone 631/324-0362
Web Site www.easthamptonchamber.com

What to See and Do

Miss Amelia's Cottage Museum. *Hwy 27A and Windmill Ln, Amagansett. Phone 631/267-3020.* This original home is part of the history of Amagansett, a quaint village on the South Fork. Mary Amelia Schellinger, who was the last of her family to live in this 1725 house, was a descendant of Jacob Schellinger, the founder of Amagansett. She lived in the home without electricity or water for years. The cottage features its original colonial furnishings, so you get a true sense of what a home looked like so many centuries ago. (June-Sept, Fri-Sun 9 am-1 pm) **DONATION**

Town Marine Museum. *300 Bluff Rd, Amagansett (11937). Bluff Rd, 1/2 mile S of Hwy 27, on ocean. Phone 631/267-6544.* Exhibits on commercial and sport fishing, offshore whaling from colonial times to present; underwater archaeology, sailing, aquaculture, commercial fishing techniques; garden; picnicking. Programs administered by the East Hampton Historical Society. (July-Aug: daily; June and Sept: weekends only) **$**

Limited-Service Hotel

★ SEA CREST ON THE OCEAN. *2166 Montauk Hwy, Amagansett (11930). Phone 631/267-3159; toll-free 800/732-3297; fax 631/267-6840. www.duneresorts.com.* 74 rooms, 2 story. Check-in 3 pm, check-out 11 am. Outdoor pool. Tennis. **$$$**

Restaurants

★ CAFE ON MAIN. *195 Main St, Amagansett (11930). Phone 631/267-2200.* American menu. Breakfast, lunch. Casual attire. **$$**

★ ★ ESTIA. *177 Main St, Amagansett (11930). Phone 631/267-6320.* American menu. Breakfast, lunch, dinner. Bar. Casual attire. **$$**

★ ★ GORDON'S. *231 Montauk Hwy, Amagansett (11930). Phone 631/267-3010.* Continental menu. Dinner. Closed Thanksgiving, Dec 25. Bar. Casual attire. Reservations recommended. **$$$**

★ LOBSTER ROLL. *1980 Montauk Hwy, Amagansett (11930). Phone 631/267-3740. www.lobsterroll.com.* Seafood menu. Lunch, dinner. Closed Nov-Apr. Children's menu. Casual attire. Outdoor seating. **$$**

Amenia

Restaurants

★ ★ CASCADE MOUNTAIN WINERY & RESTAURANT. *835 Cascade Rd, Amenia. Phone 845/373-9021.* American menu. Lunch, dinner. Casual attire. Reservations recommended. Outdoor seating. **$$**

★ ★ XE SOGNI. *5263 Rte 44, Amenia. Phone 845/373-7755.* Italian menu. Dinner. Closed Mon-Wed. Bar. Business casual attire. Reservations recommended. Outdoor seating. **$$**

Amherst

See also Buffalo

Restaurant

★ SIENA. *4516 Main St, Amherst (14226). Phone 716/839-3108; fax 716/839-3713. www.sienarestaurant.com.* Italian menu. Lunch, dinner. Closed holidays. Bar. Outdoor seating. **$$**

Amityville

See also Massapequa Park

Population 18,355
Elevation 25 ft
Area Code 631
Zip 11701
Information Chamber of Commerce, PO Box 885; phone 631/598-0695
Web Site www.amityville.com

Amityville is a town on the Great South Bay noted for antiques, craftspeople, and its many restored houses.

What to See and Do

Lauder Museum. *170 Broadway, Amityville. Phone 631/598-1486.* Permanent and changing exhibits reflect Amityville's heritage and that of surrounding communities; research library, genealogical files. (Tues, Fri, Sun) **FREE**

Amsterdam (D-9)

See also Johnstown, Schenectady

Settled 1785
Population 18,355
Elevation 450 ft
Area Code 518
Zip 12010
Information Montgomery County Chamber of Commerce, 366 W Main St, PO Box 309; phone 518/842-8200 or toll-free 800/743-7337
Web Site www.montgomerycountyny.com

Located on the Mohawk River and New York Barge Canal, this city manufactures clothing, novelties, toys, and electronic equipment.

What to See and Do

Erie Canal. *6 miles W on Hwy 5 S at Fort Hunter. Phone 518/842-8200; toll-free 800/743-7337. www.montgomerycountyny.com.* Site of last remaining section of original canal (built in 1822). **FREE**

Guy Park State Historic Site. *366 W Main St, Amsterdam (12010). Phone 518/842-8200; toll-free 800/743-7337. www.montgomerycountyny.com.* (1773) Former home of Guy Johnson, Superintendent of Indian Affairs, who remained loyal to King George III; abandoned by Johnson in 1775. Served as a tavern for many years. Exhibits on Native Americans and on the Erie Canal and its impact on westward expansion. (Mon-Fri; closed holidays) **FREE**

National Shrine of the North American Martyrs. *6 miles W on Hwy 5 S in Auriesville, Dewey Thrwy exit 27. Phone 518/853-3033.* Site of Ossernenon, 17th-century Mohawk settlement, where Father Isaac Jogues and companions, the first canonized martyrs of the United States, were put to death. Birthplace of Blessed Kateri Tekakwitha. Coliseum-type chapel seats 6,500. Native American museum; cafeteria. (Early May-early Nov, daily) **FREE**

Schoharie Crossing State Historic Site and Visitors Center. *129 Schoharie St, Fort Hunter (12069). 5 miles W, just off Hwy 5 S, in Fort Hunter. Phone 518/829-7516.* Seven arches of the Schoharie Aqueduct; remains of original canal locks; canals from 1825 and 1840s and barge canal can be seen. Park, boat launch; historic site markers, picnic tables; hiking paths; wagon rides; tours. (Mid-May-Oct, Wed-Sat, also Sun afternoons)

Walter Elwood Museum. *300 Guy Park Ave, Amsterdam (12010). Phone 518/843-5151.* Exhibits of history, natural science, and ethnology; changing exhibits in gallery; research library. (July-Aug: Mon-Thurs; rest of year: Mon-Fri; closed holidays) **DONATION**

Limited-Service Hotel

★ ★ **BEST WESTERN AMSTERDAM.** *10 Market St, Amsterdam (12010). Phone 518/843-5760; toll-free 800/328-1234; fax 518/842-0940. www.bestwestern.com.* 125 rooms, 5 story. Pets accepted, some restrictions; fee. Check-in 3 pm, check-out noon. Restaurant, bar. Indoor pool. **$**

Restaurant

★ ★ ★ **RAINDANCER STEAK PARLOUR.** *4582 State Hwy 30, Amsterdam (12010). Phone 518/842-2606; fax 518/842-2943. www.raindancerrestaurant.com.* Casual American food is served in this rustic, friendly environment that has been family owned for more than 20 years. The varied menu will suit almost anyone and features fish, chicken, pastas, and the well-known prime rib dinner and salad bar. American menu. Lunch, dinner. Closed Dec 24-25; also Super Bowl Sun. Bar. Children's menu. **$$$**

Aquebogue

See also Riverhead

Restaurant

★ **MEETING HOUSE CREEK INN.** *177 Meeting House Creek Rd, Aquebogue (11931). Phone 631/722-4220; fax 631/722-3650.* American menu. Dinner, Sun brunch. Closed Dec 25. Bar. Children's menu. Outdoor seating. **$$**

Arcade (E-3)

See also East Aurora

Population 4,184
Elevation 1,497 ft
Area Code 716
Zip 14009

What to See and Do

Arcade and Attica Railroad. *278 Main St, Arcade (14009). Phone 585/492-3100.* Steam train ride (1 1/2 hours) through scenic countryside. (Late May-Oct, Sat-Sun, and holidays; July-Aug, also Wed) **$$$**

Ardsley

Restaurant

★ ★ **THAI HOUSE.** *466 Ashford Ave, Ardsley. Phone 914/674-6633.* Thai menu. Lunch, dinner. Bar. Casual attire. Reservations recommended. **$$**

Auburn (D-5)

See also Finger Lakes, Seneca Falls, Skaneateles, Syracuse

Settled 1793
Population 28,574
Elevation 708 ft
Area Code 315
Zip 13021
Information Cayuga County Office of Tourism, 131 Genesee St; phone 315/255-1658 or toll-free 800/499-9615
Web Site www.tourauburnny.com

On Owasco Lake, Auburn is one of the largest cities in the Finger Lakes region. Harriet Tubman, whose home was a link in the Underground Railroad, lived here. A resort and farm center, Auburn's products include electronics, auto parts, air conditioners, wire, plastics, diesel engines, steel, bottles, and aviation spark plugs.

What to See and Do

Cayuga Museum/Case Research Lab Museum. *203 Genesee St, Auburn (13021). Phone 315/253-8051.* The Cayuga Museum is housed in Greek Revival Willard-Case Mansion (1836); 19th-century furnishings; local industrial history; Bundy Monumental clock; Civil War exhibit. The Case Research Lab Museum is the restored lab where T. W. Case and E. I. Sponable invented sound film; permanent exhibits of lab, Fox Movietone, and sound studio. (Tues-Sun afternoons; also Mon holidays; closed Jan) **DONATION** Adjacent is

Schweinfurth Memorial Art Center. *205 Genesee St, Auburn (13021). Phone 315/255-1553.* Classical and contemporary fine art, photography, folk art, and quilting exhibit; concerts, lectures, museum shop. (Feb-Dec, Tues-Sun; closed holidays)

Emerson Park. *3 miles S on Hwy 38A, at head of Owasco Lake. Phone 315/253-5611.* Swimming, boating (launch); ball fields, playground, picnicking. Agricultural museum. (Mid-May-mid-Sept, daily) **$** In park is

Cayuga Museum Iroquois Center. *203 Genesee St, Auburn (13021). Phone 315/253-8051.* Permanent and changing exhibits on traditional Northeast Woodlands Native people's arts and culture; emphasis on Iroquois cultures of central New York. (June: weekends; July-Aug: Wed-Sun) **FREE**

Fort Hill Cemetery. *19 Fort St, Auburn (13021). Phone 315/253-8132.*Site was used for burial mounds by Native Americans as early as AD 1100. Burial sites of William Seward and Harriet Tubman are here. (Daily) **FREE**

Harriet Tubman Home. *180 South St, Auburn (13021). Phone 315/252-2081.* Born a slave, Harriet Tubman escaped in 1849 and rescued more than 300 slaves via the Underground Railroad. She later assisted the Union Army during the Civil War and, settling in Auburn after the war, continued to pursue other humanitarian endeavors. (Tues-Sat; closed holidays) **$$$**

Seward House. *33 South St, Auburn (13021). Phone 315/252-1283. www.sewardhouse.org.* (1816-1817) Home of William Henry Seward, governor of New York, US senator, and Lincoln and Andrew Johnson's secretary of state, who was instrumental in purchasing Alaska. Civil War relics, original Alaskan artifacts, costumes, furnishings. (Feb-late June, Mid-Oct-late Dec: Tues-Sat 1-4 pm; July-mid-Oct: Tues-Sat 10 am-4 pm, Sun from 1 pm; closed holidays) **$$**

Willard Memorial Chapel & Welch Memorial Building. *17 Nelson St, Auburn (13021). Phone 315/252-0339.* (1894) These grey and red stone Romanesque Revival buildings were once part of the Auburn Theological Seminary. The chapel's interior was designed and handcrafted by the Tiffany Glass and Decoration Company, and is the only complete and unaltered Tiffany chapel known to exist. Tiffany Concert Series in the chapel (July and Aug, Wed noon). Tours. (Tues-Fri 10 am-4 pm; also Sun 1-4 pm in summer; closed holidays). **$**

Limited-Service Hotels

★ ★ HOLIDAY INN. *75 North St, Auburn (13021). Phone 315/253-4531; fax 315/252-5843. www.holiday-inn. com.* 165 rooms, 5 story. Pets accepted. Check-in 3 pm, check-out 11 am. Restaurant, bar. Fitness room. Indoor pool. **$**

★ ★ SPRINGSIDE INN. *6141 W Lake Rd, Auburn (13021). Phone 315/252-7247; fax 315/252-8096. www. springsideinn. com.* 8 rooms, 3 story. Complimen tary continental breakfast. Check-in 2 pm. Check-out noon. Restaurant. **$**

Restaurants

★ ★ LASCA'S. *252 Grant Ave, Auburn (13021). Phone 315/253-4885; fax 315/253-3895. www.lascas. com.* Italian, American menu. Lunch, dinner. Closed Mon; holidays; also first two weeks in Feb. Bar. Children's menu. **$$**

★ ★ SPRINGSIDE INN. *6141 W Lake Rd, Auburn (13021). Phone 315/252-7247; fax 315/252-8096. www.springsideinn. com.* Built in 1830. Owasco Lake opposite. Dinner, Sun brunch. Closed holidays. Bar. Children's menu. **$$**

Averill Park

Restaurant

★ ★ LA PERLA. *3016 Hwy 43, Averill Park (12018). Phone 518/674-3774. www.gregoryhouse.com.* Three formal dining rooms and a pub room make up the restaurant at this 1830s inn. Elegant five-course dinners and an award winning wine list are presented by gracious servers in the main rooms, while lighter fare, cocktails, and coffees are served in the pub room. Italian menu. Dinner. Closed Mon-Tues; also Dec 24-26. Bar. Reservations recommended. **$$**

Avon (D-4)

See also Geneseo, Letchworth State Park, Rochester

Population 6,443
Elevation 651 ft
Area Code 716
Zip 14414

Originally a health resort with sulphur springs, Avon has since become a farming, food processing, and horse-breeding center.

What to See and Do

Genesee Country Village and Museum. *1410 Flint Hill Rd, Mumford. 8 miles NW via Hwy 5 to Hwy 36. Phone 585/538-6822. www.gcv.org.* A 19th-century village representing life in the Genesee River valley. Fifty-seven buildings, including a log cabin and a Greek Revival mansion. Small-scale farm; blacksmith, pottery, print, and tinsmith shops; and a general store are in daily operation by museum guides dressed as 19th-century villagers. Replication of 19th-century baseball with ballpark and authentic teams. Permanent exhibits of antique horse carriages. Gallery of Sporting Art has over 700 pieces of wildlife art. (Mid-May-mid-Oct: Tues-Fri 10 am-4 pm, Sat-Sun, holidays to 5 pm; July-Labor Day: Tues-Sun, holidays 10 am-5 pm) **$$**

Bainbridge (E-7)

See also Deposit, Oneonta

Population 3,401
Elevation 1,006 ft
Area Code 607
Zip 13733
Information Chamber of Commerce, PO Box 2; phone 607/967-8700
Web Site www.bainbridgechamberny.org

Special Event

General Clinton Canoe Regatta. *Hwy 7, Bainbridge (13733). Phone 607/967-8700.* World championship flat water canoe race, arts and crafts show. Midway show. Entertainment. One week in late May.

Limited-Service Hotel

★ SUPER 8. *4 Mang Dr, Sidney (13838). Phone 607/563-8880; fax 607/563-8889. www.super8.com.* 39 rooms, 2 story. Check-in 1 pm, check-out 11 am. **$**

Restaurant

★ JERICHO TAVERN. *4 N Main St, Bainbridge (13733). Phone 607/967-5893; fax 607/967-5893.* Lunch, dinner. Closed Mon-Tues; Dec 25. Bar. Children's menu. **$$**

Barryville (B-1)

See also Middletown, Monticello, Port Jervis

Population 600
Elevation 600 ft
Area Code 914
Zip 12719

What to See and Do

Fort Delaware Museum of Colonial History. *On Hwy 97 in Narrowsburg. Phone 845/252-6660.* Replica of 1755 stockade, cabins, blockhouses, gardens; exhibits, film, and demonstrations depict the life of early settlers. Colonial military encampments (July-Aug). Picnic area; snacks. (Last week June-Labor Day: daily; Memorial Day-late June: Sat and Sun only)

Lander's Delaware River Trips. *1336 Hwy 97, Narrowsburg (12764). Phone toll-free 800/252-3925. www.landersrivertrips.com.* Canoe, raft, and kayak trips on whitewater and calm water; campground along river. (Mid-Apr-mid-Oct, daily) One- and two-day package plans. **$$$$**

Batavia (D-3)

See also Buffalo, Lockport, Rochester

Founded 1801
Population 16,256
Elevation 895 ft
Area Code 585
Zip 14020
Information Genesee County Chamber of Commerce, 210 E Main St; phone 585/343-7440 or toll-free 800/622-2686
Web Site www.geneseeny.com/chamber

Established at the crossing of two Native American trails by Joseph Ellicott, an agent of the Holland Land Company, which purchased 3,300,000 acres from Robert Morris, Batavia was named for a province of the Netherlands. The brisk rate of sales of this western New York State land is said to have inspired the phrase "doing a land-office business." Batavia today is a lively farm area producing potatoes, onions, fruit, and dairy products. Industrial items include heat exchange equipment, alloy castings, and shoes. The New York State School for the Blind is here.

What to See and Do

Batavia Downs Race Track. *8315 Park Rd, Batavia (14020). I-90 to exit 48. Phone 585/343-3750. www.batavia-downs.com.* The oldest pari-mutuel harness track in North America. Clubhouse, open-air and enclosed grandstands. (Early Aug-late Nov, daily) **$**

Holland Land Office Museum. *131 W Main St, Batavia (14020). Phone 585/343-4727. www.hollandlandoffice.com.* (1815) Building from which deeds to the lands in the Holland Purchase were issued. This stone office was built by Joseph Ellicott, land agent. Local Native American and pioneer artifacts, period furniture and costumes; Civil War, medical and surgical collections (Tues-Sat 10 am-4 pm; closed holidays). **DONATION**

Iroquois National Wildlife Refuge. *15 miles NW of town via Hwy 63, on Casey Rd in Alabama, NY. Phone 585/948-5445. www.iroquoisnwr.fws.gov.* Migratory waterfowl, especially geese, visit here in large numbers during the spring migration. Overlooks, trails, illustrated talks (reservation); fishing, hunting (in season). Office (Mon-Fri 7:30 am-4 pm; also Sat-Sun 9 am-5 pm in spring and summer; closed holidays).

Le Roy House. *23 E Main St, Le Roy (14482). 1/2 mile E of jct Hwys 19 and 5; 7 miles S of NY State Thrwy exit 47. Phone 716/768-7433.* Early 19th-century house with furnishings of the period; nine rooms open to the public. Also home of Le Roy Historical Society. (Tues-Fri, mid-morning-mid-afternoon; also Sun afternoons; closed holidays)

Six Flags Darien Lake. *9993 Alleghany Rd, Darien Center (14040). I-90 to exit 48A, S on Hwy 77. Phone 585/599-4641. www.sixflags.com.* Family entertainment complex is New York's largest. Features five roller coasters, a million-gallon wave pool and sun deck, 40,000-square-foot water adventure park, and performing arts center; 2,000-site campground. (Late May-early Sept: daily; Oct: weekends; hours vary) **$$$$**

Special Events

Genesee County Agricultural Fair. *E Main Street Rd, Batavia (14020). Phone 585/344-2424. www.gcfair.com.* Tractor pull, demolition derby, livestock show, entertainment. Late July-Aug. **$**

Wing Ding Weekend. *210 E Main St, Batavia (14020). Phone 585/343-7440.* Ethnic festival, block party, food, games, entertainment. Third weekend in Aug.

Limited-Service Hotel

★★ RAMADA LIMITED. *8204 Park Rd, Batavia (14020). Phone 585/343-1000; fax 585/343-8608. www.ramada.com.* 75 rooms, 2 story. Pets accepted. Check-in 2 pm, check-out noon. Restaurant, bar. Outdoor pool. **$**

Full-Service Hotel

★★ SIX FLAGS DARIEN LAKE RESORT. *9993 Allegheny Rd, Darien Center (14040). Phone 585/599-2211; fax 585/599-5124. www.sixflags.com.* 160 rooms. Check-in 3 pm, check-out 11 am. Restaurant, bar. Children's activity center. Fitness room. Outdoor pool, whirlpool. **$$**

Restaurant

★★ SUNNY'S. *Genesee Country Mall, Batavia (14020). Phone 716/343-4578.* Italian, American menu. Lunch, dinner, late-night. Closed holidays. Bar. Children's menu. Casual attire. **$**

Bay Shore (C-3)

See also Fire Island National Seashore, Robert Moses State Park, Sayville

Founded 1708
Population 23,852
Elevation 15 ft
Area Code 516
Zip 11706

What to See and Do

Bayard Cutting Arboretum. *Bayard Cutting Arboretum and Montauk Hwy, Bay Shore. 6 miles E on Montauk Hwy (Hwy 27A). Phone 631/581-1002.* Approximately 690 acres; many broadleaf trees and coniferous evergreens, wildflowers, shrubs; aquatic birds; nature walks. (Tues-Sun; closed Jan 1, Dec 25) **$$**

Sagtikos Manor. *Gardiner Dr and Manor Ln, Bay Shore (11706). 3 miles W on Montauk Hwy (Hwy 27A).* Apple Tree Wicke (1692), served as headquarters for General Henry Clinton; original kitchen, parlor; Thompson music room and dining room added circa 1890; antiques. (July-Aug: Wed, Thurs, and Sun; June and Sept: Sun only) **$$**

Bayville

Restaurant

★ ★ **STEVE'S PIER I.** *33 Bayville Ave, Bayville (11709). Phone 516/628-2153.* Lunch, dinner. Bar. Children's menu. Valet parking. Outdoor seating. On Long Island Sound. **$$**

Beacon

Restaurant

★ **PIGGY BANK.** *448 Main St, Beacon. Phone 845/838-0028. www.piggybankrestaurant.com.* American menu. Lunch, dinner. Bar. Casual attire. Outdoor seating. **$$**

Bellport

Restaurants

★ ★ **BELLPORT.** *159 S Country Rd, Bellport (11713). Phone 631/286-7550.* Dinner. Closed Tues; Dec 25. Bar. **$$**

★ **BELLPORT CHOWDER HOUSE.** *19 Bellport Ln, Bellport (11713). Phone 631/286-2343.* Lunch, dinner, Sun brunch. Closed Dec 25. Bar. Outdoor seating. **$$**

Bemus Point (F-1)

See also Chautauqua, Jamestown

Population 340
Elevation 1,320 ft
Area Code 716
Zip 14712
Web Site www.bemuspoint.com

What to See and Do

Long Point on Lake Chautauqua State Park. *Hwy 430, Bemus Point (14712). 1 mile W off Hwy 17. Phone 716/386-2722.* Swimming, fishing, boating (marina); snowmobiling, ice fishing, cross-country skiing, picnicking. (Mid-May-Columbus Day) **$$**

Limited-Service Hotel

★ ★ **LENHART HOTEL.** *20 Lakeside Dr, Bemus Point (14712). Phone 716/386-2715; fax 716/386-3232. www.hotellenhart.com.* Family-owned since 1880. 53 rooms, 4 story. Closed Sept-May. Complimentary continental breakfast. Check-in 2 pm, check-out noon. Restaurant, bar. Airport transportation available. No credit cards accepted. **$**

Restaurant

★ ★ **YE HARE N' HOUNDS INN.** *64 Lakeside Dr, Bemus Point (14712). Phone 716/386-2181; fax 716/386-2369. www.restaurant.com/hareandhounds.* International menu. Dinner. Closed Dec 24-25. Bar. Children's menu. Casual attire. Outdoor seating. **$$$**

Bethpage

See also Hempstead, Massapequa Park, Plainview

Population 16,543
Elevation 106 ft
Area Code 516
Zip 11714
Web Site www.bethpage.com

What to See and Do

Bethpage State Park. *Bethpage State Pkwy, Farmingdale (11735). E off Bethpage Pkwy. Phone 516/249-0700.* The name Bethpage may bring to mind the famous Bethpage Black golf course, but this 1,475-acre park also offers hiking and biking paths, tennis courts, bridle paths, game fields, and cross-country skiing trails in addition to its five world-class 18-hole golf courses. Pets are not allowed in the park. (Daily) **FREE** Located here is

> **Bethpage Black Course.** *Bethpage State Park, Farmingdale (11735). Phone 516/249-0700.* One of the most difficult municipal courses in the country, Bethpage Black hosted the 2002 US Open, and only Tiger Woods seemed to be able to manage its length and its deep rough. The course is so difficult that it sports a warning sign near the first tee box. It's run by the state, so its relatively inexpensive to playgreens fees are a bargain at less than $30 per round. **$$$$**

Colonial Springs Golf Course. *1 Long Island Ave, Farmingdale (11735). Phone 631/643-0051. www.longislandgolfnews.com.* Near the renowned Bethpage Black course is Colonial Springs, which offers three 9-hole layouts to choose from. The Lake course plays around the namesake feature in the center of the course, while the Valley and Pines layouts comb the edges of the grounds. Perhaps the most difficult hole is the 527-yard par-four 5th on the Valley course. A slight dogleg means that you must hit a massive drive and still hit an accurate fairway wood from more than 200 yards away to have a chance of reaching the green in two. **$$$$**

Old Bethpage Village Restoration. *Round Swamp Rd and exit 48, Bethpage. 1 mile S of Long Island Expy, exit 48. Phone 516/572-8401. www.oldbethpage.org.* More than 25 pre-Civil War buildings including carpentry and hat shops, general store, tavern, schoolhouse, church, homes; working farm and craftsmen depict life of mid-1800s; film. Picnic area. (Mar-Dec, Wed-Sun, hours vary; closed winter holidays) **$$$**

Binghamton (F-6)

See also Deposit, Endicott, Ithaca, Owego

Settled 1787
Population 47,380
Elevation 860 ft
Area Code 607
Information Broome County Convention and Visitors Bureau, 49 Court St, Box 995, 13902; phone 607/772-8860 or 607/772-8945 (recording), or toll-free 800/836-6740.
Web Site www.binghamtoncvb.com

Largest of the Triple Cities (Johnson City and Endicott branched off later), Binghamton lies at the junction of the Chenango and Susquehanna rivers. Completion of the Chenango Canal in 1837 made it an important link between the coal regions of Pennsylvania and the Erie Canal.

What to See and Do

Binghamton University, State University of New York. *Hwy 434 and Vestal Pkwy, Binghamton. Phone 607/777-2787.*(1946) (12,000 students) Anderson Center for the Arts offers performing arts events including dance, music, and theater. Foreign films, lectures, art museum (academic year, Tues-Sun; closed holidays). Tours of campus.

Chenango Valley State Park. *153 State Park Rd, Chenango Forks (13746). 13 miles NE via I-88. Phone 607/648-5251. www.reserveamerica.com.* Swimming beach, bathhouse, fishing, boat rentals; hiking, biking, nature trails, 18-hole golf (fee), cross-country skiing, picnicking, playground, concession, tent and trailer sites, cabins (closed winter).

Day of a Playwright. *The Forum, 236 Washington St, Binghamton (13901). Phone 607/778-2480.* Theater has an exhibit honoring Syracuse-born Rod Serling (1925-1975), who grew up in Binghamton and created *The Twilight Zone* TV series; includes photos and documents highlighting his career in TV and films. (Mon-Fri and during Forum performances)

Discovery Center of the Southern Tier. *60 Morgan Rd, Binghamton (13903). Phone 607/773-8661. www.thediscoverycenter.org.* Hands-on museum allows children to experience a simulated flight in an airplane, crawl through a culvert, and stand inside a bubble, in addition to exploring other interactive exhibits. (Tues-Fri 10 am-4 pm, Sat to 5 pm, Sun noon-5 pm) **$**

Roberson Museum and Science Center. *30 Front St, Binghamton (13905). Phone 607/772-0660. www.roberson.org.* Regional museum with collections in art, history, folk art, and science. Includes turn-of-the-century mansion; changing exhibits; planetarium (fee). (Daily, hours vary; closed holidays) **$$**

Ross Park Zoo. *185 Park Ave, Binghamton (13903). Phone 607/724-5461.* www.*rossparkzoo.com.* Operated by the Southern Tier Zoological Society. A 75-acre park (free); 25-acre zoo with Wolf Woods, tiger, snow leopard, spectacled bear exhibits, petting zoo, and aviary. (Apr-Nov, daily 10 am-5 pm) Playground, picnicking. **$$**

Special Events

B.C. Open PGA Golf Tournament. *En-Joie Golf Course, Endicott. Phone 607/754-2482.* July.

Balloon Rally. *351 Industrial Park Blvd, Endicott (13760). Phone 607/761-2475. www.balloonrally.com.* Early Aug. **$$**

Broome County Performing Arts Theater, the Forum. *236 Washington St, Binghamton (13901). Phone 607/778-2480.* Broadway shows, center for dramatic and musical comedy productions by professional performers.

Broome County Veterans Memorial Arena & Convention Center. *1 Stuart St, Binghamton (13901). Phone 607/778-6626. www.gobroomecounty.com.* Professional hockey (B.C. Icemen, UHL; winter); national shows and concerts. **FREE**

Limited-Service Hotels

★ COMFORT INN. *1000 Front St, Binghamton (13905). Phone 607/724-3297; toll-free 800/469-7009; fax 607/771-0206. www.choicehotels.com.* 106 rooms, 4 story. Pets accepted. Complimentary continental breakfast. Check-in 2 pm, check-out 11 am. Outdoor pool. **$**

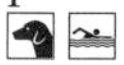

★ ★ CLARION COLLECTION GRAND ROYALE HOTEL. *80 State St, Binghamton (13901). Phone 607/722-0000; fax 607/722-7912.* This hotel, the former city hall (1897), is perfectly located in downtown Binghamton near shopping, restaurants, and entertainment. Visitors will also enjoy free use of the YMCA found only one block away. 61 rooms, 6 story. Pets accepted. Complimentary full breakfast. Check-out noon. Bar. **$$**

★ ★ HOLIDAY INN. *2-8 Hawley St, Binghamton (13901). Phone 607/722-1212; fax 607/722-6063. www.holiday-inn. com.* 241 rooms, 8 story. Pets accepted; fee. Check-out noon. Restaurant, bar. Indoor pool. Airport transportation available. **$**

Restaurants

★ ARGO. *117 Court St, Binghamton (13901). Phone 607/724-4692; fax 607/724-6470.* Italian, Greek menu. Breakfast, lunch, dinner. Closed Jan 1, Thanksgiving, Dec 25. Children's menu. **$$**

★ ★ NUMBER FIVE. *33 S Washington, Binghamton (13903). Phone 607/723-0555; fax 607/723-5885. www.number5restaurant.com.* Operating in a fire station built in 1897, this American steak and seafood house has been open since 1978. Located on the south side of downtown Binghamton and convenient to hotels, the antique-filled, fine dining atmosphere is warm and romantic. American menu. Dinner. Closed Dec 25. Bar. Children's menu. **$$**

★ SPOT. *1062 Upper Front St, Binghamton (13905). Phone 607/723-8149; fax 607/723-5844.* American, Greek menu. Breakfast, lunch, dinner, late-night. Bar. Children's menu. **$$**

Blue Mountain Lake (C-8)

See also Adirondack Park, Long Lake

Population 250
Elevation 1,829 ft
Area Code 518
Zip 12812
Web Site www.indian-lake.com

This central Adirondack resort village has mountain trails, splendid views, interesting shops, water sports, good fishing, and hunting.

What to See and Do

Adirondack Lakes Center for the Arts. *Hwy 28, Blue Mountain Lake (12812). In the village, next to the post office. Phone 518/352-7715. www.adk-arts.org.* This community center hosts concerts, films, theatrical performances, art and photography exhibits, and workshops.

Adirondack Museum. *Hwy 30, Blue Mountain Lake (12812). 1 mile N on Hwy 30. Phone 518/352-7311. www.adkmuseum.org.* On slope of Blue Mountain overlooking lakes, mountains, and village. Noted for landscaping; indoor and outdoor displays. Exhibits explore logging, transportation, boating, mining, schooling, outdoor recreation, and rustic furniture. Gift shop. (Memorial Day-mid-Oct, daily 10 am-5 pm) **$$$**

Blue Mountain. *1 1/2 miles N.* Three-mile trail to 3,800-foot summit; 35-foot observation tower overlooks Adirondack Park. Blue Mountain Lake Association has map of trails.

Limited-Service Hotel

★ ★ HEMLOCK HALL HOTEL. *Maple Lodge Rd, Blue Mountain Lake (12812). Phone 518/352-7706.* Secluded resort inn near woods on lakeshore. 22 rooms, 1 story. Closed Nov-late May. Check-out 11 am. Restaurant (public by reservation). Beach. **$**

Bolton Landing (C-9)

See also Diamond Point, Glens Falls, Lake George Area, Warrensburg

Population 1,600
Elevation 360 ft
Area Code 518
Zip 12814
Information Chamber of Commerce, Lakeshore Dr, PO Box 368; phone 518/644-3831
Web Site www.boltonchamber.com

Bolton Landing, on the shores of Lake George, has been home to musicians, artists, authors, and people of great wealth. Today most of the estates are resorts, but the cultural atmosphere lives on.

What to See and Do

Recreation. Veterans Memorial Park. *4949 Lakeshore Dr, Bolton Landing (12814). Phone 518/644-3831.* North end of town. **Rogers Memorial Park.** Center of town on NY 9 N. Beaches (parking fee), tennis, picnicking, arts and crafts instruction; swimming lessons (all free).

Limited-Service Hotel

★ ★ MELODY MANOR RESORT. *4610 Lakeshore Dr, Bolton Landing (12814). Phone 518/644-9750; fax 518/644-9750. www.melodymanor.com.* 40 rooms, 3 story. Closed Nov-Apr. Check-in 2 pm, check-out 11 am. Restaurant, bar. Beach. Outdoor pool. Tennis. **$$**

Full-Service Resort

★ ★ ★ THE SAGAMORE. *110 Sagamore Rd, Bolton Landing (12814). Phone 518/644-9400; toll-free 800/358-3585; fax 518/644-2626. www.thesagamore.com.* Experience the great American getaway at The Sagamore. This historic resort reigns over its own private 72-acre island in Lake George in the Adirondacks. Rusticate in the lap of luxury at this playground for the discerning traveler. From golf, tennis, and water sports to a myriad of winter activities, this resort is a year-round destination. Guests can even learn to be boat captains or chefs for the day in the resorts unique instructional sessions. Two types of accommodations offer visitors the choice of the classically elegant rooms at the historic hotel or the appealing cabin décor of the spacious lodges. Dining always comes with a view at the six restaurants; meals are even served aboard the resorts own replica of a 19th-century training vessel. 350 rooms, 3 story. Check-in 4 pm, check-out 11 am. High-speed Internet access. Eight restaurants, two bars. Fitness room, fitness classes available, spa. Beach. Indoor pool, whirlpool. Golf, 18 holes. Tennis. Airport transportation available. Business center. **$$$**

Restaurants

★ FREDERICK'S RESTAURANT. *Rte 9N Lakeshore Dr, Bolton Landing (12814). Phone 518/644-3484. www.fredericksrestaurant.com.* Known for authentic local specialties and an extensive raw bar. Seafood menu. Lunch, dinner. **$$**

★ ★ ★ TRILLIUM BIS. *110 Sagamore Rd, Bolton Landing (12814). Phone 518/644-9400.* www.thesagamore.com. In The Sagamore (see), a sprawling, gorgeously decorated inn on Lake George, diners will find chef George Bargisen creating a new feast daily. A typical entrée might be the roasted Maine lobster with vanilla fava bean risotto or the "just cooked" salmon. American menu. Dinner, Sun brunch. Jacket required. Reservations recommended. Valet parking. **$$$**

★ ★ VILLA NAPOLI. *4608 Lakeside Dr, Bolton Landing (12814). Phone 518/644-9047. www.melodymanor/villanapoli.com.* Italian menu. Breakfast, dinner. Closed mid-Oct-mid-May. Bar. Children's menu. Casual attire. Reservations recommended. Outdoor seating. **$$**

Boonville (C-7)

See also Rome

Population 4,572
Elevation 1,146 ft
Area Code 315
Zip 13309
Information Boonville Area Chamber of Commerce, 122 Main St, PO Box 163; phone 315/942-5112 or 315/942-6823 (recording)
Web Site www.cybervillage.com/bac

This rural community is nestled in the divide between the Mohawk and Black rivers on the southeastern portion of the Tug Hill Plateau. Pioneers cleared the forests of this area for their dairy farms; it has since become the dairy center of the region.

What to See and Do

Constable Hall. *7 miles NW via Hwy 12D, unnumbered road. Phone 315/397-2323.* (Circa 1820) Limestone Georgian residence built by William Constable, son of one of New York's most prominent merchants; he joined Alexander Macomb and William McCormick in the Macomb Purchase, which consisted of one-tenth of the state. Memorabilia of five generations of Constable family. (June-mid-Oct, Tues-Sun) **$$**

Dodge-Pratt-Northam Art and Community Center. *106 Schuyler St, Boonville (13309). Phone 315/942-5133.*Victorian mansion (1875) features changing art exhibits; tour and a variety of workshops and courses. Gift shop. (Mar-late Dec, Tues-Sat; closed Thanksgiving, Dec 25) **FREE**

Erwin Park. *On Hwy 12.* Swimming pool (June-Aug); tennis and basketball courts, picnicking, playground. (Mid-May-mid-Oct) **FREE**

Pixley Falls State Park. *11430 Hwy 46, Boonville (13309). 6 miles S on Hwy 46. Phone 315/942-4713.* Fishing; hiking, picnicking, playground, tent and trailer sites. (May-Sept) **$$**

Snow Ridge Ski Area. *Hwy 26, Turin. 11 miles N via Hwys 12D, 26. Phone 315/348-8456; toll-free 800/962-8419. www.snowridge.com.* Four double chairlifts, two T-bars, bunny tow; patrol, school, ski shop, rentals, snowmaking; babysitting, restaurant, cafeteria, bar. (Thanksgiving-Apr, daily) Cross-country trails. **$$$$**

Special Events

Boonville Oneida County Fair. *120 Schuyler St, Boonville (13309). Phone 315/942-2251. www.boonvillefair.com.* Fourth week in July.

Fall Arts Fest. Craft fair, demonstrations, art show. Second weekend in Oct.

NY State Woodsmen's Field Days. *122 Main St, Boonville (13309). Phone 315/942-4593.* Forest industry exhibits; competition. Third weekend in Aug.

Limited-Service Hotel

★ HEADWATERS MOTOR LODGE. *13524 RR 12, Boonville (13309). Phone 315/942-4493; toll-free 877/787-4606; fax 315/942-4626. www.headwatersmotorlodge.com.* 37 rooms, 2 story. Pets accepted, some restrictions. Complimentary continental breakfast. Check-out 11 am. **$**

Restaurant

★ HULBERT HOUSE. *106 Main St, Boonville (13309). Phone 315/942-4318. www.hulberthouse.com.* Early American décor; antiques; established 1812. American, seafood menu. Dinner. Closed Election Day, Dec 25. Bar. Children's menu. **$**

Brewster (B-3)

See also Mahopac, Mount Kisco, Pound Ridge, White Plains

Settled 1730
Population 2,162
Elevation 395 ft
Area Code 845
Zip 10509
Information Chamber of Commerce; phone 845/279-2477
Web Site www.brewsterchamber.com

What to See and Do

Southeast Museum. *67 Main St, Brewster (10509). Phone 845/279-7500. www.southeastmuseum.org.* Located in the 1896 Old Town Hall of Southeast. Borden dairy condensary, circus, and railroad artifacts; Trainer collection of minerals from Tilly Foster Mine; seasonal exhibits and activities. (Apr-Dec, Tues-Wed, Fri-Sat 10 am-4 pm; closed holidays) **FREE**

Thunder Ridge Ski Area. *Rte 22 and Thunder Ridge Rd, Patterson (12563). 10 miles N on Hwy 22. Phone 845/878-4100.* Three chairlifts, rope tow, Mighty Mite; patrol, school, ski and snowboard rentals; snowmaking; cafeteria, bar. Longest run 1 mile; vertical drop 500 feet. Night skiing. (Dec-Mar, daily; closed Jan 1, Dec 25 morning) Half-day rates. **$$$$**

Restaurant

★ ★ ★ ARCH. *Hwy 22, Brewster (10509). Phone 845/279-5011. www.archrestaurant.com.* So named for its windows overlooking lush, manicured gardens, this restaurant offers a lovely four-course prix fixe dinner of classic European cuisine with delicious game entrées as specials. Service is attentive and friendly. French menu. Dinner, Sun brunch. Closed Mon-Tues; Jan 1. Bar. Children's menu. Outdoor seating. **$$$$**

Bridgehampton (C-5)

What to See and Do

Bridgehampton Commons. *Montauk Hwy, Bridgehampton (11932).* Get out the credit cards and do a little damage. Actually, the prices are reasonable to a bit high at the name brand stores in the Commons shopping plaza. Shops include Eddie Bauer, Banana Republic, Victorias Secret, and Speedo. Shoppers can certainly spend a few enjoyable hours buying gifts for themselves and their friends back home.

Channing Daughters Winery. *1927 Scuttlehole Rd, Bridgehampton (11932). Phone 631/537-7224.* www. *channingdaughters.com.* This new, 30-acre winery serves up a host of wines, such as pinot grigio, cabernet franc, merlot, and chardonnay. Although small, South Forks Channing Daughters has some special features, like its unique wine club, (which offers a variety of discounts on a host of wines), and its wood sculpture garden that showcases the art of owner Walter Channing. These pieces will make an interesting addition to any art collection, but are quite pricey. And, the winery that was once a potato farm has special wine tasting classes all year-round, as well as festivals and parties. Don't pass up this place while visiting the East End. (Daily 11 am-5 pm) **FREE**

Wolffer Estate. *139 Sagg Rd, Bridgehampton (11932). Phone 631/537-5106. www.wolffer.com.* "Beautiful" is the first word that comes to mind as you enter this South Fork estate-like winery, complete with a coin-filled fountain outside. Its equally as attractive inside. The 55-acre vineyard, which opened in 1987, produces a variety of fine wines, including its very popular ros. Many special events here are held during the busy season, from May through August. These include concerts, fund raisers, and chefs tastings. Its amazing what you can do with a former potato farm, a visionary owner, and some wonderful, fertile land. Come here for the beauty, fun events, and most of all, the delectable wines. (Daily 11 am-6 pm) **FREE**

Special Event

Hampton Classic Horse Show. *240 Snake Hollow Rd, Bridgehampton. N of Hwy 27. Phone 631/537-3177. www.hamptonclassic.com.* Horse show jumping event. Celebrities, food, shopping, family activities. Last week Aug.

Restaurants

★ ★ ★ 95 SCHOOL STREET. *95 School St, Bridgehampton (11932). Phone 631/537-5555; fax 631/537-5582.* Special emphasis is placed on the local cuisine and wines of the Hamptons. American menu. Dinner. Bar. **$$**

★ ★ BOBBY VAN'S. *2393 Montauk Hwy, Bridgehampton (11932). Phone 631/537-0590.* Seafood, steak menu. Lunch, dinner. Closed Thanksgiving, Dec 25. Bar. New York City-style chop house. **$$$**

Bronx

See also New York

Area Code 718
Information Chamber of Commerce, 2885 Schley Ave, 10465

Jonas Bronck, a Swedish settler, bought 500 acres of land from the Dutch in 1639, lending his name to the future borough. Locally it is always referred to as "the Bronx," never simply "Bronx." It is the only borough in New York City on the North American continent (the others are all on islands).

What to See and Do

Bronx Museum of the Arts. *1040 Grand Concourse, Bronx (10456). At 165th St. Phone 718/681-6000. www.bxma.org.* Changing exhibits focus on contemporary art and current cultural subjects pertaining to the Bronx. Concerts, family workshops, and special events. (Wed noon-9 pm, Thurs-Sun noon-6 pm) Free admission Wed. **DONATION**

Bronx Zoo. *Fordham Rd and Bronx River Pkwy, Bronx (10460). Liberty Lines runs an express bus to the zoo gates. Catch the BXM11 Bus at designated stops on Madison Ave. Phone 718/652-8400 for the stop nearest you. Phone 718/367-1010. www.bronxzoo.com.* See the endangered snow leopards, come nose to nose with a gorilla, and encourage your kids to ride a camel at the imaginative, exciting Children's Zoo. And don't miss the Bengali Express, a 25-minute monorail ride over forests and plains that are populated by elephants, lions, tigers, and other prowling, playing wildlife. This is the largest urban zoo in the United States, the heart of the Wildlife Conservation Societys efforts to save animals and wild places. The superb and cutting-edge exhibits re-create naturalistic habitats for many of the zoos more than 4,000 animals. Be sure to see the Congo Gorilla Forest and the new habitat, Tiger Mountain. (Daily) **$$$**

City Island. *Island off the SE coast of the Bronx mainland, Bronx (10464). E of Hutchinson River Pkwy, through Pelham Bay Park, via City Island Bridge. Phone 718/829-4111. www.cityisland.com.* Referred to as "a bit of New England in the city," City Island is devoted to shipping and shipbuilding. Seafood restaurants; City Island Historical Nautical Museum (Sun).

Edgar Allan Poe Cottage. *E Kingsbridge Rd and Grand Concourse, Bronx (10458). Phone 718/881-8900.* (1812) Poe wrote *Annabel Lee, The Bells,* and *Ulalume* while living here (1846-1849). Period furniture; exhibits about the poet and his wife. Films, tours (Sat and Sun). **$$**

Fordham University. *441 E Fordham Rd, Bronx (10458). In North Bronx. Phone 718/817-4000. www.fordham.edu.* (1841) (15,000 students) All four original Gothic structures of the Rose Hill campus are designated landmarks: University Chapel (St. John's Church), St. John's Residence Hall, Administration Building, and Alumni House. A second campus is at 60th and Columbus Ave, across from the Lincoln Center for the Performing Arts.

The Hall of Fame for Great Americans. *University Ave and W 181st St, Bronx (10453). Hall of Fame Terrace, on the campus of Bronx Community College. Phone 718/289-5161.* A 630-foot, open-air colonnade provides the framework for bronze busts of great Americans; exhibits. **FREE**

Museum of Bronx History. *3266 Bainbridge Ave, Bronx (10467). At E 208th St. Phone 718/881-8900. www.bronxhistoricalsociety.org.* Valentine-Varian House (1758), site of Revolutionary War activities; exhibits on Bronx history. (Sat 10 am-4 pm and Sun 1-5 pm; tours by appointment on weekdays) **$**

The New York Botanical Garden. *200th St and Kazimiroff Blvd, Bronx (10458). Bronx Park, entrance on Southern Blvd, S of Moshulu Pkwy. Phone 718/817-8700. www.nybg.org.* One of the largest and oldest in the country, this botanical garden consists of 250 acres of natural terrain and 48 gardens. The garden also has the last 40 acres of the forest that once covered New York City. The Enid A. Haupt Conservatory has 11 distinct plant environments with changing exhibits and permanent displays, including the Fern Forest, Palm Court, and Desert Houses. Tours. Education courses. (Tues-Sun 10 am-6 pm; to 5 pm from Nov-Mar; closed Thanksgiving, Dec 25) **$$**

★ New York Yankees (MLB). *Yankee Stadium, 161st St and River Ave, Bronx (10451). Take the B/D/4 subway to 161st StYankee Stadium stop, or hop a leisurely ferry from Manhattan (800/535-3779 for information) to the stadium. Phone 718/293-6000. www.yankees.com.* If you're at all a baseball fan and you are visiting New York City during the summer, you owe it to yourself to catch a Yankees game in the house that Babe Ruth built. Watching the Bronx Bombers is the quintessential New York experience. Get tickets as early as you can, since these legendary pinstripers are popular with locals and tourists alike. The annual games between the Yankees and the New York Mets are always a very early sellout. **$$$$**

> **Yankee Stadium.** *161st St and River Ave, Bronx. Phone 718/293-4300. www.yankees.com.* Home of the New York Yankees.

Pelham Bay Park. *E of the Hutchinson River, Bronx (10475). Hutchinson River and Hutchinson River Pkwy (W); the city's northern limits; Pelham Pkwy, Burr Ave, Bruckner Expy, and Watt Ave (S); and Eastchester Bay and Long Island Sound (E) at NE corner of the Bronx. Phone 718/430-1832.*The city's largest park (2,764 acres) has Orchard Beach, 13 miles of shoreline, fishing, two golf courses (18-hole), a wildlife refuge, an environmental center, a nature trail, a visitor center, tennis courts, ball fields, a running track, riding stables and bridle paths, and picnicking. Also here near southern boundary is

> **Bartow-Pell Mansion Museum.** *895 Shore Rd, Bronx (10464). In Pelham Bay Park. Phone 718/885-1461. www.bartowpellmansionmuseum.org.* Greek Revival stone mansion (circa 1840) furnished in the Empire period; gardens (seasonal); carriage house. (Wed, Sat-Sun noon-4 pm; closed holidays) Guided tours and luncheon tours (by appointment). **$**

Van Cortlandt Golf Course. *Van Cortlandt Park S and Bailey Ave, Bronx (10463). Phone 718/543-4595.* This affordable course in the New York area has a subway stop only a block from its entrance. Former New York mayor Rudy Giuliani appropriated some $4 million in the late 1990s, which helped create 20 new tee boxes and contributed to the overall renovation of a course that was run down from heavy play. Now, its a conversation starter like it was when course architect Tom Bendelow conceived it in the late 1800s. With two par-fives of more than 600 yards each, bring your driver and swing away! **$$$$**

Arthur Avenue

Old-world charm abounds in this charming section of the Bronx, which has been the home of generations of Italian families for more than a century. Seven square blocks make up the Arthur Avenue Retail Market, an Italian-American food oasis. One of the last indoor markets in New York, opened by Mayor Fiorello LaGuardia in the 1940s, it thrives to this day as a bustling cacophony of sights, sounds, and smells. Shoppers entering through the rickety doors can only think of the possibilities lined up before them as they begin to scan the stands. Perhaps some roasted peppers? What about some cardoon fritters? It is a mecca for serious cooks. The crowded storefronts of mom-and-pop shops sell everything from fine Italian wines and homemade pastas to imported cheeses and meats to gifts and cookware.And then there are the mouthwatering restaurants, pizza parlors, and pastry shopssome dating to the 1920sto entice your palate. Have a blast with the two greengrocer brothers whose stand dominates the southern end of the market. Their knowledge of produce and preparation techniques equals any high-priced culinary education. If you are lucky enough to have a garden and are looking for heirloom seed varieties, see Joe Liberatore's Garden of Plenty (2344 Arthur Ave, phone 718/733-7690) located inside the market. They carry seeds ideal for the Italian kitchen, difficult to find elsewhere. Do not miss the fresh, locally made (farm and production in Pennsylvania) cheeses and velvety ricotta at S. Calandra & Sons (2314 Arthur Ave, phone 718/365-7572), or the pungent scent that welcomes you at Calabria Pork Store (2338 Arthur Ave, phone 718/367-5145). Be sure to look up at the gems hanging from the ceiling! The bread sold at Terranova Bakery (691 E 187th St, phone 718/733-3827) is a feast in itself. Marie's Roasted Coffee (2378 Arthur Ave, phone 718/295-0514) will make you disdain any other espresso blend. Get a pound, put it in the car, and no matter how long it takes you to get home, that fresh-ground coffee smell will be overwhelming.Forget calories when shopping here, as the Mediterranean diet is often an excellent health benefit, and you won'tbreak the bank in these reasonably priced eateries and shops. Many of the nearly 200 shops around this densely packed area do not take credit cards, so have plenty of cash on hand. If all the shopping and snooping has made you hungry, one of the best restaurants to enjoy an Italian-American meal is Roberto's (632 E 186th St, phone 718/733-9503). And if you desire a little culture with your stuffed tummy, there's even a small repertory theater, the Belmont Playhouse, dedicated to works by Italian writers. Additionally, the Italian Cultural Center, part of the New York Library, has an amazing collection of Italian books, newspapers, and films. Go ahead and poke your head in; the staff is always helpful.What is most fascinating about the evolution of this historic market is that although the products sold and the dishes served are primarily consumed by Americans of Italian descent, the area serves a nondistinct community. Fordham University students prowl at all hours for sustenance; families coming from or going to the nearby Bronx Zoo or Botanical Garden come by to stock up on tasty morsels for their picnics or for their dining tables back in Manhattan. And any foodie in the area worth his or her salt makes a regular pilgrimage.

Van Cortlandt House Museum. *Broadway and 246th St, Bronx (10025). In Van Cortlandt Park. Phone 718/543-3344. www.vancortlandthouse.org.* (1748) Georgian house is furnished in the 18th-century Dutch-English manner. (Tues-Fri 10 am-3 pm, Sat-Sun 11 am-4 pm; closed holidays) **$**

Wave Hill. *675 W 252nd St, Bronx (10471). 249th St and Independence Ave. Phone 718/549-3200. www.wavehill.org.* This Hudson River estate was, at various times, home to such notables as Mark Twain and Arturo Toscanini; it's now a public garden and cultural center featuring Wave Hill House (1843), gardens, four greenhouses, nature trails, woods, and meadows. The grounds consist of 28 acres overlooking the Hudson. Special events include concerts, dance programs, art exhibits, and education and nature workshops. (Spring-summer Tues-Sun 9 am-5:30 pm, Wed until 9 pm; fall-winter Tues-Sun 9 am-4:30 pm; closed holidays) Free admission Tues, also Sat mornings. **$**

Full-Service Inn

★ ★ ★ LE REFUGE INN. *586 City Island Ave, Bronx (10464). Phone 718/885-2478; fax 718/885-1519.*

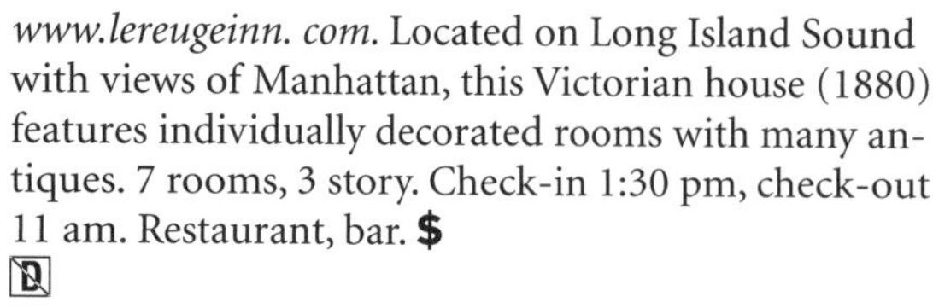

www.lereugeinn. com. Located on Long Island Sound with views of Manhattan, this Victorian house (1880) features individually decorated rooms with many antiques. 7 rooms, 3 story. Check-in 1:30 pm, check-out 11 am. Restaurant, bar. **$**

Restaurants

★ **BLACK WHALE.** *279 City Island Ave, Bronx (10464). Phone 718/885-3657. www.dineatblackwhale. com.* American menu. Lunch, dinner, Sun brunch. Bar. Children's menu. Casual attire. **$$**

★ **CHARLIE'S INN.** *2711 Harding Ave, Bronx (10465). Phone 718/931-9727.* This classic old-timer has been around since the 1930s and is still serving authentic German fare and one of the heartiest all-you-can-eat Sunday brunches in the Bronx, if not the entire city. While the menu includes stomach-filling fare like sauerbraten, Wiener schnitzel, and sausages, it is also stocked with lighter continental dishes like pasta, baked clams, fish, and chicken. In the summer, the restaurant opens its outdoor beer garden on Sundays, giving you the perfect excuse to be lazy all day long. American, German menu. Lunch, dinner, Sun brunch. Closed Mon. Bar. Children's menu. Casual attire. Outdoor seating. **$$**

★ ★ **EMILIA'S.** *2331 Arthur Ave, Bronx (10458). Phone 718/367-5915; fax 718/367-1483. arthuravenuebronx.com/emilia's.htm.* The Bronx is certainly not short on Italian food, but Emilias takes traditional fare and makes it shine, without breaking the bank. Lunch specials are the reason many locals flock here, but dinner is also a sure thing, with a generous menu of pastas, fish, and meat. Emilias serves a killer tiramisu with a healthy dose of alcohol in the sponge cake that will make you want to return and have dessert for dinner. Italian menu. Lunch, dinner. Closed Mon; Dec 25. Bar. **$$**

★ **FEEDING TREE.** *892 Gerard Ave, Bronx (10452). Phone 718/293-5025.* Feeding Tree is one of New Yorks most beloved Jamaican restaurants, located within a home runs distance from Yankee Stadium. At this friendly and lively joint, a steel drum plays in the background, and you can almost feel the Caribbean sun on your face. This is the sort of spot to tuck a napkin into your collar and fill up on jerk chicken, stewed kingfish, oxtails, curried goat, and crisp golden patties filled with spiced meatthe perfect snack to grab before a game. Caribbean menu. Breakfast, lunch, dinner. Children's menu. Casual attire. **$$**

★ ★ **JIMMY'S BRONX CAFE.** *281 W Fordham Rd, Bronx (10468). Phone 718/329-2000.* This legendary Bronx restaurant and bar from the venerable Jimmy Rodriguez has a cult following, and is especially nutty when the Yankees are playing. This is one of the few velvet rope joints in the Bronx, with a boisterous bar and a cavernous 450-seat restaurant jammed with sports, music, and celebrities. The Caribbean-Latin menu is an ode to Rodriguezs Latin-American heritage, and the kitchen turns out impressively tasty and flavorful food. Don't expect a peaceful night here; aside from the din of the crowds and the thumping beat of the music, the place is also a sports bar and boasts more than 15 televisions. Caribbean, Latin menu. Lunch, dinner, late-night. Bar. Casual attire. **$$**

★ ★ ★ **LE REFUGE INN.** *586 City Island Ave, Bronx (10464). Phone 718/885-2478. www.lerefugeinn. com.* Le Refuge Inn is, as its name suggests, a refuge. This 19th-century Victorian manor house on historic City Island is a cozy chalet of warmth, peace, and romanceperfect for melting away stress. Surrounded by the waters of the Long Island Sound, you will instantly be transported to the French countryside once tucked inside the elegant antique-filled dining room and treated to a menu of wonderful classics like bouillabaisse and duck l'orange. French menu. Dinner. Closed Mon. Bar. Children's menu. Jacket required. Reservations recommended. Outdoor seating. **$$**

★ ★ **LOBSTER BOX.** *34 City Island Ave, Bronx (10464). Phone 718/885-1952; fax 718/885-3232. www.lobsterbox.com.* The Lobster Box is a historic City Island landmark that, true to its name, offers its specialty, fresh lobster, any way you like it. Choices include broiled, steamed, stuffed, fra diavolo, or marinara, and every preparation is delicious. Pasta is also on the menu, many laden with meaty bits of lobster meat, like the lobster ravioli with sun-dried tomatoes and basil cream sauce. The Lobster Box is an easy-to-love place where the portions are generous and the expansive river views are mesmerizing. Seafood menu. Lunch, dinner. Bar. Casual attire. Valet parking. **$$**

★ ★ **ROBERTO'S TRATTORIA.** *603 Crescent Ave, Bronx (10458). Phone 718/733-9503.* Set in the Italian enclave of the Bronx, Robertos Trattoria is not high on décor or elegant atmosphere, but it is filled with terrific food prepared in the Positano style. The kitchen is surehanded and sends out home-style dishes like grilled calamari and assorted pastas, as well as heartier fare like tender short ribs. For a real treat, ask the kitchen to prepare the house specialty, a four-course meal with dishes from Robertos native Amalfi coast that will bring applause to your table. Italian menu. Lunch, dinner. Closed Mon. Casual attire. Outdoor seating. **$$**

★ VENICE RESTAURANT AND PIZZERIA. *772 E 149th St, Bronx (10455). Phone 718/585-5164.* Old-school pizza and pasta are what you'll find at Venice, a little short on décor but long on value and honest Italian-American food. Founded more than 50 years ago, this restaurant has a menu that focuses on seafood but also offers whole thin-crust pies. Italian menu, pizza. Lunch, dinner. Children's menu. Casual attire. **$$**

★ VERNON'S NEW JERK HOUSE. *987 E 223rd St, Bronx (10466). Phone 718/655-8348.* As the name suggests, Caribbean fare is the specialty of the house at Vernons New Jerk House, a lively spot in the Bronx with an easy vibe and a loyal community following. Dinner here can mean a ginger beer and a bowl of curried goat, or a plate of sweet-spiced jerk chicken with rice and beans. Take this advice: if you have never tried jerk, make a special trip; it doesn't get much better than this, at least without a plane ticket. Caribbean menu. Lunch, dinner. Bar. Casual attire. No credit cards accepted. **$**

Bronxville

Restaurant

★ ★ PANE E VINO. *124 Pondfield Rd, Bronxville (10708). Phone 914/337-3330; fax 914/337-3300. www.paneevino.net.* Italian menu. Dinner. Closed Mon; holidays. Casual attire. Reservations recommended. **$$**

Brooklyn

See also New York

Area Code 718
Information Brooklyn Historical Society, 128 Pierrepont St, 11201, phone 718/254-9830; or the NYC Convention & Visitors Bureau, phone 212/484-1200.

Many of the novels, plays, films, and television shows about New York Cityranging from *Death of a Salesman* to *The Honeymooners*are set in Brooklyn rather than Manhattan, perhaps because of the widely differing characters of these two boroughs. While Manhattan is world-class in sophistication and influence, Brooklyn is famous for such things as the hot dogs on Coney Island, and always has been quintessentially American.

Yet there is much more to Brooklyn than the popular stereotype. Manhattanites flock to performances at the renowned Brooklyn Academy of Music, and the Egyptology collection at the Brooklyn Museum compares with those in London and Cairo. Brooklyn's beautiful Prospect Park was designed by Olmsted and Vaux, who considered it more beautiful than another park they designedCentral Park in Manhattan.

As the most heavily populated borough, Brooklyn handles about 40 percent of New York City's vast shipping industry. It was pieced together from 25 independent villages and fought valiantly before allowing itself to be taken into New York City in 1898.

What to See and Do

Atlantic Avenue. *Atlantic Ave, Brooklyn (11201). Take the M/N/R subway to Court St; the 2/3/4/5 subway to Borough Hall; or the A/C/F subway to Jay St/Borough Hall.* Imagine a colorful shopping bazaar in downtown Cairo, and you've just pictured Atlantic Avenue. This area has a mix of more than 30 antiques and gift shops, ethnic food and bread stores, and savory Middle Eastern restaurants. If you crave real falafel, kebabs, and hummus at value prices, this is the neighborhood to visit. You can also enjoy a mild day by wandering around nearby Brooklyn Heights, with its quaint brownstone apartments and quiet streets.

Brooklyn Academy of Music. *30 Lafayette Ave, Brooklyn (10007). Fort Greene/Clinton Hill. Phone 718/636-4100. www.bam.org.* (1907) Founded in 1859, BAM is the oldest performing arts center in America, presenting original productions in contemporary performing arts in the Next Wave Festival each fall, noted national and international theater, dance, and opera companies, and classical and contemporary music programs.

Brooklyn Children's Museum. *145 Brooklyn Ave, Brooklyn (11213). At St. Mark's Ave. Phone 718/735-4400.* www.*bchildmus.org.* Founded in 1899, this is the world's oldest children's museum, featuring interactive exhibits, workshops, and special events. "The Mystery of Things" teaches children about cultural and scientific objects, and "Music Mix" welcomes young virtuosos. (Wed-Fri 2-5 pm, Sat-Sun 10 am-5 pm; also school holidays) **$$**

Brooklyn Heights Promenade. *The R subway goes to the nearby City Hall stop. Phone 718/965-8900.* For a peaceful stroll and a great view of Manhattan, visit this 1/3-mile-long waterfront area, stretching from Orange Street on the north to Remsen Street on the south. Pack a lunch, claim a bench, and enjoy the sights of the city skyline, Ellis Island, and Statue of Liberty. The promenade is lined with lovely homes and is a popular outdoor hangout for Brooklyn Heights yuppies during the summer. If you're in town over Independence Day weekend, this is usually a great place to view the Fourth of July fireworks. (Daily)

Brooklyn Historical Society. *128 Pierrepont St, Brooklyn Heights (11201). At the corner of Clinton and Pierrepont. Phone 718/222-4111. www.brooklynhistory.org.* This terra-cotta and pressed-brick building, designed by noted architect George Post, has been the headquarters of the Brooklyn Historical Society since 1881. Permanent and changing exhibits deal with Brooklyn history; the major exhibition, Brooklyn Works: 400 Years of Making a Living in Brooklyn, combines re-created stage set environments, authentic personal narratives, historic primary documents, and interactive media and games. Programs include performances, readings, lectures, and activities for children. (Wed-Thurs, Sat 10 am-5 pm; Fri 10 am-8 pm; Sun noon-5 pm; closed holidays) **$$**

Coney Island. *1208 Surf Ave, Brooklyn (11224). Phone 718/372-5159. www.coneyisland.com.* Although it's become a bit frayed, you can still experience a bit of old New York along Coney Island's beachfront boardwalk. Take a ride on the legendary Cyclone roller coaster at **Astroland Amusement Park** (1000 Surf Ave, 718/372-0275, www.astroland.com; open on weekends in Apr, seven days a week June-Labor Day). Afterward, grab the perfect hot dog, waffle fries, and a lemonade at Nathans Famous. For some really cheesy thrills, experience the nearby circus sideshow shown on weekends in summer. **FREE**

Discovery Tour of Brooklyn. *49 W 45th St, Brooklyn (10036). Phone 212/397-2600.*Six-hour bus tour to many of Brooklyn's sites and neighborhoods. Departs from Gray Line Bus Terminal in Manhattan. (May-Oct, Thurs and Sat) **$$$$**

Dyker Beach Golf Course. *86th St and 7th Ave, Brooklyn (11228). Phone 718/836-9722.* Easily accessible via public transit, Dyker Beach is inexpensive and should be playable for almost any golfer. Its open year-round and can be busy, but there aren't many trees, and the course offers a few nice views. Dyker Beach was built just before the turn of the 20th century and was redesigned in the 1930s. New Yorkers will tell you that its a must to play at some point if you live in close proximity to the city. **$$$$**

Gateway National Recreation Area. *Kings Hwy and Flatbush Ave, Brooklyn (11234). Phone 718/338-3338. www.nps.gov/gate.* One of the nation's first two urban national parks. A barrier peninsula across Rockaway Inlet from Coney Island via Flatbush Ave and the Marine Pkwy Bridge. This sprawling, urban recreation area consists of approximately 26,000 acres of land and water in two statesNew York and New Jersey: Floyd Bennett Field in Brooklyn (Jamaica Bay in Brooklyn and Queens), Breezy Point on the Rockaway Peninsula in Queens, Miller Field, and Great Kills Park on southeastern Staten Island and the Sandy Hook Unit in New Jersey. Jamaica Bay Wildlife Refuge in Broad Channel, Queens (9,000 acres) offers wildlife observation and hiking trails. Floyd Bennett Field has nature observation opportunities. Jacob Riis Park in Queens, with a mile-long boardwalk, offers beach and waterfront activities. Fort Tilden in Queens offers exhibits, nature walks, guided and self-guided tours of old defense batteries, sporting events, and fishing. Canarsie Pier in Brooklyn offers free weekend summer concerts and restaurants. The Staten Island Unit offers hiking trails, organized athletic programs, and recreational activities. Concession services at some units. **FREE**

New York Aquarium. *W 8th St and Surf Ave, Brooklyn (11224). Phone 718/265-3474. www.nyaquarium.org.* A varied collection of marine life that includes sharks, beluga whales, seals, seahorses, jellyfish, penguins, sea otters, and walruses. Dolphin feedings (Apr-Oct, outdoors); sea lion shows. Restaurant. (Opens daily at 10 am; closing times vary by season) **$$$**

New York Transit Museum. *Boerum Pl at Schermerhorn St, Brooklyn Heights (11201). Phone 718/243-8601. www.mta.nyc.ny.us/museum.* Exhibits on the history of the New York City transit system displayed within a 1930s subway station. Subway cars on display, including a 1903 "El" car. Photographs, maps, antique turnstiles. (Tues-Sun; closed holidays) **$$**

Prospect Park. *211 9th Ave, Brooklyn (11215). Bounded by Parkside Ave, Ocean Ave, Flatbush Ave, and Prospect Park W and SW. Phone 718/438-0100. www.prospect-park.org.* Planned by Olmsted and Vaux, designers of Central Park, its 526 acres include the impressive Grand Army Plaza with Memorial Arch (N end of park), the 90-acre Long Meadow, and a 60-acre lake. The Boathouse Visitor Center has information on park history and design; art shows (Apr-Nov). Ball fields, boating, ice rink, bridle paths, tennis courts, bandshell, historic

Brooklyn Heights

Brooklyn Heights and Atlantic Avenue provide a wonderful combination of historic Brooklyn (dating to when it was an independent city), fantastic Manhattan skyline views, and some of New York City's best ethnic food and shops.

The best start is to walk from Manhattan over the Brooklyn Bridge—about a 20-minute journey. Started in 1869 and completed in 1883, it was (at that time) the longest suspension bridge in the world (1,600 feet). It is now the oldest existing suspension bridge in America.

Coming off the bridge, follow the right-hand sidewalks onto Adams Street and Cadman Plaza. Walk the length of the Plaza onto Court Street to Brooklyn Borough Hall, a remarkable Beaux Arts building circa 1848. Free tours are offered on Tuesdays at 1 pm. Leave Borough Hall, walking back the way you came, and turn left onto Montague Street. This neighborhood was Manhattan's first "suburb." Montague is the neighborhood's main street, and it holds a potpourri of restaurants, businesses, and shops. At Clinton Street stands St. Ann's Church. The building contains 60 stained-glass windows, the first ever produced in the United States. Follow Clinton one block to Pierrepont Street, turn left, and stop in at the Brooklyn Historical Society (28 Pierrepont). This landmark building houses exhibits on the borough's past, as well as venues for performances and art exhibits.

At the end of Montague walk up onto the Promenade, the tour's highlight. It stretches north for about six blocks and offers fabulous Manhattan views. Exit the Promenade at Pineapple Street. Turn left onto Columbia Heights and walk to Fulton Landing at its end, once a ferry terminal and now the site of Barge Music, classical concerts staged on a barge moored in the river. Turn right onto Old Fulton Street. At 19 Fulton Street, right under the Brooklyn Bridge, is Patsy Grimaldi's, a.k.a. Patsy's Pizza, a family operation that serves what many have called the city's best pizza.

Continue on Old Fulton, which becomes Cadman Plaza West, and turn right on Henry Street. At this point, feel free to wander among the grid of streets—Clinton, Henry, Hicks, Willow, Cranberry, Orange, and Pineapple—to take in the townhouses and wood-framed buildings. More than half of Brooklyn Heights' structures predate the Civil War. On Henry Street, note the St. George Hotel (100 Henry St), a landmark built in 1884. Henry runs some 11 blocks before it intersects Atlantic Avenue. Turn left on Atlantic and enter a frenetic and fascinating world of Middle Eastern stores and restaurants. Be sure to visit Sahadi (187 Atlantic) for a huge choice of fruits, nuts, candies, olives, feta cheese, and grains by the pound; La Bouillabaisse (145 Atlantic) for great seafood; the Moroccan Star (205 Atlantic) for fine Middle Eastern fare; the Waterfront Ale House (155 Atlantic) for micro-brew; and, for dessert, either the Damascus Bakery (195 Atlantic)—fantastic pita bread and spinach pies and baklava—or Pete's Ice Cream (185 Atlantic), a shop with superb homemade ice cream and baked goods. For one last place to visit, turn left on Boerum Place and walk two blocks to Schermerhorn Street to the Transit Museum, which explores the city's subway and mass-transit system.

carousel, and the Lefferts Homestead, a 1783 Dutch colonial farmhouse. Directly across Flatbush Ave is

Brooklyn Botanic Garden. *1000 Washington Ave, Brooklyn (11225). Phone 718/623-7200.* For a peaceful respite away from Manhattan, hop the 1 or 2 subway to Eastern Parkway in Brooklyn and enjoy a natural wonder: the 52-acre Brooklyn Botanic Garden. It features a gorgeous Japanese garden; the Steinhardt Conservatory, which has several greenhouses filled with a variety of plants; and the Fragrance Garden, designed specifically for the blind. There are rose gardens, the annual cherry blossom festival, and many other beautiful sights to behold as well. (Apr-Sept: Tues-Fri 8 am-6 pm, Sat-Sun from 10 am; Oct-Mar: Tues-Fri 8 am-4:30 pm, Sat-Sun from 10 am; closed Jan 1, Thanksgiving, Dec 25) **$**

Brooklyn Museum of Art. *200 Eastern Pkwy, Brooklyn (11238). Phone 718/638-5000.* Although it's often overlooked by tourists, the Brooklyn Museum of Art is one of the city's foremost art institutions. Similar to the Metropolitan in some ways, it is housed in a lovely Beaux Arts building, with collections spanning virtually the entire history of art. Highlights include a large Egyptian wing, a superb Native American collection, and a major permanent assemblage of contemporary art. In addition to staging some of the more unusual and controversial exhibits in town, the museum also hosts a "First Saturday" series (the first Saturday of every month, 5-11 pm) featuring free concerts, performances, films, dances, and dance lessons. The sculpture garden, with architectural ornaments from buildings demolished in the New York City area, is a lovely spot. (Wed-Fri 10 am-5 pm, Sat-Sun 11 am-6 pm; closed Jan 1, Thanksgiving, Dec 25) **$$**

Sheepshead Bay. *2575 Coney Island Ave, Brooklyn (11223). Just E and slightly N of Coney Island via Ocean Pkwy or Shore Pkwy. Phone 718/627-6611.* This area has all the requisites of an ocean fishing community: seafood restaurants, clam bars, tackle shops, fishing boats, and some lovely views.

Full-Service Hotel

★ ★ ★ MARRIOTT BROOKLYN BRIDGE NEW YORK. *333 Adams St, Brooklyn (11201). Phone 718/246-7000; toll-free 888/436-3759; fax 718/246-0563. www.brooklynmarriott.com.* 376 rooms, 7 story. Check-in 4 pm, check-out 11 am. High-speed Internet access. Restaurant, bar. Indoor pool. Business center. **$$$**

Restaurants

★ ★ 360. *360 Van Brunt St, Brooklyn (11231). Phone 718/246-0360.* The restaurant 360 is an off-the-beaten-path neighborhood spot that may take a bit of effort to find, but those who persevere will be rewarded. The dining room is marked by artisan woodwork as well as by partner Arnaud Erharts charming ways that welcome you inside, help you make a wine selection from the mostly organic list, and ensure that your night here is memorable. But the charm doesn't just come from the dining room; the kitchen also doles out the goods in the form of a three-course prix fixe menu that changes daily, with dishes like roasted scallops with leek fondue, hanger steak, and la carte, wine-friendly bites like oysters and charcuterie. French menu. Dinner. Closed Mon-Wed. Bar. Casual attire. Reservations recommended. Outdoor seating. No credit cards accepted. **$$**

★ ★ AL DI LA TRATTORIA. *248 Fifth St, Brooklyn (11215). Phone 718/636-8888.* www.aldilatrattoria.com. Al Di La is a charming neighborhood trattoria decorated with antiques and crowded with candlelit tables of locals laughing and inhaling the delicious Venetian cuisine. It is owned by a husband-wife team (he runs the room, she is in the kitchen) who have amassed a strong fan base, making lines inevitable. But patience will pay off, as the daily changing menu from chef Anna Klinger (Lespinasse and San Francisco's La Folie) includes stunning antipasti like grilled sardines with fennel; magnificent pastas like poppy-seeded sweet beet ravioli; and savory main courses like braised rabbit over polenta and roasted monkfish with lemon-rosemary escarole. Italian menu. Dinner. Closed Sun. Bar. Casual attire. Reservations recommended. Valet parking. **$$$**

★ ★ ALMA. *187 Columbia St, Brooklyn (11231). Phone 718/643-5400. www.almarestaurant.com.* After many years as chef at Zarela (see), one of Manhattans most popular authentic Mexican restaurants, chef Gary Jacobson decided to take his soulful chile-laden fare to Brooklyn. At Alma, a bilevel restaurant and bar with a stunning lantern-lit roof deck for dining by skyline, you will find his food has remained as good as it was on Second Avenue. Guacamole; tortillas filled with braised duck; sweet, warm tamales; and tender seafood ceviche make up some of the best appetizers while generous entrées include dishes like ancho chile rellenos stuffed with shredded pork, raisins, and green olives. Mexican menu. Dinner, brunch. Bar. Business casual attire. Reservations recommended. Valet parking. Outdoor seating. **$$**

★ ★ BLUE RIBBON BROOKLYN. *280 Fifth Ave, Brooklyn (11215). Phone 718/840-0404. www.blueribbonrestaurant.com.* Set in a former grocery store in Park Slope, Blue Ribbon Brooklyn is a sleek, bustling and expansive, brick-colored bistro with a well-stocked raw barjust like its next door sibling, Blue Ribbon Sushi (see). But in addition, this branch also offers the owners (brothers Bruce and Eric Bromberg) signature overly ambitious menu filled with all sorts of deliciously comforting dishesmarrow bones, chicken liver, variations on surf and turf, famous fried chicken, and plates of golden fries piled sky-high. Like the New York branch, the restaurant is open until 4 am to satisfy all those late-night hunger pangs. American menu. Breakfast (Sun), dinner, late-night. Children's menu. Casual attire. **$$**

★ ★ **BLUE RIBBON SUSHI.** *278 Fifth Ave, Brooklyn (11215). Phone 718/840-0408. www.blueribbonrestaurant.com.* Blue Ribbon Sushi is the beloved Brooklyn sibling of the brothers Brombergs Blue Ribbon Sushi in the city. Located on a thriving strip of Fifth Avenue in Park Slope, this lively wood-accented restaurant and sushi bar offers the same winning formula the Brombergs offer in Manhattanjust to larger crowds, thanks to easier access to real estate. Expect the best raw fish in town, warm and knowledgeable service, and a tremendous selection of sakebut not a table after 7 pm without a wait. Japanese, sushi menu. Dinner, late-night. Closed Mon. Children's menu. Casual attire. **$$$**

★ ★ **BONITA.** *338 Bedford Ave, Williamsburg (11211). Phone 718/384-9500.* Although Bonita can get very crowded, you will still be happy you came to this happenin' little eatery that serves top-notch authentic Mexican fare in a lively diner-esque setting. Owned by the folks who own Diner (see), also in the youthful hipster land of Williamsburg, Bonita serves spot-on tapas-style Mexican fare including a vibrant, chile-studded guacamole, a hefty torta, and a mean mole. The vibe is cool and slick yet the service is friendly and efficient with no 'tude. Mexican menu. Lunch, dinner. Closed Mon. Bar. Casual attire. Valet parking. **$$**

★ ★ **CHESTNUT.** *271 Smith St, Brooklyn (11231). Phone 718/243-0049. www.chestnutonsmith.com.* Chestnut, a cozy newcomer to Cobble Hills restaurant row (Smith Street), is already winning fans from the hood and from Manhattan. With its wide French doors, high blond chestnut-beamed ceilings, and raw slate-tiled walls, the restaurant is a warm, lively gathering place that makes you feel like staying a long while. The talented kitchen turns out a menu of honest and delicious food with ingredients that shine, and plates that are filled with smart, creative, and well-articulated flavors. The menu features rustic dishes like chicken liver and apple toast as well as more elegant dishes like tea-smoked scallops with fingerling potatoes and sweet-hot mustard, and comforting plates like roasted organic chicken with artichokes and soft polenta. American menu. Dinner. Closed Mon. Bar. Casual attire. Reservations recommended. Outdoor seating. **$$**

★ ★ **CONVIVIUM OSTERIA.** *68 Fifth Ave, Brooklyn (11217). Phone 718/857-1833.* Convivium Osteria is a local gem serving some of the most soul-satisfying Mediterranean fare in the borough, if not all of New York City. With a setting straight out of a hillside in Tuscany, the restaurant is all aglow in candlelight and a rustic, distressed vintage design that makes you feel like it's been here forever. The menu is stocked with country-style dishes from Spain, Portugal, and Italy that focus on robust flavors in casseroles, as well as earthy pastas, slow-cooked meats, and plentiful amounts of preserved, cured, and smoked ingredientsthink salt cod and lots of delicious pig parts. Mediterranean menu. Dinner. Casual attire. Outdoor seating. **$$**

★ **DINER.** *85 Broadway, Williamsburg (11211). Phone 718/486-3077.* Williamsburg hipsters flock to Diner like ants to a picnic. Indeed, this place often feels like a zoo for young, thrift-store clad locals. Set in a loungy, refurbished dining car, this bar and restaurant is a mess hall for struggling writers, actors, musicians, and the like. The menu is a fun selection of contemporary American dishes including juicy burgers, platters of charcuterie, fresh salads, crisp and golden fries, and hearty sandwiches stuffed with seasonal ingredients. American menu. Lunch, dinner, late-night, brunch. Casual attire. **$$**

★ **GRIMALDI'S PIZZERIA.** *19 Old Fulton St, Brooklyn (11201). Phone 718/858-4300.* In Brooklyn, Grimaldi's is synonymous with pizza. And not just any old pizza by the slice, but thin-crusted, piping hot pizza pies layered with milky house-made mozzarella, bright tomato sauce, and vibrant strips of zingy basil. The restaurant is decorated in casual pizzeria style with gingham-printed tablecloths and the requisite Sinatra soundtrack playing in the background. Aside from the basic tomato, mozzarella, and basil pies, you can choose your own mess of toppings from a wide list that includes spicy sausage, house-roasted peppers, spinach, and mushrooms. Pizza. Lunch, dinner. Bar. Children's menu. Casual attire. **$**

★ ★ **M SHANGHAI BISTRO & DEN.** *129 Havenmeyer St, Brooklyn (11211). Phone 718/384-9300. www.mshanghaibistroandden.com.* M Shanghai is not your average Chinese restaurant. Decorated in a slinky style, with chocolate brown banquet tables, brick walls, and a moody soundtrack, M is a lovely den of design and food, graciously presided over by owner May Liu. The menu also sets itself apart from the fray with vibrant dishes of steamed dumplings and puffy pork buns, and deliciously flavored main courses like shredded pork with bean curd and salmon with smooth and well-seasoned tofu sauce. Once you are through with dinner, head down to the hopping downstairs lounge. Chinese menu. Dinner, late-night. Closed Mon. Bar. Casual attire. **$$**

★ ★ PATOIS. *255 Smith St, Brooklyn (11231). Phone 718/855-1535. www.patoisrestaurant.com.* Restaurant Row in Cobble Hill is Smith Street, and Patois is one of this hopping streets original destinations for flavorful French fare served in a warm bistro setting. Patois overflows with charm from its saffron-colored walls, open kitchen, and delightful Provenal-style garden. The menu is classic French (think steak frites), with a little bit of Morocco thrown in for good measure in dishes like lamb sausage with couscous and nectarine chutney. The weekend brunch is a zoo, so grab a mimosa or an espresso and get ready to wait in line. French menu. Dinner, Sun brunch. Closed Mon. Casual attire. Outdoor seating. **$$**

★ ★ ★ PETER LUGER STEAK HOUSE. *178 Broadway, Brooklyn (11211). Phone 718/387-7400; fax 718/387-3523. www.peterluger.com.* Peter Luger Steak House is the stuff legends are made of. This landmark restaurant has been serving juicy porterhouse steaks since 1887 and is still one of the citys top tables. Don't expect elegant surroundings with your expertly charred dry-aged slab of beef, though. This place is bare bones, with exposed beamed ceilings, worn tables and chairs, and waiters that are as well seasoned as the beef. In addition to the gorgeously marbled steaks, you can dig into sides like German-fried potatoes and creamed spinach. If you make it over for lunch you can wrap your hands around New Yorks best burger, made from fresh ground beef and served with slices of tearjerker raw onion and a thick beefsteak tomato. Steak menu. Lunch, dinner. Bar. Casual attire. Reservations recommended. **$$$$**

★ ★ RELISH. *225 Wythe Ave, Brooklyn (11211). Phone 718/963-4546.* At Relish, a sleek, refurbished railcar diner, you can dig into contemporary Southern fare in style. This former dining car is now a bright, stylish, windowed hang, offering regional comfort food like macaroni and cheese, hearty cheeseburgers, and rich, smoked pork loin with spiced mango chutney. Relish is also quite the popular spot on weekends, when the crowds line up for the eggs with Serrano ham and cheddar grits. American menu. Lunch, dinner. Bar. Casual attire. Outdoor seating. **$$**

★ ★ ★ RIVER CAFE. *1 Water St, Brooklyn (11201). Phone 718/522-5200; fax 718/875-0037. www.rivercafe.com.* If romance is on the evenings agenda, The River Café should be as well. Located on the Brooklyn waterfront, with the an unmatched view of the East River and the twinkling Manhattan skyline, this elegant old-timer has always been a favorite for celebrating special occasions and for creating reasons to celebrate new ones. The kitchen is skilled at sophisticated New American fare like lobster, rack of lamb, and duck, artistically plated so as to inspire oohs and aaahs. The wine list is award winning, the service is graceful and unobtrusive, and is practiced at staying away when not needed, so as to let the romance bloom. American menu. Lunch, dinner. Bar. Jacket required. Reservations recommended. Valet parking. Outdoor seating. **$$$$**

★ ★ SAUL. *140 Smith St, Brooklyn (11201). Phone 718/935-9844. www.restaurantsaul.com.* Restaurant Saul is one of those truly inviting spots that every neighborhood craves. Known for its terrific New American farecourtesy of chef/owner Saul Bolton—Saul is urbane in décor, with warm, sandy tones and exposed brick walls. The modest menu reflects Boltons training at Le Bernardin (see); expect plates adorned with stunning seasonal ingredients and simple, flavorful preparations of everything from diver scallops, to leg of lamb, duck confit, and foie gras. Don't forget to have dessert; Saul is known for its sweets, especially the classic baked Alaska. American menu. Dinner, Sun brunch. Bar. Casual attire. **$$**

★ ★ SEA. *114 N 6th St, Brooklyn (11211). Phone 718/384-8850.* Sea is known just as much for its wild Zen-inspired disco décor (complete with an in-ground pool watched over by a golden Buddha) as it is for its fiery Thai fare. Often crowded and loud, with fast servers who are interested in turning tables, Sea is not a peaceful place to dine, but it is a tasty one. The menu includes dishes like whole red snapper, rice paper-wrapped spring rolls, and a fun list of desserts like the crispy banana with green tea ice cream. The cocktail list guarantees a hangover with easy-to-imbibe drinks like the spicy pineapple-ginger martini. Thai menu. Lunch, dinner, late-night. Bar. Casual attire. Reservations recommended. **$$**

★ ★ SUPERFINE. *126 Front St, Brooklyn (11201). Phone 718/243-9005.* Located in DUBMO, Superfine is a casual neighborhood eatery with a warm, earthy vibe marked by brick walls, high ceilings, stunning flower arrangements, and views of the Manhattan Bridge. The kitchen boasts some serious skills, turning out robust Texas-style fare like seared duck breast with rutabaga and sliced shiitake mushrooms, and grilled pork chops with mashed potatoes and bitter greens. The menu of easy-to-love eats has the place packed with kids and families and hot crop of locals. On Sundays, brunch gets a pick-me-up from a bluegrass band and burritos laced with eggs, refried beans, and zesty salsa. American menu. Lunch, dinner, Sun brunch. Closed Mon. Bar. Casual attire. **$$**

★★★ **THE GROCERY.** *288 Smith St, Brooklyn (11231). Phone 718/596-3335.* When husband-wife team Charlie Kiely and Sharon Patcherchef-veterans of the New York restaurant sceneopened The Grocery, an intimate spot on Smith Street with a leafy back patio and yard, they had no idea that they would inspire a cult following. This stylish, earth-toned dining room has a serene vibe, and the delicious food coming out of the tiny kitchen makes the 13-table space all the more exquisite, with dishes that mirror the seasons. There's not a plate on the menu that won't make your mouth water. Seasons dictate the menu, but star dishes include brook trout with spinach and bacon-flecked spaetzle, ratatouille-stuffed squid, roasted beets with goat cheese ravioli, duck confit with roasted quince sauce, and pork loin with sweet potatoes and roasted pears. Get ready to fall in love with dining in Brooklyn. American menu. Dinner. Closed Sun. Bar. Casual attire. Outdoor seating. **$$$**

Buffalo (D-2)

See also Batavia, East Aurora, Niagara Falls

Population 292,648
Elevation 600 ft
Area Code 716
Information Buffalo Niagara Convention & Visitors Bureau, 617 Main St, Suite 400; phone 716/852-0511 or toll-free 888/228-3369
Web Site www.buffalocvb.org

Buffalo, at the eastern end of Lake Erie, is New York's second-largest city and one of the largest railroad centers in America. Fifteen freight depots and one passenger terminal handle more than 25,000 trains annually. Major products are metal alloys and abrasives; automobile parts and tires; aerospace and defense products; medical, dental, and pharmaceutical devices and products; chemicals and dyes; and food products.

Planned by Joseph Ellicott (agent of the Holland Land Company) in 1803-1804, the city was modeled after Washington, DC, which was laid out by his brother, Major Andrew Ellicott. Buffalo radiates from Niagara Square, dominated by a monument to President William McKinley, who was assassinated here while attending the Pan-American Exposition in 1901. The area also includes a $7 million city hall, state, and federal buildings. The Buffalo Philharmonic Orchestra, Albright-Knox Art Gallery, and many nightclubs cater to the varied interests of residents and visitors. The city is ringed with 3,000 acres of parks, which offer swimming, boating, tennis, golf, and riding.

In 1679, when Buffalo was claimed by the French, La Salle built the first boat to sail the Great Lakes, the wooden *Griffon*. During the War of 1812, Buffalo was burned by the British, but its 500 citizens returned a few months later and rebuilt. In 1816, *Walk-on-the-Water,* the first steamboat to ply the Great Lakes, was launched here. The opening of the Erie Canal in 1825 made Buffalo the major transportation break between east and west and brought trade and prosperity. Joseph Dart's invention in 1843 of a steam-powered grain elevator caused Buffalo's grain-processing industry to boom.

Since completion of the St. Lawrence Seaway in 1959, Buffalo has been one of the top Great Lakes ports in import-export tonnage.

Public Transportation

Buses and trains (Metro), phone 716/855-7211.

Airport. Buffalo/Niagara International Airport. Cash machines, gateway and baggage claim areas.

Information Phone 716/630-6000

Lost and Found Phone 716/630-6150

What to See and Do

Albright-Knox Art Gallery. *1285 Elmwood Ave, Buffalo (14222). Phone 716/882-8700. www.albrightknox.org.* Eighteenth-century English, 19th-century French and American, 20th-century American and European paintings; works by Picasso, Matisse, Monet, Renoir, and Van Gogh; sculpture from 3000 BC-present. Changing exhibits. (Tues-Sat 10 am-5 pm, Sun noon-5 pm; closed holidays) **$$**

Allentown. *Allen St.* Historic preservation district containing Victorian-era structures of every major style. Many restaurants, antique stores, art galleries, and boutiques.

Architecture in Buffalo. Among the works of famous figures in American architecture are

Frank Lloyd Wright houses. *Phone 716/829-3543.* 125 Jewett Pkwy (Darwin D. Martin House), 118 Summit (George Barton House), 285 Woodward (Gardener's Cottage), 57 Tillinghast Pl (Walter V. Davidson House), and 76 Soldiers Pl (William Heath House).

Prudential Building. *28 Church St, Buffalo (14202). Phone 716/829-3543.* (1895-1896) Designed by Dankmar Adler and Louis Sullivan, the Prudential (formerly Guaranty) Building is an outstanding example of Sullivan's ideas of functional design and terra-cotta ornament; one of America's great skyscrapers.

Boat trips. *Miss Buffalo.* *Erie Basin Marina, Buffalo. Phone 716/856-6696; toll-free 800/244-8684. www.missbuffalo.com.* Buffalo Charter Cruises. *Miss Buffalo II* (200 capacity) leaves Erie Basin Marina, for afternoon or evening cruise of harbor, Niagara River, and Lake Erie. (July and Aug: daily; June and Sept: Sat-Sun; also evening cruises) *Niagara Clipper* leaves from North Tonawanda for lunch, brunch, and dinner cruises around Grand Island. (May-Oct) **$$$$**

Buffalo & Erie County Botanical Gardens. *Olmsted's South Park, 2655 S Park Ave, Lackawanna (14218). 4 miles SE, 2 miles off NY State Thrwy I-90, exit 55 W Ridge Rd, to S Park Ave. Phone 716/827-1584. www.buffalogardens.com.* A 150-acre park with Victorian conservatory and outdoor gardens. Eleven greenhouses with desert, rainforest, and Mediterranean collections. Seasonal shows. (Mon-Tues, Thurs-Fri 9 am-4 pm, Wed 9 am-6 pm, Sat-Sun 9 am-5 pm; closed Dec 25) **FREE**

Buffalo & Erie County Historical Society. *25 Nottingham Ct, Buffalo (14216). At Elmwood Ave. Phone 716/873-9644. www.bechs.org.* A Pan-American Exposition building (1901). Exhibits include history of western New York, pioneer life; 1870 street. Pan-Am Building (Mon-Sat 10 am-5 pm, Sun noon-5 pm). Resource Center (459 Forest Ave) (Wed-Sat 1-5 pm, separate admission fee). **$$**

Buffalo & Erie County Naval & Military Park. *One Naval Park Cove, Buffalo (14202). Phone 716/847-1773.* www.*buffalonavalpark.org.* This is the largest inland naval park in the nation. Cruiser USS *Little Rock,* destroyer USS *The Sullivans,* and submarine USS *Croaker;* aircraft, PT boat, tank, and other World War II equipment; museum, video presentations; gift shop. (Apr-Oct: daily 10 am-5 pm; Nov: Sat-Sun 10 am-5 pm); Guided tours Apr-Oct: Mon-Sat 10 am and 12:30 pm). **$$**

Buffalo Bills (NFL). *Ralph Wilson Stadium, One Bills Dr, Orchard Park (14127). Phone 716/648-1800. www.buffalobills.com.*

Buffalo Museum of Science. *1020 Humboldt Pkwy, Buffalo (14211). Phone 716/896-5200. www.buffalomuseumofscience.org.* Birds of western New York, Gibson Hall of Space, Bell Hall of Space Exploration, Dinosaurs & Company, Insects Magnified World, exhibits on astronomy, botany, geology, zoology, anthropology, and natural sciences; research library, Discovery Room for children. Lectures. (Thurs-Sat 10 am-5 pm, Sun noon-5 pm; closed holidays) **$$**

Buffalo Raceway. *Hamburg Fairgrounds, 5600 McKinley Pkwy, Hamburg (14075). Thrwy (I-90) exit 56. Phone 716/649-1280. www.buffaloraceway.com.* Video gaming machines. Pari-mutuel harness racing (Feb-July). Video gaming machines. **FREE**

Buffalo Sabres (NHL). *HSBC Arena, One Seymour H. Knox III Plz, Buffalo (14203). Phone 716/855-4444. www.sabres.com.*

Buffalo State College. *1300 Elmwood Ave, Buffalo (14222). Phone 716/878-6011. www.buffalostate.edu.* (1867) (11,000 students) On campus are Burchfield Penney Art Center (Tues-Sun; closed holidays), Upton Gallery in Upton Hall (academic year, Mon-Fri).

Buffalo Zoological Gardens. *Delaware Park, 300 Parkside Ave, Buffalo (14214). Phone 716/837-3900.* www.*buffalozoo.org.* More than 2,200 animals in a 23 1/2-acre park. Features indoor and outdoor exhibits; gallery of Boehm wildlife porcelains; tropical gorilla habitat; outdoor lion and tiger exhibit; and a children's zoo. (June-early Sept: daily 10 am-5 pm; early Sept-May: daily 10 am-4 pm; closed Thanksgiving, Dec 25) **$$**

City Hall/Observation Tower. *65 Niagara Sq, 28th floor, Buffalo (14202). Phone 716/851-4200.* Panoramic view of western New York, Lake Erie, and Ontario, Canada. (Mon-Fri; closed holidays) **FREE**

Gray Line bus tours. *3466 Niagara Falls Blvd, North Tonawanda (14120). Phone 716/695-1603; toll-free 800/365-3609. www.graylinebuffalo.com.* Tours meet at Buffalo and Erie County Historical Museum (Elmwood Avenue and Nottingham Terrace, north of the Scajaquada Expressway-Hwy 198).

Q-R-S Music Rolls. *1026 Niagara St, Buffalo (14213). Phone 716/885-4600. www.qrsmusic.com.* World's largest and oldest manufacturers of player-piano rolls. Tours twice a day (Mon-Fri). Several steep stairways may pose a problem for some visitors. **$**

Shea's Performing Arts Center. *646 Main St, Buffalo (14202). Phone 716/847-1410. www.sheas.org.* (1926) Broadway shows, theater, dance, opera, music, and family programs. **$$$$**

State University of NY at Buffalo. *3435 Main St, Buffalo (14214). I-90 to Millersport Hwy, N to SUNY-Buffalo exit. Phone 716/645-2000. www.buffalo.edu.* (1846) (25,000 students) Buffalo Materials Research Center, National Center for Earthquake Research, rare library collections; art exhibits. Music, theater, dance performances. Campus tours.

Studio Arena Theatre. *710 Main St, Buffalo (14202) Phone 716/856-5650; toll-free 800/777-8243.* Regional professional theater presents world premieres, musicals, classic dramas, and contemporary works. (Sept-May, Tues-Sun evenings) **$$$$**

Theodore Roosevelt Inaugural National Historic Site. *641 Delaware Ave, Buffalo (14202). Phone 716/884-0095. www.nps.gov/thri.* (Wilcox Mansion) Theodore Roosevelt was inaugurated in this classic Greek Revival house in 1901 following the assassination of President McKinley. Audiovisual presentation; tours; Victorian herb garden. Self-guided, 2-mile architectural walking tours (fee). (Mon-Fri 9 am-5 pm, Sat-Sun noon-5 pm) **$$**

Special Events

America's Fairs. *5600 McKinley Pkwy, Hamburg (14075). NY thruway to exit 56, right onto Mile Strip Rd, left on S Park Ave. Phone 716/649-3900. www.americas-fair.com.* Mid-Aug.

Buffalo Philharmonic Orchestra. *Kleinhans Music Hall, 370 Pennsylvania St, Buffalo (14201). Phone 716/885-5000. www.bpo.org.* Classical and pop concert series; children's and family programs. Summer season also. July.

Taste of Buffalo. *Main St, Buffalo (14150). Phone 716/831-9376. www.tasteofbuffalo.com.* Hosting more than 50 local restaurants, this annual event represents some 15 ethnic and regional varieties of food, including Greek, Italian, Indian, Chinese, Middle Eastern, Mexican, Southwestern, as well as traditional American favorites, local specialties, and all manner of desserts. Each restaurant offers three menu items, ranging in price from 50 to $3. More than 400,000 people attend annually. Picking up strings of beads to take home as a reminder of the good time had by all has become a Taste tradition. Mid-July.

Limited-Service Hotels

★ ★ ADAM'S MARK. *120 Church St, Buffalo (14202). Phone 716/845-5100; toll-free 800/444-2326; fax 716/845-5377. www.adamsmark.com.* You'll find bright and attractive guest rooms at this waterfront-area hotel as well as a host of amenities to make your stay pleasant, inlcuding a complimentary newspaper, well-equipped fitness room, glass-enclosed pool, 24-hour room service, and complimentary airport shuttle. 486 rooms, 9 story. Check-in 3 pm, check-out noon. High-speed Internet access. Restaurant, bar. Fitness room. Indoor pool. Airport transportation available. Business center. **$**

★ BEST WESTERN INN - ON THE AVENUE. *510 Delaware Ave, Buffalo (14202). Phone 716/886-8333; toll-free 888/868-3033; fax 716/884-3070. www.innontheavenue.com.* The Best Western Inn - On The Avenue puts the many sights and attractions of Buffalo right at your fingertips. Comfortable and attractive guest rooms feature basics like hair dryers, ironing boards, and coffee and tea makers, while the lobby features high-speed Internet access—as well as something you most likely won't find anywhere else: a talking and whistling grey cockatoo that serves as the hotel's mascot. 61 rooms, 5 story. Pets accepted, some restrictions. Complimentary continental breakfast. Check-in 2 pm, check-out noon. High-speed Internet access. **$**

★ COMFORT INN. *901 Dick Rd, Buffalo (14225). Phone 716/633-6000; toll-free 800/517-4000; fax 716/633-6858. www.choicehotels.com.* 100 rooms, 2 story, all suites. Pets accepted, some restrictions; fee. Complimentary continental breakfast. Check-in 3 pm, check-out noon. Fitness room. Indoor pool, children's pool. Airport transportation available. **$**

★ ★ COMFORT SUITES DOWNTOWN. *601 Main St, Buffalo (14203). Phone 716/854-5500; toll-free 800/424-6423; fax 716/854-4836. www.choicehotels.com.* With tastefully decorated suites, this hotel is sure to please all of its visitors. It is located near restaurants, shopping, golf courses, and many other attractions. 146 rooms, 7 story, all suites. Complimentary continental breakfast. Check-in 3 pm, check-out noon. Wireless Internet access. Restaurant, bar. Fitness room. Airport transportation available. **$**

★ HAMPTON INN. *10 Flint Rd, Amherst (14226). Phone 716/689-4414; toll-free 800/426-7866; fax*

716/689-4382. www.hamptoninn. com. 196 rooms, 4 story. Complimentary continental breakfast. Check-in 3 pm, check-out noon. Fitness room. Indoor pool. **$**

Full-Service Hotels

★ ★ ★ BUFFALO MARRIOTT NIAGARA. *1340 Millersport Hwy, Buffalo (14221). Phone 716/689-6900; toll-free 800/334-4040; fax 716/689-0483. www. buffaloniagaramarriott.com.* Although in a quiet suburban location, the Buffalo Marriott Niagara is only a short distance from Buffalo Airport, downtown Buffalo, and Niagara Falls. Rooms are bright, elegant, and spacious, making a stay here comfortable and pleasant, as do amenities like the complimentary airport shuttle, indoor/outdoor pool, and 24-hour health club. 356 rooms, 10 story. Pets accepted, some restrictions; fee. Check-in 3 pm, check-out noon. High-speed Internet access. Restaurant, bar. Fitness room. Indoor pool, outdoor pool, whirlpool. Business center. **$$$**

★ ★ ★ HYATT REGENCY BUFFALO. *2 Fountain Plz, Buffalo (14202). Phone 716/856-1234; fax 716/852-6157. www.buffalo.hyatt.com.* This hotel is located downtown and connected to the Buffalo Convention Center. It is on the metro rail and within walking distance of shopping, restaurants, theaters, cultural and sports entertainment, and other attractions. 395 rooms, 16 story. Check-in 3 pm, check-out noon. High-speed Internet access. Two restaurants, two bars. Fitness room, fitness classes available. Indoor pool, whirlpool. Business center. **$$**

Full-Service Inn

★ ★ ★ ASA RANSOM HOUSE. *10529 Main St, Clarence (14031). Phone 716/759-2315; toll-free 800/841-2340; fax 716/759-2791. www.asaransom.com.* This inn offers nine rooms, each with its own distinct character and charm. Rooms are furnished with antiques and period reproductions. Seven of the rooms have a fireplace and most have private balconies. 9 rooms, 2 story. Closed Jan. Complimentary full breakfast. Check-in 2-10 pm, check-out 11 am (Sat-Sun noon). Restaurant. **$$**

Restaurants

★ ★ ★ ASA RANSOM HOUSE. *10529 Main St, Clarence (14031). Phone 800/841-2340; fax 716/759-2791. www.asaransom.com.* Built in 1853. Fresh herb garden. Lunch, dinner. Closed Dec 25; also Jan-mid-Feb. Children's menu. Outdoor seating. **$$$**

★ OLD MAN RIVER. *375 Niagara St, Tonawanda (14150). Phone 716/693-5558.* Overlooks Niagara River; reproduction of 18th-century sailing ship for children to play on. All counter service. Breakfast, lunch, dinner. Closed Jan 1, Thanksgiving, Dec 25. Children's menu. **$**

★ ★ ★ SALVATORE'S ITALIAN GARDENS. *6461 Transit Rd, Buffalo (14043). Phone 716/683-7990; toll-free 800/999-8082; fax 716/684-9229. www.salvatores.net.* One of Buffalo's finest Italian eateries maintains a fabulously balanced menu, which includes a "dinner for two" section (shrimp scampi, "colossal lobster tail," etc.). Also, try Salvatore's seafood medley or the several varieties of veal. American, Italian menu. Dinner. Closed holidays. Bar. Children's menu. Casual attire. **$$$**

Cairo (E-9)

See also Catskill Park, The Catskills, Hudson, Hunter, Saugerties, Windham

Population 6,355
Elevation 380 ft
Area Code 518
Zip 12413
Web Site www.caironychamber.com

What to See and Do

Durham Center Museum. *Hwy 145 and E Durham, Cairo. 9 miles on Hwy 145 just outside East Durham. Phone 518/239-8461.* Schoolhouse used from 1825 to 1940; displays of progress of the Catskill Valley; folk art; Native American artifacts; fossils; minerals; railroad and turnpike relics; antiques, household and business equipment. (Memorial Day-Columbus Day, Thurs-Sun; other times by appointment) **$$**

Zoom Flume Waterpark. *Shady Glen and Stone Bridge rds, East Durham. Exit 21 off NY State Thrwy, W on Hwy 23 to Hwy 145 W, 1 mile off Hwy 145 on Shady Glen Rd. Phone 518/239-4559.* Featuring water slides and other rides and attractions. Gift shop; restaurant, snack bar. (Mid-June-Labor Day, daily) **$$$$**

Limited-Service Hotel

★ ★ WINTER CLOVE INN ROUND TOP. *Winter Clove Rd, Round Top (12473). Phone 518/622-3267. www.winterclove.com.* Inn since 1838; antiques. 40 rooms, 4 story. Closed first three weeks of Dec. Check-in 1 pm, check-out 11 am. Restaurant (public by reservation). Children's activity center. Indoor pool, outdoor pool. Golf. Tennis. **$**

Specialty Lodging

GREENVILLE ARMS 1889 INN. *Hwys 32 and 81, Greenville (12083). Phone 518/966-5219; toll-free 888/665-0044; fax 518/966-8754. www.greenvillearms.com.* Built in 1889, this inn greets its guests with true Victorian style. Each of the rooms have comfortable furniture, antiques, a private bath, and air-conditioning. Some rooms have canopied beds or a private porch from which to enjoy the view of the grounds. 15 rooms, 2 story. Closed Nov-Apr. Children over 12 years only. Complimentary full breakfast. Check-in 2 pm, check-out 11 am. Outdoor pool. **$**

Camillus

Restaurant

★ ★ ★ INN BETWEEN. *2290 W Genessee Tpke, Camillus (13031). Phone 315/672-3166. www.inn-between.com.* Located outside Syracuse, this 1880 country house is on the outskirts of central New York wine country. Day trips to local wineries and special wine festivals in the fall are among the unique activities. American menu. Dinner. Closed Mon; Jan 1, Dec 24-25. Bar. Children's menu. **$$**

Canaan

See also Albany, Coxsackie

Population 1,820
Elevation 847 ft
Area Code 518
Zip 12029

Specialty Lodging

INN AT SILVER MAPLE FARM. *Hwy 295, Canaan (12029). Phone 518/781-3600; fax 518/781-3883. www.silvermaplefarm.com.* Converted barn and carriage house. 11 rooms. Children over 12 years only. Complimentary full breakfast. Check-in 3 pm. Check-out 11 am. **$$**

MILLHOUSE INN. *Hwy 43, Stephentown (12168). Phone 518/733-5606; toll-free 800/563-8645; fax 518/733-6025. www.themillhouseinn. com.* 12 rooms, 2 story. Closed mid-Mar-mid-May, Sept and Nov. Complimentary continental breakfast. Check-in 2:30 pm. Check-out 11 am. Outdoor pool. **$**

Canajoharie (D-8)

See also Johnstown

Settled 1730
Population 3,797
Elevation 311 ft
Area Code 518
Zip 13317

Located on the south bank of the Mohawk River, Canajoharie is in the center of the scenic and industrial Mohawk Valley. Named for a native word meaning "pot that washes itself," the town is near Canajoharie Gorge, which has a creek that winds down to a waterfall. There are many interesting buildings in the area.

What to See and Do

Fort Klock. *7203 Hwy 5, Saint Johnsville (13452). 1 mile N, then 8 miles W of NY Thrwy exit 29 on Hwy 5, in St. Johnsville. Phone 518/568-7779. www.fortklock.com.* (1750) Restored farmhouse (1750) and Native American trading post fortified during the Revolutionary War; also Dutch barn schoolhouse, blacksmith shop, carriage house, herb garden; picnicking. (Memorial Day-mid-Oct, Tues-Sun)

Fort Plain Museum. *389 Canal St, Fort Plain (13339). Hwy 5 S on Western edge of Fort Plain. Phone 518/993-2527.* Site of fort and blockhouse (1780-1786) used in defense of the Mohawk Valley during the Revolutionary War. Museum contains local history and archaeological artifacts. (May-Sept: Wed-Sun noon-5 pm, Fri-Sun 1-5 pm; rest of year: by appointment)

Library and Art Gallery. *2 Erie Blvd, Canajoharie (13317). Phone 518/673-2314.* Paintings by Sargent, Inness, Whistler, the Wyeths, Stuart; large Winslow Homer collection; Korean ceramics. (Mon-Sat; closed holidays) **FREE**

Canandaigua (D-4)

See also Finger Lakes, Geneva, Naples, Palmyra, Penn Yan, Rochester, Victor, Waterloo

Population 11,264

Elevation 767 ft
Area Code 585
Information Chamber of Commerce, 113 S Main St, 14424; phone 585/394-4400
Web Site www.canandaigua.com

This is a resort city on Canandaigua Lake (westernmost of the Finger Lakes).

What to See and Do

Canandaigua Lady. *205 Lakeshore Dr, Canandaigua (14424). Phone 585/396-7350.* Replica of 19th-century paddlewheel steamboat offers variety of cruises, including lunch, brunch, dinner, and special events. (May-Oct, daily)

Bristol Mountain Ski & Snowboard Resort. *5652 Hwy 64, Canandaigua (14424). 12 miles SW on Hwy 64. Phone 585/374-6000. www.bristolmt.com.* Two quad, two triple, double chairlifts; tow rope; patrol, school, rentals; snowmaking; cafeteria, bar. Longest run 2 miles, vertical drop 1,200 feet. (Mid-Nov-Apr, daily)

Finger Lakes Race Track. *Hwy 96 and Beaver Creek Rd*, Canandaigua. *7 miles NW on Hwy 332 at junction Hwy 96; I-90, exit 44. Phone 585/924-3232.* Thoroughbred racing (Apr-Nov, Mon-Tues, Fri-Sun). **$$**

Granger Homestead. *295 N Main St, Canandaigua (14424). Phone 585/394-1472. www.grangerhomestead.org.* (1816) and Carriage Museum. Home of Gideon Granger, Postmaster General under presidents Jefferson and Madison; nine restored rooms; original furnishings. Carriage museum in two buildings; more than 50 antique horse-drawn vehicles including coaches, cutters, surreys, sleighs, hearses. Tours (by appointment). (June-Aug: Tues-Sun 1-5 pm; late May-mid-Oct: Tues-Fri 1-5 pm) **$**

Ontario County Historical Society. *55 N Main St Canandaigua (14424). Phone 585/394-4975.* Museum and archives relating to the history of Ontario County; changing exhibits; research library for genealogical studies. Bookstore. (Tues-Sat 10 am-4:30 pm; to 9 pm on Wed; closed holidays) **$**

Sonnenberg Gardens. *151 Charlotte St, Canandaigua (14424). Off Hwy 21. Phone 585/394-4922. www.sonnenberg.org.* A 50-acre Victorian garden estate with 1887 mansion; conservatory; nine formal gardens including Italian, Japanese, colonial, rock, rose, and blue and white pansy. Tours. (June-mid-Sept: daily 9:30 am-5:30 pm; mid-late May, mid-Sept-mid Oct: daily 9:30 am-4 pm) **$$**

Special Events

Ontario County Fair. *10 County Rd, Canandaigua (14424). Phone 585/394-4987. www.ontariocountyfair.org.* July. **$**

Pageant of Steam. *Gehan Rd and Hwy 5, Canandaigua (14424). 3 miles E on Gehan Rd. Phone 585/394-8102.* Working steam engines and models; parade. Four days in Aug.

Ring of Fire. *Canandaigua Lake.* Re-enactment of Native American ceremony signifying the start of the harvest season. Sat before Labor Day.

SummerMusic. *108 East Ave, Rochester (14604). Phone 716/454-2620.* Rochester Philharmonic Orchestra, Finger Lakes Performing Arts Center. Symphonic, classical, and pops concerts. Indoor/outdoor seating. Picnic sites. July.

Specialty Lodging

ACORN INN B&B. *4508 Hwy 64, Canandaigua (14424). Phone 585/229-2834; toll-free 888/245-4134; fax 585/229-5046. www.acorninnbb.com.* Built in 1795; originally was a stagecoach inn. Federal style.4 rooms, 2 story. Children over 14 years only. Complimentary full breakfast. Check-in 3 pm, check-out 11 am. **$$**

Canastota (D-6)

See also Oneida, Rome, Syracuse, Utica

Settled 1810
Population 4,425
Elevation 420 ft
Area Code 315
Zip 13032
Web Site www.canastota.org

In 1820, when the first packetboat run was established on the Erie Canal from here to Rome, Canastota became a canal town. Some of the original structures still exist along the canal, which bisects the village.

What to See and Do

Canastota Canal Town Museum. *122 Canal St, Canastota (13032). Phone 315/697-3451.*Displays trace growth of Erie Canal and its effect on Canastota and western New York. Adjacent to state park. (Apr-Oct: Mon-Sat; closed holidays) **DONATION**

Chittenango Landing Canal Boat Museum. *7010 Lake Port Rd, Chittenanango (13037). 7 miles W via Hwy 5, on Lakeport Rd. Phone 315/687-3801.* Located on a remaining section of the Erie Canal and dedicated to the preservation of a 19th-century boat building and repair industry. Historic site has guided and self-guided walking tours, excavations, interpretive center, hands-on activities, and exhibits. (July-Aug: daily; Apr-June and Sept-Oct: weekends; rest of year: by appointment only; closed Jan 1, Dec 25) **$$**

International Boxing Hall of Fame. *1 Hall of Fame Dr, Canastota (13032). Phone 315/697-7095. www.ibhof.com.* In honor of those who have excelled in boxing and preservation of boxing heritage. (Daily; limited hours holidays; closed Easter, Thanksgiving, Dec 25) **$$**

Old Erie Canal State Park. *8729 Andrus Rd, Kirkville (13082). Accessible from Hwys 5 and 46 and I-90, exits 33, 34. Phone 315/687-7821.* This 35-mile strip of canal runs from Dewitt (canoe launching and picnicking at Cedar Bay Area) to Rome. Many features of original canal remain, including towpath, aqueducts, change bridges, culverts. Fishing, canoeing; hiking, bicycling, horseback riding, snowmobiling.

Canton (A-7)

See also Ogdensburg, Potsdam

Population 10,334
Elevation 380 ft
Area Code 315
Zip 13617
Information Chamber of Commerce, Municipal Building, PO Box 369; phone 315/386-8255
Web Site www.cantonnychamber.org

Canton, which lies on the Grass River, was settled in the early 1800s by Vermonters. Canton College of Technology is located here.

What to See and Do

Silas Wright House and Museum. *3 E Main St, Canton (13617). Phone 315/386-8133. www.slcha.org/house.* (St. Lawrence County Historical Association). Greek Revival residence (1832-1844) of the US senator and New York governor. First floor restored to 1830-1850 period; second floor gallery for temporary exhibits on local history. Gift shop. Library, archives, museum (Tues-Sat; closed holidays). **$$**

St. Lawrence University. *23 Romoda Dr, Canton (13617). Phone 315/229-5261.*(1856) (2,000 students) On campus are the Griffiths Arts Center, Gunnison Memorial Chapel, Owen D. Young Library, Augsbury-Leithead Physical Education Complex. Campus tours.

Limited-Service Hotel

★ ★ **BEST WESTERN UNIVERSITY INN.** *90 E Main St, Canton (13617). Phone 315/386-8522; toll-free 888/386-8522; fax 315/386-1025. www.bwcanton.com.* 99 rooms, 3 story. Check-in 2 pm, check-out noon. Restaurant, bar. Fitness room. Outdoor pool. **$**

Restaurant

★ **MCCARTHY'S.** *5821 Hwy 11, Canton (13617). Phone 315/386-2564; fax 315/379-9324.* **WWW.** *mccarthys.com.* Breakfast, lunch, dinner, Sun brunch. Closed holidays. Bar. Children's menu. **$$**

Carle Place

Restaurant

★ ★ **RIALTO.** *588 Westbury Ave, Carle Place (11514). Phone 516/997-5283.* Italian menu. Lunch, dinner. Closed Aug; also Mon; holidays. Bar. Casual attire. Reservations recommended. **$$$**

Catskill Park

See also Cairo, Hunter, Shandaken, Woodstock

The 705,500-acre Catskill Park includes some of the wildest country south of Maine. More than 200 miles of marked trails wind through its woods. More than 272,000 acres are owned by the state and comprise the Forest Preserve. This includes seven campgrounds: **North/South Lake**, off Hwy 23A, 3 miles NE of Haines Falls, 518/589-5058; **Devil's Tombstone**, Hwy 214, 4 miles S of Hunter, 914/688-7160; **Woodland Valley**, off Hwy 28, 6 miles SW of Phoenicia, 914/688-7647; **Mongaup Pond**, off Hwy 17, 3 miles N of DeBruce, 914/439-4233; **Little Pond**, off Hwy 17, 14 miles NW of Livingston Manor, 914/439-5480; **Beaverkill**, off Hwy 17, 7 miles NW of Livingston Manor, 914/439-4281; **Kenneth L. Wilson**, off Hwy 28, 4 miles E of Mount Tremper on County 40, 914/679-7020. Nearby is **Bear Springs Mountain** (outside Catskill Park), 5 miles SE of Walton off NY 206, 607/865-6989. Skiing at Belleayre Mountain (see SHANDAKEN), chairlift operating to 3,400 feet.

The Catskills

See also Cairo, Coxsackie, Hillsdale, Hudson, Hunter

Settled 1662
Population 11,849
Elevation 47 ft
Area Code 518
Zip 12414
Information Greene County Promotion Dept, NY Thrwy exit 21, PO Box 527; phone 518/943-3223 or toll-free 800/355-2287
Web Site www.greene-ny.com

This is the eastern entrance to the Catskill Mountains resort area. The town is at the west end of the Rip Van Winkle Bridge, over the Hudson River across from the manufacturing town of Hudson (see). The legendary Rip is said to have slept for 20 years near here.

What to See and Do

Catskill Game Farm. *400 Game Farm Rd, Catskill (12414). 8 miles W on Hwy 23, 5 miles S on Hwy 32. Phone 518/678-9595. www.catskillgamefarm.com.* Children may feed tame deer, donkeys, llamas, other animals. Rides; picnic grounds; cafeteria. (May-Oct: daily 9 am-5 pm; Jul-Aug: daily 9 am-6 pm) **$$$$**

Zoom Flume Waterpark. *E Durham and Hwy 145, Catskill. 13 miles from exit 21 off NY State Thrwy. Phone 518/239-4559; toll-free 800/888-3586. www.zoomflume.com.* Catskill's largest water park. Gift shop. Restaurant. (Mid-June-Labor Day, daily) **$$$$**

Limited-Service Hotels

★ CARL'S RIP VAN WINKLE. *810 Hwy 23B, Leeds (12451). Phone 518/943-3303; fax 518/943-2309. www.ripvanwinklemotorlogde.com.* On 160 wooded acres.68 rooms. Closed mid-Nov-mid-Apr. Check-out 11 am. Outdoor pool, children's pool. **$**

★ ★ WOLFF'S MAPLE BREEZE RESORT. *360 Cauterskill Rd, Catskill (12414). Phone 518/943-3648; toll-free 800/777-9653; fax 518/943-9335. www.wolffsresort.com.* 42 rooms, 2 story. Closed Nov-Apr. Check-in 1 pm. Check-out 11 am. Restaurant (public by reservation), bar. Children's activity center. Outdoor pool. Tennis. **$**

Full-Service Resort

★ ★ FRIAR TUCK RESORT AND CONVENTION CENTER. *4858 Hwy 32, Catskill (12414). Phone 518/678-2271; toll-free 800/832-7600. www.friartuck.com.* 525 rooms, 5 story. Check-in 3 pm, check-out noon. Restaurant, bar. Children's activity center. Fitness room. Indoor pool, two outdoor pools, whirlpool. Tennis. Business center. Theater. **$**

Cazenovia

See also Hamilton, Oneida, Syracuse

Population 6,481
Elevation 1,224 ft
Area Code 315
Zip 13035
Web Site www.cazenovia.com

What to See and Do

Chittenango Falls State Park. *2300 Rathbun Rd, Cazenovia (13036). Phone 315/655-9620.* Has 167-foot waterfall. Fishing; hiking, picnicking, playground, tent and trailer sites. (Daily)

Lorenzo State Historic Site. *17 Rippleton Rd, Cazenovia (13035). 3/4 mile S on Hwy 13. Phone 315/655-3200. www.lorenzony.org.* (1807) Elegant Federal-period mansion built by John Lincklaen; original furnishings; garden, arboretum. (May-Oct, Wed-Sun) **$$**

Toggenburg Ski Center. *Toggenburg Rd, Fabius. 6 miles W on Hwy 20, then 6 miles S on Pompey Center Rd. Phone 315/683-5842; toll-free 800/720-8644. www.skitog.com.* Triple, double chairlifts; two beginners' lifts, two T-bars; patrol, ski school, rentals; snowmaking; cafeteria, bar; nursery. Night skiing. (Dec-early Apr, daily; closed Dec 25) Cross-country trails in Highland Forest, approximately 2 miles W on Hwy 80. **$$$$**

Full-Service Inns

★ ★ ★ BREWSTER INN. *6 Ledyard Ave (Hwy 20), Cazenovia (13035). Phone 315/655-9232; fax 315/655-2130. www.thebrewsterinn. com.* Built in 1890 as the summer home of financier Benjamin B. Brewster, this inn, which overlooks the calming waters of Cazenovia

Lake, offers a carefree and relaxed setting. Guests may choose to stay in rooms in the main house or in the renovated carriage house. Massage therapists are on hand to offer a variety of experiences, from Swedish massages to medical massages. 17 rooms, 3 story. Complimentary continental breakfast. Check-in 2 pm, check-out 11 am. Restaurant, bar. Fitness room. **$**

★ ★ ★ **LINCKLAEN HOUSE.** *79 Albany St, Cazenovia (13035). Phone 315/655-3461; fax 315/655-5443. www.lincklaenhouse.com.* Since the turn of the 20th century, this property has been providing fine dining and lodging for such people as former president Grover Cleveland and John D. Rockefeller. Rooms are elegantly decorated, as is the main floor dining room. 18 rooms, 3 story. Pets accepted. Complimentary continental breakfast. Check-in 2 pm, check-out 11 am. **$**

Restaurants

★ ★ **BRAE LOCH INN.** *5 Albany St, Cazenovia (13035). Phone 315/655-3431; fax 315/655-4844. www.braelochinn. com.* American menu. Dinner, Sun brunch (Sept-June). Closed Dec 24-25. Bar. Children's menu. **$$**

★ ★ ★ **BREWSTER INN.** *6 Ledyard Ave, Cazenovia (13035). Phone 315/655-9232; fax 315/655-2130. www.thebrewsterinn. com.* This gourmet restaurant at the historic Brewster Inn offers an elegant atmosphere and house specialties like New Zealand rack of lamb, crispy boneless duck, and the Brewster Inn veal Atlantis. American, French menu. Dinner, Sun brunch. Closed holidays; open on Thanksgiving. Bar. Outdoor seating. **$$**

Chatham

See also Canaan

Restaurants

★ ★ **BLUE PLATE.** *1 Kinderhook St, Chatham (12037). Phone 518/392-7711. www.chathamblueplate.net.* American menu. Lunch, dinner. Bar. Casual attire. **$$**

Chautauqua

See also Bemus Point, Jamestown

Founded 1874
Population 4,666
Elevation 1,360 ft
Area Code 716
Zip 14722
Web Site www.tourchautauqua.com

Chautauqua Institution is a lakeside summer center for the arts, education, religion, and recreation. Programs are offered to adults and children. Summer population swells to more than 10,000.

The community began as a Sunday school teachers' training camp and developed into a cultural center that originated nationwide book clubs and correspondence schools. It has provided a platform for presidents and political leaders, as well as great musical artists and popular entertainers.

What to See and Do

Boat cruise. *Chautauqua Belle.* *Phone 716/753-2403.* Replica of a 19th-century paddlewheel steamboat cruises on Chautauqua Lake; includes narrative of history of the area and wildlife around the lake. (Memorial Day-Labor Day, daily)

★ **The Chautauqua Institution.** *1 Ames St, Chautauqua. Along Hwy 394 on the W shore of Chautauqua Lake. Phone 716/357-6200; toll-free 800/836-2787. www.ciweb.org.* Summer center for arts, education, religion, and recreation. Nine-week season (late June-late Aug, daily) features a lecture platform as well as performing arts events.

Chautauqua Amphitheater. *Bowman St and Roberts Ave, Chautauqua (14722). Phone 716/357-6200; toll-free 800/836-2787.* This 5,000-seat amphitheater, built in 1893, is the home of the Chautauqua Symphony Orchestra. It also hosts recitals, ballet, opera, lectures, and special popular musical events.

Miller Bell Tower. Campanile on the shore of Chautauqua Lake.

Norton Memorial Hall. Four operatic productions are presented in English each season by the Chautauqua Opera Company.

Palestine Park. Outdoor walk-through model of the Holy Land. Tours Mon evening, Sun afternoon.

Recreation. *Phone 716/357-6200.* Swimming, boating, sailing, fishing; tennis, 27-hole golf (fee), cross-country skiing (winter).

Full-Service Resort

★ ★ WEBB'S LAKE RESORT. *Hwy 394, Mayville (14757). Phone 716/753-2161; fax 716/753-1383. webbsworld.com.* 52 rooms, 2 story. Check-out 11 am. Restaurant, bar. Fitness room. Outdoor pool. **$**

Full-Service Inn

★ ★ ★ WILLIAM SEWARD INN. *6645 S Portage Rd, Westfield (14787). Phone 716/326-4151; fax 716/326-4163. www.williamsewardinn. com.* Southwest Chautauqua County is the perfect setting for this 1837 country inn. Various local destinations make it a year-round retreat; ski areas, Chautauqua Lake, and the well-known Chautauqua Institution for cultural and educational programs. 12 rooms, 2 story. Pets accepted, some restrictions. Children over 12 years only. Complimentary full breakfast. Check-in 2-8 pm, check-out 11 am. Restaurant. **$$**

Restaurant

★ ★ ★ ATHENAEUM. *South Lake Dr, Chautauqua (14722). Phone 716/357-4444; toll-free 800/821-1881. www.athenaeum-hotel. com.* This Victorian hotel has been serving guests since 1881 and now is listed on the National Historic Register. American menu. Breakfast, lunch, dinner. Closed Sept-May. Children's menu. Jacket required. Reservations recommended. Valet parking. Outdoor seating. **$$**

Clayton

See also Alexandria Bay, Kingston, Watertown

Population 4,817
Elevation 260 ft
Area Code 315
Zip 13624
Information Chamber of Commerce, 510 Riverside Dr; phone 315/686-3771 or phone 800/252-9806
Web Site www.thousandislands.com/claytonchamber

Clayton juts into the St. Lawrence River in the midst of the Thousand Islands resort region. Pleasure boats line the waterfront docks.

What to See and Do

Antique Boat Museum. *750 Mary St, Clayton (13624). Phone 315/686-4104. www.abm.org.* This nautical museum showcases more than 200 antique boats, including canoes, sailboats, hydroplanes, and cruisers, as well as artifacts related to boating. The museum also sponsors educational programs about boat building and boater safety. (Mid-May-mid-Oct, daily 9 am-5 pm) **$$**

Burnham Point State Park. *Hwy 12 E, Clayton. 10 miles W on Hwy 12 E. Phone 315/654-2324.* Fishing, boating (launch, dock); picnicking, playground, camping. (Mid-May-Labor Day)

Cedar Point State Park. *36661 Cedar Point State Park Dr, Clayton (13624). 6 miles W on Hwy 12 E. Phone 315/654-2522.* Swimming beach, bathhouse, fishing, boating (ramp, marina); picnicking, playground, recreation programs, camping. (Mid-May-mid-Oct)

Grass Point State Park. *Grassy Point Rd, Clayton. 6 miles E on Hwy 12, 1 mile W of I-81. Phone 315/686-4472.* Swimming beach, bathhouse, fishing, boating (launch, marina); picnicking, playground, camping. (Mid-May-late Sept)

Thousand Islands Museum. *312 James St, Clayton (13624). Old Town Hall. Phone 315/686-5794. www. timuseum.org.* History of the region; replica of turn-of-the-century Clayton. (Mid-May-Labor Day, daily) **DONATION**

Uncle Sam Boat Tours. *45 James St, Alexandria Bay (13607). Phone 315/686-3511. www.usboattours.com.* A 40-mile cruise of the Thousand Islands, traveling through Canadian and American waters, the St. Lawrence Seaway; stop at Boldt Castle and Alexandria Bay. (Mid-May-Oct, daily) **$$$$**

Special Events

Antique Boat Show. *Antique Boat Museum, 750 Mary St, Clayton (13624). Phone 315/686-4104. www.abm. org.* The show features more than 125 restored antique craft in addition to the museum's 200 antique boats, as well as sailing skiff races, a boat parade, and an auction of boats. First weekend in Aug.

Duck, Decoy, and Wildlife Art Show. *Recreation Park Arena,East Line Rd, Clayton. Phone 315/686-5794.*

Three-day event includes the Art Knapp Hunting Decoy Contest; exhibits from world championship duck decoy carvers; taxidermy exhibitors; and art auction. Third weekend in July. **$**

Model Train Show. *Recreation Park Arena, East Line Rd, Clayton.* Second weekend in Sept.

Limited-Service Hotel

★ **FAIR WIND LODGE.** *38201 Hwy 12 E, Clayton (13624). Phone 315/686-5251; toll-free 800/235-8331; fax 315/686-5253.* 24 rooms. Closed mid-Oct-mid-May. Check-out 10 am. Outdoor pool. **$**

Restaurants

★ ★ **CLIPPER INN.** *126 State St, Clayton (13624). Phone 315/686-3842; fax 315/686-2733.* American menu. Dinner. Closed Nov-Mar. Bar. Children's menu. **$$**

★ ★ **THOUSAND ISLANDS INN.** *335 Riverside Dr, Clayton (13624). Phone 315/686-3030; toll-free 800/544-4241; fax 315/686-2381. www.1000-islands.com.* Small hotel since 1897; Thousand Island dressing first created and served here. American menu. Breakfast, lunch, dinner. Closed Oct-mid-May. Bar. Children's menu. **$$$**

Cobleskill (E-8

Restaurant

★ ★ **BULL'S HEAD INN.** *105 Park Pl, Cobleskill (12043). Phone 518/234-3591; fax 518/234-3591. www.bullsheadinn.biz.* Seafood, steak menu. Dinner. Closed Jan 1, Dec 25. Bar. Historic building (1802). **$$$**

Cold Spring

Restaurants

★ ★ ★ **BRASSERIE LE BOUCHON.** *76 Main St, Cold Spring (10516). Phone 845/265-7676.* French menu. Dinner. Bar. Business casual attire. Reservations recommended. Outdoor seating. **$$**

★ ★ **HUDSON HOUSE.** *2 Main St, Cold Spring (10516). Phone 845/265-9355; fax 845/265-4532. www.hudsonhouseinn.com.* Lunch, dinner. Closed Dec 25. Bar. Children's menu. Built in 1832. Reservations recommended. **$$$**

★ ★ ★ **PLUMBUSH INN.** *1656 Hwy 9D, Cold Spring (10516). Phone 845/265-3904; fax 845/265-3997. www.plumbushinn.net.* Just across the Hudson River from West Point, this Victorian inn offers elegant dinners. The chef applies creative flair to the menu's appetizers, while offering classic entrées and desserts. American menu. Lunch, dinner, Sun brunch. Closed Mon-Tues. Bar. Valet parking. Three guest rooms available. **$$$**

★ ★ ★ **THE RIVER ROOM.** *2 Main St, Cold Spring (10516).* American menu. Dinner, brunch. Bar. Business casual attire. Reservations recommended. Outdoor seating. **$$$**

Cold Spring Harbor

Restaurants

★ ★ **105 HARBOR.** *105 Harbor Rd, Cold Spring Harbor (11724). Phone 631/367-3166; fax 631/367-3752.* French menu. Lunch, dinner, Sun brunch. Closed Dec 25. Bar. Valet parking. **$$**

★ **WYLANDS COUNTRY CAFE.** *55 Main St, Cold Spring Harbor (11724). Phone 631/692-5655; fax 631/368-8259. www.dedlandstreet.com.* American menu. Lunch. Closed Sun-Mon; holidays; also late Feb-early Mar. Children's menu. Casual attire. **$**

Congers

Restaurant

★ ★ ★ **RESTAURANT X AND BULLY BOY BAR.** *117 N Hwy 303, Congers (10920). Phone 845/268-6555. www.xaviars.com.* Chef/owner Peter Kelly started off strong, opening the nationally praised Xavier's at Garrison at the young age of 23. Now, more than 15 years and three restaurants later, he is winning kudos at this contemporary American restaurant in the woods of Rockland County. American menu. Lunch, dinner, Sun brunch. Closed Mon; Jan 1, Dec 25. Bar. Casual attire. Reservations recommended. **$$$**

Cooperstown (E-7)

See also Oneonta

Founded 1786
Population 2,032
Elevation 1,264 ft
Area Code 607
Zip 13326
Information Chamber of Commerce, 31 Chestnut St; phone 607/547-9983
Web Site www.cooperstownchamber.org

Founded by James Fenimore Cooper's father, Judge William Cooper, Cooperstown is in the center of the "Leatherstocking" country. Here in 1839, on the south end of Otsego Lake, legend has it that Abner Doubleday devised modern baseball. The National Baseball Hall of Fame and Museum is located here, on Main Street.

What to See and Do

The Farmers' Museum and Village Crossroads. *Lake Rd, Cooperstown (13326). 1 mile N on Hwy 80. Phone 607/547-1450; toll-free 888/547-1450. www.farmersmuseum.org.* Outdoor museum of rural life in early times. Craftspeople present printing, weaving, and blacksmithing in historic setting. Village of historic buildings and barn filled with exhibits. Famous "Cardiff Giant," a 10-foot statue presented to the public in 1869 as a petrified prehistoric man, is here. (Apr-Oct, daily) Special events held throughout the year. Inquire about combination ticket with Fenimore House and/or National Baseball Hall of Fame and Museum. **$$**

Fenimore Art Museum. *Hwy 80,Lake Rd, Cooperstown (13326). 1 mile N on Hwy 80. Phone 607/547-1400; toll-free 888/547-1450. www.fenimoreartmuseum.org.* Museum and headquarters of NY State Historical Association. Large American folk art collection; exhibits of Native American art and artifacts; James Fenimore Cooper memorabilia; academic and decorative arts of Romantic Era, 1800-1850; research library. (Apr-mid-May: Tues-Sun 10 am-4 pm; mid-May-mid-Oct: daily 10 am-5 pm; mid-Oct-Dec: Tues-Sun 10 am-4 pm; closed Thanksgiving and Dec 25) Inquire about combination ticket with Farmers' Museum and/or National Baseball Hall of Fame. **$$**

Glimmerglass State Park. *1527 County Hwy 31, Cooperstown (13326). 6 miles N on E Lake Rd. Phone 607/547-8662.* Swimming beach, bathhouse, fishing; hiking, biking, cross-country skiing, picnicking, playground, tent and trailer sites. (Daily; closed Jan 1, Dec 25) Standard fees. Also here is Hyde Hall, Clarke family mansion with view of Otsego Lake; Classical Revival architecture (summer daily). **$$$**

National Baseball Hall of Fame and Museum. *25 Main St, Cooperstown (13326). Phone 607/547-7200; toll-free 888/425-5633. www.baseballhalloffame.org.* Nationally known museum dedicated to the game and its players. The Hall of Fame Gallery contains plaques honoring the game's all-time greats. The museum features displays on baseball's greatest moments, the World Series, All-Star Games, ballparks, and a complete history of the game. The theater presents a special multimedia show. Gift shop. Inquire about combination ticket with Farmers' Museum and/or Fenimore House. (Early Sept-late May: daily 9 am-5 pm; late May-early Sept: daily 9 am-9 pm; closed Jan 1, Thanksgiving, Dec 25) **$$**

Special Events

Autumn Harvest Festival. *The Farmers' Museum and Village Crossroads,Lake Rd, Cooperstown (13326). Phone 607/547-1450; toll-free 888/547-1450. www.farmersmuseum.org.* Crafts, food, and entertainment. Mid-Sept. **$$**

Cooperstown Concert Series. *Sterling Auditorium, Cooperstown High School, 38 Linden Ave, Cooperstown (13326). Phone 607/547-1812.* Several performances per season by classical and jazz musicians, folk artists, dancers, actors. Sept-May.

Glimmerglass Opera. *Alice Busch Opera Theater, Hwy 80, Cooperstown (13326). Phone 607/547-2255. www.glimmerglass.org.* Four productions, 28 performances. July-late Aug.

Limited-Service Hotels

★ BEST WESTERN INN & SUITES AT THE COMMONS. *50 Commons Dr, Cooperstown (13326). Phone 607/547-7100; fax 607/547-7082. www.bestwestern.com.* 62 rooms, 2 story. Complimentary continental breakfast. Check-in 3 pm, check-out 11 am. Fitness room. Indoor pool, whirlpool. **$**

★ HICKORY GROVE MOTOR INN. *6854 Hwy 80, Cooperstown (13326). Phone 607/547-9874; toll-free 877/547-9874; fax 607/547-8567. www.*

A Baseball Kind of Town

Cooperstown is best known as the home of the Baseball Hall of Fame, and anyone who has any affinity for the game will love being immersed in it here. Not a baseball fan? Dont worry - the town also offers a variety of entertaining historic sites, activities, shops, and restaurants.

Start by picking up a copy of the self-guided walking tour at the information kiosk in the Chamber of Commerce office (31 Chestnut St). From there, turn right and walk into the heart of town. At the corner of Chestnut and Main, you'll encounter the Cooper Inn, which was built in 1813 and is surrounded by its own pocket park. Peek at the entrance hall and lobby, highlighted by paintings from the Fenimore Art Museum. Return to Main Street and walk east. On the right is Doubleday Field where, if your timing is right, a baseball game might be in progress. Both sites of Main Street are lined with shops, many of which have baseball themes. Among the baseball-themed shops to visit are Cooperstown Bat Company (66 Main St), Americas Game (75 Main St), National Pastime (81 Main St), Third Base (83 Main St), Where It All Began Bat Company (87 Main St), The Cap Company (108 Main St), Collectors World (139 Main St), and Grand Slam Collectibles (134 Main St). Other Main Street shops of note are the Cooperstown General Store (45 Main St) and Cooperstown Kid Co. (131 Main St). Take a left onto alleylike Hoffman Lane, and visit the Cooperstown Book Nook (1 Hoffman Ln). Then stop in next door for a meal at Hoffman Lane Bistro, a modern café with outdoor dining.Return to Main Street, turn left, and visit the National Baseball Hall of Fame (25 Main St); this takes some time, but daily admission allows visitors to come and go as often as they please. No food is served in the Hall, but the nearby Doubleday Café (93 Main St) serves up good homemade food in a real small-town atmosphere. Leaving the Hall, head north on First Street and follow it to the end for nice views of Otsego Lake. Head west on Lake Street for two blocks to Lake Front Park at the foot of Pioneer Streeta good spot for a picnic. From there, walk about two more blocks to the Otesaga Resort Hotelits the huge building on your right with the three-story columns guarding the entry portico. The lobby is immense and decorated with fine art. Peek into the ballroom, decorated with circa-1910 murals by Blendon Campbell, and lounge on the back veranda overlooking the lake. The food here is excellent, too.

Continue walkingor hop on the village trolleyup Lake Street (now Highway 80) for about 1/2 mile, where the Fenimore Art Museum appears on the right and the Farmers Museum is on the left. One to three hours can be spent at each of these. The Art Museum contains an outstanding collection of New York State-based art, excellent works from the Hudson River School, and an American Indian Wing. The Farmers Museum is a 19th-century living history installation and working farm. Ride the village trolley back to town and visit the art galleries on Pioneer Street: the Smithy-Pioneer Gallery and the Leatherstocking Brush and Palette Club.

hickorygrovemotorinn. com. 12 rooms. Closed mid-Oct-mid-Apr. Check-in 2 pm, check-out 11 am. Wireless Internet access. Beach. **$**

★ ★ **LAKE FRONT MOTEL.** *10 Fair St, Cooperstown (13326). Phone 607/547-9511; fax 607/547-2792. www.lakefronthotelandrestaurant.net.* 44 rooms, 2 story. Check-in 3 pm, check-out 11 am. Restaurant, bar. **$**

Full-Service Resort

★ ★ ★ **OTESAGA RESORT.** *60 Lake St, Cooperstown (13326). Phone 607/547-9931; toll-free 800/348-6222; fax 607/547-9675. www.otesaga.com.* 136 rooms. Closed Dec-mid-Apr. Complimentary continental breakfast. Check-in 3 pm, check-out 1 pm. High-speed Internet access. Two restaurants, two bars. Fitness room. Outdoor pool. Golf, 18 holes. Business center. **$$$**

Specialty Lodging

THE INN AT COOPERSTOWN. *16 Chestnut St, Cooperstown (13326). Phone 607/547-5756; fax 607/547-8779. www.innatcooperstown.com.* Former annex to Fenimore Hotel, built 1874. Victorian furnishings. 17 rooms, 3 story. Complimentary continental breakfast. Check-in 2 pm, check-out 11 am. High-speed Internet access. **$$**

Restaurant

★ ★ PEPPER MILL. *Hwy 28, Cooperstown (13326). Phone 607/547-8550; fax 607/547-6193.* Dinner. Closed Dec 25; Jan-Mar. Bar. Children's menu. **$$**

Corning (F-4)

See also Elmira, Finger Lakes ,Watkins Glen,

Settled 1833
Population 10,842
Elevation 937 ft
Area Code 607
Zip 14830
Information Chamber of Commerce, 1 Baron Steubing Pl; phone 607/936-4686
Web Site www.corningny.com

This world glass center began to grow when completion of the Chemung Canal brought plentiful Pennsylvania anthracite. In 1868, lower fuel and materials costs attracted the Brooklyn Flint Glass Works, incorporated in 1875 as the Corning Glass Works. Mass production of bulbs for Thomas A. Edison's electric light soon began. Dresser-Rand makes compressors at Painted Post, near Corning. The city's central shopping district has been restored to its 1890s appearance.

What to See and Do

Benjamin Patterson Inn Museum Complex. *59 W Pulteney St,* Corning (14830). *Phone 607/937-5281. www.pattersoninnmuseum.org.* Central attraction is a restored and furnished 1796 inn, built to encourage settlement in the Genesee Country. Includes public room and kitchen on first floor; ballroom and two bedrooms on second floor. Also on site is DeMonstoy Log Cabin (circa 1785), Browntown one-room schoolhouse (1878), Starr Barn with agricultural exhibit (circa 1860), and blacksmith shop (circa 1820). (Mon-Fri 10 am- 4 pm) **$$**

★ Corning Museum of Glass. *One Museum Way, Corning (14830). I-86, exit 46. Phone 607/937-5371; toll-free 800/732-6845. www.cmog.org.* More than 25,000 objects are on display, including outstanding pieces of both antique and modern Steuben and an 11-foot-high leaded glass window designed by Tiffany Studios in 1905. The library has the most complete collection of materials on glass in the world. The Innovations Gallery showcases optics, vessels, and windows. The Steuben Factory features skilled craftsmen transforming hot molten glass into fine crystal; only factory in the world that produces Steuben crystal. Retail stores. (Memorial Day-Labor Day: daily 9 am-8 pm; rest of year: daily 9 am-5 pm; closed Jan 1, Thanksgiving, Dec 24-25) **$$$**

Rockwell Museum of Western Art. *111 Cedar St, Corning (14830). Phone 607/937-5386. www.rockwellmuseum.org.* Here is the largest collection of American Western art in the East, including paintings by Remington, Russell, Bierstadt, Catlin, others; antique firearms; and changing exhibits. The museum is part of a combination ticket with the Corning Glass Museum. (Memorial Day-Labor Day: daily 9 am-8 pm; rest of year: daily 9 am-5 pm) **$$**

Limited-Service Hotels

★ COMFORT INN. *66 W Pulteney St, Corning (14830). Phone 607/962-1515; toll-free 877/424-6423; fax 607/962-1899. www.comfortinn. com.* A great budget-friendly option for visitors to Corning and the surrounding area, this clean, attractive motel is located near the Corning Museum of Glass and the towns historic Market Street. With a large indoor pool and complimentary continental breakfast, this is a wonderful place for families with children. 62 rooms, 2 story. Complimentary continental breakfast. Check-in 2 pm, check-out 11 am. High-speed Internet access. Fitness room. Indoor pool. **$**

★ ★ DAYS INN. *23 Riverside Dr, Corning (14830). Phone 607/936-9370; toll-free 800/329-7466; fax 607/936-0513. www.daysinn. com.* Whether you're in Corning for a visit or just passing through, this ideally located motel has everything to make your stay comfortable and enjoyable. Set next to the Museum of Glass among the shops and restaurants of charming downtown Corning, guests will never want for things to see and do. 56 rooms, 3 story. Complimentary continental breakfast. Check-in 2 pm, check-out 11 am. Restaurant, bar. Indoor pool, whirlpool. **$**

★ GATE HOUSE MOTEL. *145 E Corning Rd, Corning (14830). Phone 607/936-4131.* Within close proximity to the highway, yet set far back enough to escape traffic noise, this neat, classic brick motel has the retro feel of a roadside motor lodge. Rooms are clean and well-maintained. 20 rooms. Check-in 1:30 pm, check-out 11 am. Restaurant. **$**

★ ★ RADISSON HOTEL CORNING. *125 Denison Pkwy E, Corning (14830). Phone 607/962-*

5000; toll-free 800/333-3333; fax 607/962-4166. www. radisson.com. This upscale hotel in the heart of Corning is close to everything that the quaint town has to offer. The Rockwell Museum of Art is adjacent, while the Museum of Glass and area shopping and dining are also steps away. The lobby has a spacious, natural feel, with many trees and foliage, and the calming sounds of running water coming from an impressive waterfall fountain. 177 rooms, 3 story. Pets accepted. Check-in 3 pm, check-out 1 pm. High-speed Internet access. Restaurant, bar. Fitness room. Indoor pool, whirlpool. Business center. **$**

Specialty Lodging

ROSEWOOD INN. *134 E 1st St, Corning (14830). Phone 607/962-3253. www.rosewoodinn. com.* An ideal place for antique-lovers and those who enjoy old-fashioned hospitality, this elegant Victorian house sits among other period homes and is a short walk from the downtown area of Corning. From the moment the owner greets you at the door (in full Victorian attire, no less), to the antique linens and lace in each room, to the full, formal breakfast each morning, you know a stay at this inn will be memorable. 7 rooms, 2 story. Complimentary full breakfast. Check-in 3-7 pm, check-out 11 am. **$$**

Restaurant

★ ★ LONDON UNDERGROUND CAFE. *69 E Market St, Corning (14830). Phone 607/962-2345; fax 607/962-6603. www.londonundergroundcafe.com.* Features three levels of dining with a British theme. Desserts are homemade. American menu. Lunch, dinner. Closed Sun; Dec 25. Children's menu. Casual attire. Outdoor seating. **$$**

Corona

Restaurant

★ ★ PARK SIDE. *107-01 Corona Ave, Corona (11368). Phone 718/271-9274; fax 718/271-2454.* If you try to imagine what *My Big Fat Greek Wedding* would have been like with an Italian family, you'll get an idea of what dinner is like at Park Side, a lively, boisterous restaurant in Queens that serves hearty portions of Italian food. The waiters give the place an old-school vibe, all dressed in black suits, while the dining room feels like an ornate catering hall filled with large parties and the occasional celebrity. The menu is straight-ahead and delicious Italianthink spicy red sauce, big steaks, giant orders of fill-in-the-blank-parmigiana, and heaping bowls of risotto, in addition to a superb hot and cold antipasti selection. Italian menu. Lunch, dinner. Bar. Valet parking. Outdoor seating. **$$**

Cortland (E-6)

See also Finger Lakes, Ithaca

Settled 1791
Population 18,740
Elevation 1,120 ft
Area Code 607
Zip 13045
Information Cortland County Convention & Visitors Bureau, 34 Tompkins St; phone 607/753-8463 or toll-free 800/859-2227
Web Site www.cortlandtourism.com

Cortland lies in the midst of rich farming country. This is the home of the State University College at Cortland.

What to See and Do

1890 House Museum. *37 Tompkins St, Cortland (13045). Phone 607/756-7551.* Former mansion of industrialist Chester F. Wickwire. Built in a style known as Victorian chateauesque, the building has four stories and 30 rooms. Hand-carved cherry and oak woodwork, stained- and painted-glass windows, parquet floors, and elaborate stenciling. The house remained in the Wickwire family until 1974. (Tues-Sun 1-4 pm; closed holidays) **$$**

Cortland Country Music Park. *1804 Hwy 13, #24, Cortland (13045). On Hwy 13 N. Phone 607/753-0377. www.cortlandcountrymusicpark.com.* The self-proclaimed "Nashville of the Northeast." Hall of Fame museum, Opry Barn with large dance floor, outdoor stage, memorial garden, concerts, dinner theater, dance classes, bingo, 104 campsites.

Fillmore Glen State Park. *1686 Hwy 38, Cortland (13118). 14 miles W on Hwy 90, then 3 miles N on Hwy 38, near Moravia. Phone 315/497-0130.* Replica of President Millard Fillmore's birthplace cabin. Flow-through natural pool, bathhouse; hiking trails, picnicking, playground area, cross-country skiing, snowmobiling, tent and trailer sites, cabins (mid-May-mid-Oct).

Greek Peak. *2000 Hwy 392, Cortland (13045). 6 miles S on NY 392, off I-81. Phone 607/835-6111. www. greekpeak.net.* Eight chairlifts, one tubing lift; patrol,

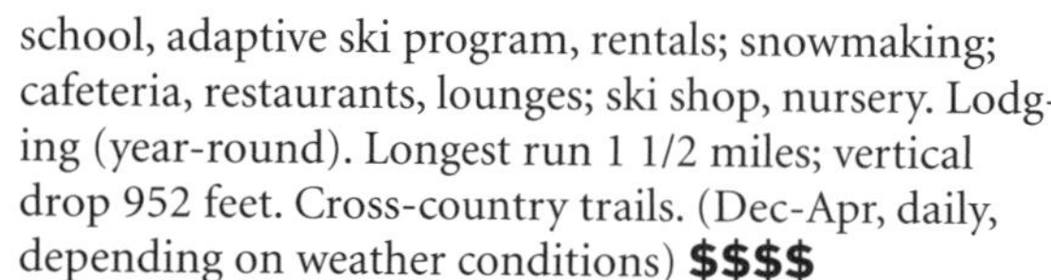

school, adaptive ski program, rentals; snowmaking; cafeteria, restaurants, lounges; ski shop, nursery. Lodging (year-round). Longest run 1 1/2 miles; vertical drop 952 feet. Cross-country trails. (Dec-Apr, daily, depending on weather conditions) **$$$$**

Labrador Mountain. *10 miles NE on Hwy 13 to Truxton, then 2 miles N on Hwy 91. Phone 607/842-6204. www.labradormtn.com.* Triple, two double chairlifts; T-bar; snowboarding; two ski shops, patrol, school, rentals; snowmaking; cafeterias, restaurant, bar; nursery. Longest run 1 1/2 miles; vertical drop 700 feet. Twenty-four slopes. (Dec-Mar, daily; closed Dec 25) **$$$$**

Song Mountain. *Approximately 15 miles N off I-81, near Preble. Phone 315/696-5711. www.songmt.com.* Double and triple chairlifts, two T-bars, J-bar; patrol, school, rentals; snowmaking; restaurant, cafeteria, bar. Longest run 1 mile; vertical drop 700 feet. (Dec-Mar, daily) Summer (mid-June-Labor Day: daily; late May-mid-June and rest of Sept: weekends only); miniature golf; water slide; some fees. **$$$$**

Suggett House Museum and Kellogg Memorial Research Library. *25 Homer Ave,* Cortland (13045). *Phone 607/756-6071. www.cortlandhistory.com.* Headquarters of the Cortland County Historical Society; museum (circa 1880) houses vignettes of home arts of 1825 to 1900; 1882 kitchen; military memorabilia, local art, children's room, and changing exhibits. Library has local history and genealogy material (additional fee per hour). (Tues-Sat 1-4 pm; library to 5 pm; other times by appointment; closed holidays) **$**

Special Events

Central New York Maple Festival. *42 Front St, Marathon (13803). 13 miles S, I-81, exit 9, in Marathon. Phone 607/849-3812. www.maplefest.org.* A variety of events showing the process of making maple syrup; also arts and crafts, hay rides, and entertainment. Early Apr.

Cortland Repertory Theatre. *Dwyer Memorial County Park Pavilion Theatre, 37 Franklin St, Cortland (13045). 10 miles N on Hwy 281 in Little York. Phone 607/753-6161. www.cortlandrep.org.* Musicals, comedies and drama. Tues-Sun evenings. Mid-June-early Sept.

Limited-Service Hotels

★ COMFORT INN. *2 1/2 Locust Ave, Cortland (13045). Phone 607/753-7721; fax 607/753-7608. www.choicehotels.com.* 66 rooms, 2 story. Pets accepted; fee. Complimentary continental breakfast. Check-in 1 pm, check-out 11 am. Wireless Internet access. Children's activity center. Fitness room. **$**

★ HAMPTON INN. *26 River St, Cortland (13045). Phone 607/662-0007; fax 607/662-0678. www.hampton-inn. com.* 111 rooms. Complimentary continental breakfast. Check-in 3 pm, check-out 11 am. High-speed Internet access. Fitness room. Indoor pool. Business center. **$**

Full-Service Inn

★ ★ ★ BENN CONGER INN. *206 W Cortland St, Groton (13073). Phone 607/898-5817; fax 607/898-5818. www.benncongerinn com.* This property is located near downtown Ithaca, wineries, antique shops, horseback riding, and more. The inn, a Greek Revival mansion and former home Benn Conger, founder of Smith Corona, features large rooms with custom mattresses and imported linens. A five-course breakfast is included during your stay.10 rooms. Pets accepted. Complimentary full breakfast. Check-in 2 pm, check-out noon. Restaurant, bar. Airport transportation available .**$$$**

Restaurant

★ ★ ★ BENN CONGER INN. *206 W Cortland St, Groton (13073). Phone 607/898-5817; fax 607/898-5818. www.benncongerinn.com.* This fine dining restaurant in the Benn Conger Inn (see)offers a wide selection of tempting Mediterranean-inspired cuisine as well as an award-winning wine list. Mediterranean menu. Dinner. Closed Mon-Tues. Bar. Children's menu. Reservations recommended. **$$$**

Coxsackie (E-9)

See also Albany, Canaan, Catskill, Hillsdale, Hudson

Population 8,884
Elevation 50 ft
Area Code 518
Zip 12051
Web Site www.coxsackie.org

What to See and Do

Bronck Museum. *Pieter Bronck Rd and Hwy 9 W, Coxsackie (12051). 4 miles S of Coxsackie Thrwy, exit 21*

B on Hwy 9 W, then right on Pieter Bronck Rd. Phone 518/731-6490. (1663) Built by Pieter, brother of Jonas Bronck, whose 500-acre "bouwerie" became New York City's Bronx. Complex of early Dutch houses dated 1663, 1685, and 1738 with outbuildings, including 13-sided barn. Antique furniture, china, glass, silver, paintings, quilts, and agricultural equipment. (Memorial Day weekend-mid-Oct, Wed-Fri noon-4 pm, Sat from 10 am, Sun from 1 pm) **$**

Crown Point (C-10)

See also Hague, Ticonderoga

Population 2,119
Elevation 200 ft
Area Code 518
Zip 12928
Information Ticonderoga Area Chamber of Commerce, 94 Montcalm, Ticonderoga 12883; phone 518/585-6619
Web Site

Located on a peninsula that forms the northernmost narrows of Lake Champlain, the Point was a strong position from which to control the trade route between New York and Canada during the French and Indian War. In the 19th century, agriculture and ironworks dominated the area.

What to See and Do

Crown Point Reservation State Campground. *Hwy 1 and Champagne Bridge, Crown Point (12928). Across highway from Crown Point State Historic Site. Phone 518/597-3603.*Fishing, boating (launch); picnic area, camping (fee). (Mid-Apr-mid-Oct) **$$**

Crown Point State Historic Site. *Bridge Rd, Crown Point. N on Hwy 9 N/22, 4 miles E at Champlain Bridge. Phone 518/597-3666.* Preserved ruins of fortifications occupied by French, British, and American forces during the French and Indian and Revolutionary wars: Fort St. Frederic (1734) and Fort Crown Point (1759). Site museum with exhibits and audiovisual presentation on history of area. Self-guided tours; events. (Grounds: May-Oct, daily 9 am-dusk; Museum: Mon, Wed-Sun 9 am-5 pm) **FREE**

Penfield Homestead Museum. *703 Creek Rd, Crown Point (12928). 6 miles W, in Ironville Historic District. Phone 518/597-3804. www.penfieldmuseum.org.* The site of the first industrial use of electricity in the United States. Museum of local history, Adirondack iron industry; self-guided tour through the ironworks ruins. (June-Oct, Thurs-Sun 11 am-4 pm) **$**

Specialty Lodging

CROWN POINT BED & BREAKFAST. *2695 Main St, Crown Point (12928). Phone 518/597-3651; fax 518/597-4451. www.crownpointbandb.com.* Victorian house built 1886 for banker; many antiques. 6 rooms, 2 story. Closed Thanksgiving, Dec 25. Complimentary continental breakfast. Check-in 3 pm. Check-out 11 am. **$**

Deposit (F-7)

See also Bainbridge, Binghamton

Settled 1789
Population 1,824
Elevation 991 ft
Area Code 607
Zip 13754
Information Chamber of Commerce, PO Box 222; phone 607/467-2556

Specialty Lodging

CHESTNUT INN AT OQUAGA LAKE. *498 Oquaga Lake Rd, Deposit (13754). Phone 607/467-2500; fax 607/467-5911.* 30 rooms, 3 story. Check-in 3 pm, check-out 11 am. Restaurant, bar. **$**

Diamond Point (C-9)

See also Bolton Landing, Glens Falls, Lake George Area, Lake Luzerne, Warrensburg

Population 400
Elevation 354 ft
Area Code 518
Zip 12824

This town is located on the southwestern shore of Lake George (see).

Limited-Service Hotel

★ **TREASURE COVE RESORT MOTEL.** *3940 Lake Shore Dr, Diamond Point (12824). Phone 518/668-*

5334; fax 581/668-9027. www.treasurecoveresort.com. 50 rooms. Closed mid-Oct-Apr. Check-in 4 pm, check-out 10 am. Children's activity center. Beach. Two outdoor pools. No credit cards accepted. **$**

Full-Service Resort

★ ★ **CANOE ISLAND LODGE.** *Lakeshore Dr, Diamond Point (12824). Phone 518/668-5592. www.canoeislandlodge.com.* Guests return to the family vacations of their youth at this 50-year-old, knotty-pine-filled resort on Lake George in the Adirondack Mountains. The namesake island is actually 1 mile offshore; a perfect escape for enjoying the Thursday night barbeque dinners during summer season. 65 rooms, 2 story. Closed mid-Oct-mid-May. Check-in 4 pm, check-out 11 am. Restaurant, bar. Children's activity center. Beach. Tennis. **$$$**

Dover Plains (F-9)

Restaurant

★ ★ ★ **OLD DROVERS INN.** *196 E Duncanhill Rd, Dover Plains (12522). Phone 845/832-9311; fax 845/832-6356. www.olddroversinn. com.* This inn, built in 1750, is located near vineyards, the Hudson Valley, and the Berkshires. Guests can visit the nearby Vanberbilt Mansion, the Culinary Institute of America, the Franklin D. Roosevelt Home, or enjoy riverboat tours on the Hudson. Lunch, dinner. Closed Wed; Dec 25. Bar. Outdoor seating. **$$**

Dunkirk (E-1)

Population 13,989
Elevation 598 ft
Area Code 716
Zip 14048
Information Northern Chautauqua Chamber of Commerce, 212 Lakeshore Dr W; phone 716/366-6200
Web Site www.tourchautauqua.com

A pleasant industrial and vacation city southwest of Buffalo on the shores of Lake Erie, about 35 miles from the Pennsylvania border, this was the birthplace of author-historian Samuel Hopkins Adams.

What to See and Do

Boating. One of three small boat harbors of refuge on Lake Erie between Erie, PA and Buffalo, NY. Launch; protected inner harbor; mooring. Breakwater.

Dunkirk Lighthouse. *1 Lighthouse Point Dr N, Dunkirk (14048). Off Hwy 5. Phone 716/366-5050.* (1875) Built in 1875; ten rooms in lighthouse with a room dedicated to each branch of the military service; also a lighthouse keeper's room; Victorian furnishings in kitchen and parlor. Guided tour includes tower and history of the Great Lakes. (June-Sept: daily 10 am-4 pm; Apr-June and Sept-Oct: Mon-Tues and Thurs-Sat 10 am-4 pm) **$$**

Evangola State Park. *10191 Old Lake Shore Rd, Irving (14081). 17 miles N on Hwy 5. Phone 716/549-1802.* Swimming, 4,000-foot sand beach, bathhouse, lifeguards, fishing; nature trails, hiking, cross-country skiing, snowmobiling, picnicking (fee), playground, game areas, tent and trailer sites (fee). **$$**

Historical Museum of the Darwin R. Barker Library. *7 Day St, Fredonia (14063). Phone 716/672-8051.* Period furniture, 1880s parlor; exhibits on Fredonia and Pomfret; documents, photos, portraits, and genealogical material; children's museum, education programs. (Tues, Thurs-Sat 2:30-4:30 pm) **FREE**

Lake Erie State Park. *5905 Lake Ave, Brocton (14716). 7 miles W on Hwy 5. Phone 716/792-9214.* Fishing; nature trails, hiking, cross-country skiing, snowmobiling, picnicking, playground, tent and trailer sites, cabins (fee). (May-mid-Oct, daily 8 am-dark) **$$**

Swimming. Point Gratiot Park Beach and Wright Park Beach. (Mid-June-Labor Day, daily) Bathhouses.

Special Event

Chautauqua County Fair. *1089 Central Ave, Dunkirk (14048). Phone 716/366-4752.* Last week in July.

Limited-Service Hotel

★ ★ **DAYS INN.** *10455 Bennett Rd, Fredonia (14063). Phone 716/673-1351; fax 716/672-6909. www.daysinn. com.* 135 rooms, 2 story. Pets accepted. Complimentary continental breakfast. Check-in 3 pm, check-out 11 am. Restaurant, bar. Indoor pool, whirlpool. **$**

Full-Service Inn

★ ★ ★ **THE WHITE INN.** *52 E Main St, Fredonia (14063). Phone 716/672-2103; toll-free 888/373-3664;*

fax 716/672-2107. www.whiteinn. com. This inn has all the comfort and charm of a country manor. It offers eloquently decorated rooms and suites, fine dining, and a location close to cultural, historical, and recreational attractions. 23 rooms, 3 story. Pets accepted. Complimentary full breakfast. Check-in 3 pm, check-out 11 am. Restaurant, bar. **$$**

Restaurant

★ ★ ★ **THE WHITE INN.** *52 E Main St, Fredonia (14063). Phone 716/672-2103; fax 716/672-2107. www. whiteinn. com.* This stately country manor with its impressive columned portico and authentic Victorian décor is the setting for elegant dining. The restaurant prides itself as one of the few surviving members of the Duncan Hines "Family of Fine Restaurants." Steak menu. Breakfast, lunch, dinner. Bar. Outdoor seating. **$$**

East Aurora (E-2)

See also Arcade, Buffalo

Population 6,673
Elevation 917 ft
Area Code 716
Zip 14052
Information Greater East Aurora Chamber of Commerce, 431 Main St; phone 716/652-8444 or toll-free 800/441-2881
Web Site www.eanycc.com

East Aurora lies very close to the large industrial and commercial center of Buffalo. In the early 1900s, Elbert Hubbard, author of *A Message to Garcia,* lived here and made it the home of the Roycrofters, makers of fine books, copper and leather ware, and furniture. The Roycroft campus is still operating, and it is the only continuous operation of its kind in America today. East Aurora is also the headquarters of Fisher-Price toys. The Baker Memorial Methodist Church, which has hand-signed Tiffany windows, is located here.

What to See and Do

The Elbert Hubbard Museum. *363 Oakwood Ave, Eas Aurora (14052). Located in the ScheideMantel House. Phone 716/652-4735.*A five-bedroom, 1910 Craftsman period home built by and for the Roycrofters. Contains Roycroft furniture, modeled leather, hammered metal, leaded glass, books, pamphlets, and other artifacts from 1895 to 1938. Also here is material on Elbert Hubbard, author of the famous essay *A Message to Garcia.* (June-mid-Oct, Wed, Sat-Sun 2-4 pm; tours by appointment)

Kissing Bridge Ski Area. *10296 State Rd, Glenwood. 9 miles W on Hwy 20A, then 17 miles S on Hwy 219 Expy S, exit at Armor Duells Rd to Hwy 240 S; follow signs. Phone 716/592-4963. www.kbski.com.* Two quad, four double chairlifts; two T-bars, J-bar, and handle tow; patrol, school, rentals; snowmaking; bars, cafe; nursery. Longest run 3,500 feet; vertical drop 550 feet. Night skiing. (Dec-Mar, daily) **$$$$**

Millard Fillmore Museum. *24 Shearer Ave, East Aurora (14052). Phone 716/652-8875.* House (circa 1825) Fillmore built for his wife contains memorabilia, furnishings. 1830s herb and rose garden. Carriage house (circa 1830) built of lumber from the former Nathaniel Fillmore farm; antique tools, Fillmore sleigh. (June-mid-Oct: Wed, Sat-Sun 2-4 pm; rest of year: by appointment) **$$**

Special Events

Roycroft Summer Festival of Arts & Crafts. *1054 Olean Rd, East Aurora (14052). Phone 716/655-7252.* Roycroft artisans and members of the art society display their arts and crafts. Last weekend in June.

Toy Festival. *636 Girard Ave, East Aurora (14052). Phone 716/687-5151. www.toytownusa.com.* Celebration commemorating Fisher-Price Toy Company's establishment here in the 1930s. Last weekend in Aug.

Full-Service Inn

★ ★ ★ **ROYCROFT INN.** *40 S Grove St, East Aurora (14052). Phone 716/652-5552; toll-free 800/267-0525; fax 716/655-5345. www.roycroftinn. com.* Visit this birthplace of the New York Arts and Crafts movement 30 minutes from Buffalo. The grounds, called the Roycroft Campus, originally housed 500 craftsmen and their shops and now are a national landmark. Rooms are breathtaking showcases of original furniture and fixtures. 22 rooms, 3 story. Complimentary continental breakfast. Check-out 11 am. Restaurant, bar. **$$**

Restaurants

★ ★ **OLD ORCHARD INN.** *2095 Blakeley Rd, East Aurora (14052). Phone 716/652-4664; fax 716/652-2250. www.oldorchardny.com.* A century-old, rustic country inn, this former hunting lodge offers hearty food in a warm atmosphere. During the summer months, enjoy its covered patio seating or wander through its woodsy 25 acres. American menu. Lunch, dinner. Closed Mon-Tues; also Jan-Apr. Bar. Casual attire. Outdoor seating. **$$$**

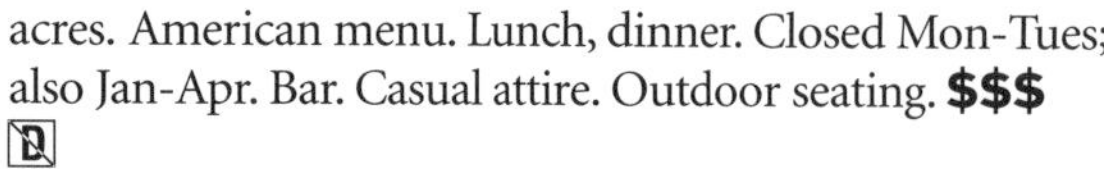

★ ★ ★ **ROYCROFT INN.** *40 S Grove St, East Aurora (14052). Phone 716/652-5552; fax 716/655-5345. www.roycroftinn. com.* This inn originally opened in 1905 to accommodate the thousands of visitors to the thriving Roycroft Arts and Crafts Community, a large, self-contained group of writers and craftspeople. Now a National Landmark that has been restored to early-1900s Arts and Crafts style, the inn preserves this rich history in its original and reproduction Arts and Crafts-style furnishings. The restaurant, a popular gathering place for locals, serves creative and fresh cuisine with continental influences, including French onion soup au gratin, rack of lamb, and sesame-encrusted tuna. A good-sized wine list, as well as a nice selection of microbrews and hand-crafted beers, ensures that diners will find suitable pairings. Choose from a fireside table or a seat on the veranda, surrounded by dogwoods and rhododendrons. American menu. Lunch, dinner, brunch. Bar. Children's menu. Casual attire. Reservations recommended. Outdoor seating. **$$**

East Bloomfield

See also Canandaigua

Restaurant

★ ★ ★ **HOLLOWAY HOUSE.** *29 State St, East Bloomfield (14443). Phone 585/657-7120; fax 585/651-4673. www.thehollowayhouse.com.* Housed in an 1808 stagecoach tavern, this seasonal restaurant has been owned by the Wayne family for over 40 years. Lunch, dinner. Closed Mon; also late Dec-Mar. Bar. Children's menu. **$$**

East Hampton (B-5)

See also Amagansett, Montauk, Sag Harbor, Shelter Island, Southampton

Settled 1648
Population 19,719
Elevation 36 ft
Area Code 631
Zip 11937
Information East Hampton Chamber of Commerce, 79 A Main St; phone 631/324-0362
Web Site www.easthamptonchamber.com

East Hampton is an old Long Island village, founded in 1648 by a group of farmers. Farming was the main livelihood until the mid-1800s, when the town began to develop into a fashionable resort.

What to See and Do

Guild Hall Museum. *158 Main St, East Hampton (11937). Phone 631/324-0806. www.guildhall.org.* Regional art exhibits; changing shows. Art and poetry lectures, classes. Library covering art and artists of the region. (June-Sept: Mon-Sat 11 am-5 pm, Sun from noon; rest of year: Thurs-Sat 11 am-5 pm, Sun from noon; closed Thanksgiving, Dec 25) **$** Also here is

> **John Drew Theater at Guild Hall.** *158 Main St, East Hampton (11937). Phone 631/324-0806.*A 382-seat theater for films, plays, concerts, lectures, and children's performances.

Historic Mulford Farm. *10 James Ln, East Hampton (11937). Adjacent to Payne House. Phone 631/324-6850.* (1680) Living history farm museum; 18th-century New England architecture; colonial history; period rooms; costumed interpretation. (July and Aug: daily; June and Sept: weekends only; rest of year: by appointment) **$** Nearby is

> **Historic Clinton Academy.** *151 Main St, East Hampton (11937). Phone 631/324-6850.*(1784) First preparatory school in New York. Now a museum housing collection of artifacts of Eastern Long Island. (July and Aug: daily; June and Sept: weekends only) **$**

Home, Sweet Home House. *14 James Ln, East Hampton (11937). Phone 631/324-0713.* Named after the popular 19th-century song, Home, Sweet Home, written by John Howard Payne, this house was originally owned by Paynes grandfather, Aaron Isaacs (the first Jewish person to settle in the area). The historic home in this historic village features beautiful antiques and china, and is dedicated to Payne, who was also an actor, playwright, and diplomat. History buffs visiting East Hampton will enjoy this attraction. (Mon-Sat 10 am-4 pm, Sun 2-4 pm) **$**

Hook Mill. *36 N Main St, East Hampton (11937).* Completely equipped 1806 windmill. Guided tours. (Memorial Day-Labor Day, Wed-Mon) **$**

Pollock-Krasner House and Study Center. *830 Fireplace Rd, East Hampton (11937). Phone 631/324-4929.* Jackson Pollock's studio and house plus a reference library on 20th-century American art. (May, Sept-Oct: Sat, by appointment only; June-Aug: Thurs-Sat, by appointment only) **$$**

Full-Service Inns

★ ★ ★ THE 1770 HOUSE. *143 Main St, East Hampton (11937). Phone 631/324-1770; fax 631/324-3504. www.1770house.com.* Restored 18th-century house; antique furnishings.7 rooms, 2 story. Children over 12 years only. Check-in 2 pm, check-out 11:30 am. Wireless Internet access. Restaurant, bar. **$$$**

★ ★ ★ MAIDSTONE ARMS. *207 Main St, East Hampton (11937). Phone 631/324-5006; fax 631/324-5037. www.maidstonearms.com.* The Osborne family built this estate as a private residence in the 1750s. It has been operating as an inn since the 1870s. Guests can enjoy the bustle of the Hamptons during the summer months or settle in by the fireplaces during winter stays. 19 rooms, 3 story. Complimentary full breakfast. Check-in 3 pm, check-out 11 am. Wireless Internet access. Restaurant, bar. **$$$**

Specialty Lodging

BAKER HOUSE 1650. *181 Main St, East Hampton (11937). Phone 631/324-4081; fax 631/329-5931. www. bakerhouse1650.com.* This stuccoed English Tudor house in the Hamptons has been refurbished into a quaint inn. Enjoy a relaxing afternoon in the cottage's living room—a perfect spot to sit and read a book. 5 rooms, 2 story. Check-in 2 pm, check-out noon. High-speed Internet access. Spa. Indoor pool. **$$$**

Restaurants

★ ★ ★ DELLA FEMINA. *99 N Main St, East Hampton (11937). Phone 631/329-6666. www.dellafemina.com.* As you approach this restaurant, you can see that extraordinary care has been taken to make it beautiful. Flower boxes adorn the windows outside; inside, the space is luminous and refined without being at all stuffy. Fresh Granny Smith apples in the entryway fill the air with their unmistakable fragrance, fueling the hunger of the diners waiting for a table. A sunken bar area complete with caricatures of famous customers invites guests to linger there before being seated. On the menu, you'll find such favorites as yellowfin tuna tartare, maple-soy pork loin chops, roasted chicken with rosemary jus, and pan-roasted day boat halibut. The sizable wine list includes many premium wines and a number of boutique and hand-crafted selections. American menu. Dinner. Closed Wed in the off-season. Bar. Casual attire. Outdoor seating. **$$$**

★ ★ ★ EAST HAMPTON POINT. *295 Three Mile Harbor, East Hampton (11937). Phone 631/329-2800; fax 631/329-2876. www.easthamptonpoint.com.* American menu. Lunch, dinner. Closed Sept-Mar. Bar. Children's menu. Casual attire. Reservations recommended. Valet parking. Outdoor seating. **$$$**

★ ★ JAMES LANE CAFE AT THE HEDGES. *74 James Ln, East Hampton (11937). Phone 631/324-7100. www.jameslanecafe.com.* In 1870s Victorian home. Italian, American, Mediterranean menu. Dinner. Closed Tues-Wed in Oct-May. Casual attire. Valet parking. Outdoor seating. **$$$**

★ ★ LAUNDRY. *341 Pantig Rd, East Hampton (11937). Phone 631/324-3199; fax 631/324-9327. www.thelaundry.com.* Once operated as a commercial laundry; courtyard, garden. American menu. Dinner. Closed Thanksgiving, Dec 25, Dec 31; Wed after Labor Day. Bar. Casual attire. Outdoor seating. **$$**

★ ★ MARYJANE'S IL MONASTERO. *128 N Main St, East Hampton (11937). Phone 631/324-8008; fax 631/324-3523.* Three dining rooms. American, Italian menu. Lunch, dinner. Closed Jan; Thanksgiving, Dec 25. Bar. Children's menu. Casual attire. **$$**

★ ★ MICHAEL'S. *28 Maidstone Park Rd, East Hampton (11937). Phone 631/324-0725; fax 631/324-8602.* Seafood, American menu. Dinner. Closed Dec 25. Bar. Casual attire.**$$**

★ ★ NICK & TONI'S. *136 N Main St, East Hampton (11937). Phone 631/324-3550; fax 631/324-7001. www.nickandtonis.org.* Mediterranean menu. Dinner, Closed Dec 25. Bar. Casual attire. Reservations recommended. **$$$**

★ ★ PALM. *94 Main St, East Hampton (11937). Phone 631/324-0411; fax 631/324-6122. www.thepalm.com.* Turn-of-the-century décor. Seafood, steak menu. Lunch, dinner. Bar. Casual attire. **$$$**

East Norwich

Restaurant

★ ★ ★ CAFE GIRASOLE. *1053 Oyster Bay Rd, East Norwich (11732). Phone 516/624-8330; fax 516/522-5240. www.canterburyalesrestaurant.com.* Italian menu. Lunch, dinner. Closed holidays. Bar. Casual attire. Reservations recommended. Outdoor seating. **$$**

East Syracuse (D-6)

Limited-Service Hotel

★ ★ **HILTON GARDEN INN.** *6004 Fair Lakes Rd, East Syracuse (13057). Phone 315/431-4800; fax 315/431-4999. www.hiltongardeninn. com.* 100 rooms. Check-in 3 pm, check-out noon. High-speed Internet access. Restaurant, bar. Fitness room. Indoor pool, whirlpool. Business center. **$**

Restaurant

★ ★ **JUSTIN'S GRILL.** *6400 Yorktown Cir, East Syracuse (13057). Phone 315/437-1461; fax 315/437-4066.* Steak menu. Lunch, dinner. Closed Sun; Jan 1, Dec 25. Bar. Children's menu. **$$**

Eastchester

Restaurant

★ ★ **PINOCCHIO.** *309 White Plains Rd, Eastchester. Phone 914/337-0044.* Italian menu. Dinner. Closed Mon. Bar. Casual attire. Reservations recommended. Outdoor seating. **$$**

Ellenville (F-8)

See also Kingston, Liberty, New Paltz

Population 4,130
Elevation 330 ft
Area Code 914
Zip 12428
Information Chamber of Commerce, PO Box 227; phone 914/647-4620
Web Site www.ellenvilleny.org

Center of the Ulster County resort area, Ellenville offers abundant scenic beauty. Hang gliding is popular here.

Full-Service Resorts

★ ★ **HUDSON VALLEY RESORT AND SPA.** *400 Granite Rd, Kerhonkson (12446). Phone 845/626-8888; toll-free 888/684-7264; fax 845/626-2595. www. hudsonvalleyresort.com.* 296 rooms, 8 story. Check-in 4 pm, check-out 11 am. Restaurant, bar. Children's activity center. Fitness room. Indoor pool, outdoor pool, whirlpool. Golf, 18 holes. Tennis. Ski in/ski out. **$**

★ ★ **NEVELE GRANDE RESORT.** *1 Nevele Rd, Ellenville (12428). Phone 800/647-6000; toll-free 800/647-6000; fax 845/647-9884. www.nevele.com.* 700 rooms, 10 story. Check-in 3 pm, check-out 1 pm. Restaurant, bar. Children's activity center. Fitness room, spa. Two indoor pools, four outdoor pools, whirlpools. Golf, 36 holes. Tennis. Ski in/ski out. Business center. **$**

Elmira (F-5)

See also Corning, Finger Lakes, Owego, Watkins Glen,

Settled 1788
Population 30,940
Elevation 859 ft
Area Code 607
Information Chemung County Chamber of Commerce, 400 E Church St, 14901; phone 607/734-5137 or toll-free 800/627-5892
Web Site www.chemungchamber.org

Elmira is on both shores of the Chemung River—on a site where, in 1779, the Sullivan-Clinton expedition found a Native American village. By the mid-19th century, the railroads and canals were opening new fields of industry; first lumber, later metalworking and textiles.

Samuel Clemens (Mark Twain) spent more than 20 summers at Quarry Farm, the Elmira country home of his wife's sister, Susan Crane. Elmira also was the birthplace of noted filmmaker Hal Roach, first United States woman space pilot Eileen Collins, and fashion designer Tommy Hilfiger.

What to See and Do

Arnot Art Museum. *235 Lake St, Elmira (14901). Phone 607/734-3697.*An 1833 mansion with three-story wing. Includes 17th- and 19th-century European paintings displayed in 1880 gallery; 19th-century American gallery; also changing exhibits. (Tues-Sun 10 am-5 pm, Sun from 1 pm; closed holidays) **$$**

Catherine Cottages. *2025 Hwy 14, Montour Falls (14865). Phone 607/535-0000. www.catharinecottages. com.* Four private cottages with private bath, heat and air conditioning, small refrigerator, table and chairs, picnic table and charcoal grill. Full housekeeping and continental breakfast included. On the banks of Catharine Creek, a trout stream. No pets.

Chemung Valley History Museum. *415 E Water St, Elmira (14901). Phone 607/734-4167. www.chemungvalleymuseum.org.* Local history displays, Mark Twain exhibit, research library; special events. (Tues-Sun; closed holidays) **$**

Elmira College. *1 Park Pl, Elmira (14901). Phone 607/735-1800; toll-free 800/935-6472. www.elmira.edu.*(1855) (1,100 students) Liberal arts. Coeducational since 1969, Elmira College was the first (1855) to grant women degrees equal to those of men. The Mark Twain Study was presented to the college by the Langdon Family in 1952; Clemens did much of his writing here, including *The Adventures of Huckleberry Finn.* Mark Twain exhibit in Hamilton Hall has memorabilia and a 20-minute video. Study and exhibit (summer: Mon-Sat; rest of year: by appointment).

Harris Hill Park. *557 Harris Hill Rd, Elmira (14903). Phone 607/732-1210. www.harnshillamusement.com.* High above the valley, this park offers picnicking, a playground, swimming pools, grills and summertime amusements including batting cages, miniature golf, and go-karts. **$**

National Soaring Museum. *51 Soaring Hill Dr, Elmira (14903). 8 miles NW in Harris Hill Park, off Hwy 17, exit 51. Phone 607/734-3128. www.soaringmuseum.org.* Features a large collection of soaring planes that depict the history of this type of flight. The simulator is a good place to test what soaring feels like before signing up for the real thing. (Daily 10 am-5 pm) **$$**

National Warplane Museum. *Elmira-Corning Regional Airport,17 Aviation Dr, Horseheads (14845). Off Hwy 17, exit 51. Phone 607/739-8200. www.warplane.org.* Dedicated to preserving the planes, engines, and memories of those who molded aviation heritage. Museum houses interactive displays, exhibits, aircrafts. Gift shop. (Mon-Fri 10 am-4 pm. Sat 9 am-5 pm, Sun 11 am-5 pm; closed Jan 1, Thanksgiving, Dec 25) **$$**

Replica Trolley Tours. *400 E Church St, Elmira (14901). Depart on E Water St. Phone 607/734-5137.* Guided tours (60 minutes) of Chemung County's tourist attractions aboard a replica trolley. (July-Labor Day; Tues-Sat) **$**

Wings of Eagles Discovery Center. *Elmira-Corning Regional Airport, 17 Aviation Dr, Horseheads (14845). Phone 607/739-8200. www.warplane.org.* Dedicated to the preservation and interpretation of military aircraft. Pretend to fly in the different planes or check out the simulator. (Mon-Fri 10 am-4 pm, Sat 9 am-5 pm, Sun 11 am-5 pm) **$$**

Woodlawn Cemetery. *233rd St and Webster Ave, Elmira. N end of Walnut St.* Graves of Samuel Clemens (Mark Twain) and Hal Roach. Nearby is

Woodlawn National Cemetery. Graves of 2,000 Confederate prisoners of war who died in Elmira.

Special Events

Baseball. *546 Luce St, Elmira (14904). www.elmirapioneers.com.* Elmira Pioneers. Affiliate of the Northeast League. Mid-May-Labor Day.

Chemung County Fair. *Horseheads, Fairview Rd and S Main St, Elmira. Phone 607/734-1203.* Early Aug.

NASCAR Race Day. *2790 County Rd 16, Watkins Glen (14891). Phone 607/535-2481.* Contests, drivers, entertainment. Early Aug.

Limited-Service Hotels

★ BEST WESTERN MARSHALL MANOR. *3527 Watkins Rd, Horseheads (14845). Phone 607/739-3891; toll-free 800/780-7234; fax 607/739-3892. www.bestwestern.com.* A charming red brick building with white pillars, this comfortable motel is set in the rolling countryside and is convenient to local wineries and a large shopping mall. The rooms here are spacious with traditional furnishings and feature oversize bathrooms.40 rooms. Pets accepted, some restrictions; fee. Complimentary continental breakfast. Check-in 1 pm, check-out 11 am. Outdoor pool. **$**

★ ★ HOLIDAY INN. *760 E Water St, Elmira (14901). Phone 607/734-4211; fax 607/734-3549. www.holiday-inn. com/elm-riverview.* Situated just off the highway, this well-maintained, family-friendly motel features a large outdoor pool and a wading pool for kids. The hotel also has a fitness room for guests, and is conveniently located near the town of Corning. 150 rooms, 2 story. Pets accepted. Check-in 2 pm, check-out noon. Restaurant, bar. Fitness room. Indoor pool, outdoor pool, children's pool. **$**

Restaurant

★ ★ HILL TOP INN. *171 Jerusalem Hill Rd, Elmira*

(14901). Phone 607/732-6728; toll-free 888/444-5867. www.hill-top-inn. com. American menu. Dinner. Closed Sun; also Nov-Feb. Bar. Children's menu. Business casual attire. Reservations recommended. Outdoor seating. **$$**

Elmsford

Restaurants

★ ★ **ANDREW'S RESTAURANT.** *86 E Main, Elmsford (10523). Phone 914/592-4213; fax 914/592-2998.* American, Italian menu. Lunch, dinner. Bar. Casual attire. Reservations recommended. Valet parking. Outdoor seating. **$$$**

★ ★ **ICHI RIKI.** *1 E Main St, Elmsford (10523). Phone 914/592-2220.* Japanese menu. Lunch, dinner. Closed Thanksgiving, Dec 25. Bar. Casual attire. Reservations recommended. **$$**

Finger Lakes (E-5)

See also Auburn, Canandaigua, Corning, Cortland, Elmira, Geneseo, Geneva, Hammondsport, Ithaca, Owego, Penn Yan, Rochester, Skaneateles, Syracuse, Waterloo, Watkins Glen

Web Site www.fingerlakes.org

Scientists say the Finger Lakes were scooped out by glaciers, resulting in one of the most delightful landscaping jobs in America. There are 11 lakes in all; Canandaigua, Keuka, Seneca, Cayuga, Owasco, and Skaneateles are the largest. The smaller lakes also have the characteristic finger shape. Seneca is the deepest at 630 feet and Cayuga the longest at 40 miles. The region has many glens and gorges with plunging streams. Hundreds of recreation spots dot the shores, offering every imaginable sport. The famous New York State wine grapes grow in the many miles of vineyards in the area. This scenic area boasts 25 state parks, many waterfalls, camping and picnicking areas, and other features.

Fire Island National Seashore (C-4)

See also Bay Shore, Riverhead

Web Site www.nps.gov/fiis

Five areas of the Fire Island National Seashore are open. Otis Pike Wilderness Visitor Center, reached via William Floyd Parkway and Smith Point Bridge (phone 516/281-3010); self-guided nature walk and boardwalk trail for the disabled. Parking (May-September, fee) and swimming at adjacent county park. Sailors Haven/Sunken Forest, reached by ferry from Sayville (begins running mid-May), has swimming, lifeguards, marina, picnicking, concession, visitor center, nature walk, self-guided tours, naturalist programs (June-Labor Day). Watch Hill, reached by ferry from Patchogue, offers the same facilities as Sailors Haven plus 26 family campsites (lottery reservations required after May 1). Fire Island Lighthouse (1858) area, reached by Robert Moses Causeway, has boardwalk leading to lighthouse; nature trail (all year); former lightkeeper's quarters are a visitor center with exhibits (April-June, Labor Day-December: weekends; July-Labor Day: Wednesday-Sunday). Parking at adjacent Robert Moses State Park (see). Headquarters is at 120 Laurel Street, Patchogue 11772.

Located on Washington Avenue in Mastic Beach is the restored estate of one of the signers of the Declaration of Independence, William Floyd (July 4-Labor Day, weekends). No pets allowed.

Fishkill (B-2)

See also Garrison, Newburgh, Poughkeepsie, Stormville

Population 20,258
Elevation 223 ft
Area Code 845
Information Dutchess County Tourism Promotion Agency, 3 Neptune Rd, Suite M-17, Poughkeepsie 12601; phone 845/463-4000 or toll-free 800/445-3131
Web Site www.dutchesstourism.com

What to See and Do

Branton Woods Golf Course. *178 Stormville Rd, Hopewell Junction (12533). Phone 845/223-1600. www.brantonwoodsgolf.com.* About 70 miles from New York City in tiny Hopewell Junction is Branton Woods, a course that makes good use of the natural wildlife. Each fairway has plenty of undulations, and golfers have three lakes to contend with from time to time. Elevation changes force difficult shots into elevated greens, and the back-to-back par-fives at 14 and 15 are quite a challenge (the 15th alone is 600 yards long). The course is beautifully manicured, and twilight golf starts early (2 pm), so play then, as the rates go down significantly and there's still plenty of daylight left to get in a leisurely round. **$$$$**

Madam Brett Homestead. *50 Van Nydeck Ave, Beacon (12508). SW on I-84, exit Hwy 52, then W 3 miles. Phone 845/831-6533.* (1709) Oldest standing structure in Dutchess County. Period furnishings of seven generations, from Dutch Colonial through Federal and Victorian eras. Garden. Occupied by same family from 1709 to 1954. (May-Dec, first Sun every month, afternoons or by appointment) **$$**

Mount Gulian Historic Site. *145 Sterling St, Beacon (12508). Off Hwy 9D N. Phone 845/831-8172.* (1730-1740) Headquarters of Baron von Steuben during the final period of the Revolutionary War; birthplace of the Order of the Society of Cincinnati, the first veteran's organization; Dutch barn and restored garden. (mid-Apr-Dec, Wed-Sun 1-5 pm; also by appointment) **$$**

Van Wyck Homestead Museum. *Jct Hwy 9 and I-84, Fishkill. S of town. Phone 845/896-9560.* (1732) Once requisitioned by the Continental Army as headquarters, orders for the army were issued from the house. Also site of court-martials, including that of Enoch Crosby, counterspy for the American forces. Notables include Washington, Lafayette, and von Steuben visited here. Library. Collection of Hudson Valley Folk Art; also changing exhibits. (Memorial Day-Oct, Sat and Sun 1-4 pm also by appointment) **$$**

Limited-Service Hotel

★ RAMADA INN. *20 Schuyler Blvd, Fishkill (12524). Phone 845/896-4995; fax 845/896-6631. www.ramada.com.* 82 rooms, 4 story. Pets accepted, some restrictions. Complimentary continental breakfast. Check-in 2 pm, check-out 11 am. Bar. **$**

Restaurant

★ ★ HUDSON'S RIBS & FISH. *1099 Hwy 9, Fishkill (12524). Phone 845/297-5002; fax 845/297-0287. www.hudsonsribsandfish.com.* Seafood menu. Dinner. Bar. Children's menu. **$$**

Floral Park

See also Garden City, Hempstead, New York, Roslyn

Population 15,967
Elevation 95 ft
Area Code 516
Web Site

John Lewis Childs started a florist and seed business here in the 1870s. He planted the village with acres of flowers, which even lined the railroad tracks for over a mile, and had the town's name changed from East Hinsdale to Floral Park.

Limited-Service Hotel

★ FLORAL PARK MOTOR LODGE. *30 Jericho Tpke, Floral Park (11001). Phone 516/775-7777; toll-free 800/255-9680; fax 516/775-0451. www.floralparkmotorlodge.com.* 107 rooms, 3 story. Complimentary continental breakfast. Check-in 3 pm, check-out noon. **$**

Restaurants

★ ★ ARTURO'S ITALIAN RESTAURANT. *246-04 Jericho Tpke, Bellerose (11001). Phone 516/352-7418; fax 516/352-2277. www.arturorestaurant.com.* Italian menu. Lunch, dinner. Closed Easter, Thanksgiving, Dec 25. Bar. **$$**

★ KOENIG'S. *86 S Tyson Ave, Floral Park (11001). Phone 516/354-2300; fax 516/354-3395. www.koenigsrestaurant.com.* German, Continental menu. Lunch, dinner. Bar. Children's menu. Casual attire. Reservations recommended. **$$**

Flushing

Special Event

US Open Tennis. *Flushing Meadows-Corona Park, USTA National Tennis Center, Flushing (11351). Take the 7 subway to the Willets Point-Shea Stadiu stop. Phone 718/760-6200. www.usopen.org.* Tennis fans from near and far flock to the US Open tennis tournament each September. You can see your favorite players, the stars of tomorrow, and a host of celebrities in the audience at this upper-crust sporting event. Tickets go on sale in late May or by the beginning of June, and those matches held closer to the finals sell out first. Purchase tickets as early as possible. Buying a ticket to the Arthur Ashe Stadium, the main court, gives you admission to all the other courts on the grounds. However, these seats tend to be more in the back, since the better seats go to corporate sponsors. Bring a pad to keep your own score, binoculars, sunscreen, and sunglasses for day games. Late Aug-early Sept.

Restaurants

★ KUM GANG SAN. *138-28 Northern Blvd, Flushing (11354). Phone 718/461-0909. www.kumgangsan.net.* Kum Gang San, a Korean barbecue, sushi, and seafood stalwart, never closes. If you'd like to perform your own *Survivor,* try to stay for all 24 hours. You could spend part of the day hanging out by the indoor waterfall while having a lunch of blistering barbecue, crisped scallion and seafood pancakes, and pungent kimchi. Then you could move over to the sushi bar for an afternoon snack, and for dinner, take a stab at plates of panchanKorean-style tapas-like crab claw with hot pepper and soy-marinated shortribs. And in the wee hours, you might join the late-night revelers and watch the fresh fish coming in from the seafood markets. Korean menu. Lunch, dinner, late-night. Casual attire. **$$**

★ ★ SICHUAN DYNASTY. *135-32 40th Rd, Flushing (11354). Phone 718/961-7500.* If you are one of those people who has trouble deciding what to order, do not go to Sichuan Dynasty. The menu contains some 60 items and will stymie even the most decisive of eaters. The key to dining here may be to go with a large group that can handle lots of fiery fare so that no dish will be left off your evenings menu. The selections run the gamut from your basic kung pao chicken and whole fish to more *Fear Factor*-style dishes like kidney in sesame oil. The setting is bright and comfortable, with colorful tabletops, wide booths, and an upper-deck bar stocked with a decent selection of California wines. Chinese menu. Lunch, dinner. Casual attire. **$$**

Frankfort

Restaurant

★ KITLAS. *2242 Broad St, Frankfort (13340). Phone 315/732-9616.* Lunch, dinner. Closed Sun; holidays. Bar. Children's menu. **$**

Freeport (C-3)

What to See and Do

Mirace Mile. *Woodcleft Ave, Freeport (11520).* A stroll along Freeports Nautical Mile on a warm, summer afternoon or night can't be beat. This revitalized 1-mile stretch of walkway in the seaport village offers a mix of restaurants, clam bars, knick-knack shops, ice cream parlors, a seaport museum, and boats for sale. Start off by eating shrimp or clams outdoors at one of the many ultra causal restaurants (some have live bands on the weekends in summer), stroll nearby and enjoy Ralphs Ices (the best around), browse at a few boats, and just take in the atmosphere. Finish off by sitting on the scenic pier at the end of the avenue and enjoying the peaceful waterfront view. The Nautical Mile is quite crowded on summer weekends and there are also many bikers in the area who rev their Harley-Davidson motorcycles up and down the avenue. Plan to spend some time, however, looking for parking.

Restaurant

★ ★ SCHOONER. *435 Woodcleft Ave, Freeport (11520). Phone 516/378-7575; fax 516/378-4869. www.theschooner.com.* Seafood, steak menu. Lunch, dinner. Closed Dec 25; also second and third weeks in Jan. Valet parking. **$$**

Fulton (D-5)

See also Oswego, Syracuse

Population 11,855
Elevation 360 ft
Area Code 315
Zip 13069
Information Chamber of Commerce, 41 S Second St, Box 148; phone 315/598-4231
Web Site

What to See and Do

Battle Island State Park. *2150 Hwy 48, Fulton (13069). N on Hwy 48. Phone 315/593-3408.* Eighteen-hole golf (fee). Cross-country skiing. Concession.

Garden City

See also Floral Park, Hempstead, New York, Westbury

Population 21,672
Elevation 90 ft
Area Code 516
Zip 11530
Information Chamber of Commerce, 230 Seventh St; phone 516/746-7724

What to See and Do

Cradle of Aviation Museum. *Charles Lindbergh Blvd, Garden City (11530). Phone 516/572-4111. www.cradleofaviation.org.* This new addition to the area celebrates aviation and space travel, and has been a big hit with both adults and children. With an emphasis on Long Islands important and colorful history in the field of aviation, the museum offers exhibits on World War I, World War II, the Jet Age, and Space Travel, to name a few. There also is an IMAX Theater, which features different films with a feel-like-you-are-there sensation. The Red Planet Café is a respite and place for a snack, and the Museum Store is a must-stop for souvenir hunters. If you or your children have any kind of interest in aviation, you will not want to miss this attraction. (Tues 10 am-2 pm, Wed-Sun 10 am-5 pm) **$$$**

Long Island Children's Museum. *Mitchel Center, 11 David Blvd, Garden City (11530). Phone 516/222-0207. www.licm.org.* This new, very popular museum located in a former military base offers many hands-on, interactive exhibits to amuse and educate the little ones. Some of these include a bubble machine that allows children to create bubbles (always a favorite for kids!), climbing ramps, and a beach exhibit that lets kids shape their own sand dune. There also are performances on weekends and programs held during the week. This is a great way to spend an afternoon and the kids are sure to enjoy it. Don't forget to stop by the gift shop for a cute trinket before you leave. The Cradle of Aviation Museum is housed here and additional museums are being planned for the future. (Wed-Sun 10 am-5 pm; also Tues in July-Aug) **$$**

Roosevelt Field. *Old Country Rd and Meadowbrook Pkwy, Garden City (11530). Phone 516/742-8000. www.simon.com.* Think of just about any item you want to buy, from big to small, inexpensive to pricey, and you can find it here at the nations fifth-largest mall. Roosevelt Field has 2.3 million square feet of space and 260 stores in a massive space that takes a road map and a tour guide to navigate. Department stores include Nordstrom, Macys, Sears, and JC Penney. There are also dozens of smaller specialty shops that sell everything from clothing and toys to jewelry and furniture to books and candy. A huge food court offers just about any kind of cheap, quick meal and snack you can imagine. Big shopping holidays (e.g. Memorial Day, and the day after Christmas) and weekends tend to get very crowded, so plan to arrive in the morning. The place is so big that valet parking is even available. (Mon-Sat 10 am-9:30 pm, Sun 11 am-7 pm) **FREE**

Full-Service Hotel

★ ★ ★ **THE GARDEN CITY HOTEL.** *45 7th St, Garden City (11530). Phone 516/747-3000; fax 516/747-3189. www.gardencityhotel. com.* 272 rooms. Check-in 3 pm, check-out noon. High-speed Internet access. Two restaurants, two bars. Fitness room. Indoor pool, whirlpool. Airport transportation available. Business center. **$$$**

Restaurants

★ ★ **AKBAR.** *1 Ring Rd, Garden City (11530). Phone 516/248-5700; fax 516/248-1835.* Indian menu. Lunch, dinner, Sun brunch. Reservations recommended. **$**

★ ★ **ORCHID.** *730 Franklin Ave, Garden City (11530). Phone 516/742-1116.* Chinese menu. Lunch, dinner. Closed Thanksgiving. Bar. Reservations recommended. **$$**

Garrison

See also Fishkill, Mahopac, Peekskill

Population 800
Elevation 21 ft
Area Code 845

What to See and Do

Foundry School Museum. *63 Chestnut St, Cold Spring (10516). 4 miles N on Hwy 9D. Phone 845/265-4010. www.pchs-fsm.org.* Old-fashioned schoolroom; West Point Foundry memorabilia, paintings, Native American artifacts, antiques; changing exhibits; genealogy and historical research library. Maintained by the Putnam County Historical Society. (Mar-Dec, Tues-Thurs 10 am-4 pm, Sat-Sun 2-5 pm; also by appointment) **$**

Full-Service Inn

★ ★ ★ **HUDSON HOUSE RIVER INN.** *2 Main St, Cold Spring (10516). Phone 845/265-9355; fax 845/265-4532. www.hudsonhouseinn. com.* Country inn (1832) on banks of Hudson River.11 rooms, 2 story. Complimentary continental breakfast. Check-in 3 pm, check-out 11 am. Restaurant, bar. **$$**

Geneseo (E-3)

See also Avon, Finger Lakes, Letchworth State Park

Population 9,654
Elevation 800 ft
Area Code 716
Zip 14454
Web Site www.geneseony.com

What to See and Do

Livingston County Historical Museum. *30 Center St, Geneseo (14454). Phone 585/243-9147. www.livingstoncountyhistoricalsociety.org.* Pioneer exhibits, antique toys, Native American artifacts housed in Cobblestone School (1838); Shaker Colony Fountain Stone, farm items; antique fire equipment. (May-Oct, Sun and Thurs 2-5 pm) **DONATION**

Geneva (D-5)

See also Canandaigua, Finger Lakes, Penn Yan, Seneca Falls, Waterloo

Settled 1788
Population 13,617
Elevation 460 ft
Area Code 315
Zip 14456
Information Chamber of Commerce, 35 Lakefront Dr, Box 587; phone 315/789-1776
Web Site www.genevany.com

In the 19th century, Geneva attracted large numbers of retired ministers and spinsters and became known as "the saints' retreat and old maids' paradise." Today, Geneva is known as a "fisherman's paradise." Located at the foot of Seneca Lake, the deepest of the Finger Lakes, the town is surrounded by rich farmland with nurseries on the outskirts of the city.

What to See and Do

Geneva Historical Society Museum. *543 S Main St, Geneva (14456). Phone 315/789-5151. www. genevahistoricalsociety.com.* (Prouty-Chew House) 1829 Federal-style home with items of local history; changing exhibits. (May-Oct : Mon-Fri 9:30 am-4:30 pm, Sat 1:30-4:30 pm, Sun in July and Aug 1:30-4:30 pm) **FREE**

Red Jacket Orchards Fruit Outlet. *957 Canandaigua Rd, Geneva (14456). Phone 315/781-2749; toll-free 800/828-9410. www.redjacketorchards.com.* Apples, apricots, peaches, plums, strawberries, raspberries, and even rhubarb are among the fruits offered at this outlet. Additionally, the company serves up fresh-squeezed juices and ciders, if you'd rather drink your fruit. Look for the big red building. (Mon-Fri 8 am-7 pm; Sat-Sun 9 am-5 pm)

Rose Hill Mansion. *E Lake Rd, Geneva. 3 miles E on NE shore of Seneca Lake on Hwy 96A, just S of Hwy 20, use NY Thrwy exit 41 or 42. Phone 315/789-3848.* (1839) Elegant country estate; Greek Revival architecture; Empire furnishings. Guided tours (May-Oct, Mon-Sat, also Sun afternoons). Grounds (Mon-Fri 10 am-4 pm, Sun 1-5 pm) **$$**

Sampson State Park. *6096 Hwy 96A, Romulus (14541). 11 miles S on Hwy 96A. Phone 315/585-6392.* Swimming beach, bathhouse, fishing, boating (launch, marina); hiking, tennis, picnicking, playground, tent and trailer sites (mid-Apr-late Nov). **$$**

Seneca Lake State Park. *1 Lakefront Dr, Geneva (14456). 1 mile E on Hwy 20. Phone 315/789-2331.* Swimming beach, bathhouse, fishing, boating (launch, marina); picnicking, playground. **$$**

Smith Opera House for the Performing Arts. *82 Seneca St, Geneva (14456). Phone 315/781-5483. www.thesmith. org.* (1894) Alternates films with theater, concerts, children's shows. Tours. (Mon-Fri 9 am-4 pm) **$$**

Special Events

National Trout Derby. *Phone 315/789-1776.* Memorial Day weekend.

Seneca Lake Whale Watch. *Lakeshore Park, 1 Lakeside Dr, Geneva (14456). Phone 315/781-0820.* Three days of music, arts and crafts, food. Aug.

Full-Service Resort

★ ★ ★ **GENEVA ON THE LAKE.** *1001 Lochland Rd; Hwy 14 S, Geneva (14456).Phone 315/789-7190;*

toll-free 800/343-6382; fax 315/789-0322. www.genevaonthelake.com. This property is found in the Finger Lakes Wine District on Seneca Lake. With 10 acres of land, this hotel offers a 70-foot pool, volleyball, 18- and 9-hole golf within a mile, and many more amenities for guests to take advantage of. 30 rooms, 3 story. Complimentary continental breakfast. Check-in 3 pm, check-out noon. Outdoor pool. **$$**

Specialty Lodging

BELHURST CASTLE. *4069 Hwy 14 S, Lochland Rd, Geneva (14456). Phone 315/781-0201. www.belhurstcastle.com.* This castle offers a unique stay for guests. Six guests rooms are in the Castle and some rooms even have their own Jacuzzi. The location is 20 minutes from shopping and close to a state park where guest can enjoy hiking, fishing, and boating. 13 rooms, 3 story. Check-in 3 pm. Check-out 11 am. Restaurant, bar. **$$**

Restaurant

★★ **BELHURST CASTLE.** *4069 Hwy 14 S, Geneva (14456). Phone 315/781-0201. www.belhurstcastle.com.* This century-old stone castle, complete with tales of a mysterious past, provides a romantic setting for an elegant dining experience. An award-winning wine list and hearty, country-inspired foodsincluding ostrich raised by the chefmake it a must-try. American menu. Breakfast, lunch, dinner, Sun brunch. Bar. Children's menu. **$$**

Glen Cove (C-3)

See also Jericho, Oyster Bay

Population 26,622
Elevation 133 ft
Area Code 516
Zip 11542
Information Chamber of Commerce, 14 Glen St, Suite 303, PO Box 721; phone 516/676-6666
Web Site www.glencovechamber.org

What to See and Do

Garvies Point Museum and Preserve. *50 Barry Dr, Glen Cove (11542). Phone 516/571-8010.* Exhibits devoted to regional geology and Native American archaeology. The preserve includes 62 acres of glacial moraine covered by forest; high cliffs along the shoreline of Hempstead Harbor. There are 5 miles of trails throughout the preserve. (Tues-Sun; closed holidays) **$**

Holocaust Memorial. *100 Crescent Beach Rd, Glen Cove (11542). Phone 516/571-8040. www.holocaust-nassau.org.* Exhibits in this small center depicting one of the most devastating events in modern history include sculptures, photographs, and paintings. You also can read accounts of survivors, attend lectures, and view portraits of children who perished during the Nazis reign of terror in Europe. This is not for the faint-hearted. The center is located on a 204-acre preserve and offers various nature trails. **FREE**

Glens Falls

See also Bolton Landing, Diamond Point, Lake George Village, Lake Luzerne, Saratoga National Historical Park, Saratoga Springs

Settled 1763
Population 14,354
Elevation 340 ft
Area Code 518
Zip 12801
Information Adirondack Regional Chambers of Commerce, 136 Warren St; phone 518/798-1761
Web Site www.glensfalls.com

The Iroquois called what is now Glens Falls "Chepontuc," a word meaning "a difficult place to get around." Surrounded by the Adirondack Mountains and adjacent to the 60-foot drop in the Hudson River, the area was settled by Abraham Wing, a Quaker.

What to See and Do

Chapman Historical Museum. *348 Glen St, Glens Falls (12801). Phone 518/793-2826. www.chapmanmuseum.org.* Victorian/Second Empire home (1868). Major portion has been redecorated as a period home reflecting 1865 and 1910. Gallery with rotating exhibits on Glens Falls, Queensbury, and the southern Adirondacks. Large photographic library featuring collection of Seneca Ray Stoddard. (Tues-Sat 10 am-4 pm; closed holidays) **$**

Cross-country skiing. *Glens Falls International Cross-Country Ski Trails, 42 Ridge St, Glens Falls (12801). Phone 518/761-3813.* **FREE**

Hyde Collection. *161 Warren St, Glens Falls (12801). Phone 518/792-1761. www.hydecollection.org.* Art museum in original collector's home. Emphasis on 15th-20th-century art, including Rembrandt, Rubens,

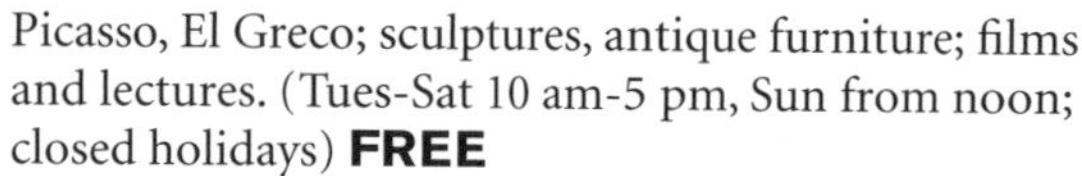

Picasso, El Greco; sculptures, antique furniture; films and lectures. (Tues-Sat 10 am-5 pm, Sun from noon; closed holidays) **FREE**

West Mountain Ski Resort. *59 West Mountain Rd, Glen Falls (12804). I-87, exit 18, 3 miles W on Corinth Rd, then 1/4 mile N on West Mountain Rd. Phone 518/793-6606. www.westmountain.com.* Triple, two double chairlifts; two rope tows; night skiing; patrol, school, rentals; snowmaking; cafeterias, bar; shop, lodge. Longest run approximately 1 1/2 miles; vertical drop 1,010 feet. (Dec-Apr, daily; closed Dec 25) **$$$$**

Limited-Service Hotels

★ BROWN'S WELCOME INN HOTEL. *932 Lake George Rd (Hwy 9), Queensbury (12804). Phone 518/792-9576; fax 518/792-8072. www.brownswelcomeinn. com.* 20 rooms. Closed mid-Oct-mid-May. Check-in 1 pm, check-out 10:30 am. Outdoor pool. **$**

★ ★ RAMADA INN. *Abby Ln, Queensbury (12804). Phone 518/793-7701; fax 518/792-5463. www.ramada.com.* 110 rooms, 2 story. Check-in 3 pm, check-out noon. Restaurant, bar. Indoor pool. **$**

Full-Service Hotel

★ ★ QUEENSBURY HOTEL. *88 Ridge St, Glens Falls (12801). Phone 518/792-1121; fax 518/792-9259. www.queensburyhotel. com.* Located central to Saratoga, Lake George, Adirondack Mountains, and minutes from historical and world famous attractions. 126 rooms, 5 story. Check-in 3 pm, check-out noon. Restaurant, bar. Fitness room. Indoor pool, whirlpool. **$**

Goshen (B-2)

See also Middletown, Monroe, Newburgh

Settled 1714
Population 12,913
Elevation 440 ft
Area Code 845
Zip 10924
Information Chamber of Commerce, 44 Park Pl, PO Box 506; phone 845/294-7741 or toll-free 800/884-2563
Web Site www.goshennychamber.com

This town, in the center of dairying and onion-growing country, has long been famous for harness racing.

What to See and Do

Brotherhood Winery. *100 Brotherhood Plaza Dr, Washingtonville (10992). NY Thrwy to exit 16, Hwy 17 W to exit 130, Hwy 208 N to Washingtonville. Phone 845/496-9101. www.brotherhoodwinery.net.* (America's Oldest Winery) Tours, wine tasting. (Daily 11 am-5 pm; closed Jan 1, Dec 25) **$$**

Goshen Historic Track. *44 Park Pl, Goshen (10924). Phone 845/294-5333.* Harness racing's oldest track dates to 1838. Self-guided walking tour. (Daily) (See SPECIAL EVENTS) **FREE**

Harness Racing Museum and Hall of Fame. *240 Main St, Goshen (10924). Phone 845/294-6330. www.harness-museum.com.* Home of the Hall of Fame of the Trotter; includes Currier and Ives trotting prints; paintings; statues; dioramas of famous horses; library. Harness racing simulator; interactive exhibits. Self-guided tours. (Daily 10 am-6 pm; closed Jan 1, Thanksgiving, Dec 25) **$$**

Special Events

Great American Weekend. *Church Park, Goshen. Phone 845/294-7741.* Arts and crafts, entertainment, rides, races. Early July.

Racing. *Goshen Historic Track, 44 Park Pl, Goshen (10924). Phone 845/294-5333.* Grand Circuit; County Fair Sire Stakes; matinee racing. Three Sat in June and four days in early July.

Great Neck (C-3)

See also New York

Population 9,538
Elevation 100 ft
Area Code 516
Information Chamber of Commerce, 643 Middleneck Rd, 11023; phone 516/487-2000
Web Site www.greatneckchamber.org

Consisting of nine villages and an unincorporated area, the population would be approximately 41,500 if added together.

What to See and Do

US Merchant Marine Academy. *300 Steamboat Rd, Kings*

Point (11024). Phone 516/773-5000. www.usmma.edu. (1943) (950 midshipmen) Memorial Chapel honoring war dead. Visitors welcome (daily 8 am-4:30 pm; closed holidays and July). Regimental Reviews (spring and fall, Sat; schedule varies). The American Merchant Marine Museum (Tues-Fri 10 am-3 pm, Sat-Sun 1-4:30 pm; closed holidays; also July) houses an extensive collection of marine art, ship models, and nautical artifacts. **FREE**

Full-Service Inn

★ ★ ★ INN AT GREAT NECK. *30 Cutter Mill Rd, Great Neck (11021). Phone 516/773-2000. www.innatgreatneck.com.* Tucked away on Long Islands Gold Coast, The Inn at Great Neck is an elegant dwelling. Sleek, sexy Art Deco décor defines this hotel in Great Neck Plaza. Surrounded by 300 shops and restaurants, this hotel is a perfect base for leisure visitors seeking retail therapy or business travelers who take the express train into New York City. The rooms and suites are comfortably sophisticated and offer updated technology. Conference and meeting facilities make this a popular spot for corporate powwows and social events. The Giraffe Room Lounge and Restaurant is the in-spot for American cuisine punctuated by Latin flavors. 85 rooms, 2 story. Pets accepted. Check-in 3 pm, check-out noon. Restaurant, bar. Fitness room. **$$**

Restaurants

★ ★ BEVANDA RISTORANTE. *570 Middle Neck Rd, Great Neck (11023). Phone 516/482-1510; fax 516/482-2659.* Italian menu. Lunch, dinner. Bar. Reservations recommended. **$$**

★ ★ BRUZELL'S. *451 Middle Neck Rd, Great Neck (11023). Phone 516/482-6600; fax 516/482-6734.* American menu. Lunch, dinner. Closed Jan 1, Dec 25. Bar. Children's menu. Valet parking. **$$**

Greene

Restaurant

★ ★ SILO RESTAURANT & CARRIAGE HOUSE. *203 Moran Rd, Greene (13778). Phone 607/656-4377; fax 607/656-4581. www.thesilorestaurant.com.* Seafood menu. Dinner, Sun brunch. Closed holidays. Bar. Overnight stays available. **$$**

Greenport

See also Riverhead, Shelter Island, Southold

Population 4,180
Elevation 10 ft
Area Code 631
Zip 11944
Web Site www.greenport.cc

Greenport is a bit of New England on Long Island. There are clean, uncrowded beaches to enjoy, as well as several wineries. This nautical, artsy, harborside village exudes charm, offering a mix of craft shops, art galleries, antique stores, restaurants, ice cream parlors, and candy shops. Stroll by the water and stop for some clams, or buy some one-of-a-kind nautical knickknacks. Take your time and take in the old-world atmosphere, especially on a warm, sunny day. Walk a little bit off Main Street and you can admire some of the old Victorian houses that are still lived in today. This area has particular appeal and ease since you can park your car and walk everywhere. Keep in mind that summer weekends can be crowded with locals.

What to See and Do

East End Seaport & Maritime Museum. *North Ferry Dock, Third St, Greenport (11944). Phone 631/477-2100. www.eastendseaport.org.* The maritime history of Long Islands East End is depicted through exhibits that include actual yachts used during World War II, a small aquarium, and submarine mock-ups. Lectures on nautical history are offered, and there are special exhibits in summerwhen the area really comes to life. There also is a maritime festival held in late September that offers a parade and various other eventsthis and the museum together make for a nice afternoon. (June-Oct, daily 11 am-5 pm) **FREE**

Orient Point, NY-New London, CT, Ferry. *41720 Hwy 25, Orient Point (11957). 8 miles NE at end of Hwy 25. Phone 631/323-2525.* Ninety-minute crossing. (Daily; closed Dec 25) One-day round trips. Reservations required for vehicle. **$$$$**

Special Event

Greenport Maritime Festival. *Main St and Hwy 48, Greenport (11944).* Wooden boat regatta, fishing tournament, whale boat race; clam chowder tasting contest. Late Sept.

Limited-Service Hotels

★ ★ SOUND VIEW INN. *58775 North Rd, Greenport (11944). Phone 631/477-1910; fax 631/477-9436. www.soundviewinn. com.* 49 rooms, 2 story. Closed Jan-early Mar. Check-in 3 pm, check-out noon. Restaurant, bar. Outdoor pool. Tennis. **$**

★ SUNSET MOTEL. *62005 Rte 48, Greenport (11944). Phone 631/477-1776. www.sunsetgreenport. com.* 18 rooms, 2 story. Closed Jan-Mar. Check-in 3 pm, check-out 11 am. **$**

Restaurants

★ CHOWDER POT PUB. *104 3rd St, Greenport (11944). Phone 631/477-1345.* Lunch, dinner. Closed Mon; also winter weekdays. Bar. Children's menu. Outdoor seating. **$$**

★ ★ CLAUDIO'S. *111 Main St, Greenport (11944). Phone 631/477-0627; fax 631/477-0894. www.claudios. com.* Seafood, steak menu. Lunch, dinner. Closed Jan-mid-Apr. Bar. Outdoor seating. **$$**

Greenwich (D-9)

See also Saratoga Springs

Population 4,896
Elevation 360 ft
Area Code 518
Zip 12834

What to See and Do

Bennington Battlefield State Historic Site. *Hwy 67, Walloomsac. 7 miles SE via Hwy 372, 6 miles S on Hwy 22, and 2 miles E on Hwy 67, E of N Hoosick.* Battlefield where militiamen under Brigadier General John Stark stopped a force of British sharpshooters, mercenaries, Loyalists, and Native Americans in Aug 1777. Hilltop view; relief map, picnic tables. View of monument in Vermont. (May-Labor Day: daily 10 am-7 pm; Labor Day-mid-Nov: Sat-Sun 10 am-7 pm) **FREE**

Willard Mountain Ski Area. *77 Intervale Rd, Greenwich (12834). 6 miles S on Hwy 40.Phone 518/692-7337; toll-free 800/457-7669. www.willardmountain.com.* Chairlift, T-bar, pony lift; patrol, school, rentals; snowmaking; bar, cafeteria, snack bar; ski shop. Longest run 3,500 feet; vertical drop 550 feet. Night skiing. (Early Dec-late Mar, daily; closed Thanksgiving, Dec 25) **$$$$**

Restaurant

★ ONE ONE ONE. *111 Main St, Greenwich (12834). Phone 518/692-8016. www.111restaurant. com.* Unique regional cuisine in an art-gallery setting. American menu. Dinner. Closed Mon-Tues. **$**

Hague (C-9)

See also Crown Point, Lake George Area, Schroon Lake, Ticonderoga

Population 854
Elevation 328 ft
Area Code 518
Zip 12836
Information Chamber of Commerce; phone 518/543-6353
Web Site www.hagueticonderoga.com

Hague is a resort community on the western shore of Lake George, near its northern tip.

What to See and Do

Rogers Rock State Public Campground. *74 Hwy 149, Hague. 3 miles N on Hwy 9 N, in Adirondack Park. Phone 518/585-6746. www.reserveamerica.com.* **$$**

Restaurant

★ ★ THE VIEW RESTAURANT AT INDIAN KETTLES. *9580 Lake Shore Dr (Hwy 9 N), Hague (12836). Phone 518/543-8038. www.indian-kettles. com.* Built in 1946 and continuously operated as a restaurant on the banks of Lake George. Known for authentic local specialties. American menu. Lunch, dinner. **$**

Hamilton (E-7)

See also Cazenovia, Norwich, Oneida

Settled circa 1794
Population 5,733
Elevation 1,126 ft
Area Code 315
Zip 13346

What to See and Do

Colgate University. *13 Oak Dr, Hamilton (13346). On Hwy 12B. Campus tours: contact Admission Office, Administration Building. Phone 315/228-7401. www.colgate.edu.* (1819) (2,650 students) A handsome campus with buildings dating from 1827. The Charles A. Dana Arts Center, designed by Paul Rudolph, houses the Picker Art Gallery (academic year, daily; closed holidays).

Rogers Environmental Education Center. *2721 Hwy 80, Sherburne. Approximately 12 miles S on Hwy 12 or Hwy 12B to Sherburne, then 1 mile W on Hwy 80. Phone 607/674-4017. www.dec.state.ny.us/website/education/rogrctr.html.* On 600 acres; trout ponds; visitor center, 350 mounted birds, outdoor exhibits, 6 miles of nature trails, cross-country skiing, observation tower, picnicking. Buildings (June-Aug: daily; rest of year: Mon-Sat). Center (daily; closed holidays). **FREE**

Limited-Service Hotel

★ ★ COLGATE INN. *1 Payne St, Hamilton (13346). Phone 315/824-2300; fax 315/824-4500. www.colgateinn. com.* 46 rooms, 3 story. Complimentary continental breakfast. Check-in 3 pm. Check-out 11 am. Restaurant, bar. Recreational facilities of Colgate University available to guests. **$**

Hammondsport (E-4)

See also Finger Lakes, Penn Yan

Population 731
Elevation 743 ft
Area Code 607
Zip 14840
Information 697/569-2989
Web Site www.hammondsport.org

This is the center of the New York State wine industry, at the southern tip of Keuka Lake. The grape growers are mainly of German and Swiss origin. They have more than a century of viniculture in New York State behind them, dating from 1829, when the Reverend William Bostwick planted the first vineyard. Glenn H. Curtiss, a pioneer aviator, was born here; most of his early experimental flights took place in this area.

What to See and Do

Glenn H. Curtiss Museum. *8419 Rte 54, Hammondsport (14840). Phone 607/569-2160. www.linkny.com/~curtiss.* Local native Curtiss, like the Wright brothers, also had a bicycle shop. His invention of the first flying boat, which took off over Lake Keuka, gave him the moniker the father of naval aviation. The museum displays the Curtiss bicycle shop and a Dawn of Aviation Gallery. (Nov-Apr: Mon-Sat 10 am-4 pm, Sun 11 am-5 pm; rest of year: Mon-Sat 9 am-5 pm, Sun 10 am-5 pm; closed holidays) **$$**

Wine & Grape Museum of Greyton H. Taylor. *8843 Greyton H. Taylor Memorial Dr, Hammondsport (14840). 2 miles N off Hwy 54A, W side of Keuka Lake. Phone 607/868-4814.* Vineyard equipment, exhibits on early champagne, wine, and brandy production; presidential wine glass collection; barrel-making housed in old area winery (1880-1920). Tours. (May-Oct, daily) **DONATION**

Limited-Service Hotel

★ DAYS INN. *330 W Morris, Bath (14810). Phone 607/776-7644; fax 607/776-7650. www.daysinn. com.* 104 rooms, 5 story. Pets accepted. Complimentary continental breakfast. Check-in 2 pm, check-out 11 am. Indoor pool. **$**

Specialty Lodging

AMITY ROSE BED & BREAKFAST. *8264 Main St, Hammondsport (14840). Phone 607/569-3402; toll-free 800/982-8818; fax 607/569-2504. www.amityrose-inn. com.* 4 rooms. Closed Jan-Mar. Complimentary breakfast. Check-in 3-6 pm, check-out 11 am. **$**

Hampton Bays (C-4)

See also Riverhead, Southampton, Westhampton Beach

Population 12,236
Elevation 50 ft
Area Code 516
Zip 11946
Web Site www.hamptonbayschamber.com

Restaurant

★ ★ VILLA PAUL. *162 W Montauk Hwy, Hampton Bays (11946). Phone 631/728-3261; fax 631/728-1017.* Late 1800s building; original woodwork in dining area. American, Italian menu. Dinner. Closed Dec 25. Bar. Children's menu. Casual attire. **$$**

Hartsdale

Population 9,830
Elevation 182 ft
Area Code 914
Zip 10530

Restaurants

★ ★ **CAFE MEZE.** *20 N Central Ave, Hartsdale (10530). Phone 914/428-2400.* American menu. Lunch, dinner. Closed holidays. Bar. Casual attire. Reservations recommended. Outdoor seating. **$$**

★ ★ **HARRY'S OF HARTSDALE.** *230 E Hartsdale Ave, Hartsdale (10530). Phone 914/472-8777; fax 914/472-1149. www.harrysofhartsdale.com.* Seafood, steak menu. Lunch, dinner. Closed Thanksgiving, Dec 25. Bar. Children's menu. Casual attire. Reservations recommended. Outdoor seating. **$$**

Hempstead (C-3)

See also Bethpage, Floral Park, Garden City, New York, Rockville Centre

Population 56,554
Elevation 60 ft
Area Code 516
Information Chamber of Commerce, 1776 Nicholas Ct, 11550; phone 516/483-2000
Web Site www.toh.li

What to See and Do

African-American Museum. *110 N Franklin St, Hempstead (11550).* Depicts the scope and depth of the story of African-American people on Long Island and their contributions to the development of its history. Collection of African-American artifacts; changing exhibits. Workshops, seminars, films. (Thurs-Sat 10 am-5 pm, Sun from 1 pm; closed holidays) **FREE**

Eisenhower Park. *Hempstead Tpke, East Hempstead (11554). Phone 516/572-0200. www.co.nassau.ny.us.* This centrally located Central Park of Nassau County offers a little bit of everything. It features an Olympic-sized pool, tennis courts, running tracks, a roller rink, batting cages, golf, miniature golf, a gourmet restaurant and catering hall, and a baseball field. There are also lots of areas to just unwind on a blanket with a good book, ride a bicycle, fly a kite on a breezy summer day, or pack a picnic and enjoy the summer sunshine. Also, free concerts are held in summer, and there are special sporting tournaments, memorial services, and dedications held from time to time. (Daily 9 am-dusk) **$$**

Hofstra University. *1000 Fulton Ave, Hempstead (11550). Phone 516/463-6600. www.hofstra.edu.*(1935) (13,400 students) The Hofstra Museum presents exhibitions in the Emily Lowe Gallery, David Filderman Gallery, Hofstra's Cultural Center, and in nine other areas on campus. (Daily; closed holidays) Concerts, lectures, drama productions, arboretum tours, and sports events. Campus tours (Mon-Fri).

Nassau Veterans Memorial Coliseum. *1255 Hempstead Tpke, Hempstead (11553). Phone 516/794-9300. www.nassaucoliseum.com.* This major sports and entertainment complex in the center of Nassau County offers a little bit of everything for just about every kind of taste and interest. Music lovers flock here to see A-list performers like Billy Joel, Elton John, and the Dixie Chicks. In addition, hockey lovers who enjoy the thrill of the sport can cheer on the New York Islanders during the ice hockey season. The Coliseum is their venue for all home games. And, the Coliseum also hosts special events, fairs, and trade shows throughout the year in its exhibit hall. Its a one-stop-shopping kind of place.

Herkimer (D-7)

See also Oneida, Utica

Settled 1725
Population 9,962
Elevation 407 ft
Area Code 315
Zip 13350
Information Herkimer County Chamber of Commerce, 28 W Main St, PO Box 129, Mohawk 13407; phone 315/866-7820
Web Site www.herkimercountychamber.com

Herkimer is a town that retains pride in its history. General Nicholas Herkimer marched from the fort here to the Battle of Oriskany, one of the Revolutionary War's bloodiest, which took place August 4, 1777. The Gillette trial, basis for Theodore Dreiser's *An American Tragedy,* was held in the Herkimer County Courthouse.

What to See and Do

Herkimer County Historical Society. *400 N Main,*

*Herkimer (13350). At Court St, on site of Fort Dayton (1776). Phone 315/866-6413.*Mansion contains exhibits of county history. (July-Aug: Mon-Sat 10 am-4 pm; rest of year: Mon-Fri; closed holidays) **FREE**

Herkimer Home State Historic Site. *200 Hwy 169, Little Falls (13365). 8 miles E on Hwy 169 off Hwy 5 S. Phone 315/823-0398. nysparks.state.ny.us.* (1764) General Nicholas Herkimer lived here; 18th-century furnishings. Family cemetery and General Herkimer Monument. Visitor center; picnic area. (Mid-May-Oct, Tues-Sat 10 am-5 pm, Sun 1-5 pm) **$**

Limited-Service Hotels

★ ★ BEST WESTERN LITTLE FALLS MOTOR INN. *20 Albany St, Little Falls (13365). Phone 315/823-4954; fax 315/823-4507. www.bestwestern.com.* 56 rooms, 2 story. Pets accepted, some restrictions. Check-in 1 pm, check-out noon. Restaurant, bar. **$**

★ HERKIMER MOTEL. *100 Marginal Rd, Herkimer (13350). Phone 315/866-0490; toll-free 877/656-6835; fax 315/866-0416. www.herkimermotel.com.* 62 rooms, 2 story. Pets accepted, some restrictions. Complimentary continental breakfast. Check-out 11 am. Fitness room. Outdoor pool. **$**

Restaurant

★ ★ CANAL SIDE INN. *395 S Ann St, Little Falls (13365). Phone 315/823-1170. www.canalsideinn.com.* Located in historic Canal Place near the Erie Canal, this restaurant has offered classic French cuisine in a modest, wood-paneled dining room for more than 15 years. Visiting for historic sightseeing or antiquing? Retire to the upstairs guest suite for a night. French menu. Dinner. Closed Sun-Mon; holidays; also Feb-mid-Mar. Bar. **$$**

Hillsdale (F-10)

See also Catskill, Coxsackie, Hudson

Population 1,744
Elevation 700 ft
Area Code 518
Zip 12529
Information Columbia County Tourism Department, 401 State St, Hudson 12534; phone toll-free 800/724-1846
Web Site www.hillsdaleny.com

What to See and Do

Catamount Ski Area. *Hwy 23 E, Hillsdale (12529). 2 miles E of Hwy 22 on Hwy 23. Phone 518/325-3200; toll-free 800/342-1840. www.catamountski.com.* Four double chairlifts, tow, J-bar; patrol, school, rentals; snowmaking; cafeteria, bar; nursery. Longest run 2 miles; vertical drop 1,000 feet. Night skiing. (Dec-Mar, daily) Half-day rates. **$$$$**

Taconic State Park. *S edge of town.* More than 4,800 acres. Bash Bish Stream and Ore Pit Pond are in the park. Swimming beach, bathhouse, fishing; hiking, picnicking (all year), cross-country skiing, tent and trailer sites. At Rudd Pond, also boating (launch, rentals); ice-skating. **$$$**

Limited-Service Hotel

★ ★ SWISS HUTTE. *Hwy 23, Hillsdale (12529). Phone 518/325-3333; fax 413/528-6201. www.swisshutte.com.* 15 rooms, 2 story. Pets accepted. Check-in 1 pm, check-out 11 am. Restaurant, bar. Outdoor pool. Tennis. **$**

Full-Service Inn

★ ★ ★ SIMMON'S WAY VILLAGE INN. *53 Main St, Millerton (12546). Phone 518/789-6235; fax 518/789-6236. www.simmonsway.com.* This inn offers Victorian elegance near the Berkshire Foothills. The inn features antiques, fireplaces, and porches. Each room is uniquely decorated, and a wonderful restaurant is also available. 9 rooms, 3 story. Complimentary full breakfast. Check-in 2 pm, check-out 11 am. Restaurant. **$$**

Restaurants

★ ★ ★ AUBERGINE. *Hwys 22 and 23, Hillsdale (12529). Phone 518/325-3412; fax 518/325-7089. www.aubergine.com.* Hearty comfort foods and seasonal game are transformed into fine cuisine that pleases the most discriminating palates at this lovely country inn. The wine cellar, once the town's county jail, stores fine vintages that perfectly complement the chef's rich dishes. American, French menu. Dinner. Closed Mon-Tues; also last week of Mar. Bar. Business casual attire. Reservations recommended. **$$$**

★ ★ ★ SIMMON'S WAY. *53 Main St, Millerton (12546). Phone 518/789-6235; fax 518/789-6236. www.simmonsway.com.* Guests travel many miles for the elegant country fare found at this restored Victorian inn. The formal dining room, complete with a cathedral ceiling and Oriental rugs, is the perfect setting for connoisseurs to sample the restaurant's fine wines and complex dishes. International/Fusion menu. Dinner, Sun brunch. Closed Mon-Tues. Bar. Outdoor seating. **$$$**

Hopewell Junction

Restaurants

★★ BLUE FOUNTAIN. *940 Rte 376, Hopewell Junction (). Phone 845/226-3570.* Italian menu. Lunch, dinner. Bar. Business casual attire. Reservations recommended. **$$**

★★★ LE CHAMBORD. *Rte 52 and Carpenter Ave, Hopewell Junction (12533). Phone 845/221-1941. www.lechambord.com.* French menu. Lunch, dinner. Bar. Business casual attire. Reservations recommended. Outdoor seating. **$$**

Hornell (E-4)

Settled 1799
Population 9,019
Elevation 1,160 ft
Area Code 607
Zip 14843
Information Hornell Area Chamber of Commerce, 40 Main St; phone 607/324-0310. A Tourist **Information** booth is located just off Hwy 17 at exit 34 and junction Hwy 36 and 21
Web Site www.hornellny.com

Also known as the "Maple City," Hornell is a scenic and popular gateway to the Finger Lakes Region. Fishing, hunting, and outdoor recreation contribute to the town's offerings. Fall foliage is especially brilliant in September and October, in and around Hornell.

What to See and Do

Almond Dam Recreation Area. *Miller St, Plattsburgh (14873). Just W of town, accessible by Hwy 21 and Hwy 36, just off County Rd 66. Phone 607/324-0539.* Includes a 125-acre lake; provides swimming, fishing, boating; hunting, camping facilities (fee). Contact Chamber of Commerce for details. **FREE**

Stony Brook State Park. *1082 Hwy 36 S, Hornell (14437). 13 miles N on Hwy 36, 3 miles S of Dansville.* Swimming beach, bathhouse; hiking, tennis, cross-country skiing, picnicking, playground, concession, tent and trailer sites (May-late-Oct). **$$$**

Swain Ski Center. *Main St and Hwy 24, Swain (14884). 8 miles N on Hwy 36, then 7 miles NW on Hwy 70. Phone 607/545-6511. www.swain.com.* Three quad, double chairlifts; patrol, school, rentals; snowmaking; restaurants, cafeteria, bar. Longest run 1 mile; vertical drop 650 feet. Night skiing. (Nov-Mar, daily) **$$$$**

Limited-Service Hotels

★ COMFORT INN. *1 Canisteo Sq, Hornell (78501). Phone 607/324-4300; toll-free 800/424-6423; fax 607/324-4311. www.choicehotels.com.* 62 rooms, 2 story. Complimentary continental breakfast. Check-in 3 pm, check-out 11 am. Fitness room. Indoor pool. **$**

★ SAXON INN. *1 Park St, Alfred (14802). Phone 607/871-2600; fax 607/871-2650. www.alfred.edu.* 26 rooms, 2 story. Complimentary continental breakfast. Check-in 2 pm, check-out 11 am. **$**

Howes Cave

See also Albany, Schenectady, Stamford

Population 150
Elevation 801 ft
Area Code 518
Zip 12092

What to See and Do

Howe Caverns. *255 Discovery Dr, Howes Cave (12092). Phone 518/296-8990. www.howecaverns.com.* Elaborately developed series of caverns with underground river and lake, unique rock formations 160-200 feet below the surface; reached by elevators; 52F in caverns. (July-Labor Day: daily 8:30 am-7pm; Sept-June: 9 am-6 pm; closed Thanksgiving, Dec 25) Tour combined with boat trip. Snack bar. Restaurant. Picnic area. **$$$$**

Old Stone Fort Museum Complex. *8 miles SE via Hwys 7, 30 in Schoharie. Phone 518/295-7192.* Church built in 1772 was fortified against raids by Tories and Native Americans during the Revolutionary War and became known as Lower Fort. Major attack came in 1780; building restored to house of worship in 1785; now houses exhibits on Revolutionary War and Schoharie

Valley history; firearms, Native American artifacts, and period furniture; local historical and genealogical library. Badgley Museum and Carriage House, annex built in style of fort. Furnishings, tools, farm implements, 1901 Rambler, fire engines. (July-Aug: daily; May-Oct: Tues-Sun 10 am-5 pm) **$$$**

Secret Caverns. *On Secret Caverns Rd. Phone 518/296-8558. www.secretcaverns.com.* Cave with natural entrance, 100-feet underground waterfalls, fossilized sea life; 50F in caverns. (June-Aug: daily 9 am-7 pm; May and Sept: daily 10 am-5 pm; mid-late Apr, Oct-Nov: daily 10 am-4 pm) 1/2 mile tour. **$$$**

Limited-Service Hotel

★ ★ BEST WESTERN INN OF COBLESKILL. *121 Burgin Dr, Cobleskill (12043). Phone 518/234-4321; fax 518/234-3869. www.bestwestern.com.* 76 rooms, 2 story. Pets accepted; fee. Check-in 3 pm, check-out 11 am. Wireless Internet access. Restaurant, bar. Indoor pool. **$**

Hudson

See also Cairo, Catskill, Coxsackie, Hillsdale, Saugerties

Settled 1783
Population 7,524
Elevation 80 ft
Area Code 518
Zip 12534
Information Columbia County Tourism Department, 401 State St; phone toll-free 800/724-1846
Web Site www.columbiacountyny.org

What to See and Do

American Museum of Firefighting. *117 Harry Howard Ave, Hudson (12534). Phone 518/822-1875. www.fasny.com/museum/museum.html.* Antique firefighting equipment including 1725 Newsham fire engine; memorabilia, art gallery. (Daily 9 am-4:30 pm; closed holidays) **FREE**

★ Clermont State Historic Site. *One Clermont Ave, Germantown (12526). Off Hwy 6, 6 miles N from intersection of Hwys 9G and 199. Phone 518/537-4240. www.nysparks.state.ny.us.* The ancestral home of Robert R. Livingston, one of five men elected to draft the Declaration of Independence, who later, as chancellor of New York, administered the oath of office to George Washington. Lived in by seven generations of the Livingston family, the grounds and mansion retain their 1930 appearance, illustrating 200 years of changing tastes. Centerpiece of a 485-acre estate on the eastern shore of the Hudson River, the home features period furnishings, restored gardens, guided tours, nature trails, and special events. Visitor center, museum store (Apr-Oct: Tues-Sun 11 am-5 pm; Nov-late Mar: Sat-Sun 11 am-4 pm). Grounds open all year for hiking, riding, cross-country skiing, picnicking. **$**

James Vanderpoel House. *16 Broad St (Hwy 9), Kinderhook (12106). 11 miles N on Hwy 9. Phone 518/758-9265.* Federal period house built around 1820, now a museum with 19th-century furnishings and art. Maintained by the Columbia County Historical Society. (Late May-early Sept: Thurs-Sat 11 am-4 pm, Sun noon-4 pm) **$$** The society also maintains

> **Luykas Van Alen House.** *Hwy 9H and Tuesday, Kinderhook (12106). Phone 518/758-9265.* (1737) Restored house is a museum of Dutch domestic culture during the 18th century. (Late May-early Sept: Thurs-Sat 11 am-5 pm, Sun 1-5 pm) **$$**

Lake Taghkanic State Park. *1528 Hwy 82, Ancram (12502). 11 miles SE via Hwys 23, 82. Phone 518/851-3631; toll-free 800/456-2267. www.nystateparks.com.* On 1,569 acres. Swimming beaches, bathhouses, fishing, boating (launch, rentals); hiking trails, cross-country skiing, snowmobiling, ice-skating, picnicking, playground, concession, tent and trailer sites, cabins, cottages. Also 177-acre lake. Camping Memorial Day-Labor Day. **$$$**

Martin Van Buren National Historic Site. *1013 Old Post Rd, Kinderhook (12106). 2 miles S of Kinderhook on Hwy 9H. Phone 518/758-9689. www.nps.gov/mava.* This is the retirement house of America's eighth president. The estate, Lindenwald, was purchased by Van Buren from General William Paulding in 1839. The house, on 20 acres, contains 36 rooms. Tours (schedule varies). Grounds (daily from 9 am-5 pm). (Mid-May-Oct, daily 9 am-4 pm) **$**

Olana State Historic Site. *5720 Hwy 9G, Hudson (12534). 5 miles S on Hwy 9G. Phone 518/828-0135. www.nysparks.state.ny.us.*(1870) A 250-acre hilltop estate with views of the Hudson River and Catskill Mountains, includes Persian/Moorish mansion and grounds landscaped in Romantic style, all designed by Hudson River School artist Frederic Edwin Church as a multidimensional work of art. Decorative Asian arts and furnishings collected by the artist; also paintings by Church. Five miles of carriage roads for walking with views planned by the artist. Grounds (daily). House Museum: entrance by guided tour only (tours limited). Reservations recommended. (Apr-Oct: daily 10 am-5 pm; Nov: daily 10 am-4 pm; Dec-Mar: Sat-Sun, by appointment) **$$**

Shaker Museum and Library. *88 Shaker Museum Rd, Old Chatham (12136). 18 miles NE via Hwy 66, County 13. Phone 518/794-9100. www.shakermuseumandlibrary.org.* One of the largest collections of Shaker culture; 26 galleries in three buildings. Exhibits include furniture, crafts, basketry, agricultural and industrial tools. Library (by appointment only). Picnic area, caf. Gift shop. (Late Apr-Oct: Mon, Wed-Sun 10 am-5 pm) **$$$**

Limited-Service Hotel

★ ★ ST. CHARLES. *16-18 Park Pl, Hudson (12534). Phone 518/822-9900; fax 518/822-0835. www.stcharleshotel. com.* Nearby shops, galleries, and picturesque mountains attract guests to this 120-year-old Hudson Valley property. 34 rooms, 3 story. Pets accepted. Complimentary continental breakfast. Check-in 4 pm, check-out noon. Restaurant, bar. **$**

Restaurants

★ EARTH FOODS. *523 Warren St, Hudson . Phone 518/822-1396.* American menu. Breakfast, lunch. Closed Tues. Children's menu. Casual attire. **$**

★ ★ MEXICAN RADIO. *537 Warren St, Hudson. Phone 518/828-7770. www.mexrad.com.* Mexican menu. Lunch, dinner. Bar. Casual attire. Reservations recommended. **$$**

★ ★ RED DOT BAR & RESTAURANT. *321 Warren St, Hudson (12534). Phone 518/828-3657.* American menu. Dinner, brunch. Closed Mon-Tues. Bar. Casual attire. Reservations recommended. Outdoor seating. **$$**

Hunter

See also Cairo, Catskill, Catskill Park, Shandaken, Windham, Woodstock

Population 490
Elevation 1,603 ft
Area Code 518
Zip 12442

Information Greene County Promotion Department, NY Thrwy exit 21, PO Box 527, Catskill 12414; phone 518/943-3223 or toll-free 800/355-2287
Web Site www.hunterchamber.org

What to See and Do

Hunter Mountain Ski Resort. *Hwy 23A. Phone 518/263-4223. www.huntermtn.com.* Three quad, two triple, five double chairlifts. Offers 53 slopes and trails. Patrol, school, rentals; snowmaking; bar, restaurant, cafeteria; nursery. Longest run 2 miles; vertical drop 1,600 feet. (Early Nov-late Apr, daily) **$$$$**

Full-Service Resort

★ ★ ★ SCRIBNER HOLLOW LODGE. *Main St, Rte 23A, Hunter (12442). Phone 518/263-4211; toll-free 800/395-4683; fax 518/263-5266. www.scribnerhollow. com.* This resort has a classical mountain lodge atmosphere with modern hotel conveniences. Visitors will find custom-decorated rooms and suites, a restaurant, and a unique underground pool with seven waterfalls, Jacuzzi and saunas. 37 rooms, 3 story. Closed Apr-mid May. Check-in 3 pm, check-out 11 am. High-speed Internet access. Restaurant, bar. Indoor pool, outdoor pool, children's pool, whirlpool. Tennis. **$$**

Specialty Lodging

EGGERY COUNTRY INN. *288 Tlatte Clove Rd, County Rd 16, Tennersville (12485). Phone 518/589-5363; toll-free 800/785-5364; fax 518/589-5774. www. eggeryinn. com.* Restored farmhouse inn built in 1900. Faces Hunter Mountain. 15 rooms, 3 story. Complimentary full breakfast. Check-in 1 pm. Check-out 11 am. High-speed Internet access. **$**

HUNTER INN. *Hwy 23A, Hunter (12442). Phone 518/263-3777; toll-free 800/270-3992; fax 518/263-3981. www.hunterinn. com.* 41 rooms, 3 story. Pets accepted, some restrictions; fee. Complimentary continental breakfast. Check-out 11 am. Fitness room. Whirlpool. **$**

Huntington (C-3)

See also Northport, Oyster Bay, Plainview, Smithtown

Settled 1653
Population 195,289
Elevation 60 ft

Area Code 631
Information Huntington Township Chamber of Commerce, 288 Main St; phone 631/423-6100
Web Site www.huntingtonchamber.com

Although the expanding suburban population of New York City has reached Huntington, 37 miles east on Long Island, it still retains its rural character. Huntington is a township including 17 communities, in which there are more than 100 industrial plants. The area has five navigable harbors and 51 miles of shorefront.

What to See and Do

Cold Spring Harbor Whaling Museum. *147 Main St, Cold Spring Harbor (11724). 2 miles W on Hwy 25A. Phone 631/367-3418. www.cswhalingmuseum.org.* Fully equipped 19th-century whale boat from the brig *Daisy* is on display. Marine paintings, scrimshaw, ship models, changing exhibit gallery. "Mark Well the Whale" permanent exhibit documents Long Island's whaling industry. Permanent exhibit "The Wonder of Whales" includes a hands-on whale bones display, a killer whale skull, and whale conservation information. (Memorial Day-Labor Day: daily; rest of year: Tues-Sun) **$$**

David Conklin Farmhouse. *2 High St, Huntington (11743). At New York Ave. Phone 631/427-7045.* (Circa 1750) Four generations of Conklin family lived here. Period rooms (Colonial, Federal, Victorian). (Tues-Fri, Sun 1-4 pm; closed holidays) **$$** Other historic buildings include

Huntington Trade School. *209 Main St, Huntington (11743). Phone 631/427-7045.*(1905) School building houses the offices of the Huntington Historical Society and a history research library. (Tues-Fri) **$$**

Kissam House. *434 Park Ave, Huntington (11743).* (1795) Federal house, barn, sheepshed, and outbuildings; home of early Huntington physicians. Period rooms (1800-1850). (By appointment only; closed holidays) **$$**

Heckscher Museum of Art. *Heckscher Park, 2 Prime Ave, Huntington (11743). Heckscher Park, Prime Ave and Hwy 25A (Main St). Phone 631/351-3250. www.heckscher.org.* Permanent collection of European and American art dating from 16th century; changing exhibits. (Tues-Fri 10 am-5 pm, Sat-Sun from 1 pm; to 8:30 pm on the first Friday of the month; closed Thanksgiving, Dec 25) **$**

Joseph Lloyd Manor House. *Lloyd Ln and Lloyd Harbor Rd, Huntington (11743). Lloyd Ln, 3 miles N in Lloyd Harbor. Phone 631/271-7760.* (1767) Large colonial manor house, elegantly furnished; 18th-century garden. (Memorial Day-mid-Oct, Sat and Sun afternoons) **$**

Sunken Meadow State Park. *Sunken Meadow Pkwy N and Hwy 25A, Huntington (11754). Approximately 9 miles E of town on Hwy 25A. Phone 631/269-4333. www.nystateparks.com.* Swimming beach, bathhouse, fishing (all year); nature, hiking, and biking trails; three 9-hole golf courses (fee). Picnicking, playground, concession. Cross-country skiing. Recreation programs. Standard fees. (Daily) **$$$**

Target Rock National Wildlife Refuge. *8 miles N via West Neck Rd, follow onto Lloyd Harbor Rd. Phone 631/286-0485. www.longislandrefuges.com.* An 80-acre refuge with hardwood forest, pond, and beach. Fishing; photography, nature trail, wildlife nature study, and environmental education. (Daily) **$$**

Walt Whitman Birthplace State Historic Site. *246 Old Walt Whitman Rd, Huntington Station (11746). Phone 631/427-5240. nysparks.state.ny.us.* The writer is well known on Long Island, where streets and malls are named for him. This simple home, which features 19th-century furnishings (including Whitmans schoolmasters desk), offers a tour with a video, as well as an exhibit that tells the story of Whitmans life. There is also a tape available of the author himself reading one of his poems. (Mon-Fri 11 am-4 pm, Sat-Sun noon-5 pm; closed holidays) **$**

Special Events

Huntington Summer Arts Festival. *Heckscher Park Amphitheater, 213 Main St, Huntington (11743). Phone 631/271-8442.* Local, national, and international artists perform dance, folk, classical, jazz, theater, and family productions. Late June-mid-Aug.

Long Island Fall Festival at Huntington. *Heckscher Park, Huntington (11743). Phone 631/423-6100.* Entertainment, carnival, sailboat regatta, food, wine tasting, family activities. Mid-Oct.

Limited-Service Hotel

★ HUNTINGTON COUNTRY INN. *270 W Jericho Tpke, Huntington Station (11746). Phone 631/421-3900; toll-free 800/739-5777; fax 631/421-5287. www.huntingtoncountryinn. com.* 61 rooms, 2 story. Complimentary continental breakfast. Check-in 3 pm, check-out noon. Fitness room. Outdoor pool. Business center. **$**

Full-Service Hotel

★ ★ ★ HILTON LONG ISLAND/HUNTINGTON. *598 Broad Hollow Rd, Melville (11747). Phone 631/845-1000; fax 631/845-1223. www.hiltonlongisland.com.* This hotel is ideally located for travelers visiting the Hamptons, Jones Beach, and New York City. Guests enter to find an atrium lobby with running waterfalls and a tropical setting. 302 rooms, 5 story. Check-in 4 pm, check-out noon. Wireless Internet access. Two restaurants, bar. Children's activity center. Fitness room. Indoor pool, outdoor pool, whirlpool. Tennis. **$$**

Hyde Park (F-9)

See also New Paltz, Poughkeepsie, Rhinebeck

Settled 1740
Population 20,851
Elevation 188 ft
Area Code 845
Zip 12538
Information Dutchess County Tourism Promotion Agency, 3 Neptune Rd, Ste M-17, Poughkeepsie 12601; phone 845/463-4000 or toll-free 800/445-3131
Web Site www.dutchesstourism.com

Hyde Park was named for Edward Hyde, Lord Cornbury, provincial governor of New York, who, in 1705, presented a parcel of land along the river to his secretary. Hyde's name was given to an estate on that property and later to the town itself. The area, noted for the varying scenery from rock outcroppings to scenic water views, is best known as the site of Springwood, the country estate of Franklin Roosevelt.

What to See and Do

Mills-Norrie State Park. *Hwy 9 and Old Post Rd, Staatsburg (12580). 4 miles N on Hwy 9. Phone 845/889-4646; reservations 800/456-2267.* Fishing, boat basin (marina, dock, launch); nature and hiking trails, 18-hole golf (fee), cross-country skiing, picnicking; tent and trailer sites, cabins. Environmental education programs, concert series. Camping (May-late Oct). In park is

Mills Mansion State Historic Site. *Hwy 9 and Old Post Rd, Staatsburg (12580). Phone 845/889-8851.* Built for Ogden Mills in 1895-1896 by prominent architect Stanford White, the Greek Revival mansion includes 65 rooms furnished in Louis XIV, Louis XV, and Louis XVI styles, with tapestries, art objects, marble fireplaces, and gilded plasterwork. Park overlooks the Hudson. (Mid-Apr-Labor Day: Wed-Sat 10 am-5 pm, Sun noon-5 pm; Labor Day-late Oct: Wed-Sun noon-5 pm; also last two weeks in Dec) **$$**

★ **Roosevelt-Vanderbilt National Historic Sites.** *1 mile S on Hwy 9. Phone 845/229-9115.*(Daily) Here is

Eleanor Roosevelt National Historic Site at Val-Kill. *56 Val-Kill Park Dr, Hyde Park (12538). 2 miles E of Roosevelt estate. Phone 845/229-9115; toll-free 800/967-2283 (reservations).* Dedicated as a memorial to Mrs. Roosevelt on October 11, 1984, the 100th anniversary of her birth, Val-Kill was her country residence from the 1920s until her death. The original house on the property, Stone Cottage (1924), is now a conference center. Her second house at Val-Kill was originally a furniture and crafts factory that Mrs. Roosevelt sponsored in an effort to stimulate rural economic development. After closing Val-Kill Industries, she had the factory remodeled to reflect her tastes and humanitarian concerns; here, she entertained family, friends, and heads of state from around the world. Film; tour. (May-Oct: daily 9 am-5 pm; Nov-Apr: Thurs-Mon 9 am-5 pm; closed Jan 1, Thanksgiving, Dec 25) Grounds (daily until sunset).

Franklin D. Roosevelt Presidential Library and Museum. *4079 Albany Post Rd, Hyde Park (12538). Phone 845/486-7770; toll-free 800/337-8474. www.fdrlibrary.marist.edu.* First of the public presidential libraries, it has exhibits covering the private lives and public careers of Franklin and Eleanor Roosevelt. Research library contains family artifacts and documents and presidential archives. Library, museum, and home. (Nov-Apr: daily 9 am-5 pm; May-Oct: daily 9 am-6 pm; closed Jan 1, Thanksgivig, Dec 25) **$$$**

Home of Franklin D. Roosevelt National Historic Site. *4097 Albany Post Rd, Hyde Park (12538). Phone 845/229-9115. www.nps.gov/hofr.* The Hyde Park estate, Springwood, was President Roosevelt's birthplace and lifelong residence. The central part of the building, the oldest section, dates from about 1826. The house was bought in 1867 by FDR's father and was extensively remodeled and expanded in 1915 by FDR and his mother, Sara Delano Roosevelt. At that time, the frame Victorian house took on its present brick and stone, neo-Georgian form. The interior is furnished exactly as it was when FDR died.

Roosevelt's grave and that of Anna Eleanor Roosevelt are in the rose garden. Home, library, and museum. Buildings (daily 9 am-5 pm; closed Jan 1, Christmas, Thanksgiving $$$). Grounds (daily 7 am-sunset). **$**

Vanderbilt Mansion National Historic Site. *Hwy 9, Hyde Park. Phone 845/229-9115. www.nps.gov/vama.* Beaux-Arts mansion (1898) designed by McKim, Mead, and White for Frederick W. Vanderbilt is a prime example of the "American-millionaire palaces" typical of the period; the interior retains most of the original furnishings as designed by turn-of-the-century decorators. The grounds offer superb views up and down the Hudson River; many ancient trees; restored formal Italian gardens. Mansion (daily 9 am-5 pm; closed Jan 1, Thanksgiving, Dec 25). Grounds (daily 7 am-sunset). **$$**

Restaurants

★ ★ AMERICAN BOUNTY. *433 Albany Post Rd, Hyde Park (12538). Phone 845/471-6608. www.ciachef.edu.* In former St. Andrew-on-Hudson Jesuit Seminary on 150 acres, high above Hudson River. American menu. Lunch, dinner. Closed Sun-Mon; holidays; also three weeks in July, two weeks in Dec. Bar. Business casual attire. **$$**

★ COCO PASTA & GRILL. *3957 Albany Post Rd, Hyde Park (12538). Phone 845/229-7969; fax 845/229-0121.* American menu. Lunch, dinner. Closed Dec 25. Bar. Children's menu. **$$**

★ ★ ★ THE ESCOFFIER. *433 Albany Post Rd, Hyde Park (12538). Phone 845/471-6608. www.ciachef.edu.* Student chefs prepare dishes that their peers serve in the dining room but some of the dishes are prepared at table. French menu. Lunch, dinner. Closed Sun-Mon; holidays; also three weeks in July, two weeks in Dec. **$$**

★ FIRESIDE BBQ. *1920 Salt Point Tpike, Salt Point. Phone 845/266-3440.* Barbecue menu. Lunch, dinner. Closed Mon. Bar. Children's menu. Casual attire. Outdoor seating. **$**

★ ★ ★ RISTORANTE CATERINA DE MEDICI. *433 Albany Post Rd (Hwy 9), Hyde Park (12538). Phone 845/471-6608.* American menu. Lunch, dinner. Closed Sat-Sun. Bar. Casual attire. Reservations recommended. **$$$**

★ ★ ST. ANDREW'S CAFE. *433 Albany Post Rd, Hyde Park (12538). Phone 845/471-6608. www.ciachef.edu.* Dining room opens onto courtyard; original regional watercolors; fireplace. American menu. Lunch, dinner. Closed Sat-Sun; holidays; also three weeks in July, two weeks in Dec. Bar. Outdoor seating. **$$**

Irvington

Restaurant

★ FUFFI OF IRVINGTON. *12 N Astor St, Irvington. Phone 914/591-0099.* Middle Eastern menu. Dinner. Closed Mon. Bar. Casual attire. **$$**

★ ★ THE RED HAT. *63 Main St, Irvington (10533). Phone 914/591-5888.* American menu. Lunch, dinner, brunch. Bar. Casual attire. Reservations recommended. **$$**

★ ★ RIVER CITY GRILLE. *6 S Broadway, Irvington (10533). Phone 914/591-2033.* American menu. Lunch, dinner. Bar. Casual attire. Reservations recommended. **$$**

Island Park

Restaurant

★ ★ COYOTE GRILL. *104 Waterview Rd, Island Park (11558). Phone 516/889-8009.* Southwestern menu. Lunch, dinner, Sun brunch. Closed Dec 25. Bar. Children's menu. Outdoor seating. **$$**

Ithaca (E-5)

See also Binghamton, Cortland, Watkins Glen, Finger Lakes

Settled 1789
Population 29,287
Elevation 405 ft
Area Code 607
Zip 14850
Information Ithaca/Tompkins County Convention & Visitors Bureau, 904 East Shore Dr; phone 607/272-1313 or toll-free 800/284-8422
Web Site www.visitithaca.com

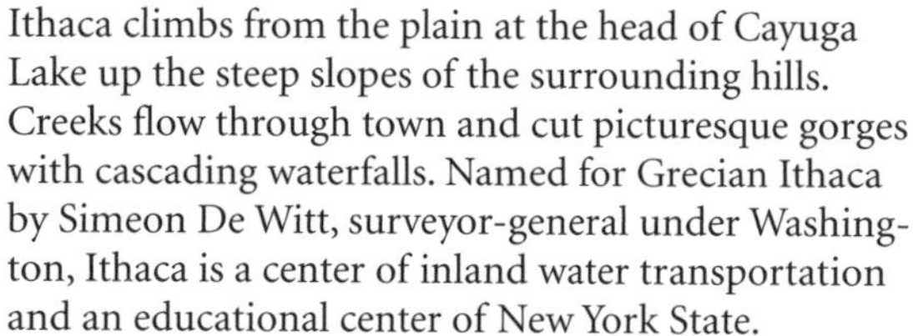

Ithaca climbs from the plain at the head of Cayuga Lake up the steep slopes of the surrounding hills. Creeks flow through town and cut picturesque gorges with cascading waterfalls. Named for Grecian Ithaca by Simeon De Witt, surveyor-general under Washington, Ithaca is a center of inland water transportation and an educational center of New York State.

What to See and Do

Allan H. Treman State Marine Park. *3 miles N on Hwy 89. Phone 607/273-3440. www.nysparks.state.ny.us/parks.* Fishing, boating (launch, marina); picnicking. (Apr-late Oct)

Buttermilk Falls. *On Hwy 13. Phone 607/273-5761. www.nysparks.com.* Swimming, bathhouse; hiking trails, picnicking, playground, from dawn to dusk, tent and trailer sites, cabins. (Mid-May-Columbus Day)

Cornell University. *E side of town. On campus are Willard Straight Hall; Laboratory of Ornithology (daily). Phone 607/254-2473. www.cornell.edu.* (1865) (20,000 students) A 745-acre campus overlooks Cayuga Lake and includes Beebe Lake, gorges, waterfalls. Founded both as a land-grant and privately endowed college by Ezra Cornell (1807-1874) and Andrew Dickson White (1832-1918). There are 13 colleges, four of which are state supported; 11 schools and colleges are in Ithaca, two in New York City.

DeWitt Historical Society & Museum. *401 E State St, Ithaca (14850). Phone 607/273-8284. www.tompkinscountyhistory.org.* Local historical exhibits; large photography collection; local history library. (Tues, Thurs, Sat 11 am-5 pm; closed holidays) **FREE**

Ithaca College. *953 Danby Rd, Ithaca (14850). 1/2 mile S on Hwy 96B. Phone 607/274-3011. www.ithaca.edu.* (1892) (6,400 students) Liberal arts and professional programs. Music, art exhibits, drama, lectures, and athletic programs. Handwerker Gallery. Campus overlooks city, Cayuga Lake. Tours of campus.

Recreation areas. *Phone 607/273-1090.* **Stewart Park.** James L. Gibbs Dr and Hwy 13. Picnicking, tennis, playground, concession. **Cass Park.** 701 Taughannock Blvd. Pool, wading pool; ice skating rink, tennis, ball fields (four lighted), playground, picnicking, concession. Fees for some activities.

Robert H. Treman State Park. *Hwys 327 and 13, Ithaca. 5 miles S on Hwy 13. Phone 607/273-3440.* Swimming, bathhouse; hiking trails, picnicking, playground, cabins, recreation programs, tent and trailer sites. Camping (Mid-May-late Nov). Standard fees. (Daily) **$$$**

Sciencenter. *601 First St, Ithaca (14850). Phone 607/272-0600. www.sciencenter.org.* There are 200 hands-on interactive science exhibits and an outdoor science park here. You can also come for lectures or special events. (Mon 10 am-5 pm (July-Aug), Tues-Sat 10 am-5 pm, Sun noon-5 pm; closed Jan 1, Thanksgiving, Dec 25) **$$** On grounds is the

> **Sagan Planet Walk.** *Sciencenter, 601 First St, Ithaca (14850). Phone 607/272-0600. www.sciencecenter.org/saganpw.* Scaled model of the solar system built in remembrance of Carl Sagan. (Daily) **FREE**

Six Mile Creek Vineyard. *1551 Slaterville Rd, Ithaca (14850). Hwy 79E. Phone 607/272-9463. www.sixmilecreek.com.* Family-operated winery. Tours, tastings (fee). Gift shop. (Daily 11 am-5 :30 pm, or by appointment) **FREE**

Taughannock Falls. *Taughannock State Park, 1785 Taughannock Blvd (Hwy 89), Ulysses (14886). 8 miles N on Hwy 89. Phone 607/387-6739. www.taughannock.com.* The falls have a drop of 215 feet, one of the highest east of the Rockies. The park also features swimming, a bathhouse, fishing, boating (marina, launch); nature trails, hiking trails, cross-country skiing, ice skating, picnicking, playground, concession, tent and trailer sites, cabins, summer concerts. Standard fees.

Special Events

Apple Harvest Festival. *Downtown Ithaca Commons, Ithaca.* This annual event features apples, cider, a craft fair, and entertainment. First weekend in Oct.

Finger Lakes Antique Show. *Women's Community Building, 100 W Seneca St, Ithaca (14850). N Cayuga and Seneca sts. Phone 607/272-1247.* First weekend in Oct.

Grassroots Festival. *Trumansburg Fairgrounds,59 E Main St, Trumansburg (14886). Approximately 10 miles N on Hwy 96 on the W side of Cayuga Lake. Phone 607/387-5098. www.grassrootsfest.org.* This four day concert features approximately 60 bands performing on four stages. Second to last weekend in July. **$$$$**

Hangar Theatre. *Cass Park,Hwy 89, Ithaca (14850). Phone 607/273-4497. www.hangartheatre.org.* Professional summer theater in park setting adjacent to Treman Marina. Five main stage productions; dramas, comedies, and musicals (Tues-Sat evenings, also Sat

Small-Town New York

Ithaca offers the best of small-town America with a college-town sophistication, plus the spectacular natural sites of Cayuga Lake and a variety of gorges and waterfalls. This walk explores Ithacas center with a stroll to nearby falls. For those who really love to hoof it, other options include the Cornell University Plantations, an arboretum and botanical gardens, and, on the other end of town, Stewart Park along Cayuga Lakes shoreline.

Start at the public parking garage on Green Street and walk west to Cayuga Street. City Hall is on the right. Stop in here to obtain visitor information and a city map. Turn right and walk 1/2 block to The Commons, home to a wide variety of shops, restaurants, cafs, and a gallery. Duck into the Susan Titus Gallery and ask about the Ithaca Art—a guide to galleries and artists studios throughout the region. Other shops of interest at the Commons are Autumn Leaves, Ithaca Books, Angleheart Designs, Handblock and Harolds Army Navy, and The Outdoor Store. The Home Dairy Bakery is a great place to grab a snack. Here, too, begins the Sagan Planet Walk. Named after astronomer Carl Sagan, this is an outdoor, scale model of the solar system that stretches 3/4 mile from the Commons to the Sciencenter on Second Street.

Leaving the west end of the Commons, turn right on Cayuga. The Clinton House Art Space is located at 116 Cayuga, and DeWitt Mall is on the next block on the right. More shopping and eating await you here; highlights include the famous Moosewood Restaurant, Calhouns Antiques, and the Sola Gallery. Continue up Cayuga past DeWitt Park, and turn left on Cascadilla Street. Go four blocks and turn right onto First Street. After two more blocks, you will reach the Sciencenter, an imaginative hands-on science exploratorium. After visiting the Sciencenter, return along First Street, and go left on Adams, which eventually merges to the right with East Lewis Street. Follow East Lewis three blocks to Tioga and turn left. The walk travels here through a pleasant residential neighborhood. After three blocks, turn right onto Falls Street, and walk two blocks to Lake Street to arrive at Ithaca Falls and Fall Creek Gorge. These falls stand almost as high as Niagara. Pause for a picnic, play on the rocks in the stream, or just admire the view. The energetic can follow the hiking trail into the upper areas of Fall Creek Gorge and onto the Cornell University campus, where a variety of trails lead to several waterfalls and Beebe Lake.

Return to Falls Street and, for diversitys sake, follow Aurora Street back into the town center. Just two blocks before arriving back at the Commons, note the William Henry Miller Inn, a circa-1880 historic home turned bed-and-breakfast, at the corner of Buffalo Street. If more walking is in order, turn left onto Court Street, and follow the trail in Cascadilla Glen (where Court meets Linn Street and University Avenue), an uphill clamber that will yield several waterfalls and views. For a more serene walk addition, drive west on Seneca Street (Highway 79), turn right onto Highways 34/13, and head into Stewart Park where miles of paths skirt Cayuga Lake. Or, simply return to the Commons for a rest and some food.

and Wed afternoons). Children's theatre (Thurs-Sat mornings). Late June-Labor Day weekend.

Ithaca Festival. *Ithaca Commons, DeWitt Park, and throughout city. Phone 607/273-3646. www.ithacafestival.org.* This four-day event features over 1,000 local musicians and performers, food, and a parade. First weekend in June. **$**

Limited-Service Hotels

★ BEST WESTERN UNIVERSITY INN. *1020 Ellis Hollow Rd, Ithaca (14850). Phone 607/272-6100; toll-free 800/780-7234; fax 607/272-1518. www.bestwesternuniversityinnithaca.com.* Just outside the Cornell University campus, this spacious motel has the feel of a lodge with vaulted ceilings in both the lobby and guest rooms. Located within walking distance of shopping and a short drive to the airport, the hotel is ideal for a visit to the university or local attractions. 101 rooms, 1 story. Pets accepted, some restrictions; fee. Complimentary continental breakfast. Check-in 3 pm, check-out noon. Wireless Internet access. Fitness room. Outdoor pool. Airport transportation available. **$**

★ ★ **HOLIDAY INN.** *222 S Cayuga St, Ithaca (14850). Phone 607/272-1000; toll-free 800/465-4329; fax 607/277-1275. www.hiithaca.com.* Set in the heart of picturesque Ithaca, this hotel is near shopping, restaurants, and the stunning Cornell University campus. Decorated with a garden theme and wrought-iron accented furnishings, the hotel has views of the surrounding hillside and is minutes from the Ithaca airport. 181 rooms, 10 story. Check-in 3 pm, check-out noon. High-speed Internet access, wireless Internet access. Restaurant, bar. Fitness room. Indoor pool. Airport transportation available. Business center. **$**

Full-Service Hotel

★ ★ ★ **STATLER HOTEL AT CORNELL UNIVERSITY.** *130 Statler Dr, Ithaca (14853). Phone 607/257-2500; toll-free 800/541-2501; fax 607/257-6432. www.statlerhotel.cornell.edu.* Because this well-appointed hotel serves as the main teaching facility for Cornell's prestigious School of Hotel Administration, no detail here has been overlooked. Boasting breathtaking views of the hills and dells of the campuss picturesque Finger Lakes location, each luxurious guest room features pillow-top mattresses and turndown service. Fresh flowers and rich wood floors are found throughout the hotels open spaces, as is a friendly and enthusiastic staff. 153 rooms, 9 story. Check-in 3 pm, check-out noon. High-speed Internet access. Restaurant, bar. Fitness room. Airport transportation available. Business center. **$$**

Full-Service Inn

★ ★ ★ **LA TOURELLE RESORT AND SPA.** *1150 Danby Rd, Ithaca (14850). Phone 607/273-2734; toll-free 800/765-1492; fax 607/273-4821. www.latourelle.com.* Offering guests a beautiful countryside setting and panoramic views of Cayuga Lake and its surrounding hill country, this inn is adjacent to state park lands with hiking trails and fishing ponds. Perfect for a romantic getaway, the inn has the overall feel of a French country estate, but also features furnishings and pieces from around the world. The location of the inn is also convenient to Ithaca College and Cornell University. 54 rooms, 3 story. Pets accepted; fee. Check-in 3 pm, check-out noon. High-speed Internet access. Restaurant. Fitness room, fitness classes available, spa. Tennis. **$$**

Restaurants

★ ★ ★ **JOHN THOMAS STEAKHOUSE.** *1152 Danby Rd, Ithaca (14850). Phone 607/273-3464; fax 607/273-4747. www.johnthomassteakhouse.net.* If your notion of a steakhouse is a slab of charred beef slammed down on a rough wooden table by a jeans-wearing server, get ready for a surprise. John Thomas Steak House, with its lamplit white-clad tables beside a blazing fire, invites fine dining. In a quaint 1850s farmhouse, spiffy waiters help you choose your favorites from the sophisticated menu. The state-of-the-art kitchen guarantees perfection every time. Best of all, you're dealt a card from a poker hand and may win free food! Steak menu. Dinner. Closed holidays. Bar. Business casual attire. Reservations recommended. **$$$**

★ ★ **MAHOGANY GRILL.** *112 N Aurora St, Ithaca (14850). Phone 607/272-1438.* A charming older building with tin ceilings and brass railings serves as the home of Mahogany Grill. Burgundy velvet drapes and local sports memorabilia decorate the dining room, giving it a cozy pub feel. The American menu offers standards like steak and seafood, and a Sunday champagne brunch is offered. American menu. Lunch, dinner, Sun brunch. Bar. Children's menu. Casual attire. Reservations recommended. Outdoor seating. **$$**

★ **MOOSEWOOD.** *215 N Cayuga St, Ithaca (14850). Phone 607/273-9610; fax 607/273-5327. www.moosewoodrestaurant.com.* This is the famous vegetarian restaurant, which has produced several cookbooks. If you're a carnivore, never fearyou may enjoy the food so much you won't realize its meat-free. Vegetarian menu. Lunch, dinner. Bar. Children's menu. Casual attire. Outdoor seating. **$$**

Jamestown (F-1)

See also Bemus Point, Chautauqua

Settled 1811
Population 31,730
Elevation 1,370 ft
Area Code 716
Zip 14701
Information Chamber of Commerce, 101 W 5th St; phone 716/484-1101
Web Site www.tourchautauqua.com

Jamestown made its mark early in the 19th century in the manufacture of metal products and furniture. These industries still flourish in this city at the southern end of Chautauqua Lake. Tourism and farming are important to the economy as well.

What to See and Do

Fenton Historical Center. *67 Washington St, Jamestown (14701). Phone 716/664-6256. www.fentonhistorycenter.org.* Home of post-Civil War governor; memorabilia of Chautauqua Lake area, Fenton family, Victorian era; re-created Victorian drawing room. Archival and genealogical library; Swedish and Italian heritage, Civil War exhibit. (Mon-Sat 10 am-4 pm; also Sun 1-4 pm from late Nov-early Jan; closed Thanksgiving, Dec 25) **$$**

Lucy-Desi Museum. *212 Pine St, Jamestown (14701). Phone 716/484-0800. www.lucydesi.com.* Interactive exhibits provide a look into the lives and careers of Lucille Ball and Desi Arnaz. Video presentation. Gift shop. (May-Oct: Mon-Sat 10 am-5:30 pm; Sun 1-5 pm; Nov-Apr: Sat 10-5:30 pm, Sun 1-5 pm) **$$**

Panama Rocks Park. *11 Rock Hill Rd, Panama (14767). 14 miles W via Hwy 394, then 6 miles S of exit 7 on I-86. Phone 716/782-2845. www.panamarocks.com.* Massive rock outcrop (25 acres) of a primeval seashore formation; cliffs, caves, crevices, and passages. Rare mosses, wildflowers, ferns; unusually shaped tree roots. Self-guided tours; hiking trail; picnicking. (May-late-Oct, daily 10 am-5 pm) (See SPECIAL EVENT) **$$$**

Special Event

Panama Rocks Folk Fair. *Panama Rocks Park, 11 Rock Hill Rd, Panama (14767). Phone 716/782-2845.* Panama Rocks Park. Second weekend in July.

Limited-Service Hotels

★ COMFORT INN. *2800 N Main St Extension, Jamestown (14701). Phone 716/664-5920; toll-free 800/453-7155; fax 716/664-3068. www.choicehotels.com.* 101 rooms, 2 story. Pets accepted; fee. Complimentary continental breakfast. Check-in 3 pm, check-out noon. Wireless Internet access. Bar. **$**

★ ★ HOLIDAY INN. *150 W Fourth St, Jamestown (14701). Phone 716/664-3400; toll-free 800/528-8791; fax 716/484-3304. www.holiday-inn. com.* 146 rooms, 8 story. Check-in 3 pm, check-out noon. Restaurant, bar. Fitness room. Indoor pool. **$**

Restaurants

★ ★ HOUSE OF PETILLO. *382 Hunt Rd, Jamestown (14701). Phone 716/664-7457.* Stein collection. Italian menu. Dinner. Closed Sun-Mon; holidays; two weeks at Easter. Bar. Casual attire. **$$**

★ ★ IRONSTONE. *516 W 4th St, Jamestown (14701). Phone 716/487-1516; fax 716/661-3870.* In 1884 building with Victorian décor. Italian menu. Lunch, dinner. Closed Sun; holidays. Bar. Children's menu. Casual attire. **$$$**

Jericho

See also Glen Cove, Oyster Bay, Plainview, Westbury

Population 13,045
Elevation 180 ft
Area Code 516
Zip 11753

Restaurants

★ ★ ★ CAPRICCIO. *399 Jericho Tpke, Jericho (11753). Phone 516/931-2727; fax 516/931-3607.* French, Italian menu. Lunch, dinner. Closed Sun; holidays. Bar. Valet parking. **$$$**

★ ★ FRANK'S STEAKS. *4 Jericho Tpke, Jericho (11753). Phone 516/338-4595; fax 516/338-4252. www.frankssteaks.com.* Seafood, steak menu. Lunch, dinner. Closed Easter, Thanksgiving, Dec 25. Bar. **$$$**

★ ★ THE MAINE MAID INN. *4 Old Jericho Tpke, Jericho (11753). Phone 516/935-6400. www.themainemaidinn.com.* Built in 1789; Federal-period décor. American menu. Lunch, dinner, Sun brunch. Closed Mon; holidays. Bar. Children's menu. Valet parking. **$$$**

★ ★ MILLERIDGE INN. *585 N Broadway, Jericho (11753). Phone 516/931-2201; fax 516/822-2381. www.milleridge.com.* American menu. Lunch, dinner, Sun brunch. Closed Dec 25. Children's menu. **$$**

Johnstown (D-8)

See also Amsterdam, Canajoharie, Schenectady

Founded 1723
Population 8,511
Elevation 691 ft
Area Code 518
Zip 12095

Information Fulton County Regional Chamber of Commerce and Industry, 2 N Main St, Gloversville 12078; phone 518/725-0641 or toll-free 800/676-3858
Web Site www.fultoncountyny.org

A center of leather tanning and related industries, Johnstown often is called a twin city to Gloversville, which it adjoins. A Revolutionary War battle was fought here six days after Cornwallis surrendered at Yorktown. Women's rights pioneer Elizabeth Cady Stanton was born here in 1815.

What to See and Do

Johnson Hall State Historic Site. *Hwy 29 W and Hall Ave, Johnstown (12095). Phone 518/762-8712.* (1763) Residence of Sir William Johnson, first baronet of New York colony; Native Americans and colonists held meetings here. Site includes hall with period furnishings; stone blockhouse; interpretation center; dioramas depicting history of the estate; tours; special events. Contact Site Manager. (Mid-May-Oct, Wed-Mon, also Sun afternoons) **$$**

Limited-Service Hotel

★ ★ HOLIDAY INN. *308 N Comrie Ave, Johnstown (12095). Phone 518/762-4686; toll-free 800/465-4329; fax 518/762-4034. www.holiday-inn. com.* 100 rooms, 3 story. Pets accepted, some restrictions. Check-in 3 pm, check-out 11 am. High-speed Internet. Restaurant, bar. Fitness room. Outdoor pool. **$**

Restaurant

★ ★ UNION HALL INN. *2 Union Pl, Johnstown (12095). Phone 518/762-3210. www.unionhallinnrestaurant.com.* American menu. Lunch, dinner. Closed Sun-Mon; holidays. Bar. **$$**

Jones Beach State Park (C-3)

See also New York

Web Site www.nysparks.state.ny.us

For millions of New Yorkers, summer means Jones Beach, a fabulous recreation area that can accommodate hundreds of thousands of people on its more than 2,400 acres.

Recreational facilities include swimming in the ocean, Zach's Bay, and freshwater pools; bathhouse, fishing in ocean and bay, boating (dock). Nature, biking trails; 18-hole pitch-and-putt golf course, miniature golf, softball fields (with permit), shuffleboard; recreation programs. Restaurant, snack bars. Gift shop. Fees vary. Phone 516/785-1600.

Special Event

Jones Beach Theatre. *Jones Beach State Park, 1000 Ocean Dr, Wantagh (11793). Phone 516/221-1000.* Concerts ranging from country to rock; top entertainers. 14,000-seat outdoor theater.

Kingston (F-9)

See also Clayton, Ellenville, New Paltz, Rhinebeck, Saugerties, Shandaken, Woodstock

Settled 1652
Population 23,456
Elevation 200 ft
Area Code 845
Information Chamber of Commerce of Ulster County, 1 Albany Ave; phone 845/338-5100
Web Site www.ulsterchamber.org

In more than 300 years, Kingston has had several names, including Esopus and Wiltwyck, and has been raided, burned, and fought over by Native Americans, Dutch, British, and Americans. It was the first capital of New York. The Delaware and Hudson Canal and then the railroads brought prosperity. A huge cement industry bloomed and died on Rondout Creek harbor in the 19th century.

What to See and Do

Delaware & Hudson Canal Museum. *Mohonk Rd and Hwy 213, High Falls (12440). 15 miles S, NY Thrwy exit 19, then S on Hwy 209, turn left on Hwy 213. Phone 845/687-9311. www.canalmuseum.org.* Dioramas, canalboat models, photographs, and memorabilia. Tours. (May-Oct Mon, Thurs-Sun; closed Nov-Apr) **$$**

Hudson River Maritime Museum. *1 Rondout Landing, Kingston (12401). At the foot of Broadway. Phone 845/338-0071.* Models, photographs, and paintings depict bygone era of river commerce; outdoor area features steam tug and a variety of antique and modern pleasure boats. (Mid-May-mid-Oct, daily 11 am-5 pm) **$**

Old Dutch Church. *272 Wall St, Kingston (12401). Main and Wall sts. Phone 845/338-6759.*(Congregation established 1659) A 19th-century church; buried on grounds is George Clinton, first governor of New York and vice president under Madison and Jefferson. Church and museum tours by appointment. **DONATION**

Senate House State Historic Site. *296 Fair St, Kingston (12401). In Stockade District. Phone 845/338-2786. nysparks.state.ny.us.* (1676) Stone residence in which the first New York State Senate met in 1777. Furnished in 18th-century Dutch style; delft tiles, Hudson Valley furniture. Paintings by John Vanderlyn and others in adjacent museum; boxwood garden. Also library of regional history (by appointment only), displays, special events. (Mid-Apr-late Oct, Mon, Wed-Sat 10 am-5 pm, Sun from 11 am) **$**

Ulster Performing Arts Center. *601 Broadway, Kingston (12401). Phone 845/339-6088. www.upac.org.* Historic Vaudeville theater (1927) presents professional Broadway touring companies, dance, contemporary music, comedy, and children's productions.

Special Event

Stone House Day. *Hwy 32 N and Broadhead Ave, New Paltz. Approximately 1/2 mile NW on Hwy 28, then 2 miles S on Hwy 209 in Hurley. Phone 845/331-4121.* Tour of eight privately owned colonial stone houses, led by costumed guides; Hurley Reformed Church and old burial ground; antique show; re-creation of Revolutionary War military encampment; country fair. Second Sat in July.

Limited-Service Hotels

★ ★ HOLIDAY INN. *503 Washington Ave, Kingston (12401). Phone 845/338-0400; toll-free 800/465-4329; fax 845/340-1908. www.holiday-inn. com.* 212 rooms, 2 story. Pets accepted; fee. Check-in 3 pm, check-out noon. Wireless Internet access. Restaurant, bar. Fitness room. Indoor pool, whirlpool. **$**

★ ★ QUALITY INN. *114 Hwy 28, Kingston (12401). Phone 845/339-3900; toll-free 800/272-6232; fax 845/338-8464. www.choicehotels.com.* 147 rooms, 2 story. Check-in 2 pm, check-out noon. Restaurant, bar. Indoor pool. **$**

Restaurants

★ ★ DOWNTOWN CAFE. *1 W Strand St, Kingston. Phone 845/331-5904. www.downtowncafekingston.com.* American menu. Lunch, dinner, brunch. Bar. Casual attire. Reservations recommended. Outdoor seating. **$$**

★ HICKORY BBQ SMOKEHOUSE. *743 Hwy 28, Kingston (12401). Phone 845/338-2424. www. hickoryrestaurant.com.* American menu. Lunch, dinner. Closed Wed. Bar. Children's menu. Casual attire. Reservations recommended. Outdoor seating.**$$**

★ ★ LE CANARD ENCHAINE. *276 Fair St, Kingston (12401). Phone 845/339-2003; fax 845/339-5923. www.lecanard-enchaine.com.* French menu. Lunch, dinner. Closed Dec 25. Bar. Outdoor seating. **$$$**

Lake George Area (C-9)

See also Bolton Landing, Diamond Point, Hague, Lake George Village, Ticonderoga

Web Site www.visitlakegeorge.com

Early explorers and settlers knew Lake George as Lac du St. Sacrement—the name given it when a Jesuit missionary, Father Isaac Jogues, reached the southern tip of the lake on the evening of Corpus Christi Day in 1646. In the foothills of the Adirondacks, the area is a center for winter as well as summer sports; there are many miles of snowmobile trails. The area is rich in memories of battles that played a major role in the future of the nation.

Lake George Village (C-9)

See also Glens Falls, Lake George Area, Lake Luzerne, Warrensburg, Adirondack Park

Population 985
Elevation 353 ft
Area Code 518
Zip 12845
Information Chamber of Commerce, PO Box 272; phone 518/668-5755 or toll-free 800/705-0059
Web Site www.visitlakegeorge.com

This village, located on the 32-mile lake, is in a popular resort area well known for fishing, swimming, boating, golf, and winter sports.

What to See and Do

Fort William Henry Museum. *48 Canada St, Lake George (12845). S edge of village on Hwy 9. Phone 518/668-5471. www.fortwilliamhenry.com/fortmus.htm.* A 1755 fort rebuilt from original plans; French and Indian War relics; military drills, musket firings, bullet molding, and cannon demonstrations. Replica of the fort used in filming of the movie *Last of the Mohicans.* Tours (July-Aug). (Daily 9 am-6 pm) **$$$**

The Great Escape and Splashwater Kingdom Fun Park. *Hwy 9, Lake George Village (12845). Hwy 9, between exits 19 and 20, off I-87. Phone 518/792-3500. www.sixflags.com/parks/greatescape.* New York's largest theme park has over 120 rides, live shows, and attractions, including numerous roller coasters, Raging River Raft Ride, All-American High-Dive Show, Storytown-themed children's area. Splashwater Kingdom water park features a giant wavepool, water slides, Adventure River, and kiddie pools. (Memorial Day-Labor Day, daily, hours vary) **$$$$**

Lake excursions. *Steel Pier Beach Rd, Lake George. Lake George Steamboat Company, Beach Rd. Phone 518/668-5777; toll-free 800/553-2628.* MV *Mohican, Lac de St. Sacrement,* and the paddlewheeler *Minne-Ha-Ha* cruise Lake George. Trips vary from one-hour shoreline cruise to 4 1/2-hour full-length cruise of Lake George; also lunch, dinner, moonlight, and Sun brunch cruises (late June-Labor Day, daily; limited schedule spring and fall). **$$$$**

Lake George Battlefield Picnic Area. *139 Beach Rd, Lake George Village (12845). 1 mile S off Hwy 9. Phone 518/668-3352.* Site of Battle of Lake George (1755); ruins of Fort George. Picnic tables, fireplaces, charcoal grills, water. (Mid-June-Labor Day: daily; May-mid-June: weekends) **$$**

Prospect Mountain State Parkway. *1/2 mile S on Hwy 9. Phone 518/668-3352.* (1969) A 5 1/2-mile paved road up Prospect Mountain (2,100 feet); buses (free) from parking lot near top to crest. (Mid-May-mid-Oct, daily) **$$**

Swimming. *Lake George Million Dollar Beach, Lake George. 1/4 mile E off Hwy 9. Phone 518/668-5755.* In Adirondack Park (see). Bathhouse, lockers, lifeguards. (Mid-June-Labor Day, daily)

Water Slide World. *Hwys 9 and 9L, Lake George. Off exit 21 of the Adirondack Northway (I-87). Phone 518/668-4407. www.adirondack.net/tour/waterslideworld.* Water fun park includes wave pool, 13 water slides, Activity Pool, Lazy River, and Toddler Lagoon play area. (Late June-Labor Day: daily 9:30 am-6 pm) **$$$$**

Special Events

Americade. *Canada St, Lake George (12845). Phone 518/668-5755. www.tourexpo.com.* This annual motorcycle touring rally includes seminars, exhibits, shows, social events, and guided scenic tours. The event attracts 50,000 motorcycle enthusiasts each year. First full week in June.

Family Festival. *Shepard Park, Canada St, Lake George (12845). Phone 518/668-5771.* Craft show, family entertainment, game booths, music, food. Third week in Aug.

Jazz Festival. *Shepard Park Bandstand, Canada St, Lake George Village (12845). Phone 518/668-5771.* Regional jazz bands; lawn seating. Mid-Sept.

Lakeside Festival. *Beach Rd, Lake George Village (12845). Phone 518/668-5771.* Juried craft show; boat show with demo rides; food, music, fireworks. Third weekend in Sept.

Winter Carnival. *Hwy 9 and Lake George Village, Lake George Village (12845). Phone 518/668-5755. www.lakegeorgewintercarnival.com.* Weekends in Feb.

Limited-Service Hotels

★ BEST WESTERN OF LAKE GEORGE. *50 Canada St, Lake George (12845). Phone 518/668-5701; toll-free 800/582-5540; fax 518/668-4926. www.bestwesternlakegeorge.com.* 87 rooms, 2 story. Complimentary continental breakfast. Check-in 2 pm, check-out 11 am. High-sped Internet. Children's activity center. Indoor pool, outdoor pool, children's pool, whirlpool. Airport transportation available. **$$**

★ COLONEL WILLIAMS MOTOR INN. *Hwy 9, Lake George (12845). Phone 518/668-5727; toll-free 800/334-5727; fax 518/668-2996. www.colonelwilliamsresort.com.* 40 rooms. Closed late Oct-mid-May. Check-out 11 am. Fitness room. Indoor, outdoor pools; whirlpool. **$**

★ ★ DAYS INN. *1454 Hwy 9, Lake George (12845). Phone 518/793-3196; toll-free 800/329-7466; fax 518/793-6028. www.daysinnlakegeorge.com.* 104 rooms,

2 story. Check-in 3 pm, check-out 11 am. Restaurant, bar. Indoor pool, whirlpool. **$**

★ ★ DUNHAMS BAY LODGE. *2999 Hwy 9L, Lake George (12845). Phone 518/656-9242; toll-free 800/795-6343; fax 518/656-9250. www.dunhamsbay.com.* 50 rooms, 2 story. Pets accepted, some restrictions. Check-in 3 pm, check-out 10 am. Restaurant, bar. Indoor pool, children's pool, whirlpool. Tennis. **$$**

★ ★ THE GEORGIAN. *384 Canada St, Lake George (12845). Phone 518/668-5401; toll-free 800/525-3436; fax 518/668-5870. www.georgianresort.com.* 165 rooms, 2 story. Check-in 3 pm, check-out 11 am. Restaurant, two bars. Beach. Outdoor pool. Airport transportation available. **$$**

★ THE HERITAGE OF LAKE GEORGE. *419 Canada St, Lake George (12845). Phone 518/668-3357; toll-free 800/883-2653; fax 518/668-9784. www.heritageoflakegeorge.com.* 39 rooms, 2 story. Closed mid-Oct-mid-May. Check-in 3 pm, check-out 11 am. Outdoor pool. **$**

★ ★ HOLIDAY INN. *Hwy 9 Canada St, Lake George (12845). Phone 518/668-5781; toll-free 800/465-5329; fax 518/668-9213. www.holiday-inn. com.* 105 rooms, 2 story. Check-in 3 pm, check-out 11 am. High-speed Internet access. Restaurant, bar. Fitness room. Indoor pool, children's pool, whirlpool. Business center. **$**

★ ★ HOWARD JOHNSON. *2 Canada St, Lake George (12845). Phone 518/668-5744; toll-free 888/843-8454; fax 518/668-3544. www.tikiresort.com.* 110 rooms, 2 story. Closed Nov-Apr. Check-in 3 pm, check-out 11 am. Two restaurants, bar. Children's activity center. Fitness room. Indoor pool, outdoor pool, children's pool. **$$**

★ LAKE CREST MOTEL. *366 Canada St, Lake George (12845). Phone 518/668-3374. www.lakecrestmotel.com.* 40 rooms, 2 story. Closed late Oct-late Apr. Check-in 2 pm, check-out 11 am. Restaurant. Beach. Outdoor pool. **$$**

★ ★ MOHICAN MOTEL. *1545 Hwy 9, Lake George (12845). Phone 518/792-0474; fax 518/761-4089. www.mohicanmotel.com.* 43 rooms. Check-out 11 am. Restaurant. Indoor pool, outdoor pool, children's pool, whirlpools. **$**

★ ★ NORDICK'S MOTEL. *2895 Lake Shore Dr, Lake George (12845). Phone 518/668-2697; toll-free 800/368-2697. www.nordicks.com.* 21 rooms. Closed late Oct-Apr. Check-out 10 am. Restaurant, bar. Outdoor pool. **$**

★ ★ ROARING BROOK RANCH & TENNIS RESORT. *Luzerne Rd, Lake George (12845). Phone 518/668-5767; toll-free 800/882-7665; fax 518/688-4019. www.roaringbrookranch.com.* Two miles from Lake George, this resort offers three pools, five tennis courts with tennis pros, 30 horses for wilderness riding, golf nearby, and so much more. The resort's conference center makes it attractive for meetings and special events. 142 rooms, 2 story. Closed Mar-mid-May and Nov-Dec. Check-in 3 pm, check-out 11 am. Restaurant, bar. Children's activity center. Fitness room. Indoor pool, two outdoor pools. Tennis. **$**

Full-Service Resort

★ ★ ★ FORT WILLIAM HENRY RESORT. *48 Canada St, Lake George (12845). Phone 518/668-3081; toll-free 800/234-6686; fax 518/668-4926. www.fortwilliamhenry.com.* 195 rooms, 2 story. Pets accepted, some restrictions; fee. Check-in 2 pm, check-out 11 am. Two restaurants, bar. Children's activity center. Indoor pool, outdoor pool, whirlpool. Airport transportation available. Business center. **$$**

Restaurants

★ ★ LOG JAM. *1484 Rte 9, Site 1, Lake George Village (12845). Phone 518/798-1155; fax 518/798-3280. www.logjam.com.* Lobster tank. American menu. Lunch, dinner. Closed Thanksgiving, Dec 25. Bar. Children's menu. Casual attire. Reservations recommended. Valet parking. **$$**

★ ★ ★ MONTCALM. *1415 Hwy 9, Lake George Village (12845). Phone 518/793-6601. www.menumart.com/montcalm.* Rich American classics such as roast rack of lamb and veal Oscar are the mainstay of this resort town restaurant. It has reasonable prices and a loyal following. Salads are prepared tableside by an attentive waitstaff. American menu. Lunch, dinner.

Closed holidays. Bar. Children's menu. Casual attire. Reservations recommended. **$$**

Lake Luzerne (D-9)

See also Diamond Point, Glens Falls, Lake George Village, Warrensburg

Population 3,219
Elevation 610 ft
Area Code 518
Zip 12846
Information Chamber of Commerce, 79 Main St, PO Box 222; phone 518/696-3500
Web Site www.lakeluzernechamber.org

Lumbering and papermaking formed the economic background of Lake Luzerne, now an all-year resort. In addition to being on the small lake for which it is named, it is near Great Sacandaga Lake, another popular area for summer and winter sports.

What to See and Do

Bow Bridge. *Phone 518/696-3500.* Parabolic bridge (1895) spans the Hudson and Sacandaga rivers. The only remaining semideck lenticular iron truss bridge, typical of the late 19th-century iron bridges in New York State.

Rockwell Falls & Chasm. *SE of town via Northway, exit 21.* Hudson River flows over rocks causing a great rush of water; joins the Sacandaga River at the end of the falls and chasm. Viewed from bridge.

Swimming, boating, fishing. *Phone 518/582-4451.* On Lake Vanare, Lake Luzerne, and Great Sacandaga Lake. Boat launching sites (free) on the Hudson River, at Fourth Lake Campground and on the Sacandaga, North Shore Rd.

Whitewater rafting. Down the Sacandaga River. Several outfitters operate in the area. Seasons usually Memorial Day-Labor Day; inquire locally.

Limited-Service Hotel

★ ★ SARATOGA ROSE. *4136 Rockwell St, Hadley (12835). Phone 518/696-2861; toll-free 800/942-5025. www.saratogarose.com.* 6 rooms, 2 story. Children over 10 years only. Complimentary full breakfast. Check-in 3 pm, check-out 11 am. Restaurant. **$**

Specialty Lodging

LAMPLIGHT INN BED & BREAKFAST. *231 Lake Ave, Lake Luzerne (12846). Phone 518/696-5294; toll-free 800/262-4668; fax 518/696-5256. www.lamplightinn.com.* Built in 1890 on a 10-acre lot, this inn offers rooms in the main house, the Brookside House and the Carriage House, all decorated in Victorian style. The inn features chesnut woodwork and a chesnut keyhole staircase crafted in England, and is surrounded by gardens, hiking and biking trails, river, lakes, and more. 17 rooms, 2 story. Children over 12 years only. Complimentary full breakfast. Check-in 3 pm, check-out 11 am. Restaurant. **$$**

Restaurants

★ CIRO'S. *1439 Lake Ave, Lake Luzerne (12846). Phone 518/696-2556; fax 518/696-4762. www.menumart.com/ciros.* Italian, American menu. Dinner. Closed Thanksgiving, Dec 25. Bar. Children's menu. **$$**

★ WATERHOUSE. *85 Lake Ave, Lake Luzerne (12846). Phone 518/696-3115; fax 518/696-2746. www.menumart.com/waterhouse.* Seafood, steak menu. Lunch, dinner. Closed Thanksgiving, Dec 25. Bar. Children's menu. Outdoor seating. **$$**

Lake Placid (B-9)

See also Saranac Lake, Tupper Lake, Wilmington

Population 2,638
Elevation 1,882 ft
Area Code 518
Zip 12946
Information Essex County Visitors Bureau, Olympic Center, 216 Main St; phone 518/523-2445 or toll-free 800/447-5224
Web Site www.lakeplacid.com

Mount Marcy, the highest mountain in New York State (5,344 feet) rises in the Adirondack peaks that surround the town. On Lake Placid, the village also partly surrounds Mirror Lake. This is one of the most famous all-year vacation centers in the East and the site of the 1932 and 1980 Winter Olympics. The Intervale Olympic Ski Jump Complex has 229-foot and 296-foot ski jumps constructed for the 1980 games, now open to the public and used for training and competition.

What to See and Do

John Brown Farm Historic Site. *115 John Brown Rd, Lake Placid (12946). 2 miles S, 1 mile off Hwy 73. Phone 518/523-3900.* Brown's final home; graves of the noted abolitionist, two sons, and ten others who died in the struggle to end slavery. Grounds (daily). House (Late May-late Oct; Mon, Wed-Sun 10 am-5 pm). **$**

Lake Placid Center for the Arts. *17 Algonquin Dr., Lake Placid (12946). At Fawn Ridge. Phone 518/523-2512. www.lpartscenter.org.* Concerts, films, art exhibits. Gallery (fall and spring: Tues-Sat 1-5 pm; summer: Tues-Fri 10 am-5 pm, Sat-Sun 1-5 pm; winter: Tues-Thurs 1-5 pm, Fri 1-9 pm). **FREE**

Lake Placid Marina. *Mirror Lake Dr and Hwy 86, Lake Placid (12946). 1 mile N on Hwy 86 to Mirror Lake Dr. Phone 518/523-9704.* One-hour scenic cruises. (Mid-May-mid-Oct) **$$$**

Olympic Arena and Convention Center. *2634 Main St, Lake Placid (12946). Phone 518/523-1655. www.orda.org.* Built for the 1932 Winter Olympics and renovated for the 1980 Winter games. Winter and summer skating shows, family shows, hockey; public skating, concerts.

Uihlein Sugar Maple Research-Extension Field Station. *60 Bear Cub Rd, Lake Placid (12946). Phone 518/523-9337. maple.dnr.cornell.edu/Uihlein/uihlein.as.*4,000-tap sugar bush; maple syrup demonstrations, exhibits in Sugar House. Owned and operated by NY State College of Agriculture at Cornell University. (July-Labor Day, Tues-Fri; mid-Sept-mid-Oct, Fri; closed July 4) Schedule may vary. **FREE**

Verizon Sports Complex (Mount Van Hoevenburg Recreation Area). *7 miles SE on Hwy 73. Phone 518/523-1655.* Site of 1980 Winter Olympic Games. Bobsled, luge, cross-country, biathlon events. Championship bobsled and luge races most weekends in winter. Cross-country trails (33 miles) open to the public when not used for racing. Bobsled rides (mid-Dec-early Mar, Tues-Sun; fee); luge rides (mid-Dec-early Mar, weekends; fee).

Limited-Service Hotels

★ ★ ADIRONDACK INN BY THE LAKE. *2625 Main St, Lake Placid (12946). Phone 518/523-2424; toll-free 800/556-2424; fax 518/523-2425. www.adirondack-inn. com.* Opposite Olympic Arena and Convention Hall. 49 rooms, 2 story. Check-in 2 pm, check-out 11 am. Restaurant, bar. Children's activity center. Fitness room. Beach. Indoor pool, whirlpool. **$**

★ ART DEVLIN'S OLYMPIC MOTOR INN. *2764 Main St, Lake Placid (12946). Phone 518/523-3700; fax 518/523-3893. www.artdevlins.com.* 41 rooms, 2 story. Pets accepted, some restrictions. Complimentary continental breakfast. Check-in 1 pm, check-out 11 am. High-speed Internet access. Outdoor pool, children's pool. **$**

★ ★ BEST WESTERN GOLDEN ARROW HOTEL. *2559 Main St, Lake Placid (12946). Phone 518/523-3353; toll-free 800/582-5540; fax 518/523-8063. www.golden-arrow.com.* 130 rooms, 4 story. Pets accepted, some restrictions; fee. Check-out 11 am. Restaurant, bar. Fitness room. Indoor pool, children's pool, whirlpool. **$**

★ ★ HOLIDAY INN. *1 Olympic Dr, Lake Placid (12946). Phone 518/523-2556; fax 518/523-9410.* 209 rooms, 4 story. Pets accepted, some restrictions. Check-in 4 pm, check-out 11 am. Restaurant, bar. Children's activity center. Fitness room. Indoor pool, whirlpool. Golf, 45 holes. Tennis. **$$**

Full-Service Resorts

★ ★ ★ HILTON LAKE PLACID RESORT. *1 Mirror Lake Dr, Lake Placid (12946). Phone 518/523-4411; toll-free 800/755-5598; fax 518/523-1120. www.lphilton.com.* All rooms at this resort offer private balconies or patios overlooking the mountains or lake. Two indoor and two outdoor pools, 72 championship holes of golf, and nearby skiing/snowboarding are just a few reasons to stay. 179 rooms, 5 story. Pets accepted; fee. Check-in 4 pm, check-out noon. Restaurant, bar. Children's activity center. Fitness room. Two indoor pools, two outdoor pools, whirlpool. Golf, 99 holes. **$$**

LAKE PLACID LODGE. *Whiteface Inn Rd, Lake Placid (12946). Phone 518/523-2700; fax 518/523-1124. www.lakeplacidlodge.com.* Nestled on the wooded shores of Lake Placid with majestic views of Whiteface Mountain, Lake Placid Lodge may be the most restful spot around. The lodge is a celebration of the simple beauty of the Adirondacks. The rooms, suites, and log and timber cabins from the 1920s reflect the regions unique style with twig and birch bark furniture and one-of-a-kind decorative accents. Every piece of artwork and furniture is attributed to a local artist or craftsman, adding to the lodges individual style. Stone fireplaces and deep-soaking tubs further enhance the rustic sophistication of the accommodations, and discriminating diners praise the restaurant's refined New American cuisine. The lakeside setting makes it ideal for water sports; during the winter months, ice skating, snowshoeing, and cross-country skiing are popular activities. The pristine setting is often experienced from the comfortable seat of a lakefront Adirondack chair. 34 rooms. Pets accepted; fee. Children over 14 years only. Complimentary full breakfast. Check-in 4 pm, check-out noon. Restaurant, bar. **$$$$**

★ ★ ★ **MIRROR LAKE INN RESORT AND SPA.** *77 Mirror Lake Dr, Lake Placid (12946). Phone 518/523-2544; fax 518/523-2414. www.mirrorlakeinn.com.* Walnut floors, marble, antiques, and stone fireplaces build a warm atmosphere in this traditional inn that also offers its guests all the amenities of a modern inn. A complete health spa and exercise facilities can be found at this property. 128 rooms, 4 story. Check-in 3 pm, check-out 11 am. Three restaurants, bar. Fitness room, spa. Beach. Indoor pool, outdoor pool, whirlpool. Tennis. **$$$**

Specialty Lodging

THE BARK EATER INN. *Alstead Hill Rd, Keene (12942). Phone 518/576-2221; toll-free 800/232-1607; fax 518/576-2071. www.barkeater.com.* Former stagecoach stop built in early 1800s; antiques. 19 rooms, 2 story. Complimentary full breakfast. Check-in 1 pm, check-out 11 am. Restaurant. **$**

Restaurant

★ ★ ★ **THE VIEW.** *5 Mirror Lake Dr, Lake Placid (12946). Phone 518/523-2544. www.mirrorlakeinn.com.* Located in the Mirror Lake Inn (see), this restaurant offers both views of the lake and the mountains. A special dinner series features theme nights that include wine dinners and many international meals. American menu. Breakfast, dinner. Bar. Children's menu. Business casual attire. Reservations recommended. Outdoor seating. **$$$**

Larchmont

Restaurants

★ ★ ★ **LUSARDI'S.** *1885 Palmer Rd, Larchmont (10538). Phone 914/834-5555.* Italian menu. Lunch, dinner. Bar. Business casual attire. Reservations recommended. **$$$**

★ ★ **WATERCOLOR CAFE.** *2094 Boston Post Rd, Larchmont (10538). Phone 914/834-2213.* American menu. Lunch, dinner. Bar. Casual attire. Reservations recommended. **$$**

Latham

Restaurant

★ ★ **DAKOTAS.** *579 Troy Schnectedy Rd, Latham (12110). Phone 518/786-1234. www.dakotarestaurant.com.* American menu. Lunch, dinner, brunch. Bar. Children's menu. Casual attire. Reservations recommended. Outdoor seating. **$$**

Letchworth State Park (E-3)

See also Avon, Castile, Geneseo

Entrances at Castile, Mount Morris, Perry, and Portageville.

Web Site www.nysparks.state.ny.us

In this 14,344-acre park are 17 miles of the Genesee River Gorge, sometimes called the Grand Canyon of the East. Sheer cliffs rise 600 feet at some points, and the river roars over three major falls, one of them 107 feet high. The park has a variety of accommodations, including an inn and motel, a 270-site tent and trailer camping area, and 82 camping cabins (ranging from one room to family size).

Located here are swimming pools with bathhouses (mid-June-Labor Day), fishing, whitewater rafting, hot air ballooning, nature and hiking trails (year-round) and outstanding fall foliage. Cross-country skiing, snowmobiling, snowtubing, picnicking at eight areas with tables, fireplaces, shelters, rest rooms, a playground, and recreation programs are also available. No pets in cabin areas and part of camping area.

The William Pryor Letchworth Museum, the grave of Mary Jemison, and a restored Seneca Indian Council House are in the park (mid-May-Oct, daily; donation).For detailed information contact Letworth State Park, 1 Letchworth State Park, Castile 14427; phone 716/493-3600.

Full-Service Inn

★ ★ ★ **GLEN IRIS INN.** *7 Letchworth State Park, Castile (14427). Phone 585/493-2622; fax 585/493-5803. www.gleniririsinn.com.* Found nestled in Letchworth State Park, this inn offers guests a comfortable stay in Victorian luxury. Guests can choose to stay in a room with a double or twin bed, or in a suite with a queen bed. 15 rooms, 3 story. Closed Nov-Mar. Check-in 3 pm, check-out noon. Restaurant, bar. **$**

Restaurant

★ ★ ★ **GLEN IRIS INN.** *7 Letchworth State Park, Letchworth State Park (14427). Phone 585/493-2622; fax 716/493-5803. www.glenirisinn. com.* Housed in an old lumber mill with spectacular views of the neighboring waterfalls, the Glen Iris Inn's fine dining restaurant offers traditional fare and reasonable prices. Try one of the fresh seafood dishes. American menu. Breakfast, lunch, dinner. Closed first weekend in Nov-Easter. Children's menu. **$$**

Lewiston

Restaurants

★ ★ **CLARKSON HOUSE.** *810 Center St, Lewiston (14902). Phone 716/754-4544; fax 716/754-2844. www.clarksonhouse.com.* Seafood, steak menu. Dinner. Closed Dec 25. Bar. Children's menu. Reservations recommended. 1818 house. **$$$**

★ ★ **RIVERSIDE INN.** *115 S Water St, Lewiston (14092). Phone 716/754-8206; fax 716/754-8352. www.riversideinn. net.* Lunch, dinner. Bar. Children's menu. Built 1871; riverboat atmosphere. Outdoor seating. **$$**

★ **VILLA COFFEE HOUSE.** *769 Cayuga St, Lewiston (14092). Phone 716/754-2660.* Breakfast, lunch, dinner. Closed Jan 1, Thanksgiving, Dec 25. Children's menu. **$**

Liberty (F-8)

See also Ellenville, Monticello, Roscoe

Population 9,632
Elevation 1,509 ft
Area Code 845
Zip 12754
Information Chamber of Commerce, PO Box 147; phone 845/292-1878

Near the junction of the Willowemoc and Beaverkill rivers and on the edge of the Catskill Forest Preserve, this area offers good hunting and trout fishing, camping, hiking, and sightseeing.

What to See and Do

NY State Catskill Fish Hatchery. *Hatchery Rd, DeBruce. 11 miles NW on Fish Hatchery Rd. Phone 845/439-4328.* Ponds featuring trout of various sizes as well as breeder trout. (Oct-mid-June: daily, mid-June-Sept: weekend mornings) **FREE**

Limited-Service Hotels

★ ★ **DAYS INN.** *52 Sullivan Ave, Liberty (12754). Phone 845/292-7600; fax 845/292-3303. www.daysinn. com.* 120 rooms, 2 story. Complimentary continental breakfast. Check-out 11 am. Bar. Indoor pool, outdoor pool. **$**

★ ★ **LANZA'S COUNTRY INN.** *839 Shandelee Rd, Livingston Manor (12758). Phone 845/439-5070; fax 845/439-5003. www.lanzascountryinn. com.* Greenhouse sitting room.8 rooms, 2 story. Complimentary full breakfast. Check-in 1 pm, check-out 11 am. Restaurant. Built in 1900. **$**

Liverpool

Special Event

Scottish Games. *Long Branch Park, Liverpool Pkwy and Hwy 370, Liverpool (13088). Phone 315/470-1800.* Mid-Aug.

Limited-Service Hotel

★ HOMEWOOD SUITES. *275 Elwood Davis Rd, Liverpool (13088). Phone 315/451-3800; fax 315/451-5838. www.homewood-suites.com.* 102 rooms, all suites. Complimentary full breakfast. Check-in 3 pm, check-out noon. Fitness room. Outdoor pool. **$**

Specialty Lodging

ANCESTORS INN AT THE BASSETT HOUSE. *215 Sycamore St, Liverpool (13088). Phone 315/461-1226; toll-free 888/866-8591. www.ancestorsinn. com.* 4 rooms. Complimentary full breakfast. Check-out 11 am. **$**

Lockport (D-2)

See also Batavia, Niagara Falls, Niagara-on-the-Lake

Settled 1816
Population 22,279
Elevation 600 ft
Area Code 716
Zip 14094
Information Chamber of Commerce, 151 W Genessee St; phone 716/433-3828
Web Site www.lockport-ny.com

The town was originally settled around a series of locks of the Erie Canal, now the New York State Barge Canal.

What to See and Do

Canal Bridge. *Cottage St.* Claimed to be one of the widest single-span bridges (399 1/2 feet) in the world. View of the locks' operation, raising and lowering barges, and pleasure craft more than 60 feet.

Colonel William Bond House. *143 Ontario St, Lockport (14094). Phone 716/434-7433.* Pre-Victorian home (1824) was built with bricks made on site. Restored, with 12 furnished rooms; of special interest are the kitchen and the children's garret. (Mar-Dec, Thurs, Sat-Sun afternoons) **FREE**

Kenan Center. *433 Locust St, Lockport (14094). Phone 716/433-2617. www.kenancenter.org.* Art gallery and recreation/sports arena. Gallery (Sept-May: daily; June-Aug: Mon-Fri and Sun); Taylor Theater (fee); garden and orchard, herb garden. **DONATION**

Niagara County Historical Center. *215 Niagara St, Lockport (14094). Phone 716/434-7433.* An 1860 brick house with antiques; Erie Canal artifacts. Pioneer Building contains Native American collection, pioneer artifacts; Washington Hunt Law Office (1835); Niagara Fire Company #1, with 1834 and 1836 pumpers. 19th-century farming equipment. (Thurs-Sun; closed holidays) **$**

Limited-Service Hotel

★ LOCKPORT MOTEL. *315 S Transit St, Lockport (14094). Phone 716/434-5595; fax 716/433-0105. www. lockportmotel.com.* 65 rooms. Check-in noon, check-out 11 am. Outdoor pool. **$**

Restaurant

★ GARLOCK'S. *35 S Transit St, Lockport (14094). Phone 716/433-5595; fax 716/434-2081. www. garlocksrestaurant.com.* In mid-1800s building with collection of decanters. Seafood, steak menu. Dinner. Closed Thanksgiving, Dec 25. Bar. Children's menu. Casual attire. **$$**

Locust Valley

Restaurant

★ ★ BARNEY'S RESTAURANT. *315 Buckram Rd, Locust Valley (11560). Phone 516/671-6300.* American menu. Dinner. Closed Mon; Dec 25. Bar. Casual attire. Reservations recommended. **$$$**

Long Island

Web Site www.licvb.com

Long Island stretches 118 miles east by northeast from the edge of Manhattan to the lonely dunes of Montauk. Much of the island is ideal resort country, with vast white beaches, quiet bays, coves, and woods.

At the eastern tip, Montauk Light stands on its headland; on the southwestern shore is Coney Island. New York City sprawls over the whole of Long Island's two westernmost countiesQueens and Kings (the boroughs of Queens and Brooklyn).

Nassau County, adjoining the city, is made up of suburbs filled with residential communities. Eastward in Suffolk County, city influence eases, and there are firms that have attracted substantial local populations. Potatoes and the famous Long Island duckling are still raised here alongside farms for horse breeding and the vineyards producing Long Island wines.

Long Island has many miles of sandy barrier beaches along the south shore, with swimming and surf casting. The bays behind these make natural small-boat harbors. On the more tranquil waters of the north shore is a series of deeper harbors along Long Island Sound, many of them with beaches and offering good sailing opportunities. The island has played a major role in US history from the early 17th century; the record of this role is carefully preserved in many buildings, some 300 years old. Few regions offer such varied interests in so small an area. The Long Island Railroad conducts tours to points of interest on the island (late May to early Nov). For information about these escorted day excursions, write to the Long Island Railroad, Sales and Promotion Department, #1723, Jamaica 11435; phone 718/217-5477. For further information and special events, contact the Long Island Convention & Visitors Bureau, 350 Vanderbilt Motor Pkwy, Suite 103, Hauppage 11788; phone 800/441-4601.

Long Island towns listed in the Mobil Travel Guide are Amagansett, Amityville, Bay Shore, Bethpage, East Hampton, Fire Island National Seashore, Floral Park, Garden City, Glen Cove, Great Neck, Greenport, Hampton Bays, Hempstead, Huntington, Jericho, Jones Beach State Park, Massapequa Park, Montauk, Northport, Oyster Bay, Plainview, Port Jefferson, Port Washington, Riverhead, Robert Moses State Park, Rockville Centre, Roslyn, Sag Harbor, Sayville, Shelter Island, Smithtown, Southampton, Southold, Stony Brook, Westbury, and Westhampton Beach.

What to See and Do

American Airpower Museum. *1300 New Hwy, Farmingdale (11735). Phone 631/293-6398. www.americanpowermuseum.com.* This museum, located in a former hangar of the Republic Aviation Company, is a must for aviation and history buffs. Original warplanes from various battles and eras of the 20th century are on display, along with equipment, vintage flying gear, and maps. The museum also hosts special events. (Thurs-Sun 10:30 am-4 pm) **$$**

Big Duck. Rte *24, Flanders. Phone 631/852-8292.* Long Islanders love their ducks! In honor of the quacking animal, this goofy South Fork gift shop and museum is visible from the road as a 20-foot-high white concrete duck (seriously!). The attraction is actually listed on the National Register of Historic Places. The museum portion has various duck items and photos on display. For sale in the shop are specialties like duck-embossed T-shirts, caps, boxer shorts, and ties-knickknacks at their silliest. Both adults and kids will get a kick out of this place. (May-Sept: daily 10 am-5 pm; weekends only through Nov)

Duck Walk Vineyards. *231 Montauk Hwy, Water Mill (11976). Phone 631/726-7555. www.duckwalk.com.* This light and airy winery on the South Fork produces some very interesting wines, including a delicately sweet blueberry port that goes great with chocolate, and a boysenberry dessert wine. Duck Walk produces other, more traditional varieties as well, such as merlot and chardonnay. The winerys tasting room sells wines, preserves, books, and other souvenirs. There are verandas overlooking the vineyards to sit, have a leisurely picnic, and enjoy music on weekends in summer. Tours are given Sat-Sun at noon, 2 pm, and 4 pm in the off-season and every day in the warmer months. (Daily 11 am-6 pm) **FREE**

Jones Beach State Park. *Ocean Dr, Wantash. Phone 516/785-1600. nysparks.state.ny.us.* Many native New Yorkers flock to this 6-mile beachfront when the mercury starts to climb. But this state park has more than a great beach. It offers two Olympic-sized pools, 14 cafeterias and snack stands, playgrounds, basketball courts, a boat basin, paddle tennis courts, a boardwalk for strolling, and softball fields. Pool admission is cheap ($1 to $3), and parking is also inexpensive and plentiful. You can even take a bus from the city if you don't have a car. Bring plenty of sunscreen and plan to spend the whole day. Note that no pets are allowed. (Daily) **$**

Quogue Wildlife Refuge and Nature Center. *3 Old Country Rd, Quogue (11959). Phone 631/653-4771. www.quoguewildliferefuge.com.* If you enjoy the beauty of nature and the pleasure of animals, this is a place that will be very special to you. The refuges 305 acres are filled with birds, ducks, geese, and flora and fauna, and include the Distressed Wildlife Complex, which takes care of hurt animals and provides care for them; its keepers have aided a number of species, including hawks and eagles. Special classes and programs are offered here, such as nature walks, field trips, and a summer day camp for children. (Nature Center: Feb-Nov, Tues-Thurs 1-4 pm; Refuge: year-round dawn-dusk) **FREE**

Science Museum of Long Island. *1526 N Plandome Rd*, Plandome (11030). *Phone 516/627-9400.* This is not a traditional museum, but rather a hands-on education center for the study of natural sciences. Children over 3 years may participate in the special workshops and programs, but pre-registration is required. The museum is located in a peaceful setting36 acres of streams and beachfront. A fun family experience will be had by all, especially the little ones. (Daily from 9 am)

Tilles Center for the Performing Arts. *CW Post Campus of Long Island University, Hwy 25A, Brookville (11545). Phone 516/299-3100. www.tillescenter.org.* From Michael Feinstein to the New York Philharmonic to the Alvin Ailey American Dance Theater, this center features a variety of music, dance, and theater performers from all walks of life. Well-known performers and lesser-known chamber music concerts and cabaret stars have all appeared at Tilles. The center also hosts local cultural organizations. In addition, it offers a jazz series and folk music festival. It tends to have something for just about every taste year after year. Both young and old will find an event to enjoy at this eclectic concert venue. Prices also vary, and can suit most budgets.

Special Event

Jones Beach Coca-Cola Concert Series. *Tommy Hilfiger at Jones Beach Theater, Ocean Dr, Wantagh (11793). Phone 516/221-1000. www.jonesbeach.com.* Combine an outdoor amphitheater right off the Atlantic Ocean in a beautiful state park, good friends or that special someone, a balmy summer night, and some of the top names in rock 'n roll, blues, and R&B, and you have one great evening at a Jones Beach concert. Performers vary from summer to summer and have included such legends as Rod Stewart, George Benson, the Moody Blues, Tina Turner, and James Taylor. The crowd is usually mellow and easy-going and varies in age, depending upon the performers. Bring a light jacket or sweater, since ocean breezes can create a slight chilleven on the warmest nights. Word of caution: performances are usually rain or shine with no refunds, so if the skies start to open up you may get drenched. But, this is the chance you take at an outdoor venue. It's worth it. June-Sept. **$$$$**

Long Island City

What to See and Do

P. S. 1 Contemporary Art Center. *22-25 Jackson Ave, Long Island City, L.I. (11101). At 46th Ave. Phone 718/784-2084. www.ps1.org.* A premier center for art on the cutting edge; specializes in the avant-garde, conceptual, and experimental; housed in a newly renovated, four-story building that was once a public school; changing exhibits. (Mon, Thurs-Sun; closed holidays) **$$**

Special Event

P. S. 1 Contemporary Arts Center–Warm Up Music Series. *22-25 Jackson Ave, Long Island City (11101) Phone 718/784-2084. www.ps1.org.* This new-wave community arts center in Queens attracts the hippest of DJs and crowds to its Saturday afternoon/evening outdoor dance parties in its courtyard. You won'tsee dance parties like these anywhere else. All ages are welcome. You'll see a variety of social butterflies and some pretty good dancers here. The center is a short subway or cab ride from Manhattan, and you can't beat the priceso join in the fun. July-Aug; Sat evenings. **$$**

Restaurants

★ ★ MANDUCATIS. *13-27 Jackson Ave, Long Island City (11101). Phone 718/729-4602; fax 718/361-0411. www.manducatis.com.* Sure, Manhattan boasts some fairly impressive Italian eateries, but one of the best-hidden treasures is located in Queens. Owned by Vicenzo Cerbone, Manducatis is a family-run operation serving the home-style dishes of Italys best mamas. The terra-cotta room has an earthy, countryside appeal, as does the menu. Expect delicate homemade pastas topped with soft pillows of milky mozzarella. The kitchen also turns out lovely fish and meat dishes and has an extensive wine list that includes many rare wines from small producers. In the winter, grab a seat by the blazing fireplace and you will be transported to the mountains of Tuscany. Italian menu. Lunch, dinner. Closed holidays; also the last two weeks in Aug. Bar. **$$**

★ ★ **TOURNESOL.** *50-12 Vernon Blvd, Long Island City (11109). Phone 718/472-4355. tournesolny.com.* Tournesol is a sunny little French bistro just across the river from Manhattan in Long Island City that could have fallen off any old charming *rue* in Paris. Filled to the gills with trappings of Parisromantic music, a sidewalk caf, bistro tables and chairs, floor-to-ceiling French doors, and vintage tin ceilingsthis cheery local favorite offers up friendly service and a rustic menu of classic French standards like rabbit stew, braised beef cheeks, frise au lardons, and country pt. Tournesol is a sweet little gem of a restaurant that offers all the romance of Paris without the hassle of transcontinental travel. French menu. Lunch, dinner, brunch. Bar. Casual attire. Reservations recommended. Outdoor seating. **$$**

★ ★ **WATER'S EDGE.** *44th Dr at the East River, Long Island City (11101). Phone 718/482-0033; fax 718/937-8817. www.watersedgenyc.com.* On the riverfront opposite the United Nations complex; views of the New York City skyline. American menu. Dinner. Bar. Business casual attire. Reservations recommended. Outdoor seating. Complimentary riverboat transportation to and from Manhattan. **$$$**

Long Lake (C-8)

See also Blue Mountain Lake, Tupper Lake

Population 852
Elevation 1,683 ft
Area Code 518
Zip 12847
Web Site www.longlake-ny.com

Located in the heart of the Adirondack Park, this area is a wilderness setting for water sports, hunting, fishing, cross-country skiing, and snowmobiling.

Limited-Service Hotels

★ **LONG LAKE MOTEL.** *Dock Rd, Long Lake (12847). Phone 518/624-2613; fax 518/624-2576. www.motellonglake.com.* 17 rooms. Closed mid-Oct-mid-May. Check-out 10:30 am; cabins 10 am. **$**

★ **SANDY POINT.** *Hwy 28 and 30, Long Lake (12847). Phone 518/624-3871. www.sandypointmotel.com.* 11 rooms, 2 story. Check-out 10:30 am. **$**

Mahopac (B-2)

See also Brewster, Garrison, Peekskill, Tarrytown, West Point, White Plains

Population 8,478
Elevation 650 ft
Area Code 845
Zip 10541
Web Site www.mahopacchamber.com

What to See and Do

Centennial Golf Club. *185 John Simpson Rd, Carmel (10512). Phone 845/225-5700. www.centennialgolf.com.* Architect Larry Nelson called the ground on which Centennial sits "the most naturally suited to golf I have ever seen." It's one in a growing trend of facilities with three nine-hole tracks, allowing players to choose any combination they like. As with many courses in the area, nonresidents can save money by playing in the twilight, when the course is half to two-thirds cheaper than at peak times. The courses have five tees, the shorter of which have been rated as some of the best around for women. A comprehensive instruction regimen is available from local professionals. (Daily 7 am-8 pm) **$$$$**

Mahopac Farm and Museum. *Hwy 6 and Baldwin Place Rd, Baldwin Place (10505). Phone 845/628-9298.* Collection of antiques and memorabilia dating from 1800s to early 1900s displayed in a barn on a 31-acre working farm. (Daily 10 am-5 pm; closed holidays) **$** Adjacent and included in admission is

> **Old Borden Farm.** Country store, museum, farm animals. (Daily; closed holidays)

Malone (A-8)

Population 14,981
Elevation 722 ft
Information Chamber of Commerce, 170 E Main St; phone 518/483-3760

What to See and Do

Franklin County Historical & Museum Society. *51 Milwaukee St, Malone (12593). Phone 518/483-2750.* Country store, craft rooms; kitchen; exhibits, Victorian parlor. Kilburn Library, genealogical collection. (Tues, Thurs, Fri 1-4 pm, Sat afternoons or by appointment)

Titus Mountain Ski Area. *215 Johnson Rd, Malone (12953). Duane Street Rd, 7 miles S. Phone 518/483-3740; toll-free 800/848-8766. www.titusmountain.com.* Two triple, five double chairlifts; handle tow; school, rentals. Snowmaking. Lodge. Twenty-six trails, longest run 3 1/2 miles, vertical drop 1,350 feet. (Nov-Apr, daily) **$$$$**

Special Event

Franklin County Fair. *Malone Fairgrounds, Raymond and Main sts, Malone. Phone 518/483-0720. www.frcofair.com.* Early-mid-Aug. **$$**

Mamaroneck

Population 28,967
Elevation 50 ft
Area Code 914
Zip 10543

Restaurant

★ TURKISH MEZE. *409 Mount Pleasant Ave, Mamaroneck (10543). Phone 914/777-3042. www.turkishmeze.com.* Mediterranean menu. Lunch, dinner. Bar. Casual attire. **$$**

Manhasset

What to See and Do

Miracle Mile. *Northern Blvd, Manhasset (11030).* This high-end stretch of stores in Nassau County features such names as Talbots, Tiffanys, and Brooks Brothers. Its a pleasant, outdoor area to shopwith ample parking, as well. If you're looking for a fine gift for yourself or a special trinket to bring home to the family, this is the place to go. Bring a couple of extra credit cards and save the bargain hunting for another time.

Restaurant

★ ★ ★ LA COQUILLE. *1669 Northern Blvd, Manhasset (11030). Phone 516/365-8422.* Under the creative direction of Chef Kevin Vincelette, dinner at this restaurant enchants guests with an array of French cuisine. Impeccable service along with delectable homemade desserts make the experience unforgettable. French menu. Dinner. Closed holidays. Reservations recommended. Valet parking. **$$$**

Massapequa Park (A-7)

See also Amityville, Bethpage

Population 17,499
Elevation 20 ft
Area Code 516
Zip 11762

What to See and Do

Tackapausha Museum & Preserve. *Washington Ave and Merrick Rd, Seaford. 4 miles SW on Washington Ave. Phone 516/571-7443.* Museum devoted to living things. Small collection of live animals. An 80-acre tract of glacial outwash plain maintained in natural state; many small mammals. (Tues-Sat, also Sun afternoons; closed holidays) **$**

Massena (A-7)

See also Potsdam

Settled 1792
Population 13,121
Elevation 210 ft
Area Code 315
Zip 13662
Information Chamber of Commerce, 50 Main St; phone 315/769-3525
Web Site www.massena.ny.us

This is the site of the largest power plant on the St. Lawrence Seaway. Massena has two aluminum plants and a major foundry.

As far back as 1903, a canal linking the Grasse River and the St. Lawrence Seaway has provided 90,000 horsepower for Massena-based Alcoa operations.

What to See and Do

Akwesasne Museum. *321 Hwy 37, Hogansburg (13662). Phone 518/358-2461.* Museum is devoted to the evolving cultural heritage of the Akwesasne Mohawk people. Includes clothing, tools, beadwork, display of Mohawk basketry. Gift shop. (Mon-Fri 9 am-4 pm) **$**

Coles Creek State Park. *13003 37 Rte, Waddington (13694). 16 miles W on Hwy 37. Phone 315/388-5636. www.nysparks.state.ny.us.* Beach swimming, fishing (all year), boating (launch, marina, dock), picnicking, playground, concession, tent and trailer sites. (Mid-May-Labor Day 8 am-10 pm)**$$$**

Eisenhower Lock. *Hwy 37 and St. Lawrence River, Massena. E on Hwy 37, then N on Hwy 131, W end of Wiley-Dondero Ship Channel. Phone 315/769-2422.* Visitors view vessels navigating the lock, lock operations, as well as the vehicular tunnel traffic under the lock. Interpretive center with films, photos. Viewing deck. Picnic tables. (May-Columbus Day, daily) **$**

The St. Lawrence Seaway. A joint project of the United States and Canada, this is one of the world's great public works and provides a route for ocean ships from more than 60 countries around the world into mid-America—a "fourth coast." Ships traverse seaway from April to December. Locks can accommodate ships 730 feet long and 76 feet wide. Ocean and lake vessels carry bulk and general cargoes of iron ore, grain, and coal to and from points along the seaway's 8,300-mile shoreline. The seaway was formally dedicated June 26, 1959, by Queen Elizabeth II and President Eisenhower.

Special Events

Folklife Festival. *Robert Moses State Park,19 Robinson Bay Rd, Massena (13662). Phone 315/769-3525.* Demonstrations, music, storytelling; ethnic foods. Second Sat in Aug.

Heritage Festival. *Massena Arena,180 Harte Haven Plz, Massena (13662). Phone 315/769-3525.* Antique and craft show; parade, entertainment, casino. First Sat in June.

Massena Car Show. *Robert Moses State Park,Main St, Massena (13662). Phone 315/769-8663.* Classic and antique car show. Late Aug.

Limited-Service Hotel

★ SUPER 8. *84 Grove St, Massena (13662). Phone 315/764-1065; toll-free 800/800-8000; fax 315/764-9710. www.super8.com.* 42 rooms, 3 story. Check-in 1 pm, check-out 11 am. **$**

Melville

What to See and Do

Crooked Lake Provincial Park. *Located 45 miles S of Yorkton. Phone 306/577-2600. www.saskparks.net.* This small, 481-acre park (195 hectares) is located in the Qu'Appelle Valley. Visitors to this park enjoy its beach, as well as a number of recreational activities, like hiking, fishing, swimming, camping, and picnicking, as well as golf at a nearby 18-hole course. Also here is the 1,000 year-old Moose Bay Burial Mound. **$$**

Middletown (B-1)

See also Barryville, Goshen, Monroe, Monticello, Newburgh, Port Jervis

Population 25,388
Elevation 500 ft
Area Code 845
Zip 10940
Information Orange County Tourism, 30 Matthews St, Suite 111, Goshen 10924; phone 845/291-2136 or toll-free 800/762-8687.
Web Site www.orangetourism.org

Special Event

Orange County Fair. *100 Carpenter Ave, Middletown (10940). Phone 845/291-2136.* Agricultural and industrial exhibits, stock-car races, entertainment. Mid-late July.

Limited-Service Hotel

★ SUPER 8. *563 Hwy 211 E, Middletown (10940). Phone 845/692-5828; fax 845/692-5828. www.super8.com.* 82 rooms, 2 story. Pets accepted; fee. Complimentary continental breakfast. Check-in 3 pm, check-out 11 am. **$**

Restaurant

★ CASA MIA. *Rte 211 E, Middletown (10940). Phone 845/692-2323.* Italian, American menu. Dinner. Closed Mon; Thanksgiving, Dec 24-25. Bar. Children's menu. **$$**

Millbrook

Restaurants

★ ★ ALLYN'S. *4258 Hwy 44, Millbrook (12545). Phone 845/677-5888; fax 845/677-3597. www.allyns.com.* Renovated church (1790); hunt motif; fireplaces. American menu. Lunch, dinner, Sun brunch. Closed Tues; Dec 25. Bar. Children's menu. Outdoor seating. **$$**

★ ★ **CAFE LES BAUX.** *152 Church St, Millbrook. Phone 845/677-8166.* French menu. Lunch, dinner, brunch. Closed Tues; holidays. Casual attire. Reservations recommended. **$$**

★ **MILLBROOK CAFE.** *Franklin Ave, Millbrook. Phone 845/677-6956.* American menu. Lunch, dinner. Closed Mon, children's menu. Casual attire. Reservations recommended. **$$$**

★ ★ **TINHORN.** *Franklin Ave, Millbrook. Phone 845/677-5600.* American menu. Lunch, dinner. Closed holidays. Bar. Business casual attire. Reservations recommended. Outdoor seating. **$$**

Mineola

Restaurant

★ ★ **CHURRASQUEIRA BAIRRADA.** *144 Jericho Tpke, Mineola (11501). Phone 516/739-3856; fax 516/739-1741. www.churrasqueira.com.* Portugese steak menu. Lunch, dinner. Closed Mon. Bar. **$$**

Monroe

See also Goshen, Middletown, Newburgh, Stony Point, West Point

Population 31,407
Elevation 679 ft
Area Code 845
Zip 10950

What to See and Do

The Golf Club at Mansion Ridge *1292 Orange Tpike, Monroe (10950). Phone 845/782-7888. www.mansionridge.com.* The first golf course in New York to be designed by Jack Nicklaus, Mansion Ridge is also the only Nicklaus course in the state that is open to the public. The course has hosted PGA pro-am tournaments as well as qualifying rounds for the tours Buick Invitational. Built on the estate of M. C. Migel, the founder of the American Foundation for the Blind, the course plays almost 6,900 yards long and also includes the Checkerboard Inn, whose construction dates to about 1730. The course is very near to West Point (see also). **$$$$**

Museum Village. *1010 Hwy 17M, Monroe (10950). Museum Village Rd, W on Hwy 17M; Hwy 6, Hwy 17 exit 129. Phone 845/782-8247.* Outdoor living history museum of over 25 buildings depicting the crafts and technology of 19th-century America. Exhibit/demonstration buildings include print shop, log cabin, drug store, general store, schoolhouse. Also view a broom maker, candle maker, blacksmith, and weaver at work. Farm animals are found here as well as historical gardens. Shops, food service, picnic area. (May-Nov, Tues-Sun; closed Thanksgiving) **$$$**

Montauk (B-5)

See also Amagansett, East Hampton

Population 3,851
Elevation 18 ft
Information Chamber of Commerce, PO Box 5029; phone 631/668-2428
Web Site www.montaukchamber.com

This is a lively fishing town on Long Island, with a big business in deep-sea fishing (tuna, shark, marlin, striped bass, and other varieties). Boats can be rented, and there are miles of uncrowded sandy beaches to enjoy.

What to See and Do

Hither Hills State Park. *Old Montauk Hwy, Montauk (11954). 3 miles W on Hwy 27. Phone 631/668-2554. www.reserveamerica.com.* Swimming beach, bathhouse, lifeguards, fishing; nature and hiking trails, picnicking, playground, concession, tent and trailer sites (mid-Apr-Nov; reservations required). Standard fees.

Montauk Lighthouse. *Montauk Point, Montauk (11954). Phone 631/668-2544. www.montauklighthouse.com.* Well, you've come as far east as you can on Long Island. Go any farther and you can start swimming toward England. In fact, Montauk Point is called "The End" by locals. What better way to end your tour of Long Island than with a trip to this historic, magnificent lighthouse that was commissioned by George Washington and completed in 1796? It is the oldest lighthouse in the state, featuring 137 winding narrow steps to the top and offering breathtaking views of the ocean from any angleeven if you're not into climbing. The lighthouse beacon still rotates and can be seen for 19 nautical miles. There also are several memorials on site, including one dedicated to fishermen lost at sea. This is an interesting attraction to see on a sunny day or a cloudy day (clouds and rain actually add to the atmosphere). (Mid-May-Oct from 10:30 am; closing times vary) **$**

Montauk Point State Park. *Old Montauk Hwy, Montauk (11954). 6 miles E on Hwy 27; easternmost tip of Long Island. Phone 631/668-2554.* Barren moor with sea view. Montauk Lighthouse, built 1795; museum, tours (summer weekends; fee). Fishing; hiking, biking, picnicking, concession. Standard fees.

Montauk Seal Watching. *Phone 631/668-3781.* This is one of the few attractions on the South Fork that takes place only in winter. Put on your warmest coat, hat, and boots and take part in a two- to three-hour guided beach walk with an expert to watch the seals in action. Check ahead to see what times the tours are being given on any specific day, which is also weather-dependent. If you are a nature or animal lover, this is a wonderful, different kind of experience unlike anything else on Long Island. Adults and children alike will enjoy this—it's something for the whole family. Don't forget to bring the camera and binoculars. (Jan-Mar, weekends) **$**

Full-Service Hotel

★ ★ ★ GURNEY'S INN RESORT AND SPA. *290 Old Montauk Hwy, Montauk (11954). Phone 631/668-2345; toll-free 800/445-8062; fax 631/668-3576. www.gurneys-inn. com.* 109 rooms, 4 story, all suites. Check-in 3:30 pm, check-out 11:30 am. Three restaurants, bar. Fitness room, fitness classes available, spa. Beach. Indoor pool, whirlpool. **$$$**

Full-Service Resort

★ ★ ★ MONTAUK YACHT CLUB. *32 Star Island Rd, Montauk (11954). Phone 631/668-3100; toll-free 800/692-8668; fax 631/668-3303. www.montaukyacht-club.com.* This property is tucked along Long Island's South Fork East End. The 60-foot lighthouse replica, built in 1928, is still a focal point, and there are abundant recreational facilities. 107 rooms, 2 story. Closed Dec-Mar. Check-in 4 pm, check-out 11 am. Two restaurants, two bars. Children's activity center. Fitness room. Beach. Indoor pool, two outdoor pools. Tennis. **$$**

Specialty Lodging

BURCLIFFE BY THE SEA. *397 Old Montauk Hwy, Montauk (11954). Phone 631/668-2880; fax 631/668-3129.* 7 rooms. Closed Dec-mid-Jan. Pets accepted, some restrictions; fee. Check-in 3 pm, check-out 10 am. **$$**

Restaurants

★ ★ CROW'S NEST. *4 Old West Lake Dr, Montauk (11954). Phone 631/668-2077. www.crowsnestrest.com.* American menu. Lunch, dinner. Bar. Children's menu. Casual attire. **$$**

★ ★ DAVE'S GRILL. *468 W Lake Dr, Montauk (11954). Phone 631/668-9190. www.davesgrill.com.* Seafood menu. Dinner. Closed Wed; also Nov-Apr. Bar. Casual attire. Outdoor seating. **$$**

★ ★ GOSMAN'S RESTAURANT. *500 W Lake Dr, Montauk (11954). Phone 631/668-5330. www.gosmans.com.* Seafood menu. Lunch, dinner. Closed mid-Oct-mid-Apr. Bar. Children's menu. Casual attire. Outdoor seating.**$$**

★ ★ HARVEST. *11 S Emory St, Montauk (11954). Phone 631/668-5574. www.harvest2000.com.* Mediterranean menu. Dinner. Closed Feb; also Thanksgiving, Dec 25. Bar. Business casual attire. Outdoor seating. Bacci courts. **$$$**

★ MONTAUKET. *88 Firestone Rd, Montauk (11954). Phone 631/668-5992.* American menu. Lunch, dinner. Bar. Children's menu. Casual attire. Outdoor seating. **$$**

★ ★ OYSTER POND. *4 South Elmwood Ave, Montauk (11954). Phone 631/668-4200. www.montaukonline.net/oysterpond.* American menu. Lunch, dinner. Closed Tues. Bar. **$$**

★ SHAGWONG RESTAURANT. *774 Montauk Hwy, Montauk (11954). Phone 631/668-3050. www.shagwong.com.* Photographs of Old Montauk and celebrity guests along the wall and an original tin ceiling (1927). American menu. Lunch, dinner, late-night. Bar. Children's menu. Casual attire. Outdoor seating. **$$**

Monticello (A-1)

See also Barryville, Liberty, Middletown

Population 6,512
Elevation 1,520 ft
Area Code 845
Zip 12701
Information Sullivan County Visitors Association, Inc, 100 North St; phone 845/794-3000 or toll-free 800/882-2287
Web Site www.scva.net

As the center of the Sullivan County Catskills resort region, Monticello offers visitors a wide selection of activities: summer theaters, children's camps, summer cottages, fishing, hunting, swimming, canoeing, skiing, tennis, golf, or just basking in the sun. Nearby lakes offer many water sports.

What to See and Do

Holiday Mountain Ski Area. *3 miles E off Hwy 17 exit 107 at 99 Holiday Mtn Rd. Phone 845/796-3161. www.holidaymtn.com.* Triple, two double chairlifts; Pomalift, two rope tows; patrol, school, rentals; snowmaking; cafeteria, bar, ski shop. Longest run 3,500 feet; vertical drop 400 feet. Night skiing. (Dec-Mar, daily) **$$$$**

Woodstock Music Festival Monument. *W on Hwy 17B to Hurd Rd.* Monument to the 1969 music festival, which was held here on Yasgur's farm.

Mount Kisco (B-2)

See also Brewster, New York, Peekskill, Pound Ridge, White Plains

Population 9,983
Elevation 289 ft
Area Code 914
Zip 10549
Information Chamber of Commerce, 3 N Moger Ave; phone 914/666-7525
Web Site www.mtkisco.com

What to See and Do

Caramoor Center for Music and the Arts. *149 Girdle Ridge Rd, Mount Kisco (10536). 5 miles NE via Saw Mill River Pkwy to Katonah-Cross River exit 6, then 1/2 mile E on Hwy 35, right onto Hwy 22 to junction with Girdle Ridge Rd; follow signs. Phone 914/232-5035. www.caramoor.org.* European-style villa built during 1930s. Collections of Chinese art, Italian Renaissance furniture; European paintings, sculptures, and tapestries dating from the Middle Ages through the 19th century; formal gardens. Tours (June-mid-Nov: Thurs, Sat, and Sun afternoons, also Wed, Fri by appointment; rest of year: by appointment). Also Summer Music Festival (late June-mid-Aug). **$**

John Jay Homestead State Historic Site. *400 J St, Katonah (10536). Phone 914/232-5651. nysparks.state.ny.us.* Estate of the first chief justice of the United States and four generations of his descendants; period furnishings, American portrait collection, gardens, farm buildings and grounds. Visits by guided tour only. (Early-Apr-Nov, Tues-Sat 10 am-4 pm, Sun from noon) **$$**

Limited-Service Hotel

★ ★ **HOLIDAY INN.** *1 Holiday Inn Dr, Mount Kisco (10549). Phone 914/241-2600; toll-free 888/452-5771; fax 914/241-4742. www.holiday-inn. com.* 122 rooms, 2 story. Pets accepted, some restrictions; fee. Check-in 3 pm, check-out 11 am. High-speed Internet access. Restaurant, bar. Fitness center. Outdoor pool. Business center. **$**

Restaurants

★ ★ **BISTRO 22.** *391 Old Post Rd (Rte 22), Bedford Village (10506). Phone 914/234-7333; fax 914/764-0239.* American, French menu. Lunch, dinner. Bar. Business casual attire. Reservations recommended. **$$$**

★ ★ ★ **CRABTREE'S KITTLE HOUSE.** *11 Kittle Rd, Chappaqua (10514). Phone 914/666-8044; fax 914/666-2684. www.kittlehouse.com.* Special services and private rooms are available for groups of up to 220 guests at this casual yet elegant restaurant. Lunch, dinner, Sun brunch. Closed Dec 25. Bar. Children's menu. Valet parking. **$$$**

★ ★ ★ **LA CAMELIA.** *234 N Bedford Rd, Mount Kisco (10549). Phone 914/666-2466; fax 914/666-0283.* This Spanish gem is located high upon a hilltop and is the perfect spot for a romantic dinner date. Share the tapas and enjoy one of the interesting Spanish selections on the wine list. Spanish menu. Lunch, dinner, Sun brunch. Closed Mon; Jan 1, Thanksgiving, Dec 25. Bar. Casual attire. Reservations recommended. Outdoor seating. **$$**

★ ★ ★ **TRAVELER'S REST.** *Hwy 100, Ossining (10562). Phone 914/941-7744; fax 914/941-6434. www.thetravelersrest.com.* Serving German-American food since the 1800s, this restaurant has stood the test of time. Enjoy seafood, beef, and poultry specialties in an old-world setting, one that has been under Langner family ownership for more than 35 years. American, German menu. Dinner. Closed Mon-Tues; Dec 24. Bar. Children's menu. **$$$**

Mount Tremper

See also Woodstock

Limited-Service Hotel

★ ★ KATE'S LAZY MEADOW MOTEL. *5191 Hwy 28, Mt. Tremper (12457). Phone 845/688-7200. www.lazymeadow.com.* 7 rooms, all suites. Check-in open, check-out open. High-speed Internet access. Whirlpool. **$$**

Restaurant

★ ★ ★ CATAMOUNT CAFE. *5368 Hwy 28, Mount Tremper (12457). Phone 845/688-2828; fax 845/688-5191.* American menu. Dinner. Closed Dec 25. Bar. Children's menu. Casual attire. Outdoor seating. **$$**

Naples (E-4)

See also Canandaigua, Penn Yan

Population 2,441
Elevation 800 ft
Area Code 585
Zip 14512
Web Site www.naplesvalleyny.com

At the south end of Canandaigua Lake, one of the Finger Lakes, Naples is the center of a grape growing, winemaking area. Many of its residents are descendants of Swiss and German winemakers.

What to See and Do

Cumming Nature Center of the Rochester Museum & Science Center. *6472 Gulick Rd, Naples (14512). Phone 585/374-6160. www.rmsc.org.* A 900-acre living museum; nature trails, natural history programs; conservation trail with operating sawmill; cross-country skiing (rentals) and snowshoeing. Visitors building with theater and exhibit hall. (Late Dec-mid-Nov, Wed-Sun) **$$**

Widmer's Wine Cellars. *1 Lake Niagara Ln, Naples (14572). Phone 585/374-6311.*Tours, wine tastings (Daily, afternoons). **$**

Specialty Lodging

THE VAGABOND INN. *3300 Sliter Hill Rd, Naples (14512). Phone 585/554-6271. www.thevagabondinn.com.* Secluded in the Bristol Mountains in the picturesque Finger Lakes region, this inn is a quiet hideaway. Travel to nearby wineries, ski areas, or the Finger Lakes Performing Arts Center.5 rooms. Children over 13 years only. Complimentary full breakfast. Check-in 2:30 pm, check-out 11:30 am. Outdoor pool, whirlpool. **$**

Restaurants

★ ★ BOB & RUTH'S VINEYARD. *204 Main St, Naples (14512). Phone 585/374-5122; fax 585/374-6011.* American menu. Breakfast, lunch, dinner. Closed Nov-Mar. Bar. Children's menu. Outdoor seating. **$$**

★ ★ NAPLES HOTEL. *111 S Main St, Naples (14512). Phone 585/374-5630. www.thenapleshotel.com.* Built in 1895; antiques. German menu. Lunch, dinner. Bar. Children's menu. **$$**

★ ★ REDWOOD. *6 Cohocton St, Naples (14512). Phone 585/374-6360.* Seafood, steak menu. Breakfast, lunch, dinner. Closed Dec 24-25. Bar. Children's menu. **$$**

New Paltz (F-9)

See also Ellenville, Hyde Park, Kingston, Newburgh, Poughkeepsie

Founded 1678
Population 12,830
Elevation 196 ft
Area Code 845
Zip 12561
Information Chamber of Commerce, 124 Main St; phone 845/255-0243 or toll-free 845/255-0411
Web Site www.newpaltzchamber.org

New Paltz was founded by a dozen Huguenots who were granted land by the colonial governor of New York. The town is surrounded by the fertile farmlands of the Wallkill River Valley, with apple orchards and vineyards.

What to See and Do

Huguenot Street Old Stone Houses. *Visitor center at DuBois Fort on Hugnenot. Phone 845/255-1660.* Six original stone dwellings (1692-1712), a reconstructed French church (1717); Jean Hasbrouck House (1694) of medieval Flemish stone architecture. All houses furnished with heirlooms of descendants. (May-Oct, Fri-Sun)

Locust Lawn. *400 Hwy 32 S, New Paltz (12561). 4 miles S on Hwy 32. Phone 845/255-1660.* Federal mansion of Josiah Hasbrouck (1814). Includes smokehouse, farmers' museum; Terwilliger Homestead (1738); bird sanctuary. (By appointment)

State University of New York College at New Paltz. *Hwy 32 S, New Paltz. On Hwy 32 S, 1 mile W of NY State Thrwy exit 18. Phone 845/257-2121.* (1828) (8,129 students) Art gallery (usually Mon-Fri, Sun); concerts, plays. Language immersion program in 15 languages (summers and weekends); Music in the Mountains, contemporary music series (summer); Repertory Theatre (see SPECIAL EVENTS). Campus tours by appointment.

Special Events

Apple Festival/Crafts Fair. *Huguenot St, New Paltz. Phone 845/255-6340.* Second Sat in Oct.

Stone House Day. *Hwy 32 N and Broadhead Ave, New Paltz. Approximately 1/2 mile NW on Hwy 28, then 2 miles S on Hwy 209 in Hurley. Phone 845/331-4121.* Tour of eight privately owned colonial stone houses, led by costumed guides; Hurley Reformed Church and old burial ground; antique show; re-creation of Revolutionary War military encampment; country fair. Second Sat in July.

SUNY College Summer Repertory Theatre. *State University of New York College at New Paltz, 1 Hawk Dr Plattekill Ave and Rte 208, New Paltz (12401). Phone 845/257-3872.* June-Aug.

Ulster County Fair. *Fairgrounds, 249 Libertyville Rd, New Paltz (12561). Fairgrounds, 2 miles SW on Libertyville Rd. Phone 845/255-1380.* Contact Ulster County Public Information Office, Box 1800, Kingston 12401. First week in Aug.

White Water Derby. *421 Old Military Rd, New Paltz (12946). Hudson River. Phone 518/251-2612.* Canoe and kayak competition. First weekend in May.

Full-Service Resort

★ ★ ROCKING HORSE RANCH RESORT. *600 Rte 44-55, Highland (12528). Phone 845/691-2927; toll-free 800/647-2624; fax 845/691-6434. www.rhranch.com.* 120 rooms, 2 story. Check-in 3 pm, check-out noon. Bar. Children's activity center. Fitness room, spa. Indoor pool, two outdoor pools, children's pool, whirlpool. Tennis. **$$**

Restaurants

★ ★ ★ DEPUY CANAL HOUSE. *Hwy 213, High Falls (12440). Phone 845/687-7700. www.depuycanalhouse.net.* American menu. Dinner, brunch. Closed Mon-Wed. Bar. Business casual attire. Reservations recommended. Outdoor seating. **$$$**

★ MAIN STREET BISTRO. *59 Main St, New Paltz (12561). Phone 845/255-7766. www.mainstreetbistro.com.* American, Vegetarian menu. Lunch, dinner, brunch. Closed holidays. Casual attire. Outdoor seating. **$$**

★ ★ ROSENDALE CAFE. *434 Main St, Rosendale (12472). Phone 845/658-9048. www.rosendalecafe.com.* Vegetarian menu. Lunch, dinner. Casual attire. Reservations recommended. Outdoor seating. **$$**

★ YANNI. *51 Main St, New Paltz (12561). Phone 845/256-0988. www.yannirestaurant.com.* Greek/Mediterranean menu. Lunch, dinner. Casual attire. Reservations recommended. Outdoor seating. **$$**

New Rochelle (C-2)

See also Mamaroneck, New York, White Plains

Population 72,182
Elevation 100 ft
Area Code 914
Information Chamber of Commerce, 459 Main St, 10801; phone 914/632-5700
Web Site www.newrochelleny.com

New Rochelle was founded in 1688 by a group of Huguenot families. Prior to the Europeans who settled here, the area was home to the Siwanoys, a part of the Mohegans stemming from the Algonquins. Boat building was the trade of many of the early settlers, who used these boats to carry goods to and from New York City and other towns and ports on the coast.

Restaurant

★ COYOTE FLACO. *273 North Ave, New Rochelle (10801). Phone 914/636-7222.* Mexican menu. Lunch, dinner. Closed Mon. Bar. Casual attire. Outdoor seating. **$$**

New York

See also Bronx, Brooklyn, Floral Park, Garden City, Great Neck, Hempstead, Mamaroneck, Mount Kisco, New Rochelle, Oyster Bay, Queens, Rockville Centre, Staten Island, Tarrytown, Westbury, White Plains

Settled 1615
Population 8,008,278
Elevation 410 ft
Area Code 212, 646, 917
Information New York City Convention & Visitors Bureau, 810 Seventh Ave, New York, NY 10019; phone 212/484-1200
Web Site www.nycvisit.com

New York is the nation's most populous city, the capital of finance, business, communications, theater, and much more. It may not be the center of the universe, but it does occupy a central place in the world's imagination. Certainly, in one way or another, New York affects the lives of nearly every American. While other cities have everything that New York hasfrom symphonies to slumsno other city has quite the style or sheer abundance. Nowhere are things done in such a grandly American way as in New York City.

Giovanni da Verrazano was the first European to glimpse Manhattan Island (1524), but the area was not explored until 1609, when Henry Hudson sailed up the river that was later named for him, searching for a passage to India. Adriaen Block arrived here in 1613, and the first trading post was established by the Dutch West India Company two years later. Peter Minuit is said to have bought the island from Native Americans for $24 worth of beads and trinkets in 1626, when New Amsterdam was foundedthe biggest real estate bargain in history.

In 1664, the Dutch surrendered to a British fleet and the town was renamed New York in honor of the Duke of York. One of the earliest tests of independence occurred here in 1734 when John Peter Zenger, publisher and editor of the *New York Weekly Journal*, was charged with seditious libel and jailed for making anti-government remarks. Following the Battle of Long Island in 1776, the British occupied the city through the Revolution, until 1783.

On the balcony of Federal Hall at Wall Street, April 30, 1789, George Washington was inaugurated as the first president of the United States, and for a time New York was the country's capital.

When the Erie Canal opened in 1825, New York City expanded vastly as a port. It has since consistently maintained its leadership. In 1898, Manhattan merged with Brooklyn, the Bronx, Queens, and Staten Island. In the next half-century several million immigrants entered the United States here, providing the city with the supply of labor needed for its growth into a major focal point. Each wave of immigrants has brought new customs, culture, and life, which makes New York City the varied metropolis it is today.

New York Fun Facts

- Gennaro Lombardi opened the first pizzeria in the country in New York City in 1895.
- Babe Ruth hit his first home run in Yankee Stadium in the first game ever played there.
- The New York Stock Exchange began in 1792 when 24 brokers met under a buttonwood tree facing 68 Wall Street.
- As late as the 1840s, thousands of pigs roamed Wall Street to consume garbage—an early sanitation system.
- Macy's, the world's largest store, covers 2.1 million square feet of space and stocks over 500,000 different items.
- The nation's largest public Halloween parade is the Greenwich Village Halloween Parade.
- There are 6,374.6 miles of streets in New York City.

New York continues to capitalize on its image as the Big Apple, attracting more than 39 million visitors each year, and its major attractions continue to thrive in style. These, of course, are centered in Manhattan; however, vacationers should not overlook the wealth of sights and activities the other boroughs have to offer. Brooklyn has Coney Island, the New York Aquarium, the superb Brooklyn History Museum, Brooklyn Botanic Garden, Brooklyn Children's Museum, and the famous landmark, Brooklyn Bridge. The Bronx is noted for its excellent Botanical Garden and Zoo and Yankee Stadium. Flushing Meadows-Corona Park, in Queens, was the site of two World's Fairs; nearby is Shea Stadium, home of the New York Mets. Uncrowded Staten Island has Richmond Town Restoration, a re-creation of 18th-century New York, rural farmland, beaches, salt marshes, and wildlife preserves.

Weather

The average mean temperatures for New York are 34° F in winter; 52° F in spring; 75° F in summer; and 58° F in fall. In summer the temperature is rarely above 90° F, but the humidity can be high. In winter the temperature is rarely lower than 10° F but has gone as low as –14° F. Average mean temperatures are listed from surveys taken at the National Weather Bureau station in Central Park.

Theater

New York is the theatrical headquarters of the United States, and theater here is an experience not to be missed. Broadway, a 36-square-block area (41st to 53rd streets and 6th to 9th avenues), offers standard full-scale plays and musicals, more than 30 of them on any particular evening. Off-Broadway, not confined to one area, is less expensive and more experimental, giving new talent a chance at exposure and established talent an opportunity to try new and different projects, such as the New York Shakespeare Festival (see SEASONAL EVENTS). Even less expensive and more daring is off-off-Broadway, consisting of dozens of small theaters in storefronts, lofts, and cellars, producing every imaginable type of theater.

There are a number of ways to obtain tickets, ranging from taking a pre-arranged package theater tour to walking up to the box office an hour before curtain for returned and unclaimed tickets. TicketMaster outlets (phone 212/307-7171), hotel theater desks, and ticket brokers will have tickets to several shows for the box office price plus a service charge. All Broadway theaters accept phone reservations charged to major credit cards. An On Stage Hotline can be reached at 212/768-1818.

The Times Square Ticket Center (a booth with large banners proclaiming "TKTS") at 47th St & Broadway has same-day tickets at half-price for most shows (daily) and for matinees (Wed, Sat-Sun). There is also a downtown branch located at the South Street Seaport, open Mon-Sat, for same-day evening performances only. Same-day half-price tickets to music and dance events may be obtained at the Music & Dance Booth, at 42nd St & Avenue of the Americas

Neighborhoods

Chinatown

The only truly ethnic neighborhood still thriving in Manhattan, Chinatown is filled with teeming streets, jostling crowds, bustling restaurants, exotic markets, and prosperous shops. Once limited to a small enclave contained in the six blocks between the Bowery and Mulberry, Canal and Worth streets (now known as "traditional Chinatown"), it has burst these boundaries in recent years to spread north of Canal Street into Little Italy and east into the Lower East Side.

Chinatown is the perfect neighborhood for haphazard wandering. In traditional Chinatown, especially, every twist or turn of the small, winding streets brings mounds of shiny fish—live carp, eels, and crabs—piles of fresh produce—cabbage, ginger root, Chinese broccoli—or displays of pretty, colorful objects—toys, handbags, knickknacks. Bakeries selling everything from moon cakes and almond cookies to "cow ears" (chips of fried dough) and pork buns are everywhere, along with the justifiably famous Chinatown Ice Cream Factory (65 Bayard St, near Mott), selling every flavor of ice cream from ginger to mango.

Chinese men, accompanied by only a handful of women, began arriving in New York in the late 1870s. Many were former transcontinental railroad workers who came to escape the persecution they were experiencing on the West Coast. But they weren't especially welcomed on the East Coast either, and soon thereafter, the violent "tong wars" between criminal Chinese gangs helped lead to the Exclusion Acts of 1882, 1888, 1902, and 1924, forbidding further Chinese immigration. Chinatown became a "bachelor society," almost devoid of women and children—a situation that continued until the lifting of immigration quotas in 1965.

Today, Chinatown's estimated population of 100,000 is made up of two especially large groups—the well-established Cantonese community, who have been in New York for over a century, and the Fujianese community, a much newer and poorer immigration group who come from the Fujian Province on the southern coast of mainland China. The Cantonese own many of the prosperous shops and restaurants in traditional Chinatown, whereas the Fujianese have set up rice-noodle shops, herbal medicine shops, and outdoor markets along Broadway and neighboring streets between Canal Street and the Manhattan Bridge.

To learn more about the history of Chinatown, visit the Museum of Chinese in the Americas (70 Mulberry St, at Bayard). To get a good meal, explore almost any street, with Mott Street—the neighborhoods main thoroughfare—holding an especially large number. Pell Street is especially known for its barber and beauty shops and for its Buddhist Temple (4 Pell St). The neighborhoods biggest festival is the Chinese New Year, celebrated between mid-January and early February; then, the streets come even more alive than usual with dragon dances, lion dances, and fireworks.

TriBeCa

Short for *Tri*angle *Be*low *Ca*nal, **TriBeCa** is a former industrial district encompassing about 40 blocks between Canal, Chambers, and West streets, and Broadway. Like SoHo, its more fashionable cousin to the north, the neighborhood discarded its working-class roots years ago and now has its share of expensive restaurants and boutiques. Upper-middle-class residents have replaced factory workers, and avant-garde establishments have replaced sweatshops.

Nonetheless, TriBeCa is much quieter than SoHo—and many other sections of Manhattanand, in parts, still retains its 19th-century feel, complete with cobblestone streets and dusty façades. After dark, especially, much of the area seems close to deserted.

TriBeCa's main thoroughfares are Broadway, West Broadway, and Church Street, three wide roads comfortable for strolling. West Broadway was originally built to relieve the congestion of Broadway and is home to a few art galleries, including the SoHo Photo Gallery (15 White St at W Broadway), a cooperative gallery featuring the work of 100-plus members. At Church and Walker streets reigns the sleek new TriBeCa Grand, the neighborhoods first upscale hotel.

Also well known is the TriBeCa Film Center, housed in the landmark Martinson Coffee Company warehouse (375 Greenwich St at Franklin St). The center was started in 1989 by actor Robert De Niro, who wanted to create a site where filmmakers could talk business, screen films, and socialize. Today, the center houses the offices of several major producers and the TriBeCa Grill, a chic eatery usually filled with more celebrity-watchers than celebrities. At Greenwich and Harrison streets stand the Harrison Houses, a group of nine restored Federal-style homes. Several were designed by John McComb, Jr., New York's first architect. East of the houses, at the northwest corner of Harrison and Hudson streets, find the former New York Mercantile Exchange. In this five-story building, complete with gables and a tower, $15,000 worth of eggs would change hands in an hour around the turn of the century. Today, TriBeCa is still the city's distribution center for eggs, cheese, and butter; a few remaining wholesalers cluster around Duane Park, one block south of the former exchange, between Hudson and Greenwich streets.

At the southern end of TriBeCa is Chambers Street, where you'll find the Borough of Manhattan Community College (199 Chambers St, near West St). At the western end of Chambers, cross over West Street via the TriBeCa Bridge to reach a public recreation center called Pier 25.

SoHo

Short for *So*uth of *Ho*uston (HOW-stun), SoHo is New Yorks trendiest neighborhood, filled with an impossible number of upscale eateries, fancy boutiques, of-the-moment bars, and, most recently, a few astronomically expensive hotels. Contained in just 25 blocks bounded by Houston and Canal streets, Lafayette, and West Broadway, SoHo attracts trend followers and tourists by the thousands, especially on weekend afternoons, when the place sometimes feels like one giant open-air bazaar.

From the late 1800s to the mid-1900s, SoHo was primarily a light manufacturing district, but starting in the 1960s, most of the factories moved out and artists—attracted by the areas low rents and loft spaces—began moving in. Soon thereafter, the art galleries arrived, and then the shops and restaurants. Almost overnight, SoHo became too expensive for the artistsand, more recently, the art galleries—who had originally settled the place, and a mecca for big-bucks shoppers from all over the world.

Nonetheless, SoHo still has plenty to offer art lovers. Broadway is lined with one first-rate museum after another, while Mercer and Greene streets, especially, boast a large number of galleries. Some top spots on Broadway include the Museum for African Art (593 Broadway), presenting an excellent array of changing exhibits and the New Museum for Contemporary Art (583 Broadway), one of the oldest, best-known, and most controversial art spaces in SoHo. To find out whos exhibiting what and where in SoHo, pick up a copy of the *Art Now Gallery Guide*, available at many bookstores and galleries.

SoHo is also home to an extraordinary number of luscious cast-iron buildings. Originally meant to serve as a cheap substitute for stone buildings, the cast-iron facades were an American invention, prefabricated in a variety of styles—from Italian Renaissance to Classical Greek—and bolted onto the front of iron-frame structures. Most of SoHos best cast-iron gems can be found along Broadway; keep an eye out for the Haughwout Building (488 Broadway), the Singer Building (561 Broadway), and the Guggenheim Museum SoHo (575 Broadway).

Top thoroughfares for shopping include Prince and Spring streets, Broadway, and West Broadway. Numerous clothing and accessory boutiques are located along all these streets; West Broadway also offers several interesting bookstores. For antiques and furnishings, check out Lafayette Street; for craft and toy stores, try Greene and Mercer streets.

Restaurants and bars line almost every street in SoHo, but one especially lively nexus is the intersection of Grand Street and West Broadway. West Broadway itself is also home to a large number of eateries, some of which offer outdoor dining in the summer.

East Village

Once considered part of the Lower East Side, the East Village is considerably scruffier and more rambunctious than its better-known sister to the West. For years, it was the refuge of immigrants and the working class, but in the 1950s, struggling writers, actors, and artists—forced out of Greenwich Village by rising rents—began moving in. First came such well-known names as Willem de Kooning and W. H. Auden, followed by the beatniks, the hippies, the yippies, the rock groups, the punk musicians, and the fashion designers.

Only in the 1980s did the neighborhood start to gentrify, as young professionals moved in, bringing with them upscale restaurants and smart shops. Ever since, New York's continuously rising rents have forced out many of the younger, poorer, and more creative types that the East Village was known for just two decades ago. Nonetheless, the neighborhood has not completely succumbed and offers an interesting mix between the cutting edge and the mainstream.

The heart of the East Village is St. Mark's Place, an always-thronging thoroughfare where you'll find everything from punked-out musicians to well-heeled business types, leather shops to sleek bistros. Many of the street's noisiest addresses are between Third and Second avenues; many of its most appealing, farther east. At the eastern end of St. Mark's Place stretches Tompkins Square Park, once known for its drug dealers, now for its families and jungle gyms. Some of the best of the many interesting little shops that fill the East Village can be found on Avenue A near the park; others line Seventh and Ninth streets east of Second Avenue.

The neighborhood's second major thoroughfare, Second Avenue, was home to many lively Yiddish theaters early in the 20th century. All are gone now, but the landmark Second Avenue Deli (at 10th St)—known for its over-stuffed sandwiches—commemorates the streets past with stars in the sidewalk. At Second Avenue and East Tenth Street is St.-Mark's-in-the-Bowery, an historic church where Peter Stuyvesant—the last of the Dutch governors who ruled Manhattan in the 1600s—is buried. The church is also known for its poetry readings, performance art, and leftist politics.

On the western edge of the East Village sprawls Astor Place, home to Cooper Union—the city's first free educational institution, now a design school—and a huge cube sculpture oddly balanced on one corner. On Lafayette Street at the southern end of Astor Place reigns the Joseph Papp Public Theater, housed in an imposing columned building that was once the Astor Library. The theater is renowned for its first-run productions and for Shakespeare in the Park, a free festival that it produces every summer in Central Park.

Greenwich Village

Although New York's fabled bohemian neighborhood has gone seriously upscale and more mainstream in recent decades, evidence of its iconoclastic past can still be found in its many narrow streets, off-Broadway theaters, cozy coffee shops, lively jazz clubs, and tiny bars. Stretching from 14th Street south to Houston Street, and from Broadway west to the Hudson River, Greenwich Village remains one of the city's best places for idle wandering, people watching, boutique browsing, and conversing over glasses of cabernet or cups of cappuccino.

Washington Square Park anchors the neighborhood to the east and, though it's nothing special to look at, is still the heart of the Village. On a sunny afternoon, everyone comes here: kids hot-dogging on skateboards, students strumming guitars, old men playing chess, and lovers entwined in each other's arms. Bordering the edges of the park are a mix of elegant townhouses and New York University buildings.

Just south and west of Washington Square, find Bleecker and MacDougal streets, home to coffee shops and bars once frequented by the likes of James Baldwin, Jack Kerouac, Allen Ginsberg, and James Agee. Le Figaro (corner of Bleecker and MacDougal) and the San Remo (93 MacDougal) were favorites back then and still attract crowds today, albeit mostly made up of tourists.

A bit farther west is Seventh Avenue South, where you'll find the Village Vanguard (178 Seventh Ave S, at 11th St)—the oldest and most venerable jazz club in the city. Also nearby are the Blue Note (131 West 3rd St, near 6th Ave), New York's premier jazz supper club, and Smalls (183 West 10th St near 7th Ave S), one of the best places to catch up-and-coming talent.

At the corner of Seventh Avenue South and Christopher Street stands Christopher Park, where a George Segal sculpture of two gay couples commemorates the Stonewall Riots, which marked the advent of the gay-rights movement. The Stonewall Inn, where the demonstration began in 1969, once stood directly across from the park at 51 Christopher, and Christopher Street itself is still lined with many gay establishments.

At the corner of Sixth Avenue and West 10th Street reigns the gothic towers and turrets of Jefferson Market Library, a stunning maroon-and-white building that dates to 1876. Across the street from the library is Balducci's (424 Sixth Ave), a famed gourmet food shop.

Chelsea

Primarily middle-class residential and still somewhat industrial, Chelsea—stretching between 14th and 30th streets, from Sixth Avenue to the Hudson River—is not the most tourist-oriented of areas. However, the neighborhood does offer an exciting, avant-garde arts scene, as well as many lovely quiet blocks lined with attractive row houses and rustling trees. A new gay community has moved in recently, bringing with it trendy cafés, shops, and bars, while an enormous, state-of-the-art sports complex, the Chelsea Piers, beckons from the river's edge (between 18th and 22nd streets).

Most of Chelsea was once owned by Captain Thomas Clarke, whose grandson, Clement Charles Clarke, laid out the residential district in the early 1800s. Clement Charles was also a scholar and a poet who wrote the famous poem beginning with the line, "Twas the night before Christmas..." Another of Clement Charles's legacies is the General Theological Seminary, a peaceful enclave of ivy-covered buildings bounded by the block between Ninth and Tenth avenues and 20th and 21st streets.

Also on the western edge of Chelsea are many of the city's foremost art galleries, which began moving here in the early 1990s as rents in SoHo—their former home—began skyrocketing. An especially large number can be found on West 21st and 22nd streets between Tenth and Eleventh avenues; among them are the Paula Cooper Gallery (534 West 21st St), the Maximum Protech Gallery (511 West 22nd St), and the Dia Center for the Arts (548 West 22nd St). One of the pioneers of the area, the Dia Center is really more a museum than an art gallery and usually hosts a variety of eye-popping exhibits, along with an open-air sculpture garden on the roof.

Most of Chelsea's thriving shops, restaurants, and bars—some of which are predominantly gay, some not—stand along Sixth and Eighth avenues between 14th and 23rd streets. Some of the neighborhood's prettiest blocks, lined with elegant row houses, are West 20th, 21st, and 22nd streets between Eighth and Tenth avenues. Also, be sure to take a gander at the Chelsea Hotel (222 W 23rd St, near Eighth Ave), a maroon-colored landmark that has all-black gables, chimneys, and balconies. Built in 1884, the Chelsea has housed dozens of artists, writers, and musicians over the years, including Arthur Miller, Jackson Pollock, Bob Dylan, and Sid Vicious.

Just north of Chelsea lies the underground Pennsylvania Station (Seventh Ave at 32nd St), topped with circular Madison Square Garden, and the General Post Office (Eighth Ave, between 31st and 33rd sts)—a gorgeous building designed by McKim, Mead & White in 1913. The Garment District, centering on Seventh Avenue in the 30s, also begins here.

Gramercy Park and Environs

Largely residential, the East Side between 14th and 34th streets is home to two inviting squares—Gramercy Park at Irving Place between 20th and 21st streets, and Union Square at Broadway between 14th and 17th streets. A long line of trendy restaurants and bars beckon along Park Avenue between 17th and 23rd streets, while a bit farther north is Little India, centered on Lexington Avenue between 27th and 29th streets. The neighborhood lacks the vibrancy of some of Manhattans better-known neighborhoods but has a quiet charm of its own, with residents ranging from young professionals to middle-class families to the upper middle class.

One of the most fashionable squares in the city, Gramercy Park is composed of elegant brownstones and townhouses surrounding an enclosed green to which only residents have the key. At the southern edge of the park stand two especially impressive buildings—the National Arts Club (15 Gramercy Park South) and the Players Club (16 Gramercy Park South). The National Arts Club was once home to New York governor Samuel Tilden, whereas the Players Club once belonged to the great thespian Edwin Booth, the brother of the man who assassinated Abraham Lincoln. Just east of Gramercy Park stands Theodore Roosevelt's Birthplace (28 East 20th St), a museum filled with the world's largest collection of Roosevelt memorabilia.

Farther south, find Union Square, a booming park surrounded by sleek megastores, upscale restaurants, and fashionable bars. The popular Farmers' Greenmarket operates in the park on Monday, Wednesday,

Friday, and Saturday mornings, and free concerts and other events sometimes take place here during the summer. To the immediate east of the square are several excellent off-Broadway theaters.

Broadway between Union Square and Madison Square (between 23rd and 26th streets, Fifth and Madison avenues) was once known as the "Ladies Mile" because of the many fashionable department stores located here. Many were housed in extravagant cast-iron buildings, which still stand, now holding more modern emporiums.

At the corner of Broadway and 23rd Street is the famous 1902 Flatiron building, built in the shape of a narrow triangle and only 6 feet wide at its northern end. Meanwhile, reigning over Madison Park to the east are the enormous Art Deco Metropolitan Life Insurance Building (Madison Avenue, between 23rd and 25th streets) and the impossibly ornate Appellate Division of the New York State Supreme Court (Madison Avenue at 25th Street).

Still farther north and east lies Little India. Though not as thriving as it once was, it still houses a number of excellent Indian restaurants, sari shops, and spice stores, which attract shoppers from all over the city.

MIDTOWN

Stretching from 34th Street to 57th Street, the Harlem River to the East River, Midtown is the heart of Manhattan. Most of the city's skyscrapers are here, along with most of its offices, major hotels, famous shops, the Empire State Building, Times Square, the Broadway theaters, the Museum of Modern Art, Rockefeller Center, Grand Central Station, and the New York Public Library.

Fifth Avenue is the center of Midtown, dividing the city into east and west. Although nothing more than a line on a map as late as 1811, the thoroughfare had become New York's most fashionable address by the Civil War. It began to turn commercial in the early 1900s and is now lined with mostly shops and office buildings.

Towering over the southern end of Midtown is the Empire State Building (350 Fifth Ave, at 34th St), one of the world's most famous skyscrapers. Built in the early 1930s, the building took just 14 months to erect and remains an Art Deco masterpiece.

Forty-Second Street is lined with one major attraction after another. On the corner of Third Avenue soars the magnificent Chrysler Building, another Art Deco masterpiece; Grand Central Station, whose magnificent concourse was recently restored to the tune of $200 million, is at Lexington Avenue. At Fifth Avenue beckons the New York Public Library, behind which spreads Bryant Park, where many free events are held during the summer months.

West of Seventh Avenue along 42nd Street begins Times Square, which stretches north to 48th Street along the Seventh Avenue-Broadway nexus. The best time to come here is at night, when the huge state-of-the-art neon lights that line the square begin to shine. Much cleaned up in recent years, Times Square is also a good place to catch street performers and, of course, Broadway theater. Many of the city's most famous theaters are located on the side streets around Times Square.

North and a little east of Times Square, Rockefeller Center reigns as an Art Deco complex stretching between 48th and 51st streets, Sixth and Fifth avenues. Built by John D. Rockefeller during the height of the Depression, Rockefeller Center is home to the landmark Radio City Music Hall, the NBC Studios, and a famed skating rink filled with outdoor enthusiasts during the winter months.

Along Fifth Avenue just south and north of Rockefeller Center, find some of the city's most famous shops—Saks Fifth Avenue, Tiffany's, Steuben Glass, and Cartier, along with Trump Tower at 56th Street. Between 50th and 51st streets soars the Gothic Saint Patrick's Cathedral, the largest Roman Catholic cathedral in the United States; the Museum of Modern Art, a must-stop for any art lover, is on 53rd Street just west of Fifth.

UPPER EAST SIDE

Long associated with wealth, much of the Upper East Side—stretching from 57th Street north to 106th Street and Fifth Avenue east to the East River—is filled with elegant mansions and brownstones, clubs, and museums. Many of the city's most famous museums—including the Metropolitan Museum of Art—are located here, along with several posh hotels and Gracie Mansion, home to New York City's mayor.

But the neighborhood is about more than just wealth. Remnants of what was once a thriving German community can be found along the 86th Street-Second Avenue nexus, while a Puerto Rican and Latin community begins in the upper 80s, east of Lexington Avenue. At the corner of 96th Street and Third Avenue is a surprising sight—the Islamic Cultural Center, a modern, gold-domed mosque flanked by a skinny minaret.

Many of the Upper East Side's cultural institutions are located on Fifth Avenue, facing Central Park, along what is known as "Museum Mile." The Frick Collection, housing the private art collection of the former 19th-century industrialist Henry Clay Frick, marks the mile's southernmost end, at 70th Street. El Museo del Barrio, dedicated to the art and culture of Latin America, marks the northernmost end, at 104th Street. In between reign the grand Metropolitan Museum of Art (at 82nd St), huge flags flapping out front, and the circular, Frank Lloyd Wright-designed Guggenheim Museum (at 88th St)—to name just two.

The Plaza Hotel beckons from the southern end of the Upper East Side (Fifth Ave, between 58th and 59th sts). This magnificent French Renaissance-style edifice was built in 1907. Directly across Fifth Avenue from the hotel, FAO Schwarz is an imaginative toy store that's as much fun for adults as it is for kids. Central Park is directly across 59th Street. Horse-drawn hansoms and their drivers congregate along the streets here, waiting hopefully for tourists interested in taking a clip-clopping tour. The small but state-of-the-art Central Park Zoo can be found in the park near Fifth Avenue and 65th Street.

Shoppers will want to take a gander at the many upscale boutiques lining Madison Avenue between 57th and 90th streets, or take a stroll over to Bloomingdale's (Lexington Ave at 59th St). Fifty-Seventh Street holds numerous world-famous galleries, including PaceWildenstein (32 E 57th St) and Andre Emmerich (41 E 57th St), as well as such popular tourist stop as Niketown (6 E 57th St). The infamous St. Patrick's Day Parade, attracting hordes of rowdy revelers, travels down Fifth Avenue from 86th Street to 44th Street every March 17th.

UPPER WEST SIDE

Primarily residential, the Upper West Side has traditionally been known as the liberal-leaning home of writers, intellectuals, musicians, dancers, doctors, lawyers, and other upper-middle-class professionals. A mix of ornate 19th-century landmarks, pre-World War II apartment buildings, and tenement houses, the Upper West Side stretches from 57th Street north to 110th Street and from Fifth Avenue west to the Hudson River. At its eastern border, between Fifth Avenue and Central Park West and 59th and 110th streets, Central Park sprawls out in a vast and beautifully landscaped expanse of green.

Anchoring the neighborhood to the south is one of its best-known addresses—the Lincoln Center for the Performing Arts (Broadway, between 62nd and 66th streets), which presents about 3,000 cultural events a year. Centering on a large, circular fountain, the 14-acre complex is home to such renowned institutions as the Metropolitan Opera House and Avery Fisher Hall. Many free outdoor concerts are presented on the plaza during the summer.

Directly across from Lincoln Center beckons a row of attractive restaurants and cafés, many with outdoor seating in summer. The Museum of American Folk Art (Broadway, between 65th and 66th streets), one of the city's smaller and more unusual museums, is also here. Another dozen or so blocks farther north, the Museum of Natural History (Central Park West, at 79th St) is packed with everything from more than 100 dinosaur skeletons to artifacts from peoples around the world. Adjoining the museum on its north side is the state-of-the-art Rose Center for Earth and Space. Completed in 2000, the center is instantly recognizable for its unusual glass architecture revealing a globe within a triangle.

The Upper West Side didn't begin developing until the late 1800s, when a grand apartment building called the Dakota was built at what is now the corner of Central Park West and 72nd Street. At the time, the building was so far north of the rest of the city that New Yorkers said it was as remote as the state of Dakotahence the name. Still standing today, the Dakota has been home to many celebrities, including Lauren Bacall, Gilda Radner, Boris Karloff, and John Lennon, who was fatally shot outside the building on December 8, 1980. In Central Park, directly across the street from the Dakota, is Strawberry Fields, a teardrop-shaped acre of land that Yoko Ono had landscaped in her husbands memory.

Central Park can be entered at major intersections all along Central Park West. Near the park's southern end, find Tavern on the Green (near Central Park West and 67th St), a glittering extravaganza of a restaurant packed with mirrors and chandeliers. A bit farther north, find an odd-shaped body of water simply known as "The Lake" (between 72nd and 77th streets); rowboats can be rented at the Loeb Boathouse at the lakes eastern edge.

Harlem

Stretching from 110th to 168th streets, between the Harlem and Hudson rivers, **Harlem** is in the midst of a renaissance. After years of being known primarily for its grinding poverty, drugs, and despair, the historic African- American neighborhood is sprucing itself up, attracting mainstream businesses such as Starbucks and Ben & Jerry's, and becoming home once again to the middle class—African-American and white.

Harlem can be divided in two: west-central Harlem, which is primarily African-American, and east Harlem, home to many Latinos and a smaller number of Italians. Between 110th and 125th streets west of Morningside Park is Morningside Heights, where Columbia University is located. Washington Heights, north of 155th Street, is home to Fort Tyron Park and the Cloisters, which houses the medieval collection of the Metropolitan Museum of Art.

First a farming community and then an affluent white suburb, Harlem began attracting African-American residents after the construction of the IRT subway in 1901, and soon became the nation's premier African-American neighborhood. The Harlem Renaissance boomed during the 1920s and 1930s, attracting writers and intellectuals such as Langston Hughes and W. E. B. DuBois, and the streets were packed with nightclubs, dance halls, and jazz clubs. Everything changed, however, with the Depression, when poverty took a stronghold that continues in many parts of the neighborhood today. When exploring Harlem, it's best to stick to the main thoroughfares.

The heart of Harlem is 125th Street, where you'll find a new Magic Johnson Theater complex, several restaurants and sweet shops offering soul food and baked goods, and the famed Apollo Theater (253 W 125th St). Nearly every major jazz, blues, R&B, and soul artist to come along performed here, and the theater still presents its famed Amateur Night every Wednesday. Just down the street from the Apollo is the Studio Museum of Harlem (144 West 125th St), a first-class fine arts institution spread over several floors of a turn-of-the-century building.

Another Harlem landmark is the Schomburg Center for Research in Black Culture (Lenox Ave at 135th St), founded by Arthur C. Schomburg, a Puerto Rican of African descent who was told as a child that his race had no history. Although primarily a library, the center also houses a large exhibit area where a wide array of changing exhibits is presented.

Not far from Columbia University, which is centered on Broadway and 116th Street, the Cathedral of St. John the Divine (Amsterdam Ave at 112th St), is the world's largest Gothic cathedral, said to be big enough to fit both Notre Dame and Chartres inside. Another major attraction nearby is Grant's Tomb (122nd St at Riverside Dr), an imposing mausoleum sitting high on a bluff overlooking the Hudson.

Brooklyn

The largest borough in population and second largest in area, Brooklyn was a city in its own right—separate from New York—up until 1898. Brooklyn had its own city hall, central park, downtown shops, and cultural attractions, which helps account for the unusual amount the borough has to offer the visitor today. Brooklyn is also home to multiple ethnic groups, socioeconomic groups, and neighborhoods, one of which—Coney Island—is world famous.

Brooklyn Heights and Williamsburg are located at the northern end of Brooklyn, closest to Manhattan. Brooklyn Heights is quiet, upper-middle-class, and dignified, filled with lovely brownstones, historic buildings, and the wide riverside Promenade, which offers magnificent views of the Manhattan skyline and New York Harbor. Williamsburg was once inhabited mostly by Jewish immigrants and is still home to the Satmarer Hasidim, a major orthodox sect. Today the area is better known for its large, young, arts-oriented population. Along Bedford Avenue, especially, find a plethora of lively, inexpensive restaurants, bars, art galleries, and shops.

Bordering Brooklyn Heights is downtown Brooklyn, home to a number of imposing government buildings that date back to the days when Brooklyn was a city in its own right. The Greek Revival Borough Hall, at the intersection of Joralemon, Fulton, and Court streets, was once Brooklyn's City Hall and is still filled with government offices. Not far away is the New York Transit Museum (Schermerhorn St at Boerum Pl), an excellent place to learn the story behind the New York subway.

Near the center of Brooklyn sprawls Prospect Park, one of the city's loveliest retreats. Spread out over 525 acres of forests and meadows, the park was designed by Frederick Law Olmsted and Calvert Vaux, the two men who also planned Central Park in Manhattan. Brooklyn's foremost cultural attractions—the Brooklyn Museum of Art (200 Eastern Pkwy, at Washington Ave) and the Brooklyn Botanic Gardens (1000 Washington Ave, near Eastern Pkwy)—are located on the eastern edge of the park. The northwestern edge is Park Slope, a genteel neighborhood filled with elegant Victorian brownstones, now mostly inhabited by urban professionals with young children.

At the far southern end of Brooklyn, you'll find three most unusual neighborhoods-Coney Island, Brighton Beach, and Sheepshead Bay. Once home to a famed amusement park, Coney Island still beckons with an idiosyncratic collection of creaky historic rides, tawdry newer ones, the first-rate Aquarium for Wildlife Conservation (West Eighth St, between the Boardwalk and Surf Ave), and a wide, windswept boardwalk that stretches along a beach. The popular Mermaid Parade, featuring eye-popping costumes, takes place here every June. Next door to Coney Island is Brighton Beach, home to a thriving a Russian community, and Sheepshead Bay, a tiny port filled with fishing boats, retirees, and seafood restaurants.

Queens

New York City's biggest borough, Queens is home to many large and vibrant ethnic neighborhoods as well as to some important cultural and historic gems. It also holds John F. Kennedy International and La Guardia airports and Shea Stadium, the ballpark of the New York Mets. At the western end of Queens stretch Long Island

City and Astoria, both just a stop or two away from Manhattan on the subway. Although largely an industrial area, Long Island City has recently become known for its burgeoning artistic community and holds a number of first-rate galleries and museums. Foremost among them are the Isamu Noguchi Garden Museum (32-37 Vernon Blvd, at 33rd Rd), containing many works of the late great sculptor, and the P.S.1 Contemporary Art Center (22-25 Jackson Ave, at 46th St), a premier showcase for art on the cutting edge.

Meanwhile, Astoria is home to a large Greek population, as well as to an increasing number of Pakistani, Italian, and Latino residents. Along 30th Avenue and Broadway between 31st and Steinway streets, you'll find many Greek restaurants, food shops, and bakeries; the American Museum of the Moving Image (34-12 36th St) is also nearby. Astoria was once the site of the Astoria Movie Studios, which produced such legends as Rudolf Valentino and Gloria Swanson; renovated and reopened in the late 1970s, the studios are now known as the Kaufman-Astoria Studios. Travel a bit farther east on the No. 7 subway line-the borough's main transportation artery-to find Jackson Heights. Nicknamed the "cornfield of Queens" in the early 1900s, Jackson Heights now holds large Colombian and Indian populations, as well as smaller Peruvian, Uruguayan, Filipino, and Thai populations. A number of excellent Colombian restaurants are located along Roosevelt Avenue near 82nd and 83rd streets; tasty Indian food can be sampled between 70th and 74th streets near Roosevelt Avenue and Broadway.

East of Jackson Heights, Flushing Meadows-Corona Park is an enormous green oasis that housed both the 1939 and 1964 World's Fairs. The park's Unisphere-a shining, 140-foot-high hollow globe-dates back to the 1964 fair, as do the buildings that now contain the Queens Museum of Art and the New York Hall of Science. The Queens Wildlife Center and Shea Stadium are also in the park.

Beyond the park, find Flushing, home to a clutch of historic buildings and large Asian communities. The historic buildings include the Bowne House (37-01 Bowne St), used for illegal Quaker meetings in the 1660s, and the 1785 Kingsland House (143-35 37th Ave), now the headquarters of the Queens Historical Society. The Asian community is centered on Main and Union streets; Asian restaurants serving delicious, authentic food are everywhere here.

The Bronx

New York City's second-smallest borough both in size and population, the Bronx is also the only one attached to the mainland. In it you'll discover such legendary New York institutions as the Bronx Zoo, the New York Botanical Gardens, Yankee Stadium, and some of the city's biggest parks.

However, in the 1970s and 1980s, the borough also garnered a reputation for urban decay, as headlining stories involving murder, drugs, and arson seemed to come out of here daily. In more recent years, though, more than $1 billion in public funds has been spent on the South Bronx—where most of the decay occurred—and the place is in better shape now than it has been in years. Elsewhere in the borough, large residential neighborhoods have always flourished, most working- and middle-class (City Island, Co-Op City), a few quite exclusive (Riverdale, Fieldston).

First settled in 1644 by a Scandinavian named Jonas Bronck, the area soon became known as "The Broncks,"and remained a predominantly agricultural community up until the late 1800s. But then the Third Avenue Elevated Railway arrived, and by 1900, the boroughs population had soared to 200,000. During the 1920s and 1930s, grand Art Deco apartment buildings sprang up along the wide thoroughfare called the Grand Concourse-a considerably more dilapidated version of which still exists today.

The New York Botanical Garden and Bronx Zoo sit adjacent to each other in the heart of the Bronx. Since they're both enormous, however, it's hard to visit them both in one day. Instead, opt for one of the two, and then head to Belmont, an Italian community just west of the zoo. One of the city's older and more established ethnic neighborhoods, it is packed with Italian restaurants, pastry shops, bakeries, butcher shops, and food markets.

Also in the Bronx is Van Cortlandt Park, which, at 2 square miles, is one of the city's largest parks. In its northernmost section sits the Van Cortlandt House Museum, a charming 18th-century mansion that once belonged to a wealthy landowner.

Across Jerome Avenue from the park stretches Woodlawn Cemetery, a lush 19th-century burial ground filled with rolling hills, meandering walkways, mausoleums, and tombs. Author Herman Melville, financier Jay Gould, and musicians Duke Ellington and Miles Davis are all buried here.

At the northern end of the Bronx reigns City Island, one of New York City's more unusual communities. A sailor's haven that had once hoped to become an important port, City Island is still home to a small shipbuilding industry. The place had only one main street-City Island Avenue-which is lined with a number of fish restaurants ranging in style from simple to old-fashioned elaborate.

STATEN ISLAND

Significantly more rural and suburban than the four other New York City boroughs, Staten Island is also predominantly white, politically conservative, and mostly working-and middle-class. Many residents own their own homes here, complete with tidy front lawns and garages-something you dont see much in the rest of the city. Unless you have access to a car, Staten Island is also quite difficult to explore. Buses run much less frequently and have more ground to cover than they do elsewhere in the city, making travel a time-consuming affair.

At 14 miles long by 7 miles wide, Staten Island was originally settled by Native Americans who successfully fought off the Dutch until 1661. Later, it became a military camp for the British during the Revolutionary War and then remained predominantly rural throughout the 1800s and early 1900s. Even as late as 1964, when the Verrazano-Narrows Bridge was completed, connecting the borough to the rest of the city, Staten Island was largely undeveloped.

The Staten Island Ferry is the borough's biggest attraction, carrying about 3 1/2 million visitors back and forth every year, with few actually disembarking to explore the Staten Island side. Rides on the ferry are free, and the views they offer of Manhattan and New York Harbor are spectacular, especially at night.

The ferry docks at St. George, a small and often empty town with many deserted storefronts. About a mile away is the Snug Harbor Cultural Center (1000 Richmond Terrace; take the S40 bus), an odd complex of buildings that was once a home for retired sailors. Today, the center holds several galleries, a botanical garden, and a Chinese scholar's garden.

In the center of Staten Island stretches the Greenbelt, a 2,500-acre nature preserve made up of several tracts of woodlands, wetlands, and open fields, interspersed with a golf course, a nature center, a considerable amount of human settlement, and a few historic sites. A favorite stop for migrating birds, the Greenbelt also supports diverse flora, thanks to a wide variety of soils deposited here by glaciers about 10,000 years ago.

South of the Greenbelt, find the Jacques Marchais Museum of Tibetan Art (338 Lighthouse Ave; take the S74 bus), the housing what is said to be the largest collection of Tibetan art in the Western world. Within walking distance of the Tibetan is Historic Richmond Town (441 Clarke Ave), a re-crated historic village filled with 29 buildings, most moved here from elsewhere on the island.

Until recently, Staten Island was also the butt of many jokes, as the city's largest dump, the Fresh Kills landfill, was located here. However, Fresh Kills was closed in early 2001.

Historic Greenwich Village

Although no longer the leading edge of the art world and radicalism, Greenwich Village remains a uniquely dynamic neighborhood. Start in Washington Square Park, lined by New York University buildings and the site of the famous arch. The park normally buzzes with street performers, in-line skaters, and families at play. Leave the park from the south side. Judson Memorial Church stands on the corner of West 4th Street and Thompson Street. Designed by Stanford White, the church is noted for its stained-glass windows and front marble work. Thompson Street is lined with chess clubs. At Bleecker Street, turn right. Look for Le Figaro Café (186 Bleecker St) and Café Borgia (185 Bleecker St), a pair of old-time coffeehouses.

Turn right onto MacDougal Street. Here stand two landmark cafés: Caff Reggio (119 MacDougal St) and Café Wha? (115 MacDougal St), as well as Minetta Tavern (113 MacDougal St), an old standby that serves good Italian food. Make a U-turn, turn right onto Minetta Lane, and then turn right onto Minetta Street, both lined with classic Village townhouses. Cross Sixth Avenue and enter the heart of Bleeckers neighborhood shopping—including some of the finest Italian bake shops in the city. Continue across Seventh Avenue and turn left onto Barrow Street. This block features a number of classic redbrick row houses (49 and 51 Barrow St are Federal style) and Chumleys Bar (86 Barrow St), once a speakeasy and a famous writers hangout. Look for 75 Barrow Street, a strange, narrow house where Edna St. Vincent Millay once lived, and 77 Barrow Street, which was built in 1799, making it the Villages oldest house. Turn right on Bedford, passing a late 19th-century horse stable (95 Bedford), an early 19th-century home with a pair of Tudor-style towers aptly named Twin Peaks (102 Bedford), and a mid-19th-century home built in the Greek Revival style (113 Bedford).

Turn right onto Christopher Street, a throbbing, busy street that's the heart of Village gay life. Go right onto Bleecker, then left onto Seventh Avenue. Sweet Basil (414 Seventh Ave) is a famed jazz club, as is Village Vanguard (178 Seventh Ave S). Turn right on Grove Street and right again on Waverly Place. At 165 Waverly Place stands the Northern Dispensary, built during the 1831 cholera epidemic. Turn left onto Sixth Avenue. The circa-1876, castlelike, Gothic-style Jefferson Market Library is located on 10th Street. Also of note on Sixth Avenue are Balduccis (424 Sixth Ave), a legendary gourmet food shop, and Bigalows (414 Sixth Ave), the citys oldest continuously operating pharmacy. Continue north and turn right onto 11th Street to minuscule Second Cemetery of the Spanish and Portuguese Synagogue, or return south and turn left onto 8th Street, another major shopping street.

At Fifth Avenue, turn right. Just before Washington Square Park is the picturesque cul-de-sac Washington Square Mews. For more shopping, continue east on 8th Street and then turn south on Broadway. These blocks, not long ago a forsaken neighborhood of old warehouses and sweatshop factory buildings, now thrive with major retail chains like Tower Records and Gap.

Midtown Manhattan

Few places pack so much to see and do into so little space as midtown Manhattan. This walk can be as short as 2 miles or as long as five or six, depending on your stamina and choice of sites.

Start at the Times Square Visitor Center at 1560 Broadway (at Seventh Ave), and pick up information on theater, dining, and sightseeing. Walk south to 42nd Street, and go right to the New Amsterdam Theatre (214 West 42nd St), currently home to the long running hit *The Lion King* but dating from 1903, the home of the Ziegfeld Follies. Guided tours are offered daily, and the daring Art Nouveau interiors are worth the time. Walk east on 42nd Street, passing the newly renovated Bryant Park, to the corner of Fifth Avenue, site of the New York Public Library Center for the Humanities branch (originally the librarys Main Branch). Tours are offered here too; however, if time doesn't allow for full tour, be sure to at least visit at main Reading Room. Its marvel of sumptuous woods and magnificent faux wood plaster ceilings with a three-part ceiling mural and massive bronzed and arched windows. Returning to 42nd Street, continue east to the Park Avenue and Grand Central Terminal, another landmark that offers guided tours. A stunning example of Beaux Arts architecture, Grand Centrals highlights is its huge central hall, lined with 33- by 66-foot windows, palatial marble staircases, and dual balconies. A new gourmet food court can be found in the lower terminal.

Return to Fifth Avenue and turn north (right). The next 15 blocks reveal the crme de la crme of premium shopping, including Saks Fifth Avenue (611 Fifth Ave), Fortunoff (681 Fifth Ave), Coca-Cola Fifth Avenue (711 Fifth Ave), Henri Bendel (712 Fifth Ave), Bergdorf Goodman (754 Fifth Ave), Tiffany & Company (727 Fifth Ave), Trump Tower (at 56th St), and FAO Schwarz (767 Fifth Ave). Rockefeller Center stands at 50th Street and Fifth Avenue, home to the famous ice rink, garden and floral displays, Radio City Music Hall, and NBC Studios. Just across from Rockefeller Center on Fifth Avenue stands St. Patricks Cathedral, the famous English/Gothic seat of the New York City Catholic Archdiocese. At 52nd Street, just a few doors west of Fifth, is the Museum of Television & Radio. On 53rd Street stands the Museum of Modern Art and its signature collection, which includes works by Picasso, Van Gogh, and Matisse, to name just three. The American Craft Museum is found just off Fifth at 40 West 53rd Street.

Turn left (east) onto West 57th Street, where the high-end shopping continues and many art galleries are found. At Seventh Avenue is Carnegie Hall, the citys premier concert hall, which also can be toured. At this point, the southern reaches of Central Park are just two blocks north. Explore the park a bit and emerge on its eastern side. Either walk back downtown or, perhaps more sensibly, hop a bus to 34th Street for a visit to the Empire State Building. Following that, walk west on 34th to Herald Square (at Seventh Avenue) and some more shopping at Macys, still the worlds largest department store. For even more shopping return to Sixth Avenue and 32nd Street for a stop at the Manhattan Mall, home to 80 stores on nine levels.

The Big Apple's Best Chefs

Manhattan is home to extraordinary restaurantsfrom tiny neighborhood places with cult followings, like Lupa and Five Points; to upscale dens of haute cuisine, like Daniel, Aquavit, and Craft; to sultry hotspots like Spice Market and Pastis in the Meatpacking District. Dining out in New York is, more than ever, exhaustingly fabulous. Every day, chefs fill the city with miraculous food, blazing a mouthwatering path into the future of American cuisine.

With the opening of the Time Warner Center, New Yorkers are officially in a culinary frenzy. **Gray Kunz**, who turned seafood into high art and left diners breathless with awe at Lespinasse, is back after many false starts on his own restaurant projects. Café Gray, a luxurious shrine to seafood, features dishes that incorporate his travels across Southeast Asia with his impeccable classical French training. Joining him in the Time Warner Center are **Jean-Georges Vongerichten** of Spice Market, 66, and, of course, Jean Georges, with his latest restaurantV Steakhouseand West Coast culinary master **Thomas Keller** of The French Laundry, whose new restaurant, Per Se, is already on the short list of every gourmand in the city.

These patriarchs of modern American cuisine are joined by pioneers like **Mario Batali**, who started out on his mission of bringing simple, seasonal Italian cuisine to the masses with Po and grew his empire to include glorious Italian eateries like Babbo, Lupa, and Esca. With Casa Mono and Bar Jamon, he brings the same sense of adventure and passion to Spanish cuisine. The spotlight also shines on **Bobby Flay** of Mesa Grill and Bolo, **Rick Moonen** of RM, **Wayne Nish** of March, and **Charlie Palmer**, whose restaurant Aureole remains one of the citys most elegant places to dine. And how could we leave out **Daniel Boulud** (Daniel, DB Bistro), **David Bouley** (Bouley), **Jonathan Waxman** (still going strong after Jams and Washington Park with the recently opened Barbuto), and **Alfred Portale** (who just celebrated 20 years at Gotham Bar and Grill)?

But these old-timers have some serious competition. A groundswell of youthful energy and creativity is bubbling up downtown, where baby-faced chefs (many age 30 and under) are turning up the heat.

The rising star spotlight shines on **Josh DeChellis** of Sumile, who serves a thrilling brand of Japanese-inspired cuisine, including mad dishes like miso-cured brook trout with blood orange pickles. Also challenging the old guard is **Galen Zamarra**, a protg of David Bouley. Zamarra is the chef/partner of Mas, where he showcases locally farmed seasonal ingredients in exquisite dishes like medallions of Cooperstown lamb wrapped in ramps with eggplant moussaka and a vibrant swoosh of tomato harissa.

Women are also getting in the game. **Sue Torres** owns the deliciously authentic regional Mexican restaurant Suenos. **Alison Vines Rushing**, the wildly talented chef at Jacks Luxury Oyster Bar, blends her spry Southern roots with classic French training to produce feisty dishes like braised pig cheeks served with collards finished with a lip-licking pepper vinegar and her signature New Orleans-style barbecued lobster. At the Spotted Pig, a West Village gastro-pub with a cult following, chef/partner **April Bloomfield**plucked from Londons lauded River Café by Spotted Pig owners Mario Batali and Ken Friedmanhas crowds lining the sidewalks for her ricotta gnudi with brown butter and sage and beautifully blistered pork sausages with arugula and lentils.

The list of talent, young and old, is always growing. The best way to keep track of the culinary goods is to get out there and dine.

MUSEUMS OF NEW YORK

New York is a city of museums. Almost everywhere you go, from the stately Upper East Side of Manhattan to the leafy reaches of Staten Island, you stumble upon them. Some are renowned worldwide: the Metropolitan Museum of Art, the Museum of Modern Art, the Museum of Natural History, the Guggenheim. Others are known only to enthusiasts: the Isamu Noguchi Garden Museum, the Tibetan Museum, the New York City Fire Museum, the Lower East Side Tenement Museum.

On these pages, find a guide to some of the city's most important, interesting, and/or offbeat museums, arranged by subject matter. If you're short on time, the must-sees are the Metropolitan Museum of Art, the Museum of Modern Art, and the American Museum of Natural History. Following not far behind are the Guggenheim, the Whitney, the Brooklyn Museum of Art, the Studio Museum in Harlem, the Cooper-Hewitt, the National Museum of the American Indian, and the Frick Collection.

Many of New York's major museums are packed with visitors on the weekends, especially in the afternoons or early evenings, because many are open late on Fridays and Saturdays. To avoid the crowds, come during the week or on weekend mornings.

MAJOR ART MUSEUMS

Any guide to the Big Apple's museums must start with that most venerable, enormous, and glorious of institutions, the **Metropolitan Museum of Art** (1000 Fifth Ave, at 82nd St; phone 212/535-7710). Housed behind an impressive Beaux Arts façade designed by Robert Morris Hunt, the museum holds collections of everything from Egyptian sarcophagi to contemporary American paintings. Equally important, it hosts at least two or three major temporary exhibits at any give time.

Founded in 1870, the Met centers on the Great Hall, a vast entrance room with a stately staircase leading to the second floor. Here you'll find the European Paintings galleries, one of the Met's most important collections. Housed in about 20 rooms are works by such masters as Rembrandt, Breughel, Rubens, Botticelli, Goya, and El Greco. Next door are the impressive 19th-century European Galleries, housing works by more modern masters such as van Gogh, Gauguin, Seurat, and Renoir.

Three sides of the Met's original buildings are flanked by modern glass wings. At the back is the Robert Lehman Collection, containing an exhibit of 19th-century French paintings, among other things. On the south side are the Rockefeller and Acheson Wings, the first holding a South Pacific collection—everything from totem poles to canoes—the second, 20th-century art. On the north side, find the Sacker Wing, best known for its 15th-century-BC Temple of Dendur, carved in faded hieroglyphics, and the American Wing, housing exhaustive galleries of decorative arts and paintings by the likes of Thomas Eakins and John Singer Sargent.

The Met's Egyptian collection is one of the largest in the world and a must-stop for history buffs. The Islamic art collection and the new South and Southeast Asian art collection are also among the world's finest. To see the museum's medieval collection, travel north to the **Cloisters** (Fort Tyron Park, 190th St at Overlook Terrace; phone 212/923-3700). Situated high on a hill with great views of the Hudson River, the Cloisters are housed in a reconstructed medieval monastery that incorporates the actual remains of four medieval cloisters.

The second stop for any serious art lover should be the Museum of Modern Art (11 W 53rd St, between Fifth and Sixth avenues; phone 212/708-9480; www.moma.org). After a major expansion that nearly doubled its size, the rejuvenated museum now sprawls more than 600,000 square feet. The six-story gallery building houses the main collection of more than 100,000 paintings, sculptures, drawings, prints, and photographs, as well as skylit galleries for temporary exhibits on the top floor. The eight-story education and research center holds an expanded library and archives, a reading room, and a 125-seat auditorium. Visitors can expect to find such masterpieces as Cézanne's *The Bather* and van Gogh's *Starry Night*, along with entire rooms devoted to Mondrian, Pollock, Matisse, and Monets *Water Lilies* and a superb photography exhibit. The enlarged Abby Aldrich Rockefeller outdoor sculpture garden will include an outdoor patio for the museum's new restaurant.

Another essential stop for modern art lovers is the **Solomon R. Guggenheim Museum** (1071 Fifth Ave, at 88th St; phone 212/423-3500). Housed in a circular building designed by Frank Lloyd Wright in 1959, the main gallery is a gentle multileveled spiral circling around a central atrium. The exhibits, all major temporary shows featuring 20th- or 21st-century artists, start at the top of the spiral and wind their way down.

Next door to the main gallery is a rotunda, housing the small but stunning Justin K. Thannhauser Collection, which includes works by such artists as Picasso, Cézanne, Modigliani, and Seurat. A ten-story tower also abuts the main gallery to the back; here, find a mix of temporary and permanent exhibits and an outdoor sculpture garden.

Not far from the Guggenheim is the **Whitney Museum of American Art** (Madison Ave, at 75th Street; phone 212/570-3676). Most of the exhibits here are temporary and feature the work of one major American artist such as Edward Hopper, Jasper Johns, or Jean-Michel Basquiat. The museum is also known for its superb permanent collection and for its controversial "Biennial" show, presented every two years to showcase the latest work of contemporary American artists.

A few blocks south of the Whitney, find the hushed **Frick Collection** (1 East 70th St, at Fifth Ave; phone 212/288-0700). The museum is housed in a lovely 1914 mansion, the former home of 19th-century industrialist Henry Clay Frick, built around a peaceful courtyard. Renowned for its permanent European art collection, the Frick boasts masterpieces by Breughel, El Greco, Vermeer, Rembrandt, and many others. Near the entrance is the Jean-Honore Fragonard Room, where all four walls are covered with *The Progress of Love,* a mural commissioned by Louis XV.

A few blocks north of the Metropolitan beckons another museum housed in a former mansion: the **Cooper-Hewitt National Design Museum** (2 E 91st St, at Fifth Ave; phone 212/849-8400). Once home to the 19th-century industrialist Andrew Carnegie, the 64-room building is now a branch of the Smithsonian Institution dedicated to design and the decorative arts. The exhibits are temporary and focus on such subjects as ceramics, furniture, textiles, and metalwork. Out back is a romantic garden, where concerts are sometimes presented.

The **Studio Museum in Harlem** (144 W 125th St, between Lenox Avenue and Adam Clayton Powell Blvd; phone 212/864-4500) is located in Harlem. Founded in 1968, the museum is the "principal center for the study of Black Art in America," spread out over several well-lit floors of a turn-of-the-century building. The permanent exhibit features works by such masters as Romare Bearden, James VanDerZee, and Jacob Lawrence; temporary exhibits present a mix of both world-renowned and emerging artists. The Studio is also known for its lively lecture and concert series, presented September through May.

Although often overlooked by tourists, the **Brooklyn Museum of Art** (200 Eastern Pkwy, at Washington; phone 718/638-5000) is one of the city's foremost art institutions. Similar to the Metropolitan in some ways, it is housed in a lovely Beaux Arts building, with collections spanning virtually the entire history of art. Highlights include a large Egyptian wing, a superb Native American collection, and a major permanent assemblage of contemporary art. In addition to staging some of the more unusual and controversial exhibits in town, the museum also hosts a "First Saturday" series (the first Saturday of every month, 5-11 pm) featuring free concerts, performances, films, dances, and dance lessons.

Smaller Art Museums

In addition to the behemoth0s above, New York City is home to scores of smaller art museums, many of which are unique gems. No matter where your art interests lie, you're bound to find something that speaks to you.

Photography buffs won't want to miss the **International Center of Photography,** which relocated from the Upper East Side to Midtown (1133 Sixth Ave, at 43rd St). In these spacious galleries, you'll find changing exhibits featuring everyone from Weegee (Arthur Fellig) to Annie Leibovitz.

Meanwhile, sculpture fans will want to visit the **Isamu Noguchi Garden Museum** in Long Island City, Queens (32-37 Vernon Blvd, at 33rd Rd; phone 718/204-7088), just a short trip from Manhattan. Housed in the sculptor's former studio, complete with an outdoor sculpture garden, the museum is filled with Noguchi stone, metal, and woodwork. The museum is open only from April through October, so you will have to time your visit accordingly.

In Murray Hill, find the **Pierpont Morgan Library** (29 E 36th St, at Madison Ave), housed in an elegant neoclassic mansion that was once financier John Pierpont Morgan's personal library and art museum. The library holds a priceless collection of illuminated manuscripts and Old Master drawings; compelling traveling exhibits are frequently on display as well.

In SoHo, the **New Museum of Contemporary Art** (583 Broadway, between Houston and Prince streets; phone 212/219-1222) hosts experimental and conceptual works by contemporary artists from all over the world. Also a premier center for art on the cutting edge is the **P.S.1 Contemporary Art Center** in Long Island City, Queens (22-25 Jackson Ave, at 46th St). On the Upper West Side, the **American Folk Art Museum** (45 W 53rd St; phone 212/595-9533) showcases everything from quilts and weathervanes to painting and sculpture; admission is always free.

History Museums

A good introduction to the history of the Big Apple can be found at the **Museum of the City of New York**

(Fifth Ave, between 103rd and 104th streets; phone 212/534-1672), an eclectic establishment filled with a vast permanent collection of paintings and photographs, maps and prints, Broadway memorabilia, and old model ships. Housed in a sprawling neo-Georgian building, the museum also hosts an interesting series of temporary exhibits on such subjects as Duke Ellington or stickball.

Also devoted to the history of New York is the **New York Historical Society** (2 W 77th St, at Central Park West; phone 212/873-3400), which recently reawakened after years of inactivity due to financial troubles. Spread out over many high-ceilinged rooms, the society presents temporary exhibits on everything from the legendary Stork Club-frequented by everyone from Frank Sinatra to JFK- the small African-American communities that once dotted Central Park.

To find out more about immigration history, visit the **Ellis Island Museum,** a trip that is usually made via ferry, in conjunction with a jaunt to the **Statue of Liberty** (for information, call the Circle Line Ferry at 212/269-5755; the ferries leave from Battery Park in Lower Manhattan). The primary point of entry for immigrants to the United States from 1892 to 1924, Ellis Island is a castlelike building, all red-brick towers and white domes, that now houses multiple exhibits on the immigrant experience, along with photographs, films, and taped oral histories. To avoid the crowds that flock here, especially during the summer, arrive first thing in the morning.

Related in theme to Ellis Island is the **Lower East Side Tenement Museum** (108 Orchard St, between Delancey and Broome streets; phone 212/431-0233; visits by guided tour only, reservations recommended). Deliberately dark and oppressive, the museum re-creates early immigrant life in Manhattan.

The **South Street Seaport Museum** is not so much a museum as it is an 11-block historic district, located in Lower Manhattan where Fulton Street meets the East River. A thriving port during the 19th century, the now-restored area is filled with commercial shops and restaurants, along with dozens of historic buildingsa boat-building shop, a former counting house—and a few historic sailing ships. The ships and some of the buildings require an entrance ticket that can be purchased at the Visitor Center (on Schermerhorn Row, an extension of Fulton Street; phone 212/748-8600).

In the East Village, find the **Merchant's House Museum** (29 E 4th St, near the Bowery; phone 212/777-1089). This classic Greek Revival home is furnished exactly as it was in 1835, when merchant Seabury Tredwell and his family lived here.

Near Gramercy Park presides **Theodore Roosevelt's Birthplace** (28 E 20th St, near Broadway; phone 212/260-1616), a handsome four-story brownstone that is an exact replica of the original. Now administered by the National Park Service, the museum houses the largest collection of Roosevelt memorabilia in the country.

Cultural Museums

As befits a city made up of many peoples, New York is home to a number of museums that focus on the culture of one country or area of the world. Some of these are major, professionally assembled institutions; others are small and homespun.

In lower Manhattan, find the George Gustav Heye Center of the **National Museum of the American Indian** (1 Bowling Green, at State St and Battery Pl; phone 212/668-6624), a branch of the Smithsonian Institution. Housed in a stunning 1907 Beaux Arts building designed by Cass Gilbert, the museum holds some of the country's finest Native American art and artifacts, ranging in date of origin from 3200 BC to the 20th century. Admission is always free.

Also in Lower Manhattan is the **Museum of Jewish Heritage** (18 First Pl, at Battery Park, Battery Park City; phone 212/968-1800), built in the shape of a hexagon, symbolic of the Star of David. Opened in 1997, the museum features thousands of moving photographs, cultural artifacts, and archival films documenting the Holocaust and the resilience of the Jewish community.

A second Jewish museum, this one devoted to the arts, culture, and history, can be found on the Upper East Side. Housed in a magnificent French Gothic mansion, the **Jewish Museum** (1109 Fifth Ave, at 92nd St, 212/423-3200) holds an outstanding permanent collection of ceremonial objects and artifacts while also hosting many major exhibits on everything from "The Dreyfus Affair" to painter Marc Chagall.

Also on the Upper East Side, find the **Asia Society** (725 Park Ave, at 59th St; phone 212/517-2742) and **El Museo del Barrio** (1230 Fifth Ave, between 104th and 105th streets; phone 212/831-7272). The former presents first-rate temporary exhibits, concerts, films, and lectures on various aspects of Asian culture and history. The latter features changing exhibits on both contemporary and historic subjects and houses a superb permanent collection of *Santos de Palo,* or carved wooden saints.

In Harlem is the **African American Wax Museum** (318 W 115th St, between Manhattan Avenue and Frederick Douglass Blvd; by appointment only), a tiny private place created and run by Haitian-born artist Raven Chanticleer. The museum is filled with wax figures of famous African AmericansFrederick Douglass, Josephine Baker, Nelson Mandela—as well as Chanticleer's own paintings and sculptures.

The **Museum of Chinese in the Americas** in Chinatown (70 Mulberry St, at Bayard St, second floor; phone 212/619-4785) is a small but fascinating place, filled with photographs, mementos, and poetry culled from nearly two decades of research in the community. Women's roles, religion, and Chinese laundries are among the subjects covered in the exhibits.

On Staten Island, find the **Jacques Marchais Museum of Tibetan Art** (338 Lighthouse Ave, at Windsor; phone 718/987-3500). Perched on a steep hill with views of the Atlantic Ocean, the museum houses the collection of Jacqueline Norman Klauber, who became fascinated with Tibet as a child. Highlights of the exhibit include a series of bright-colored masks and a large collection of golden *thangkas,* or religious images.

Natural History, Science, and Technology Museums

The must-stop in this category is the enormous **American Museum of Natural History** (Central Park West at 79th St; phone 212/769-5100), one of the city's greatest museums. Always filled with hundreds of shouting, enthusiastic kids, the museum went through a major renovation in the late 1990s and is now filled with many state-of-the-art exhibits.

At the heart of the museum are approximately 100 dinosaur skeletons, some housed in the soaring, not-to-be-missed Theodore Roosevelt Memorial Hall. Other highlights include the Mammals Wing, the Hall of Human Biology and Evolution, the Hall of Primitive Vertebrates, and the museum's many dioramas and exhibits devoted to native peoples around the world. Adjoining the museum to the north is the spanking new **Rose Center for Earth and Science,** featuring a planetarium with a Zeiss sky projector capable of projecting 9,100 stars as viewed from Earth.

The city's top pure science museum is the **New York Hall of Science** (47-01 111th St; phone 718/699-0005), located in Flushing Meadows-Corona Park, Queensbest reached from Manhattan via the 7 subway. Housed in a dramatic building with undulating walls, the museum is packed with hands-on exhibits for kids and features a large Science Playground out back, where kids can learn about the laws of physics.

Docked at Pier 86 on the western edge of Manhattan is the **Intrepid Sea-Air-Space Museum** (West 46th St at

12th Ave; phone 212/245-0072). A former World War II aircraft carrier, the museum is now devoted to military history and includes lots of child-friendly hands-on exhibits. Small aircraft and space capsules are strewn here and there, and exhibits focus on such subjects as satellite communication and spaceship design.

Also in Midtown is the **Museum of Television and Radio** (25 W 52nd St, between Fifth and Sixth avenues; phone 212/621-6800), where you can watch your favorite old television show, listen to a classic radio broadcast, or research a pop-culture question. The museum also offers traditional exhibits on such subjects as the history of animation. Be sure to arrive early if you plan to visit on the weekend and want to use one of the museum's 96 semiprivate televisions or radio consoles.

MUSEUMS FOR KIDS

In addition to the natural history, science, and technology museums, children might also enjoy visiting the **Children's Museum of Manhattan** on the Upper West Side (212 W 83rd St, between Broadway and Amsterdam Ave; phone 212/721-1223) or the **Children's Museum of the Arts in SoHo** (182 Lafayette St, between Broome and Grand streets; phone 212/274-0986). In the former, aimed at ages 2 to 10, kids can draw and paint, play at being newscasters, or explore the ever-changing play areas; the latter features an "Artists Studio", where youngsters can try their hand at sand painting, origami, sculpture, and beadwork.

Although not, strictly speaking, a children's museum, the **New York City Fire Museum** in SoHo (278 Spring St, between Varick and Houston; phone 212/691-1303) has great appeal for kids. Housed in an actual firehouse that was used up until 1959, the museum is filled with fire engines new and old, helmets and uniforms, hoses, and lifesaving nets. Retired firefighters take visitors through the museum, reciting fascinating tidbits of fire-fighting history along the way. This museum has been a particularly poignant stop since the terrorist attacks of 2001 reminded New Yorkersand all Americanswhat heroes firefighters are.

Older kids might enjoy a visit to the **Forbes Magazine Galleries** in Greenwich Village (62 Fifth Ave, near 12th St; phone 212/206-5548). Housing the collections of the idiosyncratic media tycoon Malcolm Forbes, the museum includes exhibits of more than 500 toy boats, 12,000 toy soldiers, about a dozen Fabergé eggs, and numerous historical documents relating to American history.

in Bryant Park. *The New Yorker* and *New York* magazines carry extensive listings of the week's entertainment; the Friday edition of *The New York Times* also reports weekend availability of tickets.

Additional Visitor Information

Contact the New York Convention and Visitors Bureau, 810 7th Ave, 10019; phone 212/484-1222. The bureau has free maps, "twofers" to Broadway shows, bulletins, and brochures on attractions, events, shopping, restaurants, and hotels. For events of the week, visitors should get copies of *The New Yorker* and *New York* magazines and *The New York Times.*

Public Transportation

Subway and elevated trains, buses (New York City Transit Authority), phone 718/330-3322 or 718/330-1234. The subway system, which carries more than 4 million people on weekdays, covers every borough except Staten Island, which has its own transportation system. Maps of the system are posted at every station and on every car.

Airport Information

La Guardia, in Queens 8 miles northeast of Manhattan; **Kennedy International,** in Queens 15 miles southeast of Manhattan; **Newark International,** 16 miles southwest of Manhattan in New Jersey

Driving in New York

Vehicular traffic is heaviest during weekday rush hours and on both weekdays and weekends between Thanksgiving and Christmas week—a period of almost continuous rush hour. Most Manhattan avenues and streets are one-way. Because New York traffic is very heavy and parking is both scarce and expensive, many visitors find taxis more convenient and economical than driving.

What to See and Do

Adventure on a Shoestring. *300 W 53rd St, New York (10019). Phone 212/265-2663.* Year-round walking tours of various neighborhoods, including SoHo, Haunted Greenwich Village, and Chinatown. **$**

American Bible Society Gallery/Library. *1865 Broadway, New York (10023). Phone 212/408-1500. www.mobia.org.* Changing exhibits run the gamut from stained glass in American art and architecture to the impact of the Bible on the world to religious folk art in Guatemala. Special events include lectures, workshops, and symposia. Gallery (Tues-Wed, Fri-Sun 10 am-6 pm; Thurs 10 am-8 pm; closed holidays). Library (Mon-Fri 9 am-5 pm). **FREE**

American Folk Art Museum. *45 W 53rd St, New York (10019). Phone 212/265-1040. www.folkartmuseum.org.* Folk arts of all types, including paintings, sculptures, quilts, needlework, toys, weather vanes, and handmade furniture. Changing exhibits; lectures and demonstrations. Caf; museum shop. Admission is free on Friday evenings. (Tues-Thurs, Sat-Sun 10:30 am-5:30 pm, Fri to 7:30 pm; closed holidays) **$$**

> **Eva and Morris Feld Gallery.** *66 Columbus, New York (10023). Phone 212/595-9533.* The original site of the American Folk Art Museum, reopened as a sister gallery, function space, and museum shop after renovations were completed in 2001. (Tues-Sun noon-7:30 pm) **FREE**

★ **American Museum of Natural History.** *79th St and Central Park W, New York (10024). Phone 212/769-5100. www.amnh.org.* Kids love this behemoth of a museum. Among its 36 million specimens are at least 100 dinosaur skeletons, including a huge Tyrannosaurus rex whose serrated teeth alone measure 6 inches long. You may prefer to stroll through a roomful of free-flying butterflies or examine the 563-carat Star of India sapphire. Expect to be blown away by the 4-year-old Rose Center for Earth and Space and the Hayden Planetarium. The Planetarium Space Show is only 30 minutes long, but its dazzling. Narrated by the likes of Tom Hanks and Harrison Ford, it uses the worlds largest, most powerful projector, the Zeiss Mark IX, which was built to the museums specifications. The show is one of unparalleled sophistication, accuracy, and excitement. Seating is limited, so choose a day for the museum and order tickets in advance. (Daily 10 am-5:45 pm; closed Thanksgiving, Dec 25). **$$$**

Angelika Film Center. *18 W Houston St, New York (10012). Phone 212/995-2000. www.angelikafilmcenter.com.* Get a taste of genuine SoHo living at this cultural institution that has attracted lovers of artsy movies for years. But the Angelika is even more than that. It is a special placea world away from todays overcrowded, noisy multiplexes teeming with soccer moms and screaming kids. You'll find a generally urbane crowd at the independent films shown at the theater. And the Angelika Café in the lobby area is a great little place to grab a latte and a scone before the flick or a soda and a sandwich after the movie. On Sunday mornings, you'll find locals relaxing in the caf, enjoying their coffee and *The New York Times.* Hang out here for a while and you'll feel more like a real New Yorker than a tourist. **$$$**

Asia Society and Museum. *725 Park Ave, New York (10021). At 70th St. Phone 212/288-6400; fax 212/517-8315. www.asiasociety.org.* Masterpieces of Asian art, donated by founder John Rockefeller, make up most of this museums permanent collection. Its works include sculptures, ceramics, and paintings from places like China, Korea, Japan, and India. In addition, the museum offers a schedule of films, performances, and lectures. The Asia Society also has a lovely indoor sculpture garden and caf, which make for a nice stop on a hectic day of sightseeing. (Tues-Thurs, Sat-Sun 11 am-6 pm; Fri to 9 pm; closed holidays) **$$**

Astro Minerals Gallery of Gems. *185 Madison Ave, New York (10016). At 34th St. Phone 212/889-9000. www.astrogallery.com.* Display of minerals, gems, jewelry; primitive and African art. (Mon-Wed, Fri 10 am-7 pm; Thu 10-8; Sat 11 am-6 pm; Sun 11 am-6 pm; closed Jan 1, Thanksgiving, Dec 25) **FREE**

Audubon Terrace Museum Group. *Broadway and 155th St, New York (10032).* www.*washington-heights.us.* (Audubon Terrace) Clustered around a central plaza and accessible from Broadway, this group includes the American Geographical Society, the American Academy and Institute of Arts and Letters, the American Numismatic Society, and the Hispanic Society of America. Also here are the

> **American Numismatic Society.** *96 Fulton St, New York (10038). www.numismatics.org. Phone 212/571-4470.* Society headquarters; numismatic library; "World of Coins" exhibit; changing exhibits. (Tues-Fri 9:30 am-4:30 pm, closed noon-1 pm; closed holidays) **FREE**

Hispanic Society of America. *613 W 155th St, New York (10032). Between 155th and 156th sts. Phone 212/926-2234.* Art of the Iberian Peninsula, Latin America, and the Philippines from prehistoric times to the present. Paintings, sculpture, ceramics, drawings, etchings, lithographs, textiles, and metalwork. (Tues-Sat 10 am-4:30 pm, Sun 1-4 pm; closed holidays) **FREE**

Bergdorf Goodman. *754 Fifth Ave, New York (10019). Phone 212/753-7300. www.bergdorfgoodman.com.* With its designer handbags that can set you back as much as $4,000, $700 swimsuits, and nightgowns that cost $500, Bergdorf Goodman is one of the citys grand-dame department stores. Ladies who lunch, yuppie professionals, and stylish Gen Xers with trust funds are equally at home in this shopping Mecca, located in the heart of the Midtown shopping district, which features a sophisticated selection of clothing, furs, jewelry, tableware, kitchenware, cosmetics, and lingerie. You can find items on sale, but this is not the place for bargain hunters. The selection of merchandise tends to appeal more to those whose taste borders on conservative. The sales staff is attentive and pleasant for those who need assistance in picking out just the right thing. Word to the wise: pack your platinum card. (Mon-Wed, Fri-Sat 10 am-7 pm, Thurs to 8 pm, Sun noon-6 pm)

Bloomingdale's. *1000 Third Ave,59th St and Lexington Ave, New York (10022). Phone 212/705-2000; toll-free 800/472-0788. www.bloomingdales.com.* Everyone in New York knows the name Bloomingdales and the famous Bloomies shopping bags. This world-renowned department store, loved by locals and tourists alike, sells a mix of merchandise in a sleek, modern setting. You can find designer clothing for men and women, high-quality housewares, jewelry, cosmetics, and just about everything else. Although prices are high, you can find good sales. (Mon-Thurs 10 am-8:30 pm, Fri-Sat 9 am-10 pm, Sun 11 am-7 pm; closed Thanksgiving, Dec 25)

Blue Note. *131 W 3rd St, New York (10012). Phone 212/475-8592. www.bluenotejazz.com.* For some of the worlds best names in jazz, head downtown to Greenwich Village to the Blue Note. This bastion of fine jazz has played host over the years to many well-known jazz performers, as well as rising stars. Although the cover charge is higher here than at many other venues, the acts are worth it. Monday nights can be had for around $10, when the record companies promote new releases by their artists. The club also serves a variety of food and drinks if you want to grab dinner while listening to some cool tunes. (Daily) **$$$$**

Bowling Green. *Broadway and Whitehall St, New York (10004). At the Southern end of Broadway.* Originally a Dutch market, this is the city's oldest park, said to be the place where Peter Minuit purchased Manhattan for $24 worth of trinkets. The park fence dates from 1771. You'll also find *Charging Bull* here, a 7,000-pound bronze statue that stock market investors often rub for good luck.

Bowlmor Lanes. *110 University Pl, New York (10003). Phone 212/255-8188. www.bowlmor.com.* A New York landmark since 1938, this 42-lane, two-level "more than a bowling alley" features a restored retro bar and lounge with red booths, a yellow ceiling, and a DJ on Monday nights. Richard Nixon, Cameron Diaz, and the Rolling Stones have all bowled at these lanes, where a colorful Village crowd frequents the place until all hours. Munch on anything from nachos and hamburgers to fried calamari and grilled filet mignon in the restaurant, or have your meal brought straight to your lane. Its a funky, fun hangout, even if you don't bowl. Note that no one under 21 is admitted after 5 pm. (Daily) **$$$$**

Brooklyn Bridge. *Park Row near Municipal Building, New York (10002). Take the 4, 5, or 6 subway to the Brooklyn Bridge/City Hall station, or the N or R subway to the nearby City Hall stop.* For an awesome view of lower Manhattan, Brooklyn, and the New York Harbor, take a leisurely 40-minute stroll across downtowns historic Brooklyn Bridge, the first bridge to cross the East River (actually a tidal estuary between Long Island Sound and New York Harbor) to Brooklyn. Opened on May 24, 1883, the bridge was, and still is, seen as a monument to American engineering and creativity. Two massive stone pylons, each pierced with two soaring Gothic arches, rise 272 feet to support an intricate web of cables. A particularly good time of day to take in the views is at sunset. Dress appropriately in cooler weather, since it can be very windy. At the Brooklyn end of the bridge is a lovely half-mile promenade with equally grand views. The bridge is also near the South Street Seaport (see), at the foot of Fulton Street and the East River. **FREE**

★ **Carnegie Hall.** *57th St and Broadway, New York (10019). Phone 212/247-7800. www.carnegiehall.org.* Completed in 1891, the celebrated auditorium has been home to the world's great musicians for more than a century. Guided one-hour tours ($$) (Sept-June: Mon-Fri 11:30 am, 2 pm, and 3 pm, performance schedule permitting). **$$**

Castle Clinton National Monument. *Battery Park, New York (10005). Phone 212/344-7220. www.eparks.com.* (1811) Built as a fort, this later was a place of public entertainment called Castle Garden where Jenny Lind sang in 1850 under P. T. Barnum's management. In 1855, it was taken over by the state of New York for use as an immigrant receiving station. More than 8 million people entered the United States here between 1855 and 1890; Ellis Island was opened in 1892. The castle became the New York City Aquarium in 1896, which closed in 1941 and reopened at Coney Island in Brooklyn (see). The site has undergone modifications to serve as the visitor orientation/ferry departure center for the Statue of Liberty and Ellis Island. Ferry ticket booth; exhibits on Castle Clinton, Statue of Liberty, and Ellis Island; visitor center. (Daily 9 am-5 pm; closed Dec 25) **FREE**

Cathedral Church of St. John the Divine. *1047 Amsterdam Ave, New York (10025). At 112th St. Phone 212/316-7540. www.stjohndivine.org.* (Episcopal) Under construction since 1892. When completed, this will be the largest Gothic cathedral in the world, 601 feet long and 124 feet high. Bronze doors of the central portal represent scenes from the Old and New Testaments. The great rose window, 40 feet in diameter, is made up of more than 10,000 pieces of glass. A tapestry, painting, and sculpture collection is also housed here. The cathedral and five other buildings are on 13 acres with a park and garden areas, including the Biblical Garden. No parking provided. (Daily 7:30 am-6 pm; tours Tues-Sat 11 am; also Sun at 1 pm, following last morning service; no tours religious holidays) **$$**

★ **Central Park.** *59th St and Fifth Ave (Grand Army Plaza Entrance), New York (10019). 59th to 110th sts between Fifth Ave and Central Park West. Phone 212/360-3444. www.centralparknyc.com.* Called the lungs of New York, Central Park was reclaimed in 1858 from 843 acres of swampland that were used as a garbage dump and occupied by squatters. Landscape designer Frederick Law Olmsteds dream was to bring city dwellers the kind of refreshment found only in nature. A century-and-a-half later, the park still does that; today, its a source of varied outdoor entertainment. Stop at the visitors center, called The Dairymid-park at 65th Street-for a map and a calendar of events. If you're looking for active endeavors, you can jog around the Reservoir or rent ice skates at Wollman Rink or at Lasker Rink, which becomes a swimming pool in summer. If you're looking to have a Woody Allen moment on the Lake, rent a rowboat at Loeb Boathouse. Rent a kite from Big City Kites, at Lexington and 82nd Street, and walk over to the park to catch the breeze on the Great Lawn. If you have kids, visit one of the 19 themed playgrounds, the zoo and petting zoo, the Carousel, the raucous storytelling hour at the Hans Christian Andersen statue, and the Model Boat Pond, where serious modelers race their tiny remote-controlled boats on weekends. In summer, somethings going on every night, and its free! See Shakespeare in the Park at the Delacorte Theater. Get comfortable on the Great Lawn to hear the New York Philharmonic or the Metropolitan Opera under the stars. SummerStage brings well-known artists to Rumsey Playfield for jazz, dance, traditional, and contemporary musical performances. The Band Shell is the venue for classical concerts. Take advantage of Central Park. Amble through the forested Ramble. Stroll down the venerable, elm-lined Mall and past the bronze statues of Balto the dog, Alice in Wonderland, and forgotten poets. Bring a picnic! Also in the park are

Bicycle rentals at Loeb Boathouse. *Park Dr N & E 72nd St, New York (10023). Phone 212/517-2233.* Central Park is an 843-acre oasis of calm in an otherwise chaotic city. Rent a bike for yourself and the kids and enjoy a ride through this sprawling mix of winding paths, meadows, lakes, and ponds. Take in the sight of dog walkers, kids playing softball, joggersand an occasional homeless person. The park especially comes alive on the weekends in summer. (Mar-Oct, daily 10 am-7 pm) **$$$**

The Dairy. *64th St, mid-Park, New York (10019). In the park on 65th St, W of the Central Park Wildlife Conservation Center and the carousel. Phone 212/794-6564.* Exhibition/Visitor Information Center. Video on history of the park; time-travel video; gift and book shop. (Tues-Sun 10 am-5 pm) **FREE**

Storytelling in the Park. *74th St and Fifth Ave, New York (10019). Phone 212/360-3444.* At Hans Christian Andersen statue in Central Park, near the model boat pond (June-Sept, Sat 11 am). Recommended for children 5 and older; also in certain playgrounds (July-Aug). **FREE**

Century 21. *22 Cortlandt St, New York (10007). Phone 212/227-9092. www.c21stores.com.* This is a can't-miss store if you want designer merchandise at rock-bottom prices and have time to look through aisles of items. The three-story department store sells mens, womens, and children's clothing; cosmetics; housewares; and electronics. The stores extended morning hours are a benefit for both New Yorkers who want to make purchases before work and for tourists who are early-birds. You won'tbe disappointed, and neither will your wallet or your wardrobe. But you may need to take a cab back to your hotel since you'll be so loaded down with shopping bags. (Mon-Wed, Fri 7:45 am-8 pm, Thurs to 8:30 pm, Sat 10 am-8 pm, Sun 11 am-7 pm; closed holidays)

Chelsea Piers Sports and Entertainment Complex. *24th St and West Side Hwy, New York (10011). Piers 59-62 on the Hudson River from 17th to 23rd sts. The entrance is at 23rd St. Take the C/E subway to 23rd St. Phone 212/336-6666. www.chelseapiers.com.* For the best in recreational activities all in one location, keep heading west until you hit Chelsea Piers. The 1.7-million-square-foot complex features an ice skating rink, a bowling alley, climbing walls, a driving range, basketball, in-line skating, and more. There also are pubs and restaurants where you can grab a meal after your busy day. Stop in for a cold one at the Chelsea Brewing Co., the states largest microbrewery. Make a point to visit the complex at sundown to view the beautiful sunset on the river. Both kids and adults can spend a nice few hours at this mega sports center. (Mon-Fri 6 am-11 pm, Sat-Sun 8 am-9 pm)

Children's Museum of Manhattan. *The Tisch Building, 212 W 83rd St, New York (10024). On the Upper West Side, on 83rd between Broadway and Amsterdam. Phone 212/721-1234. www.cmom.org.* Hands-on exhibits for children ages 2-10; kids can draw and paint, learn crafts, play at being newscasters, listen to stories, or explore changing play areas. (late June-mid Sept, Tues-Sun 10 am-5 pm; rest of the year, Wed-Sun 10 am-5 pm; closed holidays) **$$**

★ **Chinatown.** *Bordered by Kenmore and Delancey streets on the north, East and Worth streets on the south, Allen street on the east, and Broadway on the west. Take the J, M, N, R, 6, or Z subway to Canal St. www.chinatown-online.com.* How does the thought of 200 restaurants grab you? Or dozens of jewelry stores and gift shops? Or maybe you're into shops selling Asian antiques, feng shui items, and herbal remedies. Whatever you want to buy, from cheap and kitschy to pricey and unique, you'll find it in this noisy, crowded, and invigorating enclave of Lower Manhattan. And if you crave authentic Chinese food, you can visit this area over and over again to sample the flavorful mix of Cantonese, Szechwan, and Hunan dishes served up by mom-and-pop restaurateurs. Most of these eateries entice diners with massive meals that will suit even the most budget-conscious travelers. Tip: While many establishments close on Christmas Day, Chinatowns restaurants remain open and are usually filled with holiday diners.

Christie's Auctions. *20 Rockefeller Plz, New York (10020). At 49th St, between 5th and 6th aves. Phone 212/636-2000. www.christies.com.* Get a taste of high society at a Christie's auction. Whether you're just a spectator or you have lots of spare cash with which to purchase something wonderful, attending an auction at this institution is a thrilling, fast-paced experience. Items sold at auction at Christies have included the Master of Your Domain script from the television show *Seinfeld*, gowns worn by the late Princess Diana, and a Honus Wagner baseball card (the most expensive card ever sold). Special departments are devoted to areas like wines, cameras, and cars. Publications like *New York* magazine and *The New York Times* contain listings of upcoming events. (Mon-Fri 9:30 am-5:30 pm, Sat 10 am-5 pm, Sun 1-5 pm; closed holidays) **FREE**

Chrysler Building. *405 Lexington Ave, New York (10174). At E 42nd St. Phone 212/682-3070.* New York's famous Art Deco skyscraper. The graceful pointed spire with triangular windows set in arches is lighted at night. The impressive lobby features beautiful jazz-age detailing. (Mon-Fri 8 am-5 pm) **FREE**

Circle Line Cruises. *Pier 83, W 42nd St and 12th Ave, New York (10036). All trains (subway) stop at 42nd St. Then transfer to westbound M42 bus to pier. Phone 212/563-3200. www.circleline42.com.* Grab a seat on the port (left) side for a spectacular view of the skyline. Rest your feet and enjoy the sea air as you cruise around Manhattan. Narrated by knowledgeable, personable guides, these tours take you past the Statue of Liberty and under the Brooklyn Bridge; if you opt for the three-hour cruise, you'll also see the New Jersey Palisades, a glorious sight in autumn. Food and drinks are available on board. (Closed Tues-Wed in Jan, Tues in Mar, Jan 1, Dec 25) **$$$$**

City Center. *131 W 55th St, New York (10019). 55th St between 6th and 7th aves. Phone 212/581-1212; toll-free 877/581-1212. www.citycenter.org.* This landmark theater hosts world-renowned dance companies, including the Alvin Ailey American Dance Theater, the Paul Taylor Dance Company, and Merce Cunningham Dance Company. It also presents American music and theater events. Downstairs, City Center Stages I and II host the Manhattan Theatre Club.

City College of New York. *138th St and Convent Ave, New York (10031). Phone 212/650-7000. www.ccny.cuny.edu.*(1847) (11,000 students) One of the nation's best-known municipal colleges and the oldest in the city university system. Alumni include eight Nobel laureates, Supreme Court Justice Felix Frankfurter, and authors Upton Sinclair, Paddy Chayefsky, and Bernard Malamud. Tours (Mon-Thurs, by appointment).

City Hall Park. *Broadway and Chambers St, New York (10007). Phone 212/788-3000.*Architecturally, City Hall is a combination of American Federalist and English Georgian, with Louis XIV detailing. It is built of marble and brownstone.

Claremont Riding Academy. *175 W 89th St, New York (10024). Phone 212/724-5100.* Come to the oldest continuously operated stable in the United States to take a private or group lesson, or rent a horse and go for an unescorted walk, trot, or canter on Central Parks bridle paths. Escorted rides also are available for those with riding experience. Book as early as you can. Viewing the action from atop a beautiful horse on a mild, sunny day in the park can be quite peacefuland is quite popular. (Daily; closed Dec 25) **$$$$$**

★ **The Cloisters.** *In Fort Tryon Park, off Henry Hudson Pkwy, one exit N of George Washington Bridge. Phone 212/923-3700. www.metmuseum.org.* To escape the often frantic pace of the city, take the A train to Fort Tryon Park in upper Manhattan where The Cloisters, the medieval branch of the Metropolitan Museum, perches peacefully on a bluff overlooking the Hudson River. Funded in large part by John D. Rockefeller, Jr., The Cloisters houses an extraordinary collection of sculpture, illuminated manuscripts, stained glass, ivory, and precious metalwork, as well as the famed Unicorn tapestries. The architectural setting is as remarkable as its contents. Five cloisters (quadrangles enclosed by a roofed arcade), a chapter house, and chapels were taken from monasteries in France and Spain and reassembled stone by stone. In the Bonnefont Cloister, catch the spicy fragrance of the herb garden and take time to meditate; the sublime view of the Hudson Valley is always pristine. Donor Rockefeller also purchased the land across the river and restricted development there. (Tues-Sun 9:30 am-5:15 pm; until 4:45 pm Nov-Feb; closed Jan 1, Thanksgiving, Dec 25) **$$$**

Columbia University. *2960 Broadway*, New York (10027). *Phone 212/854-1754. www.columbia.edu.*(1754) (19,000 students) This Ivy League university was originally King's College; classes were conducted in the vestry room of Trinity Church. King's College still exists as Columbia College, with 3,000 students. The campus has more than 62 buildings, including Low Memorial Library, the administration building (which has the Rotunda and the Sackler Collection of Chinese Ceramics), and Butler Library, with more than 5 million volumes. The university numbers Alexander Hamilton, Gouverneur Morris, and John Jay among its early graduates and Nicholas Murray Butler, Dwight D. Eisenhower, and Andrew W. Cordier among its former presidents. Barnard College (1889) with 2,300 women, and the Teachers College (1887) with 5,000 students, are affiliated with Columbia. Multilingual guided tours available. (Mon-Fri except holidays and final exam period) **FREE**

Cooper Union. *Cooper Square,The Cooper Union for the Advancement, New York (10003). Third Ave at 7th St. Phone 212/353-4100. www.cooper.edu.*(1859) (1,000 students) All-scholarship college for art, architecture, and engineering. The Great Hall, where Lincoln spoke in 1861, is used as an auditorium for readings, films, lectures, and performing arts.

Dahesh Museum of Art. *IBM Building,580 Madison Ave, New York (10022). Phone 212/759-0606. www.daheshmuseum.org.* This newer museum focuses on European art from the 19th and 20th centuries, by artists who came from the academic tradition. The permanent collection, the highlights of which include paintings by Rudolf Ernst, Edwin Long, and Maurice Leloir, was started by a prominent Lebanese writer for whom the museum is named. Museum shop, caf. (Tues-Sun 11 am-6 pm; closed holidays) **$$**

The Dakota. *1 W 72nd St at Central Park W, New York (10024).* The first and most famous of the lavish apartment houses on Central Park West, The Dakota got its name because it was considered so far west that New Yorkers joked that it might as well be in the Dakotas. Planned as a turreted, chateaulike structure, it was then embellished with Wild West ornamentation. It has been the home of many celebrities, including Judy Garland, Boris Karloff, and John Lennon and Yoko Ono. On December 8, 1980, The Dakota earned its tragic claim to fame when Lennon was shot and killed by a crazed fan at its gate. Five years later, Yoko Onowho still resides herehad a section of Central Park visible from The Dakota landscaped with foliage and a mosaic with the title of Lennons song *Imagine.* Today, that area is known as Strawberry Fields.

Dean & DeLuca. *560 Broadway, New York (10012). At Prince St. Phone 212/226-6800. www.deandeluca.com.* From Portuguese cornbread to 80 percent pure cocoa and dark chocolate bars to a dozen kinds of gourmet mushrooms, Dean & DeLuca is a food lover's paradise. At this, the original outlet of the growing chain, the pastries and breads rival those of any bakery in Paris; the selection of salads, smoked fish, and meats is astounding; and the produce is so good that it puts the word *fresh* to shame. The personalized mini-cakes, available for any occasion, cost a bundlebut theyre worth every fattening bite. Come early or late, because it can get very crowded (especially on weekends), and you want to spend your time browsing and stocking up on goodies as well as cookware and kitchen accessories. Forget about your budget and let your taste buds do the shopping. (Daily 9 am-9 pm)

El Museo del Barrio. *1230 5th Ave, New York (10029). Phone 212/831-7272. www.elmuseo.org.* Dedicated to Puerto Rican and other Latin American art, this museum features changing exhibits on both contemporary and historic subjects and houses a superb permanent collection of *santos de palo,* or carved wooden saints. The museum also hosts films, theater, concerts, and educational programs. Inquire about bilingual tours. (Wed-Sun 11 am-5 pm; closed Jan 1, Thanksgiving, Dec 25) **$$**

Ellis Island Immigration Museum. *Ellis Island, New York (10004). Boat from Castle Clinton on Battery to Statue of Liberty includes a stop at Ellis Island, which has been incorporated into the monument. Phone 212/363-3206. www.nps.gov/ftoi.*The most famous port of immigration in the country. From 1892 to 1954, more than 12 million immigrants began their American dream here. The principle structure is the Main Building with its Great Hall, where the immigrants were processed; exhibits; 28-minute film; self-service restaurant. There is a fee for the round-trip ferry ride to the island. (Daily 9 am-5 pm, extended hours in the summer; closed Dec 25) **FREE**

Empire State Building. *350 5th Ave, New York (10118). Between 33rd and 34th sts. Phone 212/736-3100. www.esbnyc.com.* A beloved city symbol since it opened in 1931, the Empire State Building is where King Kong battled with airplanes in the movie classic and where visitors go for a panoramic view of Manhattan. Try going at night when the city lights compete with the stars. The slender Art Deco skyscraper is so popular that visitors are often greeted with a long line for tickets to the observation deck. Ordering them in advance from the Web site will save you time. (Daily 8 am-11:30 pm) **$$$**

ESPN Zone. *1472 Broadway, New York (10036). Phone 212/921-3776. www.espnzone.com.* Want to have fun in the city on a rainy afternoon? Hang out at the ESPN Zone in the Theater District. This family-friendly restaurant, filled with huge TV screens, sells sports-related items and gives visitors the chance to view live ESPN broadcasts. The place is loud and boisterous and is a big draw for jocks and jock wannabes; kids get a real kick out of it, too. Have a beer, grab a burger or sandwich, buy a T-shirt or two, and just relax at this sports-lovers paradise. (Mon-Tues, Thurs 11:30 am-11:30 am; Wed 11 am-11:30 pm; Fri-Sat 11 am-midnight, Sun 11 am-11 pm)

FAO Schwarz. *767 Fifth Ave, New York (10153). At Fifth Ave and 58th St. Phone 212/644-9400. www.fao.com.* Children will instantly recognize the entrance to FAO Schwarz when they see the tall, brightly colored musical clock that guards the door. Inside, two floors are crowded with live clowns, chemistry sets, train sets, Madame Alexander dolls, giant stuffed animals, child-sized motorized cars, and all the latest electronic baubles in incredible profusion and magical, mechanical display. During the holidays, shoppers often have to stand in line just to get in. (Mon-Sat 10 am-7 pm, Sun 11 am-6 pm)

Federal Hall National Memorial. *26 Wall St, New York (10005). Phone 212/825-6990. www.nps.gov/feha.*(1842) Greek Revival building on the site of the original Federal Hall, where the Stamp Act Congress met (1765), George Washington was inaugurated (April 30, 1789), and the first Congress met (1789-1790). Originally a custom house, the building was for many years the sub-treasury of the United States. The JQA Ward statue of Washington is on the Wall Street steps. (Mon-Fri 9 am-5 pm; closed holidays) **FREE**

Federal Reserve Bank of New York. *33 Liberty St, New York (10045). Phone 212/720-6130. www.newyorkfed.com.* Approximately 1/3 of the world's supply of gold bullion is stored here in a vault 80 feet below ground level; cash handling operation and historical exhibit of bank notes and coins. Tours (Mon-Fri at 9:30 am, 10:30 am, 11:30 am, 1:30 pm, and 2:30 pm; closed holidays). Student groups must be sixteen years and older; no cameras. Tour reservations required at least one week in advance. **FREE**

Forbes Magazine Galleries. *62 Fifth Ave, New York (10011). At the corner of 12th St. Phone 212/206-5548. www.forbesgalleries.com.* Housing the collections of the idiosyncratic media tycoon Malcolm Forbes, this museum includes exhibits of more than 500 toy boats, 12,000 toy soldiers, about a dozen Faberg eggs, and numerous historical documents relating to American history. (Tues-Wed, Fri-Sat 10 am-4 pm; closed holidays) **FREE**

Fordham University. *33 W 60th St, New York (10023). Across from St. Paul's Church. Phone 212/636-6000. www.fordham.edu.*Private Jesuit university founded in 1841. Other campuses are located in the Bronx and Tarrytown.

Fraunces Tavern Museum. *54 Pearl St, New York (10004). Phone 212/425-1778. www.frauncestavernmuseum.org.* (1907) The museum is housed in the historic Fraunces Tavern (1719) and four adjacent 19th-century buildings. It interprets the history and culture of early America through permanent collections of prints, paintings, decorative arts, and artifacts, changing exhibitions, and period rooms, one of which, the Long Room, is the site of George Washington's farewell to his officers at the end of the Revolutionary War (1783). The museum offers a variety of programs and activities, including tours, lectures, and films. Museum (Tues-Fri 12 pm-5 pm, Sat 10 am-5 pm). Dining room (Mon-Sat). **$**

The Frick Collection. *1 E 70th St, New York (10021). Between Madison and Fifth aves. Phone 212/288-0700. www.frick.org.* The mansion of Henry Clay Frick, wealthy tycoon, infamous strikebreaker, and avid collector of art, contains a remarkably diverse assemblage of paintings. The walls of one room are covered with large, frothy Fragonards depicting the Progress of Love. In other rooms are masterworks by Bellini, Titian, Holbein, Rembrandt, El Greco, Turner, Degas, and many others. A superb collection in a superb setting. See it in one afternoon. (Tues-Sat 10 am-6 pm, Sun 11 am-5 pm; closed holidays) No children under 10; under 16 only with adult. **$$$**

The Garment District. *6th Ave to 8th Ave and from 34th St to 42nd St.* This crowded area, heart of the clothing industry in New York, has hundreds of small shops, factories, and streets jammed with trucks and hand-pushed delivery carts. Also in this area is Macy's.

General Grant National Memorial. *122nd St and Riverside Dr, New York (10027). Phone 212/666-1640. www.nps.gov/gegr.*The largest mausoleum in North America, the General Grant National Monument is the home of Ulysses S. Grants tomb, along with that of his wife. When Grant died in 1885, he had led the North to victory in the Civil War and served two consecutive terms as President of the United States before retiring to New York City. General Grant was so popular that upon his death, more than 90,000 private citizens donated a total of $600,000 (the equivalent of over $11.5 million in todays dollars) to help in the building of his tomb. The tomb was dedicated on April 27, 1897, on the 75th anniversary of Grants birth. Located near picturesque Columbia University, the monument draws more than 75,000 visitors annually. (Daily 9 am-5 pm; closed holidays)

The George Gustav Heye Center of the National Museum of the American Indian. *One Bowling Green St, New York (10004). Phone 212/668-6624. www.nmai.si.edu.*World's largest collection of materials of the native peoples of North, Central, and South America. (Sun-Wed, Fri-Sat 10 am-5 pm, Thurs to 8 pm; closed Dec 25) **FREE**

Grand Central Station. *457 Madison Ave, New York (10017). 42nd St, between Vanderbilt and Lexington. Phone 212/935-3960. www.grandcentralterminal.com.* (1913) Built in the Beaux Arts style and recently renovated for $200 million, this is one of New York's most glorious buildings. It has a vast 125-foot-high concourse, glassed-in catwalks, grand staircases, shops, restaurants, and a star-studded aquamarine ceiling. The Municipal Art Society offers tours on Wed ($$); meet at the information booth in the center of the concourse at 12:30 pm. Terminal (daily 5:30-1:30 am).

Gray Line. *777 Eighth Ave, New York (10019). Between 47th and 48th sts. Phone 212/397-2600; toll-free 800/669-0051. www.newyorksightseeing.com.* Tours of Manhattan aboard glass-top motor coaches. Also day trips and tour packages. **$$$$**

Greenwich Village. *41 Bond St Frnt, New York (10012).* An area reaching from Broadway west to Greenwich Avenue between 14th Street on the north and Houston Street on the south. An extension of this area to the East River is known as the East Village. Perhaps most famous as an art and literary center, Greenwich Village was originally settled by wealthy Colonial New Yorkers wishing to escape to the country. Many Italian and Irish immigrants settled here in the late 19th century. Among the famous writers and artists who have lived and worked in this area are Tom Paine, Walt Whitman, Henry James, John Masefield (he scrubbed saloon floors), Eugene O'Neill, Edna St. Vincent Millay, Maximum Eastman, Arctic explorer-writer Vilhjalmur Stefansson, Franz Kline, e. e. cummings, John Dos Passos, and Martha Graham. It is a colorful area, with restaurants, taverns, book, print, art, and jewelry shops. Greenwich Village is a fashionable and expensive place to live, particularly in the vicinity of

Church of the Ascension. *5th Ave and 10th St, New York (10011). Phone 212/254-8620.*(1840) Episcopal. English Gothic; redecorated 1885-1889 under the direction of Stanford White. John La Farge's mural, *The Ascension of Our Lord*, surmounts the altar; the sculptured angels are by Louis Saint-Gaudens. (Mon-Sat)

Joseph Papp Public Theater. *425 Lafayette St, New York (10003). In the former Astor Library. Phone 212/539-8500.* Complex of six theaters where Shakespeare, new American plays, new productions of classics, films, concerts, and poetry readings are presented.

H & M. *435 Seventh Ave, New York (10018). Phone 212/643-6955. www.hm.com.* If the notion of buying affordable versions of everything you couldnt afford on Madison Avenue appeals to your wallet, then H&M is the store for you. This fast-growing international chain, which sells stylish mens, womens, young adults, and children's clothing, features its own brands at prices that suit most budgets. The shops are bright and airy, and each location has a slightly different mix of inventory. Currently there are five outlets in New York City: 435 Seventh Ave, 125 W 125th St, 1328 Broadway (34th and Herald Square), 640 Fifth Ave, and 558 Broadway (in SoHo). (Daily 9 am-10 pm; closed Thanksgiving, Dec 25)

Hamilton Grange National Memorial. *287 Convent Ave, New York (10031). At W 141st St. Phone 212/283-5154. www.nps.gov/hagr.*(1802) Federal-style residence of Alexander Hamilton. Visitor information center and museum (Fri-Sun 9 am-5 pm). **FREE**

Harlem. *451 W 151st St, New York (10031). Phone 212/757-0425.* An area reaching from 110th Street to about 165th Street and from the Harlem River to Morningside Avenue. Spanish Harlem is toward the east, although Harlem and Spanish Harlem overlap. Harlem has been called "the black capital of America." Tours offered by Harlem Spirituals, 690 Eighth Ave, phone 212/391-0900.

★ **Hayden Planetarium at the Rose Center for Earth and Space.** *American Museum of Natural History,79th St and Central Park W, New York (10024). Phone 212/769-5100. www.amnh.org/rose/haydenplanetarium.html.* Located in the four-block-long American Museum of Natural History, this exciting new planetarium will transport you to new galaxies. The planetarium is a huge sphere housed in a glass box several stories high. In the top part of the sphere is the Space Theater, which presents the awesome Space Show, a feat of sight and sound. The bottom part, called the Big Bang, re-creates the first moments of the universe in a multisensory format narrated by author and poet Maya Angelou. This is fun for the whole family that will leave everyone breathless. The admission price includes entrance to the Museum of Natural History and the rest of the Rose Center for Earth and Space, which features exhibits that cover cosmic evolution, discoveries in astrophysics, and the sizes of the universes various heavenly bodies. (Mon-Thurs, Sat-Sun 10 am-5:45 pm, Fri 10 am-8:45 pm; closed Thanksgiving, Dec 25) **$$$**

Henri Bendel. *712 Fifth Ave, New York (10019). Phone 212/247-1100.* The name Henri Bendel was synonymous with chic during the disco era. Today, the store still features hip, trendy womens designer clothes, hats, fragrances, handbags, and jewelry. Whether you're looking for a $1,200 dress or a $500 handbag, this is the shop for you. You may need to break the bank (or two!) to make a purchase, but you just may find yourself decked out in something that the girls back home wished they owned. (Mon-Sat 10 am-8 pm, Sun noon-7 pm; closed Jan 1, Thanksgiving, Dec 25)

Hogs and Heifers Saloon. *13th and Washington, New York (10014). Phone 212/929-0655. www.hogsandheifers.com.* A biker bar with celebrities bras hanging off deer antlers? Only in Manhattan. Located in the Meatpacking District (just north of Greenwich Village), this bar has hosted celebs like Julia Roberts and Drew Barrymorewho decided to leave their bras behind as eye candy for patrons. You never know who you'll run into on any given night at this wild place. In addition to downing cheap beer, you'll be treated to music and bar-top dancing. The bar also has a less-famous uptown location at 1843 First Ave, phone 212/722-8635. (Mon-Fri 11 am-4 am, Sat 1 pm-4 am, Sun 2 pm-4 am)

International Center of Photography. *6th Ave and 43rd St, New York (10036). Phone 212/857-0000. www.icp.org.* Photography buffs won't want to miss the International Center for Photography, recently relocated from the Upper East Side to Midtown. In these spacious galleries, you'll find changing exhibits featuring everyone from Weegee (Arthur Fellig) to Annie Leibovitz. (Tues-Thurs 10 am-6 pm, Fri 10 am-8 pm, Sat-Sun 10 am-6 pm; closed July 4) **$$**

***Intrepid* Sea-Air-Space Museum.** *Pier 86, 12th Ave and 46th St, New York (10036). Phone 212/245-0072. www.intrepidmuseum.org.* The famous aircraft carrier *Intrepid* has been converted into a museum with gallery space devoted to histories of the ship itself, the modern navy, and space technology. Also on display is a nuclear guided submarine and a Vietnam-era destroyer (available for boarding). Exhibits and film presentations. (Apr-late Sept: Mon-Fri 10 am-5 pm, Sat-Sun 10 am-6 pm; rest of year: Tues-Sun 10 am-5 pm; closed Thanksgiving, Dec 25) **$$$**

Jacob K. Javits Convention Center. *655 W 34th St, New York (10001). From 34th to 39th sts along the Hudson River, on 22-acre site SW of Times Square. Phone 212/216-2000. www.javitscenter.com.* One of the world's largest, most technically advanced exposition halls; 900,000 square feet of exhibit space and more than 100 meeting rooms can accommodate six events simultaneously. Designed by I. M. Pei, the center is easily recognized by its thousands of glass cubes that mirror the skyline by day.

Jewish Museum. *1109 5th Ave, New York (10128). At 92nd St. Phone 212/423-3200. www.jewishmuseum.org.* Devoted to Jewish art and culture, ancient and modern. Historical exhibits; contemporary painting and sculpture. (Sun-Wed 11 am-5:45 pm, Thurs 11 am-9 pm, Fri 11 am-3 pm; closed holidays) **$$**

Jewish Theological Seminary of America. *3080 Broadway, New York (10027). At 122nd St. Phone 212/678-8000. www.jtsa.edu.* Extensive collection of Judaica; rare book room; courtyard with sculpture by Jacques Lipchitz. Special programs. Kosher cafeteria. Tours available. (Mon-Thurs 8 am-9 pm, Fri 8 am-5 pm, Sun 9:30 am-9 pm; closed holidays) **FREE**

Jivamukti Yoga Center. *841 Broadway St, New York (10003). Phone 212/353-0214. www.jivamuktiyoga.com.* Relax and discover your inner peace at one of these soothing yoga classes (second location in Upper East Side at 853 Lexington Ave; 212/396-4200). The reasonable rates, by New York standards, make it affordable for almost anyone to take a quick break from the hectic pace of sightseeing. Book evening classes as early as you can, since they can fill up fast. A little tip: be on the lookout for possible celebrity sightings. (Daily) **$$$**

Joyce Gold History Tours. *141 W 17th St, New York (10011). Phone 212/242-5762. www.nyctours.com.* Take a walk through time with a professional who knows endless stories, both serious and frivolous, about Manhattan and its people. Since 1976, Joyce Gold has led all tours personally, rain or shine. No reservations are necessary, and tours last from 2 to 2 1/2 hours. Stops include Grand Central Terminal, Harlem, the East Village, Chinatown, and Fifth Avenue. Check the Web site for specific subjects, dates, meeting places, and departure times. **$$$**

Kitchen Arts & Letters. *1435 Lexington Ave, New York (10128). Between 93rd and 94th sts. Phone 212/876-5550.*Great cooks and novices alike can spend hours in this store, which features more than 10,000 cookbooks from all over the world. You can find the hottest new books by the most popular chefs, as well as those that have been out of print for years. Whether you want to prepare complicated desserts or perfect the art of the grilled cheese sandwich, this store will have the right cookbook for you. (Tues-Fri 10 am-6:30 pm, Mon 1-6 pm; closed holidays)

Lexington Avenue. *Take the 6 Lexington Ave subway to 28th St.* It may be only a three-block area just south of Murray Hill, but this neighborhood is brimming with the sights and sounds of India. Stores sell Indian and Pakistani spices, pastries, videos, cookware, saris, and fabrics. Restaurants cater to both Muslim and Hindu tastes, suiting both beefeaters and vegetarians. The low prices are a treat as well.

★ Liberty Helicopter Tours. *Downtown Manhattan Heliport, W 30th St and 12th Ave, New York (10004). Take the C/E subways to 34th St and Eighth Ave. Phone 212/967-6464; toll-free 800/542-9933. www.libertyhelicopters.com.* See the grand sights of the city-from the Empire State Building to Yankee Stadium to the Chrysler Buildingall from the magnificent view that only a helicopter can offer. Liberty offers six different tours on its seven-passenger helicopters, which last from five minutes for those who are a bit nervous, to as long as 30 minutes for those who want to see everything. There's even a 30-minute package that enables you to design your own course ($275 per person) and a 15-minute romance package for reserving the entire helicopter ($849), perfect for a special occasion-you even get a bottle of Champagne afterward. Just think, you can pop the question over the beautiful lights of Manhattan! A photo ID is required, and your bags will be screened. No carry-ons are allowed, except for cameras and video equipment. (Mon-Sat 9 am-6:30 pm, call for Sun tours) **$$$$**

★ Lincoln Center for the Performing Arts. *70 Lincoln Center Plz, New York (10023). At 66th St and Broadway. Phone 212/546-2656. www.lincolncenter.org.* The approach of curtain time at The Met is a glittering New York moment. People hurry across Lincoln Plaza and disappear under the ten-story marble arches that front the Opera House. The lobby empties, the director raises his baton, and the overture begins. The Metropolitan Opera House, at the heart of Lincoln Center, is home to one of the worlds greatest opera companies

and the renowned American Ballet. At the right side of the square is Avery Fisher Hall, where Lorin Maazel conducts the New York Philharmonic and an impressive roster of guest artists perform. The Philharmonics Mostly Mozart Festival in August and frequent Young Peoples Concerts for children are perennial favorites. Opposite is the New York State Theater, shared by the New York City Opera and the New York City Ballet, especially famous for its beloved holiday classic, Balanchines *The Nutcracker.* In addition to the three main buildings, the 14-acre campus contains a multitude of other venues, including the Vivian Beaumont Theater, which presents Broadway plays; Alice Tully Hall, home of the Chamber Music Society and the New York Film Festival; and the world-famous Juilliard School. Damrosch Park and its band shell offer many free summer programs, including folk, jazz, and classical concerts. To get the big picture, take a Lincoln Center Guided Tour (phone 212/875-5350), which includes stops at viewing booths when rehearsals are in session. (Daily; closed holidays) **$$$** Here is

New York Public Library for the Performing Arts. *Dorothy and Lewis B. Cullman Center, 45 Lincoln Center Plz, New York (10023). Phone 212/870-1630, www.nypl.org.* Books, phonograph record collection; exhibits and research library on music, theater, and dance; concerts, films, dance recitals. **FREE**

The Lion King. *New Amsterdam Theater,214 W 42nd St, New York (10036). Phone 212/307-4747. www.disneyonbroadway.com.* Based on the Disney animated film of the same name, this wildly popular musical is a feast for the eyes, ears, and soul. It has action, adventure, amazing costumes, and inventive characterswith performers singing and dancing their hearts out. Even though its a kids story, adults of all ages have flocked to see this musical since it opened in 1998. Because the Tony Award winner is such a spectacle to see, it is worth splurging on expensive tickets to get the best seats available. Justify the price by skimping on dinner or lunch beforehand. Book as early as you can, since this show sells out at just about any time of the year. (Daily) **$$$$**

Live TV shows. *Phone 212/664-3056. www.tvtickets.com.* For information regarding the availability of regular and/or standby tickets, contact NBC's ticket office at 30 Rockefeller Plaza, 10112 (phone 212/664-3056); CBS at 524 W 57th St, 10019 (phone 212/975-3247); or ABC at 77 W 66th St, 10023 (phone 818/753-3470). On the day of the show, the New York Convention and Visitors Bureau at 2 Columbus Circle often has tickets for out-of-town visitors on a first-come, first-served basis. Except for NBC productions, many hotels can get tickets for guests with reasonable notice. (To see an important production, write four to six weeks in advance; the number of tickets is usually limited.) Most shows are restricted to people over 18.

Loehmann's. *101 Seventh Ave, New York (10011). Phone 212/352-0856.* Women who are ravenous for famous brands of clothing at discount prices and are willing to do whatever it takes to take home the best items (near-fistfights have been witnessed) will love Loehmann's. This department store is well known to generations of New York women and still has a good reputation for bargains. The five-story store sells mostly womens clothing, jewelry, handbags, shoes, and accessories; it offers a smaller selection of mens apparel. (Mon-Sat 9 am-9 pm, Sun 11 am-7 pm)

Lower East Side. *Delancey and Essex sts, New York. Take the B or D subway to Grand St; J or M subway to Delancey St; or the F subway to Second Ave, Delancey/Essex St, or East Broadway.* Formerly a Jewish ghetto in the 19th and early 20th centuries, The Lower East Side is an ethnically mixed neighborhood with a mishmash of mom-and-pop stores and trendy boutiques that will attract those looking for good deals on clothing, accessories, and housewares. The farther east you go, the dicier the area becomes. Because some stores are owned by Orthodox Jews, they aren'topen Friday evening or on Saturday.

Lower East Side Tenement Museum. *108 Orchard St, New York (10002). Phone 212/431-0233. www.tenement.org.* The highlight at this one-of-a-kind living history museum is the guided tour of an actual tenement inhabited by real Lower East Side immigrants from the late 19th and early 20th centuries. Three apartments have been restored to their original condition. (You will need reservations for any of the guided tours, of which several are offered.) The museum also offers walking tours around the Lower East Side itself, which give you a feel for the area and what its immigrant residents had to endure upon arriving in America in search of their dreams. (Mon 11 am-5:30 pm, Tues-Fri 1-6 pm, Sat-Sun 10:45 am-6 pm) **$$**

Macy's Herald Square. *151 W 34th St, New York (10001). 34th St at Broadway. Phone 212/695-4400. www.macys.com.* "The world's largest store" has everything from international fashion collections for men and women to antique galleries. (Mon-Sat 10-9 pm, Sun 11 am-8 pm; closed Easter, Thanksgiving, Dec 25)

★ Madison Avenue. *Madison Ave and 57th St, New York. Take the 6 subway to the 77th St stop and walk south. Or take the 4, 5, or 6 subway to the 59th St stop or the N or R subway to the Lexington Ave stop and walk north.* If you are well schooled (or even a novice) in the fine art of window-shopping, this stretch of very exclusive brand-name stores along swanky Madison Avenue is calling your name. Top European designers have shops here, including Giorgio Armani (760 Madison Ave, 212/988-9191), Valentino (747 Madison Ave, 212/772-6969), and Prada (841 Madison Ave, 212/327-4200), to name a few. American designers such as Polo/Ralph Lauren (867 Madison Ave, 212/606-2100) and Calvin Klein (654 Madison Ave, 212/292-9000) also have stores along this chic Manhattan strip. Looking to buy something special for someone back home (or for yourself)? The salespeople in these light and airy stores are usually quite helpful, but don't expect to find anything remotely on the cheap side. On a mild, sunny day, window-shopping here makes for a very relaxing stroll.

Madison Square Garden. *4 Pennsylvania Plz, New York (10001). Phone 212/465-6741. www.thegarden.com.* The Garden has been the site of major sporting events, concerts, and other special events for well over a century. The present Garden, the fourth building bearing that name, opened in 1968. (The original Garden was actually on Madison Square.) It is the home of the New York Knicks and Liberty basketball teams, and New York Rangers hockey club. The Garden complex includes the 20,000-seat arena and the Theater at Madison Square Garden, which features performances of the holiday classic *A Christmas Carol* every year.

Merchant's House Museum. *29 E 4th St, New York (10003). Phone 212/777-1089. www.merchantshousemuseum.org.* This East Village home, dating back to the 1830s, offers a look into family life in the mid-19th century. The house has been totally preserved inside and out. Original furnishings, architectural details, and family memorabilia from retired merchant Seabury Tredwell and his descendants can be viewed here. The home was lived in until 1933, when it became a museum. Tours are available on weekends. (Thurs-Mon noon-5 pm) **$$**

★ Metropolitan Museum of Art. *1000 Fifth Ave, New York (10028). At 8nd St. Phone 212/535-7710. www.metmuseum.org.* Vast, exhilarating, and a little unsettling to first-time visitors because of the number and diversity of its collections, the Metropolitan Museum of Art contains more than 2 million objects spanning a period of more than 5,000 years. Even with a map and an audio guide (for which you pay extra), getting lost is not difficultit is also part of the experience. Finding the Rooftop Garden and its population of modern sculptures is easy. Stumbling across Michelangelos sketch for the Sistine Chapel or the stunning state-of-the-art Costume Gallery may be a rewarding surprise. From the ancient Roman tomb, The Temple of Dendur, to a room designed by Frank Lloyd Wright in 1912, and from Picassos powerful portrait of Gertrude Stein to the oddly surrealistic wood panel, St. Anthony in the Wilderness by an unknown Italian master, the Met presents both familiar masterpieces and intriguing hidden treasures. You could spend days here. Plan to spend enough time to see what you'll most enjoy! Call ahead or ask at the Information Desk about free tours, concerts, lectures, and films. There are always special exhibits and children's programs, but strollers are not allowed on Sundays or at special exhibits. (Sun, Tues-Thurs 9:30 am-5 pm; Fri-Sat 9:30 am-9 pm; closed Jan 1, Thanksgiving, Dec 25) **$$$**

Metropolitan Opera Company. *Metropolitan Opera House, Lincoln Center, Broadway and 64th St, New York (10023). Take the 1 or 9 subway to the 66th Street stop. Phone 212/362-6000. www.metopera.org.* This is undoubtedly one of the worlds leading opera companies. Some of the top performers can be seen on the massive, very impressive stage of the Metropolitan Opera House. Tickets go on sale in March for the upcoming season, so book in advance. While prices can be high, it is worth spending the money on the best seats you can get if you are a true opera aficionado. When the lights go down, the curtain opens, and the orchestra begins playing, you will feel like you have been transported to another world. Attending the Metropolitan Opera also gives you a chance to get really dressed up and feel like a star yourself. Add an elegant dinner beforehand at a nearby Upper West Side restaurant and drinks afterwards at a lounge or piano bar and you may have the perfect evening. (Sept-May) **$$$$**

Morris-Jumel Mansion. *Roger Morris Park,65 Jumel Terrace, New York (10032). At 160th St and Edgecomb Ave. Phone 212/923-8008. www.morrisjumel.org.* (1765) Built by Colonel Roger and Mary Philipse Morris, this was George Washington's headquarters in 1776 and later became a British command post and Hessian headquarters. Purchased by French merchant Stephen Jumel in 1810, the house was the scene of the marriage of his widow, Madame Eliza Jumel, to former Vice-President Aaron Burr in 1833. The mansion is the only remaining colonial residence in Manhattan. Period furnishings. (Wed-Sun 10 am-4 pm; closed holidays) **$**

Murray's Cheese. *254 Bleecker St, New York (10014). At Cornelia St between Sixth and Seventh aves. Phone 212/243-3289; toll-free 888/692-4339. www.murray-scheese.com.* For the best gourmet cheese selection in the city, pop into this New York institution in lower Manhattan. The shop will entice any discerning palate with its 250 varieties of domestic and imported cheeses, as well as a selection of breads, olives, antipasti, and personalized gift baskets. (Mon-Sat 8 am-8 pm, Sun 9 am-6 pm) Murrays also has a second, newer location in Midtown at 73 Grand Central Terminal.

Museum of Arts & Design. *40 W 53rd St, New York (10019). Between 5th and 6th aves. Phone 212/956-3535. www.madmuseum.org.* Dedicated to the history of American crafts, including textiles, ceramics, and glasswork. Changing exhibits. (Daily 10 am-6 pm, Thurs to 8 pm; closed holidays) **$$**

Museum of Chinese in the Americas (MoCA). *70 Mulberry St, 2nd Floor, New York (10013). Phone 212/619-4785. www.moca-nyc.org.* This cultural and historical museum in Chinatown, also known as MoCA, is a small but fascinating place, filled with photographs, mementos, and poetry culled from nearly two decades of research in the community. Women's roles, religion, and Chinese laundries are among the subjects covered in the exhibits. Free admission on Friday. (Tues-Thurs, Sat-Sun noon-6 pm, Fri noon-7 pm) **$**

Museum of Jewish Heritage-A Living Memorial to the Holocaust. *Battery Park City, 36 Battery Pl, New York (10280). Phone 646/437-4200. www.mjhnyc.org.* Opened in 1997, this museum features thousands of moving photographs, cultural artifacts, and archival films documenting the Holocaust and the resilience of the Jewish community. It's housed in a building the shape of a hexagon, symolic of the Star of David. The East Wing houses a theater, special-exhibit galleries, a memorial garden, and a caf. (Sun-Tues, Thurs 10 am-5:45 pm, Wed 10 am-8 pm, Fri and the eve of Jewish holidays 10 am-5 pm; closed Sat, Jewish holidays, and Thanksgiving) **$$**

Museum of Television & Radio. *25 W 52nd St, New York (10019). Between Fifth and Sixth aves. Phone 212/621-6800. www.mtr.org.* William Paley, the former head of CBS, founded this museum to collect, preserve, and make available to the public the best of broadcasting. View special screenings or, at a private console, hear and see selections of your own choosing from the vast archive of more than 100,000 programs. From the comedy of Burns and Allen to the Beatles in America, and from a teary-eyed Walter Cronkite reporting on President Kennedys assassination to a tireless Peter Jennings persevering through an endless 9/11, its there for the asking. (Tues-Sun noon-6 pm, Thurs to 8 pm; closed holidays) **$$**

Museum of the City of New York. *1220 Fifth Ave, New York (10029). At 103rd St. Phone 212/534-1672. www.mcny.org.* Explore unique aspects of the city in this Upper East Side mansion dating back to 1930. Displays include a toy gallery with dollhouses; collections of decorative arts, prints, and photographs; and an exhibit on Broadway, complete with costumes and set designs. Other exhibits feature slide shows, paintings, memorabilia, and sculptures, all dedicated to the fascinating history of the city up to the present day. (Tues-Sun 10 am-5 pm; closed holidays) **DONATION**

New York City Fire Museum. *278 Spring St, New York (10013). In SoHo. Phone 212/691-1303. www.nycfiremuseum.org.* Although it isn't, strictly speaking, a children's museum, the New York City Fire Museum has great appeal for kids. Housed in an actual firehouse that was used until 1959, the museum is filled with fire engines new and old, helmets and uniforms, hoses and lifesaving nets. Retired firefighters take visitors through the museum, reciting fascinating tidbits of firefighting history along the way. (Tues-Sat 10 am-5 pm, Sun 10-am-4 pm) **DONATION**

New York Giants (NFL). *Giants Stadium, 50 Hwy 120, East Rutherford (07073). Phone 201/935-8111. www.giants.com.* The Giants had sporadic success throughout the 1980s and '90s (including winning two Super Bowls), and made an improbable run for the Super Bowl in 2000 before losing to the Baltimore Ravens.

New York Historical Society. *170 Central Park W, New York (10024). Phone 212/873-3400. www.nyhistory.org.* This monument to the history of the city recently reawakened after years of inactivity due to financial troubles. Spread out over many high-ceilinged rooms, the society presents temporary exhibits on everything from the legendary Stork Clubfrequented by everyone from Frank Sinatra to JFKto the small African-American communities that once dotted Central Park. The Henry Luce III Center for the Study of American culture features 40,000 objects, including George Washington's camp bed at Valley Forge to the world's largest collection of Tiffany lamps, as well as a nice collection of paintings, sculpture, furniture, and decorative objects. (Tues-Sun 10 am-6 pm) **$$**

New York Islanders (NHL). *Nassau Coliseum, 1255 Hempstead Tpke, Uniondale (11553). Phone 516/501-6700; toll-free 800/882-4753. www.newyorkislanders.com.* Pro hockey's Islanders were the dominant team of the early 1980s, winning three Stanley Cups in a row from 1980 to 1982.

New York Jets (NFL). *Giants Stadium, 50 Hwy 120, East Rutherford (07073). Phone 516/560-8200 (tickets). www.newyorkjets.com.* The Jets began their tenure in the NFL with a bang, when "Broadway Joe" Namath guaranteed victory over the Baltimore Colts in Super Bowl III and then pulled off the feat.

New York Knicks (NBA). *Madison Square Garden, 4 Pennsylvania Plz, New York (10121). Phone 212/465-5867. www.nyknicks.com.* Knicks tickets are sometimes difficult to get because corporations and season ticket holders have snatched them up; call early to maximize your chances. Remember to be on the lookout for celebritiesWoody Allen and Spike Lee often attend games. **$$$$**

New York Liberty (WNBA). *Madison Square Garden, 4 Pennsylvania Plz, New York (10121). Phone 212/564-9622. www.nyliberty.com.* Professional women's basketball games. **$$$$**

★ **New York Mets (MLB).** *Shea Stadium,123-01 Roosevelt Ave, Flushing (11368). Take the 7 subway to the Willets Point-Shea Stadium stop, or hop a leisurely ferry from Manhattan (phone toll-free 800/533-3799 for information) to the stadium. Phone 718/507-6387. www.mets.com.* Although the Mets may not have as long and colorful a history as the Yankees, they are nonetheless a fun team to watch and offer any baseball lover a great spring or summer afternoons or evenings experience. Tickets are usually easy to get for most games, except the annual match-up against the Bronx Bombers. Bring extra cash and do the game right by noshing on hot dogs and peanuts, loading up on souvenirs, and cheering loudly for your favorite players. Don't forget sunscreen, a hat, and sunglasses for day games. (Apr-Sept)

New York Public Library. *Fifth Ave and 42nd St, New York (10018). Phone 212/930-0501. www.nypl.org.* One of the best research libraries in the world, with more than 10 million volumes. Exhibits of rare books, art materials; free programs at branches. One-hour tours of central building (Tues-Sat), library tours at 11 am and 2 pm. Many interesting collections on display at the Central Research Library and The New York Public Library for the Performing Arts (also tours). **FREE**

New York Rangers (NHL). *Madison Square Garden, 4 Pennsylvania Plz, New York (10121). Phone 212/465-6741. www.newyorkrangers.com.* If you love the thrill of ice hockey—as well as the colorful fights that break out between players and the screaming, cursing fans on the sidelines—try to catch the popular New York Rangers in action. Because the team has done so well over the years, getting tickets has become very difficult. Buy yours months in advance if you can. Avoid the temptation to buy overpriced (or worse, counterfeit) tickets from the numerous scalpers who sell their wares in front of the Garden before each game. If you just can't get tickets but still want to experience live hockey while you're visiting New York, opt for a short commute to see either the New York Islanders (phone 631/888-9000 for tickets) or the New Jersey Devils (phone 201/935-6050 for tickets).

New York Stock Exchange. *11 Wall St, New York (10005). Phone 212/656-3000. www.nyse.com.* The world's largest securities trader. Currently, the New York Stock Exchange Interactive Education Center is closed indefinitely for all tours. Call for updated information.

New York University. *22 Washington Sq N, New York (10011). Phone 212/998-4524. www.nyu.edu.*(1831) (15,584 students) One of the largest private universities in the country, NYU is known for its undergraduate and graduate business, medical, and law schools, school of performing arts, and fine arts programs. The university has graduated a large number of "Fortune 500" company executives. Most programs, including the Graduate Business Center, are located on the main campus surrounding Washington Square Park; the medical and dental schools are on the East Side. Tours (Mon-Fri except holidays, from Admissions Office at 22 Washington Sq N). In the Main Building at the northeast corner of Washington Square is the Grey Art Gallery and Study Center, with paintings, drawings, sculpture, and changing exhibits (Tues-Sat). Renaissance musical instrument collection in Waverly Building (by appointment).

★ **New York Yankees.** (SEE BRONX).

Police Museum. *100 Old Slip, New York (10005). Phone 212/480-3100. www.nycpolicemuseum.org.* Exhibits of police uniforms, badges, and equipment. (Mon-Sat 10 am-5 pm; closed holidays) **DONATION**

The Producers. *St. James Theater, 246 W 44th St, New York (10036). Phone 212/239-5800. www.producersonbroadway.com.* This show has won the most Tony Awards ever, and it's truly worth all the accolades that it has received. Based on the hysterical Mel Brooks movie of the same name, this even funnier musical brings to life the story of two producers who try desperately to stage a Broadway flop. Take that wacky premise, add even wackier characters and very funny song and dance numbers, and you have a delightful night out for lovers of musical theater. You'll laugh from start to finish and even hum some of the catchy, irreverent tunes. This show is destined to be around for a long time. Book very early, since *The Producers* is always a sell-out with both locals and tourists. (Tues-Sun) **$$$$**

Riverside Park. *475 Riverside Dr, New York (10115). W 72nd St to W 158th St along the Hudson River. Phone 212/408-0264. www.nycgovparks.org.* This city park on the Upper West Side offers a pleasant, bucolic setting that's even more laid back than Central Park. The long, narrow, breezy park has a promenade for bike riders between West 72nd and West 110th streets designed for those who want to take a nice, easy ride at a slow pace. Bike rentals are available at the nearby Toga Bike Shop (110 West End Ave, phone 212/799-9625). For even more relaxation, the 79th Street Boat Basin (phone 212/496-2105) provides a quiet respite for walking on the rivers edge. There's also a nearby café that's open in summer. The park offers some sightseeing in the way of Grants Tomb, a towering granite tomb that is one of the worlds largest mausoleums. It holds the remains of President Ulysses S. Grant and his wife, Juliaa must-see for Civil War history buffs. **FREE**

★ **Rockefeller Center.** *30 Rockefeller Plz, New York (10112). Fifth Ave to Ave of the Americas and beyond, 47th St to 51st St with some buildings stretching to 52nd St. Phone 212/632-3975. www.rockefellercenter.com.* Conceived of by John D. Rockefeller during the 1930s, Rockefeller Center is the largest privately owned business and entertainment complex in the world. Enter through the Channel Gardens (5th Avenue between 49th and 50th) and walk toward the central sunken plaza. Here, a golden statue of Prometheus sprawls benevolently beside a pool and an outdoor café that becomes an ice skating rink in winter. (Yes, you can rent skates.) The center is magical at Christmastime, when a 78,000-light tree towers over Prometheus. The backdrop of the scene is the core skyscraper, the GE Building, home to NBC Studios. You can take a studio tour (adults $17.95, seniors and children $15.50, no children under 6; phone 212/664-7174), or catch *The Today Show* being broadcast live through the street-level picture window at West 49th and Rockefeller Plaza. The 21-acre complex contains 19 buildings, most built of limestone with aluminum streamlining. But the Art Deco gem of the group is Radio City Music Hall, Americas largest theater. Tour the theater or see a showespecially if the high-kicking Rockettes are performing (www.radiocity.com; phone 212/247-4777).

Schomburg Center for Research in Black Culture. *515 Malcolm X Blvd, New York (10037). Phone 212/491-2200. www.nypl.org* .The center's collection covers every phase of black activity wherever black people have lived in significant numbers. Books, manuscripts, periodicals, art, and audiovisual materials. (Tues-Sat **FREE**

Serena. *222 W 23rd St, New York (10011). Phone 212/255-4646. www.serenanyc.com.* If you want to be a part of the scene and be seen, Serena is the bar and lounge for you. It serves food and drinks and is known as an after-hours hangout for the chic and the hip. The place has a plush, dark look to it. But, look carefully, because you may see some celebrities sipping champagne off in a corner somewhere. (Daily)

The Slipper Room. *167 Orchard St, New York (10002). Phone 212/253-7246. www.slipperroom.com.* This club features a mix of offbeat shows and music. From quiz show nights to bawdy burlesque performances to up-and-coming bands, the Slipper Room is a fun, inexpensive place to act silly and party with your friends. The club gets a mixed late-night crowd and is the kind of place that attracts fun-loving night owls who like to party until dawn. (Tues-Sat; Sun, Mon special events only) **$**

Smithsonian Cooper-Hewitt, National Design Museum. *2 E 91st St, New York (10128). At Fifth Ave. Phone 212/849-8400. www.ndm.si.edu.*Once home to 19th-century industrialist Andrew Carnegie, this 64-room 1901 Georgian mansion is now a branch of the Smithsonian Institution dedicated to design and the decorative arts. The exhibits are temporary and focus on such subjects as ceramics, furniture, textiles, and metalwork. Out back is a romantic garden, where concerts are sometimes presented. (Mon-Thurs 10 am-5 pm, Fri 10 am-9 pm, Sat 10 am-6 pm, Sun noon-6 pm; closed holidays) **$$**

SOB's. *204 Varick St, New York (10014). Phone 212/243-4940. www.sobs.com.* Lovers of the Brazilian beat, as well as hip-hop, reggae, salsa, African music, and other kinds of international sounds, have flocked since 1982 to this venerable SoHo nightclub. SOBsSounds of Brazilfeatures new performers and well-known stars who always get the crowd up and dancing. Monday nights are famous for Latin dance lessons, with an entrance fee of just $5 before 7 pm. Novices are most welcome to try out their dancing shoes during these classes. Saturday Night Samba features dancers and Brazilian performers. Every evening has a different theme and varied performers. For your dining pleasure, Latin and Brazilian cuisine are on the menu. While other clubs are quiet for the weekdays, SOBs continues to come alive. (Daily; hours vary) **$$$$**

SoHo Street Vendors. *South of Houston, New York (10012). The N/R subways stop at Canal or Prince St, or you can take the A/C/E subways to Canal St. Then wander around the general area, since street vendors change locations.* Shopping from street vendors in this hip section of the city is a fun experience largely due to the haggling, which seems to come naturally to many native New Yorkers. If you're not comfortable doing this, bring along a buddy for moral support. Never accept a first offer, and don't look for authenticity. Just have fun with it. If you see something you like, grab it, because the same vendor may not be back at the same spot the next day. Vendors peddle a multitude of treasures, including trendy clothing, cool jewelry, and paintings, drawings, and other artwork. With so many items to choose from, you're sure to come away with something you haven't seen anywhere else beforeor won'tsee until the trend hits your neck of the woods months later.

Solomon R. Guggenheim Museum. *1071 Fifth Ave, New York (10128). Between E 88th and 89th sts. Phone 212/423-3500. www.guggenheim.org.* Some say that the Guggenheim looks like a giant snail or an upside-down wedding cake. Few would deny that Frank Lloyd Wrights brilliant concept of ever-widening concrete circles around a central atrium provided an intriguing new way to display artespecially in 1959 when the museum opened. Take the elevator to the top and walk down the gently sloping spiral to view temporary exhibits that draw a diversity of viewers. Past shows have included Centre Pompidou from Paris, Norman Rockwell: Pictures for the American People, and Art of the Motorcycle. A smaller adjoining rotunda and tower hold a stunning permanent collection heavy in works by Wassily Kandinsky, Paul Klee, Francois Leger, and Marc Chagall, as well as by the French Impressionists. Pablo Picasso is well represented, especially in his early Blue Period, including *Woman Ironing,* the artists well-known depiction of labor and fatigue. Free docent-led tours are scheduled daily at noon. (Sat-Wed 10 am-5:45 pm, Fri 10 am-7:45 pm; closed holidays) **$$$**

Sotheby's Auctions. *1334 York Ave, New York (10021). Phone 212/606-7000. www.sothebys.com.* Get a taste of high society at a Sothebys auction. Whether you're just a spectator or you have lots of spare cash with which to purchase something wonderful, attending an auction at this institution is a thrilling, fast-paced experience. Sothebys has held auctions for items belonging to the Duke and Duchess of Windsor and other celebrities. It has fashion, book and manuscript, and vintage car departments, just to name a few. Sothebys Arcade features more affordable items. Publications like *New York* magazine and *The New York Times* contain listings of upcoming events. (Closed holidays) **FREE**

South Street Seaport. *19 Fulton St, New York (10038). Fulton and Water sts, at the East River. Phone 212/732-7678. www.southstreetseaport.com.* This 12-block area was restored to display the city's maritime history, with an emphasis on South Street in the days of sailing vessels. The South Street Museum piers at South and Fulton streets now moor the *Ambrose,* a lightship (1908); the *Lettie G. Howard,* a Gloucester fishing schooner (1893); the fully-rigged *Wavertree* (1885); the *Peking,* a German four-masted barque (1911); and the *Pioneer,* a schooner (1885). Permanent and changing maritime exhibits include models, prints, photos, and artifacts. If history isn't your thing, this festival marketplace has more than 100 souvenir and mall-type stores, like Abercrombie & Fitch and The Body Shop, as well as 35 mostly casual restaurants. Don't miss the three-story glass and steel Pier 17 Pavilion, which extends into the East River and offers great views of the Brooklyn Bridge and New York Harbor.

South Street Seaport Museum. *South and Fulton sts, at the East River. Phone 212/748-8600. www.southstreetseaportmuseum.org.* This eleven-block area was restored to display the city's maritime history, with emphasis on South Street in the days of sailing vessels. The museum piers now moor the *Ambrose,* a lightship (1908); the *Lettie G. Howard,* a Gloucester fishing schooner (1893); the fully-rigged *Wavertree* (1885); the *Peking,* a German four-masted barque (1911); and the *Pioneer,*a schooner (1885). Permanent and changing maritime exhibits include models, prints, photos, and artifacts. Tours. Harbor excursions. Children admitted only when accompanied by adult. (Tues-Sun 10 am-5 pm; closed Jan 1, Thanksgiving, Dec 25) **$$**

St. Patrick's Cathedral. *263 Mulberry Ave, New York (10012). Between E 50th and 51st sts. Phone 212/226-8075. www.oldsaintpatricks.com.* Irish immigrants and their descendents were largely responsible for the construction and dedication of St. Patricks Cathedral, the largest Catholic cathedral in the United States. A standout on Fifth Avenue since 1859, the white marble and stone structure dominates the surrounding skyscrapers. Twin Gothic spires reach heavenward, and some of the stained glass windows were made in Chartres. Cool and calm within, the church bestows a palpable peace on visitors as well as those attending services. It is the resting place of New Yorks deceased archbishops; they are buried in tombs under the high altar, and their hats hang from the ceiling above. The steps of St. Pats are a popular meeting place for New Yorkers. (Thurs-Tues) **FREE**

★ **Statue of Liberty National Monument.** *Liberty Island, New York (10004). Ferry tickets and departures from Castle Clinton National Monument in Battery Park. Phone 212/363-3200 (recording). www.nps.gov/stli.* This worldwide symbol of freedom is the first thing passengers see as their ships sail into New York Harbor. A gift from France in 1886 (her iron skeleton was designed by Gustave Eiffel, creator of Paris's Eiffel Tower), she stands 152 feet high on an 89-foot pedestal, indomitable and welcoming. Ellis Island, the most famous port of immigration in the United States, became part of the national monument in 1965. Between 1892 and 1954, 12 million immigrants first stepped on American soil at Ellis Island. When it closed in 1954, it had processed 40 percent of living American families. You can look for your ancestors' names on the Wall of Honor or visit the dramatic Immigrants' Living Theater and the cavernous Great Hall, where nervous immigrants awaited processing. Passing the Statue of Liberty on the return trip may prove to be a heart-stirring, thought-provoking experience. (Daily 9:30 am-5 pm; closed Dec 25) **$$** Located on the second floor in the pedestal of the Statue is

> **Statue of Liberty Exhibit.** *Liberty Island, Statue of Liberty, New York (10004). Phone 212/363-3200. www.nps.gov/stli.* Photographs, artifacts, and history dioramas with light and sound effects depict the construction of the Statue of Liberty (No admission, but there is charge for ferry ride to island; daily 8:30 am-6 pm). **FREE**

Studio Museum in Harlem. *144 W 125th St, New York (10027). Phone 212/864-4500. www.studiomuseum.org.* Founded in 1968, this museum is the "principal center for the study of Black art in America," spread out over several well-lit floors of a turn-of-the-century building. The permanent exhibit features works by such masters as Romare Bearden, James VanDerZee, and Jacob Lawrence; temporary exhibits present a mixture of both world-renowned and emerging artists. The Studio is also known for its lively lecture and concert series, presented September through May. (Wed-Fri, Sun noon-6 pm, Sat 10 am-6 pm; closed holidays) **$$**

Sullivan St Bakery. *73 Sullivan St, New York (10012). At Broome and Spring sts. Phone 212/334-9435. www.sullivanstreetbakery.com.* If bread is your passion, then enter these doors and take in the sights and smells of the Sullivan St Bakery. The bakery sells a variety of mouthwatering thin-crust Italian breads, Roman-style pizzas, biscotti, and tarts, as well as coffee to wash it all down. A second location is in Hells Kitchen at 533 W 47th Street, phone 212/265-5580. (Daily 7 am-7 pm)

Summer Events in Central Park. *14 E. 60th St, New York (10022). Events held throughout the park and at Lincoln Center. Take the #1 or #9 subway to the 66th Street stop to get to Lincoln Center. Phone 212/310-6600. www.centralpark.org.* The city comes alive in summer with a plethora of wonderful, free cultural events that run the gamut and appeal to all ages. Central Park hosts a variety of musical performances by the New York Philharmonic and the Metropolitan Opera Co. In addition, its SummerStage (212/360-2777) attracts a mix of pop, blues, and rock stars. At nearby Lincoln Center, free concerts and dance performances are held during August at its Damrosch Park outdoor area. All these events, coupled with brunch or a casual picnic in the park, are a great, budget-conscious way to spend a warm, sunny day in the Big Apple. (Daily)

Temple Emanu-El. *1 E 65th St, New York (10021). Fifth Ave and 65th St. Phone 212/744-1400. www.emanuelnyc.org.* Largest Jewish house of worship in the world; Reform Congregation founded in 1845. Romanesque temple seats 2,500; Beth-El chapel seats 350. (Sun-Thurs 10 am-4:45 pm; no visiting on High Holy Days) Tours (by appointment, upon written request).

Terence Conran Shop. *415 E 59th St, New York (10022). Phone 212/755-9079. www.conran.com.* This British-based retailer has come to the Big Apple, with a shop built right into a pavilion at the Queensboro Bridge. With international flair and a sense of style, the store sells fineand sometimes unusualhome furnishings, kitchenware, and jewelry familiar to those who read *Wallpaper* and *British Elle Décor*. If you don't blow your budget on these irresistible, ultra-modern accessories, stop for a bite next door at Gustavinos, a French-American restaurant that is just as chic as the store. (Mon-Fri 11 am-8 pm, Sat 10 am-7 pm, Sun noon-6 pm) the world. The street begins at Broadway, where you'll find Trinity Church (built in 1846 and a symbol of the citys strength when it survived the nearby September 11, 2001, terrorist attacks), and stretches east to the East River. If you walk the streets six or so blocks, you'll pass the Federal Hall National Monument, the site where George Washington took the Oath of Office and became the first President of the United States in 1789. Step inside the building to view the impressive rotunda and check out an exhibit on the Constitution. Just half a block south of Wall Street, on Broad Street, is the New York Stock Exchange, where fortunes are made and lost with every clang of the opening bell.

Washington Square Park. *W 4th St and Waverly Pl, New York (10011). Many subways stop at nearby W 4th St.* For the ultimate in daytime people-watching, head downtown to the heart and soul of Greenwich Village. The bustling 9-acre park, dating back to 1827, serves up a cacophony of jugglers, street musicians, magicians, and countless students from nearby New York University. The park hosts outdoor art fairs in spring and fall, as well as jazz performances in summer. The north end of the park features the historic Washington Memorial Arch (14 Washington Square N). This marble structure was modeled after Paris Arc de Triomphe and was erected in 1889. (Daily)

Whitney Museum of American Art. *945 Madison Ave, New York (10021). At E 75th St. Phone toll-free 800/944-8639. www.whitney.org.* Bauhaus-trained architect Marcel Breuers museum is menacingly cantilevered toward Madison Avenue. Its bold, sculptural quality makes it a fitting home for modern and contemporary art. The impressive permanent collection takes American art from the early 20th century into the 21st, showing realistic works by Thomas Hart Benton, Edward Hopper, and Georgia OKeeffe, as well as works by later artists such as Alexander Calder, Louise Nevelson, Robert Rauschenberg, and Jasper Johns. The controversial Whitney Biennial showcases the latest works of contemporary artists. (Wed-Thurs, Sat-Sun 11 am-6 pm, Fri 1-9 pm (6-9 pm pay-what-you-wish admission); closed Jan 1, Thanksgiving, Dec 25) **$$$** includes

> **Whitney Museum of American Art at Altria.** *120 Park Ave, New York (10017). At 42nd St. Phone 917/663-2453.*Gallery and sculpture court. Changing exhibits annually; free lectures, performances. Gallery tours (Wed, Fri 1 pm). Gallery (Mon-Fri 11 am-6 pm, Thurs to 7:30 pm). Sculpture court (Mon-Sat 7:30 am-9:30 pm, Sun and holidays 11 am-7 pm). **FREE**

Woolworth Building. *233 Broadway, New York (10279).* This neo-Gothic skyscraper by Cass Gilbert was the tallest building in the world (792 feet, 58 stories) when it was built. Frank W. Woolworth, the dime-store king, paid $13.5 million cash for his "cathedral of commerce" when it was completed in 1913.

World Financial Center. *200 Liberty St, New York (10281). West St between Liberty and Vesey sts. Phone 212/945-0505. www.worldfinancialcenter.com.* The center includes more than 40 shops and restaurants on and around the Winter Garden, a 120-foot-high, vaulted glass and steel atrium.

Yeshiva University. *Wilf Campus,500 W 185th St, New York (10033). Phone 212/960-5400. www.yu.edu.* (1886) (6,300 students) America's oldest and largest university under Jewish auspices. Zysmon Hall, historic main building, has elaborate stone façade and Byzantine domes. The Mendel Gottesman Library houses many specialized collections (academic year, Mon-Fri, Sun; closed holidays, Jewish holidays; tours by appointment). Part of the university is

> **Yeshiva University Museum.** *15 W 16th St, New York (10011). Phone 212/294-8330.*This teaching museum devoted to Jewish art, architecture, history, and culture has permanent exhibits, including scale models of synagogues from the 3rd to 19th centuries; reproduction of frescoes from the Dura-Europos Synagogue; ceremonial objects, rare books; audiovisual presentations; theater; changing exhibits. (Academic year, Mon-Thurs, Sun 11 am-5 pm; closed holidays, Jewish holidays) **$$**

Zabar's. *2245 Broadway, New York (10024). At 80th St. Phone 212/787-2000. www.zabars.com.* Zabars is one of those places that makes New York the yummy place that it is. This second-generation gourmet food market, considered sacred by those who enjoy fine eating, has graced Manhattans Upper West Side since 1934. Occupying close to one city block and employing 250 people, Zabars sells sinful breads and pastries, meats, cheeses, smoked fish, condiments, and cookware. The shops babka (Russian coffee cake) makes life worth living. Since Zabars is one of the rare establishments in New York that's open every day of the year, you can treat your taste buds anytime you like. Forget diets and just enjoy. (Mon-Fri 8 am-7:30 pm, Sat 8 am-8 pm, Sun 9 am-6 pm)

Special Events

Bryant Park Summer Film Festival. *42nd St be-*

tween Fifth and Sixth aves, New York (10036). Phone 212/512-5700. www.bryantpark.org. For a relaxing evening taking in the balmy breezes of summer, a picnic with your favorite foods, and an outdoor screening of a classic American film, park yourself on the lawn at Bryant Park for its weekly film showing. Hundreds come each Monday night to see a movie and hang out once the sun goes down. And you can't beat the price! Check the local newspapers to find out whats playing each week. Mon, June-Aug. **FREE**

Central Park Concerts. *72nd St and Fifth Ave, New York (10021). Phone 212/360-3456. www.centralparknyc.org/thingstodo/music.* Free performances by the New York Philharmonic and the Metropolitan Opera Company on the Great Lawn, mid-park at 81st St. June-Aug.

Chinese New Year. *Mott and Pell sts, New York (10013). Phone 212/226-1330.* Parade with lions, dragons, costumes, firecrackers. Early-mid-Feb.

Columbus Day Parade. *Fifth Ave between 45th and 86th sts, New York (10022). Phone 212/484-1222.* Oct.

Fleet Week. *Pier 88, New York. Phone 212/245-0072. www.intrepidmuseum.org/pages/fleetweek.* In a scene right out of the Gene Kelly, Navy-themed musical, *On the Town*, Navy and Coast Guard ships gather for a parade up the Hudson River that is a true spectacle of springtime in New York. After the ships dock by the museum, they are open to the public for tours. You can find some great photo opportunities here. Other fun sights for all ages include flyovers and 21-gun salutes. Expect to find Navy men all over the city, looking for a good time. Fleet Week is pure Americana that gives the city a real patriotic feeling. Late May.

Greenwich Village Halloween Parade. *Take almost any subway to W Fourth St and keep walking uptown into Chelsea. Phone 845/758-5519. www.halloween-nyc.com.* Straights, gays, men, women, kids, seniors, and everyone in between dress in the wildest of costumes for this annual Halloween tradition in the West Village. Strangers become instant friends and everyone gets into the fun spirit in what has become the largest Halloween parade in the United States. Although the crowd may get a bit wild, the event is usually quite safe due to the large police presence and general good feelings exuded by area residents. If you've ever wanted to let it all hang out and wear a costume that will shock everyone you know, this is the place to do it. Prepare to stay out late and enjoy some late-night partying at a local bar (unless you have the kids with you, of course). Late Oct.

Independence Day Harbor Festival. *East River and South St Seaport, New York (10044). Phone 212/494-4495.* This is the nation's largest July 4 celebration; fireworks; food; music. Weekend of July 4.

JVC Jazz Festival. *Park Row between Beekman and Ann sts, New York (10038). Phone 212/501-1390. www.festivalproductions.net.* World-famous musicians perform in Avery Fisher Hall, Carnegie Hall, Town Hall, and other sites throughout the city. Last two weeks in June.

Macy's Thanksgiving Day Parade. *34th and 72nd sts, New York (10001). Phone 212/494-5432. www.macysparade.com.* If you have a child or you want to feel like a kid again yourself, spend Thanksgiving Day morning enjoying this wonderful and festive New York event. Amazing floats, cheerful clowns (who are all volunteers and are either Macys employees or friends and families of Macys employees), and celebrities are all part of the parade, which starts at 9 am and ends at around noon. The atmosphere is always jovial and will put you in the holiday spirit. Since you may spend most of the time standing, wear comfortable shoes, dress in layers, bring snacks, and duck into nearby eateries for hot drinks and bathroom breaks. Keep in mind that standing for several hours may be too tiring for children under 5 (unless they spend most of the time perched atop your shoulders, which may be too tiring for you!). One of the best viewing spots is on Herald Square in front of Macys.

National Puerto Rican Day Parade. *Fifth Ave between 45th and 86th sts,* New York (10036). *Phone 718/401-0404. www.nationalpuertoricandayparade.org.* Mid-June.

New York Shakespeare Festival & Shakespeare in the Park. *81st St and Central Park W, New York (10024). Phone 212/260-2400. www.publictheater.org.* At the 2,000-seat outdoor Delacorte Theater in Central Park, near W 81st St. Tues-Sun. Free tickets are distributed on the day of the performance. June-Sept.

Ninth Avenue International Food Festival. *Ninth Ave between 37th and 57th sts, New York (10018). Take the A/C/E subway to 34th St and 8th Ave. Phone 212/581-7029. www.hellskitchennyc.com/html/9thavefest.htm.* This event epitomizes all the gastronomical diversity that is New York City. Taking place during the third weekend in May in the ethnically mixed Hells Kitchen neighborhood, the two-day festival is a 20-block extravaganza of food booths and entertainment. From burritos to jerk chicken to curried chicken, you can

Theodore Roosevelt Birthplace National Historic Site. *28 E 20th St, New York (10003). Between Broadway and Park Ave S. Phone 212/260-1616. www.nps.gov/thrb.*The reconstructed birthplace of the 26th president, who lived here from 1858 to 1872. Guided tours (every hour with the last tour at 4 pm) of five rooms restored to their 1865 appearance. Audiovisual presentation and special events. (Tues-Sat 9 am-5 pm; closed holidays) **$**

Times Square and the Theater District. *1560 Broadway, New York (10036). 6th to 8th aves and 40th to 53rd sts. Phone 212/768-1560. www.timessquarenyc.org.* Entertainment center of the city and theatrical headquarters of the country offering plays, musicals, concerts, movies, and exotic entertainments; named for the Times Tower at One Times Square, originally the home of *The New York Times.* (See THEATER in introductory copy.)

TKTS Discount Theater Tickets. *Broadway at 47th St, New York (10036). www.tkts.com.* With the price of Broadway shows closing in at $100 for the best seats in the house, TKTS is a godsend to theater lovers. The more popular TKTS booth at Times Square (just look for lots of people standing on two lines) provides up to 50 percent discounted tickets on Broadway, off-Broadway, and some musical and dance events. Tickets are sold for the day of performance for matinees and evening shows. The downtown booth (199 Water St) sells tickets for evening day-of performance and for matinees one day in advance. Generally, you will not be able to get tickets for the hottest shows in town through TKTS, but usually for ones that have been playing for a while or are not doing as well. Lines are long and you are guaranteed nothing by waiting on line. Have a first, second, and third choice in mind. Only cash and travelers checks are accepted. (Daily)

Trinity Church. *Broadway at Wall St, New York (10019). Broadway at Wall St. Phone 212/602-0800. www.trinitywallstreet.org.* (1846) The third building to occupy this site; the original was built in 1697. Its famous graveyard, favorite lunchtime spot of workers in the financial district, contains the graves of Robert Fulton and Alexander Hamilton. The Gothic Revival brownstone church houses a museum. Parish center with dining room open to the public. Services (Mon-Fri 12:05 pm, Sun 9 am, 11:15 am). Church (Mon-Fri 8 am-6 pm, Sat-Sun to 4). Churchyard (weather permitting, daily 7 am-4 pm). **FREE** Also here is

St. Paul's Chapel. *209 Broadway, New York (10007). Phone 212/602-0874.* A chapel of Trinity Church, this example of Georgian architecture, finished in 1766, is the oldest public building in continuous use on Manhattan Island. George Washington's pew is in the north aisle; chancel ornamentation by L'Enfant; Waterford chandeliers. Concerts (Mon). (Daily) **FREE**

Ukrainian Museum. *222 E 6th St, New York (10003). Between 12th and 13th sts. Phone 212/228-0110. www.ukrainianmuseum.org.* Changing exhibits of Ukrainian folk art, fine art, and history; workshops on weekends in folk crafts. (Wed-Sun 11:30 am-5 pm; closed holidays, Jan 7) **$$**

Union Square Greenmarket. *17th St and Broadway, New York (10001). The 4, 5, 6, N, and R subways stop at Union Square. Phone 212/788-7476. www.cenyc.org.* This bustling year-round farmers' market is located at Union Square between 14th and 17th streets and Broadway and Park Avenue. Its a chance to experience a bit of the country in the Big Apple, as farmers and other vendors sell fresh fruits, vegetables, cheeses, homemade pies, herbs, cut flowers, and potted plants. Plan to arrive early for the best selection. (Mon, Wed, Fri-Sat 8 am-6 pm; closed holidays)

United Nations. *First Ave at 46th St, New York (10017). First Ave from 42nd to 48th St. Phone 212/963-8687. www.un.org.* These four buildings, designed under the direction of Wallace K. Harrison, were completed between 1950 and 1952. Regular sessions of the General Assembly start on the third Tuesday in September. Tickets are occasionally available to certain official meetings on a first-come basis. The entrance is on First Avenue at 46th Street, at the north end of the General Assembly Building. An information desk and a ticket booth are in the lobby; the UN book and gift shops and the UN Post Office are in the basement, where one can mail letters bearing United Nations stamps. On the fourth floor is the UN Delegates Dining Room. The Conference Building is where the various UN Councils meet. The Secretariat Building is a 550-foot-high rectangular glass-and-steel building; here the day-to-day work of the UN staff is performed. The fourth building is the Dag Hammarskjold Library, open only to UN staff and delegations, or by special permission for serious research. Guided tours (45 minutes) leave the public entrance lobby at frequent intervals (daily; closed Thanksgiving and several days during year-end holiday season; also weekdays in Jan-Feb); no children under 5. Buildings (daily). **$$$**

Wall Street. *Between Broadway and South St.* New Yorks Wall Street stands for much more than an address: it is the symbol of American capitalism, known around find any kind of food imaginable in this ultimate of block parties. More than 1 million visitors have showed up in the past to this annual festival that's been going strong for 28 years, so prepare for crowds. Wear comfortable shoes and loose-fitting clothes so that you can pig out in total comfort. Late May.

The Nutcracker. *New York State Theater, 20 Lincoln Center, New York (10023). Phone 212/870-5570. www nycballet.com.* Taking your child (and yourself!) to the New York City Ballets performance of *The Nutcracker* is one of those magical events that both tourists and New Yorkers love to take in during the colorful, festive Christmas season. This fantasy story of the Mouse King and little Clara has delighted children for many years. The New York Ballets version of this classic is sure to please, with renowned dancers, some of the most appealing young performers, beautiful music by Tchaikovsky, and luscious sets and costumes. No ballet lover should miss a performance of *The Nutcracker* while visiting New York City during Christmas. Dec.

NYC Marathon. *Staten Island side of the Verrazano-Narrows Bridge, New York (10024). Phone 212/423-2249. www.ingnycmarathon.org.* What event attracts more than 2 million spectators, 30,000 participants from every corner of the globe, and 12,000 volunteers? None other than the grueling 26.2-mile New York City Marathon. Whether you're an experienced runner or a diehard couch potato, to stand on the sidelines and cheer on these amazing men and women during the worlds largest marathon is a thrilling and rewarding experience. The event begins on the Staten Island side of the Verrazano-Narrows Bridge, goes through all five boroughs of the city, and finishes up by Tavern on the Green restaurant in Central Park. Bring your camera, pack some bagels and coffee, and get ready to clap and holler. You'll feel really inspired afterward. First Sun in Nov.

Ringling Brothers and Barnum and Bailey Circus. *Madison Square Garden,Seventh Ave and 32nd St, New York (10001). Phone 212/465-6741. www.ringling.com.* The kids will have a ball enjoying the Greatest Show on Earth, which graces the city every spring. Expect the usual circus fare—elephants, trapeze artists, clowns, and the like. For a special treat, view the parade of circus people and animals from 12th Avenue and 34th Street to the Garden on the morning before the show opens. Mar-Apr.

San Gennaro Festival. *Little Italy,Mulberry St between Canal and Houston sts, New York (10013). Phone 212/768-9320.* More than 75 years old, this giant street festival in Little Italy salutes the patron saint of Naples with a celebratory Mass and a candlelit procession of the Statue of the Saint. More than a million people descend on Little Italy over 11 days to feast on food from the old country, watch the parades, enjoy the live music, and compete for the title of cannoli-eating champion. Mid-Sept.

South Street Seaport Events. *Phone 212/732-8257. www.southstreetseaport.com.* Throughout the year, concerts, festivals, and special events are staged in the seaport area; weather permitting, passengers are taken for a sail around the harbor aboard the *Pioneer.* The museum's Children's Center hosts a variety of special programs, workshops, and exhibits. In the fall, a fleet of classic sailing vessels is assembled to compete in a race for the Mayor's Cup.

St. Patrick's Day Parade. *Fifth Ave between 44th and 86th sts, New York (10017). www.saintpatricksdayparade.com.* New York's biggest parade; approximately 100,000 marchers.

Washington Square Art Show. *LaGuardia Pl, between Bleecker & E 4th sts, New York (10021). Phone 212/982-6255.* Outdoor art show. Weekends, late May-June and late Aug-early Sept. **FREE**

Westminster Kennel Club Dog Show. *Madison Square Garden, 4 Pennsylvania Plz, New York (10001). Phone 212/307-7171; toll-free 800/455-3647. www.westminsterkennelclub.org.* Canine lovers unite! Nearly 3,000 top dogs and their owners take part in this two-day annual extravaganza leading up to the crowning of Best in Show on the second night of competition. Whether you love big or small dogs, you will surely find this event a delight. Heres a real insiders tip: arrive two hours early each night, at about 6 pm, and go to the huge backstage area. Here, you will be able to pet, play with, and nuzzle up to the dogs that vied for Best in Breed in competitions held earlier in the day. (Always ask the owner/handler for permission before petting an animal.) The owners and handlers welcome the public since they love showing off their poochesthey may even convince you to buy a future offspring of their show dogs. This is, by far, the best part of the show. Wear comfortable shoes, since this staging area is massive. Best in Group competitions for the seven groups run from 8-11 pm each night. You can buy tickets for one or both nights. For the best deal, purchase a general-admission, two-day pass. Mid-Feb. **$$$$**

Winter and Summer Restaurant Weeks. *www.restaurantweek.com.* Many of the citys finest restaurants offer two- or three-course, fixed-price lunches at bargain prices during two weeks in summer. This is a wildly popular promotion that natives can't wait to get their hands on. Check local newspapers at the beginning of your trip to see which restaurants are participating and make a reservation ASAP. This is a great way to experience top dining at great prices. Bon apptit! Third and fourth week in June.

Limited-Service Hotels

★ ★ ALGONQUIN HOTEL. *59 W 44th St, New York (10036). Phone 212/840-6800; fax 212/944-1419. www.algonquinhotel. com.* Originally opened in 1902, this gracious hotel in the heart of Midtown and just one block from Times Square became famous as a gathering spot for writers and theatrical performers. The legendary Algonquin Round Table, which formed after World War I, included such illustrious writers as Dorothy Parker and George S. Kaufman; additional regulars included Booth Tarkington, H. L. Mencken, and Gertrude Stein. That spirit lives on in the Oak Room, the Algonquin's supper club, where guests can catch well-known cabaret acts on Tuesday through Saturday evenings, September through June. Having undergone a historical restoration in the late 1990s, the hotel (housed in a Beaux Arts building) features beautifully detailed ironwork and the original marble staircase, with antique furnishings and rich tones to suit the period. Guest rooms combine historic elegance with 21st-century conveniences. 174 rooms, 12 story. Pets accepted; fee. Check-in 3 pm, check-out noon. High-speed Internet access, wireless Internet access. Two restaurants, bar. Fitness room. Airport transportation available. Credit cards accepted. **$$$**

★ ★ AMERITANIA HOTEL. *230 W 54th St, New York (10019). Phone 212/247-5000; toll-free 888/664-6835; fax 212/751-7868. www.nychotels.com/.* 219 rooms. Check-in 3 pm, check-out noon. Bar. **$$**

★ ★ BENTLEY HOTEL. *500 E 62nd St, New York (10022). Phone 212/644-6000; toll-free 888/664-6835; fax 212/207-4800.*197 rooms, 21 story. Check-in 3 pm, check-out noon. Restaurant, bar. **$**

★ ★ COURTYARD BY MARRIOTT TIMES SQUARE SOUTH. *114 W 40th St, New York (10018). Phone 212/391-0088; toll-free 888/236-2427; fax 212/391-6023. www.courtyard.com.* Located in the heart of the fashion district and just blocks from 42nd Street, Times Square, the theater district, shopping, and corporate offices, this property is an ideal choice for both business and leisure travelers. The contemporary-style guest rooms feature high-speed Internet access, I-Pod stations, and pillowtop mattresses and upgraded pillows.244 rooms. Pets accepted, some restrictions. Check-in 3 pm, check-out noon. High-speed Internet access. Restaurant. Fitness room. Credit cards accepted. **$$$**

★ ★ DAYS HOTEL NEW YORK CITY. *790 8th Ave, New York (10019). Phone 212/581-7000; toll-free 800/544-8313; fax 212/974-0291. www.daysinn. com.* Just one block to Javits Convention Center and an easy walk to Times Square, this is a budget-friendly hotel in a busy commercial area.367 rooms, 15 story. Check-in 3 pm, check-out noon. Restaurant, bar. Fitness room. Indoor pool. **$**

★ HAMPTON INN MANHATTAN CHELSEA. *108 W 24th St, New York (10011). Phone 212/414-1000; fax 212/647-1511. www.hamptoninn. com.* 144 rooms. Complimentary continental breakfast. Check-in 3 pm, check-out noon. Fitness room. **$**

★ ★ HOTEL BEACON. *2130 Broadway at 75th St, New York (10023). Phone 212/787-1100; toll-free 800/572-4969; fax 212/724-0839. www.beaconhotel. com.* 241 rooms, 25 story. Check-in 2 pm, check-out noon. Restaurant. **$$**

★ ★ HOTEL WALES. *1295 Madison Ave, New York (10128). Phone 212/876-6000; toll-free 866/925-3746; fax 212/860-7000. www.waleshotel. com.* This restored 1902 hotel, located on Manhattan's Upper East Side, is the perfect mix of old-world elegance and modern amenities. Reminiscent of a country inn, the cozy decor features original heating pipes and fireplaces, a curved marble staircase in the lobby, oriental rugs, and antique tables. The comfortable guest rooms feature Belgian linens, fresh flowers, Aveda toiletries, and VCRs. 87 rooms, 10 story. Pets accepted; fee. Check-in 3 pm, check-out noon. High-speed Internet access, wireless Internet access. Restaurant. Fitness room. Airport transportation available. Business center. Credit cards accepted. **$$$**

★ LYDEN GARDENS. *215 E 64th St, New York (10021). Phone 212/355-1230; toll-free 800/637-8483; fax 212/758-7858. www.affinia.com.* 131 rooms, 13 story, all suites. Check-in 3 pm, check-out noon. Wireless Internet access. Fitness room. **$$$**

★ ★ THE MANSFIELD. *12 W 44th St, New York (10036). Phone 212/277-8700; toll-free 800/255-5167; fax 212/764-4477. www.mansfieldhotel. com.* Upon entering this Midtown hotel, guests will feel as if they've been transported back in time to the early 1900s. The club-like surroundings include dark woods and original terrazzo floors in the lobby. The stylish guest rooms feature ebony- stained hardwood floors; 300-count linens with down comforters, and pillow top mattresses; black-and-white photographs; chrome accent lighting; and CD players. The luxurious bathrooms feature black Cambrian marble baths, plush cotton robes, and Aveda bath products. The M Bar, with its domed skylight, mahogany bookshelves, Beaux Arts lighting, and comfortable lounge seating, is the perfect spot to end the day with an evening cocktail. 126 rooms, 13 story. Pets accepted, some restrictions. Complimentary continental breakfast. Check-in 3 pm, check-out noon. High-speed Internet access, wireless Internet access. Restaurant, bar. Fitness room. Airport transportation available. Business center. Credit cards accepted. **$$**

★ ★ RADISSON LEXINGTON HOTEL NEW YORK. *511 Lexington Ave at 48th St, New York (10017). Phone 212/755-4400; toll-free 800/448-4471; fax 212/751-4091.lexingtonhotelnyc.com.* Near Grand Central Station. 705 rooms, 27 story. Check-in 3 pm, check-out noon. High-speed Internet access. Restaurant, bar. Fitness room. Business center. **$$**

★ THE ROGER WILLIAMS. *131 Madison Ave, New York (10016). Phone 212/448-7000; toll-free 888/448-7788; fax 212/448-7007. www.hotelrogerwilliams. com.* 187 rooms, 16 story. Complimentary continental breakfast. Check-in 3 pm, check-out noon. Fitness room. Business center. **$$**

★ ★ ROOSEVELT HOTEL. *45 E 45th St and Madison Ave, New York (10017). Phone 212/661-9600; toll-free 888/833-3969; fax 212/885-6161. www.theroos-evelthotel.com.* 1,043 rooms, 19 story. Check-in 3 pm, check-out noon. High-speed Internet access. Restaurant, bar. Fitness room. Business center. **$$**

★ SALISBURY HOTEL. *123 W 57th St, New York (10019). Phone 212/246-1300; toll-free 888/692-5757; fax 212/977-7752. www.nycsalisbury.com.* 201 rooms, 17 story. Check-in 3 pm, check-out noon. **$$**

★ ★ ★ WARWICK HOTEL. *65 W 54th St, New York (10019). Phone 212/247-2700; fax 212/247-2725. www.warwickhotelny.com.* 425 rooms, 33 story. Check-out 1 pm. Restaurant, bar. Fitness room. Business center. **$$$**

Full-Service Hotels

★ ★ ★ 60 THOMPSON. *60 Thompson St, New York (10012). Phone 212/431-0400; toll-free 877/431-0400; fax 212/431-0200. www.60thompson.com.* This SoHo boutique hotel features warm and inviting rooms and suites, done in brown and gray tones accented with dark woods and full-wall leather headboards. Frette linens, in-room spa products by Philosophy, and oversized showers pamper well-heeled guests. The accommodations will surely please high-tech aficionados, as they offer high-speed Internet connections, DVD players, and CD stereo systems. Matching this in hipness are decadent marble bathrooms with oversized showers. The hotels Asian-influenced seafood restaurant, Thom, is popular with in-the-know locals. It also offers Thoms Bar, a clubby, intimate setting in which to relax and enjoy a drink.100 rooms, 8 story. Check-in 3 pm, check-out noon. High-speed Internet access. Restaurant, bar. Business center. **$$$**

★ ★ ★ THE AVALON. *16 E 32nd St, New York (10016). Phone 212/299-7000; toll-free 888/442-8256; fax 212/299-7002. www.avalonhotelnyc.com.* Stately black marble columns and a pretty mosaic floor make an elegant first impression at this Murray Hill boutique hotel located near many area attractions. The elegant lobby is warm and inviting, with the look and feel of a mini European palace. Warm chestnut tones give the place a sense of grandeur, but in a smaller setting that is part of boutique intimacy. The guest rooms feature desk chairs designed for comfort and functionality, as well as Irish cotton linens and velour bathrobes. The Avalon bills itself as a home away from home: each room also comes with a signature body pillow. 100 rooms, 12 story. Check-in 3 pm, check-out noon. High-speed Internet access. Restaurant, bar. Business center. **$$**

★ ★ ★ THE BENJAMIN. *125 E 50th St, New York (10022). Phone 212/715-2500; toll-free 800/637-8483; fax 212/715-2525. www.thebenjamin.com.* Despite the fact that it's set in a classic 1927 building, this hotel has all the high-tech amenities a business traveler could want, including high-speed Internet access and Web TV. It offers comfortable accommodations in a sophisticated setting that features beige, silver, and brown tones throughout the property and in the marble and silver two-story lobby. A particularly nice amenity is the pillow menu, which offers you a choice of ten different kinds of bed pillows and a guarantee of your money back if you do not wake well rested. The Benjamins Woodstock Spa and Wellness Center offers many services and treatments with a holistic approach. 209 rooms. Pets accepted. Check-in 3 pm, check-out noon. High-speed Internet access. Restaurant. Fitness room, spa. Business center. Credit cards accepted. **$$$$**

★ ★ ★ BRYANT PARK HOTEL. *40 W 40th St, New York (10018). Phone 212/869-0100; toll-free 877/640-9300; fax 212/869-4446. www.bryantparkhotel.com.* In the shadows of the New York Public Library and Bryant Park, this centrally located hotel offers great views and has a bit of everything. The modern, sleek, almost minimalist rooms feature hardwood floors and are decorated in white with red accents. Each room offers high-tech amenities like DSL Internet connections, making this hotel a good choice for people traveling on business. Every room has 400-thread-count linens, Tibetan rugs, Bose Wave radios, and cashmere throws, and some have deep soaking tubs.149 rooms, 25 story. Check-in 3 pm, check-out noon. High-speed Internet access. Restaurant, bar. Fitness room. Business center**. $$$**

★ ★ ★ ★ THE CARLYLE. *35 E 76th St, New York (10021). Phone 212/744-1600; fax 212/717-4682. www.thecarlyle.com.* Discreetly tucked away on Manhattans Upper East Side, The Carlyle has maintained the allure of being one of New Yorks best-kept secrets for more than 70 years. A favorite of many movie stars, presidents, and royals, The Carlyle feels like an exclusive private club with its white-glove service and impeccable taste. Its art collection is extraordinary, from Audubon prints and Piranesi architectural drawings to English country scenes by Kips. Art plays a significant role at The Carlyle, where all rooms are equipped with direct lines to Sothebys. The rooms are completed in an Art Deco décor and are enhanced by striking antiques and bountiful bouquets. Populated by power brokers and socialites, The Carlyle Restaurant defines elegance. Bemelmans Bar proudly shows off its murals by *Madeline* creator Ludwig Bemelmans, while guests have been tapping their toes to the tunes of Bobby Short for more than 30 years in the Café Carlyle. 179 rooms, 35 story. Pets accepted; fee. Check-in 3 pm, check-out noon. High-speed Internet access, wireless Internet access. Two restaurants, bar. Fitness room, fitness classes available, spa. Airport transportation available. Business center**. $$$$**

★ ★ ★ CHAMBERS. *15 W 56th St, New York (10019). Phone 212/974-5656; toll-free 866/204-5656; fax 212/974-5657. www.chambershotel.com.* Located just steps from some of New Yorks finest retail shops, the trendy hotel has a modern, open-air feel to it. The public spacesincluding the soaring lobby with a double-sided fireplaceand the loftlike guest rooms feature original works of art, including pieces by filmmaker John Waters. The spacious, high-tech rooms with hand-troweled cement walls offer amenities like slippers you can actually keep, umbrellas, Frette bathrobes, and flat-screen TVs. Baths are stocked with Bumble + Bumble amenities. Just off the lobby, Town restaurant (see) serves fine American cuisine accented with French and Asian influences; you can also enjoy a Town meal in the comfort of your room. Guests of the hotel receive complimentary passes to the New York Sports Club.77 rooms, 30 story. Pets accepted, some restrictions. Complimentary continental breakfast. Check-in 3 pm, check-out noon. Restaurant, bar**. $$$$**

★ ★ ★ CITY CLUB HOTEL. *55 W 44th Street, New York (10036). Phone 212/921-5500; toll-free 877/367-2269; fax 212/944-5544. www.cityclubhotel. com.* A world away from its former life as a gentlemens club, the City Club Hotel is all about contemporary style and elegance. From the Frette bed linens to the Hermes bath products, this intimate boutique hotel spoils its guests with luxurious amenities, not to mention attentive service. With Times Square and Fifth Avenue shopping only a block away, you won't have to go far to explore some of New Yorks most famous spots. And if you're looking for one of New Yorks best meals, you won'teven have to leave the hotelworld-renowned chef Daniel Bouluds acclaimed DB Bistro Moderne is adjacent to the hotel lobby. 65 rooms. Pets accepted, some restrictions; fee. Check-in 3 pm, check-out noon. High-speed Internet access. Restaurant, bar**. $$**

★ ★ ★ DOUBLETREE GUEST SUITES. *1568 Broadway, New York (10036). Phone 212/719-1600;*

toll-free 800/222-8733; fax 212/921-5212. www.doubletree.com. If you're looking for an all-suite hotel in Times Square, look no further; this hotel is located only steps away from the theater district.458 rooms, 43 story, all suites. Check-in 3 pm, check-out noon. Restaurant, bar. Fitness room. **$$**

★ ★ ★ **DOUBLETREE METROPOLITAN HOTEL NEW YORK CITY.** *569 Lexington Ave, New York (10022). Phone 212/752-7000; toll-free 800/222-8733; fax 212/758-6311. www.doubletree.com.* Recently renovated, this East Side business travelers hotel (formerly the Loews New York) has a casual elegance in its soft tones and king-bed rooms. The Lexington Avenue Grill serves contemporary American cuisine, and the popular Lexy Lounge features a signature cocktail called the Sexy Lexy that is a hit with locals. The business center offers everything from secretarial services to fax capabilities to workstation rentals. The premium business-class program includes a separate check-in and check-out area; private lounge with wine and cheese, continental breakfast, and snacks; and special in-room amenities like fax machines. 667 rooms, 20 story. Check-in 3 pm, check-out noon. Restaurant, bar. Fitness room. Airport transportation available. Business center. **$$**

★ ★ ★ **DYLAN HOTEL.** *52 E 41st St, New York (10017). Phone 212/338-0500; toll-free 866/553-9526; fax 212/338-0569. www.dylanhotel. com.* With a grand feeling throughout, the 1903 Beaux Arts-style building, with its ornate facade and spiraling marble staircase, used to be the home of the Chemists Club. The guest rooms are bright and airy, with 11-foot ceilings and elegant marble baths. The rooms white and blue walls, deep amethyst and steel blue carpeting, and ebony-stained furniture give them a quiet, tailored look without being austere or cold. Situated on a quiet street, the hotel contains the Dylan restaurant, which serves basic fare like burgers and pastas, and a bar for relaxing with a drink. 107 rooms, 20 story. Check-in 3 pm, check-out noon. Restaurant, bar. Fitness room. Business center. **$$$**

★ ★ ★ **EASTGATE TOWER HOTEL.** *222 E 39th St, New York (10016). Phone 212/687-8000; toll-free 866/233-4642; fax 212/490-2634. www.affinia.com.* Located on the east side of Midtown, this all-suite hotel is a convenient choice for business and leisure travelers. Grand Central Station, the United Nations, and world-class shopping are nearby. The guest suites are large and feature fully-equipped kitchens—a plus for individuals with long-term business assignments or families. The hotel's contemporary Italian restaurant, Il Sogno, features a large patio for alfresco dining. 187 rooms, 25 story, all suites. Check-in 3 pm, check-out noon. Wireless Internet access. Restaurant, bar. Fitness room. Credit cards accepted. **$$$**

★ ★ ★ ★ ★ **FOUR SEASONS HOTEL NEW YORK.** *57 E 57th St, New York (10022). Phone 212/758-5700; toll-free 800/545-4000; fax 212/758-5711. www.fourseasons.com.* The bustling world of 57th Streets designer boutiques and office towers awaits outside the doors of the Four Seasons Hotel New York, yet this temple of modern elegance provides a serene escape from city life. Designed by legendary architect I. M. Pei, the Four Seasons pays homage to the citys beloved skyscrapers as the tallest hotel in New York. The rooms and suites are testaments to chic simplicity with neutral tones, English sycamore furnishings, and state-of-the-art technology, but its the service that defines the Four Seasons experience. The staff makes guests feel completely at ease in the monumental building, with ready smiles and generous spirit. The views are terrific, too; floor-to-ceiling windows showcase the dazzling city skyline or the quietude of Central Park. Some rooms offer furnished terraces so that guests can further admire the sights. 370 rooms, 52 story. Pets accepted, some restrictions. Check-in 3 pm, check-out noon. High-speed Internet access, wireless Internet access. Restaurant, bar. Fitness room, spa. Airport transportation available. Business center. **$$$$**

★ ★ ★ **HILTON NEW YORK.** *1335 Avenue of the Americas, New York (10019). Phone 212/586-7000; toll-free 800/445-8667; fax 212/315-1374. www.hilton.com.* This large convention hotel has a bustling, urban charm. Several restaurants, shops, and services make it a convenient base from which to explore New York. 2,058 rooms, 44 story. Check-in 3 pm, check-out noon. High-speed Internet access. Two restaurants, two bars. Fitness room, spa. Business center. **$$**

★ ★ ★ **HOTEL ELYSEE.** *60 E 54th St, New York (10022). Phone 212/753-1066; toll-free 800/535-9733; fax 212/980-9278. www.elyseehotel. com.* Celebrities like Tennessee Williams, Joe Dimaggio, Ava Gardner, and Marlon Brando have called this historic hotel home over the years since it opened in the 1920s. This hotel is well-known for its library, and the Monkey Bar and Grill remains a thriving New York hotspot, serving American cuisine both in the restaurant and through hotel room service. The guest rooms have marble baths; some have terraces, solariums, or kitchenettes. 101 rooms, 14 story. Complimentary continental breakfast. Check-in 3 pm, check-out 1 pm. Restaurant, bar. **$$$$**

★ ★ ★ **HOTEL PLAZA ATHENEE.** *37 E 64th St, New York (10021). Phone 212/734-9100; toll-free 800/447-8800; fax 212/772-0958. www.plaza-athenee.com.* Hotel Plaza Athne is the perfect place to enjoy a little bit of France while visiting New York. Located between Park and Madison avenues in one of the citys most exclusive neighborhoods, this elegant hotel is a perfect hideaway with a decidedly residential feel. Celebrating its place among the boutiques of Madison Avenue, the townhouses and apartment buildings of Park Avenue, and the greenery of Central Park, the Plaza Athne indeed feels like a home away from home for its guests. A palette of blues, golds, and reds creates the French contemporary décor of the rooms and suites. Some suites have dining rooms, while others have indoor terraces or outdoor balconies. The exotic flavor of the Bar Seine, with its vibrant colors and striking furnishings, transports guests to a faraway land, while Arabelle Restaurant combines gracious French style with delicious continental cuisine. 150 rooms, 17 story. Pets accepted, some restrictions. Check-in 3 pm, check-out 1 pm. Restaurant, bar. Fitness room. **$$$$**

★ ★ ★ **INTERCONTINENTAL THE BARCLAY NEW YORK.** *111 E 48th St, New York (10017). Phone 212/755-5900; toll-free 800/327-0200; fax 212/644-0079. www.new-york-barclay.intercontinental.com.* 603 rooms, 14 story. Check-in 3 pm, check-out noon. High-speed Internet access. Restaurant, bar. Fitness room. Airport transportation available. Business center. **$$$**

★ ★ ★ **THE IROQUOIS.** *49 W 44th St, New York (10036). Phone 212/840-3080; toll-free 800/332-7220; fax 212/719-0006. www.iroquoisny.com.* This hotel underwent a $10 million renovation several years ago, having been restored to its 1923 elegance. It has the feel of a European mansion, with French décor. The guest rooms are individually decorated with works of art reflecting New York themes such as Broadway, fashion, and museums and feature luxe Frette linens and Italian marble baths. A library provides a sitting area for perusing the hotel's collection of leather-bound editions of the classics. Triomphe restaurant features French cuisine, and the Burgundy Room offers breakfast and cocktails. 114 rooms, 12 story. Check-in 3 pm, check-out noon. High-speed Internet access, wireless Internet access. Restaurant, bar. Fitness room. Airport transportation available. Business center, business center. **$$$$**

★ ★ ★ **THE KIMBERLY HOTEL.** *145 E 50th St, New York (10022). Phone 212/755-0400; toll-free 800/683-0400; fax 212/486-6915. www.kimberlyHhotel.com.* If you're looking for an elegant, spacious room designed in bold colors and warm wood furnishings that the whole family will feel comfortable in, the all-suite Kimberly Hotel is for you. The one- and two-bedroom suites feature living rooms, dining areas, and fully equipped separate kitchens. For extra comfort, the suites feature plush robes and goose down or aromatherapy pillows. Many suites also have private terraces with city views. Guests receive free use of the New York Health and Racquet Club. As an added bonus, guests can take a complimentary cruise on the hotels 75-foot yacht on weekends from May through October. 193 rooms, 30 story, all suites. Check-in 3 pm, check-out noon. High-speed Internet access, wireless Internet access. Restaurant, bar. Airport transportation available. Business center. **$$$$**

★ ★ ★ **THE KITANO NEW YORK.** *66 Park Ave, New York (10016). Phone 212/885-7000; toll-free 800/548-2666; fax 212/885-7100. www.kitano.com.* This Japanese import located in Murray Hill features modern guest rooms with soft tones of beige and tan and soundproof windows that ensure peace and quiet. The rooms also feature Web TV, duvets, large desks, and Japanese teacups and green tea. Keeping with the Asian theme are an authentic Japanese tea room, gallery, and elegant shops located off the warm mahogany and marble lobby. Original works of art and sculptures are displayed throughout the hotel. The Nadaman Hakubai restaurant specializes in gourmet Japanese cuisine, and the sun-drenched Garden Café features contemporary continental cuisine. 149 rooms, 18 story. Check-in 3 pm, check-out 11 am. High-speed Internet access. Two restaurants, bar. Business center. **$$$$**

★ ★ ★ LE PARKER MERIDIEN. *118 W 57th St, New York (10019). Phone 212/245-5000; toll-free 800/543-4300; fax 212/307-1776. parkermeridien.com.* Everything that makes New York the charismatic city that it is is just steps from Le Parker Meridien—Carnegie Hall, Broadway theaters, Fifth Avenue shops, and Central Park are nearby, and Times Squre is just a short taxi ride away. Consistent with its big city surroundings, this chic hotel is clean and contemporary with minimal but sleek decor, with rooms that feature breathtaking views, DVC/CD players, and 32" televisions. The high-tech business center, with computers, fax machines, copiers, cell phones, beepers, and pagers never made work so easy, while the Concierge assists with everything you need to make your New York trip truly relaxing.731 rooms, 42 story. Pets accepted. Check-in 3 pm, check-out noon. High-speed Internet access, wireless Internet access. Three restaurants, bar. Fitness room, fitness classes available, spa. Indoor pool. Airport transportation available. Business center. **$$$$**

★ ★ ★ LIBRARY HOTEL. *299 Madison Ave, New York (10017). Phone 212/983-4500; toll-free 877/793-7323; fax 212/499-9099. www.libraryhotel. com.* As the name suggests, this unique hotel was inspired by a librarythe famous New York City Public Library located one block away. Each of the ten floors is dedicated to one of the ten categories of the Dewey Decimal System, which include languages, literature, history, the arts, and religion. Each guest room is furnished in a modern, sleek, yet warm and inviting décor and is stocked with books and art relevant to the floor's particular topic. In keeping with this theme, the hotel features a reading room and a poetry garden with terrace for relaxing and reading. 60 rooms, 10 story. Complimentary continental breakfast. Check-in 3 pm, check-out 1 pm. High-speed Internet access. Restaurant, bar. Business center. **$$$**

★ ★ ★ THE LOMBARDY HOTEL. *111 E 56th St, New York (10022). Phone 212/753-8600; toll-free 800/637-7200; fax 212/754-5683. www.lombardyhotel. com.* An elegant Midtown hotel, the Lombardy was built in the 1920s by William Randolph Hearst. This historic hotel has oversized rooms decorated in a classic, elegant, old-world style with comfortable couches and chairs. The marble baths have oversized showers and an array of upscale toiletries. Flowers, works of art, and crystal chandeliers are featured throughout the property. Above-and-beyond personal services include a seamstress and white-glove attendant service in the elevators. The hotel also has a fully equipped business center and is close to shopping, theaters, and Central Park. 167 rooms, 21 story. Check-in 3 pm, check-out 1 pm. High-speed Internet access. Restaurant, bar. Fitness room. Airport transportation available. Business center. **$$$**

★ ★ ★ ★ THE LOWELL. *28 E 63rd St, New York (10021). Phone 212/838-1400; toll-free 800/221-4444; fax 212/319-4230. www.lowellhotel. com.* Located in a landmark 1920s building in the historic district of the Upper East Side, The Lowell provides a refreshing change of pace. Its rooms and suites capture the essence of an elegant country house with a delightful blend of English prints, floral fabrics, and Chinese porcelains. Many suites boast wood-burning fireplacesa rarity in Manhattan. All rooms are individually decorated, and The Lowells specialty suites are a unique treat. The Garden Suite takes its inspiration from English country gardens and has two terraces, one complete with a rose garden and fountain. The glamour of the 1930s silver screen is recalled in the Hollywood Suite, while the Gym Suite, originally created for Madonna, is perfect for exercise buffs. The English influences extend to the Pembroke Room, where a proper tea is served, as are breakfast and brunch. Resembling a gentlemans club, the Post House (see), a well-respected New York steakhouse, is a paradise for carnivores. 70 rooms, 17 story. Pets accepted. Complimentary continental breakfast. Check-in 3 pm, check-out 1 pm. High-speed Internet access, wireless Internet access. Two restaurants, bar. Fitness room. Airport transportation available. Business center. **$$$$**

★ ★ ★ ★ ★ MANDARIN ORIENTAL, NEW YORK. *80 Columbus Cir, New York (10019). Phone 212/399-3938; toll-free 866/801-8880; fax 212/399-7189. www.mandarinoriental.com.* One look through a window in the Mandarin Oriental, New York, could spoil guests for other New York City hotels forever. Part of the Time Warner Center, the first floor of the hotel sits high atop the city on the 35th floor of the building. Views of Central Park, the Hudson River, and the city skyline provide a dazzling backdrop to a luxurious experience. Though serene guest rooms make it tempting to laze about for hours on end, slip out to explore all that the hoteland the Time Warner Centerhas to offer. Take a swim in the surrounded-by-windows pool on the 36th floor. Indulge in a Balinese body massage or a foot and nail treatment with hot stones at the spa. Return to the room in the evening to find an orchid on the pillow. The hotel's Asian theme carries over into Asiate, which serves French and Japanese fusion cuisine, and MObar, which features drinks like the East Meets West, an innovative combination of pear and cinnamon-infused brandy, chilled champagne, and a sugar cube. Want to be dazzled by one of the world's best chefs? Call ahead to make reservations at one of the much talked-about restaurants that sit 33 floors below the hotel, including Thomas Keller's Per Se, Masa Takayama's Masa, or Jean-Georges Vongerichten's V. 251 rooms. Pets accepted. Check-in 3 pm, check-out noon. High-speed Internet access, wireless Internet access. Two restaurants, bar. Fitness room, spa. Indoor pool, whirlpool. Business center. **$$$$**

★ ★ ★ **THE MARK.** *25 E 77th St, New York (10021). Phone 212/744-4300; toll-free 800/843-6275; fax 212/744-2749. www.mandarinoriental.com.* Take a break from the shopping of Madison Avenue and the museums of the Upper East Side and enter the haven of The Mark New York, where style and comfort combine for an exceptional experience. Situated on a quiet tree-lined street, The Mark feels like an elegant private home. The hotels eclectic décor perfectly blends the clean lines of Italian design with the lively spirit of English florals. Asian decorative objects and Piranesi prints complete the look in the hotels rooms and suites. Sophisticated cuisine is highlighted at Marks Restaurant, where the Master Sommelier also offers wine-tasting courses and themed dinners. Afternoon tea at The Mark is especially notable thanks to the Tea Master, who ensures that little bits of America and the Orient are brought to this British tradition. Marks Bar, a jewel-toned bite, is particularly popular with local denizens as well as hotel guests. 176 rooms, 16 story. Pets accepted. Check-in 3 pm, check-out noon. Restaurant, bar. Fitness room. Business center. **$$$$**

★ ★ ★ ★ **THE MERCER.** *147 Mercer St, New York (10012). Phone 212/966-6060; toll-free 888/918-6060; fax 212/965-3838. www.mercerhotel. com.* Catering to a fashion-forward clientele in New Yorks SoHo, Mercer Hotel is a boutique hotel in the midst of one of the citys most exciting neighborhoods. This former artists community stays true to its roots in its many cutting-edge boutiques and galleries. The loft-style Mercer Hotel epitomizes bohemian chic with its exposed brick, steel beams, and hardwood floors. Christian Liaigre, darling of the minimalist décor movement, has designed a sophisticated look for the hotel with simple furnishings and serene neutral colors. The uncluttered look extends to the bathrooms, with clean white tiles and luxurious two-person bathtubs or spacious showers with assorted spray fixtures. The lobby also serves as a lending library stocked with favorite books and videos, and the nearby trend-setting Crunch Gym is accessible to all guests. Mercer Kitchen (see) and Bar reign as hotspots on the local scene, for both their sensational food under the direction of Jean-Georges Vongerichten and their fabulous people-watching. 75 rooms, 6 story. Pets accepted. Check-in 3 pm, check-out noon. High-speed Internet access, wireless Internet access. Restaurant, bar. Business center. **$$$$**

★ ★ ★ **THE MICHELANGELO.** *152 W 51st St, New York (10019). Phone 212/765-1900; toll-free 800/237-0990; fax 212/581-4618. www.michelangelo-hotel. com.* If you are a lover of all things Italian, plan to stay at this ornate hotel during your next visit to New York. Special touches include opera music played in public spaces, Buon Di breakfast with cappuccino and Italian pastries, and Baci chocolates at turndown. The extra-large rooms are decorated in Art Deco, country French, or neoclassical style. Cherry wood furnishings have black accents and brass mounts. The rooms also feature woven fabrics from Italy. The hotels upscale restaurant, Limoncello, serves Italian cuisine, and The Grotto offers more casual dining and a selection of fine cigars. 178 rooms, 7 story. Complimentary continental breakfast. Check-in 3 pm, check-out noon. Restaurant, bar. Fitness room. **$$$$**

★ ★ ★ **MILLENIUM HILTON.** *55 Church St, New York (10007). Phone 212/693-2001; toll-free 800/445-8667; fax 212/571-2316. www.hilton.com.* Lower Manhattan's financial district is home to the tall and sleek Millenium Hilton. Nicely appointed guest rooms offer everything to make a stay here pleasant and cozy, with warm earth toned furnishings, 42" plasma screen televisions, and Hilton's signature, "The Bed," with soft, luxurious bed linens and fluffy down comforters. 565 rooms, 55 story. Pets accepted. Check-in 3 pm, check-out noon. High-speed Internet access, wireless Internet access. Restaurant, two bars. Fitness room, spa. Indoor pool. Airport transportation available. Business center. **$$$**

★ ★ ★ **MILLENNIUM BROADWAY HOTEL NEW YORK.** *145 W 44th St, New York (10036). Phone 212/768-4400; toll-free 800/622-5569; fax 212/768-0847. www.millenniumhotels.com.* Colorful murals that evoke the 1930s adorn the lobby of this contemporary Midtown hotel. Its convenient location near Times Square, the theater district, shopping, and Central Park makes this property a smart choice for both business and leisure travelers. Each spacious guest room is tastefully appointed with a satellite TV, mini bar, high-speed Internet access, iron and ironing board, hairdryer, and breathtaking views of Manhattan. 750 rooms, 52 story. Pets accepted; fee. Check-in 4 pm, check-out noon. High-speed Internet access, wireless Internet access. Restaurant, bar. Fitness room. Airport transportation available. Business center. Credit cards accepted. **$$**

★ ★ ★ MILLENNIUM UN PLAZA HOTEL. *1 UN Plaza, New York (10017). Phone 212/758-1234; toll-free 877/866-7529; fax 212/702-5051. www.millennium-hotels.com.* With a contemporary design and dizzying views of the Easter River, the Millennium UN Plaza Hotel offers an ideal New York experience. Bright lights and big mirrors add glamour to the lobby, while rooms are modern and contemporary in design and feature amenities like satellite television, high-speed Internet access, and mini-bars. 427 rooms, 40 story. Check-in 3 pm, check-out noon. High-speed Internet access. Restaurant, bar. Fitness room, spa. Indoor pool. Tennis. Airport transportation available. Business center**. $$$**

★ ★ ★ MORGANS.*237 Madison Ave, New York (10016). Phone 212/686-0300; fax 212/779-8352.*Another in Ian Schragers collection of hotels, Morgans is so hip that the front door has no sign, and no address is even posted. The guest rooms are decorated in soft, muted tones; a contrasting black-and-white checkerboard design differentiates the ultra-sleek bathrooms. Added touches to make your stay more pleasant include down comforters and pillows, CD players, and fresh flowers in the rooms. Asia de Cuba restaurant attracts a hip air-kiss crowd. (You may see celebrities!) Complimentary breakfast and afternoon tea add to the value. 84 rooms, 19 story. Pets accepted; fee. Check-in 3 pm, check-out 11 am. Wireless Internet access. Restaurant, bar**. $$**

★ ★ ★ THE MUSE. *130 W 46th St, New York (10036). Phone 212/485-2400; toll-free 877/692-6873; fax 212/485-2900. www.themusehotel. com.* A designers dream, this hotel has restored its unique, triple-arched, limestone and brick façade to give it a dramatic feel. Adding to the drama is a 15-foot vaulted ceiling with a commissioned mural depicting the nine muses in the lobby. Original artwork celebrating the theater and the performing arts hangs in each room, decorated in a warm color scheme of rust, burgundy, pear green, and muted blue-green and cherry wood furniture. Custom linens and duvet-covered feather beds add to guests comfort. Guest baths feature green marble with stone vanities. Other distinguishing features include in-room spa services, balconies, and DVD players. 200 rooms, 19 story. Pets accepted, some restrictions. Check-in 3 pm, check-out noon. Restaurant, bar. Fitness room**. $$$$**

★ ★ ★ NEW YORK MARRIOTT FINANCIAL CENTER. *85 West St, New York (10006). Phone 212/385-4900; toll-free 800/228-9290; fax 212/227-8136. www.marriott.com.* As its name suggests, this contemporary hotel is located in the Financial District in Lower Manhattan, within walking distance to Wall Street and other financial institutions. It also offers easy access to Tribeca, the Statue of Liberty, and Battery Park. Rooms are spacious and feature Revive—a luxury bed, high-speed Internet access, marble bathrooms, and views of the Statue of Liberty and New York Harbor (in some rooms). After a long day at the office or sightseeing, Roy's New York, the renowned Hawaiian-fusion restaurant, is the perfect place for a delicious dinner. 497 rooms, 38 story. Check-in 4 pm, check-out noon. High-speed Internet access, wireless Internet access. Restaurant, bar. Fitness room. Indoor pool. Airport transportation available. Business center. Credit cards accepted. **$$$$**

★ ★ ★ NEW YORK MARRIOTT MARQUIS. *1535 Broadway, New York (10036). Phone 212/398-1900; toll-free 800/843-4898; fax 212/704-8930. www.marriott.com.* 1,946 rooms, 49 story. Pets accepted, some restrictions. Check-in 3 pm, check-out noon. High-speed Internet access. Three restaurants, four bars. Fitness room. Business center**. $$$**

★ ★ ★ ★ THE NEW YORK PALACE. *455 Madison Ave, New York (10022). Phone 212/888-7000; toll-free 800/697-2522; fax 212/303-6000. www.newyork-palace.com.* Return to the Gilded Age at The New York Palace. Marrying the historic 1882 Villard Houses with a 55-story contemporary tower, The Palace brings the best of both worlds together under one roof. Directly across from St. Patricks Cathedral, The Palace is convenient for sightseeing or conducting business. First impressions are memorable, and the grand entrance through the gated courtyard of twinkling lights is no exception. The glorious public rooms are masterfully restored and recall their former incarnations as part of the private residences of Americas wealthiest citizens at the turn of the century. Set against the backdrop of New York City, The Palaces rooms and suites are a blend of contemporary flair or period décor. The Villard Bar & Lounge captures the imagination of its patrons with its Victorian design. Home to Le Cirque 2000 (see), one of the worlds most famous restaurants, The New York Palace is in its own class. 897 rooms, 55 story. Pets accepted, some restrictions. Check-in 3 pm, check-out noon. High-speed Internet access, wireless Internet access. Restaurant, bar. Fitness room, spa. Airport transportation available. Business center. **$$$$**

★ ★ ★ OMNI BERKSHIRE PLACE. *21 E 52nd St at Madison Ave, New York (10022). Phone 212/753-5800; toll-free 800/843-6664; fax 212/754-5018. www.omnihotels.com.* A soaring atrium with a wood-burning fireplace is the focal point of the lobby of this understated hotel. The rooms are designed with an Asian aesthetic, and business travelers will find all they need for a hassle-free stay. 396 rooms, 21 story. Pets accepted, some restrictions; fee. Check-in 3 pm, check-out noon. Wireless Internet access. Restaurant, bar. Fitness room. Business center. **$$$**

★ ★ ★ PARAMOUNT HOTEL NEW YORK. *235 W 46th St, New York (10036). Phone 212/364-5500; fax 212/535-3196. www.solmelia.com.* Ian Schrager does it again. One-of-a kind, funky but comfortable furniture (such as a wood chair upholstered with a large silkscreen image of a growling dog) dots the lobby. Guest rooms are decorated in white tones, with ultra-modern furniture and Scottish lambswool throws. The Mezzanine Restaurant features a Latin-inspired tasting and tapas menu. For foodies, the hotel has a Dean & Deluca takeout shop that offers mouthwatering items you can enjoy back in your room. 567 rooms, 19 story. Pets accepted; fee. Check-in 3 pm, check-out noon. High-speed Internet access, wireless Internet access. Restaurant, two bars. Fitness room. Airport transportation available. Business center. **$$$**

★ ★ ★ ★ THE PENINSULA NEW YORK. *700 5th Ave, New York (10019). Phone 212/956-2888; toll-free 800/262-9467; fax 212/903-3949. www.peninsula.com.* Situated on Fifth Avenue in Midtown, The Peninsula is a perfect location for exploring the sights and sounds of New York City, whether you're heading for the stores, catching a concert at nearby Carnegie Hall or Radio City, or relaxing in Rockefeller Center. The lobby is magnificent with its sweeping staircase carpeted in crimson. Bellhops in crisp white uniforms escort guests to rooms and suites, where lush fabrics and warm tones create a sensual ambience. The Peninsula is known for setting standards in the industry, which is evident in the fact that guests are able to regulate the temperature, lighting, and entertainment systems from their beds with a simple touch. The fitness center, overlooking the city, brings new meaning to exercise high, while the hotels lively mood is celebrated in its bars and restaurants. With its staggering views above the city, the Pen-Top Terrace & Bar should not be missed, regardless of the prices of cocktails, which are as high as the tower itself. 239 rooms, 23 story. Pets accepted. Check-in 3 pm, check-out noon. High-speed Internet access, wireless Internet access. Two restaurants, three bars. Fitness room, fitness classes available, spa. Indoor pool, whirlpool. Airport transportation available. Business center. **$$$$**

★ ★ ★ ★ THE PIERRE NEW YORK, A TAJ HOTEL. *2 E 61st St, New York (10021). Phone 212/838-8000; toll-free 800/545-4000; fax 212/826-0319. www.tajhotels.com/pierre.* Regal and esteemed, The Pierre New York is the definition of a grand old hotel. Relishing its location across from Central Park on Fifth Avenue, The Pierre has been a city landmark since 1930. Owned by Charles Pierre and John Paul Getty, among others, The Pierre is carefully maintains the integrity of this historic building while imparting its signature service levels with mixed success. Guests linger for hours in the impressive lobby, soaking up the ambience of old-world Europe. The rooms and suites are traditional with floral prints and antique reproductions. The Rotunda, where breakfast, light lunch, and afternoon tea are served, is a magical place where the cares of the world disappear under a ceiling of *trompe loeil* murals. Influenced by Renaissance paintings, the murals depict pastoral scenes of mythological figures intertwined with icons of the 1960s, including Jacqueline Kennedy Onassis. 201 rooms, 41 story. Pets accepted. Check-in 3 pm, check-out noon. High-speed Internet access, wireless Internet access. Two restaurants, bar. Fitness room. Business center. **$$$$**

★ ★ ★ **THE PLAZA.** *768 5th Ave, New York (10019). Phone 212/546-5499; toll-free 800/257-7544; fax 212/546-5324. www.fairmont.com.* Considered by many to be the grande dame of New York City lodgings, this massive, opulent hotel filled with lush furniture, pricey stores, and chandeliers has played host to dignitaries, celebrities, and just about every rich and famous person who has lived throughout its history. The rooms are elegant, too, with crystal chandeliers, formal furnishings, and 14-foot ceilings. The Oak Room is a classic steakhouse with an equally formal feel, and the Palm Court is legendary for its high tea and overflowing Sunday brunch. Bring an extra credit card to dine at either venue. 805 rooms, 18 story. Pets accepted, some restrictions. Check-in 3 pm, check-out noon. High-speed Internet access. Four restaurants, three bars. Fitness room, spa. Whirlpool. Business center. **$$$**

★ ★ ★ **THE REGENCY HOTEL.** *540 Park Ave, New York (10021). Phone 212/759-4100; toll-free 800/233-2356; fax 212/826-5674. www.loewshotels.com/hotels/newyork.*Home of the original power breakfast, where deals are sealed and fortunes are made, The Regency consistently ranks as one of New Yorks top hotels. Combining the appearance of a library and a private club, The Regency provides attentive service that extends above and beyond the ordinary to create a memorable stay. International design influences create a warm atmosphere throughout the well-appointed rooms, while the fitness and business centers cater to guests with specific goals in mind. Creature comforts abound in the luxurious rooms and suites, from the Frette linens to the Did You Forget closet stocked with items often left at home. Pets are even welcomed in grand style with room service designed exclusively for mans best friend, as well as dog-walking services and listings of pet-friendly establishments. Unwind at Feinsteins, where Grammy-nominated Michael Feinstein entertains nightly, or savor a delectable meal at 540 Park or The Library. 351 rooms, 20 story. Pets accepted. Check-in 3 pm, check-out 1 pm. High-speed Internet access. Three restaurants, bar. Fitness room, spa. Airport transportation available. Business center. **$$$$**

★ ★ ★ **RENAISSANCE NEW YORK HOTEL TIMES SQUARE.** *714 7th Ave, New York (10036). Phone 212/765-7676; toll-free 800/468-3571; fax 212/765-1962. www.renaissancehotels.com.* You'll find many conveniences at this business hotel located just north of Times Square. The lobby, located three floors above the street, has an appealing Art Deco theme that carries into the comfortable guest rooms. 305 rooms, 26 story. Pets accepted, some restrictions; fee. Check-in 4 pm, check-out noon. Restaurant, two bars. Fitness room. Business center. **$$$**

★ ★ ★ **RIHGA ROYAL, JW MARRIOTT HOTEL.** *151 W 54th St, New York (10019). Phone 212/307-5000; toll-free 866/656-1777; fax 212/765-6530. www.rihgaroyalny.com.* You'll feel like the king of New York with the royal accommodations at the Rihga Royal. Contemporary sophistication is the theme at this Midtown gem, where each spacious suite features exquisite details like luxurious bed linens, marble bathrooms with fine bath amenities, and flat-screen televisions. And with a location in the heart of Manhattan near Central Park, theaters, shopping, Times Square, and Carnegie Hall, you couldn't ask for a better home base for your New York trip. 507 rooms, all suites. Pets accepted. Check-in 3 pm, check-out 12 pm. High-speed Internet access. Restaurant, bar. Fitness room. Business center. **$$$$**

★ ★ ★ ★ **THE RITZ-CARLTON NEW YORK BATTERY PARK.** *2 West St, New York (10004). Phone 212/344-0800; toll-free 800/241-3333; fax 212/344-3801. www.ritzcarlton.com.* Watch the world from The Ritz-Carlton New York, Battery Park. While only a 5-minute walk from Wall Street and the Financial District, The Ritz-Carlton feels light years away with its staggering views of the Hudson River, the Statue of Liberty, and Ellis Island from its location on the southern tip of Manhattan. This 38-story glass and brick tower is a departure from the traditional Ritz-Carlton European style, from the contemporary glass artwork bestowed upon the public and private spaces to the modern furnishings in rooms and suites. The service is distinctly Ritz-Carlton, however, with exceptional concierge service and Bath Butlers who create special concoctions for bath time. The view is omnipresent throughout the hotel, whether you're gazing through a telescope in a harbor view room, enjoying a cocktail while at Rise, the 14th-floor bar, or savoring a delicious meal at 2 West. 298 rooms, 39 story. Pets accepted; fee. Check-in 3 pm, check-out noon. High-speed Internet access, wireless Internet access. Restaurant, two bars. Fitness room, spa. Business center. **$$$$**

★ ★ ★ ★ ★ THE RITZ-CARLTON NEW YORK, CENTRAL PARK. *50 Central Park S, New York (10019). Phone 212/308-9100; toll-free 800/241-3333; fax 212/207-8831. www.ritzcarlton.com.* Rising above Central Park and flanked by prestigious Fifth Avenue and fashionable Central Park West, The Ritz-Carlton New York, Central Park has one of the most coveted locations in town. This genteel hotel is exquisite down to every last detail, from the priceless antiques and artwork to the bountiful floral displays. The light-filled rooms and suites are a pastel-hued paradise, with sumptuous fabrics and plush furnishings. No detail is overlooked; rooms facing the park include telescopes for closer viewing. The distinguished ambience and white-glove service make this a top choice of well-heeled travelers. The hotel's restaurant, Atelier (see), garners praise from top critics for its modern French cuisine. Dedicated to excellence in all areas, the hotel includes an outpost of the renowned European La Prairie Spa. 261 rooms, 15 story. Pets accepted; fee. Complimentary continental breakfast. Check-in 3 pm, check-out noon. High-speed Internet access, wireless Internet access. Restaurant, bar. Fitness room, fitness classes available, spa. Airport transportation available. Business center. **$$$$**

★ ★ ★ ROYALTON. *44 W 44th St, New York (10036). Phone 212/869-4400; toll-free 800/635-9013; fax 212/869-8965. www.royalton.com.* Join the "in" crowd at this Ian Schrager hotel. Designed by Philippe Starck, the Royalton raised the bar on hipness when it opened a decade ago. Every detail is just so, from the stylish vodka bar to the lobby lounge where guests recline on cushioned steps to the small, minimalist guest rooms with modern, custom-made beds. The cream-colored rooms feature fresh flowers, down comforters and pillows, VCRs, CD players, and subtle lighting. The bathrooms are right out of the future, with stainless steel and glass fixtures. Some rooms have fireplaces and round tubs for two. The lobby also has a steely, minimalist look that is clean and sleek. The restaurant 44 is popular with local movers and shakers. 169 rooms, 16 story. Pets accepted, some restrictions; fee. Check-in 3 pm, check-out noon. Restaurant, two bars. Fitness room. **$$$$**

★ ★ ★ SAN CARLOS HOTEL. *150 E 50th St, New York (10022). Phone 212/755-1800; toll-free 800/722-2012; fax 212/688-9778. www.sancarloshotel. com.* The choice for many foreign heads of state visiting New York for business at the United Nations, the San Carlos is an elegant, low-key hotel located in the center of Midtown Manhattan. Rooms are spacious and comfortable with clean, contemporary decor and soothing neutral colors. Amenities such as-wet bars, fluffy robes and bath towels, Aveda bath products, and flat-screen televisions set the stage for a luxurious experience, while the well-equipped Wi-Fi business center and large in-room desks make working less of a chore. 147 rooms. Complimentary continental breakfast. Check-in 3 pm, check-out noon. High-speed Internet access, wireless Internet access. Restaurant, bar. Fitness room. Airport transportation available. Business center. **$$$**

★ ★ ★ SHERATON NEW YORK HOTEL AND TOWERS. *811 7th Ave, New York (10019). Phone 212/581-1000; fax 212/262-4410. www.sheraton.com.* This large, comfortable hotel is one of Sheraton's flagships—good for business or pleasure. Its proximity to the theater district, world-class shopping, Times Square, and Central Park will give guests plenty of options for outdoor activities. Guests will also find plenty of options to keep them busy inside the hotel including the spa, fitness room, business center, two restaurants, and a bar. The contemporary rooms are large by New York standards and feature the pillow-top Sheraton Sweet Sleeper bed. 1,748 rooms, 50 story. Pets accepted, some restrictions. Check-in 3 pm, check-out noon. High-speed Internet access. Two restaurants, bar. Fitness room, fitness classes available, spa. Airport transportation available. Business center. Credit cards accepted. **$$$**

★ ★ ★ THE SHOREHAM HOTEL. *33 W 55th St, New York (10019). Phone 212/247-6700; toll-free 800/553-3347; fax 212/247-6190. www. shorehamhotel. com.* When the hustle and bustle of the city has taken its toll, retreat to the intimate Shoreham Hotel in Midtown. A congenial staff eager to attend to your every need awaits you here as do contemporary, luxurious accommodations. Marble and slate bathrooms are stocked with Aveda bath amenities, while soft 300-count bed linens and feathery pillow top mattresses won't make you miss your bed back home. The 24-hour, state-of-the-art fitness center includes treadmills, elliptical equipment, bicycles, and free weights to help you stay in shape as well as personalized televisions and audio technology to make your workout a little less painful. And when you need a quick pick-me-up, stop by the lobby, where The Shoreham offers complimentary cappuccino and espresso for guests. 174 rooms, 11 story. Pets accepted.

Check-in 3 pm, check-out noon. High-speed Internet access, wireless Internet access. Restaurant, bar. Business center. **$$$**

★ ★ ★ **SOFITEL NEW YORK.** *45 W 44th St, New York (10036). Phone 212/354-8844; toll-free 877/565-9240; fax 212/354-2480. www.sofitel.com.* To see all of New York's sights in one trip is next to impossible, but you can be close to many of the city's most popular attractions with a stay at the Sofitel New York. Times Square, Greenwich Village, the Guggenheim, Carnegie Hall, and Lincoln Center are all neaby, as are many of New York's fantastic restaurants. And after a busy day of sightseeing, the hotel provides a serene and comfortable place to rest your head. With the Sofitel's signature and super-luxurious MyBed, along with soundproof windows, you'll sleep like a baby—even though you are in the city that never sleeps. 398 rooms, 30 story. Pets accepted. Check-in 3 pm, check-out noon. High-speed Internet access, wireless Internet access. Restaurant, bar. Fitness room. Airport transportation available. Business center. **$$$$**

★ ★ ★ **SOHO GRAND HOTEL.** *310 W Broadway, New York (10013). Phone 212/965-3000; toll-free 800/965-3000; fax 212/965-3244. www.grandhospitality.com.* Calculated cool is the best way to describe this trendy downtown hotel. The second-floor lobby doubles as a popular lounge. The guest rooms are simple in design, with tones of black and white and clean, uncluttered baths. All rooms have stereos, and some have rocking chairs. The lobby provides a comfortable gathering place, with high ceilings, couches, and exotic plants. Each floor also features a pantry with complimentary coffee, tea, and espresso. The Grand Bar & Lounge serves a mix of dishes, from macaroni and cheese to lobster tea sandwiches to chickpea-fried rock shrimp. The lounge also features music and DJsa good place to hang out after a day of sightseeing. 363 rooms, 17 story. Pets accepted. Check-in 3 pm, check-out noon. High-speed Internet access, wireless Internet access. Restaurant, two bars. Fitness room. Business center. **$$$$**

★ ★ ★ ★ ★ **THE ST. REGIS.** *2 E 55th St, New York (10022).Phone 212/753-4500; fax 212/787-3447. www.stregis.com/newyork.*Located just steps off Fifth Avenue in the heart of Manhattan, The St. Regis reigns as New Yorks grande dame. Opened in 1904, guests glide past the revolving doors of this Beaux Arts landmark to enter the rarefied world of old New York. The St. Regis defines elegance with its gleaming marble, glittering gold leafing, and sparkling chandeliers. The guest rooms are elegantly decorated in soft pastel colors with Louis XVI-style furnishings, while personal butlers cater to every whim 24 hours a day. Set under a ceiling of magical clouds that casts a dreamlike spell over its patrons, the Astor Court is the perfect place to enjoy traditional afternoon tea. Renowned for its famous Red Snapper cocktail and bewitching Maxfield Parrish mural, the King Cole Bar is a favorite of hotel guests and locals alike.315 rooms, 20 story. Pets accepted; fee. Check-in 3 pm, check-out noon. High-speed Internet access, wireless Internet access. Restaurant, bar. Fitness room, fitness classes available, spa. Airport transportation available. Business center. **$$$$**

★ ★ ★ **SURREY HOTEL.** *20 E 76th St, New York (10021). Phone 212/288-3700; toll-free 800/637-8483; fax 212/628-1549. www.affinia.com.* Like staying at the home of a rich great-aunt, this hotel has the understated grandeur of a faded residence. You'll see old-world charm upon entering the lobby, with its 18th-century English décor, wood-paneled elevators, and leather sofas. The studio, one-bedroom, and two-bedroom suites have a similar look, with molded ceilings, beveled-glass mirrors, and antique accents. Some have kitchenettes, and others have full kitchens. Suites also offer Web TV, Nintendo, VCRs, and bathrobesall the comforts of home. The hotels best feature is its restaurantworld-renowned chef Daniel Bouluds Café Boulud serves up gourmet French cuisine (at prices to match). 132 rooms, 16 story, all suites. Pets accepted. Check-in 3 pm, check-out noon. Restaurant. Fitness room. Business center. **$$$$**

★ ★ ★ **SWISSOTEL NEW YORK, THE DRAKE.** *440 Park Ave and 56th St, New York (10022). Phone 212/421-0900; toll-free 800/637-9477; fax 212/371-4190. www.swissotel.com.* This hotel is popular with business travelers who need easy access to Midtown's many corporate offices. For vacationers, it's within walking distance of Fifth Avenue shopping and Central Park. 495 rooms, 21 story. Pets accepted; fee. Check-in 3 pm, check-out noon. High-speed Internet access, wireless Internet access. Restaurant, bar. Fitness room, spa. Airport transportation available. Business center. **$$$$**

★ ★ ★ **TRIBECA GRAND HOTEL.** *2 6th Ave, New York (10013). Phone 212/519-6600; toll-free 800/965-3000; fax 212/519-6700. www.tribecagrandhotel. com.*

Tribeca is one of the most trendy areas of New York, and the Tribeca Grand Hotel most certainly reflects this. A contemporary urban style is found throughout, from the spacious lobby that includes the hip Church Lounge, to the ultra-modern guest rooms with digital cable, iPods, and DVD/CD players. 203 rooms. Pets accepted. Check-in 3 pm, check-out noon. High-speed Internet access, wireless Internet access. Restaurant, bar. Fitness room. Airport transportation available. Business center. **$$$**

★ ★ ★ ★ **TRUMP INTERNATIONAL HOTEL & TOWER.** *One Central Park W, New York (10023). Phone 212/299-1000; toll-free 888/448-7867; fax 212/299-1150. www.trumpintl.com.* Occupying an enviable site across from Central Park on Manhattans Upper West Side, the 52-story Trump International Hotel & Tower makes guests feel like they are on top of the world. The lobbys warm brass tones and polished marble welcome visitors to the world of Trump, where attention to detail results in perfection and everyone feels like a tycoon. The guest rooms and suites are elegantly decorated with a contemporary European flavor, while the floor-to-ceiling windows focus attention on the mesmerizing views of Central Park framed by the impressive skyline. The Personal Attach service ensures that all guests are properly coddled, while the extensive fitness center caters to exercise enthusiasts. All suites and most rooms come complete with kitchens, and in-room chefs are available to craft memorable dining experiences. Room service is world-class and created by one of New Yorks top chefs, Jean-Georges Vongerichten, whose restaurant, Jean Georges (see), is located here. 168 rooms, 52 story. Pets accepted; fee. Check-in 4 pm, check-out noon. High-speed Internet access, wireless Internet access. Restaurant, bar. Fitness room, spa. Indoor pool. Airport transportation available. Business center. **$$$$**

★ ★ ★ **W NEW YORK.** *541 Lexington Ave, New York (10022). Phone 212/755-1200; toll-free 888/625-5144; fax 212/319-8344. www.whotels.com.* The chic lobby has the air of an urban ski lodge, with a sunken lobby bar that has tree trunk end tables and colorful rugs. The guest rooms have an organic feel with natural cotton linens and neutral tones. 682 rooms, 18 story. Pets accepted. Check-in 3 pm, check-out noon. High-speed Internet access, wireless Internet access. Two restaurants, bar. Fitness room, spa. Airport transportation available. Business center. **$$$$**

★ ★ ★ **W NEW YORK - TIMES SQUARE.** *1567 Broadway, New York (10036). Phone 212/930-7400; fax 212/930-7500. www.whotels.com.* 509 rooms. Pets accepted, some restrictions; fee. Check-in 3 pm, check-out noon. High-speed Internet access. Restaurant, bar. Fitness room. Business center. **$$**

★ ★ ★ **W NEW YORK - UNION SQUARE.** *201 Park Ave S, New York (10016). Phone 212/253-9119; toll-free 888/625-5144; fax 212/253-9229. www.whotels.com.* The Union Square outpost of this hip hotel chain pampers both business and leisure travelers (and their pooches, too). Its setting in the 1911 Guardian Life Building, a lovely Beaux Arts-style structure, brings a historic touch to this thoroughly modern hotel. It's one of few hotels on Union Square, which offers shops, restaurants, bars, theaters, and the famous Greenmarket. Inside, you'll find hotspots Olives (see), chef Todd English's Mediterranean restaurant, and Underbar, owned by Rande Gerber. Guest rooms, done in shades of purple, feature the W's signature feather beds with pillowtop mattresses, large work desks, and Aveda bath products. If you can't find something to satisfy your cravings in the W munchie box, room service is available 24 hours a day. 270 rooms, 25 story. Pets accepted; fee. Check-in 3 pm, check-out noon. High-speed Internet access, wireless Internet access. Restaurant, two bars. Fitness room. Airport transportation available. Business center. **$$$$**

★ ★ ★ **THE WALDORF-ASTORIA.** *301 Park Ave, New York (10022). Phone 212/355-3000; toll-free 800/925-3673; fax 212/872-7272. www.waldorfastoria.com.* Enjoy a taste of old New York at this lodging landmark. The 1931 Art Deco hotel has played host to US presidents and other luminaries and features a grand lobby that is not to be missed. It has murals, mosaics, elaborate design work, and a piano that once belonged to Cole Porter. The rooms are individually decorated, elegant, and traditional in style. The Bull & Bear steakhouse has a 1940s feel and attracts the powerful and wealthy. The ultra-exclusive Waldorf Towers, from floor 28 and above, is even more upscale and private. 1,416 rooms, 42 story. Check-in 3 pm, check-out noon. High-speed Internet access, wireless Internet access. Two restaurants, two bars. Spa. Airport transportation available. Business center. **$$$$**

★ ★ ★ **WESTIN ESSEX HOUSE ON CENTRAL PARK.** *160 Central Park S, New York (10019).*

Phone 212/247-0300; toll-free 800/937-8461; fax 212/315-1839. www.essexhouse.com. An elegant hotel on Central Park South, one of the more fabulous locations in New York City, the Essex House is full of wealth and history. The Art Deco hotel boasts many luxurious touches, as well as large rooms and spectacular views of Central Park. Don't miss the stunning elevator doors and the terrific gift shop on the ground floor. Dining options include the casual Café Botanica and the haute cuisine of Alain Ducasse (see). 601 rooms, 19 story. Pets accepted, some restrictions. Check-in 3 pm, check-out noon. High-speed Internet access. Two restaurants, bar. Fitness room (fee), spa. Business center. **$$$**

★ ★ ★ **WESTIN TIMES SQUARE.** *270 W 43rd St, New York (10036). Phone 212/201-2700; toll-free 866/837-4183; fax 212/201-2701. www.westinny.com.* Located in the center of New York's most famous district, the Westin Times Square keeps guests in the center of it all—theaters, shops, entertainment, and general buzzing of activity. Sleek and simple rooms include soundproof windows and the Westin's signature Heavenly Bed for a blissful night's sleep as well as deluxe bath robes and bath amenities. Guests looking for the ultimate in serenity can indulge in a spa-inspired room, which features amenities such as an electric massage chair, mini-bar stocked with healthy snacks, and an aromatherapy air diffuser. 863 rooms. Pets accepted, some restrictions. Check-in 3 pm, check-out noon. High-speed Internet access, wireless Internet access. Restaurant, two bars. Fitness room, spa. Business center. **$$$$**

Full-Service Inn

★ ★ ★ **INN AT IRVING PLACE.** *56 Irving Pl, New York (10003). Phone 212/533-4600; toll-free 800/685-1447; fax 212/533-4611. www.innatirving.com.* Step back in time to 19th-century New York in this intimate, romantic brownstone hideaway located in a row of 1830s townhouses just south of Gramercy Park. The high-ceilinged guest rooms feature antiques, four-poster beds, and cozy couches and chairs without sacrificing modern amenities like remote climate control and Internet access. Enjoy breakfast in bed or take it in the elegant guest parlor. Continental breakfast and afternoon high tea are served at a leisurely pace in this elegant country-style inn. The staff can arrange any special services you need, such as an in-room massage or the booking of theater tickets. 11 rooms, 3 story. Children over 12 years only. Complimentary continental breakfast. Check-in 3 pm, check-out noon. Bar. **$$$$**

Spas

★ ★ ★ ★ **FOUR SEASONS HOTEL NEW YORK SPA.** *57 E 57th St, New York (10022). Phone 212/758-5700. www.fourseasons.com.* Elegant, yet far from fussy, the spa at the Four Seasons mirrors the hotel's commitment to contemporary chic. Blonde woods, soothing accent colors, and black-and-white photography create a serene escape from the city streets, and the treatment rooms are stylish cocoons.The spa's dedication to complete surrender is easily discovered on its treatment menu, where modern technology meets aromatherapy and Asian traditions. Awaken the body with the coffee blossom treatment, or heal the skin with an omega body elixir, which uses a propolis moisturizing lotion created by honeybees in the rainforest. The Four Seasons in One treatment celebrates the seasons with a cooling scrub symbolizing winter, a floral body wrap for spring, a medley of massages for summer, and a soothing scalp treatment for fall. Let your troubles drift away during the floating sensory experience, where a heated flotation bed makes for a delightfully relaxing treatment. In addition to shiatsu, aromatherapy, and reflexology, the Four Seasons offers a full range of unique massage therapies. From the Thai ceremony massage, which uses heated herbal mushroom packs to soothe muscles, and acupressure with walking bars, where a therapist uses his or her body weight to deliver relief, to the Asian Scentao hot stone massage, a definitive Asian influence is found here. Facials harness the power of modern technology with microcurrent lifting, oxygen cellular renewal, and DNA molecular regeneration.

★ ★ ★ ★ ★ **SPA AT MANDARIN ORIENTAL NEW YORK.** *80 Coumbus Circle, New York (10019).* The Mandarin Oriental is the very definition of Zen chic. Rising above the treetops of Central Park from its prestigious Time Warner Center location, this sleek hotel marries Asian sensibilities with New York panache, and its 14,500-square-foot spa is the piece-de-la-resistance. Bamboo and natural stone are used throughout, creating a temple of serenity in this most frenetic of world capitals. Chinese, Ayurvedic, Balinese, and Thai healing therapies are the highlight of a visit to this facility, where guests are encouraged to book blocks of time, known as Time Rituals, for a comprehensive relaxation experience. The spa menu is far-reaching, offering a wide array of massage therapies, body treatments, and facials designed to purify, nurture, balance, and rejuvenate visitors. Signature therapies celebrate the spa's Eastern heritage with Lomi Lomi massage, Chakra balancing, and Ama releasing Abhyanga. This bastion of blissful quietude is capped off by a state-of-the-art fitness center, complete with a magnificent pool where swimmers can lap up the city skyline views.

★★★★ THE PENINSULA SPA AT THE PENINSULA NEW YORK. *700 Fifth Ave, New York (10019). Phone 212/903-3910; toll-free 800/262-9467. www.peninsulaspa.com.* While The Peninsula calls the heart of midtown Manhattan home, one step inside this Beaux Arts landmark, with its abundant fresh flowers and gentle hush, will have guests leaving the frenetic city pace behind. The Peninsula Spa is the embodiment of the urban oasis. This spa is defined by its city skyline views, and sleek styling adds to the cosmopolitan atmosphere. Fitness and wellness programming are a large part of The Peninsula Spa experience. Personal trainers are available in addition to group classes, including yoga, Pilates, and ballet, tap, or jazz dance classes. Water aerobics and one-on-one swim instruction are offered at the pool. The spa features a wide range of skin care, massage, and body treatments. The facial menu includes deep-cleansing, aromatherapy, and sensitive skin treatments, while the specialty facials include signature therapies using June Jacobs or Valmont products. Microdermabrasion targets lifeless skin, and the back treatment pays special attention to this often-neglected region. The body treatments are among the most appealing offerings, with treatments such as the papaya hydrating body mask, chai soy mud mask, and body champagne, which uses heated seaweed and other ingredients to give the body a bubbly sensation. Stressed-out executives head straight for the massage table to enjoy a Swedish, shiatsu, sports, deep-tissue, or aromatherapy massage. Couples and pregnancy massages are also featured here.

Restaurants

★★★ 21 CLUB. *21 W 52nd St, New York (10019). Phone 212/582-7200; fax 212/586-5065. www.21club.com.* This one-time speakeasy is now one of New York Citys most celebrated spots for lunch, dinner, and lots of drinksat least for the well-heeled Wall Street, media, and superstar regulars who frequent its best tables. The chef turns out stellar, seasonal Modern American fare, with standards that shine and inventive twists that delight. The restaurant has a distinguished air to it, with a clubby, brass-railed bar (often the sight of dealmakers clinking martini glasses), luxurious linen-lined tables, golden lighting, antique oil paintings, and old photos hung on wood-paneled walls. The deep wine list explores the world at large and works well to complement the cuisine. The Upstairs at 21 is a restaurant within a restaurant and provides a more intimate dining experience. American menu. Lunch, dinner. Closed Sun; three weeks in Aug; holidays. Bar. Jacket required in Upstairs at 21. Reservations recommended. **$$$**

★★ 'INOTECA. *98 Rivington St, New York (10002). Phone 212/614-0473; fax 212/614-0637. www.inotecanyc.com.* From Jason and Joe Denton, the owners of the tiny and irresistible wine bar ino comes inoteca, a rustic, wood-beamed Italian wine bar in the super-hip Lower East Side. The wine list is all Italianall the timeand the wonderful staff is ready, willing, and able to help walk you through it. The simply delicious menu of Italian snacks includes platters of cured meats and cheeses, panini, antipasti, and the house signature truffled egg toast. Although the fashionable crowds gather here in full force on a regular basis, the place is surprisingly attitude free. Be sure to bring your patience, because the waiting is the hardest part. Italian menu. Lunch, dinner, late-night, brunch. Bar. Casual attire. Outdoor seating. **$**

★ 88 PALACE. *88 E Broadway, New York (10002). Phone 212/941-8886; fax 212/925-6375.*If you are craving dim sum, or a perfect Chinese tea luncheon, consider stopping at 88 Palace, a bustling Chinese restaurant featuring a delicious and authentic selection of dim sum and house-made soups, fish, meats, and rice dishes. The restaurant is a favorite among Chinatown's locals, and many of the staff don't speak much English, but no matter. The point-to-order method works well. Chinese menu. Lunch, dinner. Casual attire. **$$**

★ A SALT & BATTERY. *80 Second Ave, New York (10003). Phone 212/254-6610.* Continental menu. Lunch, dinner. Casual attire. **$$**

★★★ AL BUSTAN. *827 Third Ave, New York (10022). Phone 212/759-5933; fax 212/759-0050. www.albustanny.com.* If you've ever wondered what Lebanese cuisine is like, head to Al Bustan and discover a world of aromatic and exquisite food. Many have already made the discovery, which means that Al Bustan is very popular, especially at lunch, as its Midtown location makes it a nice choice for dealmakers. But when the sun sets, Al Bustan becomes an elegant respite for dinner, offering guests a luxurious upscale Lebanese dining experience that includes some of the best bread in the city, served with a magnificent array of mezze, not to mention a full menu of authentic Lebanese dishes. Middle Eastern menu. Lunch, dinner. Bar. Casual attire. Reservations recommended. **$$$**

★ ★ ★ ★ ★ **ALAIN DUCASSE.** *155 W 58th St, New York (10019). Phone 212/265-7300; fax 212/265-5200. www.alain-ducasse.com.* When word came that the famed French wizard of gastronomy, Alain Ducasse, was opening a restaurant in New York, the citys food world began salivating. And while the excess, such as the choice of half a dozen pens to sign the bill, drew some criticism at its opening, people started to embrace the restaurant once they experienced Ducasse firsthand. Ducasse has superhuman culinary powers; food doesn't taste this way anywhere else, and it sure doesn't arrive at a table this way anywhere else. Elegant to the point of being regal, Ducasse is a restaurant designed to please every one of the senses: sight, sound, smell, taste, and touch. The room frequently fills with attractive diners. Hours later, when dinner is over and you attempt to get up and walk to the door, you receive a gift for breakfast the next morning: a gift-wrapped buttery, fruit-laced brioche that will make you swoon. If you manage not to dig into it in the cab on the way back to your hotel, you have a will of steel. But divine excess does not come without its price. Dinner at Ducasse will set you back several pretty pennies, but really, isn't paying your mortgage a dull way to spend your money? French menu. Dinner. Closed Sun; holidays. Jacket required. Reservations recommended. **$$$$**

★ ★ **ALFAMA.** *551 Hudson St, New York (10014). Phone 212/645-2500; fax 212/645-1476. www.alfamarestaurant.com.* The wonderful seaside cuisine of Alfama, an ancient village in Portugal, is on the menu at this namesake bistro decorated with authentic blue and white Portuguese tiles in Manhattans West Village. Bacalau (salt cod) is one of the most common ingredients in Portuguese cooking, and it shows up here mixed in a dish with potatoes and peppers that is alive with robust flavors. Cooking in a cataplanaa sort of open-mouth clamshell pot made from copperis another tradition in Portugal. The cataplana is filled with fish, scallops, and shrimp and studded with chorizo, potatoes, and tomatoesa Hungry Man-style bouillabaisse that is complemented by an incredible selection of Portuguese wines. To keep things like they are in the old country, soulful Fado singers perform on Wednesday nights. Spanish menu. Lunch, dinner, Sun brunch. Bar. Casual attire. Reservations recommended. **$$$**

★ ★ **AMMA.** *246 E 51st St, New York (10022). Phone 212/644-8330; fax 212/644-8250. www.ammanyc.com.* At Amma, an elegant, petite Midtown spot serving excellent Indian fare, you'll find tables jammed with eager curry lovers kvelling over dishes of Goan shrimp, piles of toothsome bhel puri, and plates of frizzled okra with tomatoes and onions. This is not your ordinary curry house, though. Amma is stylish and serene, and the service is efficient and fine. The chef, formerly of Tamarind (see), knows his way around the tandor oven, and you should by all means order several tandoori dishes like stuffed chicken breasts, crisp and spiced shrimp, or the succulent yogurt-infused lamb chops. Save room for dessert; the rasmalai dumplings are a showstopper. Indian menu. Lunch, dinner. Children's menu. Casual attire. **$$**

★ ★ ★ **ANNISA.** *13 Barrow St, New York (10014). Phone 212/741-6699; fax 212/741-6696. www.annisarestaurant.com.* At Annisa, a cozy, off-the-beaten-path gem in Greenwich Village, chef/partner Anita Lo and partner Jennifer Scism (who runs the front of the house) bring a bit of Asia and a lot of flavor and savvy style to the contemporary American table. With the restaurants golden glow and elegant, sheer-white curtains draped along the tall walls, its easy to feel like you're dining somewhere very close to heaven. The simple, approachable menu helps keep you in the celestial mood. An array of wines by the glass and a strong sommelier make pairing wine with dinner a no-brainer. American menu. Dinner. Bar. Business casual attire. Reservations recommended. **$$$**

★ ★ **AOC BEDFORD.** *14 Bedford St, New York (10014). Phone 212/414-4764; fax 212/414-4765. www.aocbedford.com.* Located on a quiet, tree-lined street in the West Village, AOC Bedford is a stylish yet rustic retreat that welcomes you in with its exposed brick walls and wood-beamed ceilings. The restaurant derives its name from the term *appellation dorigine contrle*, the official French designation for food products of the highest quality. The menu is not exclusively French, though. In fact, much of it has a Spanish flare, like the house specialty of suckling pig, served Iberian style (with the bone-in) and accompanied by a pile of dates, or the grand paella, stocked with cockles, clams, shrimp, and squidall ingredients that shine easily. French, Italian, Spanish menu. Dinner. Bar. Casual attire. Reservations recommended. **$$$**

★ ★ ★ **AQUAGRILL.** *210 Spring St, New York (10012). Phone 212/274-0505; fax 212/274-0587. www.aquagrill.com.* When the sun is out and a warm breeze is in the air, you'll find the citys hip locals lounging outside at Aquagrill, a perennial favorite for swimmingly fresh seafood (and great dry-aged steak). With its tall French doors sprung open to the street, Aquagrill has a European elegance and calm to it that makes it an irresistible spot to settle in, even if only for a glass of sparkling wine and a dozen (or two) shimmering oysters. Although the warmer months are the most fun, when there is a nip in the air, the dining room wraps you up, making you feel cozy in an instant. Seafood menu. Lunch, dinner, brunch. Closed Mon; holidays. Bar. Casual attire. Reservations recommended. Outdoor seating. **$$$**

★ ★ ★ **AQUAVIT.** *65 E 55th St, New York (10022). Phone 212/307-7311; fax 212/265-8584. www.aquavit.org.* Chef/partner Marcus Samuelsson introduced New York to his splashy brand of modern Scandinavian cuisine a decade ago at Aquavit. After ten years and a move to the ultra-modern Park Avenue Tower, the restaurant has a sleek, sophisticated vibe, and the cuisine is even more spectacular. While ingredients like herring, lamb, salmon, caviar, and dill show up with regularity on this Scandinavian-inspired menu, the food here is more uniquely Samuelsson than anything else. What this means is that every dazzling plate achieves a startlingly delicious harmony as the result of the chefs careful and creative combination of textures, flavors, temperatures, ingredients, and the cooking styles of France, Asia, and Sweden. A shot of smooth, citrus-tinged aquavit complements dinner nicely, as does a selection from the impressive wine list. Scandanavian menu. Lunch, dinner, Sun brunch. Closed holidays. Bar. Business casual attire. Reservations recommended. **$$$$**

★ ★ **ARTISANAL.** *2 Park Ave, New York (10016). Phone 212/725-8585; fax 212/481-5455. www.artisanalcheese.com.* Say cheese! Artisinal is chef/owner Terrance Brennans ode to the stuff, and it is a glorious tribute at that. (Brennan is also chef/owner of Picholine-see also.) In addition to one of the best cheese selections this side of the Atlantic, you'll find lovely brasserie standards like moules frites, gougres (warm, cheese-filled brioche puffs that melt in your mouth and are impossible to stop eating), frise au lardons, and of course, cheese fonduethe house specialty. If you are more inclined to eat a meal at the bar, Artisinals is a terrific spot to hunker down and sample some of the best cheeses from the United States and around the world, not to mention wines, all 120 of which are available by the glass. Located in the east 30s, this is also just about the best place to eat before or after a Madison Square Garden event. French bistro menu. Lunch, dinner, brunch. Bar. Casual attire. Reservations recommended. **$$$**

★ ★ ★ ★ **ASIATE.** *80 Columbus Cir, New York (10023). Phone 212/805-8800; fax 212/805-8888. www.mandarinoriental.com.* French-Asian cuisine has been given a bad name, and deservedly so. Too often, the fusion of such wide-ranging traditions results in flavors unpleasantly smushed together rather than heightened. But at its best, contact between cultures can produce unique dishes of subtlety and depth that transcend their origins. At Asiate, chef Nori Sugie challenges customers' palates. There's his Caesar salad soup, for example, and pan-roasted branzino with green papaya salad. Or Wagyu beef, the US version of high-end beef from Japan, served with smoked potato puree and oxtail sauce. Desserts also borrow from the two traditionsraspberry clafoutis comes with a sake cheesecake foam and Thai basil ice cream. This is rich food served in a rich setting. At 35 floors up, in a plush room designed by Tony Chi, the elegance and exclusivity add to the appreciation of whats on the plate. French, Japanese menu. Breakfast, lunch, dinner, brunch. Jacket required. Reservations recommended. **$$$$**

★ ★ ★ ★ **ATELIER.** *50 Central Park S, New York (10019). Phone 212/521-6146; fax 212/207-8831. www.ritzcarlton.com.* This is no run-of-the-mill hotel restaurant. This is the restaurant at The Ritz-Carlton New York, Central Park (see). Executive Chef Gabriel Kreuther, originally from Alsace, began his restaurant training at age 12 by helping out around his uncle's hotel and restaurant. Now he is considered one of America's top young chefs. Before taking over the kitchen at Atelier in early 2002, Kreuther was the chef de cuisine at the much-lauded Jean Georges. From signature dishes, including bluefin tuna and diver scallop tartare seasoned with Iranian Osetra caviar, to the exclusive china pattern made by Bernardaud, Atelier's staff takes incredible care to make sure the experience is most memorable. Even the restaurant's restrooms, featuring the same plush hand towels hotel guests enjoy, have won awards. Gentle harp, piano, or recorded music doesn't drown out voices. If the conversation flags at dinner, quick inspiration is available by looking out the restaurant windows on the horse drawn carriages that slowly roll in and out of the park. A meal at Atelier calls for a handsomely knotted tie or beautiful new outfit; those who don't dress the part risk being upstaged by the elegant setting. French menu. Breakfast, lunch, dinner, Sun brunch. Bar. Children's menu. Business casual attire. Reservations recommended. Valet parking. **$$$**

★ ★ ★ ★ **AUREOLE.** *34 E 61st St, New York (10021). Phone 212/319-1660; fax 212/755-3126. www.charliepalmer.com/aureole_ny/.* Hidden away inside a lovely brownstone on Manhattans Upper East Side, Aureole is inviting and warm and feels like a special place to dine. The waitstaffs gracious hospitality ensures that you continue to feel that way throughout your meal. The luxurious space is bathed in cream tones and warm lighting, and is furnished with overstuffed wine-colored banquettes. (An enclosed courtyard garden opens for warm-weather dining.) Diners at Aureole are generally here to celebrate something, as it is one of New Yorks most impressive eateries. The crowd is mostly middle-aged and from the upper echelon of New York society, although Aureole is not a stuffy place. It is friendly and cozy and well suited for just about any occasion, from couples looking for romance to colleagues looking to have a delightful business dinner together. Owner and celebrity chef Charlie Palmer offers his guests the delicious opportunity to dine on a wonderfully prepared menu of what he calls "Progressive American" fare. But it doesn't really matter what label you give it, because its all great. There are always two tasting menusone vegetarian and another inspired from the marketin addition to a parade of terrific la carte selections. The extensive and celebrated wine program includes bold wines from California, Spain, and Italy. American menu. Lunch, dinner. Closed Sun; holidays. Bar. Jacket required. Reservations recommended. **$$$$**

★ ★ **AVRA.** *141 E 48th St, New York (10017). Phone 212/759-8550; fax 212/751-0894. www.avrany.com.* At this terrific, airy, and elegant estiatorio, you can eat like they do on the Greek islands, feasting on fresh fish (priced by the pound) simply grilled with lemon, herbs, and olive oil; salads of fresh briny feta and tomato; and loaves of fluffy, warm pita to dip into assorted garlicky mezze like hummus and tzatziki. Save room for dessert, as the sticky-sweet honey-soaked baklava is not to be missed. Greek menu. Lunch, dinner, brunch. Bar. Casual attire. Reservations recommended. Outdoor seating. **$$$**

★ ★ **AZUL BISTRO.** *152 Stanton St, New York (10002). Phone 646/602-2004; fax 646/602-2014.* Located on a sleepy corner of Stanton Street in the now hip hood known as the Lower East Side, Azul Bistro is a seductive corner spot with raw wood accents and low lighting. Serving South American fare to the soft rhythms of tango music, Azul makes a nice substitute for a trip to Buenos Aires. While the menu focuses on Argentinean cuisine, you'll also find Latin American dishes like ceviche and empanadas. Grilled meats are a specialty, like the lamb and the juicy steak dotted with chimichurri sauce (think garlicky pesto). The watermelon sangria should get the night going on the right foot, no matter what you order. Latin American menu. Dinner. Casual attire. Reservations recommended. Outdoor seating. **$$$**

★ ★ ★ **BABBO.** *110 Waverly Pl, New York (10011). Phone 212/777-0303; fax 212/777-3365. www.babbonyc.com.* Dressed in his signature orange clogs and shorts, Mario Batali is the king of rustic authentic Italian cuisine on televisions Food Network. But before he was a star of the small screen, he was a cookand he is one celebrity chef who still is. Here in New York, you'll find him at Babbo, a charming Greenwich Village carriage house-turned-stylish duplex hotspot where celebrities, foodies, VIPs, and supermodels fill tables (and every nook of space) for the chance to feast on Batalis unique brand of robust and risky Italian fare. The man is known for serving braised pigs feet, warm lamb tongue, and testa (head cheese). Cult-status signature pastas like beef cheek ravioli and mint love lettersspicy lamb sausage ragu soothed with mint and wrapped in envelopes of fresh pastaare lick-lipping delicious and demonstrate that some culinary risks are worth taking. Italian menu. Dinner. Bar. Casual attire. **$$$**

★ ★ ★ **BALTHAZAR.** *80 Spring St, New York (10012). Phone 212/965-1785; fax 212/966-2502. www.balthazarny.com.* If you don't know what all the hype surrounding Balthazar is about, you most certainly should. Keith McNallys super-fabulous replica of a Parisian brasserie is one of those rare spots that actually deserves the buzz. From the attractive crowds at the bar to the stunning folks who squeeze into the restaurants tiny tables (you'll be seated as close to a stranger as is possible without becoming intimate), Balthazar is a dazzling, dizzying, wonderfully chaotic destination that sports a perfect menu of delicious brasserie standards like frisee au lardons, pan bagnat, steak frites, and a glistening raw bar built for royalty, not to mention the fresh-baked bread from the Balthazar bakery next door. To feel like a true New Yorker, pick up a bag of croissants, a couple of baguettes, and a dozen tarts on your way out for breakfast or lunch the next day. Balthazar is fun and loud and, in its own electric way, flawless. French menu. Breakfast, lunch, dinner, late-night, brunch. Bar. Casual attire. Reservations recommended. **$$$**

★ ★ BAO 111. *111 Avenue C, New York (10009). Phone 212/254-7773; fax 212/254-2229. www.bao111.com.* This sleek little spot on Avenue C gets major snaps for its contemporary brand of Vietnamese fare. Drawing an eclectic crowd, Bao 111 is an alluring space, marked by amber lighting and wood banquettes littered with embroidered pillows. The menu is authentic Vietnamese, tweaked for a trendy New York palate. Expect dishes like the signature short ribs skewered with lemongrass, spring rolls with mint and basil, five-spice quail, and crab and shrimp soup with noodles. Vietnamese menu. Dinner. Bar. Casual attire. Reservations recommended. **$$$**

★ ★ BAR JAMON. *125 E 17th St, New York (10003). Phone 212/253-2773; fax 212/253-5318.*Mario Batali is turning Spanish on us. After mastering the art of simple Italian fare at Babbo, Lupa, Otto (see all three), and Esca, he is taking on the Iberian Peninsula with Bar Jamon. Yes folks, a ham and wine bar set adjacent to Casa Mono (see), where he serves up a menu of Catalan small plates in a convivial setting straight out of Barcelona. A miniature spot with dark wood accents and a marble bar, this crowded watering hole features all sorts of Spanish jamon (pronounced *haahmon*), cheeses (manchego, queso de tetilla, valdeon, calabres), and olives. More exciting plates include smoked trout salad with olives and cava-soaked grapes and classics like tortilla dEspanaall perfectly suited to Spanish wine and sherry. Spanish menu. Lunch, dinner, late-night. Bar. Casual attire. **$**

★ ★ ★ BAR MASA. *10 Columbus Cir, New York (10019). Phone 212/823-9800; fax 212/823-9809. www.masanyc.com.* Japanese menu. Lunch, dinner. Closed Sun. Bar. Casual attire. **$$$**

★ ★ BARBETTA. *321 W 46th St, New York (10036). Phone 212/246-9171; fax 212/246-1279. www.barbettarestaurant.com.* Barbetta is the grand old dame of the theater district. This classic Italian restaurant opened its doors in 1906 and is still owned by the same loving family, the Maioglios. Located in a pair of historic early-19th-century townhouses, this restaurant is a classic charmer that's all about super-elegant, old-world dining. The menu doesn't aim anywhere other than where its heart isItalybut don't expect just pasta. The kitchen offers a great selection of seafood, poultry, and beef prepared with seasonal ingredients and lively flavors. The tree-lined outdoor garden is an enchanted spot to unwind over dinner or drinks. Italian menu. Lunch, dinner. Closed Sun-Mon, outdoor seating. **$$$**

★ BARNEY GREENGRASS. *541 Amsterdam Ave, New York (10024). Phone 212/724-4707; fax 212/595-6565. www.barneygreengrass.com.* If you don't mind lines that rival opening day of *The Lord of the Rings,* then you'll be fine at Barney Greengrass, an Upper West Side institution for brunch since 1908. The restaurant, still decked out like a vintage New York soda fountain, features a simple menu of eggs, waffles, pancakes, and assorted heavenly platters of smoked fish and bagels. From the menu to the waiters to the décor, Barney Greengrass hasn't really changed a whole lot in its century of doing business, and that is part of its distinct old-world charm. American menu. Breakfast, lunch, brunch. Closed Mon; Jewish holidays. Casual attire. No credit cards accepted. **$$**

★ ★ ★ BAYARD'S. *1 Hanover Sq, New York (10004). Phone 212/514-9454; fax 212/514-9443. www.bayards.com.* Fresh flowers, a rare Buddha collection, crafted ship models, stately antiques, fine china, mahogany double staircases, and hand-carved working fireplaces are just some of the charming details you will encounter at Bayardsan exquisite French-American restaurant located in the India House, a historic landmark building located at One Hanover Square, near Wall Street. To match the surroundings, executive chef Eberhard Mller delivers a magnificent menu that showcases the seasons. Indeed, most of the menus fruits and vegetables are hand-harvested from Satur Farmsthe 50-acre family farm chef Mller and his wife own in the North Fork of Long Islandmaking every bite a delicious discovery of the land. Signatures include Fishers Island oysters, served warm with champagne sauce and osetra caviar, Maine lobster with black trumpet mushrooms and pea shoots, and dry-aged New York strip steak with cipolini onions, creamed spinach, and fingerling potatoes. American, French menu. Dinner. Closed Sun. Bar. Casual attire. Reservations recommended. **$$$**

★ ★ BECCO. *355 W 46th St, New York (10036). Phone 212/397-7597; fax 212/977-6738. www.becconyc.com.* Becco, a charming Italian restaurant in the Theater District, is a delightful place to relax over a delicious Italian supper before or after the theater, or at lunch for a business meeting. Becco offers great food, gracious service, and a lovely, airy atmosphere. The pre-theater special for which it has become famous offers authentic homemade pastas in an all-you-can-eat format. You choose three pastas, and they keep dishing them out until you say Uncle! or until you can't rise from the table, whichever comes first. Italian menu. Lunch, dinner. Closed Dec 25. Casual attire. Reservations recommended. **$$$**

★ ★ ★ **BEN BENSON'S STEAKHOUSE.** *123 W 52nd St, New York (10019). Phone 212/581-8888; fax 212/581-1170. www.benbensons.com.* At this popular testosterone-infused steakhouse, you'll find yourself elbow to elbow with celebrities, politicians, sports stars, and the citys financial elite. As you might expect from a power steak spot, the menu is as big as the egos in the room and includes solid standards like salads, poultry, and seafood that are simply and impeccably prepared. But the magnetic pull here is the restaurants signature selection of USDA dry-aged prime beef, served in the form of about a dozen cuts and portion sizes. The huge steaks are matched in size by lobsters the size of small pets. Don't miss the houses signature crispy hashed browns. When the sun is shining, grab a seat outside in the sidewalk dining room, appointed in the same style as the indoor space with deep armchairs, formal white linens, and green-and-white wainscoted plantersan ideal alfresco setting. Steak menu. Lunch, dinner. Closed holidays. Bar. Business casual attire. Reservations recommended. Outdoor seating. **$$$**

★ ★ **BEPPE.** *45 E 22nd St, New York (10010). Phone 212/982-8422; fax 212/982-6616. www.beppenyc.com.* Walk into Chelsea's Beppe, and you may feel yourself leaving the city of New York and entering the lovely land of Italy. At this warm, weathered eatery filled with all the charm of an Italian farmhouse kitchen, you can sample some of chef/owner Cesare Cassellas earthy and divine pasta; a terrific selection of Tuscan-style wood-fired seafood, meat, and game; and a wine list that focuses on gems from Tuscany and Italys lesser-known regions. Italian menu. Lunch, dinner. Closed Sun. Bar. Casual attire. Reservations recommended. **$$$**

★ ★ **BEYOGLU.** *1431 Third Ave, New York (10028). Phone 212/650-0850. www.beyoglunyc.com.* There is much to love about this family-run Turkish restaurant on the Upper East Side. From the service, which is warm and friendly, to the dining room, a spacious, stylish, low-lit space, to the easygoing crowd of neighborhood folks, Beyoglu beckons you back as soon as you enter. The real star here is the food, which includes delicious warm pita bread drizzled with olive oil to start and moves on to a terrific variety of mezze and a heavenly spiced selection of fragrant rice and assorted kabobs that will leave you in want of a ticket to Istanbul ASAP. Middle Eastern menu. Lunch, dinner. Bar. Casual attire. Reservations recommended. Outdoor seating. **$$**

★ ★ **BICE.** *7 E 54th St, New York (10022). Phone 212/688-1999; fax 212/752-1329. www.bicenewyork.com.* Italian menu. Lunch, dinner. Bar. Business casual attire. Reservations recommended. Outdoor seating. **$$$**

★ ★ ★ **BILTMORE ROOM.** *290 Eighth Ave, New York (10001). Phone 212/807-0111; fax 212/807-0074. www.thebiltmoreroom.com.* Located on a nondescript block of Chelsea, The Biltmore Room appears like a mirage in the desert, its magnificent façade marked by guilded gates and marble columns that make the entranceway feel like an old palace. Once inside, the design continues to please the eye, with marble floors; a long, sexy bar; high ceilings; and loveseat-style banquettes set around the dining room like an elegant old-world parlor. The bar, where the impressive cocktails are made from the freshest ingredients, draws the beautiful people crowd, a mix of sophisticated foodies and hipsters in scant dress. As if the design and the drinks werent enough, the food, by chef/partner Gary Robbins, is already creating legions of fans. The menu features a savvy fusion style of American and Asian flavors with dishes accented with chiles, mango, lime, sweet spices, fresh mint, basil, and other savory herbs. The Biltmore Room is the rare spot that lacks pretension despite its fabulous food and design, which makes it a perfect spot for drinks, a special occasion, or a night out with friends. American menu. Dinner. Bar. Business casual attire. Reservations recommended. **$$$$**

★ ★ ★ **BLUE FIN.** *1567 Broadway, New York (10036). Phone 212/918-1400; fax 212/918-1300. www.brguestrestaurants.com.* Located in the heart of Times Square in the swanky W Times Square Hotel, Blue Fin is restaurateur Steve Hansons (Blue Water Grill, Dos Caminossee both) most elaborate seafood palace. On two levels, with a breathtaking aquatic-themed design, Blue Fin features high-end fish dishes and a stunning array of sushi, sashimi, and maki. The bar on the ground floor is always packed to the gills with suits sipping tall, cool cocktails, while the upstairs bar is more mellow but may still be a struggle for intimate conversation at peak times. Blue Fin offers terrific food in a stylish and slick setting that makes it a great spot for pre-theater, a dinner with a large group, or

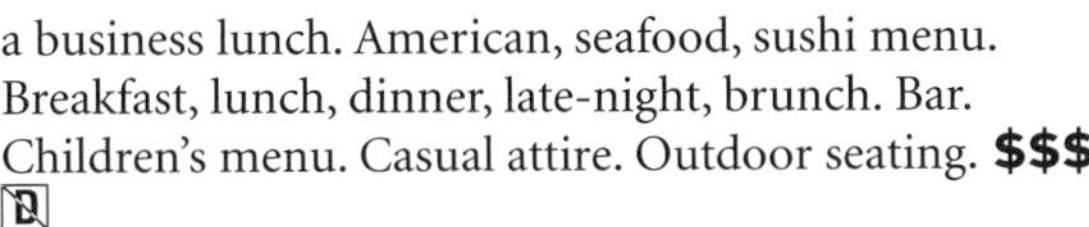

a business lunch. American, seafood, sushi menu. Breakfast, lunch, dinner, late-night, brunch. Bar. Children's menu. Casual attire. Outdoor seating. **$$$**

★ ★ ★ **BLUE HILL.** *75 Washington Pl, New York (10011). Phone 212/539-1776; fax 212/539-0959.* *www.bluehillnyc.com.* Blue Hill is a rare and lovely restaurant offering gracious hospitality, extraordinary seasonal American fare, and a stellar wine list in a warm, cozy, contemporary space that feels just right, like a page out of an upscale Pottery Barn catalog. Chocolate tones, soft lighting, and serene service make this restaurant a luxurious experience perfect for special occasions, and the truly wonderful menu by chef/owner Dan Barber ensures a delicious evening. American menu. Dinner. Bar. Casual attire. Reservations recommended. Outdoor seating. **$$$**

★ ★ **BLUE RIBBON.** *97 Sullivan St, New York (10012). Phone 212/274-0404.* *www.blueribbonrestaurants.com.* Brothers Bruce and Eric Bromberg opened Blue Ribbon on a quiet block in SoHo years ago, and it is as packed today as it was on day one. The tiny, low-lit bistro oozes fabulousness (models, moguls, and musicians are regulars) and features an eclectic menu of New York and French staples, like an icy raw bar stocked with oysters, deliriously good fried chicken (served with honey), and a perfect, meaty, and intensely flavored steak tartare garnished with cornichons, onion, egg, and coarse mustard. Blue Ribbons notoriety comes from its late-night crowd that inevitably includes superstar chefs unwinding after a night of cooking or a night on the town. International menu. Lunch, dinner. Closed holidays. Bar. Casual attire. **$$$**

★ ★ **BLUE RIBBON BAKERY.** *35 Downing St, New York (10014). Phone 212/337-0404; fax 212/242-1086.* *www.blueribbonrestaurants.com.* The brothers Bromberg first brought New Yorkers a taste of their creative culinary genius with Blue Ribbon, their hip late-night bistro. With Blue Ribbon Bakery, a rustic, wood-beamed, windowed corner spot in the West Village, they took on the task of baking bread (delicious bread) and decided to offer a menu of salads, small plates, and fresh seasonal entrées to boot. Whether for lunch, brunch, dinner, or an afternoon pick-me-up, Blue Ribbon Bakery is the perfect spot for a casual and always tasty bite. American, French menu. Lunch, dinner, brunch. Bar. Casual attire. **$$$**

★ ★ **BLUE SMOKE.** *116 E 27th St, New York (10016). Phone 212/447-7733; fax 212/576-2561.* *www.bluesmoke.com.* With elegant restaurants like Union Square Café and Gramercy Tavern (see both) in his repertoire, Danny Meyer might come as a surprise as the man behind Blue Smoke, a sleek, casual barbecue joint packed nightly with a loud and boisterous crowd. But Meyer hails from St. Louis, and barbecue has been his longtime passion. This love of cue shines through in saucy, meaty ribs; pulled pork sandwiches; and fried catfish, paired with super sides like smoky bacon-laced pit beans, messy slaw, and, for dessert, a perfect banana cream pie. American menu. Lunch, dinner, late-night. Bar. Children's menu. Casual attire. **$$**

★ ★ **BLUE WATER GRILL.** *31 Union Sq W, New York (10003). Phone 212/675-9500; fax 212/331-0354.* *www.brguestrestaurants.com.* Overlooking Union Square Park, Blue Water Grill is a buzzing shrine to seafood, with a raw bar and an extensive menu of fresh fish prepared with global accents and a terrific array of sushi, sashimi, and creative maki rolls. The dining room is massive and magnificent, with marble columns and floors, and sky-high ceilings. The crowds are always here because the food is tasty, inventive, and fun, which means the vibe is spirited and lively. Be warned that conversation may be difficult to conduct above the roar at peak times. American, Seafood menu. Lunch, dinner, Sun brunch. Bar. Casual attire. Outdoor seating. **$$**

★ ★ **BOATHOUSE RESTAURANT.** *72nd St & Park Dr N, New York (10028). Phone 212/517-2233; fax 212/517-8821.* *www.thecentralparkboathouse.com.* Central Park is one of the most wonderful places to spend a day in Manhattan. It really doesn't matter what the season. The same can be said of the Boathouse Restaurant, an open, airy, and romantic New York icon/restaurant with views of the rowboaters making their way across the unfortunately green Central Park pond. Sure, summer is the ideal time to settle in for cocktails on the patio under the cherry blossoms, but this restaurant is equally idyllic in the winter, when snow blankets the park in a soft hush. The menu at the Boathouse is New American, with steak, fish, pasta, and salads sure to please any and all culinary desires. Brunch in warmer months is a winner here, but the lines are long, so call ahead for a table. American menu. Breakfast, lunch, dinner, brunch. Bar. Children's menu. Casual attire. Reservations recommended. Outdoor seating. **$$$**

★ ★ **BOLO.** *23 E 22nd St, New York (10010). Phone 212/228-2200; fax 212/228-2239. www.bolorestaurant.com.* Chef, restaurateur, Food Network star, and author Bobby Flay is one busy celebrity chef. Lucky for us, fame hasnt gone to his head. The food at Bolo, the Spanish restaurant he opened a decade ago, keeps getting better. Since taking trips to Barcelona, Flay has reinvented the menu at Bolo, adding a delicious menu of tapas (and a nice list of sherries) to his lively, contemporary Spanish menu. While the food continues to excite, the room at Bolo could use a facelift and feels worn at the seams. Nevertheless, the bar is still alive with regulars, and the restaurant has a warm energy that makes it a wonderful place to dine. Spanish, tapas menu. Lunch, dinner. Closed Dec 25. Bar. Casual attire. **$$$**

★ ★ ★ **BOND STREET.** *6 Bond St, New York (10012). Phone 212/777-2500; fax 212/777-6530.* High-art sushi and sashimi are the calling cards of Bond Street, a hot spot and hipster hangout disguised as a modern Japanese restaurant. Famous fashionistas, celebrities, and supermodels are the typical guests at the whitewashed, airy restaurant, and down in the dark and sexy lower-level bar you'll find more of the same. For all the hype, though, Bond Street serves excellent sushi and sashimi, and the extensive and inventive modern Japanese-influenced menu stands up to the scene with impressive resolve. Japanese menu. Dinner. Bar. Business casual attire. Reservations recommended. **$$$**

★ ★ **BOOM.** *152 Spring St, New York (10012). Phone 212/431-3663; fax 212/431-3643. www.boomny.com.* Located in the heart of SoHo, Boom is a popular spot for European expats living (and shopping) in New York. The stylish crowds give Boom a hotspot vibe, but its really just a simple, cozy bistro, with wood floors, candles burning, and, through open windows, a great view of the hipsters strolling by on Spring Street. The kitchen is not breaking any culinary ground but manages to turn out a respectable and eclectic menu of tasty global dishes. American, Mediterranean menu. Breakfast, lunch, dinner, brunch. Bar. **$**

★ ★ ★ ★ **BOULEY.** *120 W Broadway, New York (10013). Phone 212/964-2525; fax 212/219-3443. www.davidbouley.com.* Acclaimed chef David Bouley is the talent behind the stoves at this temple of haute French gastronomy. Housed in the renovated and impeccably decorated space that was once his more casual bistro, Bouley Bakery, Bouley appeals to Manhattans most discerning and divine diners. The elegant and oh-so-civilized place is packed with well-heeled foodies, fashionistas, political pundits, and celebs who understand that a night in Bouleys care is nothing short of miraculous. Bouley delivers on every front: the service is charming, the seasonal ingredients are stunning, the French technique is impeccable, and his kitchen magic is nothing short of brilliant. French menu. Lunch, dinner. Jacket required. Reservations recommended. **$$$$**

★ ★ ★ **BRASSERIE.** *100 E 53rd St, New York (10022). Phone 212/751-4840; fax 212/751-8777. www.rapatina.com.* As you enter Brasserie, you may feel all eyes on you, which is probably because they are. The dining room is set down a level, and when you enter, you must walk down a futuristic glass staircase, a dramatic walkway that calls all eyes up. In case the folks at the backlit bar and seated along the long, luxurious banquettes are too busy feasting on the tasty brasserie fare (like duck cassoulet, frise aux lardons, onion soup, escargots, or goujonettes of sole) to look up and catch your entrance, 15 video screens broadcast images of incoming diners; you'll be captured on film for repeat viewing later. Its best just to get over your stage fright and relax, because its so easy to enjoy a meal here. French menu. Breakfast, lunch, dinner, late-night, brunch. Bar. Business casual attire. Reservations recommended. **$$$**

★ ★ ★ **BRASSERIE 8 1/2.** *9 W 57th St, New York (10019). Phone 212/829-0812; fax 212/829-0821. www.brasserie8andahalf.com.* Located in the sleek, Gordon Bunshaft-designed 9 building in the heart of West 57th Street, Brasserie 8 1/2 is the perfect spot for all sorts of plans. Its a great pick for a power lunch or for shimmering cocktails after work. The long, backlit bar is a mecca for stylish men and women in search of one another. Its also a wise choice for pre-theater dinner and a terrific selection for those who want to relax in a slick, modern setting and enjoy a leisurely meal of updated brasserie classics tweaked to modern attention. The kitchen incorporates accents from Asia and the Mediterranean into these classic dishes, varying each dish just enough from its original base. Be warned that the spacious banquettes are so soft and comfortable that you may never want to get up. American, French menu. Lunch, dinner, Sun brunch. Bar. Business casual attire. Reservations recommended. **$$$**

★ ★ **BRICK LANE CURRY HOUSE.** *306-308 E 6th St, New York (10003). Phone 212/979-2900; fax 212/979-8420. www.bricklanecurryhouse.com.* Brick Lane Curry House is a standout in Curry Row, a stretch of East 6th Street in the East Village that's lined with Indian restaurants. Named for Londons Little India dining district, Brick Lane opened to instant raves for its stunning well-spiced Indian cuisine and stylish, hip setting. Some of the dishes, like the phaal curry, are so fiery that the house will buy you a beer if you can finish it. May the force be with you. Indian menu. Lunch, dinner. Bar. Casual attire. Reservations recommended. **$$**

★ ★ BRYANT PARK GRILL. *25 W 40th St, New York (10018). Phone 212/840-6500; fax 212/840-8122. www.arkrestaurants.com.* Located behind the New York Public Library in the leafy tree-lined Bryant Park, the Bryant Park Grill is an airy, vaulted, and stylish spot to relax over dinner or hammer out a complex business transaction over lunch. The simple American menu features salads, steaks, fish, sandwiches, and pasta on a straightforward, seasonal menu. The bar is a zoo in the summertime, so if mingling with happy hour crowds is your thing, make Bryant Park Grill your destination. American menu. Lunch, dinner, brunch. Bar. Children's menu. Casual attire. Outdoor seating. **$$$**

★ ★ ★ BULL AND BEAR STEAKHOUSE. *301 Park Ave., New York (10022). Phone 212/872-4900; fax 212/486-5107. www.waldorf.com.* Located in the stately Waldorf-Astoria Hotel in Midtown (see), the Bull and Bear Steakhouse is a testosterone-heavy, meat-eaters haven. The street-level dining room is elegant in a clubby, macho sort of way, and the steaks, all cut from certified aged Black Angus, are fat, juicy, and the way to go, even though the menu does offer a wide variety of other choices, including chicken, lamb, pot pie, and assorted seafood. Classic steakhouse sides like creamed spinach, garlic mashed potatoes, and buttermilk fried onion rings are sinful and match up well with the rich beef on the plate. A terrific selection of red wine will complete your meaty meal nicely. American, Steak menu. Lunch, dinner. Bar. **$$$**

★ ★ ★ CAFE BOULUD. *20 E 76th St, New York (10021). Phone 212/772-2600; fax 212/772-9372. www.danielnyc.com.* Daniel Boulud is one very committed chef. So committed, in fact, that he is the chef-king of a little empire of French restaurants in New York City. Café Boulud is his less formal version of his haute temple of French gastronomy, Daniel (see). But less formal is a relative term. Café Boulud is a majestic space, perfect for quiet conversation and intimate dining. The service is helpful and unobtrusive. The chef is a whiz at pleasing the palate and offers a choice of four la carte menus: La Tradition (French Classics and Country Cooking), La Saison (The Rhythm of the Seasons), Le Potager (Vegetarian Selections from the Farmers' Market), and Le Voyage (a menu inspired from a changing international destinationMexico, Morocco, etc.). The wine program is ambitious, and the staff is unintimidating and eager to assist with pairings, making the total dining experience like a little slice of French heaven. American, French menu. Lunch, dinner. Business casual attire. Reservations recommended. Outdoor seating. **$$$**

★ ★ CAFE DE BRUXELLES. *118 Greenwich Ave, New York (10011). Phone 212/206-1830.* New Yorkers flock to this casual Greenwich Village eatery for out-of-this-world french fries and tasty mussles. Staff is charming, the menu is packed with fresh, flavorful choices, and the beer selection rivals any pub in the city. Belgian menu. Lunch, dinner, brunch. Closed holidays. Bar. Casual attire. Reservations recommended. **$$**

★ ★ ★ CAFE DES ARTISTES. *1 W 67th St, New York (10023). Phone 212/877-3500; fax 212/877-7754. www.cafenyc.com.* Café des Artistes is a timeless New York City classic. Originally fashioned after the English Ordinary, a cozy bistro with a limited menu based on food available in the market, the Café was a regular meeting place where local artists in the neighborhood would come together to discuss their creative works. Today, the restaurant remains an old-guard favorite for its luxurious, sophisticated setting, impeccable service, and menu of up-to-the-minute, yet approachable, seasonal, French bistro fare. While elegant in its art-filled décor, the restaurants menu does not try too hard, over-flourish, or over-think things. The kitchen stays true to its roots. French bistro menu. Lunch, dinner, brunch. Bar. Business casual attire. Reservations recommended. **$$$**

★ ★ CAFE FIORELLO'S. *1900 Broadway, New York (10023). Phone 212/595-5330; fax 212/496-2471. www.cafefiorello.com.* If you find yourself taking in a ballet or an opera at Lincoln Center and you don't want to break the bank on dinner because you've just spent your last dime on those tough-to-get tickets, Café Fiorello is a great choice for a reasonable, casual, and tasty meal. The convivial restaurant has a large outdoor patio for summertime seating and people-watching, while the indoor room is warm and welcoming with dark wood walls, deep red ceilings tiles, and terra cotta floor tiles, making it equally charming in the winter months. The menu offers a delicious selection of antipasti, pasta, meat, and fish prepared in the tradition of a Roman osteria, along with classic desserts like a creamy tiramisu. Northern Italian menu. Lunch, dinner, brunch. Closed Dec 25. Bar. Casual attire. Reservations recommended. **$$$**

★ CAFE HABANA. *17 Prince St, New York (10012). Phone 212/625-2001.* It's safe to say that if you don't see a crowd of models, musicians, and assorted other super-fabulous people strewn out on the sidewalk outside Café Habana, it is closed. Indeed, as soon as this Cuban diner opens, the crowds are there, like metal to a magnet. The space is decked out in vintage chrome, with a food bar and way-cool retro booths, but the draw here is the flawless menu of cheap, straight-up Cuban grub, like rice and beans, terrific hangover-curing egg dishes, fried plantains, and divine plates of classic ropa vieja. Cuban, Mexican menu. Breakfast, lunch, dinner, late-night, brunch. Casual attire. **$**

★ ★ CAFE LOUP. *105 W 13th St, New York (10011). Phone 212/255-4746; fax 212/255-2022.* Café Loup is a neighborhood favorite for simple but stylish French fare. This spacious, airy restaurant has a soothing vibe and is adorned with fresh flowers, lithographs, and photographs. If you are in the mood for attitude and a scene, head somewhere else, as this is an easy place to feel comfortable and to enjoy dinner. French bistro menu. Lunch, dinner, Sun brunch. Bar. Casual attire. **$$**

★ ★ CAFE LUXEMBOURG. *200 W 70th St, New York (10023). Phone 212/873-7411; fax 212/721-6854.* This Upper West Side gem has become a favorite of New Yorkers over the years, which explains why it's constantly abuzz with activity. The Art Deco décor with warm, cream-colored walls offers a sophisticated and stylish atmosphere, but it's the consistently good bistro fare that draws admirers. Lunch and dinner menus feature choices like steak au poivre, escargots with garlic butter, and truffle-scented risotto, while duck hash and eggs, Irish oatmeal with brown sugar and cinnamon, and smoked salmon benedict are standouts on the brunch menu. American, French menu. Breakfast, lunch, dinner, brunch. Bar. Casual attire. Reservations recommended. **$$$**

★ ★ CAFE SABARSKY. *1048 Fifth Ave, New York (10028). Phone 212/288-0665; fax 212/645-7127. www.wallse.com.* Located in the Neue Galerie, facing the magnificent Central Park on Fifth Avenue, Café Sabarsky offers a taste of Austria in a spectacular New York City setting. With sky-high ceilings, marble pillars, crystal chandeliers, and elegant brocade banquettes, Café Sabarsky feels like a royal chateau in the Austrian Alps. The divine menu, prepared by wonder-chef Kurt Gutenbrunner of Wallse, includes delicious and authentic Viennese pastries and savory Austrian dishes. The wine list is extensive and includes wonderful Austrian red and white varietals. Continental menu. Breakfast, lunch, dinner. Closed Tues. Casual attire. Reservations recommended. **$$$**

★ ★ CAFETERIA. *119 Seventh Ave, New York (10011). Phone 212/414-1717. www.cafeteria247.com.* This Chelsea restaurant is a hotspot late at nightand at all times in betweenfor its easy-to-love American menu in a minimalist whitewashed setting. Cafeteria is a sleek, ramped-up diner with good food, fun cocktails, and lots of fabulous attitude that makes it a second home to lots of size 2 babes, metrosexuals, and buff Chelsea boys. American menu. Breakfast, lunch, dinner, late-night, brunch. Bar. Children's menu. Casual attire. Outdoor seating. **$$**

★ ★ CANDELA RESTAURANT. *116 E 16th St, New York (10003). Phone 212/254-1600; fax 212/614-8626. www.candelarestaurant.com.* Located near Union Square Park, Candela is an ideal choice for a romantic dinner, a large gathering of friends, or a light bite and a drink at the long, inviting, low-lit bar. Candela, as the name suggests, is filled with ivory-pillared candles of varying sizes, giving the large dining room dressed in dark wood a sexy, amber glow. The space gets its medieval vibe from heavy hanging tapestries, beamed ceilings, and dark oak-planked floors. The menu is sort of like the Gap, offering something for everyone at reasonable prices. Expect a nice selection of Mediterranean, Italian, and Asian dishes like garlicky hummus, lobster and corn ravioli, and sushi dishes like a tempura-battered spicy tuna roll or black cod with a rich miso glaze. International menu. Dinner. Bar. Casual attire. Reservations recommended. Outdoor seating. **$$$**

★ ★ ★ CAPSOUTO FRERES. *451 Washington St, New York (10013). Phone 212/966-4900; fax 212/925-5296. www.capsoutofreres.com.* As its name suggests, Capsouto Freres is owned by the Capsouto brothers. What you may not get from its name is that this is a lovely choice for a special night on the town. Set in a restored 1891 factory in TriBeCa, it has an understated elegance, with original beam floors, exposed brick walls, magnificent open windows, and sunny floral arrangements. The restaurant is a neighborhood institution, having survived for years in this once deserted and now hip part of town. The eclectic menu features an impressive variety of choices, from calf's liver in sherry vinegar sauce to cassoulet, salmon with green herb sauce, and wild Scottish venison. If you are wandering around downtown on a Sunday, the brunch here is a great choice, with omelets and excellent French toast at reasonable prices. French menu. Lunch, dinner, brunch. Bar. Casual attire. Outdoor seating. **$$$**

★ ★ ★ **CARLYLE RESTAURANT.** *35 E 76th St, New York (10021). Phone 212/744-1600; fax 212/717-4682. www.rosewoodhotels.com.* Just one block from Fifth Avenue and Central Park, this lavishly decorated restaurant is housed in the elegant Carlyle Hotel (see). From the exquisite plush velvet wall coverings with rare 19-century prints to the crystal chandeliers and unique floral arrangements, guests will delight in this rich atmosphere. Meticulous attention is paid to the visual presentation of the gourmet dishes served by a wonderfully attentive staff. Entertainment includes a pianist and jazz trio. French menu. Breakfast, lunch, dinner, brunch. Bar. Children's menu. Business casual attire. Reservations recommended. Valet parking. Credit cards accepted. **$$$**

★ **CARMINE'S.** *2450 Broadway, New York (10024). Phone 212/362-2200; fax 212/362-0742. www.carminesnyc.com.* If you have an aversion to garlic, do yourself a favor and stay far away from Carmines, a frenetic, oversized Italian spot in the theater district. Garlic, a prominent ingredient here, reeks from the walls. But if you crave hearty portions of zesty, family-style, red-sauced Italian food at reasonable prices, this is your place. Conversation is difficult as the noise level is high. The dining room, originally a hotel ballroom, is a re-creation of a 1940s neighborhood Italian restaurant. Italian menu. Lunch, dinner. Bar. Casual attire. Reservations recommended. Outdoor seating. **$$$**

★ **CARNEGIE DELI.** *854 Seventh Ave, New York (10019). Phone 212/757-2245; toll-free 800/334-5606; fax 212/757-9889. www.carnegiedeli.com.* Sandwiches are the specialty of Carnegie Deli, and by sandwich we mean 6 inches tall with at least a pound of freshly sliced meat, cheese, cole slaw, and assorted condiments stuffed between two slices of rye bread. Take note: this is not a place for dainty eaters. The Carnegie Deli is the quintessential New York deli; a loud, hectic, and chaotic whirlwind of a place with a bustling lunch crowd that is equally crazy in the evenings, when the old-fashioned booths fill up with eager sandwich lovers. American menu. Breakfast, lunch, dinner, late-night. Casual attire. **$$**

★ **CARRY ON TEA & SYMPATHY.** *110 Greenwich Ave, New York (10011). Phone 212/807-8329; fax 212/352-0779. www.teaandsympathynewyork.com.* Anglophiles will love this small, cozy restaurant in the West Village, where everything from the décor to the food is British through and through. Walls are adorned with the Queen's portrait and royal proclamations, while the menu offers a charming assortment of English fare, such as tweed kettle pie, bangers and mash, and roast beef with Yorkshire pudding. English menu. Breakfast, lunch, dinner. Casual attire. Credit cards accepted. **$$**

★ ★ **CASA MONO.** *52 Irving Pl, New York (10003). Phone 212/253-2773; fax 212/253-5318.* With Casa Mono (which means monkey house), a snug little restaurant on the corner of 17th and Irving Place, Mario Batali has stepped off familiar Italian earth and onto the culinary and fashion hotbed known as Barcelona. Grab a seat in this cozy restaurant and watch as the chefs in the open kitchen deliver a menu that excites and invigorates in its simplicity. Popular picks include the sepia a la plancha (grilled squid), quail with quince, and oxtail-stuffed piquillo peppers. This is the sort of place that makes you smile until your face hurts. Claim your sliver of real estate and be patient. You'll soon be rewarded. Spanish menu. Lunch, dinner. Bar. Casual attire. Reservations recommended. **$$**

★ ★ **CENTOLIRE.** *1167 Madison Ave, New York (10028). Phone 212/734-7711; fax 212/794-5001. www.centolire.citysearch.com.* Fashionable Upper East Siders use Pino Luongos Centolire as their elegant dining room and watering hole. The space, soothing and all aglow in ultra-flattering light, has a serene vibe with an air of money and power subtly floating in the background. This is not to say that Centolire is pretentious, its not. The service is gracious and the Italian menu of simple, well articulated flavors is wonderful. However, if you are used to a downtown crowd, you may feel out of place among all the glitzy guests. Italian menu. Lunch, dinner, Sun brunch. Bar. Casual attire. **$$$**

★ ★ ★ **'CESCA.** *164 W 75th St, New York (10023). Phone 212/787-6300; fax 212/787-1081. www.cescanyc.com.* Chef Tom Valenti is like Santa Claus for the Upper West Sidebringing culinary treats for all the good neighbors strolling along Columbus Avenue. The follow-up to his slam hit Ouest, Cesca is an earthy and lively restaurant specializing in rustic, authentic, and often slow-cooked Italian fare like the oven-baked pasta with meat ragu and a Fred Flintstone-sized braised pork shank. If at all possible, go with an empty tummy so it can be filled all the way up. And while a reservation is nice, the warm, chocolate-toned bar, decked out in dark wood with amber lighting, is a perfect place to sit awhile, drink some wine, and nosh. Southern Italian menu. Lunch, dinner. Bar. Business casual attire. Reservations recommended. **$$$**

★ ★ ★ **CHANTERELLE.** *2 Harrison St, New York (10013). Phone 212/966-6960; fax 212/966-6143. www.chanterellenyc.com.* Long hailed as one of the most romantic restaurants in New York City, Chanterelle has been the scene of many bent-knee, velvet-box-in-hand proposals. Indeed, this restaurant is a New York dining icon. But Chanterelle, located on a sleepy corner in TriBeCa, offers much more than romance. Husband-and-wife owners David and Karen Waltuck (he is the chef, she works the room) have been serving brilliant, unfussy, modern French fare for more than 20 years. The menu, handwritten each week, reflects the best products available from local greenmarkets and regional farmers, and the award-winning wine list makes meals here even more memorable. French menu. Lunch, dinner. Closed Sun; holidays; also the first week of July. Business casual attire. Reservations recommended. **$$$$**

★ ★ **CHAT'N'CHEW.** *10 E 16th St, New York (10003). Phone 212/243-1616; fax 212/243-2895. www.chatnchewnyc.com.* Walk by Chat'n'Chew on a Saturday afternoon and you'll walk straight into a line of twentysomethings, married couples with strollers, and red-eyed partiers waiting to get inside to feast on one of the best and most reasonably priced brunch menus in the city. Filled with vintage décor and thrift store restaurant finds, this crowded Union Square diner is about quantity (portions are giant) and comfort food. There's roast turkey with gravy, mac 'n' cheese, and hearty breakfast fare like eggs, hash browns, French toast, and pancakes. Its not fancy, its inexpensive, and its all good. American menu. Lunch, dinner, brunch. Bar. Casual attire. Outdoor seating. **$**

★ ★ **CHELSEA BISTRO AND BAR.** *358 W 23rd St, New York (10011). Phone 212/727-2026; fax 212/727-2180.* Chelsea Bistro and Bar is a lovely neighborhood French bistro that goes beyond the call of the average local spot. Warm service, a charming atmosphere, wonderful food, and romantic lighting make this an ideal choice for almost any type of evening plans. A bite at the bar makes you feel like a regular even if you are from miles away. French menu. Dinner. Closed Memorial Day, July 4, Labor Day. Bar. Casual attire. Reservations recommended. **$$**

★ ★ **CHIKALICIOUS.** *203 E 10th St, New York (10003). Phone 212/995-9511. www.chikalicious.com.* Children are always fantasizing about skipping supper and just having dessert for dinner, and secretly, adults crave the same indulgence. With Chikalicious, the dream of an all-dessert-all-the-time meal has come true. At this quaint and sweetly decorated East Village cake, cupcake, cookie, brownie, and muffin depot, you can enjoy haute treats while watching the pastry chefs in action. Chikalicious opens at 3 pm, the perfect time for an afternoon snack, or for breaking the ultimate rulehaving dessert before dinner. American menu. Dinner, late-night. Closed Mon-Tues. Bar. Casual attire. **$$**

★ ★ **CHOW BAR.** *230 W 4th St, New York (10014). Phone 212/633-2212; fax 212/633-4328.* Asian fusion menu. Dinner, late-night, Sun brunch. Bar. Casual attire. Reservations recommended. **$$**

★ ★ **CHURRASCARIA PLATAFORMA.** *316 W 49th St, New York (10019). Phone 212/245-0505; fax 212/974-8250. www.churrascariaplataforma.com.* Succulent Brazilian barbecue is served in delicious abundance at Churrascaria Plataforma, a loud, high-energy eatery in the theater district. This authentic Riodizio offers grilled and skewered beef, pork, chicken, sausage, lamb, and fish in all-you-can-eat portions (you give your server the green light by flipping the small disc at your place setting, indicating "Go!"), accompanied by intoxicating caiparinastangy, lime-soaked cocktails made from cachaca, a potent alcohol similar to rum. Brazilian menu. Lunch, dinner. Closed Dec 25. Bar. Casual attire. Reservations recommended. **$$$**

★ ★ ★ **CITE.** *120 W 51st St, New York (10020). Phone 212/956-7100; fax 212/956-7157. www.citerestaurant.com.* Located in the heart of Midtown, Cit is an elegant, civilized spot for wining and dining. The restaurant is known for its wonderful prix fixe meals paired with four complimentary wines, making this power spot a meat and wine lovers paradise. The signature tender prime filet mignon (piled high with golden French fries) is a dish made for the restaurants bold reds from France, Spain, and around the world. Seafaring diners, fret not: you too can rejoice in lobster, salmon, and meaty crab cakes, with lots of crisp whites to complement them. American, French menu. Lunch, dinner. Closed holidays. Bar. Casual attire. **$$$**

★ CITY BAKERY. *3 W 18th St, New York (10003). Phone 212/366-1414; fax 212/645-0810. www.citybakerycatering.com.* Maury Rubin, the owner and creator of City Bakery, would probably have a warrant taken out on him if he ever closed City Bakery. Literally, New Yorkers would revolt and hunt him down. This hall of out-of-this-world baked goods is perpetually jammed with trendy locals craving his rich and creamy hot chocolate with house-made marshmallows, and his signature try-and-stop-at-one pretzel croissants. Aside from his selection of baked goods, he offers a dreamy buffet stocked with sandwiches, salads, antipasti, and soups made from the freshest seasonal ingredients. Just try and leave without loosening your belt buckle. American menu. Breakfast, lunch, brunch. Casual attire. **$**

★ ★ COCO PAZZO. *23 E 74th St, New York (10021). Phone 212/794-0205; fax 212/794-0208. www.cocopazzonewyork.citysearch.com.* For more than a decade, Pino Luongo has been serving the wonderful cuisine of his native Tuscany in this sunny, airy space on the Upper East Side. Your senses will be seduced upon entry by tables crowded with Italian cheeses and roasted vegetable displays. After you're seated, dense homemade breads arrive, along with vibrant green olive oil. Try to save some room for dinner, though. The kitchen masters classics like tomato bruschetta, spaghetti with meatballs, and osso bucco, and also excels in modern dishes like a seasonal salad made from goat cheese, brussels sprouts, pumpkin, and endive. Italian menu. Lunch, dinner. Closed Sun in summer; holidays. Bar. Jacket required. Reservations recommended. **$$$**

★ CORNER BISTRO. *331 W 4th St, New York (10014). Phone 212/242-9502.* Corner Bistro is known far and wide for one thing and one thing only: burgers. They are good, but the hype is a bit out of control these days. The place, a run-down little tavern with quite a bit of character, is located, as its name suggests, on a nice little corner of the West Village, and the space is far from glamorous. In a word, its a dive, but a friendly one, that serves tasty burgers on cardboard plates topped with cheese, bacon, or, if you're splurging on the Bistro Burger, bacon, raw onions, lettuce, tomato, and cheese. The Corner Bistro formula is simple: its beer, burgers, and if you're lucky, some napkins. If you want anything more, you'd better go elsewhere. American menu. Lunch, dinner, late-night. Bar. Casual attire. No credit cards accepted. **$**

★ ★ ★ CRAFT. *43 E 19th St, New York (10003). Phone 212/780-0880; fax 212/780-0666. www.craftrestaurant.com.* Craft is a restaurant for two types of people: inventive, adventurous sorts who like to build things and gourmets who appreciate perfectly executed portions of meat, fish, fowl, and vegetables. Why these two sorts of folks? Because at Craft, lovers of Legos delight in creating dinner from the listlike menu of meat, fish, vegetables, mushrooms, and condiments. You choose what two delicious morsels should come together on your plate. (Those who prefer to defer to the chef may opt for a preplanned menu.) Dinner at Craft is a unique, interactive, exciting, and delicious adventure that should be experienced at least once, with like-minded builders. American menu. Dinner. Bar. Business casual attire. Reservations recommended. **$$$**

★ ★ CRAFTBAR. *900 Broadway, New York (10003). Phone 212/780-0880; fax 212/598-1859. www.craftrestaurant.com.* After the runaway success of Craft (see), it was only a matter of time before they opened a smaller, more intimate and casual offshoot. Located right next door to its fancier sibling, craftbar is part wine bar, part Italian trattoria, and part American eatery, serving small plates like the signature fried, stuffed sage leaves and crisp fried oysters with preserved lemon, alongside beautiful salads, soups, crusty panini, game, fish, and the most extraordinary veal ricotta meatballs in the country, if not the world. The wine list is extensive, and a meal at the bar is a great way to go if you can't score a table. American, Mediterranean menu. Lunch, dinner. Bar. Casual attire. **$$$**

★ ★ CRISPO. *240 W 14th St, New York (10011). Phone 212/229-1818; fax 212/229-2918. www.crisporestaurant.com.* Named after its chef/owner Frank Crispo, this West 14th Street eatery is a staple for fans of rustic, Italian-accented cuisine, like plates of delicious hand-sliced prosciutto di Parma, simple yet stellar pastas, grilled chops, and seasonal salads. The warm, exposed-brick room gets crowded early on, so plan to reserve a table ahead of time or wait at the bar (not a bad option at all, although the bar area is small) for one of the coveted tables to open up. Italian menu. Dinner. Bar. Casual attire. Reservations recommended. Outdoor seating. **$$$**

★ ★ **CUB ROOM CAFE.** *131 Sullivan St, New York (10012). Phone 212/677-4100; fax 212/228-3425. www.cubroom.com.* The Cub Room was one of the first hotspots to open in SoHo, and it has stood the test of time thanks to chef-owner Henry Meer, who keeps the seasonal Mediterranean-accented menu fresh and fun, offering the perfect brand of upscale fare for the lively bunch that frequents this popular destination. In the chic, living room-style lounge with vintage fabric-covered sofas and a long, serpentine bar, a gregarious and gorgeous crowd sips chilly cocktails, while inside the rustic, country-style dining room, big groups and whispering couples feast on Meers solid cooking. American menu. Lunch, dinner, brunch. Closed Dec 25. Bar. Casual attire. **$$**

★ ★ ★ **DA SILVANO.** *260 Sixth Ave, New York (10014). Phone 212/982-2343; fax 212/982-2254. www.dasilvano.com.* If one thing is certain about a meal at Da Silvano, it is that before you finish your Tuscan dinner, you will have spotted at least one actor, model, musician, or other such celebrity. Da Silvano is a scene, and a great one at that. With such a loyal and fabulous following, the food could be mediocre, but the kitchen does not rest on its star-infested laurels. This kitchen offers wonderful, robust, regional Italian fare, like homemade pasta, meat, fish, and salad. The sliver of a wine bar next door, Da Silvano Cantinetta, offers Italian-style tapas paired with a wide selection of wines by the glass. But perhaps the best way to experience Da Silvano is on a warm day, where a seat at the wide, European-style sidewalk café offers prime people-watching. Italian menu. Lunch, dinner. Bar. Casual attire. Reservations recommended. Outdoor seating. **$$$**

★ ★ **DA UMBERTO.** *107 W 17th St, New York (10011). Phone 212/989-0303.* Italian menu. Lunch, dinner. Closed Sun. Bar. Business casual attire. Reservations recommended. **$$$**

★ ★ ★ ★ **DANIEL.** *60 E 65th St, New York (10021). Phone 212/288-0033; fax 212/396-9014. www.danielnyc.com.* Daniel Boulud is one of those chefs who could make scrambled eggs taste like manna from heaven. He has a magic touch that warms you from the inside out. For this reason, Daniel is a dining experience. It is not dinner. The experience starts when you enter the palatial front room, continues as you sip an old-fashioned cocktail in the romantic, low-lit lounge, and is taken to new heights when you take a seat at your table, your home for the hours you will spend as the fortunate culinary guest of Boulud. French food at other restaurants is good. With Boulud facing the stove, it is sublime. Potato-crusted sea bass is a signature. The crisp, golden coat, fashioned from whisper-thin slices of potatoes, protects the fish while it cooks and seals in its juices so that it melts on the tongue. It is wonderful. Wine service is another perk. Friendly and helpful, the staff wants you to learn and wants to help you choose the right wine for your meal and your wallet. You will have a new favorite wine before leaving. After dessert, you will think that you're free to go, but not so fast. There are petit fours, of course, and then the pice de resistance: madeleines. Daniel is famous for these delicate, fluffy, lemony little cakes served warm, just seconds out of the oven. When you are finally free to go, you may not want to. French menu. Dinner. Closed Sun. Bar. Children's menu. Jacket required. Reservations recommended. **$$$$**

★ ★ ★ ★ **DANUBE.** *30 Hudson St, New York (10013). Phone 212/791-3771; fax 212/219-3443. www.davidbouley.com.* Danube is the creation of David Bouley, the inspired and famed chef who has created many notable New York establishments. It is a stunning place to spend an evening. It has the feel of an old Austrian castle, with dark wood; deep, plush banquettes; and soft, warm lighting. It repeatedly draws a glamorous crowd that craves Bouleys masterful technique and creativity. Bouleys regal, majestic restaurant celebrates the cuisine of Austria within the framework of a New York restaurant. On the menu, you'll find a couple of Austrian-inspired dishes interspersed with lighter, modern, and truly exciting seasonal New American dishes. Bouley has a rare talent, and his food is spectacular, though not for those who are fearful of taking some risks at dinner. This is not a creamed-corn-and-roast-chicken place. The staff offers refined service, and the wine list is eclectic and extensive. As you would expect, it includes some gems from Austria. The cocktail lounge at Danube is a perfect spot to relax and get cozy before or after dinner. It is low-lit and romantic, and the bartenders serve delicious, perfectly balanced cocktails. Continental menu. Dinner. Closed Sun. Bar. Business casual attire. Reservations recommended. **$$$$**

★ ★ ★ **DAWAT.** *210 E 58th St, New York (10022). Phone 212/355-7555; fax 212/355-1735. www.restaurant.com/dawat.* Located on the eastern edge of Midtown, just a stones throw from Bloomingdales, Dawat is one of the citys first (and best) high-end Indian restaurants. Serving elegant haute cuisine in a posh, hushed townhouse setting, Dawat is one of the most popular destinations for seekers of upscale, authentic Indian cuisine, including curries, rice dishes, poori, naan, and chutneys. Indian menu. Lunch, dinner. Bar. Business casual attire. Reservations recommended. **$$$**

★ ★ ★ **DB BISTRO MODERNE.** *55 W 44th St, New York (10036). Phone 212/391-2400; fax 212/391-1188. www.danielnyc.com.* This cool, colorful, ultra-stylish bistro in Midtown is Daniel Bouluds most casual restaurant. But he succeeds in making it a hotspot for foodies and moguls of all sorts without making it ordinary. For Boulud, making a regular restaurant is simply not possible. In many dishes, Boulud has a magic touch, transforming simple into spectacular with ease. His signature DB Burger is an excellent example of his creative interpretations. He builds the fattest, juiciest round of beef and stuffs it with short ribs and sinful amounts of foie gras and truffles. He serves it on a homemade Parmesan brioche bun, with house-stewed tomato confit (instead of ketchup) and a great big vat of fries. Don't think that this will be too much food for you to eat aloneyou'll regret offering to share after the first bite. French bistro menu. Lunch, dinner. Business casual attire. Reservations recommended. **$$$**

★ **DIM SUM GO GO.** *5 E Broadway, New York (10038). Phone 212/732-0797; fax 212/964-3149.* Looking for a chic little spot to have a quick bite of inventive Chinese fare? Dim Sum Go Go is your place. This super-mod, super-hip, minimalist spot sports a terrific menu of Chinese snacks like fresh soybeans with pickled vegetables, as well as homemade noodles and bigger dishes like the Garlicky Go Go roast chicken, with a taut golden skin. On weekends, you can sample fresh steamed dumplings with fillings like shark fin and crunchy white sea fungus. Come on, live a little. Chinese menu. Lunch, dinner. Bar. Casual attire. **$$**

★ ★ **DIWAN.** *148 E 48th St, New York (10017). Phone 212/593-5425; fax 212/593-5732. www.diwanrestaurant.com.* Indian cuisine may not seem glamorous, but it is at Diwan—one of the citys most acclaimed Indian restaurants, serving amazing, upscale dishes in a swanky, newly remodeled setting smack dab in the center of Midtown. The lunchtime hour finds Diwan packed with businesspeople leaning in over tables to seal deals, while dinner is more relaxed and intimate, with an extensive menu of Bombay-inspired dishes that will satisfy your strongest craving for great Indian cuisine. Indian menu. Lunch, dinner. Casual attire. **$$**

★ ★ **DO HWA.** *55 Carmine St, New York (10014). Phone 212/414-1224; fax 212/741-1387. www.dohwanyc.com.* Do Hwa is always crowded with Village trendsetters. Its one of those perpetually hot restaurants, mostly due to the menu, which features spicy, authentic Korean food at reasonable prices. Sure, there are more elegant, refined places to dine in the city, but Do Hwa is not trying to be anything other than what it isa warm and lively restaurant that focuses on food and does it very well. Korean menu. Lunch, dinner, late-night. Bar. Casual attire. Reservations recommended. **$$**

★ ★ **DOS CAMINOS.** *373 Park Ave S, New York (10016). Phone 212/294-1000; fax 212/294-1090. www.brguestrestaurants.com.* Steve Hanson has built a New York City restaurant empire with Blue Water Grill (see), Ruby Foo's (see), and Fiamma. With Dos Caminos, he has introduced the regional cuisines of Mexico to his winning formula of hip scene, cool bar, and crowd-pleasing eats. Dos Caminos is loud and always crowded, so don't plan on intimate dining, but certainly plan on tasty food. The menu reflects the diverse regions of Mexico, including guacamole made tableside to your desired level of spiciness; warm homemade tacos filled with chile-rubbed shrimp, steak, or pulled pork; and snapper steamed in banana leaves. To wash it all down, margaritas are potent and tasty. Mexican menu. Lunch, dinner, brunch. Bar. Casual attire. Reservations recommended. **$$$**

★ **EL GAUCHITO.** *94-60 Corona Ave, New York (10306). Phone 718/271-8198.* Argentinean menu. Lunch, dinner. Closed Wed. Casual attire. **$$**

★ **THE ELEPHANT.** *58 E 1st St, New York (10003). Phone 212/505-7739; fax 212/979-7573. www.elephantrestaurant.com.* Located on the burgeoning restaurant row known as 1st Street in the East Village, The Elephant is a local hipsters hangout, perpetually crowded with trendy twenty and thirtysomethings who pile in to fill this sexy bistros cramped tables and experience the cool, dressed-down vibe as well as the Thai-French bistro fare. The Elephant is loud, it has a great buzz, and everyone is fashionably underweight. You get the picture. Thai menu. Lunch, dinner. Bar. Casual attire. Reservations recommended. Outdoor seating. No credit cards accepted. **$$**

★ **ELEPHANT AND CASTLE.** *68 Greenwich Ave, New York (10011). Phone 212/243-1400; fax 212/989-9294. www.elephantandcastle.com.* Elephant and Castle feels like a bit of London here in the Big Apple. This pub, styled like those found in rainy England, is low-lit and narrow, with dark wood paneling that gives the place a warm vibe that feels welcoming and cozy. The menu is straightforward and includes easy-to-love New York-style fare like Caesar salads, omelets, burgers, and top-notch sandwiches. The beer list is impressive as well. Continental menu. Breakfast, lunch, dinner, brunch. Casual attire. **$$**

★ ★ ★ ELEVEN MADISON PARK. *11 Madison Ave, New York (10010). Phone 212/889-0905; fax 212/889-0918. www.elevenmadisonpark.com.* Located across from the leafy, historic Madison Square Park, Danny Meyers grand New American restaurant is a wonderful, soothing spot to take respite from the frenetic pace of a day in New York City. The magnificent dining room boasts old-world charm with vaulted ceilings, clubby banquettes, giant floor-to-ceiling windows, and warm, golden lighting. The crowd is equally stunning: a savvy blend of sexy, suited Wall Street types and chic, fashion-forward New Yorkers. The contemporary seasonal menu features updated American classics as well as a smart selection of dishes that borrow accents from Spain, France, and Asia. Meyer, who also owns Gramercy Tavern and Union Square Café (see both), continues to offer his gracious brand of warmth and hospitality at Eleven Madison Park. You will feel at home in an instant. American menu. Lunch, dinner, brunch. Closed Jan 1, Labor Day, Dec 24-25. Bar. Business casual attire. Reservations recommended. **$$$**

★ ★ ELMO. *156 Seventh Ave, New York (10011). Phone 212/242-0612. www.elmorestaurant.com.* Located in the heart of Chelsea, Elmo is a convivial American eatery with a bustling bar serving comfort food that has been tweaked a bit for a fashionable New York City crowd. There are dishes as retro as Alphabet Soup with fluffy, dill-accented chicken dumplings; a hearty mac and cheese; and easy-to-love Hungry Man-type meals featuring meat and potatoes. There's even a Duncan Hines devil's food cake for dessert. Mom would be proud. American menu. Lunch, dinner, brunch. Bar. Casual attire. Outdoor seating. **$$**

★ ★ ESSEX RESTAURANT. *120 Essex St, New York (10002). Phone 212/533-9616; fax 212/533-7413. www.essexnyc.com.* Located on the Lower East Side, one of Manhattans hippest 'hoods, Essex is a warm, inviting, minimalist space marked by skylights, whitewashed brick, and sleek black tables. This is a perfect place for cocktails or a dinner date. The menu is as eclectic as the neighborhood, with dishes that pay tribute to the diverse local populationlike a potato cake napoleon (a haute version of the knish), the Essex cubano sandwich, a scallop and mango ceviche, and kasha varnishkes. Late-night, the place turns into a loud and lively DJ party, the perfect prelude to the brunch with all-you-can-drink Bloody Marys, mimosas, or screwdrivers. International menu. Dinner, late-night, brunch. Closed Mon. Bar. Casual attire. Reservations recommended. **$$**

★ ★ ★ ESTIATORIO MILOS. *125 W 55th St, New York (10019). Phone 212/245-7400; fax 212/245-4828. www.milos.ca.* Milos, as its called for short (try saying Estiatorio over and over again and you'll understand why), is a luxurious, cavernous, whitewashed eatery decorated with umbrella-topped tables and seafood market-style fish displays. Showcasing simple, rustic Greek cooking, this elegant, airy restaurant takes you from the hustle of Midtown to the shores of the Mediterranean in the whirl of a revolving door. Seafood is priced by the pound and is prepared either perfectly grilled over charcoal or in the Greek style called *spetsiota* filleted and baked with tomatoes, onions, herbs, and olive oil. Greek, Mediterranean, seafood menu. Lunch, dinner. Bar. Business casual attire. Reservations recommended. Outdoor seating. **$$$**

★ FANELLI'S CAFE. *94 Prince St, New York (10012). Phone 212/226-9412; fax 212/475-6951.* This classic SoHo eatery dressed in dark wood, with a long, tavern-style bar up front, has been around for a dogs age (since 1872). It remains one of the neighborhoods best hideaways for honest and hearty American meals like mac and cheese, big bowls of hot chili, juicy burgers, and thick steaks. Some things are better for not changing with the times; Fanellis is one of them. American menu. Lunch, dinner, late-night. Bar. Casual attire. **$$**

★ ★ ★ FELIDIA. *243 E 58th St, New York (10022). Phone 212/758-1479; fax 212/935-7687. www.lidiasitaly.com.* Celebrated chef and TV personality Lidia Bastianich is the unofficial matriarch of Italian-American cuisine. Her restaurant, Felidia (she and son Joe are partners in Becco (see), Babbo (see), and Esca as well), is warm and elegant and draws an elite New York crowd, although it remains free of pretense. The lovely dining room is bathed in golden, amber light and decorated with rich wood-paneled walls, hardwood floors, magnificent flowers, and seasonal vegetable and fruit displays. The menu focuses on a wide array of Italian dishes that you would discover if you journeyed throughout the countrys varied culinary regions. Diners are expected to eat as they do in Italy, so you'll start with a plate of antipasti or a bowl of *zuppe* (soup), move on to a fragrant bowl of fresh pasta and then to a grilled whole fish, and finally have a bit of dolci for dessert. The Italian wine list is extra-special, so be sure to pair your meal with a few glasses. Italian menu. Lunch, dinner. Bar. Business casual attire. Reservations recommended. **$$$**

★ ★ FELIX. *340 W Broadway, New York (10013). Phone 212/431-0021; fax 212/343-0278. www.felixnyc.com.* Located on a busy stretch of West Broadway in SoHo (more of a mall these days than its former renegade artsy self), Felix is one of those perfect French bistros for moules frites, steak frites, or just about anything with frites. At this beautiful people scene, you'll find statuesque lovelies sipping cocktails and nibbling on salad greens while chiseled men recline and admire them. Felix is really more about the scene than the food, but if you need a place to rest after shopping, you'll do just fine with this menu of decent bistro standards. French bistro menu. Lunch, dinner, brunch. Bar. Casual attire. Outdoor seating. **$$**

★ ★ ★ FIAMMA OSTERIA. *206 Spring St, New York (10012). Phone 212/653-0100; fax 212/653-0101. www.brguestrestaurants.com.* This upscale and stylish spot for refined Italian fare in SoHo is the first chef-driven restaurant from Stephen Hanson, the owner of hip, casual eateries like Blue Water Grill and Dos Caminos (see both). For this project, Hanson pulled out all the stops, creating one of the best Italian dining experiences in New York City. From homemade pastas to silky fish and tender grilled meats to the all-Italian cheese course to the massive wine list, this is a place to mark for impressing business associates and loved ones alike. Italian menu. Lunch, dinner. Bar. Business casual attire. Reservations recommended. **$$$**

★ ★ ★ FIREBIRD. *365 W 46th St, New York (10036). Phone 212/586-0244; fax 212/957-2983. www.firebirdrestaurant.com.* Firebird is an ode to the glamour and gluttony of St. Petersburg, sometime around its heyday in 1912. Set in a lavish, double townhouse, this restaurant and cabaret is furnished like a majestic Russian palace, with ornate antique furniture, intricate china and etched glass, old-world oil paintings, and 19th-century photographs. The extravagance extends to the food, with Russian classics like blinis with sour cream and caviar, *zakuska* (the Russian equivalent of tapas), borscht made with pork and dill, and sturgeon baked in puff pastry. Vodka flows like water in a fast-running stream, and the wine list is deep as well. Eastern European menu. Lunch, dinner. Closed Mon; holidays. Bar. Business casual attire. Reservations recommended. Outdoor seating. **$$$**

★ ★ ★ FLEUR DE SEL. *5 E 20th St, New York (10003). Phone 212/460-9100; fax 212/460-8319. www.fleurdeselnyc.com.* Located on a sleepy block of East 20th Street, Fleur de Sel sneaks up on you like a ray of sunshine through the clouds. This lovely buttercup-colored cottagelike restaurant is one of the most enchanted hideaways in the city, serving sophisticated French-American fare in a serene dining room decorated with sheer curtains, soothing creamy walls, and precious bouquets of fresh flowers. It is, quite simply, a lovely setting to enjoy a dinner of stunningly presented, delicate, and deliciously prepared food. French menu. Lunch, dinner. Closed Sun in Aug. Business casual attire. Reservations recommended. **$$$$**

★ FLORENT. *69 Gansevoort St, New York (10014). Phone 212/989-5779; fax 212/645-2498. restaurantflorent.com.* Florent is a late-night revelers institution. Located in the now-hip Meatpacking District, Florent has been there for decades. It opened way back in the day when the neighborhood was filled with seedy, unsavory characters, not haute, savory meals. It is still a hotspot, serving its menu of simple, brasserie-style French fare 24-7. You can feast on boudin with caramelized onions, steak frites, eggs, and fat, juicy burgers. The best part of Florent is strolling in after a long night of partying and sitting down to a cup of coffee, a good hot meal, and a whole lot of people-watching. You'll see drag queens, truckers, supermodels, Chelsea boys, and just about every other walk of life sitting side by side, smiling, and enjoying the wonderful world that is New York. French, American menu. Breakfast, lunch, dinner, late-night, brunch. Closed Dec 25. Bar. Children's menu. Casual attire. **$$**

★ ★ ★ ★ FOUR SEASONS RESTAURANT. *99 E 52nd St, New York (10022). Phone 212/754-9494; fax 212/754-1077. www.fourseasonsrestaurant.com.* The Four Seasons is truly a New York classic. Since 1959, it has been the de facto dining room of media powerhouses, financial movers and shakers, publishing hotshots, legal dealmakers, and the generally fabulous crowd that follows them. Lunch can be an exercise in connect-the-famous-faces, as is the bar, a must for a pre-dinner cocktail or a quick bite. As for what you'll eat when you take a break from gawking at the stars, the food at The Four Seasons is simple but well prepared and takes its cues from around the world. You'll find classic French entrées as well as more contemporary American fare accented with flavors borrowed from Asia, Morocco, and Latin America. Guests at The Four Seasons are often some of the highest rollers, and the room has an energetic buzz that epitomizes the life and breath of the city that never sleeps. It is a scene. Dining here is fun, especially at lunch, if only to be a fly on the wall as deals are made and fortunes are won and lost. American menu. Lunch, dinner. Closed Sun; holidays. Bar. Jacket required. Reservations recommended. **$$$$**

★ **FRANK.** *88 Second Ave, New York (10003). Phone 212/420-0202; fax 212/420-0699. www.frankrestaurant.com.* Do you love simple, rustic Italian food? Do you love reasonable prices and a cool downtown vibe? If you answered yes to these questions, you will fall in love with Frank in an instant, for the same reason that throngs of East Villagers are already swooning over this cramped, thrift-store-furnished spot for southern Italian cuisine. You'll find great food, cheap prices, and a happening crowd that doesn't mind waiting over an hour to get inside and sit elbow to elbow. Italian menu. Breakfast, lunch, dinner. Bar. Casual attire. Reservations recommended. Outdoor seating. No credit cards accepted. **$$**

★ ★ ★ **GABRIEL'S.** *11 W 60th St, New York (10023). Phone 212/956-4600; fax 212/956-2309. www.gabrielsbarandrest.com.* Gabriels is the creation of owner Gabriel Aiello, a charming host who knows how to make guests feel at home in this elegant Lincoln Center area spot for sumptuous Tuscan fare like gorgonzola tortelloni with a shiitake mushroom tomato sauce, lasagna Bolognese, and a daily house-made risotto. The restaurant is elegantly dressed with contemporary art cloaking the warm saffron-toned walls; wide, sleep-worthy green felt banquettes; well-spaced tables; soothing indirect lighting; and a 35-foot-long mahogany bar. While Gabriels may look like a see-and-be-seen hotspot, the restaurant is warm and welcoming, without pretension, making an evening here a delight from start to finish. Northern Italian menu. Lunch, dinner. Closed Sun; holidays. Bar. Business casual attire. Reservations recommended. **$$$**

★ ★ ★ **GALLAGHER'S.** *228 W 52nd St, New York (10019). Phone 212/245-5336; fax 212/245-5426. www.gallaghersnysteakhouse.com.* The theater district has some great longtime restaurant hotspots to choose from, and Gallaghers is one of its brightest stars. This steakhouse is a New York City landmark and former speakeasy, and remains decorated as it was the day it opened in November 1927, with plain-planked floors, red-checked tablecloths, and dark wood-paneled walls covered in old photos. Specializing in dry-aged beef, the kitchen stays true to simple American fare rather than straying off course for global flourishes that have no place in such a comfortable, back-to-basics establishment. The tried-and-true formula is winning; after all these years, Gallaghers is a perennial favorite on Theater Row. American, steak menu. Lunch, dinner. Bar. Casual attire. Reservations recommended. **$$$**

★ ★ **GASCOGNE.** *158 Eighth Ave, New York (10011). Phone 212/675-6564; fax 212/627-3018. www.gascognenyc.com.* At this charming neighborhood restaurant, the robust regional cuisine of Gascogne fills the air. Paying tribute to the southwest of France, the kitchen offers heavenly plates of fill-in-the-blank confit, Armagnac-soaked prunes and foie gras terrine, cassoulet, and monkfish casserole, and a lovely list of wines to match. This is a spot for romance, as the dining room is intimate and candlelit, and the garden out back makes you feel like you are miles from the city. French menu. Lunch, dinner. Closed holidays. Bar. Casual attire. Reservations recommended. Outdoor seating. **$$$**

★ ★ ★ **GEISHA.** *33 E 61st St, New York (10021). Phone 212/813-1112; fax 212/813-1150. www.geisharestaurant.com.* Set in a modern, posh townhouse in the east 60s, Geisha is seafood whiz kid Eric Riperts inspired translation of Japanese cuisine. While he is still manning the stoves at Le Bernardin (see), here at Geisha, his love affair with Asian-tinged seafood is in full bloom. The food at Geisha delivers Zen enlightenment in plates of coconut-marinated fluke with coconut ponzu, lime vinaigrette, and orange essence; bowls of tiger shrimp dumplings with toasted pumpkin in a green curry broth; and dishes of dayboat cod with warm pepper and snow pea salad in soy ginger butter, not to mention gorgeous platters of sushi, sashimi and signature rolls prepared by a pair of seriously skilled sushi chefs. Japanese tea and an extensive sake list will keep you well hydrated and spiritually centered. French, Japanese, sushi menu. Lunch, dinner. Closed Sun. Bar. Casual attire. Reservations recommended. Outdoor seating. **$$$**

★ ★ **GHENET RESTAURANT.** *284 Mulberry St, New York (10012). Phone 212/343-1888. www.ghenet.com.* Featuring the fragrant dishes of Ethiopia, Ghenet is a charming spot to explore a new and delicious cuisine. The menu reads like a wonderful textbook, with great explanations of all the menu items, many of which are savory rice dishes and lamb or beef stews to be mopped up with Frisbee-size rounds of homemade flatbread. Owned by a husband-and-wife team, this family-run establishment is all about hospitality, and you will feel like family when you leave. Middle Eastern menu. Lunch Tues-Sun, dinner. Bar. Casual attire. **$$**

★ ★ **GIGINO TRATTORIA.** *323 Greenwich St, New York (10013). Phone 212/431-1112; fax 212/431-1294. www.gigino-trattoria.com.* Gigino Trattoria has been a local favorite for Italian fare since 1983. Owned by Phil Suarez and Bob Giraldi (partners in Patria and Jean-Georges), this TriBeCa gem offers casual, comfortable dining and the tasty, home-style cooking of an authentic Italian trattoria. Generous bowls of pasta, brick-oven pizzas, seasonal produce, game, fish, and meats round out the appealing menu. Italian menu. Lunch, dinner. Closed Jan 1, Memorial Day, Dec 25. Bar. Casual attire. Outdoor seating. **$$$**

★ ★ ★ ★ **GILT.** *955 Madison Ave, New York (10022). Phone 212/891-8100. www.giltnewyork.com.* When the staff at New York's celebrated Le Cirque 2000 packed up their knives and left town at the tail end of 2004, foodies everywhere wondered what would take the famed restaurant's place in the New York Palace Hotel's historic Villard Mansion. Nearly a year later, they had the answer: the opulent Gilt, whose name pays homage to the late 19th-century's Gilded Age, when the mansion was created. As the opening chef, the young British culinary genius Paul Liebrandt created an ultra-formal, avant-garde dining experience that became a hit on the New York dining scene. But wanting to focus on his own venture, Liebrandt surrendered his title as top toque nine months later to Christopher Lee, formerly of Philadelphia's acclaimed Striped Bass. With Lee at the helm, the restaurant discarded its requirement for male patrons to wear jackets and created a less-formal version of his Modern American menu for bar and lounge dining. But all of this doesn't mean that Gilt is any less spectacular. The 55-seat space, with carved-wood and gilded walls, cathedral ceilings, and marble fireplaces, features contemporary elements like an illuminated purple honeycomb screen behind the fiberglass bar and leather banquettes that give the dining room a modern twist while retaining its historic beauty. Such a setting would make most any meal here memorable, but it's Chef Lee's skills behind the stove that makes Gilt stand out. Each plate that emerges from the kitchen is like a work of art, from formal dining menu options like the signature Tuna Wellington—yellowfin tuna baked in puff pastry with porcini mushrooms and flat leaf spinach and served with a red wine reduction and foie gras sauce—to bar and lounge menu choices like truffle potato fries, lobster sliders, and caviar service. Diners can dig into Chef Lee's creations via a prix fixe pre-theater menu, a three-course prix fixe dinner menu, and a five-course tasting menu. Wine is a large part of the experience, and Gilt offers an expansive—and expensive—selection to complement each dish on the Modern American menu. Continental menu. Dinner. Closed Sun, Mon. Bar. Jacket required. Reservations recommended. **$$$$**

★ ★ ★ ★ **GOTHAM BAR & GRILL.** *12 E 12th St, New York (10003). Phone 212/620-4020; fax 212/627-7810. www.gothambarandgrill.com.* Alfred Portale, the chef and owner of Gotham Bar and Grill, is an icon in New Yorks hallowed culinary circles. The leader of the tall-food movement and a passionate advocate of seasonal Greenmarket ingredients, he has been a gastronomic force from behind the stoves at his swanky, vaulted-ceilinged Gotham Bar and Grill for more than a decade. The room is loud, energetic, and packed with a very stylish crowd at both lunch and dinner. The lively bar also draws a regular crowd of black-clad after-work revelers. You'll have no problem finding a dish with your name on it at Gotham. The menu offers something for everyonesalad, fish, pasta, poultry, beef, and gameand each dish is prepared with a bold dose of sophistication. Portale is an icon for a reason. Under his care, simple dishes are taken to new heights. And while the food isn't as tall as it used to be, size really doesn't matter. His food is just terrific. American menu. Lunch, dinner. Bar. Casual attire. Reservations recommended. **$$$**

★ ★ ★ ★ **GRAMERCY TAVERN.** *42 E 20th St, New York (10003). Phone 212/477-0777; fax 212/477-1160. www.gramercytavern.com.* Dining at Gramercy Tavern is for people who don't have trouble being very well taken care of. Owner Danny Meyers perpetually bustling New York eatery oozes warmth and charm without a smidgen of pretension. Pristine, seasonal, locally sourced ingredients shine, and every bite allows the flavors to converse quietly yet speak individually as well. Though formal and elegant in tone, Gramercy Tavern is a fun place to dine. The food is so good that you can't help but have a great time, and the waitstaffs enthusiasm for the chef's talent shows, adding to the appeal. In the glorious main room, you can choose from a pair of seasonal tasting menus or a wide array of equally tempting la carte selections. And if you don't have a reservation, don't fret. Meyer is a fan of democracy and accepts walk-ins in the front Tavern Room. Stroll in, put your name on the list, and you'll have the chance to sample the spectacular food (the menu is different than in the main dining room but just as wonderful) and rub elbows with the citys sexy locals. There's a terrific house cocktail list as well, so make a nice toast while you're there. American menu. Lunch, dinner. Bar. Business casual attire. Reservations recommended. **$$$**

★ GREAT NY NOODLETOWN. *28 Bowery, New York (10013). Phone 212/349-0923.* It would be impossible to pass NY Noodletown off as your own private discovery. Anointed years ago by rave reviews, this bright corner spot continues to draw crowds all day and late into the night. Press in and enjoy the bustle. This is not the place for complicated dishes. Treat NY Noodletown like a Chinese version of your local coffee shop: avoid preparations that have more than two ingredients and you'll do well. The roast meats are top-notch, particularly the crisp-skinned baby pig. Greens are basic and fresh, and perfectly cooked noodles, naturally, are a strong point. When summer comes, the salt-baked soft-shell crab is a must, juicy and tasting of the sea, as much of a New York ritual as a trip to Coney Island. Chinese menu. Breakfast, lunch, dinner, late-night. Bar. Casual attire. No credit cards accepted. **$**

★ ★ GUASTAVINO'S. *409 E 59th St, New York (10022). Phone 212/980-2455; fax 212/980-2904. www.guastavinos.com.* Located under the Queensborough Bridge, a marvelous structure built by Guastavino, this cavernous and awesome restaurant is home to chef/owner Daniel Orrs stunning New American brasserie. The downstairs bar and lounge serves as watering hole to hundreds of sexy singles, all well dressed in swanky business attire and ready for after-work reveling. Beyond the bar, in the gorgeous, marble-arched dining room, you'll discover terrific seasonal American fare in a magnificent and alluring setting. For drinks or dinner, Guastavinos is visually mesmerizing and gastronomically pleasing. American menu. Lunch, dinner, brunch. Bar. Children's menu. Casual attire. Outdoor seating. **$$$**

★ ★ ★ HAKUBAI. *66 Park Ave, New York (10016). Phone 212/885-7111; fax 212/885-7095. www.kitano.com.* Located in the posh Kitano hotel (see), Hakubai offers authentic Japanese fare in a tranquil, Zen-like space. The menu features a myriad of traditionally prepared seafood dishes like *ika shiokara* (chopped salted squid), *karuge-su* (vinegar-marinated jellyfish), and *karei* (fried, grilled, or simmered flounder). For a special treat, call ahead and reserve a private room for the multicourse chefs choice menu ($120 to $150), or, to savor a simpler meal, choose from the restaurants swimming selection of sushi, sashimi, and maki rolls, as well as udon and soba noodle dishes. Japanese menu. Lunch, dinner. Bar. Business casual attire. Valet parking. **$$$$**

★ ★ ★ HARRISON. *355 Greenwich St, New York (10013). Phone 212/274-9310; fax 212/274-9376. www.theharrison.com.* With its amber lighting, hardwood floors, wainscoting, and inviting bar, The Harrison is one of those restaurants that makes you feel like never leaving. Owned by Jimmy Bradley and Danny Abrams, the savvy team behind The Red Cat and the Mermaid Inn (see both), this Mediterranean-accented restaurant is a charming neighborhood hotspot with a chic clientele. The signature fried clams with fried slivered rounds of lemon are a must have, whether seated at the happening bar or at one of the well-spaced, linen-topped tables. American menu. Dinner. Bar. Casual attire. Outdoor seating. **$$$**

★ ★ ★ HARRY CIPRIANI. *781 Fifth Ave, New York (10022). Phone 212/753-5566; fax 212/308-5653. www.cipriani.com.* If you are searching for a place to see and be seen by some of New Yorks most moneyed crowds, Harrys is your spot. Located across the street from Central Park, this posh restaurant features Italian cuisine and gracious service. The entire experience here is very old-world charming. Be prepared to hear the word daaahhling with alarming regularity. American, Italian menu. Lunch, dinner. Bar. Business casual attire. Reservations recommended. **$$$**

★ ★ ★ HEARTH. *403 E 12th St, New York (10009). Phone 646/602-0531; fax 646/602-0552. www.restauranthearth.com.* American menu. Dinner. Bar. Casual attire. Reservations recommended. **$$$**

★ HEARTLAND BREWERY. *35 Union Square W, New York (10003). Phone 212/645-3400; fax 212/645-8306. www.heartlandbrewery.com.* American menu. Lunch, dinner, late-night. Bar. Casual attire. Outdoor seating. **$$**

★ HOG PIT. *22 Ninth Ave, New York (10014). Phone 212/604-0092. www.hogpit.com.* Located in the Meatpacking District, the Hog Pit is a down-home barbecue spot with a roadside dive flare. This is the sort of place where licking your fingers is a must, and manners are not necessary. The menu at this rough-and-tumble watering hole includes soul food and barbecue dishes like baby-back pork ribs, and meatloaf served with sides of hush puppies, black-eyed peas, collard greens, and creamy mac and cheese. American menu. Lunch, dinner. Bar. Casual attire. **$$**

★ ★ **HOME.** *20 Cornelia St, New York (10014). Phone 212/243-9579; fax 212/647-9393. www.recipesfromhome.com.* Owned by husband-wife team David Page (he is also executive chef) and Barbara Shin, Home is one of those rare and wonderful restaurants that wraps you in warmth, hospitality, grace, and delicious cuisine. Tucked away on a sleepy block of the West Village, Home offers diners home-style American meals made from the seasons best ingredients. The restaurant has a charming outdoor garden (heated in winter) and boasts one of the most extensive all-New York State wine lists around town. (The couples own wine, Shin Merlot, made in the North Fork of Long Island was added to the list in 2004.) This gem of a restaurant should be shared with someone as special as it is. American menu. Lunch, dinner, brunch. Closed Dec 25. Casual attire. Outdoor seating. **$$**

★ ★ ★ **HONMURA AN.** *170 Mercer St, New York (10012). Phone 212/334-5253.* Honmura An is a delightful, serene escape in SoHo with minimalist decor and dramatic flower arrangements where spectacular just-made soba and udon noodles are the house specialty. Bring an appetite, because aside from the noodles, the kitchen has an in for some of the most delicious fish in the citysashimi, sushi, and maki rolls that will force you to order more even if you have reached maximum food capacity. Japanese menu. Lunch, dinner. Closed Mon. Casual attire. **$$$**

★ ★ ★ **I TRULLI.** *122 E 27th St, New York (10016). Phone 212/481-7372; fax 212/481-5785. www.itrulli.com.* i Trulli envelops you with warmth, whether in the winter with its hearth-style, wood-burning fireplace, or in the summer when the lovely outdoor courtyard garden opens up for dining under the stars. This is a true neighborhood place, with charming service that features the rustic Italian cuisine of the Apulia region. Favorites include ricotta-stuffed cannelloni, orchiette with veal ragu, and fantastically fat calzones made by hand and baked to a golden brown in the wood-burning oven. Italian menu. Lunch, dinner. Bar. Casual attire. Reservations recommended. Outdoor seating. **$$$**

★ ★ **IL BUCO.** *47 Bond St, New York (10012). Phone 212/533-1932; fax 212/533-3502. www.ilbuco.com.* While the Italian food here is some of the most honest and well executed of its kind in the city, Il Buco is all about atmosphere. The place is low-lit and warm, filled with antiques (many for sale) and sturdy farmhouse tables that give the restaurant the soft, inviting charm of an out-of-the-way farmhouse somewhere in the mountains. Romance is always a big draw, but even if you aren'tin love, go with friends. You'll have a great meal, and you'll leave feeling all warm and fuzzy inside. Italian, Mediterranean menu. Lunch Tues-Sat, dinner. Bar. Casual attire. **$$$**

★ ★ **IL CORTILE.** *125 Mulberry St, New York (10013). Phone 212/226-6060; fax 212/431-7283. www.ilcortile.com.* Il Cortile has been a pillar of Italian cuisine in Little Italy since 1975. This neighborhood tratorria, located amid the bustling streets of Little Italy and Chinatown, offers heaps of authentic Italian fareantipasti, pasta, fish, poultry, and beef, prepared with love and with a nod to the traditions of the old country. The restaurant has a sunny indoor garden room that makes you feel like you are dining somewhere on the Mediterranean. Italian menu. Lunch, dinner. Closed Thanksgiving, Dec 24-25. Bar. Casual attire. Reservations recommended. **$$$**

★ ★ ★ **IL MULINO.** *86 W 3rd St, New York (10012). Phone 212/673-3783; fax 212/673-9875. www.ilmulinonewyork.com.* If Tony Soprano were having dinner out in New York City, chances are hed love Il Mulino. Its a dark relic of an Italian spot where the service is excellent and the rich, heavy food is read from long lists of specials and served in huge portions (the herb-crusted lamb chops are built for Fred Flintstone). Tableside theatrics like making a Caesar salad and filleting a whole fish give guests even more of a show. Il Mulino is a boys club with lots of loud, brash eaters who tend to drink one too many bottles of wine. Italian menu. Lunch, dinner. Closed Sun. Bar. Reservations recommended. **$$$$**

★ ★ ★ **IL NIDO.** *251 E 53rd St, New York (10022). Phone 212/753-8450; fax 212/224-0155. www.ilnidonyc.com.* A bit more rustic than its Il Monello sister, this bistro offers a plethora of antipasti and pastas to begin its northern Italian menu, including rigatoni Toscana with tomatoes, white beans, and sage. For added entertainment, many entrées are prepared tableside. Italian menu. Lunch, dinner. Closed Sun; holidays. Bar. Business casual attire. Reservations recommended. **$$$**

★ **INO.** *21 Bedford St, New York (10014). Phone 212/989-5769. www.cafeino.com.* Jason Denton honed his skills at Mario Batalis first hit restaurant, Po, and decided to branch off on his own and open a little nook of a wine and panini bar in the West Village. Lucky for us. His itty-bitty Italian wine bar is open from breakfast until late at night, serving a mouth-watering selection of pressed sandwiches and an extensive and reasonably priced list of Italian wines by the glass. Don't miss the signature truffled egg toast, a delicious snack anytime of the day. Italian menu. Breakfast, lunch, dinner, late-night, brunch. Bar. Casual attire. **$$**

★ **JACKSON HOLE.** *1611 Second Ave, New York (10028). Phone 212/737-8788; fax 212/737-8621. www.jacksonholeburgers.com.* If you crave a thick, juicy burger and don't mind a loud crowd and a fast-paced—sometimes even frenetic—setting, then Jackson Hole is the place for you. This is a top spot to feast on burgers offered in various sizes and weights with an almost infinite variety of toppings. All are served with piles of steak fries and thick slices of red onion and ripe tomatoes. American menu. Lunch, dinner. Closed Thanksgiving, Dec 25. Bar. Children's menu. Casual attire. Outdoor seating. **$$**

★ ★ ★ ★ ★ **JEAN GEORGES.** *One Central Park W, New York (10023). Phone 212/299-3900; fax 212/299-3908. www.jean-georges.com.* Perfection is a word that comes to mind when speaking of meals at Jean-Georges. Heaven is another word and divine yet another. Located in the Trump International Hotel & Tower (see) across from Central Park, Jean-Georges is a shrine to haute cuisine. Drawing influences from around the world, the menu is conceived and impeccably executed by celebrity chef/owner (and author) Jean-Georges Vongerichten. Vongerichten is a man of meticulous discipline, and it shows on the plate. Nothing is present that shouldnt be there. Under Vongerichtens direction, ingredients shine, flavors spark, and the mouth trembles. Suffice it to say that you will be in heaven within minutes of the meals commencement. The room is sophisticated and stunning, yet remains comfortable. You'll find that its filled nightly with well-known names, high-powered financial moguls, actors, models, and local New Yorkers who are lucky enough to score reservations. Call well in advance. It is worth the time it may take you to get through. If you can't manage to secure a table, try your luck at Nougatine, the popular café in the outer bar area. It has a simpler menu but will give you a taste of what Vongerichten is capable of. The bar is also a lovely place to meet for an aperitif or a cocktail before dinner or a walk through the park. Continental, French menu. Breakfast, lunch, dinner, brunch. Bar. Jacket required. Reservations recommended. Valet parking. Outdoor seating. **$$$$**

★ ★ ★ **JEWEL BAKO.** *239 E 5th St, New York (10003). Phone 212/979-1012.* This is one restaurant that sounds like its nameit is a shoebox-sized jewel of a place, serving precious, glorious sushi and sashimi as well as more traditional Japanese meals. The tiny, intimate, and chic East Village sliver of a space is owned by a husband-wife team who make it their mission to ensure that your experience is marked by warm service and gracious hospitality. The restaurants small size and popular following make reserving a table ahead of time a good plan. Japanese, sushi menu. Dinner, late-night. Closed Sun. Casual attire. Reservations recommended. **$$$**

★ **JING FONG.** *20 Elizabeth St, New York (10013). Phone 212/964-5256.* Jing Fong is a dim sum lover's paradise. This vast banquet hall offers mountains of delicious dim sum from carts, but also allows those too hungry to wait for a cart to hover by the kitchen to snatch up plates of fresh morselsdumplings, buns, rollsas they are cooked. In addition, you can opt for a feast from a buffet of raw seafood and have it cooked to order. Don't leave without sampling one of the tiny white mochi dessertscoconut shells filled with black sesame paste that tastes like peanut butter. Chinese menu. Lunch, dinner. Casual attire. **$$**

★ **JOHN'S PIZZERIA.** *278 Bleecker St, New York (10014). Phone 212/243-1680; fax 212/243-0450. www.johnsofbleeckerstreet.com.* For many pizza aficionados, Johns is the beginning, the middle, and the end. There simply is no other. This decades-old standard, located on a congested block of Bleecker Street in Greenwich Village, is almost a dive in terms of décor, but no matter; the pizzagorgeous, piping hot, bubbling mozzarella-topped piesis divine. To wash it down, there are carafes of wine, pitchers of beer, and not much else, but what else do you really need? Italian menu. Lunch, dinner. Casual attire. No credit cards accepted. **$$**

★ ★ ★ **JOJO.** *160 E 64th St, New York (10021). Phone 212/223-5656; fax 212/755-9038. www.jean-georges.com.* Located in a charming old townhouse, JoJo was one of the first restaurants from acclaimed star-chef and restaurateur Jean-Georges Vongerichten. It has a turn-of-the-century feel, with deep jewel tones, velvet and silk fabrics, and 17th-century terra-cotta tiles. The dishes highlight Vongerichtens French-Asian style, such as goat cheese and potato terrine with chive oil, roast chicken with chickpea fries, and tuna spring rolls with soybean coulis. JoJo is a wonderful spot for elegant, restful, special-occasion dining. French menu. Lunch, dinner. Closed holidays. Bar. Business casual attire. Reservations recommended. **$$$**

★ ★ ★ ★ **KAI.** *822 Madison Ave, New York (10021). Phone 212/988-7277; fax 212/570-4500. www.itoen.com.* Take respite from the city streets at KAI, a restaurant and teahouse on the second floor of renowned tea merchant ITO EN. Located in one of New York City's toniest shopping areas, KAI offers instant transport to the peace and serenity of Japan's best teahouses. Bamboo, stone, slate, and traditional Japanese pottery are the main design elements of the spare yet elegant restaurant. Along with an afternoon tea featuring many of ITO EN's premium teas and sweets like black sesame and green tea layered cake, the restaurant is open for lunch and dinner. At lunch, diners delight in flavors and textures of soups and dishes made with noodles, tea-scented rice, vegetables, seafood, or beef. Bento boxes or sashimi lunches are also popular choices. At dinner, order la carte or a tasting menu such as the nine-course Iron Goddess, which features dishes like chilled puree of lily bulb soup and "live" unagi with seasonal vegetables and spicy miso. Make the experience last by purchasing favorite teas at ITO EN. Japanese menu. Lunch, dinner. Closed Sun; holidays. Business casual attire. Reservations recommended. **$$$**

★ **KELLEY & PING.** *127 Greene St, New York (10012). Phone 212/228-1212; fax 212/228-7341. www.kelleyandping.com.* This trendy pan-Asian eatery has been filling up with slinky hipsters since the day it opened. The menu of fiery fare served at this exposed-brick, wood-paneled teashop, noodle bar, and Asian grocery reflects many regions of Asia, including China, Vietnam, Korea, and Thailand. For those who can't make a decision about what to eat first, the menu offers combination platters that include spring rolls, chicken satay, dumplings, and duck pancakes. Pan-Asian menu. Lunch, dinner. Children's menu. Casual attire. **$$**

★ ★ **KINGS' CARRIAGE HOUSE.** *251 E 82nd St, New York (10028). Phone 212/734-5490. www.kingscarriagehouse.com.* Located on a lovely residential, tree-lined block of the Upper East Side, Kings' Carriage House is an exquisite and intimate restaurant with all the comforts of an antique-filled Irish manor house. Owned by former food stylist Elizabeth King and her husband, Paul Farell, a native of Dublin, this is indeed one of Manhattan's most enchanted and personal restaurants. Special treats include Sunday afternoon tea and the Sunday roast dinner, but the everyday menu with dishes like shrimp bisque and Irish smoked salmon is winning as well. Continental menu. Dinner. Closed Dec 25; also two weeks in late Aug. Bar. Business casual attire. Reservations recommended. **$$$**

★ ★ **KITCHEN 22.** *36 E 22nd St, New York (10010). Phone 212/228-4399; fax 212/228-4612. www.charliepalmer.com.* At this low-lit neighborhood bistro in the Flatiron neighborhood, you'll be treated to a three-course prix fixe menu of seasonal American fare for an unbelievably affordable price of $25 for dinner. This Charlie Palmer restaurant provides a winning formula for hip locals who crowd in for drinks and delicious meals in a dark, sexy setting. The crowded bar up front is a popular spot for regulars to gather and sip martinis in style. American menu. Dinner. Closed Sun. Bar. Casual attire. **$$**

★ ★ ★ **KURUMA ZUSHI.** *7 E 47th St, New York (10017). Phone 212/317-2802; fax 212/317-2803.* Kuruma Zushi is New Yorks most secreted sushi spot. Located on the second floor of a less-than-impressive Midtown building, with only a tiny sign to alert you to its presence, it is tough to find but well worth the search. Fresh, supple, mouthwatering fish is served with freshly grated wasabi and bright, fiery shavings of ginger. This sushi temple has quite a following, among them Ruth Reichl, the former *New York Times* restaurant critic and current editor of *Gourmet* magazine, who is vocal about her love of the restaurants spectacular fish. You will be dreaming about this fish for weeks after your meal has ended. While many consider this the pinnacle of sushi, it does come with quite an insane price tag. Dinner per person can easily hit the $100 mark, which may be why the restaurant, an earth-colored, minimalist room, is most popular with business people on expense accounts and true devotees. Japanese, sushi menu. Lunch, dinner. Closed Sun. Bar. Casual attire. Reservations recommended. **$$$$**

★ ★ **L'EXPRESS.** *249 Park Ave, New York (10003). Phone 212/254-5858; fax 212/254-5890. www.lexpress-nyc.com.* Open 24 hours a day for omelettes, frisee au lardons, steak frites, and other traditional bistro fare, LExpress is a perfect choice for an off-hour snack, a late-night meal, or a quiet breakfast of eggs, coffee, and a newspaper. At prime lunch and dinner hours, this replica of a French brasserie can get a bit frenetic, but if you don't mind the hustle and bustle, you'll have yourself a nice Parisian-style meal. French menu. Breakfast, lunch, dinner, late-night, brunch. Bar. Casual attire. **$$**

★ ★ ★ L'IMPERO. *45 Tudor City Pl, New York (10017). Phone 212/599-5045; fax 212/599-5043. www.limpero.com.* L'Impero arrived on the New York City dining scene in 2002, and with it, the landscape of elegant Italian cuisine was permanently changed. Chef/partner Scott Conant takes you to new heights with his interpretation of the Italian cucina. There are simple plates of pasta, like a gorgeous bowl of perfect handmade spaghetti garnished with fresh tomato and basil that will renew your love of a dish tossed aside long ago. His signature capretto (that would be goat) is moist-roasted until fork-tender and saturated with rich, delicious flavors. His takes on crudo (raw, brightly accented sashimi-style dishes of fish) are luminous. The service is flawless, the wine list is an Italian encyclopedia, and the décor is serene and civilized, warmed with chocolate and blue tones. L'Impero is a must-visit for a special occasion or for a well-deserved renewal of a love affair with Italian food. Italian menu. Lunch, dinner. Closed Sun. Bar. Business casual attire. Reservations recommended. Outdoor seating. **$$$**

★ LA BONNE SOUPE. *48 W 55th St, New York (10019). Phone 212/586-7650; fax 212/765-6409. www.labonnesoupe.com.* La Bonne Soupe is one of those restaurants that fits like an old shoe, in the best sense of the word. Comfortable and easy, the room feels like a Parisian bistro with checked tablecloths, long banquettes, and lovely French waitresses. The menu keeps the illusion of Paris alive with dishes like fluffy quiche, an excellent bouillabaisse, and of course, a delicious French onion soup capped with a thick and gooey blanket of melting Gruyre cheese. For a pre-theater meal, keep this gem in mind. French menu. Lunch, dinner. Closed holidays. Bar. Children's menu. Casual attire. Reservations recommended. Outdoor seating. **$$**

★ ★ ★ ★ LA GRENOUILLE. *3 E 52nd St, New York (10022). Phone 212/752-1495; fax 212/593-4964. www.la-grenouille.com.* Yes, frogs' legs are on the menu at La Grenouille, whose name literally means The Frog. This stunning Midtown restaurant is the epitome of a classic. If you're craving some sort of fusion hotspot with a loud crowd and a lengthy cocktail list that contains the word "cosmopolitan," you won'tbe happy here. La Grenouille is elegant and conservative in style and substance. The room is quiet, lovely, and modest; the kitchen serves authentic, sophisticated French cuisine at its finest; and the staff offers service that is refined and seemingly effortless. Now back to those frogs' legs, which appropriately are the restaurants signature. They are served sautéed, Provenal style, and are a must for adventurous diners who have never indulged in them. This is certainly the place to have your first experience with them, although it may spoil you for life. The wine list is mostly French, although some American wines have managed to make the cut as well. Indulging in a cheese course is a nice way to finish your meal, as it is in France. The restaurant is popular at lunch and is frequently crowded with well-preserved businesspeople on lunch hour, being in the heart of Midtown. It is also a wonderful spot to take a civilized siesta from hours of shopping along Fifth Avenue and recharge your batteries for the afternoon ahead. French menu. Lunch, dinner. Closed Sun-Mon; also three weeks in Aug. Bar. Jacket required. Reservations recommended. **$$$$**

★ ★ LA MANGEOIRE. *1008 Second Ave, New York (10022). Phone 212/759-7086; fax 212/759-6387. www.lamangeoire.com.* La Mangeoire is a perfect place for a business lunch or a quiet, intimate dinner. The warm dining room is charming and cozy, and the menu offers enough of a selection of contemporary French farees-cargots, Provenal fish soup, and the caramelized onion tart are signaturesto please even the most high-maintenance diners. The staff is gracious, and hospitality flows effortlessly. French menu. Lunch, dinner, Sun brunch. Closed holidays. Bar. Casual attire. Reservations recommended. Outdoor seating. **$$$**

★ ★ LA PAELLA. *214 E 9th St, New York (10003). Phone 212/598-4321.* La Paella is a lively Iberian hot spot that seems tailor made for large, loud groups of friends who are on a budget. While the room could seem claustrophobic to some, with gaggles of couples and hordes of singles sitting at candlelit tables, somehow it seems cozy and quaint. The specialty isshock-erpaella, and it is offered in five different varieties, in addition to a dozen or so hot and cold tapas. Spanish menu. Lunch, dinner. Bar. Casual attire. Reservations recommended. Outdoor seating. **$$$**

★ ★ LA PALAPA. *77 St. Marks Pl, New York (10003). Phone 212/777-2537; fax 212/777-9730. www.lapalapa.com.* In Mexico, when the blazing afternoon sun beats down on the beach, locals flock to palapas-

palm-thatched shelters where icy cervezas wash down spicy fish tacos. The seaside palapa now exists in New York City, thanks to chef/owner Barbara Sibley and her partner Margaritte Malfy, who opened La Palapa, a hacienda-style urban shelter in the East Village featuring tearfully good authentic Mexican home cooking. Expect strong, tart margaritas and plates piled high with chile-rich regional signatures like masa pockets stuffed with chicken in chipotle and grilled muscovy duck breast in a wild raspberry and ancho chile mole. Mexican menu. Lunch, dinner, brunch. Bar. Casual attire. Reservations recommended. Outdoor seating. **$$**

★ LA PARISIENNE RESTAURANT. *910 Seventh Ave, New York (10019). Phone 212/765-4591.* American, Greek menu. Breakfast, lunch, dinner. Bar. Casual attire. No credit cards accepted. **$$**

★ ★ ★ LAFAYETTE GRILL & BAR. *54 Franklin St, New York (10013). Phone 212/732-5600; fax 212/732-4144. www.lafgrill.com.* Mediterranean menu. Lunch, dinner, late-night. Closed Sun. Bar. Casual attire. Reservations recommended. **$$**

★ ★ ★ LCB BRASSERIE RACHOU. *60 W 55th St, New York (10019). Phone 212/688-6525; fax 212/258-2493.* French menu. Lunch, dinner. Bar. Business casual attire. Reservations recommended. **$$$$**

★ ★ ★ ★ LE BERNARDIN. *155 W 51st St, New York (10019). Phone 212/554-1515; fax 212/554-1100. www.le-bernardin.com.* If you crave the fruits of the sea, if you dream of lush, shimmering plates of pristine, perfectly prepared seafood, if you are a fan of soft, sinking seats, if your idea of paradise is a long, luxurious meal, you will be very happy at Le Bernardin. The restaurant, born in Paris in 1972, has been impressing foodies and novices alike since it moved across the ocean to Manhattan in 1986. After you experience the food and service, its easy to see why. Le Bernardin is elegant everythingelegant service, elegant food, elegant crowd. Its all very civilized and sophisticated, and its not the type of place to go for a quick bite. This is real dining at its finest. The sauces are light, aromatic, and perfectly balanced. The ingredients are seasonal and stunning. The presentations are museum-worthy in their perfection. All these elements combined with flawless service make dinner at Le Bernardin an experience that will stay with you for days, even months. The food is thoughtful and innovative, yet simple and approachable. It is the sort of menu that makes you want to try new things. But those craving beef need not enter. Seafood is the star at this distinguished, elegant New York restaurant, and the menu reflects the kitchens passion for this food. Mind-altering fish first courses are divided between Simply Raw and Lightly Cooked. Equally stellar entrées are completely from the sea, with a reluctant addition of meat at the end, in a section entitled Upon Request. This is not the strength of the talented kitchen. Enjoy all courses of that which once swam when you're at Le Bernardin, and you won'tregret it. French, Seafood menu. Lunch, dinner. Closed Sun; holidays. Bar. Jacket required. Reservations recommended. **$$$$**

★ ★ LE COLONIAL. *149 E 57th St, New York (10022). Phone 212/752-0808; fax 212/752-7534. www.lecolonialnyc.com.* Serving sophisticated French-Vietnamese fare, Le Colonial is a Midtown favorite for lunch and dinner. The room feels like colonial Saigon come to life, with tall bamboo, spinning ceiling fans, lazy palms, and soft lighting. The menu offers the vibrant chile-tinged signature dishes of the region and includes such treats as glossy spring rolls filled with shrimp, pork, and mushrooms; tender ginger-marinated duck with a tamarind dipping sauce; and grilled loin of pork paired with a lively mango and jicama salad. Vietnamese, French menu. Lunch, dinner. Closed July 4, Thanksgiving, Dec 25. Bar. Casual attire. Reservations recommended. **$$$**

★ ★ ★ LE PERIGORD. *405 E 52nd St, New York (10022). Phone 212/755-6244; fax 212/486-3906. www.leperigord.com.* Le Perigord is one of New Yorks old-time favorites for sophisticated French dining. The menu of classic dishes, including the restaurants signature game selection (in season), is geared for diners who define luxury in terms of impeccable, attentive service; elegant furnishings; inspired haute cuisine of the nouvelle French variety; and the quiet of a dining room filled with people enjoying a civilized meal. The food here is delicate and serene, in perfect harmony with the peaceful and majestic dining room. French menu. Lunch, dinner. Bar. Jacket required. Reservations recommended. **$$$$**

★ ★ ★ LE REFUGE. *166 E 82nd St, New York (10028). Phone 212/861-4505; fax 212/736-0384. www.lerefugenyc.com.* Located within walking distance of the Metropolitan Museum of Art and the lush greenery of Central Park, Le Refuge is a classically charming French restaurant that offers a small slice of Paris in New York, without the smoking, of course. Aside from the lack of cigarette smoke, the difference between the two is negligible. The upper crust of society gathers at

Le Refuge for its Parisian elegance and its impressive wine list that pairs up perfectly with the selection of simple, bistro-style fare, like farm-raised duck with fresh fruit and filet mignon with peppercorn sauce. Continental, French menu. Dinner. Closed holidays. Bar. Children's menu. Casual attire. Reservations recommended. Outdoor seating. **$$$**

★ ★ LE SOUK. *47 Avenue B, New York (10009). Phone 212/777-5454; fax 212/253-9485. www.lesoukny.com.* The fragrant and seductive foods of Morocco and Egypt are served with warm hospitality at this East Village hideaway. Amber lighting and hookah pipes lend an opium den quality to the dining room that doubles as a stage for belly dancers. The menu includes Moroccan specialties like chicken cooked in a tagine, moulekayaa rich and savory Egyptian stewand toasty pita bread with assorted mezze (think Middle Eastern tapas like stuffed grape leaves, hummus, baba ghanoush, and the like). A tray of deserts arrives in show-and-tell style, and the selection includes everything from chocolate mousse cake to baklava. Middle Eastern menu. Dinner. Bar. Casual attire. Outdoor seating. **$$**

★ ★ ★ LENOX ROOM. *1278 Third Ave, New York (10021). Phone 212/772-0404; fax 212/772-3229. www.lenoxroom.com.* Restaurateur Tony Fortuna has managed to bring a bit of slick, downtown style to this quiet, residential (some might say culinarily comatose) neighborhood on the Upper East Side. Thanks to Fortuna, the vibrant life inside Lenox Room more than makes up for the lack of a pulse beating at nearby eateries. At Lenox, you will find a sexy bar and lounge with cool cocktails and inventive tiers of cocktail cuisine, and a swanky, intimate dining room offering a smart New American menu. Lenox is a sure thing for a business lunch, a ladies-only cocktail outing, or a spirited dinner with friends. Not only will the food win you over, but Fortunas gracious hospitality will have you scheduling your next visit before you leave. American menu. Lunch, dinner, Sun brunch. Closed holidays. Bar. Casual attire. Reservations recommended. Outdoor seating. **$$$**

★ ★ LES HALLES. *411 Park Ave S, New York (10016). Phone 212/679-4111; fax 212/779-0679. www.leshalles.net.* Chef Anthony Bourdain (author of behind-the-scenes memoir *Kitchen Confidential*) brought Les Halles into the culinary limelight a few years back. Despite all the hype, this brasserie remains a genuine star for amazing cuts of steak and terrific takes on pork, chicken, moules, and, of course, lots of frites. The front serves as a French-style butcher shop, while the crowded bistro-style dining room feels like it just fell out of some super-fabulous arrondisement in Paris. French menu. Breakfast, lunch, dinner, Sun brunch. Bar. Casual attire. **$$**

★ ★ LES HALLES DOWNTOWN. *15 John St, New York (10038). Phone 212/285-8585; fax 212/791-3280. www.leshalles.net.* French, steak menu. Lunch, dinner, brunch. Bar. Children's menu. Casual attire. **$$**

★ ★ ★ LEVER HOUSE. *390 Park Ave, New York (10022). Phone 212/888-2700; fax 212/888-2740. www.leverhouse.com.* Designed by Mark Newsen, The Lever House is a post-modern podlike dining room filled with whiplash-worthy celebrities from Charlie Rose to Pink. Chef Dan Silverman (formerly of Union Square Cafe) honors the seasons and all sorts of appetites with dainty ladylike dishes such as silky fluke tartare, heated up with chiles and orange zest, and hearty dishes like the juicy Lever House burgera pile of recklessly flavored beef with pickled onions and sweet tomatoes on a big, puffy bun that will send Atkins groupies underground for extra carb-aversion therapy. The Lever House is a serious power spot with a heart. The service is gracious and not pretentious. The food is comfortable but spirited, not mundane. The Lever House is a class act all around and is destined to be taking A-list reservations for years to come. American menu. Lunch, dinner. Bar. Business casual attire. Reservations recommended. **$$$**

★ LOMBARDI'S. *32 Spring St, New York (10012). Phone 212/941-7994; fax 212/941-4159. www.lombardispizza.com.* Arguably the best pizza in the city is served at Lombardis, a decades-old institution in Little Italy. Straight from the coal-fired oven, these pies are served piping hot and smoky from the coals char, with thin, crispy crusts and fresh toppings. The service can be lazy but is always friendly, and the tables are tight, but who cares? This is not Mobil Four-Star dining, but Four-Star eating, and when you crave pizza and a bottle of red, nothing is better. Pizza. Lunch, dinner. Casual attire. Outdoor seating. No credit cards accepted. **$**

★ ★ LUCKY STRIKE. *59 Grand St, New York (10013). Phone 212/941-0772; fax 212/274-9365. www.luckystrikeny.com.* Lucky Strike was one of the first downtown hot spots from Keith McNally, the king of the distressed Parisian chic brasseriethink Balthazar (see), Pastis, and the latest entry, Schillers Liquor Bar (see). Filled with smoky mirrors and a dressed-down vintage French vibe, Lucky Strike is still a super-cool spot to slink down into a sexy banquette and feast on perfect bistro standards like steak frites, frise and goat cheese salad, steamed mussels, and juicy roast chicken. American, French menu. Lunch, dinner, late-night, brunch. Bar. Casual attire. **$$**

★ ★ **LUCY LATIN KITCHEN.** *35 E 18th St, New York (10003). Phone 212/475-5829; fax 212/598-3020. www.lucylatinkitchen.com.* On the ground floor of ABC Carpet & Home, just past the accessories, you will find Lucy. Swathed in white sheer curtains with wood-beamed ceilings and colorful oversized sofas, Lucy feels like a rustic, beachside hacienda. The menu is a fun and festive assortment of Oaxacan snacks like chorizo and potato quesadillas and red chile pork and grilled pineapple tacos. Try not to fill up on snacks, though, as the house specialty, Barbacoaslow-roasted lamb in avocado and hoja santa leavesis a knockout. Latin American menu. Lunch, dinner. Bar. Casual attire. Reservations recommended. **$$$**

★ ★ **LUPA.** *170 Thompson St, New York (10012). Phone 212/982-5089; fax 212/982-5490. www.luparestaurant.com.* There are several sure things about Lupa, celebrity chef Mario Batalis wonderfully rustic, Roman osteria: the line for a table will wind its way down Thompson Street. The heavenly spaghettini with spicy cauliflower ragout (chef/partner Mark Ladners signature dish since he opened the place in 1999) will leave you wondering how you ever hated cauliflower. The antipasti boarda massive butcher block piled high with house-made cured meats and sausageswill leave you unable to eat these heavenly pork products anywhere else. For all these reasons and more (like wine, atmosphere, service, and style), Lupa is, hands-down, one of the most beloved spots for earthy and satisfying Roman fare. Its worth the wait. Italian menu. Lunch, dinner. Bar. Casual attire. Outdoor seating. **$$**

★ ★ **LUSARDI'S.** *1494 Second Ave, New York (10021). Phone 212/249-2020; fax 212/585-2941. www.lusardis.com.* This well-established neighborhood staple is a favorite among Upper East Siders craving reliable Italian fare in a modest, warm setting. The menu sticks to the things Italian restaurants do bestlavish plates of antipasti, fresh composed salads, hearty bowls of pasta, olive oil-grilled fish, and tender slow-cooked meats braised in red wine. This is a lovely restaurant with a gracious staff and a wonderful wine list to complement the cuisine. Italian menu. Lunch, dinner. Closed holidays. Bar. Casual attire. Reservations recommended. **$$$**

★ ★ ★ **MALONEY & PORCELLI.** *37 E 50th St, New York (10022). Phone 212/750-2233; fax 212/750-2252. www.maloneyandporcelli.com.* Named for the restaurant owners attorneys, Maloney & Porcelli is an easy, smart choice for an urban business lunch or a simple dinner out with a group of friends who favor simple, well-executed cuisine served in a classic, clubby environment without fuss or pretense. The New American menu offers straight-ahead choices like a raw bar, thin-crust pizza, and filet mignon. The wine list contains some real gems as well, making Maloney & Porcelli a favorite for Midtown dining. American, steak menu. Lunch, dinner, brunch. Closed Jan 1, Dec 25. Bar. Business casual attire. Reservations recommended. **$$$**

★ ★ ★ **MAMLOUK.** *211 E 4th St, New York (10009). Phone 212/529-3477; fax 212/529-8516.* At Mamlouk, a cozy Middle Eastern spot in the East Village, you are taken away to an Arabic land filled with sitar music and warm, fragrant spiced meals of Middle Eastern fare. Mamlouk is an experience, from the gentle rhythmic music to the tables named "Beirut" and "Jerusalem," to the hostess who addresses everyone as "darling." While hookah smoking is now banned by New York City law, Mamlouk still manages to spirit you off to a star-filled night by the Nile. Dinner at Mamlouk is always six courses, with dishes like zatter, a flat bread topped with a paste of sesame seeds, olive oil, and thyme; vegetarian moussaka; and mjadarra, a sweet spice-flecked lentil puree served with tender grilled chicken. Middle Eastern menu. Dinner. Casual attire. Reservations recommended. Outdoor seating. **$$$**

★ ★ ★ ★ **MARCH.** *405 E 58th, New York (10022). Phone 212/754-6272; fax 212/838-5108. www.marchrestaurant.com.* Many people have issues with indulgence. Chef/owner Wayne Nish is not one of them. He believes that his guests should be indulged from the moment they enter his jewel-like, turn-of-the-century-townhouse restaurant to the moment they sadly must part. And a meal at March is just thatpure, blissful indulgence-from start to finish. For this reason (and because its one of the most romantic spots in New York City), it is truly a special-occasion place, and reservations should be secured well in advance. Nishs menu, of what he calls New York City Cuisine, is fabulous. Dishes focus on fresh, seasonal products sparked to attention with luxurious ingredients from around the world. Choose from three-, four-, five-, or six-course tasting menus; each is available with or without wine pairings. Go for the wine.

Co-owner Joseph Scalice is a gifted wine director, so you're in for a treat. Alfresco dining on the townhouses rooftop terrace and mezzanine is magical in warm months. American menu. Dinner. Closed holidays. Business casual attire. Reservations recommended. Outdoor seating. **$$$**

★ ★ **MARKT.** *401 W 14th St, New York (10014). Phone 212/727-3314; fax 212/255-8515. www.marktrestaurant.com.* Located in the Meatpacking District, the new land of the hip and fabulous set, Markt offers a taste of Belgium in a festive brasserie setting. The specialty of the house, as you might expect from a Belgian restaurant, is mussels, served in a variety of ways with crispy vats of golden fries, a nice dish to pair with one of the dozens of international beers on tap. Outdoor seating in the warmer months makes this place sizzle. Continental menu. Breakfast, lunch, dinner, brunch. Bar. Casual attire. Reservations recommended. Outdoor seating. **$$$**

★ ★ **MARY'S FISH CAMP.** *64 Charles St (W 4th St), New York (10014). Phone 646/486-2185; fax 646/486-6703. www.marysfishcamp.com.* Mary Redding, chef/owner of this downscale neighborhood seafood shack, is a smart woman. She knows that even people who don't live in New England crave that simple style of food—fat, sweet steamers; meaty lobster rolls; salt-crusted shrimp; and all sorts of daily-catch specials. At her bustling, minimalist, forever-crowded West Village restaurant, the vibe is fun and casual and the fish is swimming-fresh and delicious. Don't mind the wait—it is so worth it. Seafood menu. Lunch, dinner. Closed Sun. Bar. Casual attire. **$$**

★ ★ ★ ★ ★ **MASA.** *10 Columbus Cir, New York (10019). Phone 212/823-9800; fax 212/823-9809. www.masanyc.com.* You need deep, deep pockets to indulge at Masa, or at least a healthy expense account. Its the high rollers table for gourmands, given that you've already committed to spending $350 just by walking through the 2,500-year-old Japanese cedar doorbefore you've had a drink, tacked on tax, or made your gratuity donation. Chef/owner Masa Takayama creates a different dining experience each day based on market offerings. And what an experience it is. The ingredients that Takayama uses are precious, and his ability to present them in a simplified form is artistic. A mere shitake mushroom is raised to shrine-worthy status, attended to as if it were the last pearl of caviar from the Caspian. Every detail presented to you is aesthetically exquisite, from the tasteful sake glasses to the unusual ceramic ware. Pass on a table for this meal and perch yourself at the 23-foot-long bar where the chefs will serve you course by course and you can benefit from the calmness of their passionate devotion. Eating at Masa is theatre, and if you accept that the sticker price includes a mesmerizing display of true talent and commitment, the bite may sting a bit less. Japanese menu. Lunch, dinner. Closed Sun; also two weeks in Aug and Dec. Bar. Casual attire. Reservations recommended. **$$$$**

★ ★ ★ **MATSURI.** *369 W 16th St, New York (10011). Phone 212/243-6400; fax 212/835-5535. www.themaritimehotel.com.* Located in a sexy subterranean space in the Meatpacking Districts hot new Maritime Hotel, Matsuri is an Asian wonderland. From the bamboo and paper-lanterned movie set décor to the shimmering sushi, sashimi, and expertly plated haute Japanese stylings of chef Tadashi Ono, this restaurant is an ode to the exotic senses of the Far East. Matsuri packs in the crowds, mostly here to see and be seen rather than to dine, but serious foodies make it in as well, searching for Onos divine and wild interpretations of Japanese fare and his careful hand with glorious sushi. Japanese, sushi menu. Dinner. Bar. Casual attire. Reservations recommended. **$$$**

★ ★ **MAX.** *51 Avenue B, New York (10009). Phone 212/539-0111; fax 212/539-0237. www.maxrestaurantny.com.* Delicious and cheap are two words commonly used to describe Max, a no-frills joint for terrific red sauce, pasta, lasagna, and all sorts of dishes whose names end in parmagiana. Other words you might be tempted to throw into the mix include crowded, loud, and no reservations, all of which means that you'd better be prepared to wait, and to shout to be heard. But that's part of Maxs charm, and the food makes it worthwhile. Italian menu. Lunch, dinner. Bar. Casual attire. Outdoor seating. No credit cards accepted. **$$**

★ ★ ★ **MAYA.** *1191 First Ave, New York (10021). Phone 212/585-1818; fax 212/734-6579. www.modernmexican.com/mayany.* A native of Mexico City, Mayas chef/owner Richard Sandoval knows authentic Mexican cuisine. His popular Upper East Side outpost is perpetually packed with smart, sexy neighborhood locals who understand that Mexico does more than just refried beans and cheesy enchiladas. At Maya, you'll find a soothing hacienda-style roomwood-paneled walls accented with native art, and terra-cotta tiled floorsa comfortable, stylish place to relax for dinner. And speaking of dinner, you'll be treated to a thrilling menu of authentic regional Mexican dishes like Cordero en Mole Verdelamb shank braised in mole verde with pan-roasted potatoes, chayote squash, and baby carrots, and the house Mariscadaa mammoth bowl bobbing with sea scallops, shrimp, mussels, and clams, served with black rice and a coriander seed-red pepper emulsion. The food goes down almost as easily as the terrific selection of one hundred tequilas and mezcals. Take two aspirin before bed. Mexican menu. Dinner. Closed Jan 1, Dec 25. Bar. Business casual attire. Reservations recommended. **$$$**

★ ★ ★ **MERCER KITCHEN.** *99 Prince St, New York (10012). Phone 212/966-5454; fax 212/965-3855. www.mercerhotel. com.* Located in the ultra-chic The Mercer hotel (see) in SoHo, this exposed-brick, subterranean hotspot is constantly teeming with celebrities and those who believe that they are celebrities merely because they are dining in their glow. The Asian-influenced American menu, under the talented direction of chef/owner Jean-Georges Vongerichten, is as swanky as the crowd, with signatures like raw tuna and wasabi pizza and yellowtail carpaccio with lime, coriander, and mint. If you haven't the slightest appetite, head over to the sexy bar, where hipsters sip martinis with abandon. American, French menu. Breakfast, lunch, dinner, brunch. Closed holidays. Bar. Casual attire. Reservations recommended. **$$$**

★ ★ **MERMAID INN.** *96 Second Ave, New York (10003). Phone 212/674-5870; fax 212/674-0510. www.themermaidnyc.com.* Jimmy Bradley (of The Red Cat and The Harrisonsee both) has opened another easy-to-love restaurant with The Mermaid Inn, located in the East Village. The restaurant will take you away to the bluffs of a windswept seashore with its dark wainscoting, hurricane lamps, vintage nautical maps, and big, icy raw bar. The menu here is all seafood, all the time. The signature lobster sandwicha sort of lobster roll gone burgeris a mess of sweet, fat, juicy lobster meat, held together by just the right bit of mayo, that is served on a wide, puffy, golden brioche bun with a mountain of skinny, crispy fries dusted with Old Bay seasoning. Bradley also offers more global takes on seafood, like a flaky, moist skate, sautéed until golden and set in a nutty puddle of white gazpacho sauce made from almonds. Mermaid has a great neighborhood vibe that makes it perfect for a first date, a last date, or dinner with the girls, the guys, your parents, or heck, even your enemies. Seafood menu. Dinner. Bar. Casual attire. Outdoor seating. **$$**

★ ★ **MESA GRILL.** *102 Fifth Ave, New York (10011). Phone 212/807-7400; fax 212/989-0034. www.mesagrill.com.* In the more than ten years since the Southwestern haven known as Mesa Grill opened its tall blond-wood doors and chef/owner Bobby Flay reached stardom on cable TV's Food Network, he has, impressively, managed to keep his creative eye on this, his first restaurant. The vaulted, lively room remains a popular spot for margarita-soaked happy hours, as well as a top choice for superb Southwestern-inspired American fare. The vibrant menu changes with the seasons, but famous plates include the cotija-crusted quesadilla stuffed with goat cheese, basil, and red chiles, topped with a charred corn salsa; and the 16-spiced chicken with mango garlic sauce and cilantro-pesto mashed potatoes. Flays food is not shy, so keep a cold margarita handy to soothe the heat. Southwestern menu. Lunch, dinner, brunch. Closed Dec 25. Bar. Casual attire. **$$$**

★ ★ **MI COCINA.** *57 Jane St, New York (10014). Phone 212/627-8273. www.micocinany.com.* Authentic regional Mexican cuisine is featured at Mi Cocina, a cozy, colorful, and lively West Village favorite for outstanding dishes of our neighbor to the south. The menu offers easy-to-love dishes like crisp, savory quesadillas and soft tacos fashioned from fresh corn tortillas filled with ancho-rubbed pulled pork, as well as vibrant regional specialties like the rich, chocolate moles of Oaxaca and the lime- and chile-marinated fish from the seaside region of Veracruz. Margaritas are wonderfully tart with lots of fresh lime juice and, of course, quite a bit of tequila. This restaurant is all about fun. Mexican menu. Dinner, brunch. Closed Dec 24-25. Bar. Children's menu. Casual attire. Reservations recommended. Outdoor seating. **$$**

★ **MICKEY MANTLE'S.** *42 Central Park S, New York (10019). Phone 212/688-7777; fax 212/751-5797. www.mickeymantles.com.* Located on Central Park South, Mickey Mantles is an easy and smart choice when you want to catch a game and have a good meal minus the roar of a crowded sports bar. This elegant dining room is a good option if you're wandering around Central Park and get hungry for straightforward, tasty American fare. Burgers, steaks, seafood, and pastas are on the menu, and in season, the Yankees are always on TV here. As you'd expect, you'll also find a nice collection of baseball memorabilia and sports-themed art on the walls. American menu. Lunch, dinner, late-night, brunch. Bar. Children's menu. Casual attire. Reservations recommended. Outdoor seating. **$$**

★ ★ ★ **MOLYVOS.** *871 Seventh Ave, New York (10019). Phone 212/582-7500; fax 212/582-7502. www.*

molyvos.com. Located just steps from Carnegie Hall and City Center, Molyvos is a great choice for before or after a dance or concert, with a wonderful menu of modern Greek specialties like assorted mezze served with warm, puffy pita; grilled whole fish; stunning takes on lamb; and an impressive international wine list. The restaurant feels like it fell from the shores of the Mediterranean, with blue and white tiles and sturdy wooden tables. The lively bar and front room is ideal if you're in the mood for a light bite and a glass of wine before a show, while the more refined dining room offers leisurely diners a place to unwind without rushing. Greek menu. Lunch, dinner. Bar. Casual attire. Reservations recommended. **$$$**

★ ★ ★ **MONTRACHET.** *239 W Broadway, New York (10013). Phone 212/219-2777; fax 212/274-9508. myriadrestaurantgroup.com/montrachet.* Montrachet is the first restaurant from restaurateur Drew Nieporent. (He also owns Nobu and Tribeca Grill, among others.) It is still one of the most prized and romantic dining experiences to be had in New York City. The seasonal, modern French-American menu and the warm, attentive service remain as fresh and inspired as they were on day one. Montrachets wine list has been met with critical acclaim and marries well with the sophisticated fare, making for delightful dining. French menu. Lunch, dinner. Closed Sun; holidays. Bar. Casual attire. Reservations recommended. **$$$**

D

★ ★ ★ **MORTON'S, THE STEAKHOUSE.** *551 Fifth Ave, New York (10017). Phone 212/972-3315; fax 212/972-0018. www.mortons.com.* This steakhouse chain, which originated in Chicago in 1978, appeals to serious meat lovers. With a selection of belt-busting carnivorous delights (like the house specialty, a 24-ounce porterhouse), as well as fresh fish, lobster, and chicken entres, Mortons rarely disappoints. If you just aren'tsure what you're in the mood for, the tableside menu presentation may help you decide. Here, main course selections are placed on a cart that's rolled to your table, where servers describe each item in detail. Steak menu. Lunch, dinner. Closed holidays. Bar. Business casual attire. Reservations recommended. **$$$$**

★ ★ ★ **MR. K'S.** *570 Lexington Ave, New York (10022). Phone 212/583-1668; fax 212/583-1620. www.mrks.com.* In general, most movers and shakers in the world of finance, media, and power know of Mr. Ksit is their daily cafeteria for grease-less, elegant Chinese food. Forget what you may have ever thought about Chinese food, because Mr. Ks breaks all the rules, bringing New Yorkers wonderful, upscale, exotic dishes from the various regions of China and serving them in an ultra-elegant, posh setting filled with fresh flowers, plush cushioned banquettes, and most notably, waiters who know the meaning of service. The restaurant, which is a clone of the DC original, is a wonderful choice for a big party to celebrate a special occasion, even if its just being able to share a dazzling meal at Mr. Ks together. Chinese menu. Lunch, dinner. Bar. Business casual attire. Reservations recommended. **$$$**

★ ★ **NAM.** *110 Reade St, New York (10013). Phone 212/267-1777; fax 212/267-3781. www.namnyc.com.* The fresh, spicy flavors of Vietnam are on the menu at Nam, a chic, breezy, bamboo-accented restaurant in TriBeCa. Giving a city-slicker kick to this Asian cuisine, Nam offers Vietnamese classics like noodle dishes, soups, spring rolls, green papaya salads, and simply magnificent seafood dishes. The crispy whole red snapper is slathered in chile and lime and served with steamed jasmine rice, while the steamed sea bass is a fleshy, sweet dish, accompanied by stewed tomatoes. Vietnamese menu. Lunch, dinner. Bar. Casual attire. **$$**

★ **NEW YORK KOM TANG.** *32 W 32nd St, New York (10001). Phone 212/947-8482.* Korean menu. Breakfast, lunch, dinner, late-night. Casual attire. **$$**

★ **NHA TRANG CENTRE.** *148 Centre St, New York (10013). Phone 212/941-9292; fax 212/941-6034.* New Yorkers who are forced to serve jury duty look forward to it for one reason and one reason onlynot their chance to serve their community, but because the courthouses are near Nha Trang, a frenetic, fast-paced, cafeteria-style spot serving some of the best authentic Vietnamese fare going. The place is generally chaotic, especially at lunch (be prepared to share your table with people you don't know), but the experience is a great one nonetheless, considering that you can feast on excellent bowls of pho (noodle soup), spicy spring rolls stuffed with basil and shrimp, and delicious dishes like banh xeo, crispy yellow rice-flower pancakes wrapped around sautéed mushrooms, shrimp, and sprouts. Vietnamese menu. Lunch, dinner. Casual attire. **$**

★ **NICE.** *35 E Broadway, New York (10002). Phone 212/406-9510.*In classic Chinatown form, Nice, a Cantonese restaurant with a following, serves loads of delicious steaming dim sum out of traditional trolley carts. The crowds come out in numbers on the weekends, making this massive place feel a tad scary, so try to sneak in during the week or be prepared to feel claustrophobic. Chinese menu. Breakfast, lunch, dinner. Casual attire. **$$**

★ ★ ★ **NOBU.** *105 Hudson St, New York (10013). Phone 212/219-0500; fax 212/219-1441. www.nobu-matsuhisa.com.* There is a place in New York where folks have been known to cry when they eat because the food is so good. That place is Nobu. The lively room is decorated with seaweed-like wall coverings and bamboo poles and has a serene vibe despite the high-energy, high-fashion crowd that packs in nightly for some of famed chef Nobu Matsuhisas simply spectacular sushi and unique brand of Asian-Latin-inspired seafood. Lime, soy, chiles, miso, cilantro, and ginger are flavors frequently employed to accent many of the chefs succulent creations. A signature dish is black cod with miso, and its a signature for good reason. The fish is coated in a sweet miso glaze, and once it enters your mouth, it slowly vaporizes, melting away like ice over a flame. The omakase (chefs choice) menu is an option for those with an adventurous palate. If you can't get a reservation (call well in advance and be prepared for many busy signals), you can always try to sneak in at the sushi bar. Be warned, though; once you eat sushi here, its hard to eat it anywhere else. Japanese menu. Lunch, dinner. Closed holidays. Casual attire. Reservations recommended. **$$$$**

★ **NYONYA.** *194 Grand St, New York (10013). Phone 212/334-3669; fax 212/334-6701. www.penangusa.com.* Serving some of the best Malaysian fare in town, Nyonya is a slightly chaotic spot with a vibrant and authentic menu. While the atmosphere is not exactly elegant (it feels like a diner), this restaurant is an ideal place for a group of friends to sit down to dinner and taste the variety of refreshing Malaysian dishes on the menu. But be sure to come on an empty stomach, as the food is too good not to lick plates clean. Pacific-Rim/Pan-Asian menu. Lunch, dinner. Casual attire. Reservations recommended. No credit cards accepted. **$**

★ ★ ★ **OCEANA.** *55 E 54th St, New York (10022). Phone 212/759-5941; fax 212/759-6076. www.oceanarestaurant.com.* Oceana has been one of New Yorks most lauded seafood spots for more than a decade. Although ten years could have derailed the restaurant, it has stayed a steady course and its mission is as clear as ever: stunning, just-shy-of-swimming seafood tinged with subtle, precise flavors from around the globe. You'll find practically every glorious fish in the sea on the menu, from halibut to tuna, dorade to turbot. Scallops, lobster, and glistening oysters are also on the menu. But there's a nod to the issue of overfishing here as well. Oceana is known for serving only sustainable seafood that is not in danger of becoming extinct. The service is warm and efficient, and the cream-colored, nautical-themed room (portholes dot the walls) is peaceful and comfortable, making Oceana a perennial favorite for power lunchers and pre-theater diners. The wine list is impressive, with a good number of seafood-friendly options at a variety of price points. A signature selection of American caviar from sturgeon, paddlefish, and rainbow trout makes a strong argument for forgoing osetra, beluga, and sevruga. Seafood menu. Lunch, dinner. Closed Sun; holidays. Bar. Jacket required. Reservations recommended. Outdoor seating. **$$$$**

★ ★ **THE ODEON.** *145 W Broadway, New York (10013). Phone 212/233-0507; fax 212/406-1962. www.theodeonrestaurant.com.* Odeon is the original hipster diner. This sleek, retro space, located in TriBeCa, has been serving delicious brasserie fare like perfect frise au lardons, thick and juicy burgers, and steak frites to the masses of fabulous locals for almost two decades. Brunch is a must, but if you are in the area late at night, it is also a hotspot to grab a bite to tide you over until morning. Celebrities of the Robert De Niro caliber are bound to be tucked into booths, so keep an eye out. American, French menu. Lunch, dinner, late-night, brunch. Bar. Children's menu. Casual attire. Outdoor seating. **$$**

★ ★ ★ **OLIVES.** *201 Park Ave S, New York (10003). Phone 212/353-8345; fax 212/353-9592. www.toddenglish.com.* Celebrity chef-restaurateur Todd Englishs New York debut is a branch of his mega-successful Boston-based bistro. Located in the swanky W Union Square Hotel, the inviting and bustling restaurant has an open kitchen, with buttery walls, an open hearth fireplace, and deep, oval banquettes for luxurious relaxation all night long. The menu stars Englishs standard (but delicious) Mediterranean formula: boldly flavored, luxurious dishes that are impeccably prepared and artfully presented on the plate. His signature tart filled with olives, goat cheese, and sweet caramelized onions is a winner, but the menu offers a dish for every taste, including lamb, fish, homemade pastas, and pizzas from the wood oven. Mediterranean menu. Breakfast, lunch, dinner, brunch. Bar. Casual attire. Reservations recommended. **$$$**

★ ★ ★ **ONE IF BY LAND, TWO IF BY SEA.** *17 Barrow St, New York (10014). Phone 212/255-8649; fax 212/206-7855. www.oneifbyland.com.* This classic French restaurant, set in a restored, turn-of-the-century carriage house in Greenwich Village that was once owned by Aaron Burr, is one of New Yorks most cherished spots for romance and other love-related special occasion dining: anniversaries, engagements, and the like. Dark and elegant, the hushed, candlelit, two-story dining room is richly appointed with antique sconces, heavy velvet drapes, oriental carpets, and blazing fireplaces. The menu here is straight-ahead French, with seasonal accompaniments and modern flourishes that add sparkle to the plate. American, continental menu. Dinner. Closed holidays. Bar. Business casual attire. Reservations recommended. **$$$**

★ ★ OSTERIA AL DOGE. *142 W 44th St, New York (10036). Phone 212/944-3643; fax 212/944-5754. www.osteria-doge.com.* Osteria al Doge is a warm restaurant that feels like a seaside town near Venice. The room is decorated warmly with blue, green, and yellow and has a balcony overlooking the main dining area. The kitchen is not breaking culinary ground, but it doesn't really need to. This restaurant is a solid standby for Venetian-inspired seafood dishes like whole branzino with cherry tomatoes, olives, and potatoes; a bouillabaisse-style seafood stew; and house-made trenette pasta with crabmeat. Those craving more substantial meals can dig into veal, poultry, and beef. A good choice for pre-theater dining. Italian menu. Lunch, dinner. Closed Jan 1, Dec 25. Bar. **$$**

★ ★ ★ OSTERIA DEL CIRCO. *120 W 55th St, New York (10019). Phone 212/265-3636; fax 212/265-9283. www.osteriadelcirco.com.* Owned by Sirio Maccioni of Le Cirque 2000 fame, Osterio del Circo carries on his signature brand of homespun hospitality in a more casual, yet no less spirited, atmosphere. The rustic menu of Italian fare includes delicious homemade pastas made from Maccioni Mama Egis lick-your-plate-clean recipes, as well as thin Tuscan-style pizzas, classic antipasti, and signature main courses like salt-baked Mediterranean seabass and brick-pressed chicken. Because it's located near Carnegie Hall and City Center, its a great place to stop by before or after the theater. Italian menu. Lunch, dinner. Closed holidays. Bar. Business casual attire. Reservations recommended. Outdoor seating. **$$$**

★ ★ OTTO. *1 Fifth Ave, New York (10003). Phone 212/995-9559; fax 212/995-9052. www.ottopizzeria.com.* With Otto, celebrity chef Mario Batali has veered into casual territory, offering New Yorkers a taste of an authentic Italian pizzeria in the style of an old-fashioned European train station. Decorated with tall marble bars and dark wainscoting, this high-energy eatery is always filled with a stylish crowd that comes in for wonderful antipasti (the mussels with chile flakes is delish), cant-stop-at-one-slice prosciutto di Parma, and an amazing array of magnificent thin-crust pizzas. Gelatos are extra-special, especially the one made from olive oil that tastes like a very creamy version of heaven. Italian menu. Breakfast, lunch, dinner. Bar. Casual attire. **$$**

★ ★ OUR PLACE. *1444 Third Ave, New York (10028). Phone 212/288-4888; fax 212/288-5231. www.ourplaceuptown.com.* Our Place could be mistaken for just another neighborhood Chinese joint, but once you try their sophisticated cuisine, you'll agree it's a notch or two above. The dining room and staff are so pleasant and professional it's worth dining in, but if you must stay at home it's by far the highest-quality Chinese delivery on the Upper East Side. On weekends, don't miss their dim sum brunch for a fun change from the usual brunch destinations. Chinese menu, Dim Sum. Lunch, dinner, brunch. Closed Thanksgiving. Bar. **$$$**

★ ★ OYSTER BAR. *Grand Central Terminal, Lower Level, New York (10017). Phone 212/490-6650; fax 212/949-5210. www.oysterbarny.com.* Chaos has never been more fun than at the Oyster Bar. Packed to the gills at lunch and dinner daily, this Grand Central Station icon is a famous cocktail spot and one of the best places to gorge on all sorts of seafood. The room makes you feel as though you have gone back in time, with vaulted subway-tiled ceilings and waiters who have been working here since Nixon was in the White House. As for the grub, there are more than two dozen varieties of oysters to choose from, as well as all sorts of chowders, fish sandwiches, fish entres, and, well, you get the idea. If it swims or even sits in water, its on the menu, which changes daily based on market availability. If you're on the run, don't worry: grab a seat at the bar or at one of the old-fashioned lunch counters for a quick lunch. Seafood menu. Lunch, dinner. Closed Sun; holidays. Bar. Casual attire. **$$$**

★ ★ ★ PARK AVENUE CAFE. *100 E 63rd St, New York (10021). Phone 212/644-1900; fax 212/688-0373. www.parkavenuecafe.com.* Sophisticated and savvy New Yorkers head to Park Avenue Café for luxurious lunch meetings, intimate dinners, and large party outings. The warm, blond-wooded room is bright and airy and feels easy and comfortable. The menu of inspired seasonal dishes uses clean, simple flavors that please the palate. Desserts whipped up by famed pastry chef Richard Leach make you feel like a kid again; finger-licking may be necessary. American menu. Lunch, dinner, brunch. Closed Jan 1, Dec 25. Bar. Business casual attire. Reservations recommended. **$$$**

★ ★ PAT PONG. *244 E 13th St, New York (10009). Phone 212/505-6454; fax 212/254-8702.* Located in the East Village, Pat Pong serves a need in the local community for reasonably priced and very tasty Thai cuisine. The restaurant is spare and bright, with a variety of authentic dishes on the menu, including beef, pork, shrimp, and many vegetarian options. Thai menu. Lunch, dinner. Casual attire. Reservations recommended. **$$**

★ ★ ★ PATROON. *160 E 46th St, New York (10017). Phone 212/883-7373; fax 212/883-1118. www.patroonrestaurant.com.* Owner Ken Aretskys popular, clubby, low-lit Patroon is more than a boys' club for juicy steaks. You'll also find women feasting at Patroon, as his American restaurant has that edge that other steakhouses don'ta terrific kitchen with talent for more than just beef (although the beef is fabulous). Of the USDA Prime selections, Steak Diana (named for Aretskys wife) is a house specialty and is prepared tableside with brown butter, shallots, and wine for an arresting visual presentation. The kitchen also gussies things up with hearty dishes like pork shanks, short ribs, and lighter fare like oysters, shrimp, lump crab, and a slew of stunning seafood. A wide rooftop deck makes summertime fun with great grilled fare and chilly cocktails. American menu. Lunch, dinner. Closed Sat-Sun; holidays; also week of Dec 25. Bar. Business casual attire. Reservations recommended. **$$$**

★ PATSY'S PIZZERIA. *2287 First Ave, New York (10035). Phone 212/534-9783.* Folks in New York take their pizza seriously, and with a pizza joint on what seems like every corner, the competition is fierce. But Patsys remains a favorite among pie connoisseurs, consistently serving wonderful pizza with thin, crisp but chewy crusts, with an array of toppings for every appetite. Patsys original location in Harlem is an easy, casual place, with gingham tablecloths, wood floors, and a welcoming, seasoned waitstaff. Italian menu, pizza. Lunch, dinner. Bar. Casual attire. No credit cards accepted. **$$**

★ ★ ★ PAYARD PATISSERIE AND BISTRO. *1032 Lexington Ave, New York (10021). Phone 212/717-5252; fax 212/737-4731. www.payard.com.* Willpower must be left outside of Payard. Aside from the great selection of sandwiches, salads, and Parisian bistro staples served in this lovely, butter-yellow French pastry shop, the desserts are as tempting as they come. But this should come as no surprise considering that the baker in question is Franois Payard, a master of sweets and treats. While lunch and dinner are good choices, Payards afternoon tea is a wonderful way to get acquainted with his talents. French menu. Breakfast, lunch, dinner. Closed Sun; holidays. Bar. Business casual attire. **$$$**

★ ★ PEARL OYSTER BAR. *18 Cornelia St, New York (10014). Phone 212/691-8211; fax 212/691-8210. www.pearloysterbar.com.* Rebecca Charles, who cooked for many years in New England, offers up the steamy, rustic ocean cuisine of the Atlantic Coast to New Yorkers at her newly expanded restaurant, Pearl Oyster Bar. Named for Charles's grandmother, Pearl is known for its luscious lobster rolls, fat steamers, and fresh fried fish sandwiches. While this warm, upscale New England diner-style place is always packed, it is worth the madness. If tables are taken, the warm and friendly bar is a super place to grab a fresh fish bite with a cold ale. Seafood menu. Lunch, dinner. Closed Sun. Bar. Casual attire. **$$$**

★ ★ ★ ★ ★ PER SE. *10 Columbus Cir, New York (10019). Phone 212/823-9335; toll-free 877/825-9335; fax 212/823-9353. www.perseny.com.* Thomas Keller, the chef at Yountville, Californias The French Laundry, calls his new restaurant in the Time Warner Center Per Se because its not exactly The French Laundry, per se. Whats missing is the bucolic setting of the Napa Valley, but in its place are the finest views of any restaurant in Manhattan, a new level of urban sophistication in service and ambience, and food so pure in flavor that every meal is memorable. The best way to enjoy Per Se is to order a tasting menu and then sit back for three hours of culinary epiphanies exemplified by small dishes such as truffles and custard in an eggshell and foie gras accompanied by various salts. The kitchen excels in its use of high-end ingredients, but attention to detail is also evident in the regard given to vegetables and legumes. The quality of dining at Per Se is so superior to what is typical, even in a luxury restaurant, that Keller and his team have established the gold standard. American, French menu. Lunch, dinner. Closed two weeks in July. Bar. Business casual attire. Reservations recommended. **$$$$**

★ ★ ★ PERIYALI. *35 W 20th St, New York (10011). Phone 212/463-7890; fax 212/924-9403. www.periyali.com.* Offering authentic Greek fare in a soothing

Mediterranean-accented setting, Periyali is a wonderful place to experience the delicious seaside cuisine of Athens and beyond. Classics on the menu include octopus marinated in red wine, sautéed sweetbreads with white beans, grilled whole fish, and mezze like taramosalata (caviar mousse), melitzanosalata (grilled-eggplant mousse), and spanakopita (spinach and cheese pie). Periyali has been around for a while, but the restaurants popularity has not waned. You'll find it full of regulars most days at lunch, although at night the pace is calmer, making it a great choice for a leisurely dinner. Greek menu. Lunch, dinner. Closed Sun. Bar. Reservations recommended. **$$$**

★ ★ ★ **PETROSSIAN PARIS.** *182 W 58th St, New York (10019). Phone 212/767-1043; fax 212/245-2812. www.petrossian.com.* Caviar, caviar, and caviar are the first three reasons to head to Petrossian Paris, an elegant restaurant in Midtown with black-mirrored windows, marble walls, and Art Deco leather booths and a menu that includes, you guessed it, caviar. In addition to the great salty roe, served on perfect blinis with creme fraiche, you'll find an ultra-luxurious brand of Franco-Russian cuisine that includes classics like borscht, assorted Russian zakuska (tapas) like smoked salmon (served with cold shots of vodka—ask for Zyr, one of the best from Russia), and other glamorous plates, including foie gras prepared several different ways and, of course, beef Stroganoff. But don't miss the caviar. Continental, French menu. Lunch, dinner, brunch. Bar. Business casual attire. Reservations recommended. **$$$**

★ ★ ★ ★ **PICHOLINE.** *35 W 64th St, New York (10023). Phone 212/724-8585; fax 212/875-8979.*Located on Manhattans Upper West Side, Picholine is a great choice for dinner if you happen to be attending an opera, ballet, or play at Lincoln Center. Don't feel like you need to be heading over to Lincoln Center in order to dine here, though; chef/owner Terrance Brennans lovely, serene restaurant is easy to enjoy all by itself, which is probably why Picholine is often pleasantly packed with a savvy set of New Yorkers at both lunch and dinner, with no ticket stubs to be found. The menu changes with the seasons, and the chef uses organic and local ingredients as much as possible. Picholine is a safe bet for both adventurous diners and conservative eaters and for vegetarians and meat lovers alike. The menu runs the gamut from the exotic to the familiar, offering a wide selection of dishes from the land and the sea. Folks with a weakness for cheese are in the right place, as well. The cheese list (not to mention the great wine list) is one of the best in the city, and room must be saved to indulge in several types. The wine list, though seriously priced, offers a variety of selections to match all courses. French, Mediterranean menu. Lunch, dinner. Closed holidays. Bar. Jacket required. Reservations recommended. **$$$**

★ **PIE BY THE POUND.** *124 Fourth Ave, New York (10003). Phone 212/475-4977. www.piebythepound.com.* At Pie by the Pound, a slick little pizza joint in the East Village, pizza by the slice is taboo. Ditto for pizza by the round pie. The pizzas at Pie are long and rectangular, with scissors used to slice off just the amount you want. You can have your very own pizza party by selecting a variety of pizzas topped with fresh and tasty ingredients like crispy potato, tallegio, and walnuts or pillowy mozzarella, tomato, and basil. Once you make your selections, your slices are weighed, and you pay by the pound, not by the slice. Pizza. Lunch, dinner, late-night, brunch. Children's menu. Casual attire. **$**

★ **PIG HEAVEN.** *1540 Second Ave, New York (10028). Phone 212/744-4887; fax 212/744-2853. www.pigheaven.biz.* The name may be intimidating, but they're not guilty of false advertising one bit. The spare ribs, roast pork, and suckling pig are some of the best found outside Chinatown (the roast duck is fantastic, too). And with the delightful and contemporary decor, Pig Heaven is just as much for dining out as for dining in. Chinese menu. Lunch, dinner. Bar. Casual attire. Outdoor seating. **$$**

★ ★ **PING'S.** *22 Mott St, New York (10013). Phone 212/602-9988; fax 212/602-9992.* Be sure to pack your sense of culinary adventure when you go to Ping's, a Chinatown favorite for dim sum and gorgeous live seafood cooked up to order. The room is usually filled to capacity with Chinese families and lawyers on break from arguing at the nearby courthouses, but do not be deterred by the crowds. The steamed pork buns alone make Ping's worth the wait. Chinese, seafood menu. Lunch, dinner. Casual attire. **$$**

★ ★ **PIPA.** *38 E 19th St, New York (10003). Phone 212/677-2233; fax 646/602-3811.* Pipa, a lively and sultry restaurant and tapas bar in the Flatiron District, serves up some of the most delicious modern Spanish food in the city in a setting worthy of a designer's dream. The eclectic decor of the candlelit dining room, which features antiques, exposed brick walls, and crystal chandeliers should come as no surprise, as the restaurant occupies the ground floor of ABC Carpet & Home, one of the citys swankiest furniture and accessories stores, making it the perfect shopping pit stop. Spanish, tapas menu. Lunch, dinner. Bar. Casual attire. Reservations recommended. **$$$**

★ ★ **POETESSA.** *92 Second Ave, New York (10003). Phone 212/387-0065; fax 212/387-9942.* Italian menu. Lunch Fri-Sun, dinner, late-night, brunch. Bar. Casual attire. Outdoor seating. **$$**

★ ★ ★ **POST HOUSE.** *28 E 63rd St, New York (10021). Phone 212/935-2888. www.theposthouse.com.* New York has many steakhouses, and The Post House is one of the power lunch clubs favorites. The comfortable dining room, with a long bar, has an easy feel thanks to polished parquet floors, wooden wainscoting, and leather armchair seating. The menu sports a super selection of salads, signature appetizers like cornmeal-fried oysters, and a shimmering raw bar in addition to entrées like grilled chicken, rack of lamb, and meat-eater delights like prime rib, filet mignon, and the signature Stolen Cajun Rib Steak. An extensive wine list emphasizes California wines and some rare gems from Burgundy and Bordeaux. Steak menu. Lunch, dinner. Closed Jan 1, Dec 25. Bar. Business casual attire. Reservations recommended. **$$$**

★ ★ **PRAVDA.** *281 Lafayette St, New York (10012). Phone 212/226-4944; fax 212/226-5052. www.pravdany.com.* Vodka is the main theme at Pravda, a sexy, subterranean bar and lounge in SoHo. As for the menu, it pretty much matches what might be served at a Russian vodka bar: caviar, blinis, assorted smoked fish, and black breadperfect nibbles for late-night revelers of the waif, supermodel, or straight-ahead European expatriate variety. Pravda is dark and luxuriously decadent, and its all about the vodka. Eastern European menu. Dinner, late-night. Closed Sun July-Aug. Bar. Casual attire. **$$**

★ ★ **PROVENCE.** *38 MacDougal St, New York (10012). Phone 212/475-7500; fax 646/602-9772. www.provence.citysearch.com.* Located on a sleepy block in SoHo, Provence offers a taste of this sunny French region right here in the concrete jungle. It is a wonderfully charming restaurant, decorated with antiques and fresh flowers and warmed by delicate, soft lighting. In summer, don't miss out on the charming garden. Even in winter, this place is a simple delight, offering homey French dishes like steak au poivre, bouillabaisse, and bourrides. The menu is authentic Provenal, and all meals start with warm, crusty bread and are complemented by a terrific wine list. French menu. Lunch, dinner, brunch. Closed holidays. Casual attire. Reservations recommended. **$$**

★ ★ **PRUNE.** *54 E 1st St, New York (10003). Phone 212/677-6221; fax 212/677-6982.* Prune is one of those neighborhood restaurants that immediately seduces you. The distressed décorvery Left Bank chicis irresistible. The American bistro menu, devised by chef/owner Gabrielle Hamilton, is a list of guilty pleasures, from her signature Triscuit and canned sardine appetizer to more labor-intensive dishes like slow-cooked lamb shanks to her leftover dish of bread heels and pulled chicken. This is one of the most popular restaurants in New York for a reason. Although the tables are too close together and the waits are too long, the food is delicious, and the vibe is casual but fierce. Brunch is a must, even if you go just for the Bloody Marys. American menu. Dinner, brunch. Bar. Casual attire. Reservations recommended. Outdoor seating. **$$**

★ ★ **RADIO PERFECTO.** *190 Avenue B, New York (10009). Phone 212/477-3366; fax 212/477-4336. www.radioperfecto.com.* This hip, retro eatery in the East Village is known for its terrific juicy rotisserie chicken, but it also keeps hordes of locals happy with its spicy blend of Mexican fusion cuisine like steak with tequila mushroom sauce and kickin chile-rubbed pulled pork. This is a lively joint to hang with friends. Lines can get long, so be prepared to waitwith a killer margarita in hand. American menu. Dinner, Sun brunch. Bar. Children's menu. Casual attire. Reservations recommended. Outdoor seating. **$$**

★ ★ **RAGA.** *433 E 6th St, New York (10009). Phone 212/388-0957. www.raganyc.com.* Located on Curry Row in the East Village, Raga sets itself apart with its dark, sexy décor and truly innovative Indian menu. While you'll find straight-ahead classics, the kitchen serves a few more contemporary plates as well. Vegetable curries share menu space with ambitious dishes like roasted lamb sirloin with cranberry beans, mussels steeped in lemongrass, and wildly flavorful house samosas. The kitchen is not afraid of being fresh and innovative, making eating here an exciting and delicious experience. French, Indian menu. Dinner, late-night. Closed Mon. Casual attire. Reservations recommended. Outdoor seating. **$$**

★ ★ **RAIN.** *100 W 82nd St, New York (10024). Phone 212/501-0776; fax 212/501-9147. www.rainrestaurant.com.* Nestled in Manhattan's Upper West Side among brownstone apartments and upscale shops, Rain is a sleek and inviting Pan-Asian spot with exposed brick walls, polished wood floors, and candlelit tables. Menu selections feature delightful choices like crispy shrimp spring rolls, pad Thai, and grilled N.Y. sirloin while desserts like fried coconut ice cream and sweet sticky rice tempt. Pacific-Rim/Pan-Asian menu. Dinner. Closed Dec 25. Bar. Children's menu. Reservations recommended. **$$**

★ ★ **RAOUL'S.** *180 Prince St, New York (10012). Phone 212/966-3518; fax 212/966-0205. www.raouls.com.* Raouls is one of the most French and most romantic restaurants in the city. Opened in the mid-1970s, this intimate little bistro has managed to retain its popularity, meaning that it is constantly packed, so reservations are a must. (Specify which room you'd like to be seated inthe downstairs main dining room is dark and sultry, while the upstairs has a bit more light and feels more civilized.) Seafood dishes are especially good here, although peppercorn steak frites will not disappoint carnivores. House pt and frise with cambozola cheese are also lovely menu items. French menu. Dinner, late-night. Bar. Casual attire. Reservations recommended. Outdoor seating. **$$$**

★ ★ **RED CAT.** *227 Tenth Ave, New York (10011). Phone 212/242-1122; fax 212/242-1390. www.theredcat.com.* Jimmy Bradley, chef/owner of The Red Cat, is one of those restaurateurs who knows exactly what New Yorkers are looking for in a dining experience: a cool, hip scene? Check. An innovative and exciting menu? Check. A solid international wine list with lots by the glass and a tempting selection of sexy house cocktails? Check, check. Indeed, Bradley delivers it all at his West Chelsea haunt for inspired Mediterranean-accented fare set in a New England-chic space trimmed with white-and-red wainscoting, hurricane lamps, and deep, long banquettes. This is one place you will want to return to, even if its just to figure out how to replicate his formula in your own town. American menu. Dinner. Closed Jan 1, Dec 24-25. Bar. Casual attire. Reservations recommended. **$$**

★ ★ **REDEYE GRILL.** *890 Seventh Ave, New York (10019). Phone 212/541-9000; fax 212/245-6840. www.redeyegrill.com.* You can't miss the bright red entrance to Redeye Grill, which sits just 50 feet from Carnegie Hall. Its name comes from the dreaded overnight flight linking the West and East coasts, and that link is exactly what inspires its seafood-heavy menu as well as its design. The soaring dining room features Mission-style furnishings and is anchored by a shrimp, sushi, and smoked fish bar, flanked by giant bronze shrimp sculptures. Nightly jazz on the balcony keeps diners toes tapping. American, Seafood menu. Lunch, dinner, brunch. Bar. Business casual attire. Reservations recommended. **$$$**

★ ★ ★ **REMI.** *145 W 53rd St, New York (10019). Phone 212/581-4242; fax 212/581-7182.* The cuisine of Venice is the focus of the menu at Remi, an airy, lofty restaurant decorated with ornate Venetian blown-glass lights and murals of the Italian citys romantic canals. Remi has long been a favorite for local businesspeople to dish over lunch, but also makes a terrific choice for drinks, dinner, or a visit before or after the theater. The kitchens specialty is brilliant handmade pastas, but the menu also features contemporary Mediterranean takes on fish, beef, poultry, and game. A *ciccetti* menu of Venetian tapas is also available at the bar for nibbling while working through the restaurants impressive Italian wine list. Italian menu. Lunch, dinner. Closed holidays. Bar. Business casual attire. Reservations recommended. Valet parking. Outdoor seating. **$$$**

★ ★ **RENE PUJOL.** *321 W 51st St, New York (10019). Phone 212/246-3023; fax 212/245-5206. www.renepujol.com.* Ren Pujol is a theater district charmer, offering Gallic cuisine updated with a modern sensibility. The restaurant is warm and convivial, with butter-colored walls, a brick hearth, and snug, cozy tables. The menu offers refined takes on French dishes that are hearty and savory, like the lamb shanks with white beans, a house specialty. French menu. Lunch, dinner. Closed Sun-Mon; holidays. Jacket required. **$$$**

★ **REPUBLIC.** *37 Union Sq W, New York (10003). Phone 212/627-7172; fax 212/627-7010. www.thinknoodles.com.* Located on Union Square West, Republic is perpetually packed with trendy locals who seek out the restaurants signature Asian noodle dishes. Be ready to sit on communal picnic tables and shout above the din, but the decibels and the less-than-comfy seating vanish when the steaming bowls arrive, brimming with Thai, Japanese, and other East Asian recipes for all sorts of delicious noodles. Asian menu. Lunch, dinner. Closed Memorial Day, Dec 25. Bar. Casual attire. Outdoor seating. **$**

★ ★ ★ **RIINGO.** *206 E 45th St, New York (10017). Phone 212/867-4200. riingo.com.* Marcus Samuelsson, the heartthrob, boy-wonder chef behind the very popular contemporary Scandinavian spot Aquavit (see), is the man behind Riingo, a white-hot Asian restaurant in Midtowns Alex hotel. Japanese for apple, Riingo is a sleek and sexy bilevel space featuring dark ebony woodwork and bamboo floors, and luxurious banquettes that swallow you up in warmth. Its tough not to feel fabulous here, seated in magnificent surroundings while nibbling on Samuelssons inventive brand of Japanese-American fare. This stylish restaurant comes equipped with the requisite swanky lounge, an extensive house-infused sake list, full sushi bar, and look-at-me crowds. Riingo is the perfect apple for the Big Apple. American, Japanese, sushi menu. Lunch, dinner, brunch. Business casual attire. Valet parking. **$$$**

★ ★ **ROCK CENTER CAFE.** *20 W 50th St, New York (10020). Phone 212/332-7620; fax 212/332-7677. www.rockcentercafeny.com.* Located in Rockefeller Center, this American restaurant is an ideal place to relax under blue summer skies with cool cocktails, or to grab a seat and watch the ice skaters slip, slide, and crash all winter long under the twinkling Christmas tree. The Rock Center Café is one of those places that never fails to satisfy with a broad menu of terrific salads, sandwiches, burgers, and generously sized seasonal American entres. American, Italian menu. Breakfast, lunch, dinner, brunch. Outdoor seating. **$$**

★ ★ ★ **ROSA MEXICANO.** *61 Columbus Ave, New York (10023). Phone 212/977-7700; fax 212/977-7575. www.rosamexicano.com.* One of the first restaurants to introduce New Yorkers to authentic Mexican cuisine, Rosa Mexicano was founded by chef Josefina Howard in the early '80s and today remains an essential stop for anyone who craves strong, chilly, perfectly mixed margaritas (frozen or on the rocks), and bright, fresh, vibrant bowls of guacamole mixed tableside to your desired level of heat (mild to scorching). The menu is a beautiful tribute to the regional home-cooking of Mexico—steamy pork tamales; chicken in a rich, savory blanket of mole; terra-cotta cazuelas brimming with shrimp, tomatoes, garlic, and chiles; and a long-time entrée signature—budin Azteca, a wonderful tortilla casserole with layers of shredded chicken and cheese. The decor is just as colorful as the food, with bright hand-painted tiles and a two-story tile wall of water which descends over small white ceramic divers into a shallow pool, recalling the renowned divers of Acapulco. Mexican menu. Lunch, dinner, brunch, late-night. Bar. Casual attire. Reservations recommended. Outdoor seating. **$$**

★ ★ ★ **RUTH'S CHRIS STEAK HOUSE.** *148 W 51st St, New York (10019). Phone 212/245-9600; fax 212/245-0460. www.ruthschris.com.* Like many diners in Midtown, this New Orleans-based steak palace is an out-of-towner. Steak menu. Lunch, dinner. Closed Jan 1, Dec 25. Bar. Children's menu. Business casual attire. Reservations recommended. **$$$**

★ ★ ★ **SAKAGURA.** *211 E 43rd St, New York (10017). Phone 212/953-7253; fax 212/557-5205. www.sakagura.com.* At this subterranean hideaway in Midtown, you'll find one of the most extensive sake collections in the city, as well as a talented knife-wielding team of sushi chefs turning out some of the most delicious sashimi you've ever tasted. (There is no sushi here, as it is forbidden to serve rice with sake.) Sakagura may be a bit tough to find—you enter through the lobby of an office building and follow a small gold sign that points you toward this buried basement space. But once you have found it, you will be hesitant to leave. The space is very Zen/minimalist and is leanly decorated with bamboo plants and paper lanterns. Between the soothing atmosphere and the potent sake, you'll sleep like a baby after your evening here. Japanese menu. Lunch, dinner. Business casual attire. Reservations recommended. **$$$**

★ ★ ★ **SAN DOMENICO.** *240 Central Park S, New York (10019). Phone 212/265-5959; fax 212/399-5672. www.sandomenicony.com.* Tony Mays San Domenico is like an Armani suit—classic, elegant, and perfect for every occasion. Located on Central Park South with views of the horse-drawn carriages lined up along the edge of Central Park just outside, San Domenico is one of citys most well regarded restaurants for sophisticated, contemporary Italian cuisine. Pasta, fish, and meat dishes manage to feel rustic yet updated, as the chef teams new-world ingredients and twists with authentic old-world recipes and style. An impressive wine list from the motherland of Italy enriches every bite. Italian menu. Lunch, dinner, Sun brunch (fall-spring). Closed Jan 1, Thanksgiving, Dec 25. Bar. Jacket required. Reservations recommended. **$$$**

★ ★ ★ **SAN PIETRO.** *18 E 54th St, New York (10022). Phone 212/753-9015; fax 212/371-2337. www.sanpietro.net.* San Pietro is one of the restaurants where you walk in a customer and leave a part of the family. Located on a busy Midtown street, San Pietro is owned and run by the three Bruno brothers, who grew up on a family farm along the Amalfi Coast in the southern Italian region of Campagna. At San Pietro, the brothers pay homage to their homeland by serving traditional dishes—antipasti, pasta, poultry, fish, veal, and beef—accented with seasonal ingredients and lots of Italian charm. The wine list contains a knockout selection of southern Italian wines to complete the experience. Southern Italian menu. Lunch, dinner. Closed Sun; holidays. Bar. Business casual attire. Reservations recommended. Credit cards accepted. **$$$**

★ ★ **SARABETH'S (WEST).** *423 Amsterdam Ave, New York (10024). Phone 212/496-6280; fax 212/787-9655. www.sarabeth.com.* Sarabeths is known for some of the most delicate and delicious pastries, scones, and muffins in the city, so brunch here is a must for anyone who craves buttery cakes with coffee in the morning. Aside from the pastry arena, Sarabeths offers a wonderful brunch of wild berry pancakes, brioche French toast, and plates of fluffy eggs, as well as a seasonal American menu for dinner nightly. Don't forget to pick up some baked goods for the next morning on your way out. American menu. Breakfast, lunch, dinner, brunch. Closed Dec 25. Casual attire. Reservations recommended. Outdoor seating. **$$**

★ ★ **SARDI'S.** *234 W 44th St, New York (10036). Phone 212/221-8440; fax 212/302-0865. www.sardis.com.* This icon in the theater district, established in 1921, is one of those old-time favorites that seems to stay the same year after year. For some places, though, no change is a good thing. Sardis still serves as a cafeteria of sorts for many theater celebrities, and still offers hearty Italian signatures like stuffed cannelloni (veal, beef, or sausage), serviceable antipasti (this is not the restaurants strong suit), and solid simple dishes like rotisserie roasted chicken and grilled filet mignon. Yes, the brilliant baked Alaska is still on the menu, and its still a monstera tasty one at that. Italian menu. Lunch, dinner, late-night. Closed Mon. Bar. Casual attire. Reservations recommended. **$$$**

★ ★ **SAVORE.** *200 Spring St, New York (10012). Phone 212/431-1212; fax 212/343-2605. www.savoreny.com.* Located on a lovely block in SoHo, Savore is a quiet little gem that offers Tuscan dining in a relaxed and authentic countryside setting. At Savore, you'll feel like you are dining in Europe. Meals are not rushed, service is leisurely, and the food is simple and deliciousthe menu features earthy pastas, grilled whole fish, braised meats, and fresh salads. All you crave after dinner is a ticket to Italy. Italian menu. Lunch, dinner. Closed Dec 25. Bar. Casual attire. Outdoor seating. **$$$**

★ ★ ★ **SAVOY.** *70 Prince St, New York (10012). Phone 212/219-8570; fax 212/334-4868. www.savoynyc.com.* Peter Hoffman, the chef and an owner of Savoy, a comfortable, urban dining spot in SoHo, has been a proponent of Greenmarket cooking style for more than ten years. You'll find him with his tricycle-pulled wagon at the local farmers' markets several times a week, picking produce for his inspired menu of global faredishes taken from Spain, Latin America, France, Morocco, and Greece, as well as Americas various regionsbrought to life with simple, brilliant ingredients. The intimate dining room upstairs features an open fireplace where many of Hoffmans rustic dishes are cooked right before your eyes in the blazing hearth. American, Mediterranean menu. Lunch, dinner. Closed holidays. Bar. Casual attire. Reservations recommended. **$$$**

★ ★ **SCHILLER'S LIQUOR BAR.** *131 Rivington St, New York (10002). Phone 212/260-4555; fax 212/260-4581. www.schillersny.com.* This hipster haunt from Keith McNally, the king of the distressed vintage Parisian brasserie, Schiller's Liquor Bar is bursting at its authentic subway-tiled seams with the most up-to-the-minute stars and scene-seekers. Its safe to say that this formerly grungy corner of Rivington and Norfolk has never seen so much Prada and Paul Smith. American menu. Breakfast, lunch, dinner, late-night, brunch. Bar. Casual attire. **$$**

★ ★ **SEA GRILL.** *19 W 49th St, New York (10020). Phone 212/332-7610; fax 212/332-7677. www.theseagrillnyc.com.* The Sea Grill is home to some of the most delicious seafood in the city. This lavish, ocean-blue restaurant dressed up in aquamarine and off-white tones sports a slick bar and prime wintertime views of ice skaters twirling (and crashing) on the rink under the twinkling Christmas tree at Rockefeller Plaza. Summertime brings alfresco dining and lots of icy cool cocktails to pair up with veteran chef Ed Browns fantastic contemporary seafood menu. Crab cakes are his signature, and they deserve to be ordered at least once. Other dishessalmon, cod, halibut, skate, you name itare just as special, as Brown infuses his cooking with techniques and flavors from Asia and the world at large. Seafood menu. Lunch, dinner. Closed Sun; holidays. Bar. Casual attire. Reservations recommended. Valet parking. Outdoor seating. **$$$**

★ ★ **SERAFINA FABULOUS PIZZA.** *210 W 55th St, New York (10021). Phone 212/734-2676; fax 212/315-4312. www.serafinarestaurant.com.* At this mini-chain of velvet-roped pizza joints, you can start the evening off with a simple meal of tasty Italian fare like wood-fired pizzas, salads, antipasti, pasta, seafood, and meat and then stay and hang out in the bar to sip cool cocktails and listen to the DJs spinning tunes. Serafina is casual but hip, with a generally young and gorgeous European crowd that comes in more for the see-and-be-scene vibe than the terrific pizzas. Italian menu. Lunch, dinner. Casual attire. **$$$**

★ **SERENDIPITY 3.** *225 E 60th St, New York (10022). Phone 212/838-3531; fax 212/688-4896. www.serendipity3.com.* Most restaurants rest on their savory menus. Not at Serendipity 3, a loud, kid-in-a-candy-store sort of a place that is fashioned after a vintage soda parlor. Decorated with Tiffany lamps and stained-glass windows, with a fun boutique up front, this is one restaurant where desserts rule the roost. Sure, you can grab sandwiches, burgers, salads, and the like, but really, this is one place to have dessert for dinner. Monster-sized sundaes, gooey chocolate layer cake, mountain-size cheesecake, and the signature frozen hot chocolatea birdbath-sized chocolate seducerare great dinner dishes. Who needs protein? American menu. Lunch, dinner. Closed Dec 25. Reservations recommended. **$$**

★ ★ ★ **SHUN LEE PALACE.** *155 E 55th St, New York (10022). Phone 212/371-8844; fax 212/752-1936. www.shunleepalace.com.* The lovely, swirling décor of the Adam Tihany-designed dining room should tell you that something special awaits you at Shun Lee Palace. The large space is perfect for business luncheons or family get-togethers. Restaurateur Michael Tong's extensive haute Chinese menu makes this spot a New York favoriteso much so that a second location has opened on the West Side. Guest chefs visit frequently from Hong Kong, and the special prix fixe lunch is a deal. Chinese menu. Lunch, dinner. Closed Thanksgiving. Bar. Business casual attire. Reservations recommended. **$$$**

★ **SIAM GRILL.** *592 Ninth Ave, New York (10036). Phone 212/307-1363; fax 212/265-5383. www.siamgrillnyc.com.* At this warm and cozy Thai grill in the theater district, you'll find that it's easy to kick back and relax for dinner. The service is pleasant and prompt, and the menu is filled with tasty traditional Thai dishes like pad Thai and Bammee curry and house specialties like crispy duck in red curry and steamed fish in ginger and bean threads. The prices seem high for the fare, but considering its location, they aren't out of line. Thai menu. Lunch, dinner. Closed holidays. **$$**

★ ★ ★ **SMITH & WOLLENSKY.** *797 Third Ave, New York (10022). Phone 212/753-1530; fax 212/751-5446. www.smithandwollensky.com.* The original after which the national chain was modeled, this 390-seat, wood-paneled dining room is known for sirloin steaks and filet mignon, but also offers lamb and veal chops. Sides are huge and straightforward, with the likes of creamed spinach and hash browns. Good wines and personable service complete the experience. Steak menu. Lunch, dinner. Closed Jan 1, Thanksgiving, Dec 25. Bar. Casual attire. Reservations recommended. Outdoor seating. **$$$**

★ ★ **SOBA-YA.** *229 E 9th St, New York (10003). Phone 212/533-6966. www.sobaya-nyc.com.* Located in the East Village, Soba-Ya is a tiny, serene space that is the neighborhoods perennial favorite for Japanese noodle dishes. Noodles come both hot and cold, plus you can watch the soba and udon noodles being cut and hung to dry like in an old laundry house. Although the noodles make the best impression, the rest of the menu deserves attention as well, like tempura vegetables with spicy curry sauce and an excellent assortment of sakes, organized on the menu to pair up with the food. Japanese menu. Lunch, dinner. Casual attire. **$$**

★ ★ ★ **SPARKS STEAK HOUSE.** *210 E 46th St, New York (10017). Phone 212/687-4855; fax 212/557-7409. www.sparkssteakhouse.com.* This temple of beef is one of the standard spots for meat-seekers in New York City. The cavernous dining room has a classic old-world charm to it, with oil paintings, etched glass, and dark wood paneling, and the large bar feels like home as soon as you wrap your fingers around the stem of your martini glass. Sparks is a serious American chophouse, and only serious appetites need apply for entry. There are no dainty portions here, so come ready to feast on thick, juicy steaks, burgers, roasts, racks, and fish (if you must). Steak menu. Lunch, dinner. Closed Sun; holidays. Bar. Business casual attire. Reservations recommended. **$$**

★ ★ **SPICE MARKET.** *403 W 13th St, New York (10014). Phone 212/675-2322; fax 212/675-4551. www.jean-georges.com.* Spice Market, the first project from dynamic chef duo Jean-Georges Vongerichten and Gray Kunz, is like something out of the Kasbahan authentic jewel-toned Moroccan wonderland with raw, color-stained wood panels and benches flown in from India and waitresses decked out in saris and backless silk halter tops. As for the fare, you are in for magic on the plate. Out of the 60-foot-long open kitchen (complete with its own sultry food bar) comes fragrant, exotically spiced, family-style dishes inspired by Morocco and the Far Eastsatays and summer rolls, dosa and pho, and fragrant pulled-oxtail hot pots with coriander chutney and kumquats. Filled with the most fabulous crowds reclining on stunning banquettes in the amber glow of candles and lanterns, Spice Market is easily a contender for New Yorks hottest and tastiest scene. Pacific-Rim/Pan-Asian menu. Lunch, dinner. Bar. Casual attire. Reservations recommended. Outdoor seating. **$$$**

★ STAGE DELI. *834 Seventh Ave, New York (10019). Phone 212/245-7850; fax 212/245-7957. www.stagedeli.com.* Stage Deli is one of New Yorks most favored between-the-bread restaurants, offering lovely sandwiches crafted from rye bread, pastrami, tongue, brisket, mustard, mayo, and half-sour pickles, as well as comforting standards like chicken noodle soup. This is a hectic and bustling deli, with cafeteria-style tables, a tiny, eat-at bar, and a ton of energy that exemplifies life in the Big Apple. Deli menu. Breakfast, lunch, dinner. Bar. Casual attire. **$$**

★ ★ STEAK FRITES. *9 E 16th St, New York (10003). Phone 212/463-7101; fax 212/627-2760. www.steakfritesnyc.com.* Located down the block from the Union Square Greenmarket, Steak Frites is the perfect rest stop after shopping for the seasons best produce. Open for Saturday and Sunday brunch, it is popular on weekends, when locals grab outdoor tables and people-watch. At night, the restaurant is lively and has a rich European flair, decorated with vintage posters and long leather banquettes. This is a fun restaurant to hang out in and just have drinks, but its also an ideal spot to hunker down over a dinner of the signature steak frites with a bold red wine. The menu also offers a great selection of fish, pastas, and salads. French menu. Lunch, dinner, brunch. Closed Jan 1, Dec 25. Bar. Casual attire. Outdoor seating. **$$**

★ ★ ★ STRIP HOUSE. *13 E 12th St, New York (10003). Phone 212/328-0000; fax 212/337-0233. www.theglaziergroup.com.* If you can get over the fact that you're eating in a restaurant called Strip House (no dollar bills needed here other than to tip the folks in coat check), you will be in for some of the best beef in the city. The low-lit restaurant, swathed in deep red fabric and decorated with old black-and-white photos of burlesque stars, has a great vibe in a bordello-chic sort of way. It is sexy; tawdry it is not. The kitchen does a great job with its selection of steakhouse favorites (a half-dozen steaks and chops cooked to chin-wiping perfection) and adds some inspired sides, like truffle-scented creamed spinach, goosefat potatoes, and mixed heirloom tomatoes in season. Steak menu. Dinner. Bar. Business casual attire. Reservations recommended. **$$$**

★ ★ SUEÑOS. *311 W 17th St, New York (10011). Phone 212/243-1333; fax 212/243-3377. www.suenosnyc.com.* Walk by Sueños and you will most likely spy a crowd of people gathered on the sidewalk, looking through a large rectangular window, drooling. The porthole gives sidewalk voyeurs a bird's-eye view of the kitchen, where Mexican-cuisine diva (chef/owner) Sue Torres executes orders of her addictive modern regional Mexican cuisine. There are fat, steamy empanadas filled with fava beans and drunken goat cheese, heavenly pork tamales steamed in banana leaves and plated in a fiery lather of ancho beurre blanc, and tortilla-crusted Chilean sea bass with a chile rajas tamale. The restaurant is lively and hip, decorated in bright colors and filled with the sweet smell of fresh corn tortillas, which are made by hand in the main dining room. The margaritas are a must. Mexican menu. Dinner, brunch. Bar. Casual attire. Reservations recommended. **$$$**

★ ★ ★ ★ SUGIYAMA. *251 W 55th St, New York (10019). Phone 212/956-0670; fax 212/956-0671. www.sugiyama-nyc.com.* If you're searching for an oasis of calm in the center of Midtown Manhattan, head to Sugiyama and your blood pressure will drop upon entry. The dining room is warm and tranquil and has a Zen air to it. The spare, warm room fills up quickly at lunch with strikingly well-appointed businesspeople on expense accounts. But even filled to capacity, it maintains a soothing energy. Sugiyamas specialties are prix fixe kaiseki-style meals. Those who are not well suited to culinary adventures should search for calm somewhere else. Its not worth the visit to order only sushi. Kaiseki are multicourse meals that were originally part of elaborate, traditional Japanese tea ceremonies, but at Sugiyama they have evolved into a procession of precious little plates, holding petite portions that are as tasty as they are appealing to the eye. Lead by head chef and owner Nao Sugiyama, the chefs here have a talent for presentationevery dish is a work of art. Meals are tailored to suit your appetite and preferences and start with sakizuke (an amuse bouche) followed by a seasonal special (zensai), soup, sashimi, sushi, salad, and beef or seafood cooked over a hot stone (ishiyaki), among other sumptuous Japanese delicacies. Soups are Nao's specialty, and warm broths have never been so dynamic and exciting. Dining at Sugiyama is an unexpected adventure. The chef's enthusiasm and energy are contagious, and you can't help departing with a giant grin knowing that you've just had an experience like no other. Japanese menu. Dinner. Closed Sun-Mon. Casual attire. Reservations recommended. **$$$**

★ ★ ★ **SUMILE.** *154 W 13th St, New York (10011). Phone 212/989-7699; fax 212/989-0421. www.sumile.com.* There are some restaurants that try to please everyone, and then there are restaurants that dance to the beat of their own drum. Sumile, a spare, windowless, and soothing Zen space, is of the latter category. Filled with leggy lovelies reclining on pillowed banquettes next to assorted men in waiting, Sumile feels like a space out of a movie set with star-quality guests to match. The menu is a celebration of Japanese ingredients and contrasting textures, temperatures, and flavors. Josh DeChellis, the young avant-garde chef, dares to be true to his own culinary vision in the face of populist trends. His menu features innovative plates like sweet braised gulf shrimp in horseradish consomm, poached hamachi with pickled melon and nori salt, and seared duck in a frothy foie gras mousse blended with aged sake. This is not a place for timid eaters. Bring your sense of adventure, or stay home. Japanese menu. Dinner. Closed Sun-Mon. Bar. Casual attire. Reservations recommended. Outdoor seating. **$$$**

★ ★ **SURYA.** *302 Bleecker St, New York (10014). Phone 212/807-7770; fax 212/337-0695. www.suryany.com.* Surya is a sleek, low-lit restaurant and bote that offers the most stylish setting in the city for contemporary Indian cuisine. The lounge is a chic place to stop in for a cocktail, like the house tajmapolitan (a cosmopolitan with cinnamon). After that drink, you might want to move into the sultry dining room for dinner (beef-free), featuring a wonderful list of inspired vegetable dishes like birianyi—basmati rice perfumed with sweet spices and served with raitaand urulakilangu katrika koze, spiced potatoes and eggplant served with paratha (griddle-fried bread). In warm weather, you can dine outside in the restaurant's lovely leafy garden. Indian menu. Lunch, dinner. Bar. Casual attire. Reservations recommended. Outdoor seating. **$$**

★ ★ ★ **SUSHI OF GARI.** *402 E 78th St, New York (10021). Phone 212/517-5340.* Sushi of Gari is one of those spots frequented by New Yorkers in the know. Nobus divine, sure, but Sushi of Gari stays true to Japanese fare rather than infusing Latin ingredients. The problem is that, like Nobu, Sushi of Gari is always packed to capacity with sushi-seeking trendsetters, and at times, its hard to hear yourself order, let alone have a conversation. But try to keep your ears tuned to other tables as they order, since many regulars come in and order amazing dishes that are not on the menu. Either eavesdrop or feel free to ask your neighbors for their recommendationsNew Yorkers love to talk about food. If you're sticking to the basics, the raw fishlike the kanpachi (Japanese yellowtail) and the toro (fatty tuna)is silky and luscious. Japanese, sushi menu. Dinner. Closed Mon. Casual attire. Reservations recommended. **$$$**

★ **SWEET-N-TART.** *20 Mott St, New York (10013). Phone 212/964-0380; fax 212/571-7696. www.sweetntart.com.* In the heart of Chinatown, you will find Sweet and Tart, an authentic Hong Kong-style Chinese restaurant that offers enough variety to please an army of eaters. The space has three levels: the upper level is crowded with families, while the ground floor soda-fountain diner is more for Gen Xers. The menu sticks to impeccably prepared Cantonese classics and delicious dim sum, and also offers dishes from Thailand and Japan. Chinese, Dim Sum menu. Lunch, dinner, late-night. Casual attire. **$**

★ ★ ★ **TABLA.** *11 Madison Ave, New York (10010). Phone 212/889-0667; fax 212/889-0914. www.tablany.com.* Tabla is the Indian-inspired culinary star from restaurant tour de force Danny Meyer (Gramercy Tavern, Union Square Cafe—see both). Chef/partner Floyd Cardoz cleverly peppers his menu with the intoxicating flavors of Indiasweet and savory spices, chutneys, meats from a tandoor oven, and soft rounds of pillowy, handmade breads. The result is a delicious introduction to the sumptuous flavors of India, not a crash course that hits you over the head. The stunning, bilevel dining room has an almost mystical quality to it, with its muted jewel-toned accents, rich redwood floors, and soaring windows that face Madison Square Park. American, Indian menu. Lunch, dinner. Bar. Reservations recommended. Outdoor seating. **$$$**

★ ★ ★ **TAMARIND.** *41-43 E 22nd St, New York (10010). Phone 212/674-7400; fax 212/674-4449. www.tamarinde22.com.* The fragrant cuisine of India is served at Tamarind, an elegant restaurant in the Flatiron District with a lively bar and a serene and beautiful dining room. The attraction here is a menu of dishes showcasing perfect-pitch flavorsspicy, sweet, sour, and hot play together wonderfully on the plate. The kitchen serves stunning samosas, naan, pouri, chutneys, and traditional curries, alongside more contemporary dishes that play to the sophisticated New Yorker crowd. Indian menu. Lunch, dinner. Bar. Jacket required. Reservations recommended. **$$$**

★ ★ TASTING ROOM. *72 E 1st St, New York (10003). Phone 212/358-7831; fax 212/358-8432. www.thetastingroomnyc.com.* The Tasting Room, a charming shoebox-sized East Village restaurant, features a seasonal American menu with dishes in two sizestasting (appetizer size) and sharing (entrée size), allowing you to sample many of the gifted chefs wonderful seasonal dishes. Chef/owner Colin Alevras is dedicated to shopping from local organic producers, and his passion for local products extends to the all-American, 300-bottle wine list. Colins wife, Renee, runs the petite dining room, making you feel like you are at home in an instant. The Tasting Room is truly a jewel of a spot, perfect for intimate evenings. American menu. Dinner. Closed Sun-Mon; also one week in summer and one week in winter. Casual attire. Reservations recommended. **$$$**

★ ★ TAVERN ON THE GREEN. *Central Park at W 67th St, New York (10023). Phone 212/873-3200; fax 212/580-4265. www.tavernonthegreen.com.* Ornate, over the top, and brash, Tavern on the Green is the Cher of the New York restaurant scene. Like the one-name singer, its still popular after all these years, its had a lot of work done, and its tacky but loved anyway. If you're in the mood for a serviceable meal and extra-high prices, go for it; otherwise, you may want to steer clear of this tourist trap. The food is straightforward and fine, and the view of Central Park is romantic, but the restaurant has morphed into more of a theme park than a serious dining destination. American, Continental menu. Lunch, dinner, brunch. Bar. Children's menu. Casual attire. Reservations recommended. Valet parking. Outdoor seating. **$$$**

★ ★ ★ TERRACE IN THE SKY. *400 W 119th St, New York (10027). Phone 212/666-9490; fax 212/666-3471. www.terraceinthesky.com.* Set high in the sky on the top floor of a prewar Upper West Side building, Terrace in the Sky offers breathtaking panoramic views of the city and a rich selection of eclectic fare to match. The haute menu of seared sweetbreads, foie gras torchon, smoked salmon, lobster, and caviar make dining here seem very posh. If you have love on your mind, this is *the* place to go. Terrace in the Sky is ideal for romance with its elegant linen-topped tables, soft candlelit ambience, and views that are truly beyond compare. French, Mediterranean menu. Lunch, dinner, brunch Sun. Closed Mon. Business casual attire. Reservations recommended. Valet parking. Outdoor seating. **$$$**

★ ★ ★ TOCQUEVILLE. *1 E 15th St, New York (10003). Phone 212/647-1515; fax 212/647-7148. www.tocquevillerestaurant.com.* Owned by husband Marco Moreira (chef) and wife Jo-Ann Makovitsky (front-of-house manager), Tocqueville is a little slice of paradise in the form of a restaurant. This is the sort of place that will calm you from the moment you walk through the tall blond doors into the petite, elegant room warmed with golden light, butter-yellow walls, and stunningly appointed tabletops. The cuisine is as magical as the space. Chef Moreira offers impeccably prepared, inventive New American fare crafted with care from pristine seasonal ingredients hand-picked from local farmers and the nearby Greenmarket. Intimate and soothing, Tocqueville is a perfect spot for those seeking quiet conversation and luxurious food. American, French menu. Lunch, dinner. Bar. Business casual attire. **$$$**

★ ★ ★ TOWN. *15 W 56th St, New York (10019). Phone 212/582-4445. www.townnyc.com.* Located in the swanky Chambers hotel (see), Town is an oasis of hipness, featuring a white-hot, low-lit lounge and bar with some of the most inventive and well-made cocktails in the city. Move downstairs to the sexy, oversized-banquetted, David Rockwell-designed dining room, and you'll find it filled edge to edge with high-powered media and fashion folks digging into chef/owner Geoffrey Zakarians brilliant high-styled, modern American fare. American menu. Lunch, dinner, Sun brunch. Bar. Casual attire. Reservations recommended. **$$$**

★ ★ ★ TRATTORIA DELL'ARTE. *900 Seventh Ave, New York (10019). Phone 212/245-9800; fax 212/265-3296. www.trattoriadellarte.com.* Trattoria dellArte is the perfect choice if Carnegie Hall or a performance at City Center is on your list. Owned by Shelly Fireman, this lively and popular restaurant offers easy, approachable Italian cuisine in a comfortable, neighborly setting with bright colored walls and wicker chairs. The scene here is festive, so expect it to be loud with diners who are clearly enjoying the generous plates of homemade pastas, selections from the spectacular antipasti bar, seafood, and meats, all prepared in simple Mediterranean style. Italian menu. Lunch, dinner, brunch, late-night. Closed Thanksgiving, Dec 25. Bar. Children's menu. Casual attire. Reservations recommended. Outdoor seating. **$$$**

★ ★ ★ **TRIBECA GRILL.** *375 Greenwich St, New York (10013). Phone 212/941-3900; fax 212/941-3915. www.tribecagrill.com.* This New York icon from super-restaurateur Drew Nieporent (Nobu, Montrachetsee both) and partner Robert De Niro is a shining example of what a restaurant should offer. First, hospitalitythe service is warm, attentive, and knowledgeable without an ounce of pretension. Second, atmospherethe Grill is a comfortable, urban dining room with exposed brick walls, oil paintings by Robert De Niro, Sr., and a magnificent cherry wood, wraparound bar that looks like it fell off the set of *Cheers.* Third, foodthe kitchen features an approachable, contemporary, seasonal American menu with dishes for every type of diner, from wild foodies to simple roast chicken eaters. Finally, wine-TriBeCa Grill offers an impressive and diverse wine program led by David Gordon, who has earned the restaurant much praise and admiration near and far. TriBeCa Grill, which is more than 15 years old, remains a winner on all counts. American menu. Lunch, dinner, late-night, Sun brunch. Closed holidays. Bar. Children's menu. Casual attire. Reservations recommended. Outdoor seating. **$$$**

★ ★ **TURKISH KITCHEN.** *386 Third Ave, New York (10016). Phone 212/679-6633; fax 212/679-1830. www.turkishkitchen.com.* Be prepared to enjoy your food at this bustling Murray Hill outpost for authentic Turkish fare. The restaurant specializes in the well-spiced cuisine of this beautiful country, with dishes of tender lamb, beef, and chicken, as well as lots of warm bread for ripping off and dipping in assorted mezze. Stained a deep red, the walls and the Arabic décor give the room a warm feeling. The only drawback is the service, which is very friendly and very knowledgeable, but can be slow. Middle Eastern menu. Lunch, dinner, Sun brunch. Children's menu. Casual attire. Reservations recommended. **$$**

★ ★ **TUSCAN SQUARE.** *16 W 51st St, New York (10020). Phone 212/977-7777; fax 212/977-3144. www.tuscansquare.citysearch.com.* Restaurateur Pino Luongo is a native Italian whose airy, comfortable Tuscan Square restaurant brings his idyllic homeland to life, warding off all cases of homesickness here in the big, boisterous city. Located in Rockefeller Center, Tuscan Square is a great place to relax and unwind at lunch or dinner. It offers a taste of the Italian countryside with a sunny, frescoed dining room and impressive antipasti and homemade pastas, as well as more robust regional specialties that match up well with the deep selection of Chianti, Barbaresco, Barolo, montepulciano, Orvieto, and pinot grigio. Italian menu. Lunch, dinner. Closed Sun; holidays. Casual attire. **$$$**

★ ★ ★ **UNION SQUARE CAFE.** *21 E 16th St, New York (10003). Phone 212/243-4020; fax 212/627-2673. www.unionsquarecafe.com.* Union Square Café is the first restaurant from the man who brought New York Gramercy Tavern, Eleven Madison, Tabla, and Blue Smoke (see all): Danny Meyer. This bright, warm, cheery, bilevel restaurant and bar is still packing in locals and wooing tourists with Meyers signature hospitality, chef Michael Romanos divine New American fare, and an award-wining wine list. While the menu changes with the seasons and often features produce from the Greenmarket across the way, the chefs succulent signature grilled tuna burger should not be considered optional. If a table doesn't seem possible (reservations are tough to score), a seat at the bar is a fabulousand more authentic New Yorkeralternative. American menu. Lunch, dinner. Closed holidays. Bar. Casual attire. Reservations recommended. **$$$**

★ ★ ★ **VERITAS.** *43 E 20th St, New York (10003). Phone 212/353-3700; fax 212/353-1632. www.veritas-nyc.com.* If a passion for wine runs through your veins, then a visit to Veritas should be considered mandatory. At this stylish Gramercy Park gem, you'll find a magnificent wine list that, at last count, was over 3,000 bottles long. Despite its intimidating length, wine neophytes should not be deterred. There is no fear factor here. The staff is friendly and knowledgeable and all too happy to help you find a suitable wine to match your meal and budget. Bottles range from $20 to $6500 for a bottle of 1865 Chateau Latour. While wine is the primary draw for Veritas, the food gives the wine a run for its money. It is specifically created with wine in mind and perfectly complements the beverage of focus. The full menu is available at the sleek bar, which is a nice option if you want a quick bite and some (or lots of) wine. Whether you're seated at the bar or tucked into a snug and intimate booth, the restaurants contemporary American menu is easy to love. Robust flavors, seasonal ingredients, and a light hand in the kitchen make for magical meals. Veritas is a perfect place to explore wine and food alike. American menu. Dinner. Bar. Business casual attire. Reservations recommended. **$$$$**

★ ★ **VESPA CIBOBUONO.** *1625 2nd Ave, New York (10028). Phone 212/472-2050; fax 212/472-7566. www.barvespa.com.* Italian menu. Lunch, dinner. Closed holidays. Bar. Casual attire. Outdoor seating. **$$**

★ ★ **VICTOR'S.** *236 W 52nd St, New York (10019). Phone 212/586-7714; fax 212/333-7872. www.victorscafe.com.* Long before the mojito became as popular as the cosmopolitan, these minty rum drinks from Cuba were the cocktail of choice at Victors, a popular theater district restaurant that feels like an elegant throwback to Havana, decorated with tall palm trees and filled with the rhythmic sounds of Cuban jazz. Aside from the terrific cocktails, Victors is a festive place to feast on top-notch contemporary Cuban cuisine, like roasted marinated pork with rice and beans, picadillo, fried plantains, and tostones. Cuban menu. Lunch, dinner. Bar. Casual attire. Reservations recommended. **$$$**

★ **VIRGIL'S REAL BARBECUE.** *152 W 44th St, New York (10036). Phone 212/921-9494; fax 212/921-9631. www.virgilsbbq.com.* While everyone has an opinion about barbecue, most will agree that Virgils is a super choice. Manners are thrown to the wind at Virgils, a sprawling hog pit where ribs, juicy chicken, tomato-based pulled pork, Memphis pit beans, and spicy collard greens are gobbled up in record time. The noise can be deafening, but there really isn't time to talk once the food arrives. The warm, fluffy buttermilk biscuits usually quiet everyone down rather quickly. American menu. Lunch, dinner, late-night. Closed Dec 25. Bar. Children's menu. Casual attire. **$$**

★ ★ ★ **VONG.** *200 E 54th St, New York (10022). Phone 212/486-9592; fax 212/980-3745. www.jean-georges.com.* When Jean-Georges Vongerichten, Alsatian-born wonder chef, opened a Thai restaurant called Vong, people werent sure what to make of it. But doubts were soon dispelled as diners began to experience his exciting and exotic French riffs on fiery Thai classics, incorporating spices and flavors of the East with a New York sensibility. The restaurant feels like a wild and mystical night in the Orient, decorated with long, deep banquettes covered with silk pillows in brilliant jewel tones, walls painted crimson red and accented with gold leaf, and a long table showcasing a Buddha altar. Its a journey for all the senses. Thai, French menu. Lunch, dinner. Closed holidays. Bar. Casual attire. Reservations recommended. Outdoor seating. **$$$**

★ ★ ★ **WALLSE.** *344 W 11th St, New York (10014). Phone 212/352-2300; fax 212/645-7127. www.wallserestaurant.com.* Enter this charming restaurant, tucked in a sleepy corner of the West Village, and you are instantly transported to Vienna. Decorated with contemporary art and filled with close, square tables; antique furnishings; deep blue banquettes; and a long, romantic stretch of rich mahogany bar (where the cocktails are stellar), chef Kurt Gutenbrunners Wallse is a personal and delicious ode to the hearty yet delicate cuisine of his homeland, Austria. The thin, golden-crusted Wiener schnitzel should not be missed. A terrific selection of Austrian wines complements the meal, and a nice slice of strudel will send you off on a sweet note. Continental menu. Dinner, brunch. Bar. Casual attire. Reservations recommended. **$$$**

★ ★ ★ **WATER CLUB.** *500 E 30th St, New York (10016). Phone 212/683-3333; fax 212/696-4009. www.thewaterclub.com.* Special occasions were made for The Water Club, a lovely restaurant with romantic, panoramic views of the East River. The shiplike space features soothing, nightly live piano and an intimate, clubby lounge, perfect for relaxing before or after dinner. While poultry and beef are on the menu, The Water Club is known for its seafood; in addition to a gigantic raw bar, you'll find an impressive selection of lobster, scallops, cod, tuna, salmon, and whatever else looks good at the fish markets. On a sunny day, you can't beat brunch out on the deck with a fiery Bloody Mary in hand, watching the ships go by, feeling like you're far away from it all. American, Seafood menu. Lunch, dinner, brunch. Bar. Business casual attire. Reservations recommended. Valet parking. Outdoor seating. **$$$$**

★ ★ ★ **WD-50.** *50 Clinton St, New York (10002). Phone 212/477-2900. www.wd-50.com.* Using his kitchen as a laboratory, chef Wylie Dufresne is intent on creating his own category of American cuisine. By utilizing a multitude of ingredients and culinary techniques, nothing is as it seems at wd-50, but everything is delicious. The restaurant offers both a tasting and an la carte menugo expecting the unexpected. The cocktail and wine list are as equally impressive and adventurousexpect to sample lots of lesser-known grape varietals from all over the globe. American menu. Dinner. Bar. Business casual attire. Reservations recommended. **$$$**

★ ★ ★ **WOO LAE OAK.** *148 Mercer St, New York (10012). Phone 212/925-8200; fax 212/925-8232. www.woolaeoaksoho.com.* If you're searching for a lively spot to gather a large group for some very tasty and authentic Korean food, Woo Lae Oak is the place. This sleek, cavernous multiplex-style space offers some of the best Korean barbecue in the city. Guests grill marinated meats and seafood to a savory char on wicked-cool smokeless grill tables. The food is traditional; novices in the arena of Korean fare should seek assistance from one of the restaurants trs chic yet very friendly waiters. Meltingly creamy black cod simmered in a sweet-hot, garlicky soy sauce is a one of the restaurants most famous plates, but there isn't a bad choice on the menu. Korean menu. Lunch, dinner. Bar. Casual attire. Reservations recommended. **$$$**

★ ★ **ZARELA.** *953 Second Ave, New York (10022). Phone 212/644-6740; fax 212/980-1073. www.zarela.com.* This colorful and spirited Mexican eatery in Midtown is renowned for its killer margaritas (be careful with these) and delicious regional Mexican fare. Loud and lively, the bar is always packed with a rowdy afterwork crowd that lingers well into the evening. Upstairs, in the more intimate yet still boisterous dining room, you'll feast on some of chef/owner Zarela Martinezs vibrant dishes, from rich enchiladas to luxuriously savory moles. Mexican menu. Lunch, dinner. Closed Sat-Sun; holidays. Bar. Casual attire. **$$**
D

★ ★ **ZOE.** *90 Prince St, New York (10012). Phone 212/966-6722; fax 212/966-6718. www.zoerest.com.* Thalia and Stephen Loffredo opened Zo smack in the heart of SoHo more than ten years ago, and they have managed to maintain its chic yet comfortable American bistro vibe and, better yet, to keep the kitchen inspired. The menu is still in sync with the demanding and fickle New York palate, offering creative, sophisticated American standards painted with global accents and seasonal flourishes and an extensive, heavily American wine list. There is also a terrific cocktail list and a tempting menu of bar snacks to match, all of which makes Zo an ideal restaurant for brunch, lunch, dinner, or just wine and a bite at the inviting bar. American menu. Lunch, dinner, brunch. Closed Mon; also July 4, Dec 25. Bar. Casual attire. **$$$**

Newburgh (B-2)

See also Fishkill, Goshen, Middletown, Monroe, New Paltz, Poughkeepsie, Stony Point, West Point

Settled 1709
Population 28,259
Elevation 139 ft
Area Code 845
Zip 12550
Information Chamber of Commerce of Orange County, Inc, 47 Grand St; phone 845/567-6229 (Monroe office)
Web Site www.orangetourism.org

This manufacturing city was General George Washington's headquarters from April 1, 1782, until August 18, 1783. He announced the end of the Revolutionary War here, and officially disbanded the army.

Newburgh is the small urban center of eastern Orange County. West Point, the US Military Academy, lies 12 miles south of town (see).

What to See and Do

New Windsor Cantonment State Historic Site. *374 Temple Hill Rd (Hwy 300), Vails Gate (12584). 2 miles S of NY Thrwy exit 17. Phone 845/561-1765. www.nysparks.com.* (1782) The Cantonment was the last winter encampment (1782-1783) of the Continental Army. Featured are demonstrations of 18th-century military life, including muskets and artillery, woodworking, blacksmithing, and camp life activities. Exhibit buildings and picnic area. (Mid-Apr-Oct, Wed-Sat, also Sun afternoons) Special events. **FREE**

Storm King Art Center. *Old Pleasant Hill and Orrs Mill rds, Mountainville (10953). 6 miles S via Hwy 32. Phone 845/534-3115. www.stormking.org.* A 400-acre sculpture park and museum with permanent collection of 20th-century sculpture. Guided tours. (Apr-mid-Nov, daily). **$$$**

Washington's Headquarters State Historic Site. *84 Liberty St, Newburgh (12550). Phone 845/562-1195. www.nysparks.com.* Jonathan Hasbrouck house (1750); General George Washington's headquarters for 16 1/2 months at the close of the Revolutionary War (April 1782-August 1783). Dutch vernacular fieldstone house furnished as headquarters. Adjacent museum has permanent and changing exhibits, audiovisual program. Tours, special events. (Mid-Apr-Oct, Wed-Sun; inquire for winter schedule) **$$**

Limited-Service Hotels

★ HOWARD JOHNSON. *95 Hwy 17K, Newburgh (12550). Phone 845/564-4000; toll-free 800/446-4656; fax 845/564-0620. www.hojo.com.* 74 rooms, 2 story. Complimentary continental breakfast. Check-in 3 pm, check-out noon. Outdoor pool. Tennis. **$**

★ ★ QUALITY INN. *90 Hwy 17K, Newburgh (12550). Phone 845/564-9020; fax 845/564-9040. www.choicehotels.com.* 122 rooms, 2 story. Pets accepted; fee. Check-in 3 pm, check-out noon. Restaurant, bar. Fitness room. Outdoor pool. Airport transportation available. **$**

★ ★ RAMADA INN. *1289 Hwy 300, Newburgh (12550). Phone 845/564-4500; fax 845/564-4524. www.ramada.com.* 164 rooms, 2 story. Complimentary full breakfast. Check-out noon. Restaurant, bar. Fitness room. Outdoor pool. Airport transportation available. **$**

Restaurants

★ ★ BEEBS. *30 Plank Rd, Newburgh (12550). Phone 845/568-6102.* American menu. Lunch, dinner, brunch. Bar. Casual attire. Reservations recommended. **$$**

★ CAFE PITTI. *40 Front St, Newburgh (12550). Phone 845/565-1444.* Italian menu. Lunch, dinner. Bar. Casual attire. Reservations recommended. Outdoor seating. **$**

★ ★ COSIMO'S ON UNION. *1217 Hwy 300 Union Ave, Newburgh (12550). Phone 845/567-1556; fax 845/567-9246. www.cosimosonunion.com.* Italian menu. Lunch, dinner. Closed Easter, Thanksgiving, Dec 25. Bar. Children's menu. Casual attire. Outdoor seating. **$$**

★ ★ IL CENA'COLO. *228 S Plank Rd, Newburgh (12550). Phone 845/564-4494.*Italian menu. Lunch. Bar. Business casual attire. Reservations recommended. **$$$**

Niagara Falls (D-2)

See also Buffalo, Lockport, Niagara-on-the-Lake

Settled 1806
Population 55,593
Elevation 610 ft
Area Code 716
Information Convention & Visitors Bureau, 310 4th St, 14303; phone 716/285-2400 or toll-free 800/421-5223
Web Site www.nfcvb.com

Higher falls exist, but Niagara puts on a first-class performance. On the border with Canada, the American Falls are 184 feet high, the Canadian Horseshoe, 176 feet. The two are separated by Goat Island. For several hours in the evening, the beauty of the falls continues in a display of colored lights playing over the water.

Originally, after the glacial period, the falls were 7 miles downstream at the Niagara escarpment. Rocks have crashed from top to bottom, causing the falls to retreat at a rate averaging about 1 foot per year.

With a flow of more than 200,000 cubic feet of water per second, Niagara has a power potential of about 4 million horsepower. Electrical production is controlled by agreements between the United States and Canada so that each receives a full share while the beauty of the cataracts is preserved.

The industries nourished by these waters include aircraft, aerospace equipment (Bell), abrasives (Carborundum), food products, paper, chemicals, and a tremendous tourist business. (For border crossing regulations, see MAKING THE MOST OF YOUR TRIP.)

What to See and Do

Aquarium of Niagara. *701 Whirlpool St, Niagara Falls (14301). Phone 716/285-3575; toll-free 800/500-4609. www.aquariumofniagara.org.* More than 1,500 aquatic animals from around the world, including sharks, otters, piranha, endangered Peruvian penguins, and exotic fish. Free outdoor sea lion pool with sessions every 90 minutes; shark feedings on alternate days. (Daily 9 am-4 pm; summer until 7 pm; closed Thanksgiving, Dec 25) **$$**

Artpark. *450 S 4th St, Lewiston (14092). 7 miles N on Robert Moses Pkwy. Phone 716/754-4375; toll-free 800/659-7275. www.artpark.net.* A 150-acre state park and summer theater devoted to the visual and performing arts. Events at the 2,300-seat theater with lawn seating include musicals, classical concerts by the Buffalo Philharmonic Orchestra, dance programs, and jazz and pop music concerts.

Castellani Art Museum. *Niagara University,5795 Lewiston Rd, Niagara Falls (14109). Directly across from Devil's Hole State Park. Phone 716/286-8200. www.niagara.edu/cam.*The more than 3,000 artworks at this museum range from the Hudson River School to contemporary sculpture; first-rate Folk Arts Program, including exhibits, artist demonstrations, and performances.(Tues-Sat 11 am-5 pm; Sun 1-5 pm; closed holidays) **FREE**

Devil's Hole State Park. *Robert Moses Parkway N, Niagara Falls (14305). 1 mile N of Whirlpool State Park. Phone 716/284-5778.* View of the lower Whirlpool rapids and Power Authority generating plant, with a walkway leading along the Niagara River. Fishing; nature trails; picnicking. **FREE**

Fort Niagara State Park. *Hwy 18F, Youngstown (14174). 14 miles N on Robert Moses Pkwy. Phone 716/745-7273. www.nysparks.state.ny.us/parks.* Swimming pool with water slide (fee), fishing, boating (two launches); hiking trails, playing fields, tennis, cross-country skiing, and sledding. (Daily; closed Jan 1, Thanksgiving, Dec 25) Here is

Old Fort Niagara State Historic Site. *Robert Moses Pkwy, Youngstown (14174). 18 miles N on Robert Moses Pkwy. Phone 716/745-7611.* This restored fort, which dates to 1679 and has been held by France, Great Britain, and the United States, played an important role in the French and Indian War and in the War of 1812. The buildings on the site are the oldest in the Great Lakes region and include the "French Castle," constructed by the French in 1726. Exhibits, living history programs, re-enactments; picnicking. (Daily from 9 am; closing time varies by season) **$$**

Four Mile Creek State Park Campground. *Hwy 18 and Lake Rd, Youngstown (14174). On Lake Ontario. Phone 716/745-7273. www.nysparks.state.ny.us/parks.* Fishing, hiking, playground; 266 tent and trailer sites. (Mid-Apr-Oct)

Martin's Fantasy Island. *2400 Grand Island Blvd, Grand Island (14072). S on I-190 in Grand Island. Phone 716/773-7591. www.martinsfantasyisland.com.* An 80-acre family theme park with more than 100 attractions, including a water park, thrill rides, children's rides, a western town, and live shows. (Mid-June-early Sept, daily; also weekends mid-May-mid-June) **$$$$**

★ **Niagara Falls State Park.** *4 miles W of I-190 via Robert Moses Pkwy. Phone 716/278-1770. www.niagarafallsstatepark.com.* This park, the oldest state park in the nation, provides many views of Niagara Falls and the rapids above and below the cataract from Prospect and Terrapin points, Luna Island, and many other locations. It was designed by Frederick Law Olmsted, who also laid out New York's Central Park. Fishing; nature and hiking trails. Restaurant. Visitor center; recreation programs. **$$** In the park are

Boat ride.*Maid of the Mist.* *Phone 716/284-4233.* *Maid of the Mist* debarks from the base of the Observation Tower at Prospect Point and takes passengers close to the base of the American Falls, then to Horseshoe Falls. (June-early Sept: daily, approximately every 30 minutes) Fee includes the use of waterproof clothing. **$$$**

Cave of the Winds. *2153 Juron Dr, Niagara Falls (14304). Phone 716/278-1770.* Elevators from Goat Island take you 175 feet deep into the Niagara Gorge. From the elevator, walk over a series of wooden walkways to Hurricane Bridge, where you'll feel the spray at the base of the American Falls. Waterproof garments (including shoes) are supplied. (Mid-May-mid-Oct: daily) **$$**

Goat Island. *Phone 716/278-1762.* Goat Island separates the Canadian Horseshoe and American Falls. Drives and walks in a 70-acre park offer the closest possible views of the falls and upper rapids. Picnic areas; restaurant, snack bar. Smaller Luna Island and Three Sister Islands can be reached by footbridge. (Daily)

Niagara Gorge Discovery Center. *Robert Moses Parkway, Niagara Falls (14301). Across from the Niagara Aquarium. Phone 716/278-1780.* Showcases geological formation and history of the falls. Audiovisual presentation. Rock garden, gorge overlook. (Memorial Day-Oct: daily; rest of year: Thurs-Sun; closed Jan 1, Thanksgiving, Dec 25) **$**

Niagara Scenic Trolley. *139 Niagara St, Niagara Falls (14303). Phone 716/278-1796.* This three-hour guided train ride travels from Prospect Point to Goat Island and returns has seven stopovers, including the Cave of the Winds, the *Maid of the Mist,* Terrapin Point, and Three Sister Islands. Ride all day for one price. (Apr-Oct: daily) **$**

Niagara Falls State Park

Niagara Falls is almost an American tourist clich. But, it's still one of the most spectacular natural sites in the country, and Niagara Falls State Park (established in 1885 as Niagara Reservation State park)—the oldest state park in the United States—offers a wonderful walking opportunity. In warmer months, tickets can be purchased for a ride on the Viewmobile, which tours the entire park, so that at any given point walking can be abandoned for a respite ride.

Start at the Visitor Center to obtain maps of the park, watch a wide-screen film about the falls, and purchase a Niagara Master Pass. The Pass allows savings on all the major attractions in the park, including the Observation Tower, the geological museum, a guided walking tour, the boat tour, and more. From the Visitor Center walk toward the river to the Observation Tower (closed in winter). The tower rises some 200 feet above the base of the gorge and presents terrific views of all three falls—Horseshoe, American, and Bridal Veil. The glass elevator ride is fun, too. The elevator goes down to the dock from which the *Maid of the Mist* boat tour departs. This narrated 30-minute boat ride, in operation since 1846, goes to the base of American Falls and into the ring of Horseshoe Falls.

From the Tower, turn right and follow the pedestrian walkway to the edge of American Falls. Follow the walkway upriver and cross the Goat Island Pedestrian Bridge. On Goat Island are picnic grounds, a restaurant, a gift shop, and snack bars. Follow the path to the Bridal Veil Falls overlook. Here, too, is the Cave of the Winds attraction, a boardwalk that leads right into the Bridal Veil Falls themselves. Continue around the downriver point of the island to Terrapin Point. This overlook sits just a few yards from the top of Horseshoe Falls and reveals the full power of the rushing water. From there, walk up the side of the island and follow the pedestrian bridge onto Three Sisters Island. This trio of small islands yields an excellent view of the river's upper rapids.

Coming off Three Sisters, either turn right and continue the Goat Island loop, or turn left and follow the midisland pathways back to the pedestrian bridge. Continue back past the Visitor Center and onto Main Street. A short way up Main stands the Aquarium of Niagara (701 Whirlpool St). The aquarium houses an international collection of fish, a unique colony of endangered Peruvian penguins, and California sea lions that perform every 90 minutes. Leaving the aquarium, cross the highway via the pedestrian bridge, and visit The Schoellkopf Geological Museum (Robert Moses Parkway at Main Street), which offers a multifaceted look at the Niagara Gorge and its 12,000-year-old waterfalls. To reap the fullest experience, leave the museum along the riverside walkway and stroll across Rainbow Bridge, which leads to Canada. The bridge yields another spectacular view of all the falls.

Prospect Park Visitor Center. *Easter Pkwy and Flatbush Ave, Niagara Falls. Phone 716/278-1796.* Information desk, video displays; wide-screen theater featuring movie *Niagara Wonders;* Great Lakes Garden. (Summer: daily 8 am-10:15 pm; winter: daily 8 am-6:15 pm) **FREE**

Prospect Point Observation Tower. *Prospect Park, Robert Moses Pkwy and Niagra Falls, Niagara Falls (14303). Phone 716/278-1770.* The 282-foot tower rises adjacent to American Falls. Elevator to gorge below and *Maid of the Mist.* (Daily) **$**

Niagara Power Project Visitor Center. *5777 Lewiston Rd, (Hwy 104), Lewiston (14092). 4 1/2 miles N of the falls. Phone 716/286-6661; toll-free 866/697-2386. www.nypa.gov/vc/niagara.htm.* Glass-enclosed observation building with outdoor balcony; view of Niagara River Gorge, hydroelectric projects on both sides of river; displays explain power generation; Father Louis Hennepin mural; museum shows development of power and industry at Niagara Falls with hands-on displays. (Daily 9 am-5 pm; closed holidays) **FREE**

Niagara's Wax Museum of History. *303 Prospect St, Niagara Falls (14303). At Old Falls St. Phone 716/285-1271.* Life-size wax figures depict history of the area; historic items. (Daily) **$$**

Reservoir State Park. *Hwys 31 and 265 and Military Rd, Ogdensburg (14303). 4 miles NE at junction Hwy 31, 265. Phone 716/278-1762. nysparks.state.ny.us.*

Overlook at the Robert Moses Power Plant Reservoir. Tennis, picnicking, playground, ball field, cross-country skiing, snowmobiling. Household pets allowed caged or on a leash not more than 6 feet; not allowed in buildings or on improved walkways and boardwalks. (Daily)

Whirlpool State Park. *Robert Moses Pkwy and Niagara Rapids Blvd, Niagara Falls (14305). 3 miles N of falls on Robert Moses Pkwy. Phone 716/278-1770.* Splendid view of the famous Niagara River Gorge whirlpool and rapids. Ongiara Trail, nature and hiking trails, picnicking, playground. (Daily) **FREE**

Limited-Service Hotels

★ ★ BEST WESTERN SUMMIT INN. *9500 Niagara Falls Blvd, Niagara Falls (14304). Phone 716/297-5050; toll-free 800/404-8217; fax 716/297-0802. www.bestwestern.com.* You won't miss any of the comforts of home at the Best Western Summit Inn. Rooms at this hotel near downtown Niagara Falls feature satellite television, alarm clocks, hair dryers, coffee and tea makers, ironing boards, and high-speed Internet access. And just like mom, they don't want your busy day to start on an empty stomach; a complimentary continental breakfast of fresh fruits, cereals, bagels, muffins, danish, and coffee, tea, juice, and milk is included in your stay. 88 rooms, 2 story. Pets accepted, some restrictions; fee. Complimentary continental breakfast. Check-in 3 pm, check-out 11 am. High-speed Internet access, wireless Internet access. Fitness room. Indoor pool. **$**

★ COMFORT INN. *1 Prospect Pointe, Niagara Falls (14303). Phone 716/284-6835; toll-free 800/284-6835; fax 716/284-5177. www.choicehotels.com.* This hotel is literally at the point of the American side of the falls, and you can hear the roar of the rushing water as you approach the entrance. Like any Comfort Inn, this outlet in the chain doesn't offer a lot of amenities, but its terrific location and no-frills prices make it worth consideration if you're in town to see one of America's most amazing natural wonders. 118 rooms, 6 story. Complimentary continental breakfast. Check-in 3 pm, check-out 11 am. High-speed Internet access, wireless Internet access. Restaurant. Fitness room. **$**

★ ★ FOUR POINTS BY SHERATON. *114 Buffalo Ave, Niagara Falls (14303). Phone 716/285-2521; toll-free 800/325-3535; fax 716/285-0963. www.fourpoints.com/niagarafalls.* The kids will beg you to stay at this downton Four Points by Sheraton, which features a jungle gym and Niagara's largest game room. But with its great location, clean and comfortable rooms, and many services and amenities, you won't need any persuading. 189 rooms, 7 story. Check-in 3 pm, check-out noon. Restaurant, bar. Children's activity center. Fitness room. Indoor pool, whirlpool. **$**

★ ★ QUALITY INN. *7708 Niagara Falls Blvd, Niagara Falls (14304). Phone 716/283-0621; toll-free 800/508-8981; fax 716/283-2121. www.qualityinnfalls.com.* With the Prime Outlet Mall, The Falls, and other attractions just a short distance away, the Quality Inn is a convenient choice for guests traveling to Niagara Falls. 94 rooms, 2 story. Check-in 2 pm, check-out 11 am. Wireless Internet access. Restaurant, bar. Indoor pool. **$**

Full-Service Resort

★ ★ HOLIDAY INN. *100 Whitehaven Rd, Grand Island (14072). Phone 716/773-1111; fax 716/773-1229. www.holidayinn. com.* This hotel is located 12 miles from Niagara Falls and 10 miles from Buffalo. It offers an indoor/outdoor pool, children's pool, game room, tennis court, and more. A golf course and marina are adjacent to the hotel. 261 rooms, 6 story. Pets accepted. Check-in 3 pm, check-out noon. High-speed Internet access. Restaurant, bar. Children's activity center. Fitness room. Indoor pool, outdoor pool, children's pool, whirlpool. Tennis. **$**

Full-Service Inn

★ ★ ★ THE RED COACH INN. *2 Buffalo Ave, Niagara Falls (14303). Phone 716/282-1459; toll-free 800/282-1459; fax 716/282-2650. www.redcoach.com.* Modeled after the Old Bell Inn in England, the Red Coach Inn has been welcoming guests to historic Niagara Falls since 1923. It is situated just 1,500 feet from the falls and near many other attractions as well. The English Tudor house has antique furniture, floral curtains and linens, whirlpool tubs, and amazing views in its guest accommodations. Most suites have kitchens and fireplaces. Continental breakfast is included and champagne, fruit, and cheese await you upon arrival. The main dining room has a roaring fire in winter, and in summer the flower-filled patio is a popular spot for a snack. 19 rooms. Complimentary

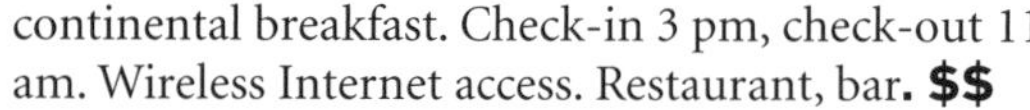

continental breakfast. Check-in 3 pm, check-out 11 am. Wireless Internet access. Restaurant, bar**. $$**

Restaurants

★ COMO RESTAURANT. *2220 Pine Ave, Niagara Falls (14301). Phone 716/285-9341; fax 716/285-9352. www.thecomorestaurant.com.* This little gem of a restaurant is located in Niagara Falls' Little Italy. Family owned and operated since 1927, the Como Restaurant is popular with locals who come for traditional and tasty Italian fare. If you're eating on the run, the on-site deli offers a selection of pasta dinners and luncheon plates as well as soups, sandwiches, and pizzas. Italian menu. Lunch, dinner. Closed Memorial Day, Labor Day, Dec 25. Bar. Children's menu. Casual attire. Reservations recommended. **$$**

★ HONEY'S-NIAGARA FALLS. *2002 Military Rd, Niagara Falls (14304). Phone 716/297-7900. www.honeysniagara.com.* With its red and yellow-striped awning, Honey's is hard to miss. Located at the Prime Outlet Mall of Niagara Falls, this restaurant is great for a post-shopping meal with the family or a fun night out with friends. American menu. Lunch, dinner, late-night. Bar. Children's menu. Casual attire. Outdoor seating. **$**

★ ★ THE RED COACH INN. *2 Buffalo Ave, Niagara Falls (14303). Phone 716/282-1459; fax 716/282-2650. www.redcoachinn. com.* Exposed beams, upholstered banquettes and chairs, and dark wood create a cozy, old-world atmosphere at The Red Coach Inn restaurant. Continental menu. Lunch, dinner. Closed Dec 25. Bar. Children's menu. Casual attire. Reservations recommended. Outdoor seating. **$$**

North Creek (C-9)

See also Schroon Lake, Warrensburg

Population 950
Elevation 1,028 ft
Area Code 518
Zip 12853
Information Gore Mountain Region Chamber of Commerce Accommodation and Visitors Bureau, 295 Main St, PO Box 84; phone 518/251-2612 or toll-free 800/880-4673
Web Site www.goremtnregion.org

What to See and Do

Garnet Hill Lodge, Cross-Country Ski Center, and Mountain Bike Center. *13th Lake Rd, North River (18256). 5 miles NW via Hwy 28, at the top of 13th Lake Rd. Phone 518/251-2444. www.garnet-hill.com.* Approximately 35 miles of groomed cross-country trails adjacent state wilderness trails; tennis courts, mountain biking (rentals), hiking trails, fishing, beach and boat rentals on 13th Lake, site of abandoned garnet mine. Restaurant. (Daily) **$$$$**

Gore Mountain. *Approximately 2 miles NW off Hwy 28. Phone 518/251-2411. www.goremountain.com.* Gondola; two quad, triple, three double chairlifts; two surface lifts; cross-country trails; patrol, school, rentals; cafeteria, restaurant, bar; nursery; lodges; snowmaking. Longest run 3 miles; vertical drop 2,100 feet. (Nov-Apr, daily; also fall weekends for gondola) **$$$$**

Gore Mountain Mineral Shop.*Barton Mine Rd. Phone 518/251-2706.* Tours of open-pit garnet mine; opportunity to collect loose gem garnets. (Mid-June-Labor Day, daily)

Rafting. Sixteen-mile whitewater rafting trips from Indian Lake to North River. (Apr-Nov) Contact Gore Mountain Region Chamber of Commerce.

Special Events

Teddy Roosevelt Celebration. *Phone 518/582-4451.* Town-wide. Sept.

White Water Derby. *421 Old Military Rd, New Paltz (12946). Hudson River. Phone 518/251-2612.* Canoe and kayak competition. First weekend in May.

Specialty Lodging

COOPERFIELD INN. *15 Chestnut St, North Creek (13326). Phone 607/547-2567; toll-free 800/348-6222. www.cooperinn.com.* 15 rooms. Closed Dec-Mar. Complimentary continental breakfast. Check-in 3 pm, check-out 11 am**. $$**

North Salem

Restaurant

★ ★ ★ AUBERGE MAXIME. *721 Titicus Rd, North Salem (10560). Phone 914/669-5450; fax 914/669-8573. www.aubergemaxime.com.* This elegantly appointed country retreat houses a romantic restaurant offering indulgent French cuisine. Duck is the celebrated specialty of the European-trained chef, and a tasting menu for two is available for a truly sumptuous meal. French menu. Lunch, dinner. Closed Tues-Wed. Bar. Casual attire. Reservations recommended. Outdoor seating. **$$$**

Northport (C-3)

See also Huntington, Smithtown, Stony Brook

Settled 1656
Population 7,606
Elevation 100 ft
Area Code 516
Zip 11768
Web Site www.northportny.com

An early English Puritan settlement, the land in and around Northport was purchased from the Matinecock.

What to See and Do

Eaton's Neck Lighthouse. *Lighthouse Rd and Huntington Bay, Northport (11798).* (1798) Second lighthouse built in the United States. A 73-foot-high beacon warns ships more than 17 miles out at sea.

Northport Historical Museum. *215 Main St, Northport (11768). Phone 516/757-9859.* Changing exhibits of local history; photographs, artifacts, costumes, and shipbuilding memorabilia. (Tues-Sun; closed holidays) Walking tours of village on some Sun afternoons in spring and summer. **DONATION**

Suffolk County Vanderbilt Museum. *180 Little Neck Road, Centerport (11721). Phone 516/854-5555. www.vanderbiltmuseum.org.* If you want to see how the other half lived, come visit this grand 24-room mansion that was used as a summer getaway for William K. Vanderbilt II. The furnishings are elegant and the grounds are masterfully maintained. The planetarium is a favorite of visitors and offers an array of special shows that will please adults and children alike. There also are special children's performances held at the mansion; check out the Web site for these events. (Hours vary) **$$** Here is

Vanderbilt Museum Planetarium. *180 Little Neck Rd, Centerport (11721). Phone 516/854-5555.* Sky shows in the 60-foot, domed Sky Theater. Space-related exhibits in the lobby include a meteorite and moon globe. (Tues-Sun)

Norwich (E-7)

See also Hamilton, Oneonta

Population 7,355
Elevation 1,015 ft
Area Code 607
Zip 13815
Information Chenango County Chamber of Commerce, 19 Eaton Ave; phone 607/334-1400 or toll-free 800/556-8596
Web Site www.norwich.net

What to See and Do

Bowman Lake State Park. *745 Bliven Sherman Rd, Oxford (13830). Hwy 220 W. Phone 607/334-2718.* This 660-acre park borders on 11,000 acres of state forest land. Swimming beach, fishing, paddleboats, rowboats (rentals); nature and hiking trails, cross-country skiing, snowmobiling, picnicking. **$$$**

Northeast Classic Car Museum. *24 Rexford St, Norwich (13815). Phone 607/334-2886. www.classiccarmuseum.org.* Features the largest collection of Franklin autos in the world; Duesenbergs, Cords, Auburns, Packards, and more. All are restored, preserved and fully operational. (Daily 10 am-5 pm; closed Jan 1, Thanksgiving, Dec 25) **$$$**

Special Events

Chenango County Fair. *Chenango County Fairgrounds, 168 E Main St, Norwich (13815). Phone 607/334-9198.* Mid-Aug.

General Clinton Canoe Regatta. *28 N Main St, Norwich (13733). Phone 607/334-9198. www.canoeregatta.org.* The start of this 70-mile flat-water endurance race is at the source of the Susquehanna River on Otsego Lake in Cooperstown; it ends at General Clinton Park in Bainbridge. Memorial Day weekend.

Limited-Service Hotel

★ ★ HOWARD JOHNSON. *75 N Broad St, Norwich (13815). Phone 607/334-2200; fax 607/336-5619. www.hojo.com.* 86 rooms, 3 story. Pets accepted, some restrictions; fee. Check-out 11 am. Restaurant, bar. Indoor pool. **$**

Restaurant

★ ★ **HANDS INN.** *S Broad St, Norwich (13815). Phone 607/334-8223.* Lunch, dinner. Closed Sun; Memorial Day, July 4, Labor Day. Bar. Children's menu. **$$**

Nyack (B-2)

See also White Plains,

Population 6,737
Elevation 70 ft
Area Code 845
Zip 10960
Information Chamber of Commerce, PO Box 677; phone 845/353-2221
Web Site www.nyackny.com

Many outstanding Victorian-style homes and an Edward Hopper art gallery grace this village.

What to See and Do

Antiques on the Hudson. *366 Hwy 9 W, Nyack (10960). W side of Tappan Zee Bridge; NY State Thrwy N exit 10 or 11; or Thrwy S exit 11. Phone 845/358-3751.*A collection of more than 75 art, crafts, and antique shops located in upper Nyack on the Hudson. (Tues-Sun)

Hudson Valley Children's Museum. *21C Burd St, Nyack (10960). Nyack Seaport. Phone 845/358-2191.* Interactive, hands-on exhibits focus on arts and sciences. Exhibits include Early Childhood, Royal Bubble Factory, Gadget Garage, Creation Station, and others with social and educational themes. Museum shop. (Mon-Sat) **$$**

Restaurants

★ ★ **KING & I.** *93 Main St, Nyack (10960). Phone 845/353-4208.* Thai menu. Lunch, dinner. Closed holidays. Bar. Casual attire. **$$**

★ ★ **RIVER CLUB.** *11 Burd St, Nyack (10960). Phone 845/358-0220; fax 845/358-0286.* American, seafood menu. Lunch, dinner. Closed Mon; Thanksgiving, Dec 25. Bar. Children's menu. Casual attire. Reservations recommended. Outdoor seating. **$$**

★ ★ **WASABI.** *110 Main St, Nyack (10960). Phone 845/358-7977.* Japanese menu. Lunch, dinner. Closed Mon. Bar. Casual attire. **$$**

Oakdale

Restaurant

★ ★ ★ **RIVERVIEW.** *3 Consuelo Pl, Oakdale (11769). Phone 631/589-2694; fax 631/589-2785.* Overlooking the Great South Bay, this elegant waterfront restaurant is a respite for weary sailors. Docks are available for any size boat, and cocktails and appetizers are served on the covered deck. The facilities are reserved on Saturday afternoons. Lunch, dinner, Sun brunch. Bar. Children's menu. Outdoor seating. **$$**

★ ★ **SNAPPER INN.** *500 Shore Dr, Oakdale (11769). Phone 631/589-0248; fax 631/589-0572. www.thesnapperinn. com.* Seafood menu. Lunch, dinner, Sun brunch. Closed Mon; Dec 25. Bar. Children's menu. Outdoor seating. **$$$**

Ogdensburg (A-7)

See also Brockville, Canton

Settled 1749
Population 12,364
Elevation 280 ft
Area Code 315
Zip 13669
Information Greater Ogdensburg Chamber of Commerce, 1020 Park St, PO Box 681; phone 315/393-3620
Web Site www.ogdensburgny.com

On the St. Lawrence Seaway, at the mouth of the Oswegatchie River, this busy port and industrial town had its beginnings as an outpost of New France, where the Iroquois were converted to Christianity. In 1837, it was the base from which American sympathizers worked "to free Canada from the yoke of England" in the abortive Patriots' War.

What to See and Do

Fort Wellington National Historic Site. *379 Van-Koughnet St, Prescott (KOE 1T0). 4 miles W of International Bridge. Phone 613/925-2896.* Built during the War of 1812 to protect the communications link between Montréal and Kingston; rebuilt in 1838-1839 in response to the Canadian Rebellions of 1837-1838. Restored blockhouse, officers' quarters, guides in period costume, demonstrations of 1846 life at the fort. (Mid-May-Sept: daily; rest of year: by appointment)

Frederic Remington Art Museum. *303 Washington St, Ogdensburg (13369). Phone 315/393-2425.* Largest single collection of paintings, sculpture, drawings by Frederic Remington, foremost artist of the Old West; re-created studio; Belter furniture, glass, china, silver. (May-Oct: daily; rest of year: Wed-Sat; closed legal holidays) **$$**

Greenbelt Riverfront Park. *State St and Riverside Ave, Ogdensburg (13669). Phone 315/393-1980.* Deep-water marina, launching ramp; picnicking, barbecue pits, lighted tennis courts. (Daily) Here is

> **War of 1812 Battlefield Walking Tour.** Walking tour along site of the Battle of Ogdensburg. 1/2 mile of paved walkways on waterfront; plaques located along the path detail the action.

Jacques Cartier State Park. *Hwy 12, Morristown. 3 miles W of Morristown. Phone 315/375-6371.* Swimming beach, bathhouse, fishing, boating (launch, anchorage); picnicking, playground, tent and trailer sites. (Late May-early Oct) Standard fees.

Ogdensburg, NY-Johnstown, Ontario International Bridge. *One Bridge Plz, Ogdensburg (13669). Connects Hwy 37 and 812 with Hwys 2, 16, and 401 in Canada. Phone 315/393-4080.* 13,510 feet long; opened September 1960. View of St. Lawrence Valley and Seaway marine terminal. Duty-free shop. **$**

Swimming Beaches. Municipal Beach. Libson Beach. *5 miles N on Hwy 37.* At Bridge Plaza. **FREE**

Special Event

International Seaway Festival. *1020 Park St, Ogdensburg (13669). Phone 315/393-3620. www.ogdensburgny.com.* Concerts, fireworks, parade, canoe race. Last full week in July.

Limited-Service Hotel

★ ★ QUALITY INN. *6765 Hwy 37, Ogdensburg (13669). Phone 315/393-4550; toll-free 800/392-4550; fax 315/393-3520. www.qualityinn. com.* 48 rooms, 2 story. Check-in 2:30 pm, check-out 11 am. Restaurant, bar. Outdoor pool. **$**

Full-Service Resort

★ ★ STONEFENCE LODGING INC. *7191 Hwy 37, Ogdensburg (13669). Phone 315/393-1545; toll-free 800/253-1545; fax 315/393-1749. www.stonefenceresort.com.* 31 rooms. Pets accepted, some restrictions; fee. Check-out 11 am. Restaurant. Outdoor pool, whirlpool. Tennis. **$**

Restaurant

★ SHOLETTE'S STEAK & ALE. *513 Linden St, Ogdensburg (13669). Phone 315/393-5172; fax 315/393-6374.* Italian, Mexican, American menu. Lunch, dinner. Closed holidays. Bar. Children's menu. **$$**

Old Forge (C-7)

See also Adirondack Park

Population 1,060
Elevation 1,712 ft
Area Code 315
Zip 13420
Information Visitor **Information** Center, Hwy 28, PO Box 68; phone 315/369-6983
Web Site www.adirondacktravel.com

In almost any season there is fun in this Adirondack resort town, located in the Fulton Chain of Lakes region—everything from hunting, fishing, snowmobiling, and skiing to basking on a sunny beach.

What to See and Do

Canoeing. *Phone 518/457-7433.* An 86-mile canoe trip to the hamlet of Paul Smiths (north of the Saranac Lakes). For information on Adirondack canoe trips contact Department of Environmental Conservation, Albany 12233-4255.

Enchanted Forest/Water Safari. *3183 Hwy 28, Old Forge (13420). 1/2 mile N on Hwy 28. Phone 315/369-6145. www.watersafari.com.* This 60-acre water theme park complex features water attractions and traditional amusement rides; circus performances twice daily. (June-Labor Day, days and hours vary) **$$$$**

Fern Park. *South Shore Rd, Old Forge (13420). 15 miles NW in Inlet. Phone 315/357-5501.* Hiking, cross-country skiing, showshoeing, biking, ice skating, baseball, volleyball, basketball; special events. **FREE**

Forest Industries Exhibit Hall. *3311 Hwy 28, Old Forge (13420). 1 mile N on Hwy 28. Phone 315/369-3078.* Samples of products of forest industries; dioramas; film on managed forests. (Late May-Labor Day: Mon,

Wed-Sat 10 am-5 pm, Sun from noon; after Labor Day-Columbus Day: weekends only) **FREE**

McCauley Mountain. *2 miles S off Hwy 28. Phone 315/369-3225.* Double chairlift, two T-bars, two rope tows, pony lift; patrol, school, rentals; snowmaking; cafeteria. Longest run 3/4 mile; vertical drop 633 feet. (Thanksgiving-Apr, Mon and Wed-Sun) Half-day rates. Chairlift to top of McCauley Mountain also operates June-Oct (daily). Picnic area. **$$$$**

Old Forge Lake Cruise. *Main St, Old Forge. Phone 315/369-6473.* Cruises on Fulton Chain of Lakes (28 miles). (Memorial Day-Columbus Day) Also show-boat and dinner cruises. **$$$**

Public beach. *On Hwy 28.* Swimming; lifeguards, bathhouse. (Early June-Labor Day, daily) Tourist Information Center is located here (daily). **$**

Limited-Service Hotel

★ BEST WESTERN SUNSET INN. *Hwy 28, Old Forge (13420). Phone 315/369-6836; fax 315/369-2607. www.bestwestern.com.* 52 rooms, 2 story. Pets accepted, some restrictions. Complimentary continental breakfast. Check-in 3 pm, check-out 11 am. Indoor pool, whirlpool. Tennis. **$**

Restaurant

★ ★ OLD MILL. *Hwy 28, Old Forge (13420). Phone 315/369-3662.* Converted gristmill. American menu. Dinner. Closed Nov-Dec. Bar. Children's menu. **$$**

Olean (F-3)

Settled 1804
Population 15,347
Elevation 1,451 ft
Area Code 716
Zip 14760
Information Greater Olean Chamber of Commerce, 120 N Union St; phone 716/372-4433
Web Site www.oleanny.com

Only seven years after the landing of the Pilgrims, a Franciscan father was led by Native Americans to a mystical spring near the present city of Olean. There he found what he called "thick water which ignited like brandy." It was petroleum. Olean (from the Latin *oleum,* meaning "oil") was once an oil-boom town; now it is a manufacturing and retail center.

What to See and Do

Friedsam Memorial Library. *Olean and Allegany,* St. *Bonaventure (14778). On campus of St. Bonaventure University. Phone 716/375-2323. www.sbu.edu/friedsam.html.* Paintings by Rembrandt, Rubens, and Bellini; works by 19th-century and contemporary artists; American Southwest and pre-Columbian pottery, porelain collection; rare books. (Sept-mid-June: Mon-Thurs 8 am-midnight, Fri to 8 pm, Sat 10 am-6 pm, Sun noon-midnight; rest of year: Mon-Fri; closed school holidays) **FREE**

Restaurants

★ ★ BEEF 'N BARREL. *146 N Union St, Olean (14760). Phone 716/372-2985; fax 716/372-3910. www.beefnbarrel.com.* American menu. Lunch, dinner. Closed Sun; holidays. Bar. Children's menu. Casual attire. **$$**

★ ★ OLD LIBRARY. *116 S Union St, Olean (14760). Phone 716/372-2226; toll-free 877/241-4348; fax 716/373-7775. www.oldlibraryrestaurant.com.* Historic landmark; former Andrew Carnegie library (1909). American menu. Lunch, dinner, late-night, Sun brunch. Closed holidays. Bar. Children's menu. Casual attire. **$$**

Oneida (D-6)

See also Canastota, Cazenovia, Hamilton, Herkimer, Rome, Skaneateles, Syracuse, Utica

Settled 1834
Population 10,987
Elevation 443 ft
Area Code 315
Zip 13421
Information The Greater Oneida Chamber of Commerce, 136 Lenox Ave; phone 315/363-4300
Web Site www.oneidachamber.com

Perhaps the best known of the 19th-century American "Utopias" was established at Oneida (o-NYE-dah) in 1848 by John Humphrey Noyes, leader of the "Perfectionists." The group held all property in common, practiced complex marriage, and undertook other social experiments. Faced with hostile attacks by the local population, the community was dissolved in

1880. In 1881, the Oneida Community became a stock corporation. The silverware factory it built remains a major industry, making "Community Plate" and William A. Rogers silver.

What to See and Do

Madison County Historical Society, Cottage Lawn Museum. *435 Main St, Oneida (13421). At Grove St. Phone 315/363-4136. www.mchs1900.org.* An 1849 Gothic Revival cottage designed by Alexander Jackson Davis. Victorian period rooms; historical and traditional craft archives; changing exhibits; 1862 stagecoach, 1853 gym, and adjacent agricultural museum. (June-Aug: Mon-Sat; Sept-May: Mon-Fri) **$**

The Mansion House. *170 Kenwood Avenue, Oneida (13421). Phone 315/361-3671. www.oneidacommunity.org.* The communal home built in the 1860s. Tours (Wed-Sat, morning and afternoon tours, also Sun afternoon tours). **$$**

Vernon Downs. *Stuhlman Rd, Vernon. 8 miles E on Hwy 5, S of I-90 exit 33, on Hwy 31. Phone 315/829-2201.* Harness racing; glass-enclosed grandstand and clubhouse. (Feb-early Nov) **$**

Verona Beach State Park. *Hwy 13 and Oneida Lake, Oneida (13162). N on Hwy 46, W on Hwy 31, then N on Hwy 13, on Oneida Lake. Phone 315/762-4463.* Swimming beach, bathhouse, fishing; hiking (all year), cross-country skiing, snowmobiling, picnicking, baseball, basketball, fishing, horse trails, playground, concession, tent and trailer sites. Standard fees. **$$**

Special Events

Craft Days. *Madison County Historical Society Museum, 435 Main St, Oneida (13421).* Traditional craftsmen demonstrate their skills; food, entertainment. First weekend after Labor Day weekend.

Madison County Hop Fest. *Madison County Historical Society Museum, 435 Main St, Oneida (13421).*

Limited-Service Hotel

★ SUPER 8. *215 Genesee St, Oneida (13421). Phone 315/363-5168; fax 315/363-4628. www.super8.com.* 39 rooms, 2 story. Complimentary continental breakfast. Check-out 11 am. **$**

Full-Service Resort

★ ★ TURNING STONE CASINO RESORT. *5218 Patrick Rd, Verona (13478). Phone 315/361-7711; toll-free 800/771-7711; fax 315/361-7999. www.turning-stone.com.* 281 rooms. Check-in 3 pm, check-out 11 am. Restaurant. Golf, 18 holes. Casino. **$$**

Oneonta (E-7)

See also Bainbridge, Cooperstown, Norwich, Stamford

Settled 1780
Population 13,292
Elevation 1,085 ft
Area Code 607
Zip 13820
Information Otsego County Chamber of Commerce, 12 Carbon St; phone 607/432-4500 or toll-free 800/843-3394
Web Site www.oneonta.net

Oneonta lies deep in the hills at the western edge of the Catskills. It was here in 1883 that the Brotherhood of Railroad Trainmen had its beginnings. A branch of the State University College of New York is located here.

What to See and Do

Gilbert Lake State Park. *Hwy 12, Laurens (13796). 7 1/2 miles N on Hwy 205 to Laurens, then County 12 to park. Phone 607/432-2114.* Swimming, fishing, boating; picnicking, playground, concession, tent and trailer sites, cabins. Standard fees. (Mid-May-mid-Oct, daily) **$$**

Hanford Mills Museum. *County Rds 10 and 12, East Meredith. 11 miles E via Hwy 23, on County 10. Phone 607/278-5744. www.hanfordmills.org.* Water-powered sawmill, gristmill, and woodworking complex dating from circa 1840. Ten-foot diameter by 12-foot width overshot waterwheel drives machinery. Demonstrations of antique machine collection, tours. Special events. Picnicking. (May-Oct, daily) **$$**

Hartwick College. *Hartwick and West sts, Oneonta (13820). Phone 607/431-4200. www.hartwick.edu.* (1797) (1,400 students) Library and archives house collections of works by Willard Yager, Judge William Cooper, and John Christopher Hartwick papers. Hall of Science with display of fresh and saltwater shells and Hoysradt Herbarium. Anderson Center for the Arts. Yager Museum contains more than 10,000 Native American artifacts and the VanEss Collection of

Renaissance and Baroque Art (Sept-May: daily; rest of year: by appointment only).

National Soccer Hall of Fame. *Wright National Soccer Campus,18 Stadium Cir, Oneonta (13820). Phone 607/432-3351. www.soccerhall.org.* Displays and exhibits range from youth, amateur, and collegiate to professional soccer; trophies, mementos, historical items, uniforms. Interactive games. Video theater with soccer films dating from 1930s. (Labor Day-Memorial Day: daily 10 am-5 pm; rest of year: daily 9 am-7 pm; closed holidays) **$$**

Limited-Service Hotel

★ ★ HOLIDAY INN. *Hwy 23 Southside, Oneonta (13820). Phone 607/433-2250; fax 607/432-7028. www. holiday-inn. com.* 120 rooms, 2 story. Pets accepted, some restrictions. Check-in 3 pm, check-out 11 am. Restaurant, bar. Outdoor pool, children's pool. **$**

Full-Service Inn

★ ★ ★ COOPERSTOWN ALL STAR VILLAGE. *4158 Hwy 23, Oneonta (13820). Phone 607/432-7483; toll-free 800/327-6790; fax 607/432-7483.* This country inn—a servants' house built in the 1930s—is located only 20 minutes from Cooperstown and the Baseball Hall of Fame. The property offers rooms and suites, and guests will enjoy the outdoor heated pool and Jacuzzi, as well as fine dining in the restaurant. 19 rooms, 2 story. Check-in 3 pm, check-out noon. Restaurant. Outdoor pool, whirlpool. **$$**

Restaurants

★ CHRISTOPHER'S. *Hwy 23, Oneonta (13820). Phone 607/432-2444; fax 607/432-1076. www. christopherslodging.com.* American menu. Lunch, dinner. Closed Dec 25. Bar. Children's menu. Guest rooms available. **$$**

★ ★ FARMHOUSE. *Hwy 7, Oneonta (13820). Phone 607/432-7374. www.farmhouserestaurant.com.* Restored farmhouse built in the 1780s. American menu. Dinner. Closed Dec 25. Bar. Children's menu. **$$**

★ ★ SABATINI'S LITTLE ITALY. *Hwy 28 Southside, Oneonta (13820). Phone 607/432-3000; fax 607/432-1076.* Italian, American menu. Lunch, dinner. Closed Thanksgiving, Dec 25. Bar. **$$**

Oswego (C-5)

See also Fulton

Population 17,954
Elevation 298 ft
Area Code 315
Zip 13126
Information Chamber of Commerce, 156 W 2nd St; phone 315/343-7681
Web Site www.oswegochamber.com

Oswego's location on Lake Ontario, at the mouth of the Oswego River, made it an important trading post and a strategic fort as early as 1722. Today, as a seaway port and northern terminus of the State Barge Canal, Oswego carries on its industrial and shipping tradition. The town has the largest US port of entry on Lake Ontario.

What to See and Do

Fair Haven Beach State Park. *Hannibal and Hwy 104A, Oswego. Approximately 15 miles SW via Hwy 104, 104A. Phone 315/947-5205.*Swimming beach, bathhouse, fishing, boating (rentals, launch, anchorage); hiking trails, cross-country skiing, picnicking, playground, concession, camping, tent and trailer sites, cabins. (Late Apr-early Nov) Standard fees.

Fort Ontario State Historic Site. *1 E 4th St, Oswego (13126). Foot of E 7th St. Phone 315/343-4711. www. fortontario.com.* The original fort was built by the British in 1755, taken by the French, and eventually used as a US Army installation (1840-1946). Strategic fort commanded the route from the Hudson and Mohawk valleys to the Great Lakes. Restored site re-creates life at a military installation during the 1860s. Exhibits; guided and self-guided tours. Picnic area. Drills (July-Labor Day). Special programs. Park (Memorial Day-Labor Day, Wed-Sun). **$$**

H. Lee White Marine Museum. *Foot of W 1st, Oswego. Phone 315/342-0480. www.hleewhitemarinemuseum. com.* Museum features 12 rooms of artifacts, models, documents, and paintings relating to 300 years of Oswego Harbor and Lake Ontario history. (Jan-mid-May: Sat 1-5 pm, Sun by appointment; mid-May-late June, Sept-Dec: daily 1-5 pm; July-Aug: daily 10 am-5 pm) **$**

Oswego County Historical Society. *135 E 3rd St, Oswego (13126). Phone 315/343-1342.* Richardson-Bates House Museum includes local historical material; period furnishings; changing exhibits. (Tues-Fri; Sat-Sun afternoons) **$$**

Selkirk Shores State Park. *7101 Hwy 3, Pulaski (13142). 17 miles NE via Hwys 104, 3. Phone 315/298-5737. nysparks.state.ny.us.* Beach, fishing, canoeing; hiking, cross-country skiing, picnicking, playground, concession, tent and trailer sites (fee), cabins. Standard fees. **$$**

State University of New York. *Hwy 104, Oswego (13126). Phone 315/341-2250. www.oswego.edu.*(1861) (8,000 students) Campus overlooks Lake Ontario. Campus tours, contact Office of Admissions.

Special Event

Oswego Speedway. *300 E Albany, Oswego (13126). Off Hwy 104 E. Phone 315/342-0646.* This is a 5/8th's asphalt racing facility. Short-track racing; supermodifieds and limited supermodifieds. Early May-Labor Day.

Limited-Service Hotels

★ BEST WESTERN CAPTAIN'S QUARTERS. *26 E 1st St, Oswego (13126). Phone 315/342-4040; fax 315/342-5454. www.bestwestern.com.* 93 rooms, 4 story. Complimentary continental breakfast. Check-in 2 pm, check-out 11 am. Fitness room. Indoor pool, whirlpool. **$**

★ DAYS INN. *101 Hwy 104, Oswego (13126). Phone 315/343-3136; fax 315/343-6187. www.daysinn. com.* 44 rooms, 2 story. Pets accepted, some restrictions. Complimentary continental breakfast. Check-out 11 am. **$**

★ OSWEGO. *180 E 10th St, Oswego (13126). Phone 315/342-6200; toll-free 800/721-7341; fax 315/343-6234. www.oswegoinn. com.* 13 rooms, 2 story. Complimentary continental breakfast. Check-in 2 pm, check-out 11 am. **$**

Owego (F-6)

See also Binghamton, Elmira, Endicott, Finger Lakes

Population 20,365
Elevation 817 ft
Area Code 607
Zip 13827
Information Tioga County Chamber of Commerce, 188 Front St; phone 607/687-2020
Web Site www.tiogachamber.com

What to See and Do

Tioga County Historical Society Museum. *110 Front St, Owego (13827). Phone 607/687-2460. www.tiogahistory.org.* Native American artifacts, folk art; pioneer crafts; exhibits on early county commerce, industry, and military history. (Tues-Sat 10 am-4 pm; closed holidays) **FREE**

Tioga Gardens. *2217 Hwy 17C, Owego (13827). Phone 607/687-5522. www.tiogagardens.com.* Tropical plant conservatory with solar dome. Greenhouses; 2-acre water garden with water lilies; Japanese garden. (Daily) **FREE**

Tioga Scenic Railroad. *25 Delphine St, Owego (13827). Phone 607/687-6786. www.tiogascenicrailroad.com.* Scenic rail excursions available. (Early May-late Oct) **$$$$**

Special Events

Owego Strawberry Festival. *210 Front St, Owego (13827). Phone 607/687-6305.* Mid-June.

Tioga County Fair. *114 Main St, Owego (13827). Phone 607/687-1308.* Mid-July.

Limited-Service Hotel

★ ★ OWEGO TREADWAY INN. *1100 Hwy 17C, Owego (13827). Phone 607/687-4500; fax 607/687-2456. www.owegotreadway.com.* 96 rooms, 2 story. Check-out noon. Restaurant, bar. Fitness room. Indoor pool. **$**

Oyster Bay

See also Glen Cove, Huntington, Jericho, New York

Settled 1653
Population 6,826
Elevation 20 ft
Area Code 516
Zip 11771
Information Chamber of Commerce, 120 South St, PO Box 21; phone 516/922-6464
Web Site www.oysterbayli.com

What to See and Do

Planting Fields Arboretum. *Planting Fields Rd, Oyster Bay (11771). 1 1/2 miles W, off Hwy 25A. Phone 516/922-9200. www.plantingfields.org.* A 400-acre estate of the late William Robertson Coe. Landscaped plantings (150 acres); large collections of azaleas and rhododendrons; self-guided tour; guided tours available; nature trails; greenhouses. (Daily 9 am-5 pm; closed Dec 25) **$$** Located in center of Arboretum is

> **Coe Hall.** *Lexington Ave and Mill River Rd, Oyster Bay (11771). Phone 516/922-0479.* (1918) Tudor-revival mansion (65 rooms) was a country estate for Coe and his family. Various 16th- and 17th-century furnishings imported from Europe contribute to its atmosphere of a historic English country house. Guided tours. (Apr-late Sept: daily noon-3:30 pm) **$**

Raynham Hall Museum. *20 W Main St, Oyster Bay (11771). Phone 516/922-6808. www.raynhamhallmuseum.org.* Historic colonial house museum with Victorian wing. Home of Samuel Townsend, a prosperous merchant; headquarters for the Queens Rangers during the Revolutionary War. Victorian garden. (July-Labor Day: Tues-Sun noon-5 pm; rest of year: 1-5 pm) **$**

★ Sagamore Hill National Historic Site. *Phone 516/922-4447. www.nps.gov/sahi.* For a price that you simply can't beat, take a 45-55-minute tour of the historic home of former President Theodore Roosevelt. The 23-room mansion has been painstakingly preserved, and shows off the many animal trophies that Roosevelt caught in his legendary hunting trips. The home also features exotic gifts that Roosevelt received from his overseas trips, as well as original furnishings and paintings. Nearby is the Theodore Roosevelt Sanctuary, which cares for injured birds and offers nature walks. The whole experience is a must for history buffs and fans of this colorful, larger-than-life president. (Daily 9:30 am-4 pm; closed Mon and Tues, Oct-May) **$**

Theodore Roosevelt Sanctuary & Audubon Center. *134 Cove Rd, Oyster Bay (11771). Phone 516/922-3200. ny.audubon.org/trsac.htm.* Owned by the National Audubon Society, the memorial contains 12 acres of forest and nature trails. The sanctuary serves as a memorial to Theodore Roosevelt's pioneering conservation achievements. Museum contains displays on Roosevelt and the conservation movement; bird exhibits. Adjacent in Young's Cemetery is Theodore Roosevelt's grave. Trails, bird-watching, library. (Daily) **FREE**

Special Events

Friends of the Arts Long Island Summer Festival. *Planting Fields Arboretum, Planting Fields Rd, Oyster Bay. Phone 516/922-0061. www.fotapresents.org.* For the ultimate evening in great music and relaxation at prices as low as $20 for lawn seats, venture out to this beautiful 409-acre Gold Coast estate. The annual festival specializes in blues, jazz, and easy listening concerts, and has offered up such artists as Michael Feinstein, David Sanborn, David Benoit, and Natalie Cole. Forget the more expensive pavilion seats and buy lawn seats. This way you can bring a picnic with your favorite wines and cheeses. And don't forget your blanket, chairs, plenty of bug repellent, a light jacket, and, of course, that special someone. The crowd tends to be a bit more mature, but very mellow and polite. Arrive at least 1 1/2 hours before the concert starts to scope out your spot on the lawn and to spend some time admiring the flower gardens. One negative: the concerts go on rain or shine. Evenings in June-Sept. **$$$$**

Oyster Festival. *120 South St, Oyster Bay (11771). Phone 516/922-6464.* Street festival, arts and crafts. Usually the weekend after Columbus Day.

Limited-Service Hotel

★ EAST NORWICH INN. *6321 Northern Blvd, East Norwich (11732). Phone 516/922-1500; toll-free 800/334-4798; fax 516/922-1089. www.eastnorwichinn.com.* Located on Long Island's north shore, this quaint property is ideal for a weekend away from the city. 65 rooms, 2 story. Complimentary continental breakfast. Check-out noon. Fitness room. Outdoor pool. **$**

Restaurants

★ CANTERBURY ALES OYSTER BAR & GRILL. *46 Audrey Ave, Oyster Bay (11771). Phone 516/922-3614; fax 516/922-3730.* Historic Teddy Roosevelt library in rear includes photos. Seafood menu. Lunch, dinner, Sun brunch. Closed Thanksgiving, Dec 25. Bar. Children's menu. **$$**

★ ★ ★ MILL RIVER INN. *160 Mill River Rd, Oyster Bay (11771). Phone 516/922-7768; fax 516/922-4978.* The menu at this creative American restaurant changes weekly. Though the experience is upscale, the dress is business casual. American menu. Dinner. Closed Dec 25. Bar. Reservations recommended. **$$$**

Palisades Interstate Parks

See also New York, Yonkers

Reached via Palisades Interstate Pkwy, starting at the New Jersey end of the George Washington Bridge; Hwy 9 W, Hwy 17, Dewey Thrwy exit 13. Phone 914/786-2701.

Web Site www.pipc.org

This 81,067-acre system of conservation and recreation areas extends along the west side of the Hudson River from the George Washington Bridge at Fort Lee, New Jersey, to Saugerties, New York. Its main unit is the 51,679-acre tract of Bear Mountain and Harriman (NY) state parks; the two are contiguous.

Bear Mountain (5,066 acres) extends westward from the Hudson River opposite Peekskill. Only 45 miles from New York City via the Palisades Interstate Parkway, this is one of the most popular recreation areas, with year-round facilities, mostly for one-day visits. The area includes a swimming pool (Memorial Day-Labor Day; fee), bathhouse, fishing, boating on Hessian Lake; game fields, nature trails, ice skating (late Oct-mid-Mar; fee), square dances in July and August. Cafeteria, inn.

Perkins Memorial Drive leads to the top of Bear Mountain, where there is a picnic area and a sightseeing tower. Near the site of Fort Clinton, just west of Bear Mountain Bridge, is the Trailside Museum, with exhibits of local flora, fauna, geology, and history (daily; fee).

Harriman (46,613 acres), southwest of Bear Mountain, includes much wilder country with several lakes. Swimming beaches (Lakes Tiorati, Welch, and Sebago), fishing, boating; hiking, biking, picnicking, miles of scenic drives, tent camping (Lake Welch), cabins (Lake Sebago).

Alpine Area (12 acres). This area has fishing, boat basin; hiking, picnicking, concession (seasonal). Outdoor concerts in summer. (Daily, weather permitting) Off Henry Hudson Drive, east of Alpine.

Many smaller parks are located in the New Jersey section of the park system.

What to See and Do

Englewood-Bloomers Area. This 13-acre area offers fishing, boat basin; hiking, picnicking, concession (seasonal). (Daily, weather permitting) Off Henry Hudson Drive, east of junction Palisades Interstate Pkwy and Hwy 505 in Englewood Cliffs.

Fort Lee Historic Park. This 33-acre facility in Hudson Terrace (phone 201/461-1776) presents the story of Washington's retreat from Fort Lee in 1776. Visitor's Center/Museum (Mar-Dec, Wed-Sun) offers two floors of exhibits; audiovisual displays; a short film; general information; special events. On the grounds (daily during daylight hours) are an 18th-century soldiers' hut, reconstructed gun batteries, a rifle parapet; overlooks with scenic views of the George Washington Bridge, the Palisades, the Hudson River, and the New York skyline. Gift shop. Parking fee (May-Sept: daily; Apr and Oct-mid-Nov: weekends and holidays). No pets, bicycles, or fires. **$**

Ross Dock. Near the southern end of the park system, this 14-acre area has fishing, boat-launching ramp; hiking, picnicking, playgrounds. (Apr-mid-Nov, daily, weather permitting) Off Henry Hudson Dr, north of George Washington Bridge.

There are fees for parking and special events. For further information about the New Jersey section, contact the Palisades Interstate Park Commission, PO Box 155, Alpine 07620; phone 201/768-1360. Further information on the New York section can be obtained from Palisades Interstate Park Commission, Administration Building, Bear Mountain, NY 10911; phone 914/786-2701.

Palmyra (D-4)

See also Canandaigua, Rochester, Victor

Founded 1789
Population 7,672
Elevation 472 ft
Area Code 315
Zip 14522
Web Site www.palmyrany.com

In 1820, in the frontier town of Palmyra, 15-year-old Joseph Smith had a vision that led to the founding of a new religious group—the Church of Jesus Christ of Latter-Day Saints, better known as the Mormon Church.

What to See and Do

Alling Coverlet Museum. *122 William St, Palmyra (14522). Phone 315/597-6737.* Largest collection of American Jacquard and handwoven coverlets in the country. (June-Sept, daily 1-4 pm or by appointment) **FREE**

Mormon Historic Sites and Bureau of Information. *603 Hwy 21 S, Palmyra (14522). Hill Cumorah, 4 miles S on Hwy 21, near I-90 exit 43. Phone 315/597-5851.* Guides. (Daily) **FREE** Includes

> **Book of Mormon Historic Publication Site.** *217 E Main St, Palmyra (14522). Phone 315/597-5982.* Between June 1829 and March 1830, the first edition of 5,000 copies of the *Book of Mormon* was printed here at a cost of $3,000. (Daily; also summer evenings)
>
> **Hill Cumorah.** *603 Hwy 21 S, Palmyra (14522). Phone 315/597-5851.* Where the golden plates from which Joseph Smith translated the Book of Mormon were delivered to him. A monument to the Angel Moroni now stands on the hill. Visitors center has religious exhibits and films. (Daily; also summer evenings)
>
> **Joseph Smith Home.** *29 Stafford Rd, Palmyra (14522). Phone 315/597-4383.* Where Smith lived as a young man; period décor (1820-1830). Nearby is the Sacred Grove where he had his first vision.

Palmyra Historical Museum. *132 Market St, Palmyra (14522). Phone 315/597-6981. www.historicpalmyrany.com.* Display of 19th-century items including furniture, toys, and household items. (June-Sept, Sat and Sun afternoons, or by appointment) **$**

Phelps General Store Museum. *140 Market St, Palmyra (14522). Phone 315/597-6981.* Contains displays of turn-of-the-century merchandise and household furnishings. (June-Sept, Sat-Sun afternoons, or by appointment) **$**

Special Event

The Hill Cumorah Pageant. *603 Hwy 21 S, Palmyra (14522). Phone 315/597-6808.* At Hill Cumorah; seating for 6,500. Early-mid-July.

Limited-Service Hotel

★ ★ QUALITY INN. *125 N Main St, Newark (14513). Phone 315/331-9500; fax 315/331-5264.* On barge canal. 107 rooms, 2 story. Pets accepted, some restrictions; fee. Check-in 1 pm, check-out 11 am. Restaurant, bar. Indoor pool. **$**

Pawling

Restaurant

★ BIG W ROADSIDE BAR-B-Q. *22 Oak Shadow Ln, Pawling. Phone 845/855-0454.* American menu. Lunch, dinner. Children's menu. Casual attire. Outdoor seating. **$**

Peekskill (B-2)

See also Garrison, Mahopac, Mount Kisco, Stony Point, Tarrytown, West Point

Population 22,441
Elevation 132 ft
Area Code 914
Zip 10566
Information Peekskill/Cortlandt Chamber of Commerce, 1 S Division St; phone 914/737-3600
Web Site www.ci.peekskill.ny.us

This city is named for Jan Peek, a Dutchman who set up a trading post on the creek that runs along the northern edge of town.

Limited-Service Hotels

★ ★ BEAR MOUNTAIN INN. *Bear Mountain Complex, Bear Mountain (10911). Phone 845/786-2731; fax 845/786-2543. www.bearmountaininn. com.* 60 rooms. Complimentary continental breakfast. Check-out 11 am. Restaurant, bar. Outdoor pool. **$**

★ ★ PEEKSKILL INN. *634 Main St, Peekskill (10566). Phone 914/739-1500; toll-free 800/526-9466; fax 914/739-7067.* 53 rooms, 2 story. Pets accepted; fee.

Complimentary continental breakfast. Check-out 11 am. Restaurant, bar. Outdoor pool. **$**

Restaurants

★ ★ CRYSTAL BAY. *5 John Walsh Blvd, Peekskill (10566). Phone 914/737-8332. www.crystal-bay.com.* On the Hudson River. International menu. Lunch, dinner, Sun brunch. Closed Dec 25. Bar. Children's menu. Casual attire. Reservations recommended. Outdoor seating. **$$**

★ ★ ★ MONTEVERDE RESTAURANT AT OLDSTONE. *Hwys 6 and 202 W, Cortlandt Manor (10566). Phone 914/739-5000; fax 914/739-5342. www.monteverderestaurant.com.* The Van Cortlandt family originally built this 18th-century mansion overlooking the Hudson River. The current owners have offered guests fantastic views and Italian-influenced French cuisine for more than 20 years. The interior features Victorian furnishings and wrought-iron lamps and chandeliers, while the outdoor terrace overlooks the Hudson River. French menu. Lunch, dinner. Closed Tues. Bar. Outdoor seating. **$$$**

★ ★ SUSAN'S. *12 N Division St, Peekskill (10566). Phone 914/737-6624. www.susansinnpeekskill.com.* Susans Restaurant is not your typical country restaurant. While this charming establishment does have the requisite country French décor, its menu spans the globe for inspiration. From Maine to Louisiana and Turkey to Thailand, the dishes show off distinctive flavors, and the homemade desserts are not to be missed. American menu. Lunch, dinner. Bar. Casual attire. Reservations recommended. **$$**

Penn Yan (E-5)

See also Canandaigua, Finger Lakes, Geneva, Hammondsport, Naples, Watkins Glen

Founded 1787
Population 5,219
Elevation 737 ft
Area Code 315
Zip 14527
Information Yates County Chamber of Commerce, 2375 Hwy 14A; phone 315/536-3111 or toll-free 800/868-9283
Web Site www.yatesny.com

Legend has it that the first settlers here, Pennsylvanians and Yankees, could not agree on a name for their town and finally compromised on Penn Yan. The town lies at the north end of Y-shaped Keuka Lake, in resort country; nearby is Keuka College.

What to See and Do

Keuka Lake State Park. *3370 Pepper Rd, Bluff Point (14478). 6 miles SW off Hwy 54A. Phone 315/536-3666.* Swimming beach, bathhouse, fishing, boating (launch); hiking, cross-country skiing, playground, tent and trailer sites (May-Oct). **$$**

Oliver House Museum. *200 Main St, Penn Yan (14527). Phone 315/536-7318. www.yatespast.com.* (1852) Brick house that originally belonged to the Oliver family, distinguished by three generations of physicians. Now headquarters for the Yates County Genealogical and Historical Society, operated as a local history museum. Includes period rooms, changing local history exhibits, research room. (Mon-Fri 9:30 am-4:30 pm; Sat by appointment) **DONATION**

The Outlet Trail. *Keuka St in Penn Yan to Seneca St, in Dresden.* Six-mile trail that follows an abandoned railroad path built in 1884. The Outlet drops almost 300 feet between Keuka and Seneca lakes, with waterfalls, wildlife, and remains of early settlements and mills to be found along the way.

Specialty Lodging

FOX INN. *158 Main St, Penn Yan (14527). Phone 315/536-3101; toll-free 800/901-9779. www.foxinnbandb.com.* This Greek Revival inn, located in the winery-spotted countryside of the Finger Lakes region, has a stately white-pillared entrance and brick façade. 5 rooms, 2 story. Complimentary full breakfast. Check-in 3 pm, check-out noon. **$**

Piermont

See also Garrison

Restaurant

★ ★ ★ XAVIARS AT PIERMONT. *506 Piermont Ave, Piermont (10968). Phone 845/359-7007; fax 845/424-3124. www.xaviars.com.* This eccentric restaurant is located in a country club. Although the sparse room and "banquet hall" feel are odd, there is something appealing about its quirkiness. Luckily, the Contemporary American food is good and mostly well prepared. American menu. Lunch, dinner. Closed Mon-Tues; holidays. Bar. Business casual attire. Reservations recommended. **$$$**

Pittsford

Restaurants

★ ★ ★ RICHARDSON'S CANAL HOUSE. *1474 Marsh Rd, Pittsford (14534). Phone 585/248-5000; fax 585/248-9970. www.canalhouse.org.* This is the oldest working tavern on the Erie Canal and is on the National Register of Historic Buildings. The bright yellow structure, dating back to the early 1800's, houses a New American dining room and a pub for more casual fare. American menu. Dinner. Closed Sun; holidays. Bar. Historic inn. Outdoor seating. **$$$**

★ VILLAGE COAL TOWER. *9 Schoen Pl, Pittsford (14534). Phone 585/381-7866.* Breakfast, lunch, dinner. Closed holidays. Children's menu. In turn-of-the-century coal storage structure used to service boats on Erie Canal. Outdoor seating. **$**

Plattsburgh (A-9)

Population 18,816
Elevation 135 ft
Area Code 518
Zip 12901
Information Plattsburgh-North Country Chamber of Commerce, 7601 Hwy 9, PO Box 310; phone 518/563-1000
Web Site northcountrychamber.com

The Cumberland Bay area of Lake Champlain has been a military base since colonial days. Plattsburgh, at the mouth of the Saranac River, has a dramatic history in the struggle for US independence. The British won the Battle of Lake Champlain off these shores in 1776. Here, in 1814, Commodore Thomas Macdonough defeated a British fleet from Canada by an arrangement of anchors and winches that enabled him to swivel his vessels completely around, thus giving the enemy both broadsides. While this was going on, US General Alexander Macomb polished off the Redcoats on shore with the help of school boys and the local militia. Today, Plattsburgh accommodates both industry and resort trade.

What to See and Do

Alice T. Miner Colonial Collection. *9618 Main St, Chazy. 12 miles N on Hwy 9. Phone 518/846-7336.* Antiques, colonial household items and appliances in 1824 house; sandwich glass collection; gardens. (Feb-late Dec, Tues-Sat 10 am-4 pm; closed Jan, Dec 25) **$$**

Boat excursion. M/V *Juniper. Phone toll-free 800/388-8970.* Leaves from the foot of Dock Street and cruises Lake Champlain, circling Valcour Island. (May-Sept, two daily departures; also sunset and dinner cruises nightly). Contact Heritage Adventures Inc, 69 Miller St.

Champlain Monument. *Cumberland Ave and Lorraine, Plattsburgh (12901).* Statue of the explorer.

Kent-Delord House Museum. *17 Cumberland Ave, Plattsburgh (12901). Phone 518/561-1035.* (1797) Historic house; British officers' quarters during the Battle of Plattsburgh (War of 1812); period furnishings. Tours (Mar-Dec: Tues-Sat afternoons; rest of year: by appointment only; closed Jan 1, Thanksgiving, Dec 25). **$$**

Macdonough Monument. *41 City Hall Pl, Plattsburgh (12901). Phone 518/563-7701.* Obelisk commemorates the naval encounter.

State University of New York College at Plattsburgh. *101 Broad St, Plattsburgh (12901). Phone 518/564-2000. www.plattsburgh.edu.*(1889) (6,400 students) On campus is SUNY Plattsburgh Art Museum, comprised of Meyers Fine Arts Gallery and Winkel Sculpture Court; also Rockwell Kent Gallery, with extensive collection of paintings, drawings, prints, and book engravings by American artist Rockwell Kent, famous for his illustrated Shakespeare and *Moby Dick* (Mon-Thurs, Sat-Sun).

Swimming. Municipal Beach. *1 1/4 miles N on Hwy 9, 1 mile E on Hwy 314. Phone 518/563-4431.* **AuSable Point State Park.** 12 miles S on Hwy 9. Beach, fishing, boating; camping. Phone 518/561-7080. **Cumberland Bay State Park.** Adjacent to Municipal Beach. Phone 518/563-5240. All areas (Memorial Day-Oct). Admission fee. Bathhouse, lifeguard; picnicking, concession.

Limited-Service Hotels

★ ★ BEST WESTERN THE INN AT SMITHFIELD. *446 Cornelia St, Plattsburgh (12901). Phone 518/561-7750; toll-free 800/243-4656; fax 518/561-*

9431. www.bestwestern.com. 120 rooms, 2 story. Pets accepted. Check-out noon. Restaurant, bar. Fitness room. Indoor pool. **$**

★ **DAYS INN & SUITES.** *8 Everleth Dr, Plattsburgh (12901). Phone 518/561-0403; fax 518/561-4192. www. daysinn. com.* 112 rooms, 3 story. Complimentary continental breakfast. Check-in 2 pm, check-out noon. High-speed Internet access. Fitness room. Indoor pool, whirlpool. **$**

★ ★ **HOLIDAY INN.** *412 Hwy 3, Plattsburgh (12901). Phone 518/561-5000; fax 518/562-2974. www. holiday-inn. com.* 102 rooms, 4 story. Check-out noon. Restaurant, bar. Fitness room. Indoor pool, children's pool, whirlpool. **$**

Restaurant

★ ★ ★ **ANTHONY'S.** *538 Hwy 3, Plattsburgh (12901). Phone 518/561-6420; fax 518/561-6421. www. anthonysrestaurantandbistro.com.* American menu. Lunch, dinner. Closed holidays. Bar. Children's menu. Casual attire. **$$**

Port Jefferson (B-3)

See also Smithtown, Stony Brook

Population 7,527
Elevation 50 ft
Area Code 631
Zip 11777
Information Greater Port Jefferson Chamber of Commerce, 118 W Broadway; phone 631/473-1414
Web Site www.portjeffchamber.com

What to See and Do

Ferry to Bridgeport, CT. *102 W Broadway, Port Jefferson (11777). Phone 631/473-0286; toll-free 888/443-3779. www.bpferry.com.* Car and passenger service. (Daily) See Web site for fees and schedule. **$$$**

Strolling though Port Jefferson. This Suffolk County waterfront village epitomizes quaint. You can easily spend a day strolling down its streets that are filled with seafood restaurants, ice cream and candy shops, and cute stores that sell everything from puppies (the Yuppy Puppy is the place for all dog lovers) to funky clothing to motorcycle paraphernalia. Danfords Inn on the water is a lovely hotel to spend the night at or maybe cap off your afternoon with a hearty dinner (make reservations on the weekends). Or, sit on a bench and watch the ferries as they leave for Connecticut. Keep in mind that the area gets quite crowded on weekends in summers, with locals who are taking in their own scenery.

Thompson House. *93 N Country Rd, Setauket (11733). 4 miles W on Hwy 25A, on N Country Rd. Phone 631/692-4664.* (Circa 1700) Historian Benjamin F. Thompson was born in this saltbox house in 1784; authentically furnished to depict 18th-century life on rural Long Island. Herb garden. (Memorial Day-Columbus Day, Sat-Sun 1-5 pm; also Fri in July-Aug) **$**

Limited-Service Hotel

★ ★ **DANFORDS ON THE SOUND.** *25 E Broadway, Port Jefferson (11777). Phone 631/928-5200; toll-free 800/332-6367; fax 631/928-3598. www.danfords. com.* On Long Island Sound.86 rooms, 3 story. Check-in 4 pm, check-out 11 am. High-speed Internet access. Restaurant, bar. Fitness room, spa. **$$$**

Restaurants

★ ★ **25 EAST AMERICAN BISTRO.** *25 E Broadway, Port Jefferson (11777). Phone 631/928-5200; fax 631/473-0195. www.danfords.com.* Built in 1890 as a chowder house. Breakfast, lunch, dinner, Sun brunch. Bars. Children's menu. Outdoor seating. **$$**

★ **PAPA JOES.** *111 W Broadway, Port Jefferson (11777). Phone 631/473-5656; fax 631/473-0195.* American, German menu. Lunch, dinner. Bar. Children's menu. Outdoor seating. **$$**

★ **VILLAGE WAY.** *106 Main St, Port Jefferson (11777). Phone 631/928-3395; fax 631/928-3458.* Lunch, dinner, Sun brunch. Closed Thanksgiving, Dec 25. Bar. Children's menu. Outdoor seating. **$$**

Port Jervis (B-1)

See also Barryville, Middletown

Population 8,860
Elevation 440 ft
Area Code 845
Zip 12771
Information Tri-State Chamber of Commerce, 5 S

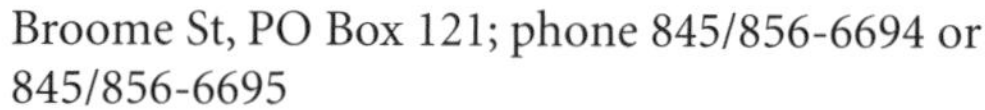

Broome St, PO Box 121; phone 845/856-6694 or 845/856-6695
Web Site www.tristatechamber.org

Port Jervis is a popular area for whitewater canoeing and rafting. Fishing, nature trails, and hot-air ballooning are highlights of the area.

What to See and Do

Gillander Glass Factory Tours and Store. *Erie and Liberty sts, Port Jervis (12771). Phone 845/856-5375.* Observe skilled craftsmen at work as they transform molten glass into beautiful glass objects. Tours, museum, store. (Mon-Fri; weekends seasonal; closed holidays) **$$**

Restaurant

★ ★ CORNUCOPIA. *176 Hwy 209, Port Jervis (12771). Phone 845/856-5361; fax 845/856-4498.* Country inn built in 1892; chalet décor. Guest rooms available. American, Continental menu. Lunch, dinner. Closed Mon. Bar. Children's menu. Casual attire. **$$**

Potsdam (A-7)

See also Canton, Massena, Ogdensburg

Founded 1802
Population 15,957
Elevation 433 ft
Area Code 315
Zip 13676
Information Chamber of Commerce, PO Box 717; phone 315/265-5440
Web Site www.potsdam.ny.us

What to See and Do

Potsdam College of the State University of New York. *44 Pierrepont Ave, Potsdam (13676). Phone 315/267-2000.* (1816) (4,450 students) Founded as St. Lawrence Academy. Gibson Art Gallery; Crane School of Music; planetarium; summer programs. Campus tours.

Potsdam Public Museum. *Civic Center, Park and Elm sts, Potsdam. Phone 315/265-6910.* Collection of English pottery; local history and decorative arts displays; changing exhibits. Walking tour brochures available. (Memorial Day-Labor Day: Tues-Fri afternoons, rest of year: Tues-Sat afternoons; closed holidays) **FREE**

Full-Service Inn

★ ★ THE CLARKSON INN. *1 Main St, Potsdam (13676). Phone 315/265-3050; toll-free 800/790-6970; fax 315/265-5848. www.clarksoninn. com.* Old-fashioned style combines with modern conveniences at this inn, which is located along the Racquette River. Visitors will enjoy the fireside sitting room and a tea room where breakfast is served each morning. New renovations allow this inn to facilitate small meetings and functions.40 rooms, 2 story. Check-out 11 am. Restaurant**.** **$**

Restaurant

★ TARDELLI'S. *141 Market St, Potsdam (13676). Phone 315/265-8446.* Italian menu. Dinner. Closed Sun; holidays. Bar. Children's menu. **$$**

Poughkeepsie (F-9)

See also Fishkill, Hyde Park, Newburgh, New Paltz, Rhinebeck

Settled 1687
Population 29,871
Elevation 176 ft
Area Code 845
Information Poughkeepsie Area Chamber of Commerce, 1 Civic Center Plaza, 12601; phone 845/454-1700
Web Site www.pokchamb.org

Many people know this Hudson River town as the site of Vassar College, founded in 1861 by a brewer named Matthew Vassar. The Smith Brothers also helped put Poughkeepsie (p'KIP-see) on the map with their cough drops, once made here. For a brief time during the Revolutionary War, this town was the state capital. It was here in 1788 that New York ratified the Constitution.

What to See and Do

Bardavon Opera House. *35 Market St, Poughkeepsie (12601). Phone 845/473-5288. www.bardavon.org.* (1869) The oldest operating theater in the state presents various dance, theatrical, and musical performances; also Hudson Valley Philharmonic concerts. (Sept-June)

James Baird State Park. *122 D Freedom Rd, Pleasant Valley (12569). 9 miles E on Hwy 55, then 1 mile N on Taconic Pkwy. Phone 845/452-1489. www.nysparks. state.ny.us/parks.*An 18-hole golf course and driving range, tennis, hiking trails, cross-country skiing, picnicking (shelters), playground, restaurant, nature center (June-Labor Day). Household pets allowed caged or on a leash no more than 10 feet. **FREE**

Locust Grove. *2683 South Rd (Hwy 9), Poughkeepsie (12601). 2 miles S of Mid-Hudson Bridge. Phone 845/454-4500. www.morsehistoricsite.org.* (Young-Morse Historic Site) (Circa 1830) Former house of Samuel F. B. Morse, inventor of the telegraph; remodeled by him into a Tuscan villa in 1847. Antiques; Morse Room, telegraph equipment and memorabilia; alternating exhibits of dolls, fans, costumes, books, and souvenirs acquired by Young family (owners following Morse); paintings, art objects, and American furnishings. Wildlife sanctuary and park (150 acres) with hiking trails, picnic area. Tours (May-Nov: daily 10 am-3 pm). Visitor center (May-Nov: daily 10 am-5 pm; closed holidays). Gardens and grounds (daily 8 am to dusk; closed holidays). **$$**

Mid-Hudson Children's Museum. *75 N Water St, Poughkeepsie (12601). Phone 845/471-0589. www.mhcm.org.* Interactive children's museum featuring more than 50 exhibits including gravity roll, IBM's Da Vinci inventions, virtual reality, climb-thru-the-heart. (Tues-Sun 11 am-5 pm; closed holidays) **$$**

Vassar College. *124 Raymond Ave, Poughkeepsie (12604). Phone 845/437-7000. www.vassar.edu.* (1861) (2,400 students) A 1,000-acre campus; coeducational (since 1969) liberal arts college. Art gallery. **FREE**

Windsor Vineyards. *26 Western Ave, Marlboro (12542). Approximately 7 1/2 miles S on Hwy 9 from Mid-Hudson Bridge, right on Western Ave, at Marlboro-on-the-Hudson. Phone 845/236-4233; toll-free 800/333-9987. www.windsorvineyards.com.* Makers of California and New York State wines and sparkling wines. Wine tasting (Mon, Thurs-Sat 10 am-5 pm; Sun noon-5 pm). **FREE**

Limited-Service Hotels

★ ★ COURTYARD BY MARRIOTT. *2641 South Rd, Poughkeepsie (12601). Phone 845/485-6336; fax 845/485-6514. www.marriott.com.* 149 rooms, 3 story. Check-in 3 pm, check-out noon. High-speed Internet access. Restaurant, bar. Indoor pool, whirlpool. Business center. **$**

★ HOLIDAY INN EXPRESS. *2750 South Rd, Poughkeepsie (12601). Phone 845/473-1151; fax 845/485-8127. www.holiday-inn. com.* 121 rooms, 4 story. Complimentary continental breakfast. Check-in 3 pm, check-out noon. High-speed Internet access. Fitness room. Outdoor pool. Airport transportation available. **$**

Full-Service Hotel

★ ★ ★ POUGHKEEPSIE GRAND HOTEL. *40 Civic Center Plz, Poughkeepsie (12601). Phone 845/485-5300; toll-free 800/216-1034; fax 845/485-4720. www.pokgrand.com.* Located adjacent to the Civic Center in the heart of the Hudson Valley, this hotel boasts plenty of meeting space and can accommodate 360 theater-style. Energize at the fitness center, and later take time to enjoy the local historic attractions. 195 rooms, 10 story. Check-out noon. High-speed Internet access. Restaurant, bar. Fitness room. **$**

Full-Service Inns

★ ★ ★ OLD DROVERS INN. *Old Rte 22, Dover Plains (12522). Phone 845/832-9311; fax 845/832-6356. www.olddroversinn.com.* This historic inn was built in 1750 and may be the oldest continuously operated inn in the United States. Each room is delicately decorated with fine antiques. 4 rooms. Pets accepted, some restrictions; fee. Complimentary continental breakfast. Check-in 3 pm, check-out 11 am. Restaurant. **$$**

★ ★ ★ TROUTBECK INN. *Leedsville Rd, Amenia (12501). Phone 845/373-9681; toll-free 800/978-7688; fax 845/373-7080. www.troutbeck.com.* This English country-style inn and conference center sits on 600 acres near the Berkshire foothills. 42 rooms, 2 story. Pets acceted; fee. Complimentary continental breakfast. Check-in Fri 5 pm, check-out Sun 2 pm. Restaurant, bar. Fitness room. Indoor pool, outdoor pool. Tennis. Business center. **$$**

Specialty Lodging

INN AT THE FALLS. *50 Red Oaks Mill Rd, Poughkeepsie (12603). Phone 845/462-5770; toll-free 800/344-1466; fax 845/462-5943. www.innatthefalls.com.* Romance and relaxation are imparted by the charm of this intimate and stylish inn. Different period furnishings are found in every room. 36 rooms, 2 story. Pets acceted; fee. Complimentary continental breakfast. Check-in 3 pm, check-out noon. **$$**

Restaurants

★ 96 MAIN. *96 Main St, Poughkeepsie (12601). Phone 845/454-5200.* International menu. Lunch, dinner. Closed Sun. Bar. Casual attire. Outdoor seating. **$$**

★ ★ AROMA OSTERIA. *114 Old Post Rd (Hwy 9), Wappingers (12570). Phone 845/298-6790.* American, Italian menu. Lunch, dinner. Closed Mon; holidays. Bar. Casual attire. Reservations recommended. Outdoor seating. **$$**

★ ★ BEECH TREE GRILL. *1-3 Collegeview Ave, Poughkeepsie (12603). Phone 845/471-7279. www.beechtreegrill.com.* American menu. Lunch, dinner. Bar. Casual attire. Reservations recommended. **$$**

★ ★ ★ CHRISTOS. *155 Wilbur Blvd, Poughkeepsie (12603). Phone 845/471-3400; fax 845/471-6430. www.christoscatering.com.* Internationally influenced American cuisine is served in this elegant, wood-paneled dining room lit by sparkling chandeliers. Smooth service from tuxedo-clad waiters and a golf course view combine for a relaxing ambience. The wine list includes excellent selections for all price ranges. American menu. Lunch, dinner. Closed Sun-Mon; also Jan and Aug. Bar. Casual attire. Reservations recommended. **$$**

★ ★ COSIMO'S TRATTORIA & BAR. *120 Delafield St, Poughkeepsie (12601). Phone 845/485-7172. www.cosimosrestaurantgroup.com.* American, Italian menu. Lunch, dinner. Bar. Children's menu. Casual attire. Reservations recommended. Outdoor seating. **$$**

★ COYOTE GRILL. *2629 Hwy 9, Poughkeepsie (12603). Phone 845/471-0600. www.coyotegrillny.com.* Mexican menu. Lunch, dinner. Bar. Children's menu. Casual attire. Reservations recommended. **$$**

★ ★ LE PAVILLON. *230 Salt Point Tpke, Poughkeepsie (12603). Phone 845/473-2525; fax 845/471-0758. www.lepavillonrestaurant.com.* This longstanding, family-run establishment is a reliable spot for those seeking traditional French-American food and a little romance. Its location in the theater district, cozy neighborhood décor, and reasonable prices make it quite a find. American, French menu. Dinner. Closed Sun-Mon; holidays. Bar. Casual attire. Reservations recommended. Outdoor seating. **$$**

Pound Ridge (B-3)

See also Brewster, Mount Kisco, Norwalk, Stamford, White Plains

Population 4,726
Elevation 600 ft
Area Code 914
Zip 10576
Web Site www.townofpoundridge.com

What to See and Do

Muscoot Farm. *Hwys 35 and 100, Somers (10589). Phone 914/864-7282.* This 777-acre park is a turn-of-the-century farm that includes farm animals, buildings, and a 28-room main house. Demonstrations of sheep-shearing, blacksmithing, beekeeping, harvesting, and bread-baking (daily). Programs (Sun). Tours (groups only). **FREE**

Ward Pound Ridge Reservation. *Hwy 121 S, Cross River. About 4 miles NW on Hwy 137, then 3 1/2 miles N on Hwy 121 S, just S of jct Hwy 35. Phone 914/864-7317.* In 4,700-acre park is Trailside Nature Museum (Wed-Sun). Cross-country ski trails, picnicking, playground, camping in lean-tos (fee). Reservation (daily; closed Jan 1, Thanksgiving, Dec 25). **$$$**

Restaurants

★ ★ INN AT POUND RIDGE. *258 Westchester Ave, Pound Ridge (10576). Phone 914/764-5779; fax 914/764-0034. www.innatpoundridge.com.* House built in 1833; antiques, fireplaces. Lunch, dinner, brunch. Bar. Children's menu. Valet parking. **$$**

★ ★ ★ L'EUROPE. *407 Smithridge Rd, South Salem (10590). Phone 914/533-2570; fax 914/533-2487.* French menu. Lunch, dinner. Closed Mon. Bar. Outdoor seating. **$$**

Queens

See also New York

Area Code 718

By far the largest borough geographically, Queens occupies 121 square miles of Long Island. Like Brooklyn, it was assembled from a number of small towns, and each of these neighborhoods has retained a strong sense of identity. Parts of the borough are less densely settled than Brooklyn, and the majority of Queens's population are homeowners. Many manufacturing plants, warehouses, and shipping facilities are in the portion called Long Island City, near the East River. Forest Hills, with its West Side Tennis Club, at Tennis Place and Burns Street, is a world-famous center for tennis. Flushing Meadows Corona Park has been the site of two world's fairs; many facilities still stand.

Public Transportation

Subway and elevated trains, buses (New York Transit Authority), phone 718/330-3322 or 718/330-1234.

Airport LaGuardia. Cash machines, upper level Main Terminal, Finger 4, Delta Terminal.

Information Phone 718/476-5000

Lost and Found Phone 718/533-3988

Airport John F. Kennedy International Airport.

Information Phone 718/656-4444

Lost and Found Phone 718/244-3225

What to See and Do

American Museum of the Moving Image. *35th Ave and 36th St, Astoria (11106). Phone 718/784-0077. www.ammi.org.* On the site of historic Astoria Studios, where many classic early movies were filmed. Museum is devoted to the art and history of film, television, and video and their effects on American culture. Permanent and changing exhibitions; two theaters with film and video series (screenings weekends). (Wed-Thurs noon-5 pm, Fri to 8 pm, Sat-Sun 11 am-6:30 pm; closed holidays). **$$**

Astoria. *At the NW tip of Queens. Phone 718/286-2667. www.queens.nyc.us.* Experience your own Big Fat Greek Wedding in this Hellenic community, just 15 minutes from Midtown Manhattan, which offers the best Greek food this side of Athens. Astoria has an estimated Greek population of 70,000the largest community outside of Greecewhich means that the area is alive with music, culture, and melt-in-your mouth saganaki and baklava. Food markets, gift shops, bakeries, restaurants, and intimate cafs await your shopping and dining pleasure. Finish your excursion by relaxing on a nice, sunny day with a cup of Greek coffee in nearby Astoria Park and take in a great view of upper Manhattan. If you want to combine this Greek experience with other area attractions, the American Museum of the Moving Image(phone 718/784-0077) and the historic Kaufman Astoria Motion Picture Studios (phone 718/392-5600) are located in Astoria. This fun neighborhood proves that there is life in the outer boroughs of New York City.

Bowne House. *37-01 Bowne St, Flushing (11354). Phone 718/359-0528.* (1661) One of the oldest houses in New York City was built by John Bowne, a Quaker who led a historic struggle for religious freedom under Dutch rule; 17th- to 19th-century furnishings. (Tues, Sat, and Sun afternoons; closed Easter and mid-Dec-mid-Jan) Under 12 admitted only with adult. **$**

Clearview Golf Course. *202-12 Willets Point Blvd, Flushing (11360). Phone 718/229-2570.* Clearview is recognized as a good course for beginners in the New York area, and because of this its very popular. You can expect your round to take a little longer than normal, but the price won't break the bank. The rough is deep, but if you can keep your shots straight, you can avoid it. A par-70 course, Clearview plays just over 6,200 yards from the back tees, but that belies the challenge of the narrow fairways. Enjoy an inexpensive round of golf with your friends, as you'll have some time to chat while you wait for the group ahead of you. **$$$$**

Flushing Meadows-Corona Park. *Flushing and Metropolitan aves, Flushing (11368). Grand Central Pkwy to Van Wyck Expy and Union Tpke to Northern Blvd. Phone 718/217-6034.* Originally a marsh, this 1,255-acre area became the site of two World's Fairs (1939-1940 and 1964-1965). It is now the home of the United States Tennis Association National Tennis Center, where the US Open is held annually (phone 718/760-6200). The park is also the site of some of the largest cultural and ethnic festivals in the city. Facilities include an indoor ice rink, carousel, 87-acre Meadow Lake, and the Playground for All Children, designed for disabled and able-bodied children. Park rangers conduct occasional weekend tours. Also on the grounds are

New York Hall of Science. *47-01 111th St, Flushing (11368). 111th St and 48th Ave. Phone 718/699-0005.* Exhibition hall with hands-on science and technology exhibits. (Sept-June: Tues-Thurs 9:30 am-2 pm, Fri to 5 pm, Sat-Sun noon-5 pm; Jul-Aug: Mon 9:30 am-2 pm, Tues-Fri to 5 pm, Sat-Sun 10:30 am-6 pm; closed holidays) Free admission Thurs and Fri afternoons. **$$$**

The Queens Museum of Art. *New York Building, 25th Ave and 76th St, Flushing (11368). New York City Building. Phone 718/592-9700.* Interdisciplinary fine arts presentations, major traveling exhibitions; permanent collection includes 9,000-square-foot panorama of New York City, the world's largest three-dimensional architectural model. (Sept-June: Wed-Fri 10 am-5 pm, Sat-Sun from noon, Jul-Aug: Wed-Sun 1-8 pm; closed holidays) **$**

Shea Stadium. *126th St and Roosevelt Ave, Flushing (11368). Phone 718/507-6387.*Home of the New York Mets. **$$$$**

Isamu Noguchi Garden Museum. *36-01 43rd Ave, Long Island City (11101). Phone 718/204-7088. www.noguchi.org.* Sculpture fans will want to visit the Isamu Noguchi Museum, just a short trip from Manhattan. Housed in the sculptor's former studio, complete with an outdoor sculpture garden, the museum is filled with Noguchi stone, metal, and woodwork. (Apr-Nov; Mon, Thurs-Fri 10 am-5 pm; Sat-Sun 10 am-6 pm; closed Tues-Wed) **DONATION**

Queens Botanical Garden. *43-50 Main St, Flushing (11355). Phone 718/886-3800. www.queensbotanical.org.* Collections include large rose, herb, Victorian wedding, bee, woodland, and bird gardens and an arboretum. (Tues-Sun) **DONATION**

John F. Kennedy International Airport. *Belt Pkwy and Van Wyck Expy, Queens (11430).* The airport's 4,930 acres cover an area roughly one-third the size of Manhattan. Much of the air traffic going overseas is handled through here. (See PUBLIC TRANSPORTATION)

LaGuardia Airport. *Grand Central Pkwy and 94th St, Queens. Phone 718/565-5100.* (see PUBLIC TRANSPORTATION)

Union Street. *Union and Main sts, Flushing (11367). Take the 7 subway to Main Street, the last stop.* This section of Flushing, located one long block past Main Street, is home a large, culture-rich Korean community. Tiny shops feature American and Korean clothing and wedding gowns from both cultures. Gift shops sell miniature collectibles, and food markets offer exotic foods and spices. Korean restaurants serve traditional barbecue dishes and other items. In addition to being easy on the wallet, many eateries are open 24 hours a day to satisfy late-night cravings.

Special Events

Aqueduct. *11000 Rockaway Blvd, South Ozone Park (11420). Take the A train to the Aqueduct stop. Phone 718/641-4700. www.nyra.com/aqueduct.* Yes, people actually do take the A train! Hop on the subway for a short ride out to Queens for an afternoon of thoroughbred races, held from late October through early May. Races take place Wednesday through Sunday and begin at 1 pm. The track also has pretty lawns and gardens that come alive in spring. You can't beat the cheap admission price, so splurge a little and place some bets. Gates open at 11 am. **$**

Belmont Park. *2150 Hempstead Tpke, Elmont (11003). Just outside of Queens in Nassau County, on Cross Island Pkwy via Hempstead Tpke and Plainfield Ave. Phone 516/488-6000. www.nyra.com/belmont.* This 430-acre racetrack is the home of the third jewel in horse racings Triple Crown, the Belmont Stakes. This major spectacle is held in June and attracts gamblers, horse lovers, and spectators from all walks of life. Its one of the oldest annual sporting events in the nation, so make your plans in advance and reserve seats early. Hopefully, you will get a good-weather day on which to enjoy this event. The regular season racing at Belmont Park is from May through July and from September through October. Sundays are Family Fun Days; kids can play in the playground in the Backyard area. (Wed-Sun, May-July and Sept-Oct) **$**

US Open Tennis. *Flushing Meadows-Corona Park, USTA National Tennis Center, Flushing (11351). Take the 7 subway to the Willets Point-Shea Stadium stop. Phone 718/760-6200. www.usopen.org.* Tennis fans from near and far flock to the US Open tennis tournament each September. You can see your favorite players, the stars of tomorrow, and a host of celebrities in the audience at this upper-crust sporting event. Tickets go on sale in late May or by the beginning of June, and those matches held closer to the finals sell out first. Purchase tickets as early as possible. Buying a ticket to the Arthur Ashe Stadium, the main court, gives you admission to all the other courts on the grounds. However, these seats tend to be more in the back, since the better seats go to corporate sponsors. Bring a pad to keep your own score, binoculars, sunscreen, and sunglasses for day games. Late Aug-early Sept.

Limited-Service Hotel

★ ★ HOLIDAY INN. *14402 135th Ave, Jamaica (11436). Phone 718/659-0200; toll-free 800/692-5359; fax 718/322-2533. www.jfkhihotel. com.* 360 rooms, 12 story. Check-out noon. Restaurant, bar. Fitness room. Indoor pool, whirlpool. Airport transportation available**. $$**

Full-Service Hotel

★ ★ ★ CROWNE PLAZA HOTEL NEW YORK-LAGUARDIA AIRPORT. *104-04 Ditmars Blvd, East Elmhurst (11369). Phone 718/457-6300; toll-free*

800/227-6963; fax 718/672-8295. www.crowneplaza.com. 358 rooms, 7 story. Check-in 4 pm, check-out noon. Restaurant, bar. Fitness room. Indoor pool. **$$**

Restaurants

★ ★ CAVO. *4218 31st Ave, Astoria (11103). Phone 718/721-1001.* Joining the ranks of the non-Greek restaurants in Astoria, Cavo is a sprawling Mediterranean spot with a stone patio and a wonderful, wide garden that will leave you wanting to set up camp in the backyard and never leave. The menu features all the wonders of the Mediterranean, from assorted savory pastas to whole fish with lemon and herbs, rack of lamb, and assorted mezze to start. Cavo attracts a local crowd but also pulls in guests from the city, giving new meaning to "Bridge and Tunnel." Mediterranean menu. Dinner, late-night. Bar. Casual attire. Reservations recommended. Outdoor seating. **$$**

★ ★ CHRISTOS HASAPO-TAVERNA. *41-08 23rd Ave, Astoria (11105). Phone 718/726-5195. www.christossteakhouse.com.* Christos Hasapo is a restaurant with dual personalities, and both are wonderful. By day, locals crowd into this butcher shop to purchase their day's beef. But at night, the shop turns into a Greek steakhouse, serving Astoria's finest selection of beef, prepared simply and perfectly every time. This lovely Greek taverna makes you feel like you are in Athens, and the wine list is surprisingly terrific, making a trip from the city a great idea. Greek menu. Lunch, dinner. Bar. Casual attire. Outdoor seating. **$$$**

★ ★ CINA. *45-17 28th Ave, Astoria (11103). Phone 718/956-0372.* If you've ever wondered what sort of dinners people have in Romania, this Romanian bistro, with a lively staff and a convivial vibe, will answer all your questions. First on the menu would be steak—and lots of it—grilled to juicy perfection. Then there might be some polenta topped with sour cream and perhaps some grated feta. Cina features both of these dishes and more, like sausages, spicy stuffed cabbage, and, for fearless eaters, a deep-fried Cornish hen. And if you thought American donuts were good, try the papanasi—fried lumps of yeasty dough topped with, you guessed it, sour cream. Romanian menu. Lunch, dinner. Casual attire. Reservations recommended. **$$**

★ ★ COOKING WITH JAZZ. *12-01 154th St, Whitestone (11357). Phone 718/767-6979. www.cwj.net.* Cooking with Jazz is a spirited restaurant that brings a bit of New Orleans to the modest hamlet known as Queens. From the vibrant and festive décor to the enthusiastic and well-informed staff to the creative Cajun menu, this homey freestanding restaurant is bursting with energy and robust cooking. The chef/owner is a Paul Prudhomme protégé, and his training shows in classics like chicken jambalaya, a rich and smoky stew stocked with blackened chicken and meaty Andouille sausage. If you're feeling adventurous, try some alligator, which can be found in fritters or in sausage. Cajun/Creole menu. Dinner. Closed Sun-Mon. Casual attire. No credit cards accepted. **$$**

★ ELIAS CORNER. *24-02 31st St, Astoria (11102). Phone 718/932-1510.* Elias Corner is not easy on the eyes. The restaurant, a cult favorite, is a bit garish, decked out in all turquoise, and is far from subtle in the décor department. But the blinding color scheme does not seem to deter the herds of folks who come here to feast on the restaurant's standout Greek fare. If you can stand the wait (the line is usually out the door), you will be treated to a wonderful meal, cooked from whatever is in the refrigerated deli case at the front of the restaurant. Usually, that includes some sort of fish, lamb, and, of course, a selection of mezze with warm, puffy pita. Greek menu. Dinner. Casual attire. Outdoor seating. No credit cards accepted. **$$**

★ ★ IL TOSCANO. *42-05 235th St, Douglaston (11363). Phone 718/631-0300; fax 718/225-5223.* Italian menu. Dinner. Closed Mon, Dec 25. Bar. Casual attire. Reservations recommended. Valet parking. **$$$**

★ JACKSON DINER. *37-47 74th St, Jackson Heights (11372). Phone 718/672-1232.* Bright, open, and airy, the Jackson Diner has been a Queens favorite for years, serving authentic Indian cuisine in a bright and casual setting. The enormous buffet lunch is a steal, and the à la carte dinner menu is a terrific taste of the kitchen's talents: yogurt-marinated lamb chops, assorted dosas, and tasty appetizers to share among the table, like coconut-flecked chicken, fried fish, and flaky samosas. Indian menu. Lunch, dinner. Casual attire. No credit cards accepted. **$**

★ KABAB CAFE. *25-12 Steinway St, Astoria (11103). Phone 718/728-9858.* Kabab Café may not look like much from the outside, but on the inside, it's a different story. For instance, it takes your basic mezze trio—baba ganoush, hummus, and tahini—and makes them shine. Creamy, spicy, zesty, and ridiculously good, the mezze here are truly remarkable, reaching beyond the ordinary trio to more exotic treats like eggah (an Egyptian omelette), foul (a white bean salad with puréed tomatoes, lemon juice, spices, and olive oil), and a crunchy fava bean falafel. In addition to the stellar spreads (served with delicious fresh-from-the-oven bread), you can feast on larger dishes like slow-cooked lamb shank and sautéed calf's liver. Middle Eastern menu. Lunch, dinner. Closed Mon. Casual attire. No credit cards accepted. **$**

★ KHAO HOMM. *39-28 61st St, Woodside (11377). Phone 718/205-0080; fax 718/205-0048.* This fresh and fun Thai restaurant comes complete with a spirited menu, a talented and accommodating kitchen, gracious service, karaoke machines, and a loyal clientele. What sets Khao Homm apart, though, is perhaps its willingness to cook dishes that are not on the menu. But more than likely, you won't have to bother the kitchen, as the menu offers tasty options like fried whole fish topped with papaya, roasted cashews, and a sweet-and-sour vinegar sauce and pad kee mao—broad noodles coated in chiles and basil. Thai menu. Lunch, dinner. Casual attire. **$**

★ KUM GANG SAN. *138-28 Northern Blvd, Flushing (11354). Phone 718/461-0909.* Kum Gang San, a Korean barbecue, sushi, and seafood stalwart, never closes. If you'd like to perform your own *Survivor,* try to stay for all 24 hours. You could spend part of the day hanging out by the indoor waterfall while having a lunch of blistering barbecue, crisped scallion and seafood pancakes, and pungent kimchi. Then you could move over to the sushi bar for an afternoon snack, and for dinner, take a stab at plates of panchan—Korean-style tapas-like crab claw with hot pepper and soy-marinated shortribs. And in the wee hours, you might join the late-night revelers and watch the fresh fish coming in from the seafood markets. Korean menu. Lunch, dinner, late-night. Casual attire. **$$**

★ ★ MANDUCATIS. *13-27 Jackson Ave, Long Island City (11101). Phone 718/729-4602; fax 718/361-0411.* Sure, Manhattan boasts some fairly impressive Italian eateries, but one of the best-hidden treasures is located in Queens. Owned by Vicenzo Cerbone, Manducatis is a family-run operation serving the home-style dishes of Italy's best mamas. The terra-cotta room has an earthy, countryside appeal, as does the menu. Expect delicate homemade pastas topped with soft pillows of milky mozzarella. The kitchen also turns out lovely fish and meat dishes and has an extensive wine list that includes many rare wines from small producers. In the winter, grab a seat by the blazing fireplace and you will be transported to the mountains of Tuscany. Italian menu. Lunch, dinner. Closed holidays; also the last two weeks in Aug. Bar. **$$**

★ ★ MOMBAR. *2522 Steinway St, Astoria (11103). Phone 718/726-2356.* Mombar is a warm, family-owned Egyptian restaurant with a big heart. Owned by artist and chef Moustafa El Sayed and run by his wife and family, the restaurant is decorated with his stunning handmade tile work, mix-and-match wooden tables, and comfy, pillow-filled banquettes. El Sayed is there all the time, to cook, to chat, and to guide you through a meal you will never forget. While his menu changes daily, you can't go wrong with the mezze plate or any of his clay pot stews: Moulekaya, an aromatic stew made from Egyptian greens with braised rabbit or chicken, or the fragrant, soft lamb pulled from a tagine filled with a messy stew of raisins, almonds, and olives. Meals end with tea—served in old-world tea glasses—and dense little powdered sugar-coated nut cookies. Middle Eastern menu. Dinner. Closed Mon. Children's menu. Casual attire. No credit cards accepted. **$$**

★ ★ PARK SIDE. *107-01 Corona Ave, Corona (11368). Phone 718/271-9274; fax 718/271-2454.* If you try to imagine what *My Big Fat Greek Wedding* would have been like with an Italian family, you'll get an idea of what dinner is like at Park Side, a lively, boisterous restaurant in Queens that serves hearty portions of Italian food. The waiters give the place an old-school vibe, all dressed in black suits, while the dining room feels like an ornate catering hall filled with large parties and the occasional celebrity. The menu is straight-ahead and delicious Italian—think spicy red sauce, big steaks, giant orders of fill-in-the-blank-parmigiana, and heaping bowls of risotto, in addition to a superb hot and cold antipasti selection. Italian menu. Lunch, dinner. Bar. Valet parking. Outdoor seating. **$$**

★ ★ ★ PICCOLA VENEZIA. *42-01 28th Ave, Astoria (11103). Phone 718/721-8470; fax 718/721-2110. www.piccola-venezia.com.* There are only a few reasons to leave the island of Manhattan. One is baseball. (Yankees and Mets games both require a trip through a bridge or tunnel.) Another is Piccola Venezia, an old-world trattoria offering authentic northern Italian fare in the humble borough of Queens. Located in Astoria since 1973, Piccola Venezia is a family-run operation that features delicious homemade pastas and a generous menu of salads, antipasti, seafood, meat, and game prepared with imported ingredients and a strong nod to the wonderful culinary traditions of northern Italy. Italian menu. Lunch, dinner. Closed Tues; Jan 1, Dec 25; also late July-late Aug. Valet parking. **$$$**

★ ★ PING'S SEAFOOD. *83-02 Queens Blvd, Elmhurst (11373). Phone 718/396-1238.* This old-time favorite for Chinese cuisine is a straightforward spot to dine on fresh fish infused with the bright flavors of Asia. As you might expect, Ping's specializes in fish, but not just any old fish. Bring along a sense of culinary adventure if you decide to dine here, as the restaurant features tanks filled with all sorts of wild sea creatures for you to experiment with at dinner. The restaurant also offers dim sum, including steamed pork buns and shrimp dumplings. Chinese menu. Lunch, dinner. Closed Sun. **$$**

★ ★ RESTAURANT 718. *35-01 Ditmars Blvd, Astoria (11105). Phone 718/204-5553.* While Astoria was once all about Greek restaurants, the recent influx of Manhattanites fleeing rent hikes has brought about a shift in the culinary landscape. Restaurant 718 marks the official arrival of the French bistro to the Big Fat Greek scene. This sweet, cozy Parisian bistro offers standards like duck terrine and steak frites, but also features Spanish-accented plates like grilled tuna with chorizo and soy-cherry sauce, roasted duck with Serrano ham, and, in a respectful nod to the neighborhood, tzatziki with endive. French menu. Dinner, brunch. Bar. Casual attire. Reservations recommended. **$$**

★ S'AGAPO TAVERNA. *34-21 34th Ave, Astoria (11106). Phone 718/626-0303.* At this neighborhood taverna, a taste of the Greek Isles is served up with charm every night of the week. The service is warm and welcoming, as you would expect from a local gathering place. The restaurant specializes in swimmingly fresh grilled seafood as well as classic mezze like tangy, garlicky tzatziki. The only potential downside to S'Agapo is that the place can get cramped at times, as tables are snuggled up right next to one another. But if you don't mind cozy dining, you should be fine. Greek menu. Lunch, dinner. Casual attire. **$$**

★ ★ SICHUAN DYNASTY. *135-32 40th Rd, Flushing (11354). Phone 718/961-7500.* If you are one of those people who has trouble deciding what to order, do not go to Sichuan Dynasty. The menu contains some 60 items and will stymie even the most decisive of eaters. The key to dining here may be to go with a large group that can handle lots of fiery fare so that no dish will be left off your evening's menu. The selections run the gamut from your basic kung pao chicken and whole fish to more *Fear Factor*-style dishes like kidney in sesame oil. The setting is bright and comfortable, with colorful tabletops, wide booths, and an upper-deck bar stocked with a decent selection of California wines. Chinese menu. Lunch, dinner. Casual attire. **$$**

★ SRIPRAPHAI. *64-13 39th Ave, Woodside (11377). Phone 718/899-9599.* Sripraphai serves the sort of food you might get in Thailand. But instead of hopping on a jet plane, all you have to do is grab the number 7 train out to Queens. The only problem is that you may have to wait in the line that stretches out the door to get your table. The menu is filled with authentic Thai dishes like noodle bowls, green papaya salad, chile-rubbed pork, and fire-breathing dishes of green curry that will set your mouth ablaze with spice. If you have issues with heat, make sure to let your waiter know. Thai menu. Lunch, dinner. Closed Wed. Casual attire. Outdoor seating. No credit cards accepted. **$**

★ ★ TOURNESOL. *50-12 Vernon Blvd, Long Island City (11109). Phone 718/472-4355. tournesolny.com.* Tournesol is a sunny little French bistro just across the river from Manhattan in Long Island City that could have fallen off any old charming *rue* in Paris. Filled to the gills with trappings of Paris—romantic music, a sidewalk café, bistro tables and chairs, floor-to-ceiling French doors, and vintage tin ceilings—this cheery local favorite offers up friendly service and a rustic menu of classic French standards like rabbit stew, braised beef cheeks, frisée au lardons, and country pâté. Tournesol is a sweet little gem of a restaurant that offers all the romance of Paris without the hassle of transcontinental travel. French menu. Lunch, dinner, brunch. Casual attire. Reservations recommended. Outdoor seating. **$$**

★ UBOL'S KITCHEN. *24-42 Steinway St, Astoria (11103). Phone 718/545-2874.* This neighborhood Thai restaurant gets consistent "wows" from locals who head over for vibrant fare with a generous amount of heat. The menu includes many standard curry and noodle dishes, but also makes an effort to woo vegetarians with dishes like mock duck. In a neighborhood that is inundated with a slew of ubiquitous Thai restaurants of the same formula, Ubol's remains a spicy favorite. Thai menu. Lunch, dinner. Casual attire. **$**

★ ★ WATER'S EDGE. *44th Dr at the East River, Long Island City (11101). Phone 718/482-0033; fax 718/937-8817. www.watersedgenyc.com.* On the riverfront opposite the United Nations complex; views of the New York City skyline. Seafood menu. Lunch, dinner. Closed Sun. Bar. Reservations recommended. Valet parking. Outdoor seating. Complimentary riverboat transportation to and from Manhattan. **$$**

Rhinebeck (F-9)

See also Hyde Park, Kingston, Poughkeepsie

Settled 1686
Population 7,762
Elevation 200 ft
Area Code 845
Zip 12572
Information Chamber of Commerce, 19 Mill St, Box 42; phone 845/876-4778
Web Site www.rhinebecknychamber.org

Rhinebeck was once known as "violet town" because it claimed to produce more hothouse violets than any other town in the United States.

What to See and Do

Hudson River National Estuarine Research Reserve. *N on Hwy 9G to Annandale, 1 1/4 miles N of Bard College Main Gate. Phone 845/758-5193.* The Hudson River is an estuary, running from Manhattan to Troy, NY; over 4,000 acres of this estuarine land have been reserved for the study of its life and ecosystems. The Reserve includes Piermont Marsh and Iona Island in Rockland County, Tivoli Bays in Dutchess County, and Stockport Flats in Columbia County. Reserve's headquarters has lectures, workshops, special exhibits, and public field programs.

Montgomery Place. *River Rd and Annendale Rd, Rhinebeck (12571). N on Hwy 9G. Phone 845/758-5461.* Estate along Hudson River. Mansion (1805) was remodeled in the mid-1800s in the Classical-revival style. Also on grounds are a coach house, visitor center, greenhouse with rose, herb, perennial, and woodland gardens, museum, and garden shop. Scenic trails and view of cataracts meeting the Hudson. (Apr-Oct: Mon, Wed-Sun; Mar and Nov-Dec: weekends) **$$**

Old Rhinebeck Aerodrome. *42 Stone Church Rd, Rhinebeck (12572). About 3 miles NE via Hwy 9. Phone 845/758-8610. www.oldrhinebeck.org.* Museum of antique airplanes (1900-1937). Planes from World War I and earlier are flown in air shows (fee) (mid-June-mid-Oct, Sat and Sun). Aerodrome (mid-May-Oct, daily). Picnicking. Barnstorming rides. **$$$**

Special Event

Dutchess County Fair. *Dutchess County Fairgrounds, Hwy 9, Rhinebeck (12572). Phone 845/876-4001. www.dutchessfair.com.* Harness racing, livestock shows, farm machinery exhibits. Late Aug.

Full-Service Hotel

★★★ **BEEKMAN ARMS.** *6387 Mill St, Rhinebeck (12572). Phone 845/876-7077; toll-free 800/361-6517; fax 845/876-7077. www.beekmanarms.com.* In a historic walking village, this distinctive inn emanates romance. Savor fine cuisine, take enchanted walks, and visit the many local attractions: Roosevelt estate, Vanderbilt estate, Culinary Institute of America, or the Rhinebeck Aerodrome's World War I Air Show. 67 rooms, 3 story. Pets accepted. Check-in 3 pm, check-out 11 am. Restaurant, bar. **$$**

Restaurants

★ **AGRA TANDOOR.** *5856 Hwy 9, Rhinebeck (12572). Phone 845/876-7510.* Indian menu. Lunch, dinner. Casual attire. Reservations recommended. Outdoor seating. **$$**

★★ **CALICO CALICO RESTAURANT AND PATISSERIE.** *6384 Mills St, Rhinebeck (12572). Phone 845/876-2749. www.calicorhinebeck.com.* French menu. Lunch, dinner, brunch. Bar. Casual attire. Reservations recommended. **$$$**

★★ **DIASPORA.** *1094 Hwy 308, Rhinebeck (12572). Phone 845/758-9601.* Greek menu. Dinner. Bar. Reservations recommended. Outdoor seating. **$$**

★★ **GIGI TRATTORIA.** *6422 Montgomery St, Rhinebeck. Phone 845/876-1007.* Italian menu. Lunch, dinner. Closed Mon. Bar. Business casual attire. Reservations recommended. Outdoor seating. **$$**

★★ **OSAKA.** *22 Garden St, Rhinebeck (12572). Phone 845/876-7338.* Japanese, sushi menu. Lunch, dinner. Closed Tues. Casual attire. **$$**

Riverhead (B-4)

See also Fire Island National Seashore, Greenport, Hampton Bays, Southampton, Southold, Westhampton Beach

Population 27,680
Elevation 19 ft
Area Code 631
Zip 11901

Information Chamber of Commerce, 542 E Main St, PO Box 291; phone 631/727-7600
Web Site www.riverheadchamber.com

Suffolk County's thousands of acres of rich farmland, first cultivated in 1690, have made it one of the leading agricultural counties in the United States. Potatoes, corn, and cauliflower are abundant here.

What to See and Do

Atlantis Marine World. *431 E Main St, Riverhead (11901). Phone 631/208-9200. www.atlantismarineworld.com.* This aquarium offers children and adults alike the chance to observe marine life up close and personaland safely. You'll see sharks swimming in a 120,000-gallon tank, playful sea lions, and a live coral reef display. Marine World also houses the Riverhead Foundation for Marine Research and Preservation (phone 631/369-9840), where you can witness marine animals nursed back to health. (Daily 10 am-5 pm; closed Dec 25) **$$$**

Briermere Farms. *4414 Sound Ave, Riverhead (11901). Phone 631/722-3931.* Forget the calorie count when you walk into this small roadside farmstand and bakery. The many varieties of homemade fruit and cream pies are worth every delectable bitein fact, they are the closest thing to grandmas recipe that you will find. From traditional flavors like cherry and peach to more exotic tastes such as blackberry apple and blueberry cream, the pies are so chock full of fresh fruit that they are actually heavy to carry. But don't stop there: also indulge in Briermeres home-baked breads, muffins, and cookies. For healthier interests, they also sell fresh fruits and vegetables. Insiders tip: go early in the day for the best selection, and be ready to wait in line on just about any day in the summer. (Daily 9 am-5 pm)

Brookhaven National Laboratory. *William Floyd Parkway, County Road 46, Upton (11973). 14 miles W of Riverhead via Hwys 24 and 495. Phone 631/344-2345.* The Exhibit Center Science Museum is housed in the world's first nuclear reactor built to carry out research on the peaceful aspects of nuclear science. Participatory exhibits, audiovisual presentations, and historic collections. Tours (Mid-July-Aug, Sun; closed holiday weekends). **FREE**

Palmer Vineyards. *108 Sound Ave, Riverhead (11901). Phone 631/722-. www.palmervineyards.com.* Opened in 1986, this 55-acre winery is one of the most award-winning wineries on the North Fork, with an interesting, eclectic variety of wines. Palmer offers everything from Cabernet Franc to Chardonnay to special Reserve wines that have a unique, rich flavor. Pack a picnic, enjoy a tasting and a tour, and buy some wine to enjoy with lunch and to bring home to friends and family. Save some money for the gift shop, too. (June-Oct: daily 11 am-6 pm; Nov-May: daily 11 am-5 pm)

Pindar Vineyards. *Hwy 25, Peconic (11958). Phone 631/734-6200. www.pindar.net.* Even though Long Islands wine country does not have the reputation of Napa Valley, this well-known winery and its smaller counterparts in this lovely agricultural area are making a name for themselves. No trip to Long Island's wine country is complete without a stop at Pindar. On 550 lush acres, it is the North Forks largest winery and one of the most established. Founded in 1979, it offers free tastings of the 16 varieties of wine it produces. They include more common types such as merlot, chardonnay, and cabernet sauvignon and lesser-known varieties such as syrah and viognier. The winery is airy and comfortable and provides daily guided tours. Don't forget to visit the gift shop and pick up some goodies to bring home. **FREE**

Splish Splash. *2549 Splish Splash Dr, Riverhead (11901). Phone 631/727-3600. www.splishsplashlongisland.com.* Considered one of the top five water parks in the United States, this 64-acre delight for children (and adults as well) has everything wet, from tubing on a river to a mammoth speed slide to a wild roller coaster water ride. For the very young, there are kiddie rides and baby pools. Plan to buy lunch or snacks, since no outside food is allowed in the park. Also, arrive before the park opens to beat some of the crowds, and try going on an overcast day when more people will stay away and you'll have your pick of rides. (Mid-June-Labor Day, daily 9:30 am-7 pm) **$$$$**

Suffolk County Historical Society. *300 W Main St, Riverhead (11901). Phone 631/727-2881. www.riverheadli.com.* Dating back to 1886, this museum chronicles Suffolk Countys colorful history and rich traditions in farming, whaling, and Native American culture. Displays include furniture, tools, antique bicycles and carriages, and a pottery collection, and features a library containing newspapers, books, and photographs relating to Suffolk and its people. (Tues-Sat 12:30 pm-4:30 pm) **FREE**

Tanger Outlet Center. *1770 W Main St, Riverhead (11901). Phone 631/369-2732. www.tangeroutlet.com.* Welcome, all bargain hunters. This outdoor outlet mall is a great place to pick up almost any kind of merchandise you can think ofclothes, china, jewelyat below retail prices. The mall has nearly 200 stories, most of them name brands such as Banana Republic and Gap. Sometimes you'll have to do some digging to find the best possible prices, but its worth it if you want well-known brands. Keep in mind that weekends tend to be more crowded, so consider a weekday jaunt to this East End destination. (Mon-Sat 9 am-9 pm, Sun 10 am-7 pm)

Vintage Tours. *Phone 631/765-4689. www.northfork.com/tours.* If you and your traveling companion(s) would like to imbibe, relax and leave the driving to someone else. For a reasonable price, Vintage Tours will pick you up at your hotel in a comfortable 15-passenger van and take you to at least three wineries in a four- to five-hour jaunt. Also included are wine tastings, behind-the-scene winery tours, a gourmet picnic lunch suited to your tastes, and stops at the North Forks wonderful farm stands for the best in fresh vegetables and fruit. The company operates Friday-Sunday, but weekday trips can be arranged. **$$$$**

Special Event

Riverhead Country Fair. *200 Howell Ave, Riverhead (11901). Downtown. Phone 631/727-1215.* Agricultural, needlecraft exhibits and competitions; farm animal exhibit; entertainment, midway, music. Mid-Oct.

Limited-Service Hotel

★ ★ BEST WESTERN EAST END. *1830 Hwy 25, Riverhead (11901). Phone 631/369-2200; toll-free 800/528-1234; fax 631/369-1202. www.bestwesterneastend.com.* 100 rooms, 2 story. Pets accepted. Complimentary continental breakfast. Check-in 3 pm, check-out 11 am. High-speed Internet access. Restaurant, bar. Fitness room. Outdoor pool. Business center. **$$**

Robert Moses State Park (C-3)

See also Bay Shore, New York

On Fire Island, off south shore of Long Island, reached via pkwys.

Reached by the Robert Moses Causeway, the park consists of 875 acres of choice sand at the western end of a 50-mile barrier beach along the south shore of Long Island. The park includes beach swimming, bathhouses; picnic shelter, playground, surf and bay fishing, and a pitch-putt golf course. Headquarters is at Belmont Lake State Park, Babylon, Long Island 11702. For information phone 631/669-1000.

Rochester (D-4)

See also Avon, Batavia, Canandaigua, Finger Lakes, Palmyra, Victor

Founded 1803
Population 219,773
Elevation 515 ft
Area Code 585
Information Greater Rochester Visitors Association, 45 East Ave, Suite 400, 14604; phone 585/546-3070 or toll-free 800/677-7282
Web Site www.visitrochester.com

Rochester is a high-tech industrial and cultural center and the third largest city in the state. Its educational institutions include the University of Rochester with its Eastman School of Music and Rochester Institute of Technology with its National Technical Institute for the Deaf. The Vacuum Oil Company, a predecessor of Mobil Oil Corporation, was founded here in 1866. The city also has a symphony orchestra and professional theatre.

Rochester has its share of famous citizens too: Susan B. Anthony, champion of women's rights; Frederick Douglass, black abolitionist and statesman; George Eastman, inventor of flexible film; Hiram Sibley, founder of Western Union; and musicians Mitch Miller, Cab Calloway, and Chuck Mangione.

The city is on the Genesee River, near its outlet to Lake Ontario, in the midst of rich fruit and truck-gardening country.

Public Transportation

Buses (Regional Transit Service), phone 585/288-1700.

What to See and Do

Genesee Country Village & Museum. *1410 Flint Hill Rd, Mumford (14511). 20 miles SW via Hwy 36 (see AVON). Phone 585/538-6822. www.gcv.org.*

George Eastman House. *900 East Ave, Rochester (14607). Phone 585/271-3361. www.eastman.org.* Eastman's 50-room mansion and gardens contain restored rooms with their original 1920s furnishings and décor; exhibit on the house's restoration project; audiovisual shows about George Eastman and the film processes used by

Eastman Kodak. Adjacent to house is the archive building; eight exhibit spaces display extensive collection of 19th- and 20th-century photography representing major photographers of the past 150 years. Chronological display presents evolution of photographic and imaging industries. Interactive displays present history of imaging with touch-screens, video stations, and programmed audiovisual shows. Museum tours (Tues-Sat 10:30 am and 2 pm, Sun 2 pm). (May: daily 10 am-5 pm; rest of year: Tues-Wed, Fri-Sat 10 am-5 pm, Thurs to 8 pm, Sun 1-5 pm; closed Jan 1, Thanksgiving, Dec 25) **$$**

Hamlin Beach State Park. *1 Camp Rd, Hamlin (14464). 25 miles W on Lake Ontario State Pkwy. Phone 585/964-2462. www.nysparks.state.ny.us/parks.* Swimming beach (mid-June-Labor Day), fishing; nature, hiking, and biking trails; cross-country skiing, snowmobiling, picnicking, playground, concession, tent and trailer area. Recreation programs. Pets allowed in some camping areas. Standard fees. (Daily 6 am-10 pm)

★ **High Falls in the Brown's Race Historic District.** *60 Brown's Race, Rochester (14614). Phone 585/325-2030.* This is the area between Inner Loop and Platt and State streets, along the Genesee River Gorge. One of Rochester's earliest industrial districts has been renovated to preserve the area where flour mills and manufacturers once operated and Eastman Kodak and Gleason Works originated. Today, the district still houses businesses in renovated historic buildings such as the Eastman Technologies Building. Center at High Falls, on Brown's Race Street, is an interpretive museum with hands-on interactive exhibits on the history of the area as well as information on other attractions to visit in Rochester. Brown's Race Market has been transformed from a maintenance facility of the Rochester Gas and Electric Corporation into three levels of attractions including a night club, a jazz club, and a restaurant. A laser light show can be viewed from the pedestrian bridge that crosses the Genesee River. **DONATION**

The Landmark Center (Campbell-Whittlesey House Museum). *123 S Fitzhugh St, Rochester (14608). Phone 585/546-7029.* (1835) Greek Revival home, Empire furniture. Also Hoyt-Potter House with gift shop and exhibit area. (Mar-Dec; Thurs-Fri noon-3 pm) **$**

Memorial Art Gallery (University of Rochester). *500 University Ave, Rochester (14607). Phone 585/473-7720. mag.rochester.edu.* The permanent collection spans 50 centuries of art and includes masterworks by Monet, Matisse, and Homer; changing exhibitions. Café, gift shop. Tours (Thurs 6:30 pm, Fri and Sun 2 pm). (Tues-Wed, Fri 10 am-4 pm, Thurs 10 am-9 pm, Sat 10 am-5 pm, Sun noon-5 pm; closed holidays) **$$**

Rochester Historical Society. *485 East Ave, Rochester (14607). Phone 585/271-2705. www.rochesterhistory.org.* Headquarters is "Woodside," Greek Revival mansion (1839). Collection of portraits, memorabilia, costumes. Reference library, manuscript collection. Garden. (Mon-Fri 10 am-3 pm, also by appointment; closed holidays) **DONATION**

Rochester Institute of Technology. *One Lomb Memorial Dr, Rochester (14623). Jefferson Rd at E River Rd. Phone 585/475-2411. www.rit.edu.* (1829) (15,000 students) Seven colleges, National Technical Institute for the Deaf on campus. Also on campus are the Bevier Gallery (academic year, daily; summer, Mon-Fri) and Frank Ritter Memorial Ice Arena. Tours of campus available.

Rochester Museum & Science Center. *657 East Ave, Rochester (14607). At Goodman St. Phone 585/271-4320. www.rmsc.org.* Complex featuring regional museum of natural science, anthropology, history, and technology. Changing and permanent exhibits. (Mon-Sat 9 am-5 pm, Sun noon-5 pm; closed Thanksgiving, Dec 25) **$$** Located here is

> **Strasenburgh Planetarium of the Rochester Museum and Science Center.** *657 East Ave, Rochester (14607). Phone 585/271-1880.* Star Theatre shows, CineMagic 870 screen with special shows (call for times), educational exhibits. (Daily; hours vary) **$$**

Seneca Park Zoo. *2222 St. Paul St, Rochester (14621). At junction Hwy 104. Phone 585/336-7200. www.senecazoo.org.* Animals from all over the world; free-flight bird room, reptiles, Children's Discovery Center. Rocky Coasts features underwater viewing of polar bears and seals. (Daily 10 am-5 pm) **$$**

Stone-Tolan House. *2370 East Ave, Rochester (14610). 4 miles SE off I-490. Phone 585/546-7029.* (Circa 1790) Restored pioneer homestead and tavern; 4 acres of gardens and orchards. (Mar-Dec: Fri-Sat, noon-3 pm; closed holidays) **$**

Strong Museum. *One Manhattan Sq, Rochester (14607). Phone 585/263-2700. www.strongmuseum.org.* This children's learning center features hands-on exhibits, 25,000 toys, dolls, miniatures, and more. There is also an interactive 3-D exhibit based on the Children's Television Workshop program, *Sesame Street.* The glass atrium features a historic street scene with an operating 1956 diner and 1918 carousel. (Mon-Thurs 10 am-5 pm, Fri 10 am-8 pm, Sat 10 am-5 pm, Sun noon-5 pm; closed Thanksgiving, Dec 25) **$$**

Susan B. Anthony House. *17 Madison St, Rochester (14608). Phone 585/235-6124. www.susanbanthonyhouse.org.* Susan B. Anthony lived here for 40 years; she was arrested here for voting illegally in the 1872 presidential election. Mementos of the women's suffrage movement; furnishings. (Labor Day-Memorial Day: Wed-Sun 11 am-4 pm; Memorial Day-Labor Day: Tues-Sun 11 am-5 pm; closed holidays) **$$**

University of Rochester. *River Campus, Wilson Blvd, on Genesee River. Phone 585/275-2121. www.rochester.edu.*(1850) (7,700 students) Medical Center, 601 Elmwood Ave, off Mount Hope Ave. Seven colleges and schools. Tours by appointment. On campus are

CEK Mees Observatory. *6604 S Gannett Hill Rd, Naples (14512). In the Bristol Hills. Phone 585/275-4385.* For information on Friday and Saturday (June-August) sunset tours, contact the Physics and Astronomy Department. **FREE**

Eastman School of Music of the University of Rochester. *26 Gibbs St, Rochester (14604). Phone 585/274-1000.* Concerts, recitals, opera in Eastman Theatre, Howard Hanson Recital Hall, and Kilbourn Hall. **$$$**

Laboratory for Laser Energetics. *250 E River Rd, Rochester (14623). Phone 585/275-5286.* Pioneering multidisciplinary teaching and research unit in laser and energy studies. Tours by appointment.

Rush Rhees Library. *University of Rochester, Rochester (14627). Located at the head of the quad. Phone 585/275-4478.*University of Rochester's central library on River campus. Extensive collection of rare books, manuscripts. (Daily; closed holidays) **FREE**

Victorian Doll Museum. *4332 Buffalo Rd, North Chili (14514). W via I-490, exit 4 (Hwy 259), N to Buffalo Rd (Hwy 33), turn right (E) 1/2 block. Phone 585/247-0130.* More than 3,000 dolls from the mid-1800s to the present. Toy circus, puppet show, and dollhouses. Gift shop. (Feb-Dec: Tues-Sat 10 am-4:30 pm; closed holidays) **$**

Special Events

Clothesline Festival. *Memorial Art Gallery, 500 University Ave, Rochester (14607). Phone 585/473-7720. mag.rochester.edu/visit/clothesline.* Outdoor art show. Mid-Sept.

Comedies, dramas, and musicals. *GeVa Theatre, 75 Woodbury Blvd, Rochester (14607). Phone 585/232-4382. www.gevatheatre.org.* Resident professional theater. Aug-June. (Tues-Sun evenings; Sat-Sun matinees)

Corn Hill Arts Festival. *133 Fitzhugh St S, Rochester (14608). Phone 585/262-3142. www.cornhill.org.* Arts and crafts; entertainment. Mid-July.

Lilac Festival. *Highland Park, Between South Ave and Goodman St, Rochester. Phone 585/256-4960. www.lilacfestival.com.* This ten-day festival features more than 500 varieties of lilacs. Parade, art show, entertainment, and tours. Mid-May.

Monroe County Fair. *Monroe County Fairgrounds, 2695 E Henrietta Rd, Rochester (14467). Phone 585/334-4000. www.mcfair.com.* Agricultural exhibits and displays, amusement rides, games, and entertainment. Late July-early Aug.

Rochester Philharmonic Orchestra. *Eastman Theater, Main and Gibbs, Rochester (14604). Phone 585/454-7311. www.rpo.org.* Symphonic concerts. Oct-May.

SummerMusic. *108 East Ave, Rochester (14604). Phone 716/454-2620.* Rochester Philharmonic Orchestra, Finger Lakes Performing Arts Center. Symphonic, classical, and pops concerts. Indoor/outdoor seating. Picnic sites. July.

Limited-Service Hotels

★ ★ CLARION HOTEL. *120 E Main St, Rochester (14604). Phone 585/546-6400; toll-free 888/596-6400; fax 585/546-1341. www.choicehotels.com.* 465 rooms, 15 story. Check-in 3 pm, check-out noon. Restaurant, bar. Fitness room. Outdoor pool. **$**

★ COMFORT INN. *1501 Ridge Rd W, Rochester (14615). Phone 585/621-5700; toll-free 800/892-9348; fax 585/621-8446. www.choicehotels.com.* 83 rooms, 5 story. Pets accepted, some restrictions; fee. Complimentary continental breakfast. Check-in 3 pm, check-out noon. **$**

★ HAMPTON INN. *717 E Henrietta Rd, Rochester (14623). Phone 716/272-7800; toll-free 800/426-7866; fax 716/272-1211. www.hamptoninn.com.* 112 rooms, 5 story. Complimentary continental breakfast. Check-in 3 pm, check-out noon. Airport transportation available. **$**

★ ★ HOLIDAY INN. *911 Brooks Ave, Rochester (14624). Phone 585/328-6000; toll-free 800/465-4329; fax 585/328-1012. www.holiday-inn.com.* 280 rooms,

2 story. Pets accepted, some restrictions. Check-in 3 pm, check-out noon. High-speed Internet access. Restaurant, bar. Fitness room. Indoor pool, whirlpool. Business center. **$**

★ ★ **RAMADA INN.** *800 Jefferson Rd, Rochester (14623). Phone 585/475-9190; toll-free 800/888-8102; fax 585/424-2138. www.ramada.com.* 143 rooms, 3 story. Pets accepted. Complimentary full breakfast. Check-in 3 pm, check-out noon. Restaurant, bar. Fitness room. Indoor pool. **$**

Full-Service Hotels

★ ★ **BROOKWOOD INN.** *800 Pittsford-Victor Rd, Pittsford (14534). Phone 585/248-9000; toll-free 800/396-1194; fax 585/248-5869. www.hudsonhotels.com.* This property is located in Bushnell's Basin on the canal. A walking path along the canal is easily accessible. 108 rooms, 4 story. Check-out noon. Restaurant, bar. Fitness room. Indoor pool, whirlpool. Airport transportation available. **$**

★ ★ ★ **CROWNE PLAZA.** *70 State St, Rochester (14614). Phone 585/546-3450; toll-free 800/227-6963; fax 585/546-8714. www.rochestercrowne.com.* 362 rooms, 7 story. Pets accepted, some restrictions. Check-in 3 pm, check-out noon. Wireless Internet access. Restaurant, bar. Fitness room. Outdoor pool. Airport transportation available. Business center. **$**

★ ★ ★ **HYATT REGENCY ROCHESTER.** *125 E Main St, Rochester (14604). Phone 585/546-1234; toll-free 800/633-7313; fax 585/546-6777. www.hyatt.com.* A skywalk connects the hotel to the convention center, which is located near area corporations, shopping, entertainment and cultural activities, wineries, and the airport. Guests will find well-appointed rooms and a health club, extraordinary meeting space, and exceptional service by friendly staff. 336 rooms, 25 story. Check-in 3 pm, check-out noon. Restaurant, bar. Fitness room. Indoor pool, whirlpool. Business center. **$**

★ ★ ★ **STRATHALLAN HOTEL.** *550 East Ave, Rochester (14607). Phone 585/461-5010; toll-free 800/678-7284; fax 585/461-3387. www.strathallan.com.* This European-style hotel offers warm and spacious studios and one-bedroom suites. Located in a stately residential neighborhood, the property is convenient to area attractions and business destinations and is handy for those on extended business trips or traveling with a family. The restaurant offers a variety of dishes to please all in a country club setting, and the bar is a quiet place to relax. 156 rooms, 9 story, all suites. Check-in 3 pm, check-out noon. Restaurant, bar. Fitness room. Airport transportation available. **$$**

Specialty Lodging

DARTMOUTH HOUSE BED AND BREAKFAST INN. *215 Dartmouth St, Rochester (14607). Phone 585/271-7872; fax 585/473-0778. www.dartmouthhouse.com.* This bed-and-breakfast, a 1905 English Tudor, is situated in a quiet residential neighborhood near Rochesters main sights. Guests feast on a six-course breakfast by candlelight, featuring such goodies as baked blueberry blintz souffl and raspberry fudge truffle bars. The guest rooms are spacious, with antiques, comfy chairs and couches on which to relax. The living room area is warm and cozy, with a fireplace, beamed ceilings, window benches, and a piano. It's a great setting for an romanticand affordableweekend getaway.4 rooms, 3 story. Closed late Dec-early Mar. Children over 12 years only. Complimentary continental breakfast. Check-in 3-6 pm, check-out 11 am. **$$**

Restaurants

★ **DINOSAUR BAR-B-QUE.** *99 Court St, Rochester (14604). Phone 585/325-7090; fax 585/325-7125. www.dinosaurbarbque.com.* Barbecue menu. Lunch, dinner. Closed Sun. **$$$**

★ ★ ★ **THE GRILL AT STRATHALLAN.** *550 East Ave, Rochester (14607). Phone 585/461-5010; fax 716/325-5004. www.grill175.com.* A welcomed arrival in the old downtown area, this sophisticated yet casual Mediterranean dining room serves fresh, creative, and elegantly prepared food paired with a magnanimous wine cellar. For serious eaters and wine lovers alike, restaurateurs Andrea and Mike Tadich hit the mark. Steak menu. Lunch, dinner. Closed Sun. Jacket required. **$$$**

★ ★ ★ **MARIO'S VIA ABRUZZI.** *2740 Monroe Ave, Rochester (14618). Phone 585/271-1111; fax 585/271-1149. www.mariosviaabruzzi.com.* Natives of Abruzzi, Italy, the village for which the restaurant is named, would feel right at home in Marios Via Abruzzi. This charming villa, surrounded by ample parking, is built and decorated in authentic central Italian style.

Mario declares, "You're not a customer. You're my personal guest." Visiting celebrities whose signed photos adorn the walls have gotten the message. So have locals who flock here from throughout the region to enjoy a special meal or a festive event. Mario's unique Italian cuisine is served impeccably and includes a popular children's menu. The Sunday brunch has won many accolades. Italian menu. Dinner, Sun brunch. Closed Memorial Day, July 4, Labor Day. Bar. Children's menu. Casual attire. Outdoor seating. **$$**

★ ★ **OLIVE TREE.** *165 Monroe Ave, Rochester (14607). Phone 585/454-3510; fax 585/454-1396. www.olivetreerestaurant.com.* The Greek fare in this restaurant is served in a restored dry good store dating from 1864. Greek menu. Lunch, dinner. Closed Sun; holidays. Bar. Casual attire. Reservations recommended. Outdoor seating. **$$**

★ ★ ★ **ROONEYS.** *90 Henrietta St, Rochester (14620). Phone 585/442-0444; fax 585/461-4817. www.rooneysrestaurant.com.* Any date could be a success at this atmospheric downtown spot, with the intimate mood lighting and white silk table cloths. It is housed in an 1860 tavern, and the original bar is still in use. Many of the meat dishes are wood grilled; there's even venison. Dinner. Closed holidays; Sun in summer. Bar. **$$**

★ ★ **SCOTCH 'N SIRLOIN.** *3450 Winton Pl, Rochester (14623). Phone 585/427-0808; fax 585/427-8503.* Seafood, steak menu. Dinner. Closed Mon; holidays. Bar. Children's menu. **$$$**

Rockville Centre

See also Hempstead, Island Park, New York

Population 24,568
Elevation 25 ft
Area Code 516
Zip 11570
Information Chamber of Commerce, PO Box 226; phone 516/766-0666
Web Site www.rockvillecentrechamber.com

Incorporated in 1893, Rockville Centre maintains Long Island atmosphere in the midst of a thriving commercial district. The town boasts 200 acres of parkland and is a short ride from several fine beach areas.

What to See and Do

Rock Hall Museum. *199 Broadway, Lawrence (11559). 5 miles SW on Broadway from Sunrise Hwy W. Phone 516/239-1157.* (1767) Historic house with period furnishings and exhibits. (Sat-Sun afternoons) **FREE**

Restaurants

★ ★ **ESTORIL.** *191B N Long Beach Rd, Rockville Centre (11577). Phone 516/763-0800.* Mediterranean, Spanish menu. Lunch, dinner. Bar. Casual attire. **$$**

★ ★ **GEORGE MARTIN.** *65 N Park Ave, Rockville Centre (11570). Phone 516/678-7272; fax 516/594-9356. www.georgemartingroup.com.* American menu. Lunch, dinner. Closed Easter, Thanksgiving, Dec 25. **$$**

Rome (D-7)

See also Boonville, Canastota, Oneida, Utica

Settled 1786
Population 34,950
Elevation 462 ft
Area Code 315
Zip 13440
Information Rome Area Chamber of Commerce, 139 W Dominick St; phone 315/337-1700
Web Site www.when-in-rome.com

Originally the site of Fort Stanwix, where, during the Revolutionary War, tradition says the Stars and Stripes were first flown in battle. The author of the "Pledge of Allegiance," Francis Bellamy, is buried in Rome. Griffiss Air Force Base is located here.

What to See and Do

Delta Lake State Park. *8797 Hwy 46, Rome (13440). 6 miles NE off Hwy 46. Phone 315/337-4670. nysparks.state.ny.us.* Swimming beach (Memorial Day weekend-mid-June, limited days; mid-June-Labor Day, full-time), bathhouse, fishing, boating (ramp); tent and trailer sites, hiking, biking, cross-country skiing, picnicking, playground. Standard fees.

Erie Canal Village. *5789 New London Rd, Rome (13440). 2 1/2 miles W on Hwy 49. Phone 315/337-3999; toll-free 888/374-3226. www.eriecanalvillage.com.* Trips on restored section of the Erie Canal aboard mule-drawn 1840 canal packetboat, *The Chief Engineer.* Buildings of 1840s canal village include church, blacksmith shop, train station, museums, schoolhouse, Victorian home, stable, settlers house; hotel; orientation center; picnic area, and restaurant. (Mid-May-Labor Day, daily; call for extended schedule) **$$$**

Fort Rickey Children's Discovery Zoo. *3 miles W via Hwy 49. Phone 315/336-1930. www.fortrickey.com.* Restoration of 1700s British fort is site of a zoo that emphasizes animal contact. Wide variety of wildlife. Picnic facilities. (Mid-May-mid-June: Mon-Fri 10 am-2 pm, Sat-Sun 10 am-4 pm; late June-Labor Day: daily 10 am-5:30 pm) **$$**

Fort Stanwix National Monument. *Phone 315/336-2090.* Reconstructed earth-and-log fort on location of 1758 fort; here the Iroquois signed a treaty opening territory east of Ohio River to colonial expansion. In 1777, the fort was besieged by British; General Benedict Arnold forced their retreat. Costumed guides; film; museum. (Apr-Dec, daily; closed Thanksgiving, Dec 25) **FREE**

Tomb of the Unknown Soldier of the American Revolution. *201 N James St, Rome (13440).* Designed by Lorimar Rich, who also designed the tomb at Arlington National Cemetery.

Woods Valley Ski Area. *Dopp Hill Rd, Westernville. 8 miles N on Hwy 46. Phone 315/827-4721.* Two double chairlifts, T-bar; patrol, snowmaking, school, rentals; bar, cafeteria. Longest run 4,000 feet, vertical drop 500 feet. (Dec-Mar, Tues-Sun; closed Dec 25) Some evening rates. **$$$$**

Special Event

World Series of Bocce. *1412 E Dominick St, Rome (13440). Phone 315/339-3609.* Italian lawn bowling. Mid-July.

Limited-Service Hotels

★ ★ INN AT THE BEECHES. *7900 Turin Rd (Hwy 26 N), Rome (13440). Phone 315/336-1776; toll-free 800/765-7251; fax 315/339-2636. www.thebeeches.com.* 75 rooms, 2 story. Pets accepted, some restrictions; fee. Check-out 11 am. Restaurant. Outdoor pool. Business center. 52 acres with pond. **$**

★ ★ QUALITY INN. *200 S James St, Rome (13440). Phone 315/336-4300; fax 315/336-4492. www.choicehotels.com.* 103 rooms, 2 story. Check-in 3 pm, check-out 11 am. Restaurant. Outdoor pool. **$**

Restaurants

★ ★ THE BEECHES. *7980 Turin Rd (Hwy 26), Rome (13440). Phone 315/336-1700; fax 315/336-7270.* Lunch, dinner, Sun brunch. Closed Mon. Bar. Children's menu. **$$**

★ ★ SAVOY. *255 E Dominick St, Rome (13440). Phone 315/339-3166; fax 315/339-6840.* American, Italian menu. Lunch, dinner. Closed Thanksgiving, Dec 25. Bar. Children's menu. **$$**

Roscoe (F-8)

See also Liberty

Population 597
Elevation 1,300 ft
Area Code 607
Zip 12776
Information Roscoe-Rockland Chamber of Commerce, Box 443; phone 607/498-6055
Web Site www.roscoeny.com

Dutch settlers conquered the wilderness in this Catskill area, but in the process did not destroy it, a practice continued by those who followed. Small and large game abound in the area, and the Willowemoc and Beaverkill rivers provide excellent trout fishing. Four unusual and interesting covered bridges are located in the surrounding countryside.

What to See and Do

Catskill Fly Fishing Center & Museum. *1031 Old Rte 17, Roscoe (12758). Between Roscoe and Livingston Manor. Phone 914/439-4810. www.ccfm.org.* Fishing, hiking, demonstrations, programs, and events. Interpretive exhibits featuring the heritage, science, and art of the sport. Explore the lives of legendary characters who made angling history. Displays of rods, reels, flies; video room, library, hall of fame. Visitor center; gift shop. (Apr-Oct: daily; Nov-Mar: Tues-Sat) **$$**

Specialty Lodging

THE GUEST HOUSE. *408 Debruce Rd, Livingston Manor (12758). Phone 845/439-4000; fax 845/439-3344. www.theguesthouse.com.* Come visit this 40-acre estate on the Willowemoc River for the nearby outdoor activities. 7 rooms, 2 story. Pets accepted; fee. Complimentary full breakfast. Check-in 11 am, check-out noon. Fitness room. Indoor pool, whirlpool. Ten-

nis. Airport transportation available. **$$**

Roslyn

See also Floral Park, Westbury

Population 2,570
Elevation 38 ft
Area Code 516
Zip 11576
Web Site www.historicroslyn.org

What to See and Do

Nassau County Museum of Art. *One Museum Dr, Roslyn (11576). Phone 516/484-9337. www.nassaumueseum.com.* This museum is housed in a mansion that was once owned by poet William Cullen Bryant, and later steel tycoon Henry Clay Frick. Temporary exhibits have covered a wide range of topics, from Napoleon, the Civil War and American Revolution, to the surrealist art of Dali. The museum's permanent collection showcases works of many 19th- and 20th-century American and European artists. Art lovers will also enjoy the museum's outdoor sculpture garden, which features works by such artists as Auguste Rodin and Roy Lichtenstein. Call ahead, because the museum closes when it changes exhibits. (Tues-Sun 11 am-5 pm) **$$**

Restaurants

★ ★ ★ BRYANT & COOPER STEAK HOUSE. *2 Middleneck Rd, Roslyn (11576). Phone 516/627-7270; fax 516/627-7827. www.bryantandcooper.com.* Relax with a cigar and a glass of wine at this classic steakhouse. Have a drink at the bar, or feast in the dark wood and marble-accented dining room. Steak menu. Lunch, dinner. Closed Dec 25. Bar. Valet parking. **$$$**

★ ★ ★ GEORGE WASHINGTON MANOR. *1305 Old Northern Blvd, Roslyn (11576). Phone 516/621-1200; fax 516/621-7018. www.georgewashingtonmanor.com.* This historic building was once the home of Roslyn founder Hendrick Onderdonk, host to President Washington during his 1790 Long Island visit. American continental cuisine is served in colonial décor complete with six fireplaces, original wood beams, and antique furnishings. American menu. Lunch, dinner, Sun brunch. Closed Dec 25. Bar. Valet parking. **$$**

★ ★ ★ L'ENDROIT. *290 Glen Cove Rd, Roslyn (11577). Phone 516/621-6630; fax 516/621-6744. www.lendroitrestaurant.org.* The comfortably formal décor of this restaurant is shaded in burgundy and plum tones with blond wood and fresh flowers. French menu. Lunch, dinner. Closed Sun. Bar. Reservations recommended. **$$$**

Rye

See also White Plains

Restaurant

★ ★ ★ LA PANETIERE. *530 Milton Rd, Rye (10580). Phone 914/967-8140; fax 914/921-0654. www.lapanetiere.com.* Set in a charming 19th-century house in lower Westchester County, La Panetiere feels like home. Once you have dinner, you will wish it were yours. La Panetiere opened in 1985 and has been a stunning standby for wonderful contemporary French fare ever since. The kitchen focuses on local, seasonal ingredients, searching out nearby farmers for fish, poultry, and produce. The quality of the ingredients shows in every bite. The kitchen respects the ingredients and lets them remain the stars. The palate is also respected. It is not assaulted, just massaged with delicious flavors. La Panetiere draws a quiet crowd, and its the perfect spot for romance. The dining room has its original wood-beamed ceiling that gives it a rustic warmth that is balanced with elegant tapestries and beautiful 19th-century furnishings. The room envelops you like a cashmere blanket. Its a place you want to snuggle into and stay a while. Lunch, dinner. Bar. Valet parking. **$$$**

Rouses Point (A-10)

See also Plattsburgh

Population 2,277
Elevation 103 ft
Area Code 518
Zip 12979

A border town on a main route to Montréal, Rouses Point is a busy customs inspection point. A bridge across Lake Champlain goes to Vermont.

What to See and Do

Fort Lennox. *1 61st Ave, St. Paul Delile Auxnoix (J0J*

1G0). 10 miles N off Hwy 223. Phone 450/291-5700. Large stone fort built 1819-1829 on an island in the Richelieu River. Tours; picnic area, cafe; ferry (mid-May-early Sept, daily; fee). (For border-crossing regulations, see MAKING THE MOST OF YOUR TRIP.) **$$**

Sackets Harbor C-4)

See also Watertown

Settled 1800
Population 1,386
Elevation 278 ft
Area Code 315
Zip 13685
Web Site www.sacketsharborny.com

This is a lakeside resort area for the eastern Lake Ontario region. Two major battles of the War of 1812 occurred here. In the first skirmish, the British warships invading the harbor were damaged and withdrew; a landing force was repulsed in the second battle.

What to See and Do

Sackets Harbor Battlefield State Historic Site. *505 W Washington St, Sackets Harbor (13685). Overlooking lake. Phone 315/646-3634. www.sacketsharborny.com.* War of 1812 battlefield; Federal-style Union Hotel (1818); Commandant's House (1850) (fee); US Navy Yard (1812-1955); visitor center, exhibits; demonstrations; tours. (Mid-May-early Sept: Tues-Sat 10 am-5 pm, Sun from 11 am; late Sept-Columbus Day: Fri-Sat 10 am-5 pm, Sun from 11 am) **$**

Westcott Beach State Park. *12224 Hwy 3, Sackets Harbor. Phone 315/938-5083. nysparks.state.ny.us.* Swimming beach, bathhouse, fishing, boating (launch); hiking and nature trails, cross-country skiing, snowmobiling, picnicking, playground, concession, tent and trailer sites. (Mid-May-Columbus Day weekend) Standard fees.

Limited-Service Hotel

★ ONTARIO PLACE HOTEL. *103 General Smith Dr, Sackets Harbor (13685). Phone 315/646-8000; toll-free 800/564-1812; fax 315/646-2506. www.ontarioplacehotel.com.* With beautiful red leather booths, dark woods, and polished wood floors, this downtown Seattle restaurant offers a hip, urban environment in which to enjoy the ultimate in fresh seafood. 38 rooms, 3 story. Pets accepted; fee. Check-out 11 am. **$**

Sag Harbor (B-5)

See also Amagansett, East Hampton, Shelter Island, Southampton

Settled 1660
Population 2,313
Elevation 14 ft
Area Code 631
Zip 11963
Information Chamber of Commerce, PO Box 2810; phone 631/725-0011
Web Site www.hamptons.com

This great whaling town of the 19th century provided prototypes from which James Fenimore Cooper created characters for his sea stories. Sheltered in a cove of Gardiners Bay, the economy of Sag Harbor is still centered around the sea.

What to See and Do

Custom House. *161 Main St, Cold Spring Harbor (11724). Phone 631/692-4664.* Served as custom house and post office during the late 18th and early 19th centuries; antique furnishings. (July-Aug: Tues-Sun; May-June and Sept-Oct: Sat-Sun) **$$**

Elizabeth A. Morton National Wildlife Refuge. *784 Noyac Rd, Sag Harbor (11963). Phone 631/286-0485. refuges.fws.gov.* At one time, Native American tribes inhabited this area. Today, a variety of birdssome endangeredcall this 187-acre refuge home at different times of the year. Both adults and children alike will enjoy observing our feathered friends in the peaceful surroundings, or walking on the nature trail that stretches onto part of a beach.(Daily, 1/2 hour before sunrise to 1/2 hour after sunset) **$**

Sag Harbor Whaling and Historical Museum. *200 Main St, Sag Harbor (11963). Phone 631/725-0770. www.sagharborwhalingmuseum.org.* Listed on the National Register of Historic Places, this museum, housed in a mansion, celebrates Sag Harbors long history of whaling. It features items such as the tools used to capture whales, a replica of a whaleboat, whale teeth and bones, and other materials associated with whaling. Captain Ahab would have been proud of such a fine testament to the sea and its mammoth mammals! (May-Oct, daily 10 am-5 pm, Sun 1-5 pm) **$**

Restaurants

★ ★ ★ **AMERICAN HOTEL.** *Main St, Sag Harbor (11963). Phone 631/725-3535; fax 631/725-3573. www.theamericanhotel.com.* Located at the rear of the hotel lobby, this restaurant boasts a romantic atrium dining room filled with ivy, antiques, whaling memorabilia, and framed maps and paintings. The daily-changing menu reflects the fresh catch and seasonal ingredients. American, French menu. Lunch, dinner. Closed Dec 24-25. Bar. Business casual attire. Reservations recommended. Valet parking. Outdoor seating. **$$$**

★ ★ **ESTIA'S LITTLE KITCHEN.** *1615 Sag Harbor, Sag Harbor (11930). Phone 631/725-1045.* American menu. Breakfast, lunch, dinner. Closed Tues. Casual attire. Reservations recommended. **$$**

★ ★ **IL CAPUCCINO.** *30 Madison St, Sag Harbor (11963). Phone 631/725-2747; fax 631/725-5783. www.ilcapuccino.com.* Italian menu. Dinner. Closed Thanksgiving, Dec 25. Bar. Children's menu. Casual attire. **$$**

★ ★ **SPINNAKER'S.** *63 Main St, Sag Harbor (11963). Phone 631/725-9353; fax 631/725-7340.* Dining room has dark wood and brass accents. American, International menu. Lunch, dinner, Sun brunch. Closed Thanksgiving. Bar. Children's menu. Casual attire. Reservations recommended. Valet parking. **$$**

Saint James

Restaurants

★ ★ **LOTUS EAST.** *416 N Country Rd, Saint James (11780). Phone 631/862-6030.* Chinese menu. Lunch, dinner. Bar. Casual attire. **$$**

★ ★ ★ **MIRABELLE.** *404 N Country Rd, Saint James (11780). Phone 631/584-5999; fax 631/584-3090. www.restaurantmirabelle.com.* With a seasoned French chef and former food writer as proprietors, this Long Island restaurant rivals many in the city. Menu items are a twist on classical French fare, accented with the freshest herbs, and the wine list features highlights from local vintners. French menu. Lunch, dinner. Closed Mon; July 4, Thanksgiving, Dec 25. Bar. Business casual attire. Reservations recommended. Valet parking. **$$$$**

Saranac Lake (B-9)

See also Lake Placid, Tupper Lake, Wilmington

Settled 1819
Population 5,041
Elevation 1,534 ft
Area Code 518
Zip 12983
Information Chamber of Commerce, 30 Main St; phone 518/891-1990 or toll-free 800/347-1997
Web Site www.saranaclake.com

Surrounded by Adirondack Park, the village of Saranac Lake was first settled in 1819 when one Jacob Moody, who had been injured in a sawmill accident, retired to the wilderness, built a log cabin at what is now Pine and River streets, and raised a family of mountain guides. The qualities that attracted Moody and made the town a famous health resort in the 19th century continue to lure visitors in search of fresh, mountain air and a relaxing environment.

What to See and Do

Fishing. More than 130 well-stocked ponds and lakes, plus 600 miles of fishing streams.

Meadowbrook State Public Campground. *4 miles E on Hwy 86, in Adirondack Park. Phone 518/891-4351.* Tent sites, picnicking. (Mid-May-mid-Oct) **$$$**

Mount Pisgah Veterans Memorial Ski Center. *3 miles NE on Hwy 86. Phone 518/891-0970. www.saranaclake.com/pisgah.shtml.* Five slopes, T-bar; patrol, school, snowmaking; snacks. Longest run 1,800 feet, vertical drop 300 feet. (Mid-Dec-mid-Mar, Thurs-Sun) **$$$$**

Robert Louis Stevenson Memorial Cottage. *44 Stevenson Ln, Saranac Lake (12983). Phone 518/891-1462. www.pennypiper.com.* Where Robert Louis Stevenson lived while undergoing treatment for what is believed to have been tuberculosis, 1887-1888; mementos. (July-mid-Sept: Tues-Sun 9:30 am-noon, 1-4:30 pm; daily by appointment) Schedule may vary. **$**

Six Nations Indian Museum. *Adirondack Park, Buck Pond Rd, Onchiota (12989). Off Country Rd 60. Phone 518/891-2299.* Indoor and outdoor exhibits portray the life of the Native American, with a council ground, types of fires, ancient and modern articles; lecture on Native American culture and history. (July-Labor Day: Tues-Sun 10 am-6 pm; May-June, Sept-Oct: by appointment) **$**

Special Events

Adirondack Canoe Classic. *39 Main St, Saranac Lake (12983). The race begins at Adirondack Marina in Long Lake. Phone 518/891-2744; toll-free 800/347-1992. www.saranaclake.com/acc.shtml.* Ninety-mile, three-day race from Old Forge to Saranac Lake for 250 canoes, kayaks, and guideboats. Early Sept.

Willard Hanmer Guideboat, Canoe, and War Canoe Races. *Lake Flower and Saranac River. Phone 518/891-1990.* Early July.

Winter Carnival. *30 Main St # 2, Saranac Lake (12983). Phone 518/891-1990.* Parade; skating, ski, snowshoe, and snowmobile racing. Early Feb.

Limited-Service Hotel

★ ★ HOTEL SARANAC OF PAUL SMITH'S COLLEGE. *100 Main St, Saranac Lake (12983). Phone 518/891-2200; toll-free 800/937-0211; fax 518/891-5664. www.hotelsaranac.com.* Historic hotel (1927); lobby replica of foyer in Danvanzati Palace in Florence, Italy. 88 rooms, 6 story. Pets accepted; fee. Check-in 3 pm, check-out 11 am. Two restaurants, bar. **$**

Full-Service Resort

★ ★ ★ SARANAC INN GOLF & COUNTRY CLUB. *125 Hwy 46, Saranac Lake (12983). Phone 518/891-1402; fax 518/891-1309. www.saranacinn.com.* 10 rooms. Closed Nov-Apr. Check-out 11 am. Restaurant, bar. Golf. **$$**

Full-Service Inn

★ ★ ★ ★ ★ THE POINT. *Hwy 30, Saranac Lake (12983). Phone 518/891-5674; toll-free 800/255-3530; fax 518/891-1152. www.thepointresort.com.* Well-heeled travelers seeking a gentlemans version of "roughing it" head straight for The Point. This former great camp of William Avery Rockefeller revives the spirit of the early 19th century in the Adirondacks, when the wealthy came to rusticate in this sylvan paradise. No signs direct visitors to this intimate and discreet country house hotel, and a decidedly residential ambience is maintained. The resort enjoys a splendid location on a 10-acre peninsula on Upper Saranac Lake. Adirondack twig furnishings, regional decorative objects, and antiques finish the rustic yet sophisticated décor in the accommodations. From snowshoeing and cross-country skiing to water sports and trail hikes, a variety of outdoor activities beckon. Thoughtful touches include morning bread baskets delivered to guests doors; everyone feels cosseted here. Gourmet dining figures largely in the experience, and with a nod to the patrician past, guests don black-tie attire twice weekly. 11 rooms, 1 story. Pets accepted, no children allowed. Complimentary full breakfast. Check-in 3-6 pm, check-out 11 am. Restaurant, bar. Beach. Tennis. **$$$$**

Saratoga National Historical Park (D-9)

See also Glens Falls, Saratoga Springs

30 miles N of Albany on Hwys 4, 32.

Web Site www.nps.gov/sara

In two engagements, September 19 and October 7, 1777, American forces under General Horatio Gates defeated the army of General John Burgoyne in the Battles of Saratoga. This brought France into the war on the side of the colonies. The battle is regarded as the turning point of the Revolutionary War. The scene of this historic event is the rolling hill country between Highways 4 and 32, 5 miles north of Stillwater. Park folders with auto tour information are available at the Visitor Center. (Daily; closed Jan 1, Thanksgiving, Dec 25). **$$**

What to See and Do

Battlefield. *Stillwater.* Living history demonstrations (Feb-Oct).

General Philip Schuyler House. *Schuylerville. 8 miles N on Hwy 4.* (1777) Home of patriot officer who commanded Northern Army before Gates. (Mid-May-Labor Day, Wed-Sun) **FREE**

John Neilson House. *Stillwater.* Restored American staff headquarters. (Usually June-Sept)

Saratoga Monument. *Burgoyne Rd, W of Hwy 4, Schuylerville.* Granite 155-foot obelisk commemorates surrender of Crown forces under Burgoyne to American forces under Gates on Oct 17, 1777. (Mid-May-Labor Day, Wed-Sun) **FREE**

Tour road. *Stillwater.* Self-conducted; 9 miles long; ten stops where exhibits interpret history. (Early Apr-Nov, weather permitting)

Visitor Center and Museum. *Stillwater.* Visitor orientation. Exhibits and film program explain the battles. **FREE**

Saratoga Springs (D-9)

See also Glens Falls, Greenwich, Saratoga National Historical Park, Schenectady

Settled 1773
Population 26,186
Elevation 316 ft
Area Code 518
Zip 12866
Information Saratoga County Chamber of Commerce, 28 Clinton St; phone 518/584-3255
Web Site www.saratoga.org

Saratoga Springs is a resort city that is rural yet cosmopolitan. Much of the town's Victorian architecture has been restored. Saratoga Springs boasts the springs, geysers, and mineral baths that first made the town famous; internationally recognized harness and thoroughbred racing and polo; respected museums; as well as the Saratoga Performing Arts Center.

What to See and Do

High Rock Spring. *Rock St and High Rock Ave, Saratoga Springs.* Now inactive; the original Saratoga Spring.

Historic Congress Park. *Canfield Casino and Union Ave, Saratoga Springs (12866). On Broadway. Phone 518/584-6920.* The Museum of the Historical Society and the Walworth Memorial Museum are housed in the old casino (1870). The museums trace the history of the city's growth, highlighting the springs, hotels, gambling, and personalities; also gift shop. Museums (Memorial Day-Labor Day: daily; rest of year: call for hours). Park (daily). **$$**

National Bottle Museum. *76 Milton Ave, Ballston Spa (12020). 6 miles S via Hwy 50. Phone 518/885-7589.* Antique bottles, jars, stoneware, and related items; research library on bottle collecting. (June-Oct: daily; rest of year: Mon-Fri) **$**

National Museum of Dance. *99 S Broadway, Saratoga Springs. Phone 518/584-2225. www.dancemuseum.org.* Dedicated to American professional dance. Exhibits, hall of fame, museum shop. (Late May-Labor Day: Tues-Sun 10 am-5 pm; Oct-late May: Sat-Sun 10 am-5 pm) **$$**

National Museum of Racing and Hall of Fame. *191 Union Ave, Saratoga Springs (12866). Across from Saratoga Race Course. Phone 518/584-0400. www.racingmuseum.org.* Exhibitions on the history and mechanics of Thoroughbred racing; the stories of racing champs Man o' War, Secretariat, Seattle Slew, and Affirmed; exhibits on Saratoga's gambling heydey. Training track tours in summer (fee). (Mon-Sat 10 am-4 pm, Sun from noon; closed holidays) **$$$**

Petrified Sea Gardens. *42 Petrified Sea Gardens, Saratoga Springs (12866). 3 miles W, off Hwy 29.* Reefs of fossilized organisms; glacial crevices and potholes; sundials, museum. Picnic, hiking, and recreation areas. (Early May-Nov, daily)

Saratoga Gaming and Racing. *Crescent Ave, Saratoga Springs. Phone 518/584-2110.* Video gaming machines; harness racing (Feb-Nov).

Saratoga Lake. *30 Pine Rd, Saratoga Springs. 3 miles E on Hwy 9P.* Boating, fishing, water-skiing. Fee.

★ **Saratoga Spa State Park.** *19 Roosevelt Dr, Saratoga Springs (12866). S Broadway, 1 mile S on Hwy 9 or SW on Hwy 50. Phone 518/584-2535.*This 2,200-acre park is home to the performing arts center, mineral bath houses, golf, and many other recreational facilities. Visitor center. (Daily) **$$** Here are

> **Lincoln and Roosevelt Baths.** *S Broadway, Saratoga Spa State Park. Phone 518/584-2011.* Treatments with the mineral waters. Baths, massage, hot packs. Roosevelt (all year, Wed-Sun); Lincoln (July and Aug, daily).
>
> **Recreation Center.** Swimming, diving, wading pools (June-Labor Day, daily), Victoria Pool, Peerless Pool complex, mineral springs and geysers; two golf courses (Mid-Apr-Nov), picnicking.
>
> **Saratoga Performing Arts Center.** *Hwy 50, Saratoga Springs.* Amphitheater in natural setting seats 5,000 under cover with space for more on the lawn. The Little Theatre is a 500-seat indoor showcase for chamber music. (See SPECIAL EVENTS)

Yaddo Gardens. *Union Ave, Saratoga Springs. Between the Saratoga Race Course and I-87. Phone 518/584-0746.* An artists' retreat since 1926, this Victorian Gothic mansion's famous residents have included Flannery O'Connor, Leonard Bernstein, and John

Cheever. The mansion is closed to the general public, but landscaped gardens are open to all. (Daily) **FREE**

Special Events

Polo. Saratoga Polo Association. *Whitney Field, Bloomfield and Denton Rd, Saratoga Springs (12866). Phone 518/584-8108. www.saratogapolo.com.* June-Aug.

Saratoga Performing Arts Center. *Saratoga Spa State Park and Hwy 50, Saratoga Springs (12866). Phone 518/587-3330.* New York City Opera, June; New York City Ballet, July. The Philadelphia Orchestra and Saratoga Chamber Music Festival, Aug. Jazz festival, summer.

Saratoga Race Course. *Union Ave and Hwy 9P, Saratoga Springs (12866). 1/4 mile SW from exit 14 off I-87. Phone 518/584-6200.* Thoroughbred racing. Late July-early Sept.

Limited-Service Hotels

★ GRAND UNION MOTEL. *120 S Broadway, Saratoga Springs (12866). Phone 518/584-9000; fax 518/584-9001. www.grandunionmotel.com.* Victorian-style lobby. 64 rooms. Pets accepted; fee. Check-in 1 pm, check-out 11 am. Outdoor pool. Airport transportation available. **$$**

★ ★ HOLIDAY INN. *232 Broadway, Saratoga Springs (12866). Phone 518/584-4550; fax 518/584-4417. www.spa-hi.com.* 168 rooms, 4 story. Pets accepted. Check-in 2 pm, check-out 11 am. High-speed Internet access. Restaurant, bar. Fitness room. Indoor pool, outdoor pool. **$$**

★ ★ PRIME SARATOGA SPRINGS HOTEL. *534 Broadway, Saratoga Springs (12866). Phone 518/584-4000; fax 518/584-7430. http:// www.primehotelsandresorts.com.* In this mineral springs region, there's plenty for the mind, body, and soul. Take in horse races, music, museums, performing arts, nature walks, mineral baths, and more. 240 rooms, 5 story. Check-in 3 pm, check-out 11 am. High-speed Internet access. Restaurant, bar. Fitness room. Indoor pool**. $$$**

★ ★ ROOSEVELT INN & SUITES. *2961 Hwy 9, Ballston Spa (12020). Phone 518/584-0980; toll-free 800/524-9147; fax 518/581-8472. www.rooseveltsuites.com.* 51 rooms, 2 story. Complimentary continental breakfast. Check-in 2 pm, check-out 11 am. Restaurant, bar. Fitness room. Indoor pool, outdoor pool, whirlpool. Tennis. **$$**

Full-Service Hotel

★ ★ ★ GIDEON PUTNAM RESORT AND SPA. *24 Gideon Putnam Rd, Saratoga Springs (12866). Phone 518/584-3000; fax 518/584-1354.* 120 rooms, 5 story. Check-in 4 pm, check-out noon. Three restaurants, bar. Two outdoor pools. Golf, 18 holes. Tennis. Airport transportation available**. $$$**

Full-Service Inn

★ ★ ★ THE INN AT SARATOGA. *231 Broadway, Saratoga Springs (12866). Phone 518/583-1890; toll-free 800/274-3573; fax 518/283-2543. www.theinnatsaratoga.com.* Established in 1881. 42 rooms, 3 story. Pets accepted, some restrictions. Complimentary full breakfast. Check-in 3 pm, check-out 11 am. Restaurant, bar**. $$$**

Specialty Lodging

WESTCHESTER HOUSE BED & BREAKFAST. *102 Lincoln Ave, Saratoga Springs (12866). Phone 518/587-7613; toll-free 888/302-1717; fax 518/583-9562. www.westchesterhousebandb.com.* 7 rooms, 2 story. Closed Jan. Complimentary continental breakfast. Check-in 4 pm. Check-out 11 am. Queen Anne Victorian house (1885) in historical residential area**. $$$**

Restaurants

★ ★ ★ CHEZ PIERRE. *979 Hwy 9, Gansevoort (12831). Phone 518/793-3350; fax 518/798-1165.* Guests have been returning for years to experience Joe and Pierrette Baldwin's romantic French restaurant. Dine on the famous dishes, surrounded by murals painted by a local artist and framed pictures of the owner's homeland. French menu. Dinner. Closed Dec 24-25. Bar. Children's menu. **$$**

★ ★ THE INN AT SARATOGA. *231 Broadway, Saratoga Springs (12866). Phone 515/583-1890; fax 515/583-2543. www.theinnatsaratoga.com.* American.

Historic Downtown Saratoga Springs

Saratoga Springs was founded in the early 1800s as a high-society spa and gambling resort. The modern downtown holds a multitude of stunning historic buildings, many of which now house shops, cafs, and restaurants.

Begin at the Saratoga Springs Urban Cultural Park Visitor Center (297 Broadway), once a trolley station and later a "drinking hall." Pick up information, brochures, and maps here, or sign up for a guided walking tour. Cross the street and enter Congress Park. Walk to the Canfield Casino, a resplendent Italianate building that was once the height of fashionable gambling spots and is now home to the Saratoga Historical Museum. Seeing the grand ballroom alone is worth a visit. Returning to Broadway, turn right and browse the many shops. Buildings of particular note include the Rip Van Dam Hotel (353 Broadway), an 1840s Federal-style building, and the Adelphi Hotel (365 Broadway), a classic Victorian edifice. Farther along, at 473 Broadway, the Adirondack Trust Building was built in 1916 in the Classic Revival style. Shops of interest along Broadway include: Symmetry (348 Broadway), offering glass artworks; Ye Olde Wishin' Well (353-355 Broadway) for antiques; Impressions of Saratoga (368 Broadway), which sells fine art and collectibles for horse lovers; Celtic Treasures (456 Broadway), offering Irish goods and gifts; and Legends (511 Broadway), a fine art gallery set in an elegant Victorian brownstone showing the work of regional, national, and internationally known artists. Grab a sandwich and dessert at Mrs. London's bakery (464 Broadway), or stop at 43 Phila Bistro, just off Broadway, for excellent, but causal, fine dining. Also on Phila Street, visit the Ballad Bookstore and Café Lena, the oldest continuously run coffeehouse in America, founded in 1960.

Turn back south on Broadway at Lake Street and return past Congress Park. The National Museum of Dance is on the right about three blocks up. This is the only museum in the United States dedicated exclusively to American professional dance. If a break is in order, stop next door at the Lincoln Mineral Baths, offering mineral baths, massages, and herbal wraps; or try The Crystal Spa at 120 South Broadway. Continue south on Broadway to Saratoga State Park, site of the Saratoga Performing Arts Center, which hosts many summer concerts and is the summertime home to the Philadelphia Orchestra and the New York City Ballet. An expansive green space, the park offers abundant walking paths. Or, return north on South Broadway, turn right onto Circular Street, and follow it to Union Avenue. Turn right again and stroll four blocks to the National Museum of Racing and Hall of Fame, where horse racing is celebrated through displays, paintings, trophies, memorabilia, and interactive activities. The famous Saratoga Race Course lies across the street from the museum, and the Oklahoma Training Track is just a block farther up Union on the left. Also nearby is Bruno's Restaurant (237 Union), a 50s diner that's lots of fun.

Dinner. Bar. Casual attire. Reservations recommended. Outdoor seating. **$$**

★ **OLDE BRYAN INN.** *123 Maple Ave, Saratoga Springs (12866). Phone 518/587-2990; fax 518/587-4316. www.oldebryaninn. com.* Seafood menu. Dinner. Closed holidays. Bar. Children's menu. Outdoor seating. **$$**

Saugerties (F-9)

See also Cairo, Hudson, Kingston, Woodstock

Population 19,868
Elevation 155 ft
Area Code 845
Zip 12477
Web Site saugerties.hvnet.com

At the confluence of Esopus Creek and the Hudson River, Saugerties was a port of call for riverboats. The town was famous for building racing sloops and for the production of fine paper, leather, and canvas.

What to See and Do

Opus 40 & Quarryman's Museum. *50 Fite Rd, Saugerties (12477). Phone 845/246-3400.* Environmental sculpture rising out of an abandoned bluestone quarry. More than 6 acres of fitted bluestone constructed over 37 years by sculptor Harvey Fite. Site of Sunset Concert series and other programs. Quarryman's Museum houses collection of tools of quarry workers and others. (Memorial Day-Columbus Day, Fri-Sun; some Sat reserved for special events) **$$$**

Limited-Service Hotel

★ COMFORT INN. *2790 Hwy 32 N, Saugerties (12477). Phone 845/246-1565; fax 845/246-1631. www.choicehotels.com.* 66 rooms. Pets accepted; fee. Complimentary continental breakfast. Check-in 2 pm, check-out 11 am. **$**

Restaurants

★ ★ CAFE TAMAYO. *89 Partition St, Saugerties (12477). Phone 845/246-9371. www.cafetamayo.com.* This friendly, bistro-style establishment features French-and Italian-influenced fare made with local farm-fresh ingredients, including goat cheese, herbs, and various game. American menu. Dinner. Closed Mon-Wed; holidays. Bar. Casual attire. Reservations recommended. Guest rooms available. **$$$**

★ ★ MEDITERRANEAN KITCHEN. *91 Partition St, Saugerties (12477). Phone 845/246-0112.* Mediterranean menu. Dinner, brunch. Closed Wed; holidays. Bar. Business casual attire. Reservations recommended. Outdoor seating. **$$**

★ ★ NEW WORLD HOME COOKING. *1411 Hwy 212, Saugerties. Phone 845/246-0900.* American, International menu. Lunch, dinner. Closed holidays. Casual attire. Reservations recommended. Outdoor seating. **$$**

★ ★ RED ONION. *1654 Hwy 212 and Glusco Tpike, Saugerties. Phone 845/679-1223.* American, International menu. Dinner, brunch. Closed Wed; holidays. Bar. Business casual attire. Reservations recommended. Outdoor seating. **$$**

Sayville (C-3)

See also Bay Shore

Population 16,735
Elevation 20 ft
Area Code 631
Zip 11782
Information Chamber of Commerce, Montauk Hwy and Lincoln Ave, PO Box 235; phone 631/567-5257
Web Site www.sayville.com

What to See and Do

Long Island Maritime Museum. *86 W Ave, West Sayville (11796). 1 mile W on Montauk Hwy, West Ave. Phone 631/854-4974.* Local maritime exhibits; oyster cull house (circa 1870); Frank E. Penny Boatshop (1900); tug boat *Charlotte* (1888); oyster vessel *Priscilla* (1888); oyster sloop *Modesty* (1923). (Mon-Sun; closed holidays) **$$**

Limited-Service Hotels

★ COMFORT INN. *2695 Hwy 112, Medford (11763). Phone 631/654-3000; toll-free 800/626-7779; fax 631/654-1281. www.choicehotels.com.* 76 rooms, 2 story. Complimentary continental breakfast. Check-in 2 pm, check-out 11 am. Fitness room. Outdoor pool. **$**

★ ★ HOLIDAY INN. *3845 Veterans Memorial Hwy, Ronkonkoma (11779). Phone 631/585-9500; toll-free 800/422-9510; fax 631/585-9550. www.holiday-inn.com/ronkonkomany.* 289 rooms, 2 story. Check-in 2 pm, check-out noon. High-speed Internet access. Restaurant, bar. Fitness room. Outdoor pool. Airport transportation available. **$$**

Schenectady (D-9)

See also Albany, Amsterdam, Howes Cave, Johnstown, Saratoga Springs, Troy

Settled 1661
Population 61,821
Elevation 224 ft
Area Code 518
Information Schenectady County Chamber of Commerce, 306 State St, 12305; phone 518/372-5656 or toll-free 800/962-8007
Web Site www.sayschenectady.org

Schenectady offers a unique blend of the old and the new, from row houses of the pre-Revolutionary War stockade area to the bustle and vitality of the downtown area.

What to See and Do

The Historic Stockade Area. *32 Washington Ave, Sche-*

nectady (12305). Downtown. Phone 518/374-0263. www.historicstockade.com. Privately owned houses, some dating to colonial times, many marked with historic plaques. Schenectady County Historical Society offers guided tours of their building and folder describing walking tour. The society also maintains a historical museum with a collection of Sexton and Ames paintings; also 19th-century dollhouse, Shaker collection, genealogical library (fee). (Mon-Sat, afternoons). **$**

Proctor's Theatre. *432 State St, Schenectady (12305). Phone 518/346-6204.*(1926) Former movie/vaudeville palace is a regional performing arts center hosting Broadway touring shows, dance, opera, and plays. 1931 Wurlitzer theater organ. Seats 2,700. Built by F. F. Proctor and designed by Thomas Lamb, its interior incorporates elegance and grandeur; pastoral mural by A. Lundberg. Free tours by appointment.

The Schenectady Museum & Planetarium and Schenectady Heritage Area. *15 Nott Terrace Hts, Schenectady (12308). Off Nott Terrace. Phone 518/382-7890. www.schenectadymuseum.org.* Exhibits and programs on art, history, science, and technology. (Tues-Fri 10 am-4:30 pm, Sat-Sun noon-5 pm; closed holidays) Planetarium shows and children's planetarium shows (summer: Tues-Sun; rest of year: Sat-Sun) **$$**

Union College. *807 Union St, Schenectady (12308). Union Ave and Union St. Phone 518/388-6000. www.union.edu.* (1795) (2,000 students) Country's first planned campus; original buildings (1812-1814) by French architect Joseph Jacques Rame. Nott Memorial (1875), only 16-sided building in the Northern Hemisphere. Also on campus is Jackson Garden, 8 acres of landscaped and informal plantings. Tours of campus.

Special Events

Festival of Nations. *15 Nott Terrace Hts, Schenectady (12308). Phone 518/382-7890.* Second Sat in May.

Walkabout. Walking tour of six houses and three churches in the Historic Stockade Area. Last weekend in Sept.

Limited-Service Hotel

★ ★ HOLIDAY INN. *100 Nott Terrace, Schenectady (12308). Phone 518/393-4141; fax 518/393-4174. www.holiday-inn. com.* 184 rooms, 4 story. Pets accepted, some restrictions. Complimentary full breakfast. Check-out noon. Restaurant, bar. Fitness room. Indoor pool, whirlpool. Airport transportation available. **$**

Full-Service Inn

★ ★ ★ GLEN SANDERS MANSION INN. *1 Glen Ave, Scotia (12302). Phone 518/374-7262; fax 518/374-7391. www.glensandersmansion.com.* This inn is a 1995 addition to the Glen Sanders Mansion restaurant, which is housed in the original historic residence. From business people to brides, varied clientele are drawn to the combination of historic style and 20th-century comforts along the Mohawk River. 22 rooms, 2 story. Complimentary continental breakfast. Check-in 3 pm, check-out 11 am. Restaurant. **$**

Restaurant

★ ★ ★ GLEN SANDERS MANSION. *1 Glen Ave, Scotia (12302). Phone 518/374-7262; fax 518/374-7391. www.glensandersmansion.com.* Located in a lovely old mansion, the dining room is small and cozy with two crackling fireplaces. There is something on the menu for everyone in the party. Don't miss the made-on-premises desserts! American menu. Lunch, dinner. Closed holidays. Bar. Children's menu. Business casual attire. Reservations recommended. Outdoor seating. **$$$**

Schroon Lake (C-9)

See also Hague, North Creek

Population 1,759
Elevation 867 ft
Information Chamber of Commerce, PO Box 726; phone 518/532-7675 or toll-free 888/724-7666
Web Site www.schroonlake.org

The village extends for 2 miles along the west shore of Schroon Lake. A popular summer resort area, 70 lakes and ponds are within a 5-mile radius. Outdoor recreation activities are popular all year long.

What to See and Do

Natural Stone Bridge and Caves. *535 Stone Bridge Rd, Pottersville (12860). 8 miles S on I-87, exit 26, then 2 miles W. Phone 518/494-2283. www.stonebridgeandcaves.com.* Self-guided tour; underground river, rock formations, caves; picnicking. (Memorial Day-Columbus Day, daily) **$$**

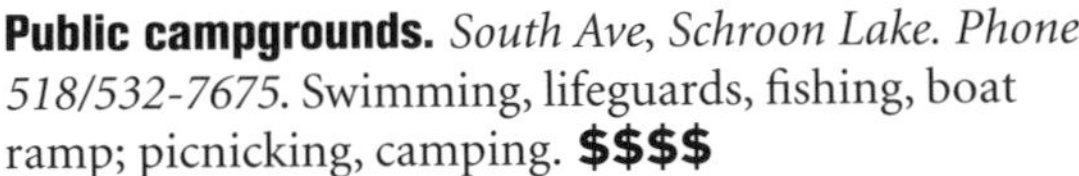

Public campgrounds. *South Ave, Schroon Lake. Phone 518/532-7675.* Swimming, lifeguards, fishing, boat ramp; picnicking, camping. **$$$$**

Eagle Point. *8 miles S on Hwy 9, N of Pottersville in Adirondack Forest Preserve. Phone 518/494-2220.* Also bathhouse. (Mid-May-early Sept) **$$$$**

Paradox Lake. *On Hwy 74, 2 miles E of Severance. Phone 518/532-7451.* Also boat launch, bathhouse. (Mid-May-mid-Nov) **$$$**

Seneca Falls (D-5)

See also Auburn, Geneva, Skaneateles, Waterloo

Settled 1787
Population 9,347
Elevation 469 ft
Information Seneca County Chamber of Commerce, Hwys 5 and 20 W; phone 315/568-2906 or toll-free 800/732-1848
Web Site www.senecachamber.org

The first convention of the US Women's Suffrage Movement met in July 1848, in Seneca Falls. The town was the home of Amelia Jenks Bloomer, who drew international attention to women's rights by advocating and wearing the costume that bears her name. The two great leaders of the movement, Elizabeth Cady Stanton and Susan B. Anthony, also worked in Seneca Falls. The Stanton home has been preserved.

A 50-foot drop in the Seneca River provided power for local industry. The rapids have been replaced by the New York State Barge Canal.

What to See and Do

Cayuga Lake State Park. *2678 Lower Lake Rd, Seneca Falls (13148). 3 miles E on Hwy 89. Phone 315/568-5163. nysparks.state.ny.us.* Swimming, beach, bathhouse, fishing, boating (launch, dock); picnicking, playground, tent and trailer sites, cabins (late Apr-late Oct). **$$**

Montezuma National Wildlife Refuge. *5 miles E on Hwys 20, 5. Phone 315/568-5987.* Federal wildlife refuge; visitor center. Peak migration for shorebirds (fall), Canada geese and ducks (spring and fall). Refuge (daily daylight hours). Office (Mon-Fri; closed holidays). **FREE**

National Women's Hall of Fame. *76 Fall St, Seneca Falls (13148). Phone 315/568-2936. www.greatwomen.org.* Museum and education center honors famous American women, past and present. (May-Sept: Mon-Sat 10 am-4 pm, Sun from noon; Oct-Apr: Wed-Sat 10 am-4 pm) **$$**

Seneca Falls Historical Society Museum. *55 Cayuga St, Seneca Falls (13148). Phone 315/568-8412.* A 19th-century, 23-room Victorian/Queen Anne mansion with period room, local history exhibits; research library, and archives. Museum shop. Tours (July-Aug, daily). **$**

State Barge Canal Locks #2 and #3. Observation point on south side, off E Bayard St to Seneca St. (May-early Nov)

Women's Rights National Historical Park. *136 Fall St, Seneca Falls (13148). Phone 315/568-2991.* Visitor center with exhibits and film; talks scheduled daily during summer. (Daily 9 am-5 pm) **$$** Included in the park are the Wesleyan Chapel and the

Elizabeth Cady Stanton House. *32 Washington St, Seneca Falls (13148).* (Circa 1830) In Women's Rights National Historical Park. House where Stanton worked and lived from 1847 to 1862. Artifacts include original china, books, and furniture. Changing exhibits. Tours (daily). **$**

Special Event

Convention Days Celebration. *115 Fall St, Seneca Falls (13148). Phone 315/568-2906.* Commemorates first women's rights convention, held July 19 and 20, 1848. Weekend closest to July 19 and 20.

Shandaken (F-8)

See also Catskill Park, Hunter, Kingston, Woodstock

Population 3,235
Elevation 1,070 ft
Area Code 845
Zip 12480

This Catskill Mountain town carries the Iroquois name meaning "rapid waters." Shandaken is a town with the combination of being in the Catskills and having easy access to New York City. Shandaken is home of the highest peak in the Catskills, Slide Mountain. It is also the home of Esopus Creek, one of the finest wild trout fisheries in the East, also noted for tubing. Skiing, hiking, and hunting are popular in this area of mountains and streams.

What to See and Do

Belleayre Mountain. *8 miles W, just off Hwy 28 at Highmount. Phone 845/254-5600. www.belleayre.com.* Two quad, triple, two double chairlifts; three handle tows; 41 runs; patrol, school, rentals; snowmaking; cafeterias; nursery. Longest run 2 1/4 miles; vertical drop 1,404 feet. (Nov-early Apr, daily) Half-day rates. Over 5 miles of cross-country trails. **$$$$**

Full-Service Hotel

★ ★ ★ **THE COPPERHOOD INN & SPA.** *70-39 Hwy 28, Shandaken (12480). Phone 845/688-2460; fax 845/688-7484. www.copperhood.com.* A European-style oasis with elegant, inviting rooms and helpful staff. Dine with variety of healthy and tasty meals. Guests can take advantage of an extensive range of spa services and recreational activities, or simply lounge and enjoy nature that abounds. 20 rooms, 2 story. Check-in 3 pm, check-out 11 am. Fitness room, spa. Indoor pool, whirlpool. Tennis. **$$$**

Specialty Lodging

BIRCH CREEK INN. *Hwy 28, Box 323, Pine Hill (12465). Phone 845/254-5222; fax 845/254-5812. www.abirchcreekinn.com.* Built in 1896; in Catskill Mountain forest. 6 rooms, 2 story. Complimentary full breakfast. Check-in 3 pm, check-out 11 am. Outdoor pool. **$$**

Shelter Island (B-4)

See also East Hampton, Greenport, Sag Harbor

Settled 1652
Population 1,234
Elevation 50 ft
Area Code 631
Zip 11964
Information Chamber of Commerce, PO Box 598; phone 631/749-0399
Web Site www.shelter-island.org

Quakers, persecuted by the Puritans in New England, settled Shelter Island in Gardiners Bay off the east end of Long Island. The island is reached by car or pedestrian ferry from Greenport, on the north fork of Long Island, or from North Haven (Sag Harbor), on the south. There is a monument to the Quakers and a graveyard with 17th-century stones plus two historical museums; the 18th-century Havens House and the 19th-century Manhanset Chapel. Also here is the 2,200-acre Nature Conservancy's Mashomack Preserve, with miles of trails for hiking and educational programs. The island offers swimming, boating off miles of sandy shoreline, biking, hiking, tennis, and golfing.

Limited-Service Hotel

★ ★ **PRIDWIN BEACH HOTEL AND COTTAGES.** *81 Shore Rd, Shelter Island (11964). Phone 631/749-0476; toll-free 800/273-2497; fax 631/749-2071. www.pridwin.com.* 40 rooms, 3 story. Closed mid-Oct-Apr. Complimentary full breakfast. Check-out noon. Restaurant, bar. Outdoor pool. Tennis. **$$**

Restaurants

★ ★ ★ **CHEQUIT INN.** *23 Grand Ave, Shelter Island (11964). Phone 631/749-0018; fax 631/749-0183. www.shelterislandinns.com.* This casual Victorian inn dishes up seafood delights and classic Continental cuisine for guests and visitors to the Shelter Islands. The homestyle Atlantic cod fish and chips with fresh tartar sauce is a proprietary specialty. The inn was originally built (circa 1870) around a maple tree that, now enormous, still shades the terrace that overlooks Deering Harbor. Continental menu. Lunch, dinner. Bar. Children's menu. Casual attire. Reservations recommended. Outdoor seating. **$$**

★ ★ ★ **RAM'S HEAD INN.** *108 Ram Island Dr, Shelter Island (11965). Phone 631/749-0811; fax 631/749-0059. www.shelterislandinns.com.* Continental menu. Dinner, brunch. Closed Nov-Apr. Bar. Children's menu. Casual attire. Reservations recommended. Outdoor seating. **$$$**

Skaneateles (D-5)

See also Auburn, Finger Lakes, Oneida, Seneca Falls, Syracuse

Settled 1794
Population 7,323
Elevation 919 ft
Area Code 315
Zip 13152
Web Site www.skaneateles.com

Skaneateles (skany-AT-les) was once a stop on the Underground Railroad. Today it is a quiet resort town at the north end of Skaneateles Lake.

What to See and Do

Boat trips. *11 Jordan St, Skaneateles (13152). Depart Clift Park dock. Phone 315/685-8500; toll-free 800/545-4318.* A 32-mile cruise along shoreline of Skaneateles Lake (July-Aug, Mon-Sat). Lunch cruise (Mon-Fri), dinner cruises (nightly), 3-hour excursion (Sun), sightseeing cruise (daily). Contact Mid-Lakes Navigation Co, PO Box 61-M. (May-Sept) **$$$$**

Special Event

Polo Matches. *Skaneateles Polo Club Grounds, 813 Andrews Rd, Skaneateles (13152). 1 mile S, just off Hwy 41A. Phone 315/685-7373.* Sun in July-Aug.

Limited-Service Hotel

★ THE BIRD'S NEST. *1601 E Genesee St and Hwy 20, Skaneateles (13152). Phone 315/685-5641; toll-free 888/447-7417. www.thebirdsnest.net.* 30 rooms. Pets accepted, some restrictions; fee. Check-in 3 pm. Check-out noon. Outdoor pool, whirlpool. Duck pond. **$**

Full-Service Hotel

★ ★ ★ MIRBEAU INN & SPA. *851 W Genesee St, Skaneateles (13152). Phone 315/685-5006; toll-free 877/647-2328; fax 315/685-5150. www.mirbeau.com.* Tucked away in the lush Finger Lakes, Mirbeau Inn & Spa captures the essence of the enchanting French countryside. This lovely 12-acre country estate, filled with ponds, herb and rose gardens, and woodlands, seems to have leapt off the canvases of Claude Monet. Together with the Arcadian setting, the European-style spa attracts world-weary visitors in need of relaxation and rejuvenation. At once modern and charming, the spas massage treatment rooms feature fireplaces and individual stereo systems. Vichy showers and kurs highlight the facilitys dedication to European approaches, while fitness classes scan the world for inspiration and include yoga and Pilates, among other techniques. Delightful Provenal fabrics and French country furnishings in the accommodations warm the hearts of Francophiles. With winsome views of the lily pond and footbridge and the fresh-from-the-garden taste of the dishes, the restaurant truly transports diners. 34 rooms, 2 story. Check-in 4 pm, check-out noon. High-speed Internet access. Restaurant, two bars. Fitness room, fitness classes available, spa. Whirlpool. **$$$**

Full-Service Inn

★ ★ ★ SHERWOOD INN. *26 W Genesee St, Skaneateles (13152). Phone 315/685-3405; toll-free 800/743-7963; fax 315/685-8983. www.thesherwoodinn.com.* Beautifully furnished with an aura of refinement, this 1807 inn, a former stage coach stop, displays fantastic views of the lake during all seasons. The staff, cuisine, and common and guest room appointments are as refreshing as the country lake breezes. 24 rooms, 3 story. Complimentary continental breakfast. Check-in 3 pm, check-out noon. Wireless Internet access. Two restaurants, bar. **$$**

Specialty Lodgings

THE ARBOR HOUSE INN. *41 Fennell St, Skaneateles (13152). Phone 315/685-8966; toll-free 888/234-4558. www.arborhouseinn.com.* 8 rooms. Complimentary full breakfast. Check-in 3 pm, check-out 11 am. **$$**

HOBBIT HOLLOW BED & BREAKFAST. *3061 W Lake Rd, Skaneateles (13152). Phone 315/685-2791; fax 315/685-3426. www.hobbithollow.com.* This colonial Revival building with country décor is set on 300 acres in the Finger Lakes region. Guests will enjoy views of Skaneateles Lake and a charming town full of stately homes, restaurants, and shops. The region's many wineries are a short drive away. 5 rooms. Children over 18 years only. Complimentary full breakfast. Check-in 3 pm, check-out noon. **$$$**

HUMMINGBIRDS HOUSE B&B. *4273 W Genesee St, Skaneateles (13152). Phone 315/685-5075; toll-free 866/207-1900.* 4 rooms. Complimentary full breakfast. Check-in 3 pm, check-out 11 am. Whirlpool. **$$**

LADY OF THE LAKE. *2 W Lake St, Skaneateles (13152). Phone 315/685-7997; toll-free 888/685-7997. www.ladyofthelake.net.* The Lady of the Lake, a beautiful 1899 Queen Anne Victorian house located across from Skaneateles Lake, is an elegant choice for your stay in Skaneateles. With a large front porch, décor that includes period furnishing and antiques, and rooms named after the ladies who previously owned the house, this bed-and-breakfast is filled with the character and charm of days gone by. But time has not completely stood still here; plenty of modern comforts are offered, including high-speed Internet access, cable television, and air conditioning, as well as a refrigerator stocked with complimentary soft drinks, bottled water, and beer. 3 rooms. Pets accepted. Children over 8 years only. Complimentary full breakfast. Check-in 3 pm, check-out 11 am. **$$**

Spa

★★★ **MIRBEAU SPA.** *851 W Genessee St, Skaneateles, (13152). Phone 315/685-5000.* For those who have ever wanted to leap into the pages of a fairy-tale book as a child, you've finally gotten your chance. The quaint central New York town of Skaneateles is home to The Mirbeau Inn and Spa, a glorious French country estate whose soaring spruce trees, colorful gardens, and picture-perfect ponds make for an idyllic storybook retreat. But the fairy-tale experience doesn't stop with its picturesque setting. Inside, the Mirbeau Spa features elegant surroundings and relaxing treatments that will make you feel like a princess (or prince!) for a day. Ten-thousand square-feet of tranquility awaits you at The Spa, whose breathtaking natural surroundings serve as the inspiration for everything from the herbal-infused steam rooms to body wraps and facials. After some pre-treatment relaxation in the resting area—complete with heated foot pools—you're ready to head to one of 14 treatment rooms for an experience as soothing as The Spa's Monet-like setting. Indulge in the A Rose Is A Rose Is A Rose body wrap. Taking inspiration from the gardens outside, this treatment uses a warm linen wrap that combines essential oils of the Bulgarian rose with natural honey to soften and hydrate the skin. More than just a massage, the Monet's Favorite Fragrance massage blends essential oils of herbs and flowers from the Finger Lakes region to create an aromatherapy treatment that stimulates the senses as the body is soothed with a Swedish massage. The Fields of Lavender manicure/pedicure is so luxurious that even Cinderella, herself, wishes she could have been treated to it before the ball. Here, you'll experience a warm wildflower-scented soak followed by an exfoliation that uses Turkish salts and lavender oil for the feet or a vegetal exfoliant for the hands. Whether it's a luxuriant spa treatment or an invigorating workout in the expansive fitness center, Mirbeau Spa will send you on your way to live happily ever after.

Restaurant

★★★ **THE DINING ROOM.** *851 W Genessee St, Skaneateles (13152). Phone 315/685-5006. www.mirbeau.com.* Want to visit Provence without bringing along a passport? Try the Mirbeau Inn & Spa's (see) Dining Room. After being pampered like royalty at the spa, you can waltz right into the casually elegant Dining Room in your cushy spa robe, where the pampering continues. Mirbeau rests on the outskirts of charming Skaneateles, graced with a pristine lake. The Dining Room's world-class service, food, and ambience attract guests from around the world. The chef and spa management work together to match guests' tastes and personal preferences with the best of French cuisine. Each dish is unique and unforgettable. American, French menu. Breakfast, lunch, dinner. Bar. Business casual attire. Reservations recommended. Outdoor seating. **$$$**

Smithtown

See also Huntington, Northport, Port Jefferson, Stony Brook

Population 115,715
Elevation 60 ft
Area Code 631
Zip 11787
Web Site www.smithtowninfo.com

Smithtown includes six unincorporated hamlets and three incorporated villages. The village of Smithtown is situated near several state parks.

Full-Service Hotels

★★★ **MARRIOTT ISLANDIA LONG ISLAND.** *3635 Express Dr, Hauppauge (11788). Phone 631/232-3000; fax 631/232-3029. www.marriott.com.* 278 rooms, 10 story. Check-in 3 pm, check-out noon. High-speed Internet access. Restaurant, bar. Fitness room. Indoor pool, whirlpool. Airport transportation available. **$**

★★★ **SHERATON LONG ISLAND HOTEL.** *110 Vanderbilt Motor Pkwy, Smithtown (11788). Phone 631/231-1100; toll-free 800/325-3535; fax 631/231-1143. www.longislandsheraton.com.* Local businesses and industrial parks draw corporate clientele, but ocean and sound beaches are also nearby. 209 rooms, 6 story. Pets accepted. Check-in 3 pm, check-out noon. Two restaurants, bar. Children's activity center.

Fitness room. Indoor pool, whirlpool. Airport transportation available. **$$**

Southampton (C-4)

See also East Hampton, Hampton Bays, Riverhead, Sag Harbor

Settled 1640
Population 54,712
Elevation 25 ft
Area Code 631
Zip 11968
Information Chamber of Commerce, 76 Main St; phone 631/283-0402
Web Site www.southamptonchamber.com

Southampton has many colonial houses. The surrounding dunes and beaches are dotted with luxury estates.

What to See and Do

Conscience Point National Wildlife Refuge. *North Sea Rd, Southampton (11968). Phone 631/286-0485.* With 60 acres, this refuge is known for its maritime grasslands. A host of birds and fowl call this area home in the colder months, and a different variety migrate here in the warmer season. The refuge opened in 1971, and over the years has played host to many guests, both feathered and non-feathered. Conscience Point, itself overlooks the North Sea Harbor and is a quiet area. This refuge is for those who want such peace and quiet while they are touring. (Hours vary)

Old Halsey House. *249 S Main St, Southampton (11968). Phone 631/283-2494.* (1648) Oldest English frame house in the state. Furnished with period furniture; colonial herb garden. (Mid-July-mid-Sept, Tues-Sun) **$**

Parrish Art Museum. *25 Jobs Ln, Southampton. Town center. Phone 631/283-2118.* Includes 19th- and 20th-century American paintings and prints; repository for William Merritt Chase and Fairfield Porter; Japanese woodblock prints; collection of Renaissance works; changing exhibits; arboretum; performing arts and concert series; lectures; research library. (Mid-June-mid-Sept: Mon-Tues and Thurs-Sat, also Sun afternoons; rest of year: Mon and Thurs-Sun; closed holidays) **$**

Shinnecock Indian Outpost. *Old Montauk Hwy, Southampton (11968). Phone 631/283-8047. www.shinnecocktradingpost.com.* This funky shop sells tax-free cigarettes, American Indian crafts, clothes, and glassware. The prices are reasonable, and you can do your browsing and shopping quite early in the morning, should you wish to avoid too many crowds. There also is a deli, where you can get your morning coffee and bagel. The Outpost makes for a quick and easy stop before you begin your day of sightseeing. (Daily 6:30 am-6 pm)

Southampton College of Long Island University. *239 Montauk Hwy, Southampton (11968). Montauk Hwy (Hwy 27A). Phone 631/283-4000. www,southampton.liu.edu.* (1963) (1,200 students) Liberal arts, marine science research. Tour of campus.

Southampton Historical Museum. *17 Meeting House Ln, Southampton (11968). Phone 631/283-2494.* This mansion, built in 1843, depicts Southamptons colorful history. It has some original furnishings, American Indian items, photos, and quilts. In addition to the house, the museums grounds include a one-room schoolhouse, drugstore, paint shop, blacksmith shop, and carpentry store. There also are special exhibits at different times of the year. (Tues-Sat 11 am-5 pm, Sun 1-5 pm) **$**

Water Mill Museum. *41 Old Mill Rd, Water Mill (11976). Phone 631/726-4625. www.watermillmuseum.org.* Restored gristmill, 18th century, houses old tools, other exhibits; craft demonstrations. (Mon, Thurs-Sat 11 am-5 pm, Sun from 1 pm) **$**

Special Events

Hampton Classic Horse Show. *240 Snake Hollow Rd, Bridgehampton. N of Hwy 27. Phone 631/537-3177. www.hamptonclassic.com.* Horse show jumping event. Celebrities, food, shopping, family activities. Last week in Aug.

Powwow. *Shinnecock Indian Reservation, Southampton. Off Hwy 27A. Phone 631/283-6143.* Dances, ceremonies, displays. Labor Day weekend.

Limited-Service Hotel

★★ **SOUTHAMPTON INN.** *91 Hill St, Southampton (11968). Phone 631/283-6500; toll-free 800/732-6500; fax 631/283-6559. www.southamptoninn.com.* 90 rooms, 2 story. Pets accepted, some restrictions; fee. Check-in 4 pm. Check-out 11 am. Restaurant, bar. Children's activity center. Outdoor pool. Tennis. **$$**

Specialty Lodging

THE VILLAGE LATCH INN. *101 Hill St, Southampton (11968). Phone 631/283-2160; fax 631/283-3236. www.villagelatch.com.* 67 rooms, 3 story. Pets accepted, some restrictions; fee. Complimentary full breakfast. Check-in 4 pm. Check-out 11 am. Outdoor pool. Tennis. **$$$**

Restaurants

★ ★ **COAST GRILL.** *1109 Noyack Rd, Southampton (11968). Phone 631/283-2277; fax 631/287-4493.* American, seafood menu. Dinner. Closed Mon-Thurs. Bar. Casual attire. **$$**

★ **GOLDEN PEAR.** *99 Main St, Southampton (11968). Phone 631/283-8900; fax 631/283-7719.* American menu. Breakfast, lunch. Casual attire. **$$**

★ ★ **JOHN DUCK JR.** *15 Prospect St, Southampton (11968). Phone 631/283-0311; fax 631/283-0282.* Established 1900; 4th generation of ownership. American, German menu. Lunch, dinner. Closed Mon; Dec 24-25. Bar. Children's menu. Casual attire. **$$**

★ ★ **LE CHEF.** *75 Jobs Ln, Southampton (11968). Phone 631/283-8581; fax 631/283-0601. www.lechef-bistro.com.* French menu. Lunch, dinner, brunch. Bar. Casual attire. **$$**

★ ★ **LOBSTER INN.** *162 Inlet Rd, Southampton (11968). Phone 631/283-1525; fax 631/283-8159.* American, seafood menu. Lunch, dinner. Closed Thanksgiving, Dec 24-25. Bar. Children's menu. Casual attire. Outdoor seating. **$$**

★ ★ **MIRKO'S.** *Water Mill Sq, Water Mill (11976). Phone 631/726-4444; fax 631/726-4472. www.mirkos restaurant.com.* American menu. Dinner. Closed Tues; also Jan. Bar. Reservations recommended. Outdoor seating. **$$$**

Southold (B-4)

See also Greenport, Riverhead

Settled 1640
Population 20,599
Elevation 32 ft
Area Code 631
Zip 11971
Information Greenport-Southold Chamber of Commerce, 1205 Tuthill Rd Extension, 11971; phone 631/765-3161
Web Site www.northfork.com

What to See and Do

Greenport Pottery. *64725 Main Rd, Southold (11971). Phone 631/477-1687.* For a great selection of homemade pottery, this is the place to go on the North Fork. The owner creates beautiful, softly-colored lamps, vases, mugs, dishes, decorative plates, and other items in his shop. You can custom order items, and he will ship just about anywhere. In addition to the fine craftsmanship, the pottery is extremely reasonably pricedjust a fraction of what comparable shops in the tonier Hamptons would charge. For these prices, you can buy a few items for yourself and bring some gifts for your favorite family members and friends back home. Tip: Drive slowly, because the place is small and you just might breeze past it. (Wed-Mon 10 am-5 pm)

Horton Point Lighthouse & Nautical Museum. *Lighthouse Park, 54325 Main Rd, Southold (11971). Phone 631/765-5500.* (Memorial Day-Columbus Day, Sat and Sun 11:30 am-4 pm) **DONATION**

The Old House. *Cases Ln and Hwy 25, Cutchogue. On Hwy 25, on the Village Green. Phone 631/734-7122.* (1649) Example of early English architecture; 17th and 18th-century furnishings. Also on Village Green are the Wickham Farmhouse (early 1700s) and the Old Schoolhouse Museum (1840). (July-Labor Day: Sat-Mon; Sept-Oct: by appointment)

Southold Indian Museum. *1080 Bayview Rd, Southold (11971). Phone 631/765-5577. www.southoldindianmuseum.org.* This museum celebrates Long Islands Native American history and features displays of artifacts like weapons, tools, and pottery, as well as other items used by the Long Island Algonquins. Special exhibits change regularly, with some featuring Indian music and dance. Also on display are artifacts from South, Central, and Western American Indians. (Sun 1:30-4:30 pm; also Sat in Jul-Aug; other times by appointment) **$**

Limited-Service Hotel

★ ★ **SANTORINI BEACHCOMBER RESORT MOTEL.** *3800 Duck Pond Rd, Cutchogue (11935). Phone 631/734-6370; fax 631/734-5579. www.santorinibeach.com.* 50 rooms, 2 story. Closed mid-Oct-Memorial Day. Pets accepted, some restrictions. Check-out 11 am. Beach. Outdoor pool, children's pool. **$**

Restaurant

★ ★ **SEAFOOD BARGE.** *62980 Main Rd, Southold (11971). Phone 631/765-3010; fax 631/765-3510. www.seafoodbarge.com.* Seafood menu. Lunch, dinner. Bar. **$$**

Spring Valley (B-2)

See also Tarrytown

Population 25,464
Elevation 420 ft
Area Code 845
Zip 10977

What to See and Do

Historical Society of Rockland County. *20 Zukor Rd, New City (10956). 3 miles N via Hwy 45, then 3 miles E on New Hempstead Rd, then 2 miles N on Main St to Zukor Rd. Phone 845/634-9629.*Museum and publications on county history; Jacob Blauvelt House (1832 Dutch farmhouse), barn. (Tues-Sun afternoons; closed holidays) **DONATION**

Limited-Service Hotels

★ **FAIRFIELD INN.** *100 Spring Valley Marketplace, Spring Valley (10977). Phone 845/426-2000; toll-free 800/228-9290; fax 845/426-2008. www.fairfieldinn. com.* 105 rooms, 4 story. Complimentary continental breakfast. Check-in 3 pm, check-out noon. Outdoor pool. **$**

★ ★ **HOLIDAY INN.** *3 Executive Blvd, Suffern (10901). Phone 845/357-4800; fax 845/918-1475. www.holiday-inn.com.* 241 rooms, 3 story. Pets accepted; fee. Check-out noon. Restaurant, bar. Fitness room. Indoor pool, whirlpool. Business center. **$**

Full-Service Hotel

★ ★ ★ **HILTON PEARL RIVER.** *500 Veterans Memorial Dr, Pearl River (10965). Phone 845/735-9000; fax 914/735-9005. www.hiltonpearlriver.com.* French chateau style; on 17 acres.150 rooms, 5 story. Check-out noon. Restaurant, bar. Fitness room. Indoor pool, whirlpool. Business center. **$$**

Stamford (E-8)

See also Howes Cave, Oneonta, Pound Ridge, White Plains

Population 1,943
Elevation 1,827 ft
Area Code 518
Zip 12167
Web Site www.delawarecounty.org

Stamford, located along the west branch of the Delaware River, has a large historical district from the Victorian era.

What to See and Do

Lansing Manor. *Hwys 30 and 23, North Blenheim (12131). 8 miles SE on Hwy 23, then 8 miles N on Hwy 30. Phone 518/287-6000; toll-free 800/724-0309.*A 19th-century manor house depicting life of an Anglo-Dutch household of the mid-1800s. (Memorial Day-Columbus Day, Mon, Wed-Sun) **FREE** Adjacent is

Visitors Center. *Phone toll-free 800/724-0309.* Remodeled dairy barn with hands-on exhibits, display on electricity, video presentation, and computers. (Daily; closed Jan 1, Dec 25)

Mine Kill State Park. *Hwy 30, North Blenheim. SE on Hwy 23, 4 miles N on Hwy 30. Phone 518/827-6111.* Swimming pool (late June-early Sept; fee), bathhouse, fishing, boating; hiking and nature trails, cross-country skiing, snowmobiling, picnicking, playground, concession. Recreation programs. Standard fees.

Zadock Pratt Museum. *1828 Homestead, Prattsville. 13 miles SE via Hwy 23. Phone 518/299-3395. www.prattmuseum.com.* Period furnishings and memorabilia. Tours, exhibits. (Memorial Day-Columbus Day, Wed-Sun afternoons) **$** Nearby is

Pratt Rocks. Relief carvings in the cliff face depicting Pratt, his son George, and the tannery. Scenic climb; picnicking; pavilion.

Staten Island (C-2)

See also New York

Area Code 718
Information Staten Island Chamber of Commerce, 130 Bay St, 10301; phone 718/727-1900; or the NYC Convention & Visitors Bureau

Staten Island, twice the size of Manhattan with only one twenty-fourth the population, is the most removed, in distance and character, from the other boroughs. At one time, sightseers on the famous Staten Island Ferry rarely disembarked to explore the almost rural character of the island. The completion of the Verrazano Bridge to Brooklyn, however, brought growth and the beginning of a struggle between developers and those who would preserve the island's uncrowded appeal.

What to See and Do

Conference House. *7455 Hylan Blvd, Staten Island (10307). Phone 718/984-6046.* Built in the mid-1680s by an English sea captain, this was the site of an unproductive meeting on Sept 11, 1776, between British Admiral Lord Howe, Benjamin Franklin, John Adams, and Edward Rutledge to discuss terms of peace to end the Revolutionary War. The meeting helped to produce the phrase the "United States of America." Rose, herb gardens; open-hearth cooking; spinning and weaving demonstrations. (Apr-Nov, Fri-Sun) **$**

The Greenbelt/High Rock. *200 Nevada Ave, Egbertville. 7 miles from Verrazano Bridge via Richmond Rd. Phone 718/667-2165.*An 85-acre nature preserve in a 2,500-acre park. Visitor center, trails. Environmental programs, workshops. Self-guided tours. Urban park ranger-guided tours (by appointment). (Daily 8 am-5 pm) No picnicking or camping. **FREE**

Historic Richmond Town. *441 Clarke Ave, Staten Island (10306). Phone 718/351-1611. www.historicrichmondtown.org.* This outdoor museum complex depicts three centuries of history and culture of Staten Island and the surrounding region. Daily life and work of a rural community is shown in trade demonstrations and tours of shops and buildings. Among the restoration's 27 historic structures are the Historic Museum; Voorlezer's House (circa 1695), the oldest surviving elementary school in the United States; general store; and trademen's shops. Special events and demonstrations. (Wed-Sun afternoons; extended hours July-Aug; closed Jan 1, Thanksgiving, Dec 25) **$**

Jacques Marchais Museum of Tibetan Art. *338 Lighthouse Ave, Staten Island (10306). Between New Dorp and Richmondtown. Phone 718/987-3500. www.tibetanmuseum.com.* Perched on a steep hill with views of the Atlantic Ocean, this museum houses the collection of Jacqueline Norman Klauber, who became fascinated with Tibet as a child. Highlights of the exhibits include a series of bright-colored masks and a large collection of golden *thangkas,* or religious images, plus terraced sculpture gardens and a koi pond. (Wed-Sun 1-5 pm) **$**

Snug Harbor Cultural Center. *1000 Richmond Terrace, Staten Island (10301). Phone 718/448-2500. www.snug-harbor.org.* Founded in 1833 as a seamen's retirement home, Snug Harbor is now a performing and visual arts center with 28 historic buildings featuring Greek Revival and Victorian architecture; art galleries (Wed-Sun, fee); children's museum (Tues-Sun afternoons); botanical garden, sculpture, 83 acres of parkland. (Daily; closed Thanksgiving, Dec 25)

Staten Island Zoo. *614 Broadway, W New Brighton (10310). Barrett Park, between Broadway and Clove Rd. Phone 718/442-3100. www.statenislandzoo.org.* Maintained by the Staten Island Zoological Society. Large collection of native and exotic reptiles, varied species of rattlesnakes, amphibians, marine reef fishes, mammals, birds. Children's center includes a miniature farm. (Daily 10 am-4:45 pm; closed Jan 1, Thanksgiving, Dec 25) Free admission on Wed afternoon, inquire for hours. **$$**

Stony Brook (B-3)

See also Northport, Port Jefferson, Smithtown

Settled 1655
Population 13,727
Elevation 123 ft
Area Code 631
Zip 11790
Web Site www.stonybrookvillage.com

Originally part of the Three Village area first settled by Boston colonists in the 17th century, Stony Brook became an important center for the shipbuilding industry on Long Island Sound in the 1800s.

What to See and Do

The Museums at Stony Brook. *1200 N Country Rd, Stony Brook (11790). On Hwy 25A. Phone 631/751-0066.* Complex of three museums. The Melville Carriage House exhibits 90 vehicles from a collection of horse-drawn carriages. The Art Museum features changing exhibits of American art. The Blackwell History Museum has changing exhibits on a variety of historical themes as well as exhibits of period rooms and antique decoys. Blacksmith shop, schoolhouse, other period buildings. Museum store. (Wed-Sun and

Mon holidays; closed other holidays) **$$**

State University of New York at Stony Brook. *Hwy 97, Stony Brook (11794). Phone 631/689-6000. www.stonybrook.edu.* (1957) (17,500 students) Academic units include College of Arts and Sciences, College of Engineering and Applied Sciences, and Health Sciences Center. Museum of Long Island Natural Sciences has permanent displays on Long Island natural history. Art galleries in the Melville Library, Staller Center, and the Student Union. On campus is

> **Staller Center for the Arts.** *Nicholas Rd and Hwy 347, Stony Brook (11794). Phone 631/632-7235.* On SUNY campus. Houses 1,049-seat main theater, three experimental theaters, art gallery, 400-seat recital hall, and electronic music studio. Summer International Theater Festival. Events all year.

Full-Service Inn

★ ★ ★ **THREE VILLAGE INN.** *150 Main St, Stony Brook (11790). Phone 631/751-0555; toll-free 888/384-4438; fax 631/751-0593. www.threevillageinn.com.* Step back in time with elegance at this harborside inn. Taste buds will dance with delectable meals and homemade breads! Enjoy village shopping and museums; nearby Stonybrook University and Hospital. 26 rooms, 2 story. Check-in 3 pm, check-out noon. Restaurant, bar. **$$**

Restaurants

★ ★ ★ **COUNTRY HOUSE.** *Hwy 25A, Stony Brook (11790). Phone 631/751-3332. www.countryhouse.com.* A top choice for American cuisine on the island. The romantic and elegant setting is perfect for special-occasion dining. American menu. Lunch, dinner. Closed Jan 1, July 4, Dec 25. Bar. Business casual attire. Reservations recommended. **$$$**

★ ★ **THREE VILLAGE INN.** *150 Main St (NY 25A), Stony Brook (11790). Phone 631/751-0555; fax 631/751-0593. www.threevillageinn.com.* Colonial homestead built in 1751. Attractive grounds; country dining. American menu. Breakfast, lunch, dinner, brunch. Closed Dec 25. Bar. Business casual attire. Reservations recommended. **$$$**

Stony Point (B-2)

See also Monroe, Newburgh, Peekskill, West Point

Population 14,244
Elevation 126 ft
Area Code 845
Zip 10980

What to See and Do

Stony Point Battlefield State Historic Site. *Hwy 9 W and Main St, Stony Point (10980). 2 miles N of town center, off Hwy 9 W, on Park Rd. Phone 845/786-2521.* Site of Revolutionary War battle in which General "Mad Anthony" Wayne successfully stormed British fortifications, July 15-16, 1779, ending the last serious threat to Washington's forces in the North. Oldest lighthouse (1826) on the Hudson River. Museum with exhibits, audiovisual program. Musket demonstrations. Self-guided walking tour and guided tour. Special events (fee). Picnic area. (Mon, Wed-Sat 10 am-4:30 pm, Sun noon-4:30 pm) **FREE**

Syracuse (D-6)

See also Auburn, Canastota, Cazenovia, Finger Lakes, Fulton, Oneida, Skaneateles

Settled 1789
Population 147,306
Elevation 406 ft
Area Code 315
Information Convention & Visitors Bureau, 572 S Salina St, 13202; phone 315/470-1910 or toll-free 800/284-4797
Web Site www.syracusecvb.org

Syracuse began as a trading post at the mouth of Onondaga Creek. Salt from wells was produced here from 1796 to 1900. Industry began in 1793, when Thomas Wiard began making wooden plows. Shortly after 1800, a blast furnace was built that produced iron utensils and, during the War of 1812, cast shot for the Army. When the Erie Canal reached town in the late 1820s, Syracuse's industrial future was assured. Today the city has many large and varied industries.

What to See and Do

Beaver Lake Nature Center. *8477 E Mud Lake Rd, Baldwinsville (13027). 12 miles NW via I-690. Phone*

315/638-2519. A 600-acre nature preserve that includes 10 miles of trails and boardwalks, a 200-acre lake that serves as a rest stop for migrating ducks and geese, and a visitor center that features exhibits. In the winter the preserve is also used for cross-country skiing and snowshoeing. Other programs include maple sugaring and guided canoe tours. (Daily 8 am-4 pm) **$**

Erie Canal Museum. *318 Erie Blvd E, Syracuse (13202). Phone 315/471-0593. www.eriecanalmuseum.org.* Indoor and outdoor exhibits detail the construction and operation of the Erie Canal; 65-foot reconstructed canal boat from which exhibits are seen; research library and archives. (Tues-Sat 10 am-5 pm, Sun to 3 pm) **FREE** Museum also houses

> **Syracuse Heritage Area Visitor Center.** *Weighlock Building, 318 Erie Blvd E, Syracuse (13202). Erie Blvd E and Montgomery St. Phone 315/471-0593.* Video presentation and exhibits here introduce visitors to area attractions.

Everson Museum of Art. *401 Harrison St, Syracuse (13202). Phone 315/474-6064. www.everson.org.* First I. M. Pei-designed museum, permanent collection of American art; collection of American ceramics; home of the Syracuse China Center for the Study of American Ceramics; changing exhibits. (Mon-Fri, Sat from 10 am, Sun noon-5 pm; closed holidays) **DONATION**

Green Lakes State Park. *7900 Green Lakes Rd, Fayetteville (13066). 10 miles E via Hwy 5. Phone 315/637-6111.* Swimming beach, bathhouse, boat rentals, fishing; hiking and biking trails, 18-hole golf, cross-country skiing, picnicking, playground, concession, tent and trailer sites (late May-Columbus Day weekends), cabins. **$$**

Landmark Theatre. *362 S Salina St, Syracuse (13201). Phone 315/475-7980. www.landmarktheatre.org.* Built in 1928 as Loew's State Theatre in the era of vaudeville-movie houses. The interior architecture is filled with carvings, chandeliers, and ornate gold decorations. Theater houses concerts, comedy, plays, dance, and classic movies.

New York State Canal Cruises. *100 Hillside Rd, Syracuse (13207). Phone 315/685-8500; toll-free 800/545-4318.* Depart Albany, Syracuse, and Buffalo (June-Oct). Also three-hour dinner cruises (nightly), three-hour excursions (Sun), sightseeing cruises.

Onondaga Historical Association Museum. *321 Montgomery St, Syracuse (13202). Phone 315/428-1864.* Changing and permanent exhibits illustrate history of central New York Wed-Sun; including exhibits on sports history, transportation, military history, and industry. (Wed-Fri noon-4 pm, Sat-Sun 11 am-4 pm) **FREE**

Onondaga Lake Park. *Vine St, Liverpool. 2 1/2 miles NW via I-81 to Liverpool exit. Phone 315/453-6712.* Boat launch and marina; picnicking, concession, bicycle rentals, exercise trail, tram rides, children's play area. (Daily dawn-dusk) **FREE** On grounds are

> **Salt Museum.** *Hwy 30, Liverpool (13088). Phone 315/453-6767.* Re-created 19th-century salt "boiling block"; artifacts and exhibits of Onondaga salt industry. Starting point for history and nature trail around lake. (May-Oct, daily 1-6 pm) **FREE**

Ste. Marie Among the Iroquois. *Phone 315/453-6767.* A 17th-century French mission living history museum. Blacksmithing, cooking, carpentry, and gardening activities. Special programs. (May-Nov: Wed-Sun; Dec-Apr: Tues-Sun)

Rosamond Gifford Zoo at Burnet Park. *1 Burnet Park Dr, Syracuse (13204). S Wilbur Ave. Phone 315/435-8511. www.rosamondgiffordz00.org.* Zoo traces origin of life from 600 million years ago; exhibits on animals' unique adaptations and animal/human interaction; gift shop. (Daily 10 am-4:30 pm; closed Jan 1, Thanksgiving, Dec 25) **$$**

Syracuse University. *University Ave at University Pl, Syracuse (13244). Phone 315/443-1870. www.syr.edu.* (1870) (18,000 students) Major, private graduate-level research and teaching institution. Noted for the Maxwell School of Citizenship and Public Affairs, Newhouse School of Public Communications, College of Engineering, and 50,000 seat Carrier Dome. On the 650-acre campus is

> **Lowe Art Gallery.** *Shaffer Art Building, 572 S Salina St, Syracuse (13202). Phone 315/443-3127.* Shows, paintings, sculpture, other art. **FREE**

Special Events

Balloon Festival. *Jamesville Beach Park, Apulia Rd, Jamesville (13078). Phone 315/435-5252.* Mid-June.

Golden Harvest Festival. *Beaver Lake Nature Center, 8477 E Mud Lake Rd, Baldwinsville (13027). Phone 315/638-2519.* Old-time harvest activities. Weekend after Labor Day.

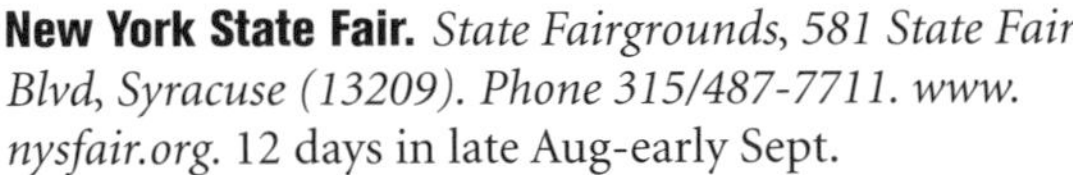

New York State Fair. *State Fairgrounds, 581 State Fair Blvd, Syracuse (13209). Phone 315/487-7711. www.nysfair.org.* 12 days in late Aug-early Sept.

Open-air concerts. *412 Spencer St, Syracuse (13204). Phone 315/473-4330.* In city parks, downtown, and throughout city. Early July-late Aug.

Scottish Games. *Long Branch Park, Liverpool Pkwy and Hwy 370,* Liverpool (13088). *Phone 315/470-1800.* Mid-Aug.

Syracuse Stage. *820 E Genesee St, Syracuse (13210). Phone 315/443-3275. www.syracusestage.org.* Original, professional theatrical productions. Sept-May.

Limited-Service Hotels

★ ★ BEST WESTERN MARSHALL MANOR. *Hwys 80 and 11, Tully (13159). Phone 315/696-6061; fax 315/696-6406. www.bestwestern.com.* 44 rooms, 2 story. Check-out 11 am. Restaurant, bar. **$**

★ ★ COURTYARD BY MARRIOTT. *6415 Yorktown Cir, East Syracuse (13057). Phone 315/432-0300; fax 315/432-9950. www.courtyard.com.* 149 rooms, 3 story. Check-in 3 pm, check-out noon. High-speed Internet access. Restaurant. Fitness room. Indoor pool, whirlpool. **$**

★ ★ EMBASSY SUITES. *6646 Old Collamer Rd, Syracuse (13057). Phone 315/446-3200; toll-free 800/362-2779; fax 315/437-3302. www.embassy-suites.com.* Waterfalls and streams in the center atrium set the tone of relaxation, while complimentary hot or cold breakfast sets the tone of efficiency. Just outside the city, the hotel is in close proximity to downtown and all points of interest.215 rooms, 5 story, all suites. Complimentary full breakfast. Check-in 4 pm, check-out noon. Restaurant, bar. Children's activity center. Fitness room. Indoor pool, whirlpool. Airport transportation available. **$**

★ FAIRFIELD INN. *6611 Old Collamer Rd, East Syracuse (13057). Phone 315/432-9333; toll-free 800/228-2800; fax 315/432-9197. www.fairfieldinn.com.* 135 rooms, 3 story. Complimentary continental breakfast. Check-in 3 pm, check-out noon. Outdoor pool. **$**

★ ★ HOLIDAY INN. *6555 Old Collamer Rd S, East Syracuse (13057). Phone 315/437-2761; toll-free 800/465-4329; fax 315/463-0028. www.holiday-inn.com.* 203 rooms, 2 story. Pets accepted; fee. Complimentary full breakfast. Check-in 3 pm, check-out noon. Restaurant, bar. Children's activity center. Fitness room. Indoor pool, whirlpool. **$**

★ ★ HOLIDAY INN. *441 Electronics Pkwy, Liverpool (13088). Phone 315/457-1122; toll-free 800/465-4329; fax 315/451-1269. www.holiday-inn.com.* 280 rooms, 6 story. Pets accepted. Check-in 4 pm, check-out 1 pm. Restaurant, bar. Fitness room. Indoor pool, whirlpool. Airport transportation available. **$**

Full-Service Hotels

★ ★ ★ GENESEE GRANDE HOTEL. *1060 E Genesee St, Syracuse (13210). Phone 315/476-4212; toll-free 800/365-4663; fax 315/471-4663. www.geneseegrande.com.* Befitting its name, the Genesee Grande is a beautiful and luxurious hotel in the University Hill section of downtown Syracuse. A sense of opulence is found throughout the hotel, from the lobby with its soaring ceilings; dramatic draperies, elegant furnishings; and koi pond, to the rooms with soft, comfortable beds and flat-screen televisions. Complementing these grand surroundings is gracious service—the helpful concierge will assist you in every way imaginable, from obtaining concert or special event tickets to delivering or picking up dry cleaning. 159 rooms, 2 story. Pets accepted, some restrictions; fee. Complimentary continental breakfast. Check-in 3 pm, check-out noon. High-speed Internet access, wireless Internet access. Restaurant, bar. Fitness room, fitness classes available. Airport transportation available. **$**

★ ★ ★ THE MARX HOTEL AND CONFERENCE CENTER. *701 E Genesee St, Syracuse (13210). Phone 315/479-7000; fax 315/472-2700. www.marxsyracuse.com.* Located in downtown Syracuse, The Marx is a chic, contemporary hotel that's perfect for both business and leisure travelers. Soothing earth-toned rooms feature well-lit desks with ergonomic seating, high-speed Internet access, and 27 televisions with 80 channels, while the fully equipped fitness center offers plenty of ways to keep fit. Those on a working vacation can order room service for breakfast, lunch, or dinner, and the complimentary van service transports sightseers to and from points of interest in the downtown area. 280 rooms. Pets accepted; fee. Check-in 3 pm, check-out noon. High-speed Internet access, wireless Internet access. Restaurant, two bars. Fitness room. Business center. **$**

★ ★ ★ SHERATON UNIVERSITY HOTEL AND CONFERENCE CENTER. *801 University Ave, Syracuse (13210). Phone 315/475-3000; toll-free 800/395-2105; fax 315/475-3311. www.sheratonsyracuse.com.* Bordering Syracuse University and hospitals, this is a perfect choice for campus visits or area business. Within easy walking distance to downtown civic centers, restaurants, entertainment arenas, and other attractions, the hotel provides convenience along with friendly, helpful service. 236 rooms, 9 story. Pets accepted, some restrictions; fee. Check-in 3 pm, check-out noon. High-speed Internet access. Restaurant, bar. Fitness room. Indoor pool. Airport transportation available. Business center. **$$**

★ ★ ★ WYNDHAM SYRACUSE HOTEL. *6301 Hwy 298, Syracuse (13057). Phone 315/432-0200; fax 315/433-1210. www.newyorkhotels.com.* 250 rooms, 7 story. Check-in 3 pm, check-out noon. High-speed Internet access. Restaurant, bar. Fitness room. Indoor pool, outdoor pool, whirlpool. Airport transportation available. **$**

Specialty Lodging

DICKENSON HOUSE ON JAMES. *1504 James St, Syracuse (13203). Phone 315/423-4777; toll-free 888/423-4777; fax 315/425-1865. www.dickensonhouse.com.* Built in 1924; English Tudor décor. 4 rooms. Complimentary full breakfast. Check-in 3 pm, check-out 11 am. **$**

GIDDINGS GARDEN B&B. *290 W Seneca Tpke, Syracuse (13207). Phone 315/492-6389; toll-free 800/377-3452. www.giddingsgarden.com.* 4 rooms. Complimentary full breakfast. Check-in 3-7 pm, check-out noon. **$**

Restaurants

★ BROOKLYN PICKLE. *2222 Burnet Ave, Syracuse (13206). Phone 315/463-1851; fax 315/463-4969.* Deli menu. Lunch, dinner. Closed Sun; holidays. Casual attire. Outdoor seating. **$**

★ ★ COLEMAN'S. *100 S Lowell Ave, Syracuse (13204). Phone 315/476-1933; fax 315/476-5922. www.colemansirishpub.com.* American menu. Lunch, dinner, late-night. Closed Dec 25. Bar. Children's menu. Casual attire. Outdoor seating. **$**

★ ★ GLEN LOCH MILL. *4626 North St, Jamesville (13078). Phone 315/469-6969; fax 315/469-0126. www.glenloch.net.* Converted feed mill; built in 1827. Glen setting, waterwheel. Seafood, steak menu. Dinner, Sun brunch. Closed Dec 25. Bar. Children's menu. Outdoor seating. **$$**

★ ★ ★ PASCALE. *204 W Fayette St, Syracuse (13202). Phone 315/471-3040; fax 315/471-3060.* For eclectic international dining in a contemporary setting with a seasonally changing menu, Pascale is the perfect choice. It's centrally located in Armory Square, a revitalized sector of downtown Syracuse, equally popular with the business community and with merry-makers. A booster of the local scene, Pascale features the work of local artists. While many other dining establishments have come and gone, this well-established restaurant recently celebrated its 20th anniversary with a complete renovation and retains its original ownership. Its elegant yet welcoming atmosphere reflects the staff's desire for guests to feel comfortable. American menu. Lunch, dinner. Closed Sun; Jan 1, Dec 25. Bar. Children's menu. Casual attire. Valet parking. Outdoor seating. **$$**

★ PLAINVILLE FARMS. *8450 Brewerton Rd, Cicero (13039). Phone 315/699-3852; fax 315/699-3852. www.plainvillefarms.com.* American menu. Lunch, dinner. Closed Dec 25. Children's menu. **$**

Tarrytown (B-2)

See also Mahopac, New York, Peekskill, Spring Valley, White Plains, Yonkers

Population 11,090
Elevation 118 ft
Area Code 914
Zip 10591
Information Sleepy Hollow Chamber of Commerce, 54 Main St, 10591-3660; phone 914/631-1705
Web Site www.sleepyhollowchamber.com

The village of Tarrytown and the neighboring villages of Irvington and Sleepy Hollow were settled by the Dutch during the mid-1600s. The name Tarrytown was taken from the Dutch word "Tarwe," meaning wheat. Here, on September 23, 1780, the British spy Major John Andr was captured while carrying the detailed plans for West Point given to him by Benedict Arnold. The village and the area were made famous by the writings of Washington Irving, particularly *The Legend of Sleepy Hollow,* from which this region takes its name.

What to See and Do

The Historical Society Serving Sleepy Hollow and Tarrytown. *1 Grove St, Thornwood (10594). Phone 914/631-8374.* Victorian house includes parlor, dining room; artifacts from archeological dig; Native American room; library, map, and photograph collection; children's room. (Tues-Thurs, Sat afternoons 2-4 pm; closed holidays) **FREE**

Kykuit, The Rockefeller Estate. *Hwy 9 N and N Broadway, Sleepy Hollow (10591). Accessible only by shuttle bus from Philipsburg Manor. Phone 914/631-9491.* This six-story stone mansion was home to three generations of the Rockefeller family; principal first-floor rooms open to the public. Extensive gardens with spectacular Hudson River views feature an important collection of 20th-century sculpture acquired by Governor Nelson A. Rockefeller; carriage barn with collection of antique cars and horse-drawn vehicles. Scheduled tours lasting 2 1/2 hours depart approximately every 15 minutes from Philipsburg Manor (mid-Apr-Oct, Mon and Wed-Sun from 9 am). **$$$$**

Lyndhurst. *635 S Broadway, Tarrytown (10591). 1/2 mile S of Tappan Zee Bridge on Hwy 9. Phone 914/631-4481. www.lyndhurst.org.* (1838) Gothic Revival mansion built for William Paulding, mayor of New York City in the 1830s. Approximately 67 landscaped acres overlooking the Hudson. Contains books, art, and furnishings. Tours. (Mid-Apr-Oct: Tues-Sun 10 am-5 pm; rest of year: Sat-Sun 10 am-4 pm) **$$**

Marymount College. *100 Marymount Ave, Tarrytown (10591). Phone 914/631-3200.* (1907) (800 women) On 25-acre hilltop campus overlooking the Hudson River. Tours of campus.

Music Hall Theater. *13 Main St, Tarrytown (10591). Phone 914/631-3390. www.tarrytownmusichall.org.* (1885) One of the oldest remaining theaters in the county; now serves as a center for the arts.

Old Dutch Church of Sleepy Hollow. *42 N Broadway, Tarrytown (10591). Broadway and Pierson (Hwy 9). Phone 914/631-1123.* (1685) Church building of Dutch origins built on what was the Manor of Frederick Philipse. Restored, includes a replica of the original pulpit. Tours by appointment. (May-Oct, Tues-Sun)

Philipsburg Manor. *381 N Broadway, Sleepy Hollow (10591). On Hwy 9, 2 miles N of NY Thrwy exit 9. Phone 914/631-3992.* Colonial farm and trading site (1720-1750); also departure point for tour of Kykuit. Manor house, barn, animals; restored operating gristmill, wooden millpond bridge across Pocantico River. A 15-minute film precedes tours. Reception center; exhibition gallery; museum shop; picnic area. (Mar-Dec, Mon, Wed-Sun; closed Thanksgiving, Dec 25) **$$$**

Sleepy Hollow Cemetery. *42 N Broadway, Sleepy Hollow (10591). Adjacent to Old Dutch Church. Phone 914/631-0081.*Graves of Washington Irving, Andrew Carnegie, William Rockefeller.

Sunnyside. *W Sunnyside Ln, #9, Tarrytown (10591). W of Hwy 9, 1 mile S of NY Thrwy exit 9. Phone 914/591-8763.* Washington Irving's Hudson River estate (1835-1859). Contains much of his furnishings, personal property, and library. Museum shop. Landscaped grounds; picnic area. (Mar-Dec: Mon and Wed-Sun; rest of year: weekends; closed Jan 1, Thanksgiving, Dec 25) **$$$**

Van Cortlandt Manor. *525 S Riverside Ave, Croton on Hudson (10520). At Croton Point Ave exit on Hwy 9, 10 miles N of NY Thrwy exit 9. Phone 914/271-8981.* Post-Revolutionary War estate of prominent Colonial family. Elegantly furnished manor house; ferry house inn and kitchen building on old Albany Post Rd; "Long Walk" with flanking 18th-century gardens; picnic area. Frequent demonstrations of open-hearth cooking, brickmaking, weaving. Museum shop. (Apr-Dec, Mon and Wed-Sun 10 am-5 pm; closed Thanksgiving, Dec 25) **$$$**

Special Events

Candlelight Tours. *150 White Plains Rd, Tarrytown (10591). Phone 914/631-8200.* At Sunnyside, Philipsburg Manor, and Van Cortland Manor. English Christmas Celebration. Dec.

Heritage & Crafts Weekend. *Van Cortlandt Manor, South Riverside Ave, Croton-on-Hudson (10520). Phone 914/271-8981.* Demonstrations and hands-on exhibits of 18th-century crafts and activities. Columbus Day weekend.

Sunset Serenades. *635 S Broadway, Tarrytown (10591). Phone 914/631-4481. www.lyndhurst.org.* On Lyndhurst grounds. Symphony concerts (Sat). July.

Limited-Service Hotel

★ ★ COURTYARD BY MARRIOTT. *475 White Plains Rd, Tarrytown (10591). Phone 914/631-1122; fax 914/631-1357. www.courtyard.com.* 139 rooms, 3 story. Check-in 3 pm, check-out noon. High-speed Internet access. Restaurant. Fitness room. Indoor pool, whirlpool. **$$**

Full-Service Hotels

★ ★ ★ CASTLE ON THE HUDSON. *400 Benedict Ave, Tarrytown (10591). Phone 914/631-1980; toll-free 800/616-4487; fax 914/631-4612. www.castleattarrytown.com.* The Castle on the Hudson is a royal getaway only 25 miles north of New York City. This authentic castle, built between 1897 and 1910, is impressive without being intimidating. The highest point for many miles, the Castles hilltop perch affords panoramic views of the Hudson River and the historic Hudson Valley. The rooms and suites are romantically furnished with four-poster or canopied beds. The luscious grounds are meticulously maintained and are perfect for strolling, while tennis courts and a pool provide diversion. History buffs delight in the areas rich treasures, from antique shops to magnificent mansions. Equus restaurant (see) is a destination in its own right, and its three rooms suit a variety of moods. The Tapestry and Oak rooms reflect the glory of a European castle with stone fireplaces and beamed ceilings, while the conservatory style of the Garden Room is notable for its scenic river views. 31 rooms, 4 story. Check-in 4 pm, check-out noon. Restaurant, bar. Fitness room. Outdoor pool, whirlpool. Airport transportation available. Business center. **$$$**

★ ★ ★ DOLCE TARRYTOWN HOUSE. *E Sunnyside Ln, Tarrytown (10591). Phone 914/591-8200; fax 914/591-3131. www.dolce.com.* This lovely estate was built in the late 1800s and has a magnificent view overlooking the Hudson River Valley. Located just 24 miles from the heart of bustling Manhattan, this is a favorite destination for everyone. 212 rooms, 2 story. Complimentary full breakfast. Check-in 4 pm, check-out 11 am. High-speed Internet access. Restaurant. Fitness room. Indoor pool, outdoor pool, whirlpool. Tennis. Business center. **$**

★ ★ ★ DOUBLETREE HOTEL TARRYTOWN. *455 S Broadway, Tarrytown (10591). Phone 914/631-5700; fax 914/631-0075.* This 40-year-old hotel is located near the woods made famous by Washington Irving's *The Legend of Sleepy Hollow.* 250 rooms, 2 story. Check-out noon. Restaurant, bar. Fitness room. Indoor pool, outdoor pool, children's pool, whirlpool. Tennis. Airport transportation available. Business center. **$$$**

Restaurants

★ ★ ★ ★ BLUE HILL AT STONE BARNS. *630 Bedford Rd, Pocantino Hills (10591). Phone 914/366-9600.* An extension of Blue Hill in Manhattan and set in the Pocantino Hills, Blue Hill at Stone Barns is not only a restaurant, but a working farm and educational center dedicated to sustainable food production. The dining room is a former barn that has been converted to a lofty, modern space with vaulted ceilings, dark wood accents, and earthy tones. The menu, a "create your own" concept, offers guests to choose two, three, or four courses from a combination of menu sections with such titles as "The Greenhouse" and "Ocean." For those who have some time on their hands, a five-course "Farmers Feast" is offered, but everyone should stay for dessert, which may include such decadent items as chocolate croquettes and warm chocolate bread pudding. American menu. Dinner, Sun brunch. Closed Mon-Tue. Bar. Business casual attire. Reservations recommended. **$$$**

★ ★ CARAVELA. *53 N Broadway, Tarrytown (10591). Phone 914/631-1863; fax 914/631-1958.* Brazilian, Spanish menu. Lunch, dinner. Closed Thanksgiving, Dec 25. Bar. Casual attire. Reservations recommended. Outdoor seating. **$$**

★ ★ ★ EQUUS. *400 Benedict Ave, Tarrytown (10591). Phone 914/631-3646; fax 914/631-4612. www.castleattarrytown.com.* Choose from three distinct and charming dining rooms at this restaurant located in The Castle on the Hudson (see). It has become a favorite special-occasion dining spot for Manhattanites that wish to escape the bustle of the city for a night. French, American menu. Lunch, dinner. Bar. Jacket required. Valet parking. **$$$**

★ ★ SANTA FE. *5 Main St, Tarrytown (10591). Phone 914/332-4452; fax 914/631-5823.* Mexican menu. Lunch, dinner. Closed Easter, Thanksgiving, Dec 25. Bar. Casual attire. **$$**

Thousand Islands (B-6)

Along the eastern United States-Canadian border.

Web Site www.thousandislands.com

This group of more than 1,800 islands on the eastern US-Canadian border, at the head of the St. Lawrence River, extends 52 miles downstream from the end of Lake Ontario. Slightly more than half the islands are in Canada. Some of them are 5 miles wide and extend more than 20 miles in length. These rocky slivers of land are noted for their scenery and numerous parks, including St. Lawrence Islands National Park. The Thousand Islands Bridge and highway (7 miles long) between the New York and Ontario mainlands crosses several of the isles and channels. Many of the Islands were settled during the early 1900s by American millionaires, whose opulent summer residences and private clubs made the area renowned throughout the world.

The Seaway Trail, a 454-mile national scenic byway, runs through the Thousand Islands region along the southeastern shore of Lake Ontario and beside the St. Lawrence area.

Uncluttered villages, boat tours, museums, walks, water sports, and abundant freshwater fishing make the Islands a popular vacation center. For details on recreational activities, contact the Thousand Islands Regional Tourism Development Corporation, PO Box 400, Alexandria Bay 13607; phone 315/482-2520 or toll-free 800/847-5263 in United States and Canada.

Listed here are the towns and parks in the Thousand Islands included in *Mobil Travel Guide:* Alexandria Bay, Clayton, Ogdensburg in New York; Brockville, Gananoque, Kingston, and St. Lawrence Islands National Park in Ontario.

Ticonderoga (C-10)

See also Crown Point, Hague

Founded 1764
Population 5,167
Elevation 154 ft
Area Code 518
Zip 12883
Information Ticonderoga Area Chamber of Commerce, 121 Montcalm St; phone 518/585-6619

Web Site www.ticonderogany.com

This resort area lies on the ancient portage route between Lake George and Lake Champlain. For almost two hundred years it was the site of various skirmishes and battles involving Native Americans, French, British, Canadians, Yankees, and Yorkers.

What to See and Do

Boating. Launching sites, 2 miles E on Hwy 74, on Lake Champlain; Black Point Rd, on Lake George.

★ **Fort Ticonderoga.** *Rte 74, Ticonderoga. 2 miles E on Hwy 74. Phone 518/585-2821.* (1755) The fort was built in 1755 by the Quebecois, who called it Carillon, and was successfully defended by the Marquis de Montcalm against a more numerous British force in 1758. It was captured by the British in 1759 and by Ethan Allen and the Green Mountain Boys in 1775 (known as the first victory of the Revolutionary War). The stone fort was restored in 1909; the largest collection of cannons in North America is assembled on the grounds. The museum houses collections of weapons, paintings, and articles of daily life of the soldiers garrisoned here during the Seven Year and Revolutionary wars. Costumed guides give tours; cannon firings daily; fife and drum corps parade (July and Aug); special events. Museum shop; restaurant; picnic area. Scenic drive to the summit of Mount Defiance for 30-mile view. (Early May-mid-Oct, daily)

Fort Ticonderoga Ferry. *Crosses Lake Champlain to Shoreham, VT. Phone 802/897-7999.* (May-Oct, daily 8 am-7:45 pm)

Heritage Museum. *Montcalm St and Tower Ave, Ticonderoga. Phone 518/585-2696.* Displays of civilian and industrial history of Ticonderoga. Children's workshop. (Late June-Labor Day: daily; Labor Day-mid-Oct: weekends) **DONATION**

Putnam Pond State Public Campground. *Rte 74 and Adirondack Park, Ticonderoga (Lake George Area) (12818). 6 miles W off Hwy 74, in Adirondack Park. Phone 518/585-7280.*Boating (launch), bathhouse, lifeguards, fishing; hiking, picnicking, tent and trailer sites. (Mid-May-Labor Day)

Replica of Hancock House. *3 Wicker St, Ticonderoga (Lake George Area) (12883). Montcalm St, at Moses Cir. Phone 518/585-7868.* The home of the Ticonderoga Historical Society is a replica of the house built for John Hancock on Beacon Street in Boston. It is maintained as a museum and research library. The rooms display

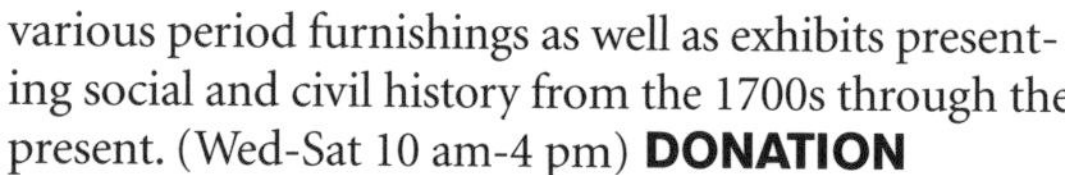

various period furnishings as well as exhibits presenting social and civil history from the 1700s through the present. (Wed-Sat 10 am-4 pm) **DONATION**

Limited-Service Hotel

★ CIRCLE COURT. *440 Montcalm St W, Ticonderoga (12883). Phone 518/585-7660.* 14 rooms. Pets accepted, some restrictions. Check-out 11 am. **$**

Restaurants

★ CARILLON RESTAURANT. *61 Hague Rd, Ticonderoga (12883). Phone 518/585-7657. www.carillonrestaurant.com.* Chef owned restaurant in historic district of Ticonderoga. American menu. Dinner. Closed Wed. **$**

★ HOT BISCUIT DINER. *428 Montcalm St, Ticonderoga (12883). Phone 518/585-3483.* American menu. Lunch, dinner, brunch. Closed holidays. Children's menu. Casual attire. **$$**

Tivoli

Restaurants

★ ★ THE BLACK SWAN. *66 Broadway, Tivoli. Phone 845/757-3777.* American menu. Dinner. Bar. Business casual attire. Reservations recommended. **$$**

★ ★ MILAGROS. *73 Broadway, Tivoli. Phone 845/757-5300.* American menu. Breakfast, lunch, dinner, brunch. Bar. Children's menu. Business casual attire. Reservations recommended. Outdoor seating. **$$**

Troy (E-9)

See also Albany, Schenectady

Settled 1786
Population 49,170
Elevation 37 ft
Area Code 518
Information Rensselaer County Chamber of Commerce, 31 Second St, 12180; phone 518/274-7020
Web Site www.renscochamber.com

What to See and Do

Grave of Samuel Wilson. *Oakwood Cemetery, 50 101st St, Troy (12180). Phone 518/272-7520. www.oakwoodcemetery.org.* Meat supplier to the Army in 1812. Because the initials "US" were stamped on his sides of beef that were shipped to Union soldiers, this supplier is regarded as the original "Uncle Sam." By an act of the 87th Congress, a resolution was adopted that saluted Wilson as the originator of the national symbol of "Uncle Sam." (Daily 9 am-4:30 pm)

Junior Museum. *105 8th St, Troy (12180). Phone 518/235-2120. www.juniormuseum.org.* Science, natural history, Iroquois, and art exhibits; settlers' cabin, marine aquarium, animals, diorama of beaver pond environment, planetarium shows, "Please Touch" family gallery plus other permanent and changing exhibits. Birthday parties and tours (by appointment). (Thurs 10 am-2 pm, Fri-Sun to 5 pm; closed holidays) **$$**

Rensselaer County Historical Society. *57 2nd St, Troy (12180). Phone 518/272-7232. www.rchsonline.org.* An 1827 town house, the Hart-Cluett Mansion, has period rooms furnished with decorative and fine arts; Troy stoves and stoneware. Research library, museum shop. Directions for walking tour of downtown area can also be obtained here. (Tues-Sat noon-5 pm; closed holidays; late Dec-late Jan) **$**

Rensselaer Polytechnic Institute. *110 8th St, Troy (12180). 15th St, 1/4 mile S off Hwy 7. Phone 518/276-6216. www.rpi.edu.* (1824) (6,000 students) Tours begin at Admissions Office in Admissions and Financial Aid Building (Sept-Apr: Mon-Sat; rest of year: Mon-Fri).

Riverspark Visitor Center. *251 River St, Troy (12180). Phone 518/270-8667. www.troyvisitor.org.* Offers visitor information, hands-on exhibits, slide presentation. Driving and walking tour information available. (Tues-Sat 10 am-5 pm) **FREE**

Russell Sage College. *45 Ferry St, Troy (12180). At 2nd St. Phone 518/244-2214. www.sage.edu.*(1916) (1,000 women) Established by Margaret Olivia Slocum Sage. Campus tours. Gallery features student art work and changing exhibits. The movie *The Age of Innocence* was filmed in part in the historic brownstones on campus.

Troy Savings Bank Music Hall. *32 2nd St, Troy (12180). State and 2nd St. Phone 518/273-0038. www.troymusichall.org.* (1875) Victorian showplace in Italian Renaissance building. Presents a wide variety of concerts. Tours by appointment (Sept-May).

Special Event

Stars and Stripes Riverfront Festival. Concerts, fireworks, carnival rides, military equipment displays, arts and crafts, food. Mid-June.

Limited-Service Hotel

★ FAIRFIELD INN. *124 Troy Rd, East Greenbush (12061). Phone 518/477-7984; toll-free 888/236-2427; fax 518/477-2382. www.marriott.com.* 105 rooms, 4 story. Complimentary continental breakfast. Check-in 3 pm, check-out 11 am. Outdoor pool. **$**

Restaurant

★ ★ MONUMENT SQUARE CAFE. *254 Broadway, Troy (12180). Phone 518/274-0167.* Seafood menu. Dinner. Closed Sun. Bar. **$$**

Tupper Lake (B-8)

See also Lake Placid, Long Lake, Saranac Lake

Settled 1890
Population 3,935
Elevation 1,600 ft
Area Code 518
Zip 12986
Information Chamber of Commerce of Tupper Lake and Town of Altamont, 60 Park St; phone 518/359-3328 or toll-free 888/887-5253
Web Site www.tupperlakeinfo.com

In the heart of the Adirondack resort country and surrounded by lakes, rivers, and mountains, Tupper Lake offers hunting, fishing, boating, mountain climbing, skiing, camping, snowmobiling, golf, tennis, and mountain biking amid magnificent scenery.

What to See and Do

Boating. State launching sites on Hwy 30, S of town, and on the Raquette River, via Hwys 3, 30. **FREE**

Camping. Fish Creek Pond State Public Campground. *Phone 518/891-4560.* Boating (rentals, launch), swimming, bathhouse, lifeguards, fishing; hiking, tent and trailer sites, picnicking. (Apr-Nov) 12 miles E on Hwy 30, in Adirondack Park (see). Phone 518/891-4560. **Rollins Pond State Public Campground.** 12 miles E pm Hwy 30, use Fish Creek entrance. Phone 518/891-3239. 288 campsites, most on waterfront. Same activities as Fish Creek. (Mid-May-early Sept) **Lake Eaton State Public Campground.** 20 miles S on Hwy 30. Phone 518/624-2641. 135 campsites, half on waterfront. Boating (ramp, rentals), swimming, bathhouse, lifeguards, fishing. Fee for some activities. (Mid-May-early Sept)

Historic Beth Joseph Synagogue. *Miller and Lake sts, Tupper Lake (12896). Phone 518/359-7229.* Built in 1905, this is the oldest synagogue in the Adirondacks and the only synagogue outside of New York City listed in The Register of New York State Historic Buildings. All fixtures and furnishings are the original contents of the building; the two stained-glass rose windows have been restored. (June-Sept, Tues-Fri 11 am-3 pm and holidays; limited hours) **DONATION**

Raquette River Outfitters. *1754 Hwy 30, Tupper Lake (12986). Phone 518/359-3228. www.raquetteriveroutfitters.com.* Canoe and kayak outfitting, sales, and rentals in the Adirondack Mountains; guided tours. (Daily 8 am-5 pm)

Special Events

Flatwater Weekend. *Hwys 3 and 30, Tupper Lake (12986).* Annual canoe races. Mid-June.

Tinman Triathlon. *60 Park St, Tupper Lake (12986). Phone 518/359-3328.* Swimming, biking, running. Mid-June.

Woodsmen's Days. *19 Front St, Tupper Lake (12986). Phone 518/359-9444.* Second weekend in July.

Limited-Service Hotels

★ SHAHEEN'S. *314 Park St, Tupper Lake (12986). Phone 518/359-3384; toll-free 800/474-2445; fax 518/359-3384. www.shaheensmotel.com.* 31 rooms, 2 story. Complimentary continental breakfast. Check-out 11 am. Outdoor pool. **$**

★ TUPPER LAKE MOTEL. *255 Park St, Tupper Lake (12986). Phone 518/359-3381; toll-free 800/944-3585; fax 518/359-8549. www.tupperlakemotel.com.* 18 rooms. Complimentary continental breakfast. Check-out 11 am. Outdoor pool. **$**

Unadilla

Restaurant

★ **UNADILLA HOUSE.** *188 Main St, Unadilla (13849). Phone 607/369-7227.* Restored 19th-century hotel. American menu. Lunch, dinner. Closed Sun; holidays. Bar. Children's menu. **$$**

Utica (D-7)

See also Canastota, Herkimer, Oneida, Rome

Population 60,651
Elevation 423 ft
Area Code 315
Information Oneida County Convention & Visitors Bureau, PO Box 551, 13503; phone 315/724-7221 or stop at the Information Booth, just off NY Thrwy exit 31
Web Site www.oneidacountycvb.com

Near the western end of the Mohawk Trail, Utica has been a manufacturing and trading center since its early days. By 1793 there was stagecoach service from Albany. The opening of the Erie Canal brought new business. The first Woolworth "five and dime" was opened here in 1879.

What to See and Do

Children's Museum. *311 Main St, Utica (13501). Phone 315/724-6128. www.museum4kids.net.* Hands-on exhibits teaching history, natural history, and science. Iroquois exhibit includes section of Long House; local history displays; dress-up area; Playspace; outdoor railroad display; special weekend programs. (Mon, Thurs-Sun 9:45 am-3:45 pm; closed holidays) **$$**

F.X. Matt Brewing Company. *Court and Varick sts, Utica (13502). Phone 315/732-0022; toll-free 800/765-6288.* Includes plant tour, trolley ride, and visit to the 1888 Tavern. Free beer or root beer. (Daily; closed holidays) Children only with adult. **$$**

Munson-Williams-Proctor Institute. *310 Genesee St, Utica (13502). Phone 315/797-0000. www.mwpai.org.* Museum of Art has collection of 18th-20th-century American and European paintings and sculpture; European, Japanese, and American prints; American decorative arts. Adjacent is Fountain Elms, a Victorian house museum, with five mid-19th-century rooms; changing exhibits. (Tues-Sun; closed holidays) Also School of Art Gallery featuring exhibits by visiting artists, faculty, and students. (Mon-Sat; closed holidays) **FREE**

Oneida County Historical Society. *1608 Genesee St, Utica (13502). Phone 315/735-3642.* Museum traces Utica and Mohawk Valley history; reference library (fee); changing exhibits. (Tues-Fri 10 am-7 pm; closed holidays) **FREE**

Utica College of Syracuse University. *1600 Burrstone Rd, Utica (13502). Phone 315/792-3006. www.utica.edu.* (1946) (2,200 students) Campus tour. **FREE**

Utica Zoo. *99 Steel Hill Rd, Utica (13501). Phone 315/738-0472. www.uticazoo.org.* More than 250 exotic and domestic animals. Children's Zoo (Apr-Oct, daily; included with admission). Snack bar, picnicking. (Daily 10 am-5 pm; closed Jan 1, Thanksgiving, Dec 25) **$**

Limited-Service Hotels

★ **BEST WESTERN GATEWAY ADIRONDACK INN.** *175 N Genesee St, Utica (13502). Phone 315/732-4121; fax 315/797-8265. www.bestwestern.com.* 89 rooms, 2 story. Pets accepted. Complimentary continental breakfast. Check-in 3 pm, check-out 11 am. Fitness room. **$**

★★ **HOLIDAY INN.** *1777 Burrstone Rd, New Hartford (13413). Phone 315/797-2131; fax 315/797-5817. www.holiday-inn.com.* 100 rooms, 2 story. Pets accepted. Check-in 3 pm, check-out noon. High-speed Internet access. Restaurant, bar. Fitness room. Outdoor pool, whirlpool. **$**

★★ **RADISSON HOTEL-UTICA CENTRE.** *200 Genesee St, Utica (13502). Phone 315/797-8010; fax 315/797-1490. www.radisson.com.* This hotel has an indoor heated pool and fitness facilities as well as a sauna and whirlpool. There are 13 meeting rooms available totaling nearly 15,000 square feet, including a conference center for 50 people and 2 dedicated board rooms. 158 rooms, 6 story. Pets accepted, some restrictions; fee. Check-out noon. High-speed Internet access. Restaurant, bar. Fitness room. Indoor pool. **$**

Restaurants

★★★ **HORNED DORSET.** *Hwy 8, Leonardsville*

(13364). Phone 315/855-7898; fax 315/855-7820. www.horneddorset.com. Apple orchards and farmland create a strangely fitting backdrop for the first-class French foods and impeccable European service found at this historic inn. The restaurant's consistency and ambiance continues to attract visitors from miles away. French menu. Dinner. Closed Mon; Jan 1, Dec 25. **$$$**

★ KITLAS. *2242 Broad St, Frankfort (13340). Phone 315/732-9616.* Lunch, dinner. Closed Sun; holidays. Bar. Children's menu. **$**

Victor (D-4)

See also Canandaigua, Palmyra, Rochester

Population 2,433
Elevation 587 ft
Area Code 585
Zip 14564
Web Site www.victorchamber.com

What to See and Do

Valentown Museum. *7377 Valentown Sq, Victor. 4 miles N on Hwy 96 to Valentown Sq, in Fishers; 1/4 mile N of I-90, exit 45, opposite Eastview Mall. Phone 585/924-4170. www.valentown.org.* A three-story structure built as a community center and shopping plaza in 1879. General store, harness maker and cobbler shops, bakery, schoolroom; Civil War artifacts. (May-Oct, Wed-Sun) **$**

Limited-Service Hotel

★ HAMPTON INN. *7637 Hwy 96, Victor (14564). Phone 585/924-4400; toll-free 800/426-7866; fax 585/924-4478. www.hamptoninn.com.* 123 rooms, 3 story. Complimentary continental breakfast. Check-in 3 pm, check-out noon. Fitness room. Indoor pool, whirlpool. **$**

Warrensburg (C-9)

See also Bolton Landing, Diamond Point, Lake George Village, Lake Luzerne, North Creek

Population 4,255
Elevation 687 ft
Area Code 518
Zip 12885
Information Chamber of Commerce, 3847 Main St; phone 518/623-2161
Web Site www.warrensburgchamber.com

Warrensburg, near Lake George, is an old-time village in the heart of a year-round tourist area and is a center for campgrounds, dude ranches, and antique shops. Activities include canoeing, fishing, golf, swimming, tubing, skiing, horseback riding, and biking, among others. The fall foliage is beautiful here.

What to See and Do

Hickory Ski Center. *Hwy 418 and Hickory Hill Rd, Warrensburg (12027). 3 miles W on Hwy 418. Phone 518/623-2825.* Two Pomalifts, T-bar, rope tow; school, rentals; snack bar. Longest run 1 1/4 miles; vertical drop 1,230 feet. (Dec-Apr, Sat, Sun, holiday weeks) **$$$$**

Warrensburg Museum of Local History. *47 Main St, Warrensburg (12885). Phone 518/623-2928.* Exhibits detail the history of Warrensburg from the time it became a town to the present. Artifacts of livelihood, business, industry, and general living of the residents. (July-Aug, Tues-Sat) **FREE**

Special Events

Arts & Crafts Festival. *Main St and Stewart Farrar Ave, Warrensburg. Phone 518/623-2161.* July 4 weekend.

World's Largest Garage Sale and Foliage Festival. *All of Main St and side streets. Phone 518/623-2161.* Late Sept-early Oct.

Full-Service Inn

★ ★ ★ FRIENDS LAKE INN. *963 Friends Lake Rd, Chestertown (12817). Phone 518/494-4751; fax 518/494-4616. www.friendslake.com.* A stay at this restored 19th century inn offers guests cross-country skiing, a private beach, and canoeing on Friends Lake. 17 rooms, 3 story. Check-in 2 pm, check-out 11 am. Restaurant. Outdoor pool. **$$$**

Restaurants

★ ★ FRIENDS LAKE INN. *963 Friends Lake Rd, Chestertown (12817). Phone 518/494-4751; fax 518/494-4616. www.friendslake.com.* Built in 1860. Seafood menu. Breakfast, dinner. Bar. **$$$**

★ ★ ★ MERRILL MAGEE HOUSE. *3 Hudson St, Warrensburg (12885). Phone 518/623-2449. www.merrillmageehouse.com.* Continental menu. Dinner.

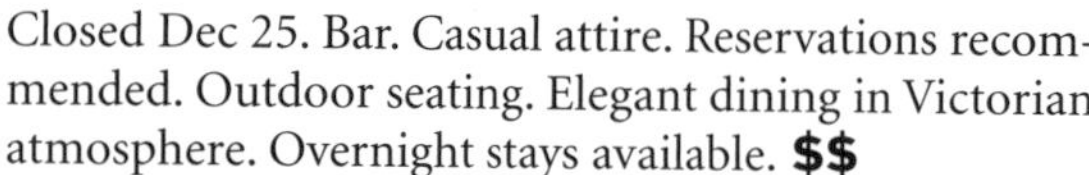

Closed Dec 25. Bar. Casual attire. Reservations recommended. Outdoor seating. Elegant dining in Victorian atmosphere. Overnight stays available. **$$**

Waterloo (D-5)

See also Canandaigua, Finger Lakes, Geneva, Seneca Falls

Settled 1800
Population 7,866
Elevation 455 ft
Area Code 315
Zip 13165
Web Site www.waterloony.com

The Church of Jesus Christ of Latter-day Saints (Mormons) was founded by Joseph Smith and five other men in a small log cabin here on April 6, 1830. The site is commemorated at the Peter Whitmer Farm.

What to See and Do

McClintock House. *14 E Williams St, Waterloo (13165). Phone 315/568-2991.*(1835) Home of the McClintocks, a Quaker family who were active in the planning of the first Women's Rights Convention. Tour (Sat-Sun). **$**

Peter Whitmer Farm. *1451 Aukst Rd, Waterloo (14521). 3 1/2 miles S via Hwy 96. Phone 315/597-5851.* This site is where the Church of Jesus Christ of Latter-day Saints (Mormons) was organized in 1830; period furnishings. Tours (20 to 30 minutes), video presentations. (Daily) **FREE**

Terwilliger Museum. *31 E Williams St, Waterloo (13165). Phone 315/539-0533.* Historical museum housing collections dating from 1875; Native American displays; authentic full-size vehicles and a replica of a general store provides a glimpse of life as it was in the 1920s. Also five rooms, each furnished to depict a specific era. (Tues-Fri, 1-4 pm) **DONATION**

Waterloo Memorial Day Museum. *35 E Main St, Waterloo (13165). Phone 315/539-9611.* Mementos of Civil War, World War I, World War II, the Korean conflict, Vietnam, and the first Memorial Day in this 20-room mansion furnished in 1860-1870 period. (July-Labor Day, Mon and Thurs afternoons, also Sat late morning-early afternoon; closed July 4) Under 12 years only with adult. **DONATION**

Limited-Service Hotel

★★ **HOLIDAY INN.** *2468 Mound Rd, Waterloo (13165). Phone 315/539-5011; fax 315/539-8355. www.holidayinn.com.* 148 rooms, 2 story. Pets accepted, some restrictions. Check-in 3 pm, check-out noon. Restaurant, bar. Fitness room. Outdoor pool, whirlpool. Tennis. **$**

Watertown (C-6)

See also Clayton, Sackets Harbor

Settled 1799
Population 26,705
Elevation 478 ft
Area Code 315
Zip 13601
Information Chamber of Commerce, 230 Franklin St; phone 315/788-4400
Web Site www.watertownny.com

Watertown lies along the Black River, 11 miles east of Lake Ontario and 22 miles south of the St. Lawrence. Within the city, the river falls more than 100 feet, providing an opportunity for whitewater rafting. During a county fair here in 1878 young Frank W. Woolworth originated the idea of the five-and-ten-cent store.

What to See and Do

American Maple Museum. *Main St, Croghan. 30 miles SE via Hwys 12 and 812. Phone 315/346-1107.* Displays of maple syrup production; equipment; history of maple production in North America; lumberjack display. (July-mid-Sept: Mon-Sat; mid-May-June and mid-Sept-mid-Oct: Mon, Fri, Sat; mid-Oct-Nov: by appointment) **$**

Jefferson County Historical Society Museum. *228 Washington St, Watertown (13601). Phone 315/782-3491.* Paddock mansion (1876); Victorian mansion with period rooms, military rooms; Native American artifacts, changing and regional history exhibits; Victorian garden. (Mon-Fri; closed holidays) **FREE**

Long Point State Park. *7495 State Park Rd, Three Mile Bay (13693). NW on Chaumont Bay, via Hwy 12 E, 8 miles W of Three Mile Bay. Phone 315/649-5258.* Fishing, boating (launch, dock); picnicking, tent and trailer sites. (May-mid-Sept) Standard fees.

Roswell P. Flower Memorial Library. *229 Washington St, Watertown (13601). Phone 315/788-2352. www.*

flowermemoriallibrary.org. Neo-Classic marble building houses murals of local history, French furniture; miniature furniture; geneology and local history. (Mid-June-Labor Day: Mon-Thurs 9 am-9 pm, Fri to 5 pm; rest of year: Mon-Tues, Thurs 9 am-9 pm, Wed, Fri-Sat to 5 pm; closed holidays) **FREE**

Sci-Tech Center. *154 Stone St, Watertown (13601). Phone 315/788-1340.* Hands-on science and technology museum for families. More than 40 exhibits, including laser display and discovery boxes; science store. (Tues-Sat; closed holidays) **$**

Special Event

Jefferson County Fair. *Coffen Street, Watertown (13601). Phone 315/782-8612.* Agriculture, livestock, art exhibits; held annually for more than 150 years. Mid-July.

Limited-Service Hotels

★ ★ BEST WESTERN CARRIAGE HOUSE INN. *300 Washington St, Watertown (13601). Phone 315/782-8000; fax 315/786-2097. www.bestwesternwatertownny.com.* 160 rooms, 3 story. Pets accepted; fee. Check-out noon. Restaurant, bar. Indoor pool. **$**

★ DAYS INN. *1142 Arsenal St, Watertown (13601). Phone 315/782-2700; fax 315/782-9877. www.daysinn.com.* 135 rooms, 6 story. Check-out 11 am. Restaurant, bar. Fitness room. Indoor pool. **$**

★ THE INN. *1190 Arsenal St, Watertown (13601). Phone 315/788-6800; toll-free 800/799-5224; fax 315/788-5366.* 96 rooms, 2 story. Pets accepted, some restrictions; fee. Check-out noon. Outdoor pool. **$**

Restaurants

★ BENNY'S STEAK HOUSE. *1050 Arsenal St, Watertown (13601). Phone 315/788-4110; fax 315/788-6103.* American, Italian menu. Lunch, dinner. Bar. Children's menu. **$$**

★ ★ PARTRIDGE BERRY INN. *26561 Hwy 3, Watertown (13601). Phone 315/788-4610; fax 315/782-6469. www.partridgeberryinn.com.* American menu. Lunch, dinner, brunch. Closed Mon. Bar. Children's menu. **$$**

Watkins Glen (E-5)

See also Corning, Elmira, Finger Lakes, Ithaca, Penn Yan

Population 2,149
Elevation 550 ft
Area Code 607
Zip 14891
Information Schuyler County Chamber of Commerce, 100 N Franklin St; phone 607/535-4300 or toll-free 800/607-4552
Web Site www.schuylerny.com

Watkins Glen is situated at the southern end of Seneca Lake, where the famous tributary gorge for which it is named emerges in the middle of the town. Several estate wineries offering tours and tastings are located on the southern shores of the lake, near town.

What to See and Do

Captain Bill's Seneca Lake Cruises. *1 N Franklin, Watkins Glen (14891). First and Franklin sts. Phone 607/535-4541. www.senecaharborstation.com/cruise.* Two tour boats. Sightseeing, lunch, dinner, and cocktail cruises. (Mid-May-mid-Oct, daily) **$$$$**

Cool-Lea Campground. *Rte 228, Odessa (14869). Phone 607/594-3500. www.coolleacamp.com.* This campground is on Cayuta Lake. 60 sites, convenience store, fishing, boat rentals.

Famous Brands Outlet. *412 N Franklin St, Watkins Glen (14891). Phone 607/535-4952. www.famousbrandsoutlet.com.* This is a popular spot for finding deals on such brand names as Carhartt, Dockers, and Woolrich. (Mon-Sat 9 am-8 pm, Sun 10 am-5 pm)

International Motor Racing Research Center at Watkins Glen. *610 S Decatur St, Watkins Glen (14891). Phone 607/535-9044. www.racingarchives.org.* The center features a wonderful display of all things racing, including cars. The broad collection also includes books, films, fine art, photographs, documents, magazines, programs, and memorabilia with a motor sports theme. (Mon-Sat 9 am-5 pm; also some Sun race days) **FREE**

Montour Falls. *408 W Main St, Montour Falls. 2 miles S on Hwy 14. Phone 607/535-7367.* Small community with seven glens nearby; fishing for rainbow trout in Catharine Creek. Chequaga Falls (156 feet) plunges into a pool beside the main street. Municipal marina,

N of town, has access to barge canal system. Trailer site (fee).

Seneca Grand Prix Family Fun Center. *2374 Hwy 414, Watkins Glen (14891). Phone 607/535-7981. www.sgpfun.com.* This park features Formula 1 go-karts, bumper boats, miniature golf, and a huge balloon giraffe (named Jerry) for the kids to jump into. (Mon-Fri 4-8 pm, Sat-Sun 1-9 pm)

Seneca Lodge. *State Rte 329, Watkins Glen (14891). Off Rte 329, at the south entrance to Watkins Glen State park. Phone 607/535-2014. www.senecalodge.com.* This place is very popular with race fans, many of whom reserve a year in advance and return year after year. On site is the historic Seneca Lodge Restaurant. The bar has NASCAR memorabilia; the mechanics hang out here. Cabins, A-frames, and motel rooms available. The cabins have a private toilet and shower. The A-frames have complete housekeeping facilities and a TV. The motel offers less Spartan rooms.

Thunder Road Tours. *The Shop, 2 N Franklin St, Watkins Glen (14891). Phone 607/535-2338.* See what it's like to be in the driver's seat as you follow the pace car for a few laps around the track. (Late May-late Oct: daily from noon) **$$$$**

Watkins Glen State Park. *State Rte 329, S Entrance, Watkins Glen. Near S end of Seneca Lake, off Hwy 14. Phone 607/535-4511. nysparks.state.ny.us.* Stairs and bridges lead upward through Watkins Glen Gorge, past the cataracts and rapids, rising some 600 feet in 1 1/2 miles. Olympic-size pool (mid-June-Labor Day, daily), bathhouse; picnicking, playground, concession; 305 campsites, trailer dumping stations, camper recreation programs (July-Aug). (Early-May-Oct) **$$$** On grounds are

> **Watkins Glen Gorge.** *State Rte 329, Watkins Glen (14891). Off Rte 14. Phone 607/535-4511.* The gorge features 19 waterfalls along this stretch. Park in town to avoid the fee ($$) at the entrance on Franklin. Guided walks by naturalists (Aug: Tues, Thurs, Sat 11 am; Sun 4:30). Climb 800 stone steps. **FREE**

Watkins Glen/Corning KOA. *Rte 414 S, Watkins Glen (14891). Phone toll-free 800/562-7430. www.koa.com/where/ny/32161.htm.* 105 sites, 26 cabins. Propane station, laundry services, ice, wood. Pool, miniature golf, bike rentals. Pets accepted.

Winery tours. Twenty-two wineries dot the hillsides of Seneca Lake. Follow Hwys 14 or 414 for tastings and tours. Contact the Seneca Lake Wine Trail for more information.

> **Glenora Wine Cellar.** *5435 Rte 14, Dundee (14837). N on Hwy 14. Phone 607/243-5511.*Winery on Seneca Lake; tastings. (Daily) **FREE**

Special Events

NASCAR Race Day. *2790 County Rd 16, Watkins Glen (14891). Phone 607/535-2481.* Contests, drivers, entertainment. Early Aug.

Watkins Glen International. *2790 County Rd 16, Watkins Glen (14891). 4 miles SW on County 16. Phone 607/535-2481. www.theglen.com.* IMSA and NASCAR Winston Cup racing. Late May-Sept.

Restaurants

★ ★ CASTEL GRISCH. *3380 County Rd 28, Watkins Glen (14891). Phone 607/535-9614; fax 607/535-2994. www.fingerlakes-ny.com/castelgrisch.* Alpine, American menu. Closed Jan-Mar. Outdoor seating. Guest rooms available. **$$**

★ ★ WILDFLOWER CAFE. *301 N Franklin St, Watkins Glen (14891). Phone 607/535-9797.* This restaurant, next door to the lively Crooked Rooster, offers a sedate atmosphere with American fareincluding sandwiches, burgers, and other entresat great prices. The microbrewery on the premises serves light and dark beers. American menu. Lunch, dinner. Closed holidays. Bar. **$$**

West Point (US Military Academy) (B-2)

See also Mahopac, Monroe, Newburgh, Peekskill, Stony Point

Established 1802
Population 7,138
Elevation 161 ft
Area Code 845
Zip 10996
Web Site www.usma.edu

West Point has been of military importance since Revolutionary days; it was one of four points on the mid-Hudson fortified against the British. In 1778, a great chain was strung across the river to stop British ships. The military academy was founded by an act of Congress in 1802. Barracks, academic, and administration buildings are closed to visitors.

What to See and Do

Battle Monument. *Thayer and Washington rds, West Point (10996). Phone 845/938-4011.* Memorial to the 2,230 officers and men of the Regular Army who fell in action during the Civil War. Nearby are some links from the chain used to block the river from 1778 to 1782.

Cadet Chapel. *Ruger Rd and Cadet Dr, West Point (10996). Phone 845/938-4011.*(1910) On hill overlooking the campus. Large pipe organ and stained glass. (Daily)

Michie Stadium. *Mills Road, West Point (10996). Phone 845/938-4011.* Seats 42,000. Army home football games.

Parades. *Hwy 9W and Hwy 218, West Point. Phone 845/938-2638.* Inquire at Visitors Center. (Late Apr-May, Sept-Nov)

Visitors Center. *Just outside Thayer Gate. Phone 845/938-2638.* Displays on cadet training, model cadet room, films shown, tours. Photo ID required. (Daily; closed Jan 1, Thanksgiving, Dec 25)

West Point Museum. *Hwy 218 (Main St) and Mountain Ave, Highland Falls (10996). In the Pershing Center at the Visitors Center, just outside Thayer Gate. Phone 845/938-2203.* Exhibits on history and ordnance. (Daily; closed Jan 1, Thanksgiving, Dec 25) **FREE**

Limited-Service Hotel

★ ★ THE THAYER HOTEL. *674 Thayer Rd, West Point (10996). Phone 845/446-4731; toll-free 800/247-5047; fax 845/446-0338. www.thethayerhotel.com.* This Hudson Valley hotel overlooking the riverthe only full-service hotel in the areais a National Historic Landmark. Sitting at the south entrance to West Point, the Gothic building was built in 1926 to accommodate US Military Academy personnel and their guests and has seen many famous faces cross its threshold, including General Douglas MacArthur and President John F. Kennedy. Today, it caters especially to groups for weddings, meetings, corporate retreats, and the like, although it's still a fine choice for individual guests. The lovely Dining Room is known for its elaborate buffet brunch (reservations required). 151 rooms, 5 story. Check-in 3 pm, check-out 11 am. Restaurant, bar. Fitness room. **$**

Specialty Lodging

CROMWELL MANOR INN. *174 Angola Rd, Cornwall (12518). Phone 845/534-7136. www.cromwellmanor.com.* 13 rooms, 2 story. Complimentary full breakfast. Check-in 4 pm, check-out 11 am. Airport transportation available. Built in 1820 by descendant of Oliver Cromwell; 7 acres of woodlands/gardens. **$$**

Restaurants

★ ★ CANTERBURY BROOK INN. *331 Main St, Cornwall (12508). Phone 845/534-9658; fax 845/446-0078. www.canterburybrookinn.com.* American menu. Dinner. Closed Sun-Tues; Dec 25. Bar. **$$**

★ PAINTER'S. *266 Hudson St, Cornwall-on-Hudson (12520). Phone 845/534-2109; fax 845/534-8428. www.painters-restaurant.com.* Seafood menu. Lunch, dinner, Sun brunch. Closed holidays. Bar. Children's menu. Outdoor seating. **$$**

Westbury

See also Garden City, Jericho, New York, Roslyn

Population 14,263
Elevation 100 ft
Area Code 516
Zip 11590
Web Site

What to See and Do

Clark Botanic Garden. *193 I. U. Willets Rd, Albertson (11507). Phone 516/484-8600. www.clarkbotanic.org.* The 12-acre former estate of Grenville Clark. Includes Hunnewell Rose Garden; ponds, streams; bulbs, perennials, annuals; wildflower, herb, rock, rhododendron, azalea, and daylily gardens; children's garden; groves of white pine, dogwood, and hemlock. (Daily 10 am-4 pm) **$**

Old Westbury Gardens. *71 Old Westbury Rd, Old Westbury (11030). Phone 516/333-0048. www.oldwestburygardens.org.* Step back in time to this grand estate, with a historic mansion that dates back to 1906. The 66-room house features grand paintings, magnificent furniture, and wonderful trinkets of all kinds. The gardens, which are delightful to stroll through, are a main attraction. They have a variety of flora and fauna that change with the seasons. Save this attraction for a pleasant sunny day in any season except winter. (Mon, Wed-Sun 10 am-5 pm; winter hours vary) **$$**

Westbury Music Fair. *960 Brush Hollow Rd, Westbury (11590). Phone 516/334-0800. www.musicfair.com.* This concert series offers a unique chance to see performances in the theater-in-the-round style. Most of the stars are a bit from yesteryear, and have included Paul Anka, Ringo Starr, Aaron Neville, and Tony Bennett. But, you're sure to have an enjoyable evening. The crowd is usually a bit older and pretty sedate.

Restaurants

★ ★ BENNY'S RISTORANTE. *199 Post Ave, Westbury (11590). Phone 516/997-8111.* Italian menu. Lunch, dinner. Closed Sun; holidays; also the last two weeks in Aug. Reservations recommended. **$$$**

★ ★ CAFE BACI. *1636 Old Country Rd, Westbury (11590). Phone 516/832-8888; fax 516/222-0769.* Italian, American menu. Lunch, dinner. Bar. Casual attire. **$$**

★ ★ GIULIO CESARE RISTORANTE. *18 Ellison Ave, Westbury (11590). Phone 516/334-2982.* Italian menu. Lunch, dinner. Closed Sun; holidays. Bar. **$$$**

Westhampton Beach

See also Hampton Bays, Riverhead

Population 1,902
Elevation 10 ft
Area Code 631
Zip 11978
Information Greater Westhampton Chamber of Commerce, 173 Montauk Hwy, PO Box 1228; phone 631/288-3337
Web Site www.whbcc.org

Surrounded by water, this resort area offers fishing and water sports. Nearby are hiking and nature trails.

What to See and Do

Main Street in Westhampton Beach. *Main St, Westhampton Beach.* This is a very pleasant in shopping jaunt during the summer months. You can buy funky, stylish beachwear (and lots of it); children's clothing; homemade ice cream; ceramics; and booksjust to name a few things. Park the car and let your feet do the rest. Tip: Try to make it out here on a weekday in summer; weekends are quite crowded.

Wertheim National Wildlife Refuge. *Approximately 10 miles W on Hwy 80 to Smith Rd S. Phone 631/286-0485.* A 2,600-acre refuge for wildlife including deer, fox, raccoon, herons, hawks, ospreys, and waterfowl. Fishing, boating, canoeing; walking trail, photography. Environmental education. (Daily 8 am-4 pm) **FREE**

White Plains (B-2)

See also Brewster, Hartsdale, Hawthorne, Mahopac, Mamaroneck, Mount Kisco, New Rochelle, New York, Nyack, Pound Ridge, Stamford, Tarrytown, Yonkers

Settled 1735
Population 53,077
Elevation 236 ft
Area Code 914
Information Westchester County Office of Tourism, 222 Mamaroneck Ave, 10605; phone 914/995-8500 or toll-free 800/833-9282
Web Site www.cityofwhiteplains.com

In October 1776, General George Washington outfoxed General Lord Howe here. Howe, with a stronger, fresher force, permitted Washington to retreat to an impregnable position; Howe never could explain why he had not pursued his overwhelming advantage.

What to See and Do

Miller Hill Restoration. *Dunlap Way and White Plains, White Plains (10603).* Restored earthworks from the Battle of White Plains (Oct 28, 1776). Built by Washington's troops. Battle diagrams.

Monument. *S Broadway and Mitchell Pl, White Plains (10603).* Here the Declaration of Independence was adopted July 1776, and the state of New York was formally organized.

Washington's Headquarters. *140 Virginia Rd, N White Plains (10603). Phone 914/949-1236.* (1776) Revolutionary War relics; demonstrations, lectures. (By appointment) **FREE**

Limited-Service Hotel

★ WELLESLEY INN. *94 Business Park Dr, Armonk (10504). Phone 914/273-9090; fax 914/273-4105. www.*

wellesleyonline.com. 140 rooms, 2 story. Check-out noon. High-speed Internet access. Restaurant, bar. Fitness room. Outdoor pool. Airport transportation available. **$**

Full-Service Hotels

★ ★ ★ HILTON RYE TOWN. *699 Westchester Ave, Rye Brook (10573). Phone 914/939-6300; fax 914/939-5328. www.hilton.com.* 437 rooms, 2 story. Pets accepted, some restrictions; fee. Check-in 3 pm, check-out noon. High-speed Internet access. Restaurant, bar. Children's activity center. Fitness room. Indoor pool, outdoor pool, children's pool, whirlpool. Tennis. Business center. **$$**

★ ★ ★ RENAISSANCE WESTCHESTER HOTEL. *80 W Red Oak Ln, White Plains (10604). Phone 914/694-5400; fax 914/694-5616. www.renaissancehotels.com.* 350 rooms, 6 story. Check-in 3 pm, check-out 1 pm. High-speed Internet access. Restaurant, bar. Fitness room. Indoor pool, whirlpool. Tennis. Business center. **$$**

Restaurants

★ ★ LE JARDIN DU ROI. *95 King St, Chappaqua. Phone 914/238-1368.* French menu. Breakfast, lunch, dinner, brunch. Casual attire. Outdoor seating. **$$**

★ ★ TAKAYAMA JAPANESE RESTAURANT. *95 King St, Chappaqua. Phone 914/238-5700; toll-free 888/870-1313; fax 914/238-5732.* Japanese menu. Lunch, dinner. Bar. Casual attire. Reservations recommended. **$$**

Whitehall

Restaurant

★ FINCH & CHUBB RESTAURANT & INN. *82 N Williams St, Whitehall (12887). Phone 518/499-2049. www.whitehall.com.* Chef-owned establishment with regional cuisine and views of Whitehall Harbor. American menu. Lunch, dinner. **$**

Williamsville

Restaurant

★ ★ ★ DAFFODIL'S. *930 Maple Rd, Williamsville (14221). Phone 716/688-5413; fax 716/688-2113. www.daffodilsrestaurant.com.* Fireplaces, paintings, and book-lined walls create a library-esque atmosphere at this long-standing Buffalo establishment. Lunch, dinner. Bar. Children's menu. Victorian décor. Valet parking. **$$$**

★ ★ RED MILL INN. *8326 Main St, Williamsville (14221). Phone 716/633-7878; fax 716/633-7897. www.redmillinn.com.* Located on the edge of Buffalo, this unique landmark restaurant was built in 1858 as a dairy farm. The restaurant keeps this historic theme with décor that includes antique farm implements and an authentic New York Central railroad caboose as part of the dining room. The farms original kitchen now serves as the Brickroom Bar, where Happy Hour takes place Monday through Friday from 4 pm to 7 pm. A menu of varied American favorites is served at the Red Mill Inn, such as seafood and steak as well as salads and sandwiches. American menu. Lunch, dinner, Sun brunch. Closed Dec 25. Bar. Children's menu. Casual attire. Reservations recommended. Valet parking. Outdoor seating. Caboose and Union Pacific dining cars. Fireplaces; country inn built in 1858. **$$**

Wilmington (B-9)

See also Lake Placid, Saranac Lake

Population 1,131
Elevation 1,020 ft
Area Code 518
Zip 12997
Information Whiteface Mtn Regional Visitors Bureau, Hwy 86, PO Box 277; phone 518/946-2255 or toll-free 888/944-8332
Web Site www.whitefaceregion.com

Gateway to Whiteface Mountain Memorial Highway, Wilmington is made-to-order for skiers and lovers of scenic splendor.

What to See and Do

High Falls Gorge. *Rte 86, Wilmington. 5 miles S on Hwy 86. Phone 518/946-2278.* Deep ravine cut into the base of Whiteface Mountain by the Ausable River.

Variety of strata, rapids, falls, and potholes can be viewed from a network of modern bridges and paths. Photography and mineral displays in main building. (Memorial Day-mid-Oct, daily) **$$$**

Santa's Home Workshop. *Hwy 431 and Whiteface Mountain, North Pole (12946). 1 1/2 miles W on Hwy 431. Phone 518/946-2211. www.northpoleny.com.* "Santa's home and workshop," Santa Claus, reindeer, children's rides and shows. (Late-June-mid-Oct, Mon-Wed; Sat, Sun) Reduced rates weekdays spring and fall. **$$$$**

Whiteface Mountain Memorial Highway. *3 miles W on Hwy 431. Phone toll-free 800/462-6236.* A 5-mile toll road to top of mountain (4,867 feet). Trail or elevator from parking area. Views of St. Lawrence River, Lake Placid, and Vermont. Elevator (Late May-mid-Oct, daily, weather permitting).

Whiteface Mountain Ski Center. *3 miles SW on Hwy 86. Phone 518/946-7171; toll-free 800/462-6236. www.whiteface.com.* Gondola; two triple, seven double chairlifts; snowmaking; patrol, school, rentals; cafeteria, bar, nursery. Longest run 2 1/2 miles; vertical drop 3,350 feet. Chairlift (mid-June-mid-Oct; fee). Lift-serviced mountain biking center; rental, repair shop, guided tours (late June-mid-Oct). (Mid-Nov-mid-Apr, daily) **$$$$**

Limited-Service Hotels

★ HUNGRY TROUT MOTOR INN. *Rte 86, Wilmington (12997). Phone 518/946-2217; toll-free 800/766-9137; fax 518/946-7418. www.hungrytrout.com.* 20 rooms. Closed Apr, Nov. Pets accepted, some restrictions; fee. Check-out 11 am. Bar. Outdoor pool, children's pool. On Ausable River. **$**

★ LEDGE ROCK AT WHITEFACE. *Hwy 86, Wilmington (12997). Phone 518/946-2302; toll-free 800/336-4754; fax 518/946-7594. www.ledgerockatwhiteface.com.* 18 rooms, 2 story. Pets accepted; fee. Check-out 11 am. Outdoor pool, children's pool. **$**

Restaurant

★ WILDERNESS INN II. *Hwy 86, Wilmington (12997). Phone 518/946-2391; fax 518/946-7290.* American menu. Dinner. Closed Wed (in winter). Bar. Children's menu. Outdoor seating. Guest cottages available. **$$**

Windham

See also Cairo, Hunter

Population 1,660
Area Code 518
Zip 12496
Web Site www.windhamchamber.org

What to See and Do

Ski Windham. *Clarence D. Lane Rd, Windham. 25 miles W on Hwy 23, exit 21. Phone 518/734-4300; toll-free 800/729-4766. www.skiwindham.com.* High-speed detachable quad, double, four triple chairlifts; surface lift; patrol, ski school, rentals; snowmaking; nursery, ski shop, restaurant, two cafeterias, bar. Snowboarding. Longest run 2 1/4 miles; vertical drop 1,600 feet. (Early Nov-early Apr, daily) **$$$$**

White Birches Campsite. *Princess Navoo Rd, Windham. 2 1/2 miles NE. Phone 518/734-3266.* Approximately 400 acres of Catskill Mountain wilderness, lake. Summer activities include lake swimming, canoeing (rentals), paddleboats (fee); camping (hookups), mountain biking, archery (fee). **$$$**

Limited-Service Hotels

★ HOTEL VIENNA. *107 Hwy 296, Windham (12496). Phone 518/734-5300; toll-free 800/898-5308; fax 518/734-4749. www.thehotelvienna.com.* 30 rooms, 2 story. Closed Apr-mid-May. Complimentary continental breakfast. Check-in 2 pm, check-out 11 am. Indoor pool, whirlpool. **$**

★ ★ WINDHAM ARMS HOTEL. *Hwy 23, Windham (12496). Phone 518/734-3000; fax 518/734-5900. www.windhamarmshotel.com.* 51 rooms, 3 story. Pets accepted; fee. Check-out 10 am. Restaurant. Fitness room. Outdoor pool. Tennis. **$**

Specialty Lodging

ALBERGO ALLEGRIA. *Hwy 296, Windham (12496). Phone 518/734-5560; fax 518/734-5570. www.albergousa.com.* This Victorian inn, furnished with antiques, has 16 bedrooms with down comforters, full private baths, TVs with VCRs, and telephones. There are twelve guest rooms named after the 12 months of the year and four suites named after the four seasons.16 rooms, 2 story. Complimentary full breakfast. Check-in 2 pm, check-out noon. **$$**

Woodstock (F-9)

See also Hunter, Kingston, Saugerties, Shandaken

Population 6,241
Elevation 512 ft
Area Code 845
Zip 12498
Information Chamber of Commerce and Arts, PO Box 36; phone 845/679-6234
Web Site www.woodstock-online.com

Woodstock has traditionally been known as an art colony. In 1902 Ralph Radcliffe Whitehead, an Englishman, came from California and set up a home and handcraft community (Byrdcliffe, north of town). The Art Students' League of New York established a summer school here a few years later. In 1916 Hervey White conceived the Maverick Summer Music Concerts, the oldest chamber concert series in the country. Woodstock was the original site chosen for the famous 1969 Woodstock Music Festival; however, when the event grew bigger than anyone imagined, it was moved 60 miles southwest to a farmer's field near Bethel (see MONTICELLO). Nevertheless, the festival gave Woodstock notoriety.

What to See and Do

Woodstock Artists Association Gallery. *24 Tinker St, Woodstock (12498). At Village Green. Phone 845/679-2940. www.woodstockart.org.* Center of the community since 1920. Changing exhibits of works by regional artists. Nationally recognized permanent collection. **DONATION**

Special Event

Maverick Concerts. *Maverick Rd, between Hwys 375 and 28. Phone 845/679-8217. www.maverickconcerts.org.* Chamber music concerts. Sun June-early Sept. **$$$$**

Specialty Lodging

LA DUCHESSE ANNE. *1564 Wittenberg Rd, Mount Tremper (12457). Phone 845/688-5260; fax 845/688-2438. www.laduchesseanne.com.* 10 rooms, 2 story. Complimentary continental breakfast. Check-in 3-11 pm. Check-out noon. Restaurant, bar. Built as a guest house in 1850. **$**

TWIN GABLES OF WOODSTOCK. *73 Tinker St, Woodstock (12498). Phone 845/679-9479; fax 845/679-5638. www.twingableswoodstockny.com.* 9 rooms, 2 story. Check-in noon, check-out 11:30 am. **$**
D

Spa

★ ★ ★ ★ THE SPA AT EMERSON PLACE. *146 Mt Pleasant Rd, Mount Tremper (12457). Phone 845/688-7900. www.theemerson.com.* Asian serenity-chic style greets guests of the Emerson Spa. Sleek rattan furnishings, bamboo decorative objects, and soothing tones are used throughout the public and private spaces. Eight treatment rooms are available, in addition to a fitness facility with resistance pool, relaxation lounge, and Vichy shower and hydrotherapy bath. Asian influences extend to the spa treatment menu, where several Ayurvedic treatments are offered. Indian head massage, dosha balancing massage, and abhyanga massage, involving two therapists in unison, are some of the bodywork offerings, while shirodhara and bindi herbal body treatments round out the Ayurvedic menu. The Emerson Spa also looks to nature for much of its inspiration. From aromaessence facials and sea salt body scrubs to warm mud wraps, many of the treatments use natural ingredients for cleansing, detoxifying, and healing the skin. The Vichy shower and hydrotherapy bath are terrific stress and bloat reducers. Expectant mothers are pampered with the prenatal tonic, a combination of a massage, facial, and pedicure, or the mother-to-be indulgence, a combination of body exfoliation and a body shaping mask. Men are also regally pampered with massage, body treatments, and facials designed especially for their skin care needs.

Restaurants

★ ★ BEAR CAFE. *295A Tinker St, Woodstock (12409). Phone 845/679-5555; fax 845/679-3306. www.bearcafe.com.* American menu. Lunch, dinner. Bar. Casual attire. Outdoor seating. **$$$**

★ ★ BLUE MOUNTAIN BISTRO. *Rte 212 and Glusco Tpike, Woodstock. Phone 845/679-8519.* Mediterranean menu. Dinner. Closed Mon; holidays. Bar. Casual attire. Reservations recommended. Outdoor seating. **$$**

★ ★ VIOLETTE RESTAURANT & WINE BAR. *85 Mill Rd, Woodstock (12498). Phone 845/679-5300.* American menu. Lunch, dinner, brunch. Closed Wed;

holidays. Bar. Casual attire. Reservations recommended. Outdoor seating. **$$**

Yonkers (B-2)

See also Mamaroneck, Tarrytown, White Plains

Settled 1646
Population 196,086
Elevation 16 ft
Area Code 914
Information Chamber of Commerce, 20 S Broadway, Suite 1207, 10701; phone 914/963-0332
Web Site www.yonkerschamber.com

Yonkers, on the New York City line, was originally puchased by Adriaen van der Donck in the early 1600s. His status as a young nobleman from Holland gave him the nickname "DeJonkeer," which underwent many changes until it became "the Yonkers land" and finally Yonkers.

What to See and Do

St. Paul's Church National Historic Site. *897 S Columbus Ave, Mount Vernon (10550). 10 miles SE via Hutchinson River Pkwy exit 8 (Sandford Blvd). Phone 914/667-4116. www.nps.gov/sapa.*Setting for historical events establishing basic freedoms outlined in the Bill of Rights. The event that made this site famous, the Great Election of 1733, led to the establishment of a free press in colonial America. Before completion, the fieldstone and brick Georgian St. Paul's Church (1763) served as a military hospital for the British and Hessians during the Revolutionary War. Building was completed after the war and served not only as a church but also as a meeting house and courtroom where Aaron Burr practiced law on at least one occasion. Tours (Mon-Fri, by appointment; closed Jan 1, Thanksgiving, Dec 25). (Mon-Fri 9 am-5 pm) **FREE** Also here is

Bill of Rights Museum. *897 S Columbus Ave, Mt Vernon (Westchester) (10550). Phone 914/667-4116.* Exhibits include a working model of an 18th-century printing press and dioramas depicting John Peter Zenger, whose trial and acquittal for seditious libel in 1735 helped establish freedom of the press in America. A series of panels detail the history of the site, including the Anne Hutchinson story, the Great Election of 1733, and the Revolutionary period. (Same days as St. Paul's Church) (Mon-Fri 9 am-5 pm) **FREE**

The Hudson River Museum of Westchester. *511 Warburton Ave, Yonkers (10701). Phone 914/963-4550. www.hrm.org.* Includes Glenview Mansion (1876), an Eastlake-inspired Hudson River house overlooking the Palisades; Andrus Planetarium; regional art, history, and science exhibits; changing exhibits of 19th- and 20th-century art in the Glenview galleries and contemporary wing. Changing exhibits, planetarium shows, lectures, jazz festival in summer. (Wed-Sun noon-5 pm, Fri to 8 pm; closed holidays) **$**

Yonkers Raceway. *810 Central Ave, Yonkers (10704). Phone 914/968-4200. www.yonkersraceway.com.* Yonkers Raceway hosts harness racing at its 98-acre location. Unlike most other New York City area horse racing venues, Yonkers is open year-round. Enjoy an evening of gambling in this suburban raceway that's always popular with locals. Because taking public transportation involves both a subway and bus, you may want to rent a car for the day. (Mon-Tues, Thurs-Sat; closed holidays) **$**

Restaurant

★★ J.J. MANNION'S. *640 McLean Ave, Yonkers (10705). Phone 914/476-2786; fax 914/476-2788.* American, Irish menu. Lunch, dinner. Closed Dec 25. Bar. Children's menu. Casual attire. **$$**

Toronto, ON

Founded 1793
Population 3,400,000
Elevation 569 ft (173 m)
Area Code 416
Information Convention & Visitors Association, Queens Quay Terminal at Harbourfront, 207 Queens Quay W, M5J 1A7; phone 416/203-2500 or toll-free 800/363-1990
Web Site www.torontotourism.com

Toronto is one of Canada's leading industrial, commercial, and cultural centers. From its location on the shores of Lake Ontario, it has performed essential communications and transportation services throughout Canadian history. Its name derives from the native word for "meeting place," as the area was called by the Hurons who led the first European, Etienne Brule, to the spot. In the mid-1800s, the Grand Trunk and Great Western Railroad and the Northern Railway connected Toronto with the upper St. Lawrence; Portland, Maine; and Chicago, Illinois.

After French fur traders from Qubec established Fort Rouille in 1749, Toronto became a base for further Canadian settlement. Its population of Scottish, English, and United States emigrants was subject to frequent armed attacks, especially during the War of 1812 and immediately thereafter. From within the United States, the attackers aimed at annexation; from within Canada, they aimed at emancipation from England. One result of these unsuccessful threats was the protective Confederation of Lower Canada, which later separated again as the province of Québec, and Upper Canada, which still later became the province of Ontario with Toronto as its capital.

Toronto today is a cosmopolitan city with many intriguing features. Once predominantly British, the population is now exceedingly multicultural--the United Nations deemed Toronto the world's most ethnically diverse city in 1989. A major theater center with many professional playhouses, including the Royal Alexandra Theatre, Toronto is also a major banking center, with several architecturally significant banks. Good shopping can be found throughout the city, but Torontonians are most proud of their Underground City, a series of subterranean malls linking more than 300 shops and restaurants in the downtown area. For professional sports fans, Toronto offers the Maple Leafs (hockey), the Blue Jays (baseball), the Raptors (basketball), and the Argonauts (football). A visit to the Harbourfront, a boat tour to the islands, or enjoying an evening on the town should round out your stay in Toronto.

Additional Visitor Information

For further information contact Tourism Toronto, Queens Quay Terminal at Harbourfront, 207 Queens Quay W, M5J 1A7; phone 416/203-2500 or toll-free 800/363-1990 (US and Canada). Toronto's public transportation system is extensive and includes buses, subways, streetcars, and trolley buses; for maps phone 416/393-4636.

Airport Information

Airport Toronto Pearson International Airport.

Information 416/776-3000

Web Site www.lbpia.toronto.on.ca

Airlines Aeroflot Russian, Aeromexico, Aerosvit Airlines, Air Canada, Air Canada Jazz, Air France, Air Jamaica, Air New Zealand, Air Transat, Alaska Airlines, Alitalia, All Nippon Airways, Allegro, American Airlines, American Eagle, America West Airlines, Atlantic Southeast, Austrian Airlines, British Airways, British Midland Airways (BMI), BWIA International, CanJet Airlines, Cathay Pacific, Comair, Continental Airlines, Continental Express, Cubana Airlines, Czech Airlines, Delta Air Lines, EL AL Israel, Finnair, HMY Airlines, Japan Air Lines, Jetsgo, KLM Royal Dutch Airlines, Korean Airlines, LanChile, LOT Polish Airline, LTU International Airways, Lufthansa, Malev Hungarian, Martinair Holland, Mesa Airlines, Mexicana Airlines, Midway Airlines, Midwest Connect, MyTravel Airways, Northwest Airlines, Olympic Airways, Pakistan International, Piedmont PSA Airlines, Qantas, Royal Jordanian, SAS Scandinavian Airlines, SATA Express, Singapore Airlines, Skyservice Airlines, Skyway Airlines, TACA/Lacsa Thai International Airways, United Airlines, US Airways, Varig Brazil, Westjet, ZOOM Airlines.

What to See and Do

Art Gallery of Ontario. *317 Dundas St W, Toronto (M5T 1G4). Phone 416/977-0414. www.ago.net.* Changing exhibits of paintings, drawings, sculpture, and graphics from the 14th to 20th centuries include the Henry Moore Collection; a permanent Cana-

Toronto Theater

Theater buffs won't suffer for lack of culture while visiting Toronto. The city has a diverse and lively performing arts scene with something for everyone, from Broadway musicals to stand-up comedy and opera to dance. Toronto has the status of third-largest theater center in the English-speaking world, after London and New York.There are performance venues throughout the city; however, three areas contain the largest concentration of theater activity. The downtown Entertainment District contains larger venues hosting touring or more lavish productions. Venues include the Canon, Royal Alexandra, Princess of Wales, and Elgin & Winter Garden theaters. Roy Thomson Hall and Massey Hall host symphony and choral events. The East End contains several venues on Front Street, east of Younge Street. Here you'll find the Canadian Stage Company, The Lorraine Kisma Theatre of Young Peoples, the St. Lawrence Centre for the Arts, and the citys largest venue, the Hummingbird Centre, home of the National Ballet of Canada and the Canadian Opera Company. The Annex is devoted to mid-size, alternative, and homegrown theater. This is where the Tarragon Theatre, Theatre Passe Muraille, and the Factory Theatre are located. Today, there are more than 90 theater venues in Toronto, and over 200 professional theater and dance companies, producing more than 10,000 live performances a year.

dian Collection and Contemporary Galleries; films, lectures, concerts. (Thurs-Fri 10 am-9 pm, Sat-Sun 10 am-5:30 pm; closed Jan 1, Dec 25) Free admission Wed evenings. **$$**

Bata Shoe Museum. *327 Bloor St W, Toronto (M5S 1W7). Phone 416/979-7799.www.batashoemuseum.ca.*When Mrs. Sonja Batas passion for collecting historical shoes began to surpass her personal storage space, the Bata family established The Bata Shoe Museum Foundation. Architect Raymond Moriyamas award-winning five-story, 3,900-square-foot (362-square-meter) building now holds more than 10,000 shoes, artfully arranged in four galleries to celebrate the style and function of footwear throughout 4,500 years of history. One permanent exhibition, All About Shoes, showcases a collection of 20th-century celebrity shoes; artifacts on exhibit range from Chinese bound-foot shoes and ancient Egyptian sandals to chestnut-crushing clogs and Elton Johns platforms. Talk about standing toe-to-toe with history. (Tues-Sat 10 am-5 pm; Thurs to 8 pm, Sun noon-5 pm; June-Aug: Mon 10 am-5 pm) **$$**

Black Creek Pioneer Village. *1000 Murray Ross Pkwy, Downsview (M3J 2P3). 2 miles (3 kilometers) N on Hwy 400, E on Steeles, then 1/2 mile (1 kilometer) to Jane St. Phone 416/736-1733.* Step back in time to a village in 1860s Ontario, when life was much simpler if you were hearty enough to handle it. In the village of Black Creek, workers wearing period costumes welcome you into 35 authentically restored homes, workshops, public buildings, and farms, and demonstrate skills such as open-hearth cooking, bread-making, looming, milling, blacksmithing, sewing, and printing. (Hours vary by month; call for schedule; closed Dec 25) **$$$**

Bloor/Yorkville area. *Bounded by Bloor St W, Ave Rd, Davenport Rd, and Yonge St. www.toronto.com.* If the last time you visited Toronto was 30 years ago, and you still have images of flower children handing out flowers on Bloor Street, you're in for a surprise. The barefoot girl who gave you a daisy is now a 40-year-old who shops at the very spot where she used to stand. The Bloor/Yorkville area is one of Toronto's most elegant shopping and dining sections, with art galleries, nightclubs, music, designer couture boutiques, and first-rate art galleries. The area itself is fun to walk around, with a cluster of courtyards and alleyways. There's also a contemporary park in the heart of the neighborhood with a huge piece of granite called The Rock. It was brought here from the Canadian Shield, a U-shaped region of ancient rock covering about half of Canada, causing the first part of North America to be permanently elevated above sea level.

Bruce Trail/Toronto Bruce Trail Club. *Phone 416/763-9061.* Canada's first and longest footpath, the Bruce Trail runs 437 miles (703 kilometers) along the Niagara Escarpment from Niagara to the Bruce Peninsula. It provides the only public access to the Escarpment, a UNESCO World Biosphere Reserve. While the Toronto Bruce Trail Club is the largest and, some say, the best organized of the many biking and hiking clubs in the area, you can contact the Toronto Convention and

Visitors Bureau (phone 416/203-2600) for Toronto access and the names of organizations that offer activities on the trail. *Note:* Although the Toronto Bruce Trail Club has members, most of its activities can be attended by the general public. (Call for information on meeting places for hikes.)

Canada's Sports Hall of Fame. *160 Princes' Blvd, Toronto (M6K 3C3). Phone 416/260-6789.* Erected to honor the country's greatest athletes in all major sports, Canada's Sports Hall of Fame features exhibit galleries, a theater, a library, archives, and kiosks that show videos of Canada's greatest moments in sports. Don't miss the Heritage Gallery (lower level), which contains artifacts showcasing the development of 125 years of sport. Also, stop in at the 50-seat Red Foster Theatre, which projects highlights from films that highlight Canadian sports, such as *The Terry Fox Story.* (Mon-Fri 10 am-4:30 pm) **FREE**

Canadian Trophy Fishing. *80 The Boardwalk Way, Suite 320, Markham (L6E 1B8). Docked at Bluffers Park in Scarborough; near the corner of Brimley Rd and Kingston Rd. Phone 905/642-8002. www.cdntrophyfishing.com.* Start working out now; you don't want the fish to win. Chinook salmon might weigh as much as 40 pounds. But for the weaker among us, consider coho salmon, Atlantic salmon, rainbow trout, brown trout, lake trout, whitefish...And it doesn't get much easier than this. Canadian Trophy Fishing supplies the equipment and facilities, will arrange for a fishing license (required), brings equipment and lifejackets, and will even pick you up at your hotel. They suggest you bring a large cooler to take home all of your catches, but for an extra fee they will smoke, fillet, freeze, and ship. Ice fishing season is Jan-mid-Mar. **$$$$**

Casa Loma. *1 Austin Terrace, Toronto (M5R 1X8). 1 1/2 miles (2 kilometers) NW of downtown. Phone 416/923-1171. www.casaloma.org.* Grab an audio cassette and a floor plan and take a self-guided tour of this domestic castle, built in 1911 over three years at a cost of $3.5 million. As romantic as he was a shrewd businessman, Sir Henry Pellatt—who immediately realized the profitability potential when Thomas Edison developed steam-generated electricity, and founded the Toronto Electric Light company—had an architect create this medieval castle. Soaring battlements, secret passageways, flowerbeds warmed by steam pipes, secret doors, servants rooms, and an 800-foot (244-meter) tunnel are just some of the treats you'll discover. (Daily 9:30 am-5 pm; closed Jan 1, Dec 25) **$$$** Adjacent is

Spadina Historic House and Garden. *285 Spadina Rd, Toronto (M5R 2V5). Phone 416/392-6910.* Built for financier James Austin and his family, this 50-room house has been restored to its 1866 Victorian glory and is open to those who want to see how the upper most of the city's upper crust spent quiet evenings at home. It's filled with the family's art, artifacts, and furniture, and until 1982 it was filled with the family itself; that's when the last generation of Austins left, and the house was turned over to public ownership. Docents tend to the glorious gardens and orchard, which are open to the public in the summer. Tours are given every 15 minutes. (Jan-Mar: Sat-Sun noon-5 pm; Apr-Dec: Mon-Fri noon-4 pm, Sat-Sun to 5 pm; holidays to 5 pm)

City parks around Toronto. *100 Queen St W, Toronto (M5H 2N2). Phone 416/392-1111.* Listed below are some of Toronto's many parks. Contact the Department of Parks and Recreation.

Allan Gardens. *19 Horticultural Ave, Toronto (M5A 2P2). W side of Sherbourne St to Jarvis St between Carlton St and Gerrard St E. Phone 416/392-7288.* Indoor/outdoor botanical displays, wading pool, picnicking, concerts. (Daily 10 am-5 pm) **FREE**

Edwards Gardens. *777 Lawrence Ave E, Toronto (M5A 2P2). NE of Downtown, at Leslie Ave E and Lawrence St. Phone 416/392-8186.* Civic garden center; rock gardens, pools, pond, rustic bridges. (Daily) **FREE**

Grange Park. *Dundas and Beverly sts, Toronto (M5H 2N2).* Wading pool, playground. Natural ice rink (winter, weather permitting). (Daily) **FREE**

High Park. *Bloor St W and Keele sts, Toronto (M5H 2N2). Between Bloor St W and The Queensway at Parkside Dr, near lakeshore. Phone 416/392-1111.* If you want a low-key adventure after a few days of sightseeing, High Park is your respite. Financier John T. Colborne, who built the mansion next door, also purchased 160 acres (65 hectares) of land intending to develop a satellite village for Toronto. But he couldn't sell his before-his-time concept of a subdivision, so he donated the land to the city. Today, High Park is an urban oasis, with expanses of grasses for sports, picnicking, and cycling; a large lake that freezes in the winter; a small zoo, a swimming pool, tennis courts, and bowling greens. (Daily dawn-dusk) **FREE**

Ice Skating at Grenadier Pond. *Phone 416/392-6916.* One of the most romantic ice skating spots you'll find is Grenadier Pond in High Park, one of 25 parks offering free artificial rinks throughout the city. In addition to vendors selling roasted chestnuts, theres a bonfire to keep Jack Frost from nipping at your nose. Other free ice rinks include Nathan Phillips Square in front of City Hall and an area at Harbourfront Centre. Equipment rentals are available on site. **FREE**

Queen's Park. *College and University, Toronto (M7A 1A2). Queen's Park Crescent. Phone 416/325-7500.* Ontario Parliament Buildings are located in this park. (Daily) **FREE**

Riverdale Park. *Broadway Ave, Toronto (M5H 2N2). Between Danforth Ave and Gerrard St E. Phone 416/392-1111.* Summer: swimming, wading pools; tennis, playgrounds, picnicking, band concerts. Winter: skating; 19th-century farm. (Daily)

Toronto Island Park. *9 Queens Quay, Toronto (M5H 2N2). S across Inner Harbour. Phone 416/392-8186.* Just seven minutes by ferry from Toronto lie 14 beautiful islands ripe for exploration. The land was originally a peninsula, but a series of storms in the mid-1800s caused a part of the land to break off into islands. The three major ones are Centre, Wards, and Algonquin, with Centre being the busiest. This is partly because it's home to Centreville, an old-fashioned amusement park, with an authentic 1890s carousel, flume ride, turn-of-the-century village complete with a Main Street, tiny shops, a firehouse, and even a small working farm. But the best thing to do on Centre Island or any of the 14, is to rent a bike and explore the 612 acres (248 hectares) of park and shaded paths. Try to get lost; that's half the fun. **FREE**

★ **CN Tower.** *301 Front St W, Toronto (M5V 2T6). Phone 416/868-6937. www.cntower.ca.* Is it the Sears Tower in Chicago? The Petronas Towers in Kuala Lumpur? The Ostankino Tower in Moscow? No. The tallest freestanding structure in the world is Toronto's CN Tower. At 1,815 feet (553 meters) from the ground to the tip of its communications aerial, it towers over the rest of the city. If you'd like to see Toronto from a bluejay's view, take the elevator to the top, where on a clear day it's said you can see the spray coming off Niagara Falls 62 miles (100 kilometers) away. But any level provides spectacular views. (Sun-Thurs 9 am-10 pm, Fri-Sat to 10:30 pm; closed Dec 25) **$$$$**

Colborne Lodge. *Colborne Lodge Dr and The Queensway, Toronto (M5H 2N2). Phone 416/392-6916. www.city.toronto.on.ca/culture/colborne.htm.* The successful 19th-century architect John Howard was just 34 when he completed this magnificent manor, named for the architect's first patron, Upper Canada Lieutenant Governor Sir John Colborne. It stands today as an excellent example of Regency-style architecture, with its stately verandas and lovely placement in a beautiful setting. (Jan-Apr: Sat-Sun noon-4 pm; May-Dec: Tues-Sun noon-5 pm; closed Mon; also Jan 1, Good Friday, Dec 25-26) **$**

Dragon City Shopping Mall. *280 Spadina Ave, Toronto (M5T 3A5). Phone 416/596-8885. www.shiupong.com.* Located in the heart of Chinatown, the Dragon City Shopping Mall consists of more than 30 stores and services that allow you to immerse yourself in Chinese culture. Buy Chinese herbs, look at quality Asian jewelry, browse chic Chinese housewares and gifts, or admire Oriental arts and crafts. After your admiration has grown and your wallet has, perhaps, contracted, treat yourself to a meal at Sky Dragon Cuisine in the Dragon City tower, an upscale Chinese restaurant with a beautiful view of the Toronto skyline. (Daily 10 am-8 pm)

Easy and The Fifth. *225 Richmond W, Toronto (M5V 1W2). Phone 416/979-3000. www.easyandthefifth.com.* A dance club for the over-25 crowd, the music is tango to Top 40, the dress code is upscale casual, and the atmosphere is loft-apartment-open, with two bars and several specialty bars (such as The Green Room, where you can shoot pool, play craps, and smoke a cigar to the accompaniment of live jazz). On Thurs from 6-10 pm, enjoy cocktail hour with a complimentary buffet. (Thurs 6 pm-2 am; Fri-Sat from 9 pm) **$$$**

Eaton Centre. *220 Yonge St, Toronto (M5B 2H1). Phone 416/598-8700. www.torontoeatoncentre.com.* Yes, a shopping mall is Toronto's top tourist attraction. And, with due respect to The Sony Store, The Canadian Naturalist, Grouchos Cigars, Sushi-Q, Baskits, London Style Fish & Chips, and the other 285 shops in the mall, it has to do with more than just goods and services. This 3 million-square-foot (278,709-square-meter) building is a masterpiece of architecture and environment. Its glass roof rises 127 feet (39 meters) above the malls lowest level. The large, open space contains glass-enclosed elevators, dozens of long, graceful escalators, and porthole windows. A flock of fiberglass Canadian geese floats through the air. Even if it usually makes you break out in hives, this is one window-shopping experience worth making. (Mon-Fri 10 am-9 pm; Sat 9:30 am-7 pm; Sun noon-6 pm)

Elgin & Winter Garden Theatre Centre. *189 Yonge St, Toronto (M5B 1M4). Phone 416/872-5555.* The 80-year history of the two theaters speaks more volumes than one of its excellent productions. Built in 1913, it was designed as a double-decker theater complex with the Winter Garden Theatre built seven stories above the Elgin Theatre. Each theater was a masterpiece in its own right: The Elgin was ornate, with gold leaf, plaster cherubs, and elegant opera boxes; the walls of the Winter Garden were hand-painted to resemble a garden, and its ceiling was a mass of beech bows and twinkling lanterns. Through the years, the stages saw the likes of George Burns and Gracie Allen, Edger Bergen and Charlie McCarthy, Milton Berle, and Sophie Tucker before the complex fell into disrepair. A 2 1/2-year, $30 million restoration began in 1987, and included such things as cleaning the walls of the Winter Garden with hundreds of pounds of raw bread dough to avoid damaging the original hand-painted water color art work. The Ontario Heritage Foundation offers year-round guided tours on Thursdays at 5 pm and Saturdays at 11 am.

Exhibition Place. *Lakeshore St, Toronto (M6K 3C3). S off Gardener Expy. Phone 416/393-6000. www.explace.on.ca.* Designed to accommodate the Canadian National Exhibition (see SPECIAL EVENTS), this 350-acre (141-hectare) park has events year-round, as well as the Marine Museum of Upper Canada. (Aug-Sept, daily)

First Canadian Place. *100 King St W,1 First Canadian Pl, Toronto (M5X 1A9). Phone 416/862-8138. www.firstcanadianplace.com.* If only you worked here. You'd have access to a personal shopper to buy your groceries or pick up that asymmetrical slit skirt; and a concierge to plan your business meetings or take care of entertaining out-of-town CEOs. As it is, you can only take advantage of 120 unique shops and boutiques, unusual restaurants, massage or spa services, and ever-interesting ongoing art exhibits. Between 10 am and 2 pm there are special promotions, sidewalk sales, and performances as diverse as Opera Ateliers staging of *The Marriage of Figaro* highlights, to the dancing monks of the Tibetan Dikung Monastery. (Mon-Fri 10 am-6 pm; some shops and restaurants open Sat-Sun)

George R. Gardiner Museum of Ceramic Art. *111 Queen's Park, Toronto (M7A 1A2). Phone 416/586-8080.* One of the world's finest collections of Italian majolica, English Delftware, and 18th-century continental porcelain. (Daily; closed Jan 1, Dec 25) **DONATION**

Gibson House. *5172 Yonge St, North York (M2N 5P6). Phone 416/395-7432. www.toronto.ca/gibsonhouse.* Home of land surveyor and local politician David Gibson; restored and furnished to 1850s style. Costumed interpreters conduct demonstrations. Tours. (Tues-Sun; closed holidays) **$**

Gray Line bus tours. *123 Front St W, Toronto (M5A 4N3). Phone 416/594-3310.*

Harbourfront Centre. *235 Queens Quay W, Toronto (M5J 2G8). Phone 416/973-3000; fax 416/973-6055. www.harbourfront.on.ca.* This 10-acre (4-hectare) waterfront community is alive with theater, dance, films, art shows, music, crafts, and children's programs. Most events are free. (Daily)

Hazelton Lanes. *55 Avenue Rd, Toronto (M5T 3L2). www.hazeltonlanes.com.* Stores that look like movie sets. Stores that sell stunning, $850 gold vermeil, sterling silver, and Swarovski crystal hair clips. Stores that have entire floors devoted to pens. This is Hazelton Lanes, one of Toronto's most exclusive shopping centers, with shops, boutiques, and services designed to turn blood blue. Even if you arent in the mood (yawn) to buy, take a stroll anyway, and see if you can spot a celeb or two; Whoopi Goldberg, Kate Hudson, Alanis Morrisette, Samuel L. Jackson, and Harrison Ford have all been known to walk by and buy. (Mon-Wed, Fri 10 am-6 pm, Thurs to 7 pm, Sat to 5 pm, Sun noon-5 pm)

Historic Fort York. *100 Garrison Rd, Toronto (M5V 3K9). Phone 416/392-6907. www.city.toronto.on.ca/culture/fort_york.htm.* It may not have seen a lot of actionjust one battle during the War of 1812but Fort Yorks place in Toronto's history is secure. It is the birthplace of modern Toronto, having played a major role in saving Yorknow Torontofrom being invaded by 1,700 American soldiers. Todays Fort York has Canada's largest collection of original War of 1812 buildings and is a designated National Historic Site. (Daily; closed Jan 1, last two weeks in Dec) **$$**

Hummingbird Centre for the Performing Arts. *1 Front St E, Toronto (M5E 1B2). Phone 416/393-7469; fax 416/393-7454. www.hummingbirdcentre.com.* Stage presentations of Broadway musicals, dramas, and concerts by international artists. Home of the Canadian Opera Company and National Ballet of Canada. Pre-performance dining; gift shop.

Huronia Historical Parks. *63 miles (101 kilometers) N via Hwy 400, then 34 miles (55 kilometers) N to Midland on Hwy 93. Phone 705/526-7838. www.hhp.*

on.ca. Two living history sites animated by costumed interpreters. (Daily) **$$$** Consists of

Discovery Harbour. *196 Jury St, Penetanguishene (L9M 1G1). Phone 705/549-8064. www.hhp.on.ca.* Marine heritage center and reconstructed 19th-century British Naval dockyard. Established in 1817, the site includes a 19th-century military base. Now rebuilt, the site features eight furnished buildings and orientation center. Replica of 49-foot (15-meter) British naval schooner, the HMS *Bee*; also HMS *Tecumseth* and *Perseverance.* Costumed interpreters bring the base to life, circa 1830. Sail training and excursions (daily). Audiovisual display; free parking, docking, picnic facilities. Theater; gift shop, restaurant. (Victoria Day-Labor Day: Mon-Fri; after Labor Day-Sept: daily) **$$$**

Ste.-Marie among the Hurons. *E of Midland on Hwy 12. www.hhp.on.ca.* (1639-1649) Reconstruction of 17th-century Jesuit mission that was Ontario's first European community. Twenty-two furnished buildings include native dwellings, workshops, barn, church, cookhouse, hospital. Candlelight tours, canoe excursions. Café features period-inspired meals and snacks. Orientation center, interpretive museum. Free parking and picnic facilities. (Victoria Day weekend-Oct, daily) World-famous Martyrs' Shrine (site of papal visit) is located across the highway. Other area highlights include pioneer museum, replica indigenous village, Wye Marsh Wildlife Centre. **$$$**

Kensington Market. *College St and Spadina Ave, Toronto. Extends from Spadina Ave on the E to Bathurst St to the W, and from Dundas St on the S to College St on the N.* Want to take a trip around the world in a few blocks? It's possible in this maze of narrow streets lined with food shops, vintage clothing stores, restaurants, and jewelry vendors. There are bargain hunters haggling, café owners enticing diners, and little stores brimming with items from Asia, South America, the Middle East, and Europe. Music fills the air, spices scent it, and Toronto's multicultural mix has never been so richly displayed. (Daily)

Kortright Centre for Conservation. *9550 Pine Valley Dr, Woodbridge (L4L 1A6). 12 miles (19.3 kilometers) NW via Hwy 400, Major MacKenzie Dr exit, then 2 miles (3 kilometers) W, then S on Pine Valley Dr. Phone 905/832-2289.* Environmental center with trails, beehouse, maple syrup shack, wildlife pond, and plantings. Naturalist-guided hikes (daily). Cross-country skiing (no rentals); picnic area, café; indoor exhibits and theater. (Daily; closed Dec 24-25) **$$**

Little Italy. *W of Bathurst St between Euclid Ave and Shaw St, Toronto. www.torontotourism.com.* After the British, Italians make up the largest cultural group in Toronto. They settled around College Street, just west of Bathurst between Euclid and Shaw, in what became Toronto's first Little Italy. Although the Italian community moved north as it grew, the atmosphere of Little Italy remains. During the day, the coffee shops, billiard halls, and food markets are filled with animated discussions about politics, family, and soccer; when night falls, the area becomes one of the hippest places in Toronto. Restaurants and bars open onto the sidewalks, fashionable cafés are everywhere, color splashes the area, music fills the airand theres not a bad meal to be had. Two items of note: Café Diplomatico (594 College St), called The Dip by locals, is often used as a set by filmmakers. And anyone looking for a little political humor need go just one block south of The Dip, where you'll find the intersection of Clinton and Gore streets.

Lorraine Kimsa Theatre for Young People. *165 Front St E, Toronto (M5A 3Z4). Phone 416/862-2222; fax 416/363-5136. www.lktyp.ca.* Professional productions for the entire family. (Oct-May: Sat-Sun)

Mackenzie House. *82 Bond St, Toronto (M5B 1X2). Phone 416/392-6915. www.toronto.ca/mackenzie-house.* Restored 19th-century home of William Lyon Mackenzie, first mayor of Toronto; furnishings and artifacts of the 1850s; 1840s print shop. Group tours (by appointment). (Tues-Sun, afternoons; closed holidays) **$$**

Market Gallery. *95 Front St E, Toronto (M5E 1B4). Phone 416/392-7604. www.stlawrencemarket.com.* Exhibition center for Toronto Archives; displays on city's historical, social, and cultural heritage; art, photographs, maps, documents, and artifacts. (Wed-Sat, also Sun afternoons; closed holidays) **FREE**

Martin Goodman Trail. *You can pick up the trail almost anywhere along the waterfront, but it is best to contact Toronto Parks and Recreation for succinct directions. Phone 416/392-8186. www.city.toronto.on.ca/parks.* Leave it to fitness-conscious Toronto not just to have a beautifully maintained waterfront, but to build a trail that takes you from one end to the other. The Martin Goodman Trail is a public jogging, biking, hiking, and in-line skating path that connects all the elements of the waterfront, traversing 13 miles (21 kilometers). It also runs past several spots for bike and skate rentals, so if you start out walking and change your mind, no worries.

McMichael Canadian Art Collection. *10365 Islington Ave, Kleinburg (L0J 1C0). Phone 905/893-1121. www.mcmichael.com.* Works by Canada's most famous artiststhe Group of Seven, Tom Thomson, Emily Carr, David Milne, Clarence Gagnon, and others. Also Inuit (Eskimo) and contemporary indigenous art and sculpture. Restaurant; book, gift shop. Constructed from hand-hewn timbers and native stone, the gallery stands in 100 acres (40 hectares) on the crest of Humber Valley; nature trail. (June-early Nov: daily; rest of year: Tues-Sun; closed Dec 25) **$$$**

Medieval Times. *Exhibition Place, Dufferin Gate, Toronto (M6K 3C3). Phone 416/260-1234. www.medievaltimes.com.* If you or anyone in your family would like to play the part of an honored guest of the King of Spainwhich means eating a hearty meal with your fingers while watching knights of old joust on hard-charging stallionsyou've come to the right place. This 11th-century castle was created to replicate an 11th-century experience, complete with knightly competitions and equestrian displays. As for the eating with your hands part, not to worrytheres not a spaghetti strand in sight. (Wed-Thurs 7 pm, Fri-Sat 7:30 pm, Sun 3:30 pm) **$$$$**

Mount Pleasant Cemetery. *375 Mount Pleasant Rd, Toronto (M4T 2V8). Phone 416/485-9129.* One of the oldest cemeteries in North America, the Mount Pleasant Cemetery is the final resting place of many well-known Canadians, including Sir Frederic Banting and Charles Best, the discoverers of insulin; renowned classical pianist Glenn Gould; and Prime Minister William Lyon Mackenzie King, who led Canada through World War II. The grounds hold rare plants and shrubs as well as a Memorial Peony Garden, and its many paths are used frequently by walkers and cyclists and those who just want a few quiet moments. (Daily 8 am-dusk)

Old City Hall. *100 Queen St W, Toronto (M5H 2N2). www.city.toronto.on.ca/old_cityhall.* The story of Toronto's Old City Hall begins as a story of how an important building begins life as a plan and suddenly becomes a Plan. It took three years to design, ten years to build, and came in at $2 million over budget when it opened in 1889. But everyone agreed it was gorgeous. Over the years it fell into disrepair and was saved from the wrecking ball and declared a National Historic Site by the Historic Sites and Monuments Board of Canada in 1989. It now stands as a majestic, living tribute to 100 years of history and architecture. (Mon-Fri 9 am-5 pm) **FREE**

Ontario Parliament Buildings. *Queen's Park,111 Wellesley St W, Toronto (M7A 1A2). Phone 416/325-7500.* Guided tours of the Legislature Building and walking tour of grounds. Gardens; art collection; historic displays. (Victoria Day-Labor Day: daily; rest of year: Mon-Fri; closed holidays) **FREE**

Ontario Place. *955 Lakeshore Blvd W, Toronto (M6K 3B9). Phone 416/314-9811; fax 416/314-9993. www.ontarioplace.com.* A 96-acre (39-hectare) cultural, recreational, and entertainment complex on three artificial islands in Lake Ontario. Includes an outdoor amphitheater for concerts, two pavilions with multimedia presentations, Cinesphere theater with IMAX films (year-round; fee); children's village. Three villages of snack bars, restaurants, and pubs; miniature golf; lagoons, canals, two marinas; 370-foot (113-meter) water slide, showboat, pedal and bumper boats; Wilderness Adventure Ride. (Mid-May-early Sept, daily) Parking fee. **$$$$**

Ontario Science Centre. *770 Don Mills Rd, Toronto (M3C 1T3). Phone 416/696-1000. www.ontariosciencecentre.ca.* This is a high-tech playground in Learning Command Centraland—it's really for kids. Ten huge exhibition halls in three linked pavilions are filled with exhibits on space and technology. You can stand at the edge of a black hole, watch bees making honey, test your reflexes, your heart rate, or your grip strength, use pedal power to light lights or raise a balloon, hold hands with a robot, or land a spaceship on the moon. Throughout the museum there are slide shows and films that demonstrate various aspects of science, and two Omnimax theaters show larger-than-life films. Plan to spend the whole day. (Daily 10 am-5 pm; closed Dec 25) **$$$**

Parachute School of Toronto. *Baldwin Airport, 5714 Smith Blvd, Baldwin (L0E 1A0). toll-free 800/361-5867. www.parachuteschool.com.* There is growing evidence that learning vacations are gaining in popularity. If this is the sort of learning that makes you feel smart-erjump on it. First, you'll have morning instruction. In the afternoon, you'll jump. See how easy? Be sure to call ahead to make sure the schools plane is flying that day. Sometimes they know things about the weather you don't. **$$$$**

Paramount Canada's Wonderland. *9580 Jane St, Vaughan (L6A 1S6). Phone 905/832-7000. www.canadaswonderland.com.* This 300-acre (121-hectare) theme park is situated 30 minutes outside Toronto, and if you ask the locals, they'll tell you it's better than Disneyland. It features more than 140 attractions (with more added every year), including a 20-acre (8-hectare) water park, a participatory play area for the kids, live shows, and more than 50 rides. Specialties among the rides are the parks roller coasters, from creaky old-fashioned wooden ones to "The Fly," a roller coaster designed to make every seat feel as if it's the front car. (June 1-25: Mon-Fri 10 am-8 pm, Fri-Sat to 10 pm; June 26-Labor Day: daily 10 am-10 pm; late May, early Sept-early Oct: Sat-Sun 10 am-8 pm) **$$$$**

Pier: Toronto's Waterfront Museum. *245 Queen's Quay W, Toronto (M5J 2G8).* Original 1930s pier building on Toronto's celebrated waterfront includes two floors of hands-on interactive displays, rare historical artifacts, re-creations of marine history stories, art gallery, boat-building center, narrated walking excursions, children's programs. (Mar-Oct, daily) **$$**

Queen Street West. *A downtown stretch from University Ave to Bathurst St.* If your style is cool and happening, welcome to Mecca. Here you'll find vintage clothing stores, trendy home furnishings, hip styles, and stylish funk that used to be original grunge and street vendor bohemia. You'll also find the handiwork of many up-and-coming fashion designers. In between the boutiques are antique stores, used bookstores, and terrific bistros and cafés. But beware of the heaps of pasta served with heaps of attitude.

Rivoli. *332-334 Queen St W, Toronto (M5V 2A2). Phone 416/596-1908.* This offbeat, artsy performance club opened in 1982 on the site of Toronto's 1920s Rivoli Vaudeville Theatre. The focus is on eclectic and cutting-edge music and performances and includes everything from grunge and rock to poetry readings and comedy. The Indigo Girls, Tory Amos, and Michelle Shocked all made their Toronto debuts here. Don't forget to check out the 5,000-square-foot (465-square-meter) skylit pool hall with its 13 vintage tables, including an 1870s Brunswick Aviator and a 1960s futuristic AMF seen in the Elvis movie *Viva Las Vegas*. (Schedule varies; cover $-$$$)

Rogers Centre. *1 Blue Jays Way, Toronto (M5V 1J3). Phone 416/341-2770; fax 416/341-3110. www.rogerscentre.com.* Many people go to see the Toronto Blue Jays play a great game of baseball, others go to see Canada's Argonauts take to the gridiron. But others go to see the place where the two hometown teams play: the Rogers Centre (formerly the SkyDome), the first stadium in the world with a retractable roof. It takes 20 minutes and costs $500 every time somebody wants the sun in. But who wants to watch a baseball game under a roof? (Tours given daily) **$$$**

Royal Ontario Museum. *100 Queen's Park, Toronto (M5S 2C6). Phone 416/586-5549. www.rom.on.ca.* When the ROM opened its doors to the public in 1914, its mission was to inspire wonder and build understanding of human cultures and the natural world. And its collectionsin archaeology, geology, genealogy, paleontology and sociologyhave moved in that direction ever since. Today the museum houses 6 million objects, with 67,000 added each year. One of the most-visited galleries is the Nubia Gallery, built in 1998 after a ROM team discovered a new archaeological culture in the Upper Nubia region of Northern Sudan, unearthing the remains of a settlement dating to 1000-800 BCE. The discovery has been officially recognized by UNESCO as "Canada's contribution to the United Nations Decade for Cultural Development." (Mon-Thurs, Sat 10 am-6 pm, Fri to 9:30 pm, Sun 11 am-6 pm; closed Jan 1, Dec 25) **$$$$**

Scarborough Civic Centre. *150 Borough Dr, Scarborough (M1P 4N7). Phone 416/396-7216.* Houses offices of municipal government. Guided tours (daily; closed Dec 25). Concerts Sun afternoons.

Second City. *51 Mercer St, Toronto (M5V 2G3). Phone 416/343-0011. www.secondcity.com.* The Toronto branch of the famous Improv Club has turned out its own respectable list of veterans. Among those who have trained here are Gilda Radner, Mike Meyers, Martin Short, Ryan Stiles, and dozens of others who have set the standards for improvisational comedy. The nightly shows are topical and frequently hilarious, but don't leave; the post-show improv sessions are the ones that will have you trying to keep your sides from splitting. (Mon-Sun 8 pm; Sat 8 and 10:30 pm)

St. Lawrence Centre for the Arts. *27 Front St E, Toronto (M5E 1B4). Phone 416/366-7723. www.stlc.com.* Performing arts complex features theater, music, dance, films, and other public events.

St. Lawrence Market. *92 Front St E, Toronto (M5E 1B4). Phone 416/392-7219.* In 1803, Governor Peter Hunt designated an area of land to be market block. Today, the St. Lawrence Market provides a good snippet of the way Toronto used to be, with enough of the character of the original architecture to make you feel as though the old city were alive and well. Some of the wide avenues, too, are reminiscent of European cities. The market itself, Toronto's largest indoor market, sells 14 different categories of foods, which include incredibly fresh seafood, poultry, meat, organic produce, baked goods, gourmet teas and coffees, plus fruit and flowers. And you'll be hard-pressed to find a better selection of cheese in all of Toronto. (Tues-Thurs 8 am-6 pm, Fri 8 am-7 pm, Sat 5 am-5 pm)

Taste of the World Neighbourhood Bicycle Tours and Walks. *Phone 416/966-1550. www.torontowalksbikes.com.* This established tour company offers walking tours that foodies will love. Every Saturday, a group of no more than 12 meets in front of Old City Hall to explore the old and new local traditions of the historic St. Lawrence Farmers Market. Equal parts fact and food, the tour walks visitors through a forgotten hanging square, a hidden gallery, and a lost pillory site. The eats include East Indian treats with new twists, decadent offerings with Belgian chocolate, sandwich samples at Carousel Bakery, and a spread at St. Urbain Bagel. On Sundays, a different tour focuses on the contributions of 200 years of immigrant activity in the Kensington market, exploring Jewish and East Indian snacks, Lebanese treats, and, of course, chocolate truffles. Different times of the year feature different food-focused themes (fall tours feature harvest traditions; December tours feature holiday festivities of different cultures, etc.). The tour company suggests a light breakfast with the St. Lawrence Tour and no breakfast with the Kensington tour. (Daily 9:30 am-1 pm) **$$$$**

Todmorden Mills Heritage Museum & Arts Centre. *67 Pottery Rd, Toronto (M5E 1C3). 2 1/4 miles (4 kilometers) N, off Don Valley Pkwy in East York between Broadview and Bayview aves. Phone 416/396-2819.* Restored historic houses; Parshall Terry House (1797) and William Helliwell House (1820). Also museum; restored 1899 train station. Picnicking. (Tues-Sun) **$**

Toronto Blue Jays (MLB). *Rogers Centre, 1 Blue Jays Way, Toronto (M5V 1J3). Phone 416/341-1000; fax 416/341-1177. www.bluejays.com.* Professional baseball team.

Toronto Maple Leafs (NHL). *Air Canada Centre, 40 Bay St, Toronto (M5J 2X2). Phone 416/815-5700; fax 416/359-9213. www.mapleleafs.com.* Professional hockey team.

Toronto Music Garden. *475 Queen's Quay W, Toronto (M5J 2G8). Phone 416/973-3000. www.city.toronto.on.ca/parks/music_index.htm.* In the mid-1990s, internationally renowned cellist Yo-Yo Ma worked with several other artists to produce a six-part film series inspired by the work of Johann Sebastian Bachs "Suites for Unaccompanied Cello." The first film was entitled *The Music Garden*, and used nature to interpret the music of Bachs first suite. Toronto was approached to create an actual garden based on *The Music Garden*, and the result Toronto Music Gardennow graces the waterfront, a symphony of swirls and curves and wandering trails. In the summertime, free concerts are given. Tours are offered, with a guide or self-guided with a handheld audiotape. The Toronto Music Garden is the only one of its kind in the world. **$**

Toronto Raptors (NBA). *Air Canada Centre, 40 Bay St, Ste 400, Toronto (M5J 2X2). Phone 416/366-3865. www.raptors.com.* Professional basketball team.

Toronto Stock Exchange. *130 King St W, Toronto (M5X 1J2). Phone 416/947-4676. www.tse.com.* The Stock Market Place visitor center has multimedia displays, interactive games, and archival exhibits to aid visitors in understanding the market. **FREE**

Toronto Symphony. *60 Simcoe St, Toronto (M5H 1K5). Phone 416/593-4828; fax 416/598-3375. www.tso.ca.* Classical, pops, and children's programs; Great Performers series. Wheelchair seating, audio enhancement for the hearing impaired.

Toronto Tours Ltd. *145 Queens Quay W, Toronto (M5J 2G8). Phone 416/869-1372. www.torontotours.com.* Four different boat tours of Toronto Harbour. **$$$$**

★ **Toronto Zoo.** *361A Old Finch Ave, Scarborough (M1B 5K7). N of Hwy 401 on Meadowvale Rd. Phone 416/392-5900. www.torontozoo.com.* There are more than 5,000 animals representing just over 450 species at the Toronto Zoo, which was awarded Best Family Outing in Toronto.coms first annual poll. Well-designed and laid out, four large tropical indoor pavilions and several smaller indoor viewing areas, plus numerous outdoor exhibits compose 710 acres (287 hectares) of zoogeographic regions, which can be explored on 6 miles (9.6 kilometers) of walking trails. And when you're tired of walking, sit down for a refreshment, or take a ride on a pony, a camel, or a safari simulator. The Zoo also takes pride in its collection of plants and vegetation, which is valued at $5 million.(Daily; closed Dec 25) **$$$$**

University of Toronto. *25 King's College Cir, Toronto (M5S 1A1). Downtown, W of Queen's Park. Phone 416/978-5000. www.utoronto.ca.* (1827) (55,000 students) Largest university in Canada. Guided walking tours of magnificent Gothic buildings begin at Hart House and include an account of campus ghost (June-Aug, Mon-Fri; free).

Waddington McLean & Company. *111 Bathurst St, Toronto (M5V 2R1). Phone 416/504-9100. www.waddingtons.ca.* The largest and oldest auction house in Canada, Waddingtons professional services have stayed the same for more than 150 years. They do appraisals, consultation, and valuation. But the real fun comes every Wednesday, when the Canadian-owned house holds weekly estate/household auctions. Twice a year, in spring and fall, they host a fine art auction with catalogued items up for bid. (Mon-Fri 8:30 am-5 pm)

Woodbine Racetrack. *555 Rexdale Blvd, Rexdale (M9W 5L2). 15 miles (24 kilometers) N via Hwy 427. Phone 416/675-7223; fax 416/213-2123. www.woodbineentertainment.com.* The only track in North America that can offer both standardbred and thoroughbred racing on the same day, Woodbine is home to Canada's most important race course events. It hosts the $1 million Queens Plate, North Americas oldest continuously run stakes race; the $1 million ATTO; the $1.5 million Canadian International, and the $1 million North America Cup for Standardbreds. It also has an outstanding grass course; it was here, in 1973, that Secretariat bid farewell to racing with his win of the grass championship. Woodbine has 1,700 slot machines, and many different dining options for those times when you might need intake instead of outgo. **FREE**

Special Events

Beaches International Jazz Festival. *Queen St E, Toronto (M4L 1H8). Phone 416/698-2152. www.beachesjazz.com.* For four days every summer since 1989, the Beaches community of Toronto has resonated with the sound of world-class jazz at the Beaches International Jazz Festival, a musical wonder that attracts nearly a million people to the waters edge. More than 40 bands play nightly, with over 700 musicians casting their spell over a crowd that includes children waving glow sticks, toe-tapping seniors, and just about everyone in between. In addition to international artists (with a focus on Canadians), the Festival also serves as a springboard for talented amateurs. Mid-late July. **FREE**

Bloor Yorkville Wine Festival. *Events held throughout the city. www.santewinefestival.net.* In the late 1990s, three separate organizations, among them the Wine Council of Ontario, began a festival that has grown to include more than 70 wineries from 11 countries. Activities include five days of international wine tastings, dinners, parties, and discussions that are held at various restaurants, bars, and hotels all over town. There is also a strong educational element to the festival, with seminars held throughout the week. If you're truly a wine aficionado you'll definitely want to wait until Saturday, the last day of the festival, which includes eight specially designed wine- and food-related seminars. And if you're a novice, sign up for the Pre-Tasting Seminar to learn how to swish, sip, and savor like the pros.

Canadian International. *Woodbine Racetrack, 555 Rexdale Blvd,* Rexdale *(M9W 5L2). Phone 416/675-7223.www.woodbineentertainment.com.* World-class thoroughbreds compete in one of Canada's most important races. Mid-late Oct.

Canadian National Exhibition. *Exhibition Place, Lake Shore Blvd and Strachan Ave, Toronto (M6K 3C3). Phone 416/393-6000. www.explace.on.ca.* This gala celebration originated in 1879 as the Toronto Industrial Exhibition for the encouragement of agriculture, industry, and the arts, although agricultural events dominated the show. Today sports, industry, labor, and the arts are of equal importance to CNE. The "Ex," as it is locally known, is so inclusive of the nation's activities that it is a condensed Canada. A special 350-acre (141-hectare) park has been built to accommodate the exhibition. Hundreds of events include animal shows, parades, exhibits, a midway, and water and air shows. Virtually every kind of sporting event is represented, from frisbee-throwing to the National Horse Show. Mid-Aug-Labor Day.

Caribana. *Exhibition Place, Lake Shore Blvd and Strachan Ave, Toronto (M6K 3C3).* Caribbean music, grand parade, floating nightclubs, dancing, costumes, and food at various locations throughout city. Late July-early Aug.

Celebrate Toronto Street Festival. *Yonge St, between Lawrence Ave and Dundas St, Toronto (M5H 2N2). Phone 416/395-0490. www.city.toronto.on.ca/special_events/streetfest.* Each July, on the first weekend after Canada Day, Toronto's Yonge Streetthe longest street in the worldis transformed into more than 500,000 square feet (46,452 square meters) of free entertainment, with something for people of all ages and tastes. Each of five intersections along Yonge Street runs its own distinctive programming mix; one has nothing but family entertainment, another has world music, a third has classic rock, and so forth. Jugglers, stilt-walkers, and buskers enliven street corners; spectacular thrill shows captivate pedestrians. Opening ceremonies, on Friday night of this weekend event, are usually at the intersection of Yonge and Eglinton; call for schedule. Early July. **FREE**

CHIN International Picnic. *Exhibition Place,Lake Shore Blvd and Strachan Ave, Toronto (M6K 3C3). Phone 416/531-9991. www.canadas-wonderland.com.* Contests, sports, picnicking. First weekend in July.

Designs on Ice. *100 Queen St W, Toronto (M5H 2N2). Phone 416/395-0490. www.city.toronto.on.ca.* Not only do you have to be handy with a pick, you have to be awfully quick. This ice sculpture competition gives contestants exactly 48 hours to chisel a block of ice into a winter work of art. Each year brings a different theme. A recent one, for example, was J. R. R. Tolkiens epic *The Lord of the Rings*, which brought forth a wonderland of hobbits, dwarves, trolls, orcs, wizards, and elves. The public chooses the winners, and the awards ceremony is part of a family skating party with live music. The sculptures stay up as long as the weather cooperates. Which, in Toronto, might be a very long time indeed. Last weekend in Dec. **FREE**

Outdoor Art Show. *Nathan Phillips Square, Queen and Bay sts, Toronto (M5H 2N2). Phone 416/408-2754. www.torontooutdoorart.org.* Mid-July.

Royal Agricultural Winter Fair. *Coliseum Building, Exhibition Place, Lake Shore Blvd and Strachan Ave, Toronto (M6K 3C3). Phone 416/263-3400.* World's largest indoor agricultural fair exhibits the finest livestock. Food shows. Royal Horse Show features international competitions in several categories. Early Nov.

Sunday Serenades. *5100 Yonge St, Toronto (M3N 5V7). Phone 416/338-0338. www.city.toronto.on.ca.* See if moonlight becomes you, and play Fred and Ginger under the stars at Mel Lastman Square. Each Sunday evening in June and July you can Lindy Hop, Big Apple, and Swing to live big band and swing music from the 30s, 40s and 50s. It's free and easyand lots of fun. Mid-July-mid-Aug. **FREE**

Toronto International Film Festival. *Eaton Centre, 220 Yonge St, Toronto (M5B 2H1). Phone 416/968-3456.* Celebration of world cinema in downtown theaters; Canadian and foreign films, international moviemakers, and stars. Early Sept.

Toronto Kids Tuesday. *100 Queen St W, Toronto (MH5 2N1). www.city.toronto.on.ca.* For four consecutive Tuesdays in July and August, Nathan Philips Square is turned into a kids fantasyland where everyone and everything is devoted to them. Theres entertainment, face painting, coloring, chalk art, make-and-take crafts, make your own t-shirts, build-a-kite; it depends on who is entertaining and what the theme of the day is. The Stylamanders brought zany choreography and championship yo-yo tricks for their popular song Hop, Skip and Jump, which was followed by a high-energy day of play, including interactive games with the Toronto Maple Leafs. No matter who entertains or what the theme, you'll be sure to find a crowd of happy kids. July-Aug. **FREE**

Toronto Wine and Cheese Show. *6900 Airport Rd, Mississauga (L4V 1E8). Phone 416/229-2060. www.towineandcheese.com.* Heres your chance to try award-winning wines without the award-winning price tags. A mainstay since 1983, the Toronto Wine and Cheese Festival brings a world of top-tier wines, beers, lagers, ales, single malt whiskies, cheeses, and specialty food to town. There are also famous chefs sharing their recipes, an exquisite collection of cigars to sample, tips on buying the perfect bottle of wine, and free seminars by well-known food and wine experts presented for both education and enjoyment. It's a great family event, as long as your family is all post-teen; no one under the age of 19 is admitted. Mid-Apr. **$$$$**

Limited-Service Hotels

★ ★ DELTA TORONTO EAST. *2035 Kennedy Rd, Scarborough (M1T 3G2). Phone 416/299-1500; fax 416/299-8959. www.deltahotels.ca.* This property allows its guests to explore the Toronto area from outside the downtown core.368 rooms, 14 story. Pets accepted; fee. Check-out noon. Restaurant, bar. Children's activity center. Fitness room. Indoor pool, children's pool, whirlpool. **$$**

★ HOLIDAY INN EXPRESS. *50 Estates Dr, Scarborough (M1H 2Z1). Phone 416/439-9666; toll-free 800/465-4329; fax 416/439-4295. www.hiexpress.com.* 138 rooms, 3 story. Complimentary continental breakfast. Check-in 3 pm, check-out 11 am. **$**

★ ★ INN ON THE PARK. *1100 Eglinton Ave E, Toronto (M3C 1H8). Phone 416/444-2561 ; toll-free 800/465-4329 ; fax 416/446-3308. www.innonthepa-rktoronto.com.* This upscale sister of the Holiday Inn Don Valley is perfect for a weekend getaway even if you live in the city. The Inn is a traditional resort-type hotel offering inconspicuous but attentive service; some staff members have been with the inn since it opened in 1963. The rich woods inside echo the 600 acres of woods and parkland outside. You can stroll through the park or choose from several nearby courses if golf is your game.269 rooms, 23 story. Check-in 3 pm, check-out noon. Restaurant, bar. Children's activity center. Fitness room. Indoor pool, whirlpool. Business center. **$$**

★ ★ QUALITY SUITES TORONTO AIRPORT. *262 Carlingview Dr, Etobicoke (M9W 5G1). Phone 416/674-8442; toll-free 800/424-6423; fax 416/674-3088. www.qualityinn.com.* 254 rooms, 12 story. Pets accepted. Check-in 1 pm, check-out 11 am. Restaurant, bar. Fitness room. **$**

★ ★ RADISSON HOTEL TORONTO EAST. *55 Hallcrown Pl, North York (M2J 4R1). Phone 416/493-7000; toll-free 800/333-3333; fax 416/493-0681. www.radisson.com.* 228 rooms, 9 story. Check-in 3 pm, check-out noon. High-speed Internet access. Restaurant, bar. Indoor pool, whirlpool. **$**

★ ★ RADISSON PLAZA HOTEL ADMIRAL. *249 Queens Quay W, Toronto (M5J 2N5). Phone 416/203-3333; toll-free 800/333-3333; fax 416/203-3100. www.radisson.com.* You can't beat the location of this downtown hotel on Queen's Quay at the heart of the harbor. Choose a room with a view of the city or a view of the lakeor go overboard and survey the lake as you bask around the outdoor pool. Situated right on the water, the hotel's nautical theme seems appropriate. The theme is carried out in meeting rooms and public areas and through the restaurants and bar.157 rooms, 8 story. Check-in 3 pm, check-out noon. High-speed Internet access. Two restaurants, bar. Fitness room. Outdoor pool, whirlpool. Business center. **$$**

Full-Service Hotels

★ ★ ★ DELTA CHELSEA. *33 Gerrard St W, Toronto (M5G 1Z4). Phone 416/595-1975; toll-free 800/268-1133; fax 416/585-4375. www.deltachelsea.com.* 1,590 rooms, 26 story. Pets accepted, some restrictions. Check-in 3 pm, check-out 11 am. High-speed Internet access. Two restaurants, two bars. Fitness room. Indoor pool, whirlpool. Airport transportation available. Business center. **$$$**

★ ★ ★ FAIRMONT ROYAL YORK. *100 Front St W, Toronto (M5J 1E3). Phone 416/368-2511; toll-free 800/527-4727; fax 416/860-5008. www.fairmont.com.* In 1929, the largest hotel in the British Commonwealth opened on the site of the old Queens Hotel, which had been an integral part of Toronto's boomtown. It was also rumored to have been the site of Sir John Macdonalds meeting with American Civil War sympathizers who plotted retaliation. The Royal York became known as a city within a city, with its 1.5 acres (.6 hectares) of public rooms including a 12-bed hospital, a 12,000-book library, a concert hall with a 50-ton pipe organ, its own bank, and ten ornate passenger elevators. A $100 million project from 1988 to 1993 restored the guest rooms and public spaces to their original elegance and added a health club. Still, many of the hotel's original features are intact, such as the marvelous hand-painted ceilings, travertine pillars, ornate furnishings, and wall hangings. Even if you aren't a guest of the hotel, take a walk through it and think about the illustrious guests who have walked before you. And don't forget to sneak a peak at ornate elevator #9, the designated lift for Her Majesty Queen Elizabeth II.1,365 rooms, 22 story. Pets accepted, some restrictions; fee. Check-in 3 pm, check-out noon. High-speed Internet access. Five restaurants, four bars. Fitness room. Indoor pool. Business center. **$$$**

★ ★ ★ ★ FOUR SEASONS HOTEL TORONTO. *21 Avenue Rd, Toronto (M5R 2G1). Phone 416/964-0411; toll-free 800/819-5053; fax 416/964-2301. www.fourseasons.com.* The standard-setting Four Seasons Hotel has a stylish home in Toronto. The headquarters is located in the Yorkville District, a fashionable and dynamic neighborhood filled with specialty shops and galleries. The guest rooms are sublimely comfortable and feature fine furnishings and impressive artwork. Guests stay on track with fitness regimes while staying here, with both a fitness center and an indoor-outdoor pool. The spa offers a variety of massages, all of which are also available in the privacy of your guest room. Toronto's dining scene is well represented at the Four Seasons, with four sensational restaurants. The eclectic décor and the striking glass art make the Studio Café a favorite place for casual dining, while the contemporary, sleek style of Avenue attracts the chic. No visit is complete without dining at Truffles (see), where a mouthwatering menu transports diners to the French countryside. 380 rooms, 32 story. Pets accepted, some restrictions. Check-in 3 pm, check-out noon. High-speed Internet access. Two restaurants, two bars. Fitness room. Indoor pool, outdoor pool, whirlpool. Business center. **$$$$**

★ ★ ★ HILTON TORONTO. *145 Richmond St W, Toronto (M5H 2L2). Phone 416/869-3456; toll-free 800/445-8667; fax 416/869-3187. www.toronto.hilton.com.* Guests will enjoy the location of this hotel in Toronto's financial and entertainment districts. 601 rooms, 32 story. Pets accepted; fee. Check-in 3 pm, check-out noon. High-speed Internet access, wireless Internet access. Two restaurants, two bars. Fitness room. Indoor pool, outdoor pool, whirlpool. Business center. **$$**

★ ★ ★ HOTEL LE GERMAIN. *30 Mercer St, Toronto (M5V 1H3). Phone 416/345-9500; toll-free 800/858-8471; fax 416/345-9501. www.hotelboutique.com.* Sleek lines, modern architecture, and a two-level lobby define this new hotel, located in Toronto's entertainment district. Wood, metal, glass, and ceramics enhance the décor, while facilities such as a massage room, two rooftop terraces, and a library with an open-hearth fireplace enhance guests stays. Four suites have fireplaces and private terraces. 122 rooms. Pets accepted, some restrictions; fee. Check-in 3 pm, check-out noon. High-speed Internet access. Restaurant, bar. Fitness room. **$$**

★ ★ ★ INTERCONTINENTAL HOTEL TORONTO CENTRE. *225 Front St W, Toronto (M5V 2X3). Phone 416/597-1400; toll-free 800/422-7969; fax 416/597-8128. www.torontocentre.intercontinental.com.* Boasting the ultimate in location and amenities, the downtown outpost of the InterContinental caters to business travelers who need meeting space, business support, and proximity to the adjacent Metro Toronto Convention Centre, as well as to leisure travelers who want to stay in the heart of the city close to theater, dining, and shopping venues. Recent renovations transformed the entrance and lobby into a downtown showpiece. For pampering, indulge in a visit to the Victoria Spaone of the best in Toronto for an extensive variety of soothing treatments.586 rooms, 25 story. Check-in 3 pm, check-out noon. High-speed Internet access. Restaurant, bar. Fitness room, spa. Indoor pool. Business center.**$$$$**

★ ★ ★ INTERCONTINENTAL TORONTO. *220 Bloor St W, Toronto (M5S 1T8). Phone 416/960-5200; toll-free 888/567-8725; fax 416/960-8269. www.intercontinental.com.* A rich, elegant atmosphere permeates this thoroughly up-to-date hotel located in the exclusive Yorkville neighborhood. Rich woods and fresh-cut flowers greet you in the lobby, and well-appointed rooms await upstairs. The guest rooms are designed to be both inviting and efficient, and each has a bay window that actually opens. Catering especially to business travelers, rooms on the two Business floors include a fax/printer/copier/scanner. In addition, the hotel offers an international newspaper service and will print a copy of any major newspaper you request.210 rooms, 8 story. Pets accepted; fee. Check-in 3 pm, check-out noon. High-speed Internet access. Restaurant, bar. Fitness room. Indoor pool. Business center. **$$**

★ ★ ★ LE ROYAL MERIDIEN KING EDWARD. *37 King St E, Toronto (M5C 1E9). Phone 416/863-3131; toll-free 800/543-4300; fax 416/367-5515. www.lemeridien-kingedward.com.* Le Royal Meridien King Edward is the grande dame of Toronto. Named in honor of King Edward VII, who also granted the hotel his seal of approval, this historic landmark opened to the public in 1903. It has been hosting the worlds elite ever since, and its enviable guest list includes everyone from the Duke of Windsor to the Beatles. Influenced by Edwardian sensibilities, the interiors are luminous. The accommodations are posh, yet comfortable. Guests staying on Le Royal Club floor are entitled to exclusive privileges, making for an exceptional visit. Sharing the hotels affinity for England in their décor, the Café Victoria and Consort Bar are essential elements of the superb King Edward experience.292 rooms, 16 story. Pets accepted. Check-in 3 pm, check-out noon. High-speed Internet access. Two restaurants, bar. Fitness room, spa. Business center. **$$$**

★ ★ ★ MARRIOTT BLOOR YORKVILLE. *90 Bloor St E, Toronto (M4W 1A7). Phone 416/961-8000; toll-free 800/859-7180; fax 416/961-4635. www.marriottbloor.com.* Situated in the fashionable Yorkville neighborhood, this hotel's creative and artistic décor makes it fit right in. Although it's located at perhaps the city's busiest intersection, the hotel feels tucked away. The staff offers efficient service to help you make the most of both the hotel's amenities (including valet parking) and the attractions of the tourist-friendly neighborhood. Close to the business district, the hotel draws a faithful business clientele that makes use of the state-of-the-art facilities.258 rooms, 6 story. Check-in 3 pm, check-out 1 pm. High-speed Internet access. Restaurant, bar. Fitness room. Business center. **$$$**

★ ★ ★ MARRIOTT TORONTO AIRPORT. *901 Dixon Rd, Toronto (M9W 1J5). Phone 416/674-9400; toll-free 800/905-2811; fax 416/674-8292. www.marriott.com.* 424 rooms, 9 story. Pets accepted; fee. Check-in 3 pm, check-out noon. Two restaurants, bar. Fitness room. Indoor pool, whirlpool. Airport transportation available. Business center. **$$**

★ ★ ★ **MARRIOTT TORONTO EATON CENTRE.** *525 Bay St, Toronto (N5G 2L2). Phone 416/597-9200; toll-free 800/905-0667; fax 416/597-9211. www.marriotteatoncentre.com.* In the financial district and near the theater district, this property attracts all types of visitors with its extensive offerings. There is a top-floor pool overlooking the city. 459 rooms, 18 story. Check-in 3 pm, check-out noon. Restaurant, bar. Fitness room, spa. Indoor pool, whirlpool. Business center. **$$**

★ ★ ★ **METROPOLITAN HOTEL TORONTO.** *108 Chestnut St, Toronto (M5G 1R3). Phone 416/977-5000; toll-free 800/668-6600; fax 416/977-9513. www.metropolitan.com.* All of Toronto is within easy reach from the Metropolitan Hotel, making it an obvious choice for discerning travelers. Not far from the financial district, the hotel also enjoys close proximity to world-renowned shopping, art galleries, and museums. The hotel has the services of a large property and the intimacy of a private residence. Blond woods, earth tones, and simple furnishings deliver a calming sense to guests. The accommodations are a dream, featuring the latest technology, from faxes, laser printers, modems, and multiline telephones to stereo equipment. Fully-staffed fitness and business centers are also on hand to assist all guests with their goals. The beige and black dining room of Lai Wah Heen (see) is a serene setting for its luscious Cantonese cuisine. Considered an excellent example of authentic dim sum, this restaurant is a local sensation.422 rooms, 26 story. Pets accepted, some restrictions. Check-in 3 pm, check-out noon. Two restaurants, bar. Fitness room. Indoor pool, whirlpool. Business center. **$$$$**

★ ★ **NOVOTEL TORONTO CENTER.** *45 The Esplanade, Toronto (M5E 1W2). Phone 416/367-8900; fax 416/360-8285. www.novoteltorontocenter.com.* This hotel has a great location near the CN Tower, the Eaton Center, and other attractions, restaurants, and stores.262 rooms, 9 story. Pets accepted. Check-in 3 pm, check-out 1 pm. High-speed Internet access. Restaurant, bar. Fitness room. Indoor pool, whirlpool. **$$**

★ ★ ★ **PANTAGES SUITES HOTEL AND SPA.** *210 Victoria St, Toronto (M5S 2R3). Phone 416/362-1777; toll-free 866/852-1777; fax 416/368-8214. www.pantageshotel.com.* What distinguishes a boutique hotel? Unique amenities and services such as a complimentary meditation channel, yoga mats, 400-thread-count Egyptian cotton linens, 27-inch flat-screen TVs, and in-room European kitchens. Some rooms have Jacuzzi tubs. Guests are close to The Eaton Centre mall and other Toronto attractions and just two minutes from the subway and Toronto's PATH underground walkway.111 rooms, all suites. Complimentary continental breakfast. Check-in 3 pm, check-out 11 am. High-speed Internet access, wireless Internet access. Fitness room. Whirlpool. Business center. **$$$**

★ ★ ★ ★ **PARK HYATT TORONTO.** *4 Avenue Rd, Toronto (M5R 2E8). Phone 416/925-1234; toll-free 800/977-4197; fax 416/324-1569. www.parktoronto.hyatt.com.* The Park Hyatt Toronto calls the stylish Yorkville area home. Located at the intersection of Avenue Road and Bloor Street, this hotel has some of the worlds leading stores just outside its doors. The hotel echoes its fashionable neighborhood in its interiors. The Art Deco lobby is at once soothing and vibrant with its soft, yellow light and gleaming marble floors. The public and private spaces have a rich feeling completed with handsome furnishings, and a clean, modern look dominates the rooms and suites. The demands of the world dissipate at the Stillwater Spa, where blissful and innovative therapies are offered. Step inside this spa and your cares will be lifted away almost immediately. Overlooking the lobby and the streets of Yorkville, the Mezzanine is a popular gathering place for locals and hotel guests alike. International dishes are the specialty at Annona, while the grilled steaks and seafood of Mortons of Chicago are always a tasty treat. 346 rooms, 18 story. Check-in 3 pm, check-out noon. High-speed Internet access. Restaurant, bar. Fitness room, spa. Business center. **$$$**

★ ★ **RENAISSANCE TORONTO HOTEL DOWNTOWN.** *1 Blue Jays Way, Toronto (M5V 1J4). Phone 416/341-7100; toll-free 800/237-1512; fax 416/341-5091. www.renaissancehotels.com.* Modern and up-to-date are terms that describe this hotel well. The hotel is designed around ease and comfort, with lively colors and whimsical features. Connected to the Rogers Centre, where the Toronto Blue Jays play baseball, you can watch a game from your window if you book one of the 70 rooms overlooking the field. If you're into sports other than baseball, the hotel has meeting rooms named for Toronto's Maple Leafs hockey team and Raptors basketball team and offers golf and cruise packages as well as baseball tickets. 348 rooms, 11 story. Check-in 3 pm, check-out noon.

High-speed Internet access. Restaurant, bar. Fitness room, fitness classes available. Indoor pool, whirlpool. Business center. **$$$**

★ ★ ★ SHERATON CENTRE HOTEL. *123 Queen St W, Toronto (M5H 2M9). Phone 416/361-1000; toll-free 800/325-3535; fax 416/947-4854. www.sheratoncentretoronto.com.* This towering edifice in the heart of downtown does everything on a grand scale. It offers more than 1,300 guest rooms and more than 80,000 square feet of conference and reception rooms. Possibly the most impressive feature, though, would be the waterfall gardens with, yes, an actual waterfall amid 2 1/2 acres of gardens bursting with flowers and greenery. The indoor/outdoor pool bridges the gap between hotel and garden, and decks and terraces give you options in relaxation. 1,382 rooms, 43 story. Pets accepted, some restrictions. Check-in 3 pm, check-out noon. Restaurant, bar. Fitness room, spa. Indoor pool, outdoor pool, whirlpool. Business center. **$$**

★ ★ ★ SHERATON GATEWAY HOTEL. *Toronto International Airport, Terminal 3, Toronto (L5P 1C4). Phone 905/672-7000; toll-free 800/325-3535; fax 905/672-7100.www.sheraton.com.*If you want to stay really close to the airport, you can't do better than the Sheraton Gateway. The hotel is connected to Terminal 3 at Toronto International Airport via a climate-controlled walkway. First-class soundproofing and Sheraton Sweet Sleeper beds help ensure a good night's sleep before an early flight. This glass-walled hotel is thoroughly modern, with every imaginable facility for the business traveler and supreme comfort and convenience for the leisure traveler. 474 rooms, 8 story. Pets accepted, some restrictions. Check-in 3 pm, check-out noon. Restaurant, bar. Fitness room. Indoor pool, whirlpool. Business center. **$$**

★ ★ ★ SOHO METROPOLITAN HOTEL. *318 Wellington St W, Toronto (M5V 3T4). Phone 416/599-8800; fax 416/599-8801. www.sohomet.com.* Little black books everywhere have a notation for the SoHo Metropolitan Hotel Toronto. This boutique hotel earns high marks for its urban chic interiors, stylish food, central location, and smart technology. The accommodations appeal to design buffs with clean, simple lines and light wood furnishings. The black-and-white photography and soft beige and cream tones create an atmosphere of pure serenity. Technology adds a luxurious element to the rooms and suites, with heated floors and bedside panels that control lighting and temperature. The SoHo Metropolitans Senses Bakery & Restaurant offers the contemporary gourmet experience to diners with its artfully designed and creatively prepared cuisine. Stop for a drink at the hip Senses Bar and ask for a snack of green tea-dried spaghetti with sea salt. From the wireless Internet access available throughout the hotel to the complete fitness center with sun deck, this hotel was designed with modern road warriors in mind. 366 rooms, 26 story. Pets accepted, some restrictions. Check-in 3 pm, check-out noon. Wireless Internet access. Two restaurants, bar. Fitness room. Indoor pool, whirlpool. Airport transportation available. Business center. **$$$**

★ ★ ★ THE SUTTON PLACE. *955 Bay St, Toronto (M5S 2A2). Phone 416/924-9221; fax 416/924-1772. www.suttonplace.com.* Expect the height of luxury from the time you hand your car over to an exceptionally gracious valet at this centrally located hotel. You get an old Europe feel from the rich surroundings, including mahogany trim in the meeting rooms and crystal chandeliers, and from the detail-oriented service from the staff. Original art and antiques grace the guest rooms and suites. For an extended stay, the hotel offers La Grande Residence, which couples the benefits of living in your own apartment with the amenities of a first-class hotel. 292 rooms, 33 story. Pets accepted; fee. Check-in 3 pm, check-out noon. High-speed Internet access. Restaurant, bar. Fitness room, spa. Indoor pool. Business center. **$$**

★ ★ ★ THE WESTIN PRINCE TORONTO. *900 York Mills Rd, North York (M3B 3H2). Phone 416/444-2511; toll-free 800/228-3000; fax 416/444-9597. www.westin.com.* Located in the center of downtown Toronto, this hotel is just minutes from both the Ontario Science Centre and the Ford Centre for the Performing Arts. 381 rooms, 22 story. Check-in 3 pm, check-out noon. Restaurant, bar. Fitness room. Outdoor pool, whirlpool. Tennis. Business center. **$$**

★ ★ ★ WESTIN HARBOUR CASTLE. *1 Harbour Sq, Toronto (M5J 1A6). Phone 416/869-1600; toll-free 800/228-3000; fax 416/869-0573. www.westin.com/harbourcastle.* The striking towers of this hotel are among the most recognized landmarks in the city. The glass-walled foyer offers a wide, clear view of Lake Ontario. You can request a room with a harbor view or go for a cityscape instead. Stay here to be near a host of tourist attractions, including the Air Canada Centre, the CN Tower, the Eaton Centre, and the theater district. If you're traveling for business, you're near the financial centers and attached to the Westin Harbour Castle Conference Centre. 977 rooms, 20 story. Pets accepted, some restrictions. Check-in 3 pm, check-out noon. Two restaurants, two bars. Children's activity center. Fitness room, spa. Indoor pool, whirlpool. Tennis. Business center. **$$$$**

★ ★ ★ WINDSOR ARMS HOTEL. *18 St. Thomas St, Toronto (M5S 3E7). Phone 416/971-9666; toll-free 877/999-2767; fax 416/921-9121. www.windsorarmshotel.com.* Behind the castlelike façade of the Windsor Arms Hotel is one of Toronto's chicest lodgings. Edgy, yet classic, it is a well-heeled hipster's dream. The accommodations in this intimate and stylish hotel are sleek, modern, and sublime, with mahogany or birch furnishings, frosted glass screens, and Frette linens. Guilty pleasures include the extraordinary 24-hour butler service. This hotel is truly a slice of the good life. The Tea Room serves a traditional tea by day, and at night is transformed into Toronto's only champagne and caviar bar. The stunning décor of the Courtyard Café attracts the fashionable set; Club 22 entertains with piano entertainment and live bands; and the Cigar Lounge offers decadent treats. Guests feeling a bit overindulged head for the fitness center and spa to work off their gastronomical sins and escape the worries of the world. 28 rooms, all suites. Pets accepted. Complimentary continental breakfast. Check-in 3 pm, check-out noon. Restaurant, bar. Fitness room, spa. Indoor pool. **$$$**

★ ★ ★ WYNDHAM BRISTOL PLACE HOTEL. *950 Dixon Rd, Etobicoke (M9W 5N4). Phone 416/675-9444; toll-free 877/999-3223; fax 416/675-2037. www.wyndham.com.* 287 rooms, 15 story. Check-in 3 pm, check-out 1 pm. High-speed Internet access. Restaurant. Fitness room. Indoor pool. Airport transportation available. Business center. **$$**

Full-Service Inns

★ ★ ★ THE MILLCROFT INN & SPA. *55 John St, Alton (L0N 1A0). Phone 519/941-8111; toll-free 800/383-3976; fax 519/941-9192. www.millcroft.com.* This former knitting mill (1881) is situated on 100 acres (40 hectares) on the Credit River. 52 rooms, 2 story. Complimentary continental breakfast. Check-in 4 pm, check-out noon. Restaurant, bar. Fitness room, spa. Outdoor pool, whirlpool. Tennis. **$$**

★ ★ ★ OLD MILL INN AND SPA. *21 Old Mill Rd, Toronto (M8X 1G5). Phone 416/236-2641; toll-free 866/653-6455; fax 416/236-2749. www.oldmilltoronto.com.* This Tudor-style inn and the adjacent meeting and conference facility exude old-world charm. In summer and winter, the setting is spectacular. The inn sits 15 minutes northwest of downtown Toronto in the Humber River Valley, which offers opportunities for hiking, biking, and in-line skating. Common areas feature dark woods, beamed ceilings, and stone walls, while the guest rooms are light and airy, with fireplaces, 32-inch TVs, separate deep-soaking whirlpool tub and shower, and stereo system. Afternoon tea is served daily, and dinner and dancing are available six nights a week. This is a terrific place for a small wedding or a corporate retreat, with on-site facilities that can accommodate more than 100 people. 60 rooms. Complimentary continental breakfast. Check-in 4 pm, check-out noon. High-speed Internet access. Two restaurants, bar. Fitness room, spa. Business center. **$$$**

Spa

★ ★ ★ ★ STILLWATER SPA AT PARK HYATT TORONTO. *4 Avenue Rd, Toronto (M5R 2E8). Phone 416/926-2389. www.stillwaterspa.com.* The Park Hyatt Toronto's sensational Stillwater Spa beckons urban warriors weary of the daily rat race. With its cool, crisp interiors—complete with a fireplace in the Tea Lounge and waterfalls and streams throughout the facility—and fabulous mind and body relaxation therapies, this sanctuary offers you an escape from the hectic pace just outside its doors. Whether you spend a few hours or an entire day here, you will experience tranquility. Among the spa's menu of body treatments is the lavender lush body glow, which includes an exfoliation with sea salts and fragrant lavender oils. Another delicious body buffing therapy is the mandarin-honey body glow, which gently exfoliates skin with honey-infused mandarin juices and French sea salts before moisturizing with a tangerine body crème. If you feel like you're carrying the weight of the world on your shoulders, try an anti-stress and mental clarity body treatment. A 30-minute massage targets stiff shoulders, back, and neck, and then a warm mud mask purifies your back before a full-body Vichy treatment completely calms your nerves. With an extensive massage therapy menu, Stillwater Spa promises to help you unwind. The signature Stillwater massage customizes an aromatherapy blend to accompany a relaxing bodywork combination of Swedish massage, trigger-points pressure, and stretching techniques. Heated neck and eye pillows and warm booties add luxurious touches. Revel in the warmth of an aroma blanket wrap, where milk and the essential oils of melissa, lavender, and orange are massaged into your skin before you are cocooned in a comfortable blanket. Another signature is the Stillwater aqua therapy, where a therapist stretches, moves, and massages your body while you float in water.Revitalize your skin's appearance with a vitamin C, Q-10, or multivitamin power treatment, or battle the effects of harsh environments and climates with an urban element facial. From men's and express facials to a back treatment and a therapy that incorporates rare yeasts used to produce Champagne, the Stillwater Spa's facials deliver softer, more radiant skin.

Restaurants

★ ★ ★ **360.** *301 Front St W, Toronto (M5V 2T6). Phone 416/362-5411; fax 416/601-4895. www.cntower.ca.* As the name suggests, this restaurant completes a 360-degree rotation, offering a breathtaking view from the CN Tower. The scenery inside is attractive as well, with colorful décor and a fresh, seasonal menu. International menu. Lunch, dinner, Sun brunch. Closed Dec 25. Bar. Business casual attire. Reservations recommended. **$$$**

★ ★ **ARKADIA HOUSE.** *2007 Eglinton Ave E, Scarborough (M1L 2M9). Phone 416/752-5685.* Greek menu. Dinner. Closed Dec 24. Bar. Children's menu. **$$**

★ ★ ★ **AUBERGE DU POMMIER.** *4150 Yonge St, Toronto (M2P 2C6). Phone 416/222-2220; fax 416/222-2580. www.aubergedupommier.com.* Located north of the city, this restaurant in an industrial park manages to feel like it is actually in rural France. The attentive service and comfortable décor are pleasing. French, American menu. Lunch, dinner. Closed Sun; holidays. Bar. Children's menu. Reservations recommended. **$$$**

★ ★ **BAROOTES.** *220 King St W, Toronto (M5H 1K4). Phone 416/979-7717; fax 416/979-0292. www.barootes.com.* International menu. Lunch, dinner. Closed Sun. Bar. Children's menu. Casual attire. Reservations recommended. **$$**

★ ★ ★ **BIAGIO.** *155 King St E, Toronto (M5C 1G9). Phone 416/366-4040; fax 416/366-4765.* Located in the historic St. Lawrence Hall near the theater district, this modern Italian restaurant serves specialties from the north. An ornate ceiling and a lovely patio with a fountain add to the ambience. Italian menu. Lunch, dinner. Closed Sun; holidays. Bar. Casual attire. Outdoor seating. **$$$**

★ **BUMPKINS.** *21 Gloucester St, Toronto (M4Y 1L8). Phone 416/922-8655; fax 416/922-0240. www.bumpkins.ca.* French menu. Lunch, dinner, brunch. Casual attire. Reservations recommended. Outdoor seating. **$$**

★ ★ ★ ★ **CANOE.** *66 Wellington St W, Toronto (M5K 1H6). Phone 416/364-0054; fax 416/364-4273.* Canoe is a tranquil place to dine. During the day, warm light streams in through the tall windows, filling the elegantly minimalist restaurant with golden tones. At night, a warm glow comes from the rooms perfect amber-hued lighting, and the dining room swells with a chic crowd; the sexy cocktail list makes the bar quite popular. Whether you're having lunch or dinner, Canoe, one of restaurateur Oliver Bonacinis many stylish Toronto eateries (others include Jump and Auberge du Pommier), is a stunning venue in which to experience creative, satisfying regional Canadian cuisine. While dazzling ingredients tend to be sourced from wonderful local producers, many organic, the kitchen borrows flavors and techniques from the world at large, including Asia, France, and the American South. The end product is inventive food and an equally original room that take your breath away. Canadian menu. Lunch, dinner. Closed Sat-Sun. Bar. Business casual attire. Reservations recommended. **$$$**

★ ★ **CARMAN'S CLUB.** *26 Alexander St, Toronto (M4Y 1B4). Phone 416/924-8558; fax 416/924-7638.* Steak, seafood menu. Dinner. Closed Sun; Good Friday, Dec 25. Casual attire. **$$$**

★ ★ ★ **CENTRO GRILL & WINE BAR.** *2472 Yonge St, Toronto (M4P 2H5). Phone 416/483-2211; fax 416/483-2641. www.centro.ca.* A lot of tastes are rolled into one destination at this contemporary European restaurant with a downstairs sushi and oyster bar. The wood floors; red, high-backed chairs; white tablecloths; and silver-accented décor create a colorful, New Age-style dining room, and the worldly menu is never a bore with novelties like caribou chop with juniper berry oil, Alsatian spatzle, and Arctic cloudberry sauce. International menu. Dinner. Closed

Sun; holidays. Bar. Casual attire. Reservations recommended. Valet parking. **$$$**

★ ★ ★ ★ **CHIADO.** *864 College St, Toronto (M6H 1A3). Phone 416/538-1910; fax 416/588-8383. www.chiadorestaurant.com.* Albino Silva is the chef/owner and loving force behind Chiado, a charming, authentic Portuguese bistro named after the oldest neighborhood in his native Lisbon. Enter the cozy dining room and you are instantly hungry: the air is heavy with the scent of seafood, garlic, and herbs, and a cutting board overflowing with Silvas fresh-baked bread stares you down as you enter the front room. Paying homage to the old seaside town but updating dishes for a more modern sensibility, Chiado features what might best be described as "nouvelle Portuguese cuisine." No matter what title you give it, the food is first-rate and fabulous. You'll find an oceans worth of fresh fish, simply prepared with olive oil and herbs, as well as innovative takes on pheasant, game, and poultry. To add to the authenticity of the experience, Chiado has the largest collection of fine Portuguese wines in North America and a superb selection of vintage ports. Spanish menu. Lunch, dinner. Bar. Casual attire. Reservations recommended. Valet parking. **$$$**

★ ★ **DAVID DUNCAN HOUSE.** *125 Moatfield Dr, North York (M3B 3L6). Phone 416/391-1424; fax 416/391-5302. www.davidduncanhouse.com.* Dark oak, dim lighting, and stained-glass windows help create the luxurious setting of this acclaimed restaurant. But what is most noteworthy is the richness of its cuisine. Dinner. Bar. Jacket required. Valet parking. **$$$**

★ ★ ★ **THE DOCTOR'S HOUSE.** *21 Nashville Rd, Kleinberg (L0J 1C0). Phone 905/893-1615; fax 905/893-0660.* American menu. Dinner, Sun brunch. Bar. Children's menu. Outdoor seating. **$$$**

★ ★ **DYNASTY CHINESE.** *131 Bloor St W, Toronto (M5S 1R1). Phone 416/923-3323; fax 416/923-1826. www.toronto.com/dynasty.* Chinese menu. Lunch, dinner. Casual attire. Reservations recommended. **$$$**

★ ★ ★ ★ **THE FIFTH.** *225 Richmond St W, Toronto (M5V 1W2). Phone 416/979-3005; fax 416/979-9877. www.thefifthgrill.com.* It takes work to make it to The Fifth. First, an alley entrance leads you to The Easy, an upscale nightclub and former speakeasy. Once inside The Easy, you are directed onto a Persian rug-lined vintage freight elevator. There, an old-school attendant takes you to floor number five. Exit, and you have finally arrived at The Fifth, a treasured contemporary French restaurant and supper club. Truly special in every sense, The Fifth is a stunning, intimate, living roomlike space with a stone fireplace, blond hardwood floors, picture windows, white linen-draped tables and chairs, and soft candle lighting. The food is of the delicious updated French variety, and the dishes are perfectly prepared, beautifully presented, and easily devoured. In warm weather, retire to the outside deck and enjoy the smooth sounds of live jazz under the stars. French menu. Dinner. Closed Sun-Wed. Bar. Business casual attire. Reservations recommended. Outdoor seating. **$$$$**

★ **GRANO.** *2035 Yonge St, Toronto (M4S 2A2). Phone 416/440-1986; fax 416/440-1996. www.grano.ca.* Italian menu. Breakfast, lunch, dinner. Closed Sun. Bar. Casual attire. Outdoor seating. **$$**

★ ★ **GRAZIE.** *2373 Yonge St, Toronto (M4P 2C8). Phone 416/488-0822; fax 416/488-0565. www.grazie.ca.* Italian menu. Lunch, dinner, late-night. Closed holidays. Bar. Casual attire. **$$**

★ ★ ★ **HEMISPHERES.** *108 Chestnut St, Toronto (M5G 1R3). Phone 416/599-8000; fax 416/977-9513. www.metropolitan.com/hemis.* Hemispheres is a star on the Toronto dining scene. This worldly restaurant elevates hotel dining to a whole new level with its stylish interior design and international fusion cuisine. Located within the hip Metropolitan Hotel Toronto (see), this restaurant is a magnet for a fashionable crowd who frequent this downtown spot for its innovative food and terrific people watching. Its laid-back sophistication is appealing to patrons who want both style and substance. The sexy space is curvy and contemporary, and an exhibition kitchen is the jewel in the crown. Diners may even book the chefs table for an insiders look at the whirlwind behind the scenes. The menu includes European and Continental classics, many with an Asian bent, and seafood accounts for a large part of the selections. The exhaustive dessert list will delight those with a sweet tooth, while wine lovers will appreciate the well-rounded and extensive cellar. International menu. Breakfast, lunch, dinner. Bar. Children's menu. Reservations recommended. Valet parking. **$$**

★ ★ **IL POSTO NUOVO.** *148 Yorkville Ave, Toronto (M5R 1C2). Phone 416/968-0469; fax 416/968-2329.www.ilposto.ca.* Italian menu. Lunch, dinner. Bar. Casual attire. Reservations recommended. Outdoor seating. **$$$**

★ ★ ★ **JOSO'S.** *202 Davenport Rd, Toronto (M5R 1J2). Phone 416/925-1903; fax 416/925-6567.* *www.josos.com.* The walls are covered with the chef's racy art and celebrity pictures at this popular restaurant, which offers unique but excellent Mediterranean cuisine. Mediterranean menu. Lunch, dinner. Closed Sun; holidays. Outdoor seating. **$$$**

★ ★ ★ **LA FENICE.** *319 King St W, Toronto (M5V 1J5). Phone 416/585-2377; fax 416/585-2709.* *www.lafenice.ca.* The stark, modern dining room of this downtown restaurant recalls the chic design aesthetic of Milan. Italian menu. Lunch, dinner. Closed Sun. Business casual attire. Reservations recommended. **$$$**

★ ★ ★ **LAI WAH HEEN.** *108 Chestnut St, Toronto (M5G 1R3). Phone 416/977-9899; fax 416/977-8027.* *www.laiwahheen.com.* Lai Wah Heen, meaning "luxurious meeting place," is truly luxurious with its two-level dining room featuring black granite, 12-foot (3.6-meter) ceilings, and solarium-style glass wall. Exotic herbs and spices, skillful use of tropical fruits, and seafood dishes of exquisite refinement make for a sumptuous Cantonese menu rich with Pacific Rim flair. For an intimate dinner, dim sum, or banquet, Lai Wah Heen delivers a true Hong Kong experience in the heart of Toronto. Cantonese, Chinese menu. Lunch, dinner. Business casual attire. Reservations recommended. Valet parking. **$$**

★ **MATIGNON.** *51 Ste. Nicholas St, Toronto (M4Y 1W6). Phone 416/921-9226; fax 416/921-2119.* *www.matignon.ca.* French menu. Dinner. Closed Sun. Business casual attire. Reservations recommended. **$$**

★ ★ **MILLCROFT INN.** *55 John St, Alton (L0N 1A0). Phone 519/941-8111; fax 519/941-9192. www.millcroft.com.* A restaurant with a substantial reputation for fine dining makes any occasion a time to celebrate, especially during the holidays, when they offer special menus. Be sure to sample their vintage wines. French menu. Dinner, Sun brunch. Bar. Valet parking. **$$$**

★ **MILLER'S COUNTRY FARE.** *5140 Dundas St W, Etobicoke (M9A 1C2). Phone 416/234-5050; fax 416/233-6747.* Lunch, dinner, brunch. Closed Dec 25. Bar. Children's menu. **$$**

★ ★ ★ **MISTURA.** *265 Davenport Rd, Toronto (M5R 1J9). Phone 416/515-0009; fax 416/515-7931.* *www.mistura.ca.* Italian menu. Dinner. Closed Sun; holidays; also Victoria Day. **$$**

★ ★ ★ ★ **NORTH 44 DEGREES.** *2537 Yonge St, Toronto (M4P 2H9). Phone 416/487-4897; fax 416/487-2179.* *www.north44restaurant.com.* Style, serenity, and elegance infuse every aspect of North 44 Degrees. From the recently renovated loftlike dining room awash in muted, sandy tones to the world-class New Continental cuisine created nightly by chef/owner Mark McEwan, North 44 Degrees is a sublime and sexy dining experience. A sophisticated crowd fills the restaurant, named for the citys latitude, on most nights, happily gathering in this airy space to dine on inventive and beautiful culinary creations. From behind the stoves, McEwan enlists the finest local produce, fish, poultry, and meats to support his cross-cultural menu, expertly blending the bright flavors of Asia with those of Italy, France, and Canada. The service is smooth, refined, and in perfect harmony with the cool space and stellar cuisine. International menu. Dinner. Closed Sun. Bar. Business casual attire. Reservations recommended. Valet parking. **$$$$**

★ ★ ★ **OLD MILL.** *21 Old Mill Rd, Toronto (M8X 1G5). Phone 416/236-2641; toll-free 866/653-6455; fax 416/236-2749.* *www.oldmilltoronto.com.* International menu. Breakfast, lunch, dinner, Sun brunch. Bar. Jacket required (weekend dinner). Reservations recommended. Valet parking. Outdoor seating. Cover charge (Fri-Sat from 8 pm). **$$$**

★ ★ ★ **OPUS RESTAURANT.** *37 Prince Arthur Ave, Toronto (M5R 1B2). Phone 416/921-3105; fax 416/921-9353.* *www.opusrestaurant.com.* This plush Yorkville restaurant is elegant, romantic, and filled with the energy of Toronto's powerful and moneyed elite. International menu. Dinner. Closed Jan 1, Dec 24-26. Bar. Casual attire. Reservations recommended. Outdoor seating. **$$$**

★ ★ ★ **ORO.** *45 Elm St, Toronto (M5G 1H1). Phone 416/597-0155.* *www.ororestaurant.com.* This restaurant has changed hands and names many times since it opened in 1922 and is famous for its patrons, who have included Ernest Hemingway and Prime Minister Jean Chrtien. The décor is contemporary and elegant, as is the food. International menu. Lunch, dinner. Closed Sun; holidays. **$$$**

★ ★ ★ **PANGAEA.** *1221 Bay St, Toronto (M5R 3P5). Phone 416/920-2323; fax 416/920-0002.* *www.pangaearestaurant.com.* This modern eatery's industrial façade doesn't do its interior space justice. Once guests enter, they'll relish the softer, calming effects of the dining room's vaulted ceiling and exotic floral arrangements. The chef creates sophisticated continental cuisine using the wealth of each season's harvest. Tired Bloor Street shoppers will find this a great place to break for lunch or tea. International menu. Lunch, dinner. Closed Sun. Bar. Business casual attire. Reservations recommended. **$$$**

★★ **PASTIS.** *1158 Yonge St, Toronto (M4W 2L9). Phone 416/928-2212; fax 416/928-1632.* Skilled preparation and artful presentation characterize this sophisticated bistro environment. This midtown restauant is popular with business professionals and a local favorite among the well-heeled. French menu. Dinner. Closed Sun-Mon. **$$**

★★ **PIER 4 STOREHOUSE.** *245 Queen's Quay W, Toronto (M5J 2K9). Phone 416/203-1440; fax 416/203-6292. www.pier4rest.com.* Seafood menu. Dinner. Bar. Children's menu. Casual attire. Reservations recommended. Outdoor seating. **$$$**

★★ **PROVENCE.** *12 Amelia St, Toronto (M4X 1A1). Phone 416/924-9901; fax 416/924-9680. www.provencerestaurant.com.* French menu. Lunch, dinner, Sat-Sun brunch. Closed Dec 25. Bar. Casual attire. Outdoor seating. **$$$**

★★ **RODNEY'S OYSTER HOUSE.** *469 King St W, Toronto (M5V 1V4). Phone 416/363-8105; fax 416/363-6638. www.rodneysoysterhouse.com.* Seafood menu. Lunch, dinner. Closed Sun. Bar. Casual attire. Reservations recommended. Outdoor seating. **$$**

★★ **ROSEWATER SUPPER CLUB.** *19 Toronto St, Toronto (M5C 2R1). Phone 416/214-5888; fax 416/214-2412. www.libertygroup.com.* This stylishly retro restaurant and nightclub is a three-level extravaganza, complete with Persian carpets, elaborate Victorian crown mouldings, and cathedral-style windows. The food and wine compete with the setting and the beautiful crowd for attention. The main floor and mezzanine both serve lunch and dinner; on the lower level, you'll find a slinky torch singer draped over a baby grand piano, purring the old romantic standards. If you'd prefer just to listen, turn your eyes to the three-story waterfall that flows over the top of the entryway. The club has two lounges: the Front Lounge welcomes casual diners who come for a light bite and to hear live jazz, and the Ember Lounge is where up to 40 people can top off an evening with a cognac or brandy and a cigar from the selection in the Rosewaters well-stocked humidor. French menu. Lunch, dinner. Closed Sun. Bar. Business casual attire. Reservations recommended. Outdoor seating. **$$$**

★★★★ **SCARAMOUCHE.** *1 Benvenuto Pl, Toronto (M4V 2L1). Phone 416/961-8011; fax 416/961-1922. www.scaramoucherestaurant.com.* Up on a hillside overlooking the dazzling downtown lights, Scaramouche is the perfect hideaway for falling in love with food (or your dining companion). This modern, bilevel space is known for its fantastic contemporary French fare and is often jammed with dressed-up, savvy locals. The restaurant is divided between a formal dining room upstairs and a modestly priced pasta bar downstairs. The latter is a casual bistro offering a selection of stunning handmade pastas as well as non-noodle standards like steak frites. The more elegant dining room is where you'll be treated to the restaurants famed contemporary French fare. While the menu changes seasonally, specialties of the house may include squab, lobster, and filet, plus a coconut cream pie that is as memorable and fantastic as the view. French menu. Dinner. Closed Sun. Bar. Casual attire. Reservations recommended. Valet parking. **$$$$**

★★ **SENATOR.** *249 Victoria St, Toronto (M5B 1T8). Phone 416/364-7517; fax 416/364-3784.* Seafood, steak menu. Dinner. Closed Mon; holidays. Bar. Casual attire. **$$$**

★★★★ **SPLENDIDO.** *88 Harbord St, Toronto (M5S 1G5). Phone 416/929-7788; fax 416/929-3501. www.splendido.ca.* Located in the middle of the University of Toronto, this restaurant is a popular pick for parents' weekends when kids get a chance to go out for "real food." International menu. Dinner. Closed Mon; July-Aug Sun; holidays. Bar. Casual attire. Reservations recommended. Valet parking. **$$$**

★★★ **SUSUR.** *601 King St W, Toronto (M5V 1M5). Phone 416/603-2205. www.susur.com.* International menu. Dinner. Closed Sun. Business casual attire. Reservations recommended. **$$$**

★★ **TA KE SUSHI.** *22 Front St W, Toronto (M5J 1N7). Phone 416/862-1891; fax 416/862-2356.* Japanese, sushi menu. Lunch, dinner. Closed Sun. Bar. Casual attire. Reservations recommended. **$$**

★ **THAI FLAVOUR.** *1554 Avenue Rd, Toronto (M5M 3X5). Phone 416/782-3288.* Thai menu. Lunch, dinner. Closed Jan 1, Dec 25. **$**

★★★★ TRUFFLES. *21 Avenue Rd, Toronto (M5R 2G1). Phone 416/964-0411; fax 416/964-8699. www.fourseasons.com.* Filled with light and luxury, Truffles' dining room feels like the parlor room of a fabulous art collector with impeccable taste. Soaring ceilings, rich wood moldings, large bay windows, and deep-chocolate velvet seating set an airy, sophisticatedbut minimaliststage for the works of a talented group of local artisans, sculptors, and artists that are on display. Located in the Four Seasons Hotel Toronto(see), Truffles is known for its distinct, stylized brand of modern Provenal-style cuisine. As the name suggests, the coveted mushrooms do indeed show up on the menu; the restaurant's signature dish is spaghettini with Perigord Black Gold and a light truffle froth. Often the chosen locale for power dinners, Truffles is also ideal for intimate conversation. Smooth service and an extensive wine list make Truffles a truly inspired dining event. French menu. Dinner. Closed Sun. Bar. Jacket required. Reservations recommended. Valet parking. **$$$$**

★ UNITED BAKER'S DAIRY RESTAURANT. *506 Lawrence Ave W, Toronto (M6A 1A1). Phone 416/789-0519; fax 416/789-4022.* Jewish menu. Breakfast, lunch, dinner. **$**

★★ VILLA BORGHESE. *2995 Bloor St W, Etobicoke (M8X 1C1). Phone 416/239-1286; fax 416/245-4870.* Italian menu. Lunch, dinner. Closed Mon; Easter, Dec 25. Bar. **$$**

Index

D

E

M

S

Chain Restaurants

New York

Albany

Hooters, One Crossgates Mall Rd, Albany, NY, 12203, (518) 862-9000, 11 am-midnight

Uno Chicago Grill, 120 Washington Ave Ext, Crossgates Mall Rd, Albany, NY, 12203, (518) 869-3100, 11 am-12:30 am

Amherst

Chili's, 1145 Niagara Falls Blvd, Amherst, NY, 14226, (716) 832-3730, 11 am-10 pm

Don Pablo's, 1591 Niagra Falls Blvd, Amherst, NY, 14228, (716) 832-8007, 11 am-10 pm

Fuddruckers, 4300 Maple Rd, Amherst, NY, 14226, 11 am-9 pm

Hooters, 4350 Maple Rd, Amherst, NY, 14226, (716) 833-0856, 11 am-midnight

Old Country Buffet, Media Play Shopping Center, 3048 Sheridan Dr, Amherst, NY, 14226, (716) 832-1773, 11 am-9 pm

Smokey Bones, 4120 Maple Rd, Amherst, NY, 14226, (716) 834-0148, 11 am-10 pm

Uno Chicago Grill, 4125 Maple Rd, Amherst, NY, 14226, (716) 834-6200, 11 am-12:30 am

Auburn

Godfather's Pizza, 68 N St, Auburn, NY, 13021, (315) 253-9118

Bainbridge

Godfather's Pizza, 117 State Hwy 7, Bainbridge, NY, 13733, (607) 563-9616

Baldwin Place

Chili's, 80 Rte 6, Ste 208, Baldwin Place, NY, 10505, (914) 621-0216, 11 am-10 pm

Bay Shore

Old Country Buffet, 1701 Sunrise Hwy, Bay Shore, NY, 11706, (631) 969-3943, 11 am-9 pm

The Ground Round, Montauk Hwy &†Saxon Ave, Bay Shore, NY, 11706, (631) 665-5643, 11 am-11 pm

Chili's, 2020 Sunrise Hwy, Bay Shore, NY, 11706, (631) 665-2777, 11 am-10 pm

Bayside

Uno Chicago Grill, 39-02 Bell Blvd, Bayside, NY, 11361, (718) 279-4900, 11 am-12:30 am

Bethpage

Chili's, 4100 Hempsted Turnpike, Bethpage, NY, 11714, (516) 579-0053, 11 am-10 pm

Binghamton

Cracker Barrel, 876 Front St, Binghamton, NY, 13905, (607) 722-5006, 6 am-10 pm

Bohemia

Godfather's Pizza, 3072 Veterans Memorial Hwy, Bohemia, NY, 11716, (631) 737-2752

www.mobiltravelguide.com

Brockport

Godfather's Pizza, 995 Transit Way, Brockport, NY, 14420, (585) 637-0280

Bronx

Uno Chicago Grill, 71 Metropolitan Oval, Bronx, NY, 10462, (718) 824-8667, 11 am-12:30 am

Sizzler, 2375 E Tremont Ave, Bronx, NY, 10462, (718) 892-5200, 11 am-10 pm

Brooklyn

Uno Chicago Grill, 9201 4th Ave, Brooklyn, NY, 11209, (718) 748-8667, 11 am-12:30 am

Central Valley

Uno Chicago Grill, 20 Centre Dr, Central Valley, NY, 10917, (845) 783-6560, 11 am-12:30 am

Cheektowaga

Fuddruckers, 2013 Walden Ave, Cheektowaga, NY, 14225, 11 am-9 pm

Smokey Bones, 2007 Walden Ave, Cheektowaga, NY, 14225, (716) 683-0724, 11 am-10 pm

Cicero

Cracker Barrel, 8400 Pardee Rd, Cicero, NY, 13039, (315) 698-4311, 6 am-10 pm

Clarence

Chili's, 4153 Transit Rd, Clarence, NY, 14221, (716) 634-0505, 11 am-10 pm

Old Country Buffet, Clarence Mall, 4401 Transit Rd, Clarence, NY, 14221, (716) 634-1893, 11 am-9 pm

Clifton Park

Cracker Barrel, 4 Tower Way, Clifton Park, NY, 12065, (518) 373-8156, 6 am-10 pm

Godfather's Pizza, 1513 Crescent Rd, Clifton Park, NY, 12065, (518) 348-0696

Ninety Nine Restaurant & Pub, 306 Clifton Park Center Rd, Clifton Park, NY, 12065, (518) 348-1499, 11:30 am-11 pm

Chili's, 5 Northside Dr, Clifton Park, NY, 12065, (518) 383-4289, 11 am-10 pm

Colonie

Chili's, 60 Wolf Rd, Colonie, NY, 12205, (518) 489-4664, 11 am-10 pm

Smokey Bones, 1557 Central Ave, Colonie, NY, 12205, (518) 464-9971, 11 am-10 pm

Romano's Macaroni Grill, 1 Metro Park Rd, Colonie, NY, 12205, (518) 446-9190, 11 am-10 pm

Ninety Nine Restaurant & Pub, 107 Wolf Rd, Colonie, NY, 12205, (518) 446-9909, 11:30 am-11 pm

Golden Corral, 1901 Central Ave, Colonie, NY, 12205, (518) 862-1520, 11 am-9 pm

Dewitt

Chili's, 3691 Erie Blvd E, Dewitt, NY, 13214, (315) 445-2200, 11 am-10 pm

Old Country Buffet, Hechinger Plz, 3179 Erie Blvd E, Dewitt, NY, 13214, (315) 449-2229, 11 am-9 pm

East Greenbush

Cracker Barrel, 122 Troy Rd, E. Greenbush, NY, 12061, (518) 479-3646, 6 am-10 pm

East Meadow

Hooters, 1740 Hempstead Turnpike, E. Meadow L.I., NY, 11554, (516) 357-9545, 11 am-midnight

East Northport

Chili's, 4000 Jericho Turnpike, East Northport, NY, 11731, (631) 462-2070, 11 am-10 pm

Elmira

Old Country Buffet, Northwest Consumer Square, 821 County Rte 64, Elmira, NY, 14903, (607) 796-6369, 11 am-9 pm

Elmont

Sizzler, 1710 Hempstead Turnpike, Elmont, NY, 11003, (516) 328-7950, 11 am-10 pm

Farmingdale

Dave and Buster's, 261 Airport Plz Blvd, Farmingdale, NY, 11735, (631) 249-0708, 11:30 am-midnight

Fayetteville

Uno Chicago Grill, 520 Towne Dr, Fayetteville, NY, 13066, (315) 637-8667, 11 am-12:30 am

Fishkill

Cracker Barrel, 4 Merritt Blvd, Fishkill, NY, 12524, (845) 896-4194, 6 am-10 pm

Godfather's Pizza, 2599 Rt 9 & Snook Rd, Fishkill, NY, 12524, (845) 897-2590

Charlie Brown's Steakhouse, 18 Westage Dr, Ste 22, Fishkill, NY, (845) 896-2666, 11 am-midnight

Floral Park

Sizzler, 287 Jericho Turnpike, Floral Park, NY, 11001, (516) 354-8554, 11 am-10 pm

Flushing

The Ground Round, 196-50 Northern Blvd, Flushing, NY, 11358, (718) 224-3998, 11 am-11 pm

Forest Hills

Sizzler, 100-27 Metropolitan Ave, Forest Hills, NY, 11375, (718) 544-4376, 11 am-10 pm

Uno Chicago Grill, 107-16 70th Rd, Forest Hills, NY, 11375, (718) 793-6700, 11 am-12:30 am

Garden City Park

Charlie Brown's Steakhouse, 2349 Jericho Tpke, Garden City Park, NY, (516) 294-7320, 11 am-midnight

Gates

Godfather's Pizza, 2328 Chili Ave, Gates, NY, 14624, (585) 247-6750

Glenmont

Chili's, 382 Rte 9W, Glenmont, NY, 12077, (518) 436-4320, 11 am-10 pm

Guilderland

Ninety Nine Restaurant & Pub, 1470 Wern Ave, Guilderland, NY, 12203, (518) 452-1999, 11:30 am-11 pm

Henrietta

Cracker Barrel, 2075 Hylan Dr, Henrietta, NY, 14623, (585) 321-3230, 6 am-10 pm

Romano's Macaroni Grill, 760 Jefferson Rd, Henrietta, NY, 14467, (585) 427-8230, 11 am-10 pm

Uno Chicago Grill, 1000 Hylan Dr, Henrietta, NY, 14467, (585) 272-8667, 11 am-12:30 am

Hicksville

On the Border, 1401 BRdway Mall, Hicksville, NY, 11801, (516) 942-4044, 11 am-10 pm

Highland

Godfather's Pizza, 491 New York State Rte 299, Highland, NY, 12528, (845) 691-2090

Godfather's Pizza, 3572 Rte 9 N, Highland, NY, 12528, (845) 691-6014

Holtsville

Charlie Brown's Steakhouse, 45 Middle Ave, Holtsville, NY, (631) 289-3320, 11 am-midnight

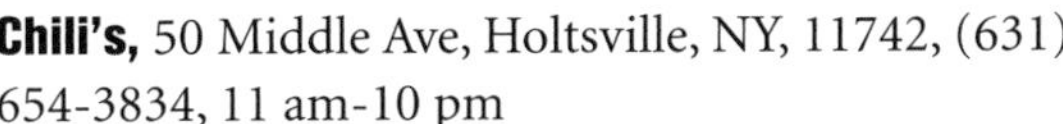

Chili's, 50 Middle Ave, Holtsville, NY, 11742, (631) 654-3834, 11 am-10 pm

Horseheads

Chili's, 3347 Chambers Rd South, Horseheads, NY, 14845, (607) 739-8437, 11 am-10 pm

Islandia

Dave and Buster's, Veterans Memorial Hwy, Islandia, NY, (631) 582-6615, 11:30 am-midnight

Hooters, 3701 Expressway Dr N, Islandia, NY, 11749, (631) 582-2599, 11 am-midnight

Ithaca

Chili's, 608 S Meadow St, Ithaca, NY, 14850, (607) 272-5004, 11 am-10 pm

Godfather's Pizza, 366 Elmira Rd, Ithaca, NY, 14850, (607) 273-4073

Johnson City

Godfather's Pizza, 709 Harry L Dr, Johnson City, NY, 13790, (607) 798-1653

Johnstown

Godfather's Pizza, 285 N Comrie, Johnstown, NY, 12095, (518) 762-6214

Kingston

Ninety Nine Restaurant & Pub, 53 Massa Dr, Kingston, NY, 12401, (845) 336-4399, 11:30 am-11 pm

Latham

Old Country Buffet, Latham Circle Mall, 800-677 New Loudon Rd, Latham, NY, 12110, (518) 783-3472,
11 am-9 pm

Uno Chicago Grill, 601 Troy-Schenectady Rd, Latham, NY, 12110, (518) 782-7166, 11 am-12:30 am

Levittown

Old Country Buffet, 3023 Hempstead Turnpike, Levittown, NY, 11756, (516) 731-4533, 11 am-9 pm

The Ground Round, 2716 Hempstead Turnpike, Levittown, NY, 11756, (516) 796-7900, 11 am-11 pm

Liverpool

Godfather's Pizza, 1075 7th N St, Liverpool, NY, 13088, (315) 461-0448

Godfather's Pizza, 4803 W Taft Rd, Liverpool, NY, 13088, (315) 453-7345

Hooters, 3873 State Rt 31, Ste 100, Liverpool, NY, 13090, (315) 652-8846, 11 am-midnight

Smokey Bones, 4036 State Rte 31, Liverpool, NY, 13090, (315) 652-7824, 11 am-10 pm

Uno Chicago Grill, 3974 State Rte 31, Liverpool, NY, 13090, (315) 622-0718, 11 am-12:30 am

Chili's, 3954 Rte 31, Liverpool, NY, 13090, (315) 652-6799, 11 am-10 pm

Long Island City

Uno Chicago Grill, 37-11 35th Ave, Long Island City, NY, 11101, (718) 706-8800, 11 am-12:30 am

Lynbrook

Charlie Brown's Steakhouse, 161 Union Ave, Lynbrook, NY, (516) 256-3273, 11 am-midnight

Uno Chicago Grill, 693 Sunrise Hwy, Lynbrook, NY, 11563, (516) 593-0100, 11 am-12:30 am

Manhasset

Benihana, 2105 Nern Blvd, Manhasset, NY, 11030, (516) 627-3400, 11:30 am-10 pm

Manorville

Godfather's Pizza, 285 Wading River Rd, Manorville, NY, 11949, (631) 395-5017

Massapequa

Sizzler, 45 Carmans Rd, Massapequa, NY, 11758, (516) 795-2293, 11 am-10 pm

Middletown

Charlie Brown's Steakhouse, 505 Schutt Rd, Middletown, NY, (845) 342-0601, 11 am-midnight

Chili's, 33 Crystal Run Rd, Middletown, NY, 10941, (845) 692-4478, 11 am-10 pm

Mohegan Lake

Charlie Brown's Steakhouse, 1745 E Main St, Mohegan Lake, NY, (914) 528-0074, 11 am-midnight

Monroe

Chili's, 320 Larkin Dr, Monroe, NY, 10950, (845) 774-8217, 11 am-10 pm

Nanuet

Chili's, 255 E Rte 59, Nanuet, NY, 10954, (845) 623-6305, 11 am-10 pm

Nesconset

Uno Chicago Grill, 2950 Middle Country Rd, Nesconset, NY, 11767, (631) 863-1900, 11 am-12:30 am

New Hartford

Uno Chicago Grill, 8645 Clinton St, New Hartford, NY, 13413, (315) 736-8323, 11 am-12:30 am

Ninety Nine Restaurant & Pub, 8675 Clinton St, New Hartford, NY, 13413, (315) 736-9699, 11:30 am-11 pm

The Ground Round, 8562 Seneca Turnpke, New Hartford, NY, 13413, (315) 724-5671, 11 am-11 pm

New York

Benihana, 47 W 56th St, New York, NY, 10019, (212) 581-0930, 11:30 am-10 pm

Bubba Gump Shrimp, 1501 Broadway, New York, NY, 10036, (212) 391-7100, 11 am-10 pm

Chevy's, 243 W 42nd St, New York, NY, 10036, (212) 302-4010, 11 am-10 pm

Chevy's, 101 N End Ave, New York, NY, 10282, (212) 786-1111, 11 am-10 pm

Dave and Buster's, 234 W 42nd St, 3rd Floor, New York, NY, 10036, (646) 495-2015, 11 am-midnight

Del Frisco's, 1221 Ave of the Americas, New York, NY, 10020, (212) 575-5129, 11 am-midnight

Haru, 1329 Third Ave, New York, NY, 10021, (212) 452-2230, 11:30 am-10 pm

Haru, 1327 Third Ave, New York, NY, 10021, (212) 452-1028, 11:30 am-10 pm

Haru, 433 Amsterdam Ave, New York, NY, 10024, (212) 579-5655, 11:30 am-10 pm

Haru, 280 Park Ave, New York, NY, 10017, (212) 490-9680, 11:30 am-10 pm

Haru, 205 W 43rd St, New York, NY, 10036, (212) 398-9810, 11:30 am-10 pm

Haru, 220 Park Ave S, New York, NY, 10003, (646) 428-0989, 11:30 am-10 pm

Hooters, 211 W 56th St, New York, NY, 10019, (212) 581-5656, 11 am-midnight

Todai, 6 E 32nd St, New York, NY, 10016, (212) 725-1333, 11:30 am-9 pm

Uno Chicago Grill, 55 3rd Ave, E Village, New York, NY, 10003, (212) 995-9668, 11 am-12:30 am

Uno Chicago Grill, 391 6th Ave, W Village, New York, NY, 10014, (212) 242-5230, 11 am-12:30 am

Uno Chicago Grill, 432 Columbus Ave, New York, NY, 10024, (212) 595-4700, 11 am-12:30 am

Uno Chicago Grill, 89 S St, Seaport, New York, NY, 10038, (212) 791-7999, 11 am-12:30 am

Uno Chicago Grill, 220 E86th St, New York, NY, 10028, (212) 472-5656, 11 am-12:30 am

Newburgh

The Ground Round, 1401 Rte 300, Newburgh, NY, 12550, (845) 564-1201, 11 am-11 pm

Godfather's Pizza, 1215 Rt 300, Newburgh, NY, 12550, (845) 567-6509

Niagara Falls

Old Country Buffet, 8215 Niagara Falls Blvd, Niagara Falls, NY, 14304, (716) 283-4910, 11 am-9 pm

Northport

The Ground Round, 747 Fort Salonga Rd, Northport, NY, 11768, (631) 754-4191, 11 am-11 pm

Plattsburgh

Ninety Nine Restaurant & Pub, 446 Rte 3, Plattsburgh, NY, 12901, (518) 566-9900, 11:30 am-11 pm

The Ground Round, 32 Smithfield Blvd, Plattsburgh, NY, 12901, (518) 561-2897, 11 am-11 pm

Port Jefferson

The Ground Round, Nesconset Hwy & Jayne Blvd, Port Jefferson, NY, 11776, (631) 928-0654, 11 am-11 pm

Poughkeepsie

Chili's, 2016 S Rd, Poughkeepsie, NY, 12601, (845) 296-1375, 11 am-10 pm

Uno Chicago Grill, 842A Main St, Poughkeepsie, NY, 12603, (845) 452-4930, 11 am-12:30 am

Queensbury

Godfather's Pizza, 756 Quaker Rd, Queensbury, NY, 12804, (518) 761-0310

Ninety Nine Restaurant & Pub, 578 Aviation Rd at the Aviation Mall, Queensbury, NY, 12804, (518) 798-0699, 11:30 am-11 pm

Uno Chicago Grill, 880 State Rte 9, Queensbury, NY, 12804, (518) 792-5399, 11 am-12:30 am

Rego Park

Sizzler, 95-25 Queens Blvd, Rego Park, NY, 11374, (718) 896-4600, 11 am-10 pm

Rochester

Hooters, 945 Jefferson Rd, Rochester, NY, 14623, (585) 475-9464, 11 am-midnight

Uno Chicago Grill, 300 Center Pl Dr, Rochester, NY, 14615, (585) 663-0720, 11 am-12:30 am

Old Country Buffet, South Town Plz, 3333 W Henrietta Rd, Rochester, NY, 14623, (585) 427-9140, 11 am-9 pm

Godfather's Pizza, 1954 Lyell Ave, Rochester, NY, 14606, (585) 254-3340

Don Pablo's, 780 Jefferson Rd, Rochester, NY, 14623, (585) 424-6860, 11 am-10 pm

Godfather's Pizza, 933 W Ridge Rd, Rochester, NY, 14615, (585) 581-5660

Old Country Buffet, Stone Ridge Plz, 1512 Ridge Rd West, Rochester, NY, 14615, (585) 581-2020, 11 am-9 pm

Ronkonkoma

Smokey Bones, 5012 Expy Dr South, Ronkonkoma, NY, 11779, (631) 580-2675, 11 am-10 pm

Roslyn

The Ground Round, 1024 Northern Blvd, Roslyn, NY, 11576, (516) 621-9375, 11 am-11 pm

Rotterdam

Ninety Nine Restaurant & Pub, 93 W Campbell Rd, Rotterdam, NY, 12306, (518) 374-7799, 11:30 am-11 pm

Godfather's Pizza, 1911 Curry Rd, Rotterdam, NY, 12306, (518) 356-9034

Saratoga Springs

Uno Chicago Grill, 3008 State Rte 50, Saratoga Springs, NY, 12866, (518) 587-4270, 11 am-12:30 am

Golden Corral, 15 Old Gick Rd, Saratoga Springs, NY, 12866, (518) 580-0682, 11 am-9 pm

Ninety Nine Restaurant & Pub, 3073 Rte 50 Wilton Mall, Saratoga Springs, NY, 12866, (518) 584-9906, 11:30 am-11 pm

Schenectady

Old Country Buffet, 2320-2326 Watt St, Schenectady, NY, 12304, (518) 347-0396, 11 am-9 pm

Smithtown

Sizzler, 133 W Main St, Smithtown, NY, 11787, (631) 361-8899, 11 am-10 pm

South Setauket

Chili's, 280 Pond Path, South Setauket, NY, 11720, (631) 580-2842, 11 am-10 pm

Staten Island

Hometown Buffet, 1501 Forest Ave, Staten Island, NY, 10302, (718) 815-7666, 11 am-8:30 pm

Chili's, 1497 Richmond Ave, Staten Island, NY, 10314, (718) 697-0883, 11 am-10 pm

Chevy's, 2690 Hylan Blvd, Staten Island, NY, 10306, (718) 667-0600, 11 am-10 pm

Charlie Brown's Steakhouse, 1001 Goethals Rd, Staten Island, NY, (718) 983-6846, 11 am-midnight

Syracuse

Hooters, 9824 Carusel Center, Syracuse, NY, 13290, (315) 466-0066, 11 am-midnight

Old Country Buffet, 3667 W Genesee St, Syracuse, NY, 13219, (315) 484-7104, 11 am-9 pm

Uno Chicago Grill, 9558 Carousel Center, Syracuse, NY, 13290, (315) 466-8667, 11 am-12:30 am

Vestal

Hooters, 3605 Vestal Pky, Vestal, NY, 13850, (607) 644-9464, 11 am-midnight

Old Country Buffet, Town Square Mall, 2433 Vestal Pkwy East, Vestal, NY, 13850, (607) 770-6116, 11 am-9 pm

Uno Chicago Grill, 2503 Vestal Pkwy, Towne Square Plz, Vestal, NY, 13850, (607) 770-7000, 11 am-12:30 am

Victor

P.F. Changs, 820 Eastview Mall, Eastview Mall, Victor, NY, 14564, (585) 223-2410, 11 am-10 pm

Uno Chicago Grill, 7724 Victor-Pittsford Rd, Valentown Corner Plz, Victor, NY, 14564, (585) 223-6100, 11 am-12:30 am

Wappingers Falls

Hometown Buffet, Wappingers Plz, 1488 Rt9, Wappingers Falls, NY, 12590, (845) 297-5187, 11 am-8:30 pm

Uno Chicago Grill, 1794 S Rd, Rte 9, Wappingers Falls, NY, 12590, (845) 297-6770, 11 am-12:30 am

Watertown

Cracker Barrel, 1289 Coffeen St, Watertown, NY, 13601, (315) 782-2460, 6 am-10 pm

Webster

Uno Chicago Grill, 931 Holt Rd, Webster, NY, 14580, (585) 872-4760, 11 am-12:30 am

West Nyack

Chili's, 4 434 Palisades Center Dr, West Nyack, NY, 10994, (845) 353-9774, 11 am-10 pm

Dave and Buster's, Palisades Center, West Nyack, NY, (845) 353-1555, 11:30 am-midnight

Stir Crazy, 4422 Palisades Center Dr, West Nyack, NY, 10994, (845) 727-2002, 11 am-9:30 pm

Cheesecake Factory, 1612 Palisades Center Dr, West Nyack, NY, 10994, (845) 727-1000, 11:30 am-11 pm

Westbury

Benihana, 920 Merchant's Concourse, Westbury, NY, 11590, (516) 222-6091, 11:30 am-10 pm

Cheesecake Factory, 1504 Old Country Rd, Westbury, NY, 11590, (516) 222-5500, 11 am-11:30 pm

Chili's, 1205 Corporate Dr, Westbury, NY, 11590, (516) 222-7001, 11 am-10 pm

Cozymel's Mexican Grill, 1177 Corporate Dr, Westbury, NY, 11590, (516) 222-7010, 11 am-10 pm

Dave and Buster's, 1504 Old Country Rd, Westbury, NY, 11590, (516) 542-8501, 11 am-1 am

P.F. Changs, 1504 Old Country Rd, The Source, Westbury, NY, 11590, (516) 222-9200, 11 am-10 pm

Romano's Macaroni Grill, 1195 Corporate Dr, Westbury, NY, 11590, (516) 683-8611, 11 am-10 pm

White Plains

Sizzler, 409 Tarrytown Rd, White Plains, NY, 10607, (914) 761-0070, 11 am-10 pm

Uno Chicago Grill, 14 Martine Ave, White Plains, NY, 10606, (914) 684-7040, 11 am-12:30 am

Cheesecake Factory, One Maple Ave , White Plains, NY, 10601, (914) 683-5253, 11 am-11 pm

P.F. Changs, 125 Westchester Ave, White Plains, NY, 10601, (914) 997-6100, 11 am-10 pm

Williamsville

Cracker Barrel, 6643 Transit Rd, Williamsville, NY, 14221, (716) 635-9542, 6 am-10 pm

Dave and Buster's, 4545 Transit Rd, Ste 220, Williamsville, NY, 14221, (716) 932-2515, 11:30 am-midnight

Don Pablo's, 6727 Transit Rd, Williamsville, NY, 14221, (716) 633-0933, 11 am-10 pm

Yonkers

Charlie Brown's Steakhouse, 1820 Central Ave, Yonkers, NY, (914) 779-7227, 11 am-midnight

Sizzler, 2368 Central Park Ave, Yonkers, NY, 10710, (914) 793-4000, 11 am-10 pm

Uno Chicago Grill, 2650 Central Park Ave, Central Plz, Yonkers, NY, 10710, (914) 779-7515, 11 am-12:30 am

Notes

Notes

Notes

Notes

Notes

Notes

Notes

Notes

Notes